John Owen and English Puritanism

OXFORD STUDIES IN HISTORICAL THEOLOGY

THE UNACCOMMODATED CALVIN
Studies in the Foundation of a Theological Tradition
Richard A. Muller

THE CONFESSIONALIZATION OF HUMANISM IN REFORMATION GERMANY
Erika Rummell

THE PLEASURE OF DISCERNMENT
Marguerite de Navarre as Theologian
Carol Thysell

REFORMATION READINGS OF THE APOCALYPSE
Geneva, Zurich, and Wittenberg
Irena Backus

WRITING THE WRONGS
Women of the Old Testament among Biblical Commentators from Philo through the Reformation
John L. Thompson

THE HUNGRY ARE DYING
Beggars and Bishops in Roman Cappadocia
Susan R. Holman

RESCUE FOR THE DEAD
The Posthumous Salvation of Non-Christians in Early Christianity
Jeffrey A. Trumbower

AFTER CALVIN
Studies in the Development of a Theological Tradition
Richard A. Muller

THE POVERTY OF RICHES
St. Francis of Assisi Reconsidered
Kenneth Baxter Wolf

REFORMING MARY
Changing Images of the Virgin Mary in Lutheran Sermons of the Sixteenth Century
Beth Kreitzer

TEACHING THE REFORMATION
Ministers and Their Message in Basel, 1529-1629
Amy Nelson Burnett

THE PASSIONS OF CHRIST IN HIGH-MEDIEVAL THOUGHT
An Essay on Christological Development
Kevin Madigan

GOD'S IRISHMEN
Theological Debates in Cromwellian Ireland
Crawford Gribben

REFORMING SAINTS
Saint's Lives and Their Authors in Germany, 1470-1530
David J. Collins

GREGORY OF NAZIANZUS ON THE TRINITY AND THE KNOWLEDGE OF GOD
In Your Light We Shall See Light
Christopher A. Beeley

THE JUDAIZING CALVIN
Sixteenth-Century Debates over the Messianic Psalms
G. Sujin Pak

THE DEATH OF SCRIPTURE AND THE RISE OF BIBLICAL STUDIES
Michael C. Legaspi

THE FILIOQUE
History of a Doctrinal Controversy
A. Edward Siecienski

ARE YOU ALONE WISE?
Debates about Certainty in the Early Modern Church
Susan E. Schreiner

EMPIRE OF SOULS
Robert Bellarmine and the Christian Commonwealth
Stefania Tutino

MARTIN BUCER'S DOCTRINE OF JUSTIFICATION
Reformation Theology and Early Modern Irenicism
Brian Lugioyo

CHRISTIAN GRACE AND PAGAN VIRTUE
The Theological Foundation of Ambrose's Ethics
J. Warren Smith

KARLSTADT AND THE ORIGINS OF THE EUCHARISTIC CONTROVERSY
A Study in the Circulation of Ideas
Amy Nelson Burnett

John Owen and English Puritanism

Experiences of Defeat

CRAWFORD GRIBBEN

OXFORD
UNIVERSITY PRESS

Oxford University Press is a department of the University of Oxford. It furthers the University's objective of excellence in research, scholarship, and education by publishing worldwide.Oxford is a registered trade mark of Oxford University Press in the UK and certain other countries.

Published in the United States of America by Oxford University Press
198 Madison Avenue, New York, NY 10016, United States of America.

First issued as an Oxford University Press paperback, 2017

Library of Congress Cataloging-in-Publication Data
Gribben, Crawford.
John Owen and English Puritanism : experiences of defeat / Crawford Gribben.
pages cm
Includes bibliographical references and index.
ISBN 978–0–19–979815–5 (hardcover); 978–0–19–086079–0 (paperback)
1. Owen, John, 1616–1683. 2. Dissenters, Religious—England—Biography.
3. Owen, John, 1616–1683—Influence. I. Title.
BX5207.O88G75 2015
285′.9092—dc23
[B]
2015030026

For Murray Pittock

Fathers and prophets have but their season, and they are not. . . . They are placed of God in their station, as a sentinel in his watch-tower; and they have their appointed season, and are then dismissed from their watch. The great Captain of their salvation comes, and saith, Go thou thy ways: thou hast faithfully discharged thy duty; go now unto thy rest. Some have harder service, – some have harder duty than others. Some keep guard in winter, – a time of storms and temptations, trials and great pressures; others in the sunshine, the summer of a more flourishing estate and condition. Yet duty they all do; – all attend in the service, – all endure some hardship, and have their appointed season for their dismission: and be they never so excellent at the discharging of their duty, they shall not abide one moment beyond the bounds which he hath set them.[1]

Contents

Preface

"FEW BOOKS MAKE good their titles," observed the subject of this biography.[1] But this book does try to do so. *John Owen and English Puritanism: Experiences of Defeat* sets out to document and describe the intellectual habits of one of the most significant religious authors and activists in early modern England while commenting on his interaction with the literary cultures of his various environments, and, which is perhaps its greatest challenge, to do so within reasonable limits. The subject of this book is formidable, and I have written this book with more than normal trepidation. Owen was, after all, a man who complained about the "needless multiplying of books (whose plenty is the general customary complaint of all men versed in them)," and who was particularly concerned by the actions of those who "bear up their own names by standing upon the shoulders of others, to deport themselves authors when indeed they are but collectors and translators."[2] Owen wanted "less writing, and more praying."[3] He knew that the writings of "all men not divinely inspired" will be "part of that stubble which shall burn at the last day."[4] He was famously guarded about the details of his own life. I am not sure that he would have approved of this project.

Modern historical writing is necessarily collaborative, nevertheless, and I am acutely conscious that I am "standing upon the shoulders of others" in my attempt to grapple with the extraordinary subject of this book. *John Owen and English Puritanism* builds on the best of the existing biographical work on its subject, including accounts by Peter Toon (1971), Sarah Gibbard Cook (1972), and Richard L. Greaves (2004), as well as the renaissance of theological reflection on Owen that appears to be precipitated by the four hundredth anniversary of his birth (2016). This book goes beyond these accounts to advance a contextual method similar to that developed in my earlier volume in this series, *God's Irishmen: Theological debates in Cromwellian Ireland* (2007), by developing a rounded religious and theological biography of its subject, paying attention to change as well as continuity in Owen's thinking;

by considering the form as well as the content of his writing, while drawing upon the methodological cautions issued by Quentin Skinner, among others; by describing Owen's ideas in their changing cultural, political, economic, institutional, ecclesiastical, literary, and personal contexts; and by situating its narrative among the conclusions of recent writing on the period.

This book has been a long time in the making. I began reading Owen almost twenty years ago, during my doctoral studies at the University of Strathclyde, under the supervision of Michael Bath and with the encouragement of Murray Pittock, then head of department, Neil Keeble, who became my external examiner, and the Reverend Maurice Roberts. But this project formally began in May 2008, after a conversation with Nigel Smith, in which he observed that Owen's broader historical significance had never really been addressed. Throughout this project, Professor Smith's advice has been invaluable, and I am extremely grateful to him and to Paul Muldoon for their hospitality during a visit to Princeton University in March 2010 in which I presented some early research on relevant contexts. Professor Smith's approach has certainly influenced my own: his biography of Andrew Marvell (2010) has been beside me as I have written, alongside other models of generic excellence provided by Richard L. Greaves's biography of John Bunyan (2002), Francis J. Bremer's biography of John Winthrop (2003), George M. Marsden's biography of Jonathan Edwards (2004), John Coffey's biography of John Goodwin (2006), Alan Ford's biography of James Ussher (2007), Paul Gutjahr's biography of Charles Hodge (2011), and Tim Cooper's superlative account of John Owen, Richard Baxter, and the formation of nonconformity (2011). These writers have taught me a great deal about the value and possibility of intellectual, religious, and theological biography.

It has been a special pleasure to write this book as a member of the School of English in Trinity College Dublin and the School of History and Anthropology in Queen's University Belfast. I have learned a great deal from my colleagues, and am especially grateful to record thanks to Darryl Jones, who as head of School granted the semester of leave that made possible a first burst of writing (2011), to Eve Patten, who as head of School permitted the semester of leave funded by the IRCHSS Collaborative Project (2012), as well as to Peter Gray and John Thompson, who as head of School and founding director of the Institute for Collaborative Research in the Humanities welcomed me to my new disciplinary and institutional home in Belfast (2013). Among these colleagues I am especially grateful for books, advice, and ideas to Ian Campbell, Philip Coleman, Sean Connolly, Scott Dixon, David Hayton, Andrew Holmes, Jarlath Killeen, Keith Lilley, David Livingstone, Chris Marsh, Ian Campbell Ross, and Joe Webster. Outside these institutions, I have learned a great deal from reading work by and talking to fellow students of Owen, particularly John Coffey and Tim Cooper, whose provision of important sources at a critical stage in the project was generous almost to a fault, as well as Martyn Cowan, Sinclair Ferguson, Lee Gatiss, Neil Keeble, Joel Halcomb, Kelly Kapic, Ryan Kelly, Paul Lim, Greg McManus, Hunter Powell, and Sebastian Rehnman with the superb students who attended my week of lectures on Owen in London Theological Seminary during April 2015. Selby Whittingham offered invaluable advice on Greenhill's portrait of Owen (1668). I am delighted to acknowledge the support of a wider circle of colleagues, including Robert Armstrong, Francis Bremer, Mark Burden, Elizabeth Clarke, David Dickson, George Ella, Kenneth Fincham, Raymond Gillespie, Jerome de Groot, Jeremy Gregory, Darryl Hart, Michael Haykin, Paul Helm, Kevin Herlihy, Ariel Hessayon, Mark Jones, Jeff Jue, Pavlos Karageorgi, Kathleen Lynch, Jason McElligott, Gráinne McLaughlin, David Manning, John Morrill, Graeme Murdock, David Norbrook, Micheál Ó Siochrú, Jane Ohlmeyer, Andrew Pettegree, James Renihan, Michael Renihan, Stephen Roberts, Dion Smythe, Scott Spurlock, and Mark Sweetnam. I have learned a great deal from the community of doctoral students and post-doctoral fellows who have worked on early modern religion in Dublin and Belfast, including Matt Bingham, Chris Caughey, Andrew Crome, Sonya Cronin, Kathleen Middleton, Kathleen Miller, Anne Sappington, Joshua Searle, and David Seip. Stephen Williams and John Webster advised on several theological points, and a number of colleagues read drafts of all or parts of the work, including Ian Campbell, Ian Clary, Philip Coleman, Matthew Cox, Scott Dixon, Paul Helm, James Renihan, Stephen Rees, and Tim Cooper, who read everything in draft and whose comments improved the final version in myriad ways. I owe the cover to Tim Cooper and John Coffey, who bumped into this long-forgotten Owen portrait in Dr. Williams's Library just days before I submitted the final typescript. The portrait is reproduced here due to the kindness of the Dr. Williams's Library trustees and staff, particularly Jane Giscombe and David Wykes.

That this project has advanced is also due to the generosity of a number of institutions involved in supporting research. A number of colleagues have hosted seminars and conferences in which I have been able to develop some key ideas. I am grateful in this regard to Michael Brown (University of Aberdeen); Emily Michelson and Roger Mason (University of St. Andrews); Scott Spurlock (University of Glasgow); Ariel Hessayon and Jason Peacey (Institute for Historical Research); Graeme Murdock (Trinity College Dublin); Anne Dunan-Page (Dr. Williams's Library); David Norbrook (University of Oxford); Clare Jackson, David Smith, and Alex Walsham (University of Cambridge); Michael Haykin (Southern Baptist Theological Seminary); and

John Coffey and Martin Dzelzainis (University of Leicester). I am grateful to the administrators of several funding schemes, particularly the Trinity College Dublin Arts and Social Sciences Benefactions Fund (2010 and 2011), and the IRCHSS Collaborative Research Scheme (2012–2013), which sponsored one semester of research leave for the writing of this book, with three weeks of research assistance by Kathleen Miller in the Folger Shakespeare Library. I am especially grateful to the libraries in which research was conducted, including the Andersonian Library, University of Strathclyde; the British Library; Chetham's Library, Manchester, especially Michael Powell; Christ Church Archives, University of Oxford, especially Judith Curthoys; the Folger Shakespeare Library, Washington, DC, especially Kathleen Lynch; the Gamble Library, Union Theological College, Belfast, especially Margaret Ollivier and Stephen Gregory, recently retired; Glasgow University Library; the John Rylands University Library, Manchester, especially Graham Johnson; the McClay Library, Queen's University Belfast, especially Deirdre Wildy; New College, Edinburgh; Marsh's Library, Dublin, especially Muriel McCarthy, now retired, and Jason McElligott; Trinity College Library, Dublin, especially Charles Benson, now retired, and the remaining staff of the Early Printed Books department; the University Library, Cambridge; and Dr. Williams's Library, London, especially David Wykes. And I am grateful to Ian Clary and Steve Weaver for permission to reuse material from my chapter in *The pure flame of devotion: The history of Christian spirituality* (2013), and similarly to David Norbrook, editor of the special issue of *Seventeenth Century* (2015), and Jeremy Gregory, editor of *Literature & History* (2011). I am by now immeasurably in debt to Cynthia Read, my editor at Oxford University Press, who has supervised this project with characteristic patience and generosity.

A word on citation conventions: much of the recent Owen scholarship continues to refer to the Goold edition of his *Works* (1850–1855), all but one volume of which has been kept in print by the Banner of Truth since 1967. More recently, Stephen Westcott led a team of university classicists in a translation of Owen's mammoth *Θεολογουμενα παντοδαπα* (1661) and other of his Latin texts, which I frankly admit that I find indispensable.[5] Recognizing that most readers of Owen will access his work by means of Goold and Westcott, my notes will refer to these editions and, where appropriate, to the relevant early modern editions and to translations from Owen's Latin and Greek, paying attention to those moments when the Banner of Truth reprint of Goold rearranges his material. Unless otherwise noted, all biblical quotations are taken from the Authorised Version, which Owen seems to have used routinely.

It is now a commonplace to acknowledge that no historian writes as an entirely neutral observer of data. My research for this book has been carried out in the context of communities in which Owen's theological legacy continues to be critically appreciated. Matthew Brennan, Colin Campbell, Martin Grubb, Shaun McFall, Stephen Rees, Stephen Roger, and David Shedden deserve special thanks for their encouragement over many years. I am also grateful to colleagues who for many years have shared with me their expertise in early modern and Reformed theology, especially Chris Caughey, Darryl Hart, Richard Muller, and David McKay.

Whatever else he might have thought of this project, Owen would have appreciated this long list of names. He admitted that "prefaces for the most part are . . . needless," but also understood that bookish appreciations served multiple purposes.[6] Some of these notes were intended to "express a gratitude for respects and favours received," others were aimed to "obtain countenance and approbation unto their endeavours . . . from names of more esteem, or at least more known than their own," while others served to "advance repute by a correspondency in judgement with men of such esteem."[7] Not much has changed in the four centuries since that observation was made. But Owen also allowed that a preface might append to its long list of obligations a special commendation to a particular reader. The "dedication of books to the names of men worthy and of esteem in their generation" is justified by a "catholic and ancient" tradition, he noted, and in that spirit I dedicate this book to an outstanding scholar, "worthy and of esteem," whose always timely advice has made possible this project and so much else.[8] Finally, as always, my greatest debts are owed to my family, and especially to Pauline and our children, Daniel, Honor, Finn, and Samuel, who understand better than anyone else why this "weak endeavour" must be, as Owen wrote of his first book, the "undigested issue of a few broken hours, too many causes, in these furious malignant days, continually interrupting the course of my studies," an experience that has regularly tested his conviction that "God gives us enough time for all that he requires of us"[9]: I could not have completed this project without them.

Despite the valiant efforts of many friends and colleagues, this project retains many shortcomings. For I am compelled to admit that Owen has defeated me. The contest was always going to be one-sided, but I had hoped to provide a more comprehensive, technical, and balanced survey of his work than here appears. In the following chapters, I represent Owen's growth as a theologian, as his thinking developed in the volatile, contingent, and often dangerous environments of English Puritanism, focusing on the period before he became the grand old man of nonconformity, the "Atlas of the Independents," whose links with Marvell, Shaftesbury, and even the dissolute heir of John Lord Lovelace did so much to shape and defend the fortunes of the erstwhile revolutionaries.[10] Like other discussions of Owen's life, I have focused on his work in the 1640s, 1650s, and early 1660s, principally because this part of my account differs most obviously from that of earlier biographers. I hope in future work to fill out the complexities of the later period. *John Owen and English Puritanism* considers Owen's life in toto, but emphasizes the ways in which he emerged as the intellectual leader of nonconformists in the early years of the Restoration, zooming in and out to examine in detail specific moments that seem to be of greater significance.

For Owen was extraordinary. He had to be. His work was driven by a commitment to describe the work of "God, the eternal spring of all beauty," "Christ, the love, desire, and hope of all nations," and "the Spirit, the great beautifier of souls."[11] But he achieved so much more than theological sublimity. Having failed to effect the changes he wanted in church and state during a decade of revolution, Owen became the religious leader of a marginalized community that refused to admit defeat, the intellectual father of the evangelical movement that would emerge in the 1730s to dominate global Christianity, and a seminal contributor to discussions about the religious condition of modernity, suggesting solutions to the very modern problem of finding public voices for private faith. Of course, Owen would have expected his ideas to have unintended consequences, for, he recognized, God is "present with every person in the world; holds his breath and all his ways in his hand; disposes of his life, death, and all his concernments, as he pleaseth."[12] Owen knew that God executes his purposes by things "contingent and accidental," that the study of history is the study of providence by means of second causes, and that "the day is coming when all his works will praise him."[13] In this, at least, we are alike. *Glóir go deo leis.*

Crawford Gribben
Tulaigh na Mullán, June 2015

John Owen and English Puritanism

Introduction

THIS BOOK IS about John Owen (1616–83) and the texts, cultures, and contexts of English Puritanism in the middle and late seventeenth century.[1] Owen was an extraordinary figure, "one of the towering theologians of the Calvinist heritage," whose life and writing negotiated and contributed to some of the most unpredictable moments in English history.[2] Born in humble circumstances during the reign of James I, and ordained as an Anglican priest under Charles I, Owen became preacher to the Long Parliament (from 1646), preacher of the regicide (1649), chaplain to Oliver Cromwell on the invasions of Ireland and Scotland (1649–50), dean of Christ Church (1651–60) and vice chancellor of the University of Oxford (1652–57), principal mover in the Cromwellian religious settlement, and active agent in the downfall of Richard Cromwell's administration (1659). The changing legal and cultural circumstances of the reign of Charles II forced Owen to withdraw from public life and facilitated the re-energizing of his already prolific publishing career in defense of high Calvinist theology and the toleration of Protestant dissenters: Owen wrote more than half of his work in the twenty years before his death, while making significant contributions to the careers of John Bunyan and Andrew Marvell, among others. Sedentary and political, and often burdened by ill health, Owen was at times frustrated with his physical inability to facilitate the life of his mind. "I have hated the feeble powers of my body," he complained in October 1657, as he stepped down from his role as vice chancellor of the University of Oxford, "nearly uncapable of keeping pace with my designs."[3] Whatever else he was, Owen was a thinker.

Owen's ideas have long dominated his readers' sense of his importance. He has been most often remembered as a theologian—and his written output was prodigious. His eight and a half million words were published in eighty books spanning a variety of genres, including sermons, theological treatises, and an encyclopedic account of redemptive history. His work appeared in a variety of lengths, ranging from a Latin poem of sixteen lines to a commentary on the epistle to the Hebrews published in "four hefty tomes exceeding 2,000 folio pages and over two million words," a text that became "one of the largest expositions of the post-Reformation era if not the entire history of biblical interpretation."[4] Owen's publications addressed a variety of audiences, from the unlearned families of his first parish in Essex to his undergraduate students in Oxford, from politicians in London and Edinburgh to his international scholarly peers. His readers did not always find his arguments convincing, but they were often impressed by his gifts. Richard Baxter, his most enduring opponent, admitted that Owen's "great ... Worth and Learning" were "too well known (to need my proof)."[5] Vincent Alsop, a Presbyterian satirist, described Owen as "Judicious, Wise, and Learned," and claimed that even those who dismissed his conclusions had copies of his books in their "Studies and Libraries" and could not afford to be without them.[6]

But, as Owen must have been one of the busiest writers of the later seventeenth century, it is unlikely that the "Studies and Libraries" of many of his earliest readers held a complete run of his works. In fact, it is possible that Owen himself did not possess a copy of everything he had published: *Bibliotheca Oweniana* (1684), the catalogue for the posthumous auction of his library of some three thousand volumes, included only a handful of his titles.[7] Owen may not have been a typical early modern reader—his amassing a library of this size qualifies Rolf Engelsing's influential argument that most reading in this period was "intensive," as individuals read repeatedly a small number of texts—but his library was not unusually large among the clerical and scholarly elite.[8] Modern readers, by contrast, have easy access to almost all his corpus. The standard edition of Owen's works, edited by William H. Goold (1850–55), runs to 24 volumes, each around 650 pages. This edition continues to be in print, but it is not complete: three volumes of auditor's notes of Owen's preaching remain in manuscript in Dr. Williams's Library, for example.[9] Some of Owen's books have gone through multiple editions, and have become established as classics of evangelical devotion, including *Of communion with God* and *On temptation*, which have been translated into multiple languages and now regularly appear in "modernized" English.[10] But many other of Owen's books, including his massive commentary on Hebrews, which he regarded as the capstone of his career and his most important contribution to the world of letters, have largely disappeared from the gaze of the scholarly and religious reading publics that continue to consume his work.[11]

Of course, many of Owen's readers have found his work difficult to admire. Owen is a challenging writer—in style, as well as in content—with firm opinions about the optimal character of theological language. He resisted those polemicists who reveled in "rhetorical flourishes," he explained, and he was determined that his work would demonstrate a "fixed and absolute disregard for all elegance and ornaments of speech."[12] The responses of several generations of readers would suggest that he realized this goal. Baxter found some parts of Owen's work confusing, and at times frankly admitted that he could not "well understand Mr. Owens minde."[13] And Baxter's response has not been unusual. Many readers attempted to deal with Owen's difficulty by subdividing his works into units of argument. Some copies of Owen's works held in early books repositories indicate the care with which his first readers parsed out his arguments, numbering points in the margins and encoding the process of interpretation with complex series of marks.[14] The copy of *A discourse concerning liturgies* (1662) that was held by Chichester Cathedral, for example, was used by a particularly energetic reader who inscribed numbers in page margins to indicate the structure of Owen's argument.[15] Later readers also found Owen's work demanding. Andrew Thomson, his nineteenth-century biographer, suggested that Owen's writing moved with an "elephant's grace and solid step, if sometimes also with his ungainly motion."[16] William H. Goold, editor of the edition that did more than any other to establish Owen's modern reputation, admitted that his style is "deficient in grace and vivacity" and that his arguments are "often tedious and prolix." He explained that Owen's imagination was "little cultivated and developed; and his chief excellence as an author, it must be admitted, consists in '*non in flosculis verborum,—sed in pondere rerum*' "—in weight, that is, rather than in floridity.[17] The old *Dictionary of National Biography* (1885–1900) described Owen's writing as "tortuous."[18] Even the introduction to the volume that began the modern revival of interest in Owen admitted that his style is "heavy and hard to read" and provided readers with methods to circumvent his "lumbering literary gait."[19] Some of this difficulty has been exacerbated by Owen's habit of English and Greek neologism—the "self-coined pretences" that he abhorred in his antagonists but which became a notable feature of his own writing, as this book will occasionally observe.[20] Ironically, Owen worried about the compositional habits of his antagonists. Quakers, he complained, "toy with words and their meanings and definitions, and they all invent totally new and unheard-of expressions in order to impress or overawe unlearned men."[21] After all, obfuscation and misdirection were theological vehicles for those religious writers who "can mean either anything at all, or nothing at all," and whose "skill and art lies in speaking so laboriously and convolutedly as to prevent all possibility of the accident of being understood."[22] Language, Owen believed, was ineluctably theological.

It is possible that some of Owen's readers have made similarly uncharitable estimations of his work. Not every one of his readers has managed to remain attentive. Many early copies of Owen's publications have been preserved in excellent condition and contain suspiciously few evidences of use.[23] James Ussher routinely annotated the texts he studied, similarly, but left unmarked his copy of *Salus electorum, sanguis Jesu: or, The death of death in the death of Christ* (1648).[24] Chetham's Library, Manchester, holds the copy of *Exercitations concerning the name, original, nature, use and continuance of a day of sacred rest* (1671) that belonged to the poet John Byrom, and it is possible that the volume's spare marginal notations were his. Not all of Owen's readers were stereotypically godly. Samuel Jeake of Rye recorded his interaction with Owen's works in his "astrological diary," evidencing the variety of cultures within which Puritan writing operated.[25] Other early copies reflect the thought processes of those with limited powers of concentration: one early reader of *Σύνεσις πνευματική: Or the causes, waies & means of understanding the mind of God as revealed in his word* (1678) inscribed its margins with a list of bonnets and cravats.[26] Some references to the ubiquity of Owen's work suggest that it was being put to uses other than those of spiritual edification. One correspondent complained that he could "scarce visit a Tavern, or Country Ale-house, but forth comes some of the Learned Works of John Owen"—though, he added, the pages were being used to wrap tobacco.[27] Owen has never lacked detractors, and, as George Hunsinger has recently noted, "no one has accused [him] of making matters easy for his readers."[28] Yet there may be less evidence than they might expect for the one conclusion his admirers and detractors have tended to share: rumors of Owen's difficulty may have been greatly exaggerated.

I

It is almost certainly true that, at the beginning of the twenty-first century, Owen is attracting a wider readership than ever before. Owen's public has been growing since his death. His work was repeatedly reprinted through the eighteenth and nineteenth centuries, and was occasionally translated into Welsh and Dutch.[29] Descriptive and analytical interest in Owen began in the early twentieth century, with the publication of *The golden book of John Owen* (1904), an anthology prepared by the future Bible translator James Moffatt. Moffatt lamented the fact that Owen's works had "dropped into the cells of oblivion," but blamed this on his subject's "restriction of outlook and interest."[30] Owen's ideas were given a more sympathetic treatment in Reginald Kirby's *The threefold bond* ([1936]), though the Australian Baptist did little more than exposit central themes in *Of communion with God*. While Owen had an important but perhaps underestimated status in W. K. Jordan's *The development of religious toleration in England* (1932–40), the modern revival of interest in Owen began in earnest in the late 1950s, as part of the resurgence of postwar evangelicalism, and gathered pace after the Banner of Truth Trust, a conservative Protestant publisher, repackaged the Goold edition of *Salus electorum, sanguis Jesu* (1648) as *The death of death* (1959). The republished text was introduced by J. I. Packer, then a young Anglican theologian, whose writings would go on to shape in profound ways the evolution of evangelicalism in the succeeding half-century.[31] Packer's foreword advanced a robust Calvinism, which his later writing would moderate, at least rhetorically.[32] He used Owen's work to launch a blistering attack on the "twisted half-truths" of evangelical theological norms, describing Owen's treatise as a "polemical work" challenging the conviction shared almost universally among mid-twentieth century evangelicals that the death of Jesus Christ was intended to provide for the salvation of all humanity.[33] Instead, Packer argued, Owen had proven that this doctrine of "universal atonement" was "unscriptural and destructive of the gospel." The only answer to the "perplexity and unsettlement" of the evangelical movement was its "recovery of the gospel," Packer claimed, and a new appropriation of Owen was to be central to that task.[34] This republication of *Salus electorum, sanguis Jesu* proved to be successful, although, as we will see, it was in several important respects unrepresentative of Owen's mature conclusions, and increasingly unreflective of those of Packer, who had so highly recommended it.[35] Within ten years, the Banner of Truth Trust had republished the Goold edition, with the exception of one volume of writings in Latin, which were published in English translation some thirty years later by another conservative Protestant publisher.[36] By the early 1970s, nevertheless, readers had been provided with the texts that would facilitate the Owen revival.

As conservative Protestants renewed their appreciation of Owen's devotional writing, scholars began more seriously to analyze his ideas. John Wilson's description of Owen's significance in *Preachers in Parliament* (1969) anticipated some of the conclusions of Peter Toon's editions of Owen's correspondence (1970), university orations (1971), and biography (1971), which represented the first fruits of what would become a minor scholarly industry. Toon's biographical account of Owen focused on the period before the Restoration, and appeared as Sarah Gibbard Cook completed her Harvard doctoral thesis on Owen's political thought (1972). Scholarly interest in Owen continued through the 1980s, with important treatments, including that of Christopher Hill in *The experience of defeat* (1984), largely repeating the principal themes of the earlier biographical accounts.[37] Owen began to be more widely appreciated by historians of religious ideas after Richard Muller's *Post-Reformation Reformed dogmatics* (1987; second edition, 2003) called attention to the intellectual vitality of Protestant scholasticism, and as Sinclair B. Ferguson offered a groundbreaking systemization of one of that tradition's most important representatives in *John Owen on the Christian life* (1987). Owen became a central figure in the confessionally driven debate about the relationship between "Calvin and the Calvinists" in the late 1980s and early 1990s. Alan C. Clifford's *Atonement and justification: English evangelical theology, 1640–1790* (1990) advanced the claim that Owen's Aristotelianism had obscured the simpler biblicism of Calvin's earlier delineation of the gospel, but the opposite case was made by Joel R. Beeke's *Assurance of faith: Calvin, English Puritanism and the Dutch Second Reformation* (1991), and was clinched in Carl Trueman's *The claims of truth: John Owen's Trinitarian theology* (1998) and Steve Griffiths's *Redeem the time: Sin in the writings of John Owen* (2001), which assumed a basic continuity of thought balanced by recognition of the changing circumstances of its articulation. The debate having been settled to the satisfaction of the majority of its participants, later work tended to follow Ferguson's lead by approaching Owen's theology on its own terms and outside these larger historiographical debates. The concern to systematize Owen's thinking continued in such impressive works as Randall C. Gleason's *John Calvin and John Owen on mortification* (1995), the chapters collected in *John Owen: The man and his theology* (2002), Richard Daniels's *The Christology of John Owen* (2004), Brian Kay's *Trinitarian spirituality: John Owen and the doctrine of God in western devotion* (2007), Alan Spence's *Incarnation and inspiration: John Owen and the coherence of Christology* (2007), J. V. Fesko's *Beyond Calvin: Union with Christ and justification in early modern Reformed theology (1517–1700)* (2012), and Ryan McGraw's *A heavenly directory: Trinitarian piety, public worship and a reassessment of John Owen's theology* (2014). This purposefully theological approach has been organized by Stephen P. Westcott in *By the Bible alone! John Owen's theology for today's church* (2010), a compendious and committed attempt to have Owen's writing shape a systematic theology, and *A puritan theology: Doctrine for life* (2012), a comprehensive exposition of Puritan accounts of Reformed theological loci by Joel R. Beeke and Mark Jones; usefully developed in the essays contained in *Drawn into controversie: Reformed theological diversity and debates within seventeenth-century British Puritanism* (2011), in which Owen features regularly; and institutionalized in *The Ashgate research companion to John Owen's theology* (2012), a volume that brings together contributions by many of Owen's most careful readers, collecting essays which tend to foreground his texts above their cultures and contexts.[38]

Other recent work has preferred to read Owen within the evolving discursive fields of the seventeenth century, and in both national and international contexts.[39] One of the most important of these recent contributions is Sebastian Rehnman's *Divine discourse: The theological methodology of John Owen* (2002). Rehnman's work offered a compelling and convincing study of Owen's theological prolegomena—his theological presuppositions—as being indicative of his wider intellectual enterprise. Rehnman was perhaps the first of Owen's readers to identify him as a "typical Renaissance man," a Reformed Catholic standing appreciatively at the conclusion of the medieval scholastic tradition.[40] Rehnman's portrait of Owen is that of a thinker struggling with the genre of theological writing, unsatisfied by the *loci* method of the sixteenth-century reformers, building upon his doctrine of Scripture to adopt an organization of theology that reflected more closely the chronological order of the divine revelation it recorded. Rehnman's work initiated a new wave of Owen scholarship, attentive to generic nuance and pursuing richer contextual detail. His recognition of the importance of the medieval and Catholic tradition was reinforced by the conclusions of Trueman's *John Owen: Reformed Catholic, Renaissance man* (2007) and Christopher Cleveland's *Thomism in John Owen* (2013). Rehnman's recognition of the importance of Protestant and contemporary contexts was significantly advanced by Kelly M. Kapic's *Communion with God: Relations between the divine and the human in the theology of John Owen* (2007), Edwin Tay's analysis of *The priesthood of Christ: Atonement in the theology of John Owen* (2014), Sinclair B. Ferguson's reflective study of *The Trinitarian devotion of John Owen* (2015), Matthew Barrett and Michael A. G. Haykin's *Owen on the Christian life* (2015), and by an increasing number of articles in scholarly journals. Donald Leggett's Cambridge MPhil thesis offered a groundbreaking account of Owen's work as a religious advisor to Cromwell (2006), and Sarah Mortimer's *Reason and religion in the English revolution* (2010) described how Owen's theology was driven by his politics. Some of the richest of the recent contextual studies have moved beyond theological and political issues to focus on Owen's creative writing, such as the accounts of Owen's Latinity provided by Edward Holberton (2008) and Gráinne McLaughlin (2013).[41] There are still significant debates within Owen studies in which this study will not intervene—for example, on the nature of Owen's Trinitarianism, in which Alan Spence, Brian Kay, and Robert Letham have contributed important, if not mutually confirming, arguments.[42] But work on Owen is only now beginning to escape the almost exclusive emphasis on doctrine, which has characterized so much of the scholarship on Puritans and Puritanism.[43] Owen is no longer, as Trueman claimed in his pioneering study of 1998, the "forgotten man of English theology."[44] But he may still be, as J. I. Packer recently put it, "Puritanism's theological Everest."[45]

Perhaps the most significant recent studies of Owen have focused on his contribution to the intellectual world of European Protestantism. Of course, many of these publications reflect the extraordinary impact of the work of Richard A. Muller, whose analyses of post-Reformation Protestant orthodoxy has propelled this intellectual domain to the forefront of early modern historical concern. Muller has described Reformed orthodoxy in seventeenth-century England as the "codification and institutionalization of the Reformation . . . consisting in the confessional character of its theology and piety . . . in continuity and also discontinuity with strands in the religious past, all with elements of response and adaptation to the changing political, social, and intellectual contexts of Puritanism."[46] This conveys Muller's attention to the nuances of ideas in terms of the evolving contingencies of the relevant interpretive contexts. Yet in much of the scholarship influenced by Muller's approach, Owen is represented as rather a static figure within a grid that underplays the extent to which his thinking evolved. Owen did change his mind, and was not ashamed of admitting it: "he that can glory that . . . he hath not altered or improved in his conception of some things . . . shall not have me for his rival."[47] And Owen changed his mind on issues with which he has become particularly identified.

There were two key periods in which Owen revised his thinking. The first was in the 1640s, in the period immediately after he became assured that he possessed saving faith and began his pastoral career. During that period, Owen backed away from his earlier belief that assurance was of the essence of saving faith.[48] This was a significant development, not least because it allowed Owen to reconstitute his spiritual biography. His earlier argument that true Christians could not doubt their spiritual state had been made, paradoxically, during a long period of acute concern about the reality of his own salvation. Thus his new affirmation that true faith could exist in the absence of certainty as to its saving value allowed him to backdate his sense of when he had been regenerated, so permitting him to identify his earlier experience of anxiety and doubt as that of a true child of God. Owen also changed his mind about the shape of the church: the Presbyterian system of church government that his earlier publications had defended rapidly gave way to a Congregational position from which, some scholars have claimed, he may have reverted very late in his life.[49] And Owen also reconsidered the nature and intention of the atonement. His early work had rejected the idea that Christ's death was necessary for the forgiveness of sins, and had argued that God could have forgiven sin by an act of sheer will. In the late 1640s, however, Owen adopted the view that was becoming normative among English Reformed theologians: that a sacrifice of propitiation would in fact be required by God if sinners were to be forgiven.[50]

These changes of opinion can be explained through different paradigms. On one hand, they show that Owen was moving away from positions held by Calvin to those that were becoming normative for mid-century English Puritans, some of which were being codified in the Westminster Confession of Faith (1647). But the movement was not all one-way, for Owen moved closer to Calvin as he reconsidered other key doctrines. This was most obvious in Owen's reformulation of the extent of the atonement. Owen continually argued that Christ's death was limited in its efficiency—that is, that it was effective in achieving salvation only for those who had saving faith. But during the late 1640s he moved from arguing that Christ's death was limited in its sufficiency to claim instead that it was unlimited in its sufficiency—that is, that its merit was sufficient to satisfy God's justice for an infinite number of people. This change allowed him to make a stronger defense of the notion of human responsibility—it was due to no lack of provision on the part of God that any human being should be lost—but it also brought Owen into line with the conclusions of the international synod of Protestant divines that had been convened at Dort (1618–19).[51] The question of whether Owen moved toward or away from Calvin's position on these subjects is therefore misleading: throughout the late 1640s, as later chapters will illustrate, Owen was moving from an eclectic and eccentric combination of theological positions to endorse the perspectives outlined in documents that were to become the manifestos of English Puritanism, while always retaining a number of minority positions. Among these minority positions, for example, was his increasing tendency toward preterism. In January 1649, preaching after the regicide, he described 2 Peter 3 as referring not to the destruction of the "material heavens and earth," but to the "political heights and splendour, the popular multitudes and strength, of the nations of the earth," which "are thus to be shaken."[52] Thirty years later, in his commentary on Hebrews 10:25, he had changed his mind, arguing that the renovation of the heavens and earth which many of his contemporaries expected to take place at the end of time had already taken place in the destruction of the "Mosaical ordinances" in 70 A.D.[53]

Owen passed through another period of acute self-doubt in the early 1660s. Reeling in the aftermath of the Restoration from the "experience of defeat," and negotiating the circumstances of a new, confusing, and dangerous world, Owen appears to have experienced some kind of political and theological collapse. Backing away from his hopes and disappointments, Owen's rejection of his aspirations and achievements in and after the civil wars became almost pathological—and at this distance it is impossible to know whether he was merely changing his mind, persuading himself in the process of accommodating his new circumstances, or even systemically misleading his readers. Few of those who had sat in Owen's lectures in Oxford could have expected his sudden rejection of scholastic method in *Θεολογουμενα παντοδαπα* (1661). Many of those MPs who had listened to his sermon after the execution of Charles I would have been surprised by his eulogizing of "our late king, of glorious memory" and his expressions of gratitude for the godliness of Charles II in his writings from the early 1660s.[54] Many of those who had ridden with Owen in the militia he raised for the defense of Oxford in 1655, or who had gathered in his home for the illegal conventicle from which government forces confiscated six or seven cases of pistols in 1661, would have been surprised to discover in 1664 that he "doth, and ever did, abhor swords, and guns, and crusades, in matters of religion and conscience, with all violence."[55] And none of those who had negotiated with him the terms of the Cromwellian religious settlement could have expected his abrupt dismissal of confessions of faith. These regulating statements of doctrine by which Christians should be reduced "to the same opinion in all things" were, he concluded, no more than "a Procrustes' bed." Owen felt sure that the effort to impose a confession of faith would be "vain and fruitless," for, "when Christians had any unity in the world, the Bible alone was thought to contain their religion," nor "will there ever, I fear, be again any unity among them until things are reduced to the same state and condition."[56] And yet this hesitation about theological manifestos might not have been entirely unexpected: this was, after all, the argument of the man who did more than any other to prepare the Savoy Declaration of Faith (1658), a platform of Congregational and perhaps national orthodoxy to which his writings would hardly ever refer.[57]

Owen's thinking was never static, therefore, despite the methodological assumptions of some of his best recent readers. The "freeze-frame" approach has perhaps been made possible because so much recent scholarship on Owen has developed around particular foci in particular periods, and so little of it has offered a general account of his thinking or has shown how his articulation of individual themes in theology evolved across time. But the triumph of this static view has been assisted by Owen himself. In his millions of published words, he almost never called attention to his many, sometimes significant, changes of position. Always a guarded writer, he never reflected upon his intellectual or theological journey. Continually deflecting attention away from himself, he never apologized, and never explained. Admitting that he had changed his mind on certain topics, he hesitated to explain when, where, and why. Of course, in the suddenly and dangerously changing contexts of the mid-seventeenth century, this policy of self-abnegation may have been less indicative of exemplary Christian humility than of a very human aspiration simply to survive. But the key question is that of motive—and it is in this respect that much of the available writing on Owen becomes less helpful. For while these recent and detailed accounts of Owen's thinking have offered acute and substantial readings of particular themes in his system, they have advanced far beyond the published accounts of his life. For, as Alec Ryrie properly notes, "Christians are more than creedal statements on legs."[58] Modern readers of Owen, schooled in an approach to his writing that emphasizes texts above contexts, may find themselves as surprised as Andrew Marvell did to discover that "this *J. O.* . . . had a Head, and a Mouth with a Tongue and Teeth in it, and Hands with Fingers and Nails upon them," that he was "a very Man as any of us are."[59]

II

Scholars have long felt the need for an adequate life of Owen. Cotton Mather believed that "the church of God is wronged, in that the life of the great John Owen is not written," reprinting Owen's full epitaph in a chapter dedicated to his memory in *Magnalia Christi Americana* (1702).[60] Succeeding generations of admirers attempted to redress the error. Two accounts of Owen's life were prepared in the early eighteenth century. The first biography appeared anonymously as part of the prefatory material for *Seventeen sermons* (1720). Owen's life was a "Subject which deserves the best Pen of the Age," the account began, and continued by insisting that it was to be "lamented" that "none of his Reverend and Learned Brethren have attempted it long e'er now." The sources of the anonymous account were a "Person of Quality, who was long Intimate with the Doctor, and a Member of his Congregation; with some Memoirs from others of the Doctor's Friends, and what cou'd be collected from his own Writings, and the occasional Characters given of him both his Friends and Enemies."[61] For all of its attempt at crowd sourcing, the anonymous account included a number of errors, among them a misstatement of the year of Owen's birth.[62] This account was almost immediately followed by another. *Memoirs of the life of John Owen* (1721) was prepared by John Asty, who was clearly frustrated by having been so rudely anticipated by a competing text.[63] Despite the fact that Asty's links to Owen went back almost eighty years to his father's involvement in the congregation in Coggeshall, his account was also brief and inaccurate, but it superseded the earlier narrative and, as preserving the recollections of Owen's friends, dominated discussions of his life for a century.[64] It was effectively replaced by the new biography prepared by William Orme for the twenty-eight-volume edition of Owen's works, which was edited by Thomas Russell (1826). Orme's work was the first credible biography of its subject, while occasionally evidencing "careless scholarship," and it provided the basis for the next of the Owen biographies, written by Andrew Thomson, which was published in the first volume of the Goold edition (1850).[65] Thomson's biography developed beyond Orme's conclusions and corrected a number of his mistakes, but it offered its own uncertainties, occasionally debating with Goold's explanatory annotations within the confines of the same edition.[66] These accounts remained current until Peter Toon's *God's statesmen: The life and work of John Owen* (1971) and R. Glynne Lloyd's *John Owen: Commonwealth puritan* (1972) brought to a conclusion the hagiographical tradition of Owen biography. Toon's work, the more reliable and more widely circulated of the two accounts, ought to have been superseded by Sarah Gibbard Cook's Harvard PhD thesis (1972), which intended to be compendious, referring to "nearly every known or commonly alleged fact of Owen's life." Cook's principal contribution was her sidestepping of Owen's theological engagement—which, she admitted, had been "more competently and comprehensively treated by other biographers"—to concentrate instead on his politics.[67] This change of focus was certainly important, for while Toon had cast Owen as an emerging republican, Cook's careful study of his political interventions offered a different conclusion, upon which later chapters in this book will reflect.[68] But Cook's work was never published, and its focus on politics was not developed, except in Donald Leggett's fine Cambridge MPhil thesis (2006), leaving so much of the best work on Owen's theology depending on sometimes limited accounts of his life and isolated from an adequate narrative of his times. Nevertheless, Cook's approach was compressed and combined with elements of theological biography in Richard L. Greaves's expansive entry in the *Oxford Dictionary of National Biography* (2004), which, while not the most extensive, remains the most definitive account of Owen's life to date.

Owen's biographical fortunes have risen in the decade since Greaves's account was published. In part this can be explained by Owen's status in the "new Calvinism" that is exercising increasing influence on global evangelicalism and which, according to a *Time* magazine cover story in March 2009, may become one of the key indicators of cultural change in the new millennium.[69] Evangelical publishers have offered a telling signal of Owen's newly talismanic status in their beginning to market biographies of Owen for children. These accounts are not always well grounded in the existing biographical literature. Irene Howatt's account of Owen (2003) described her subject as being soundly converted while a student at Oxford, where he objected to the "Romanist innovations" of the Laudian regime, and gaining the appreciation of an elder in St. Giles, Edinburgh, after the Cromwellian invasion of Scotland had destroyed its Presbyterian infrastructure: these claims do not accord with the likelihoods of Owen's biographical narrative.[70] A more recent, fuller, and more factual account by Simonetta Carr (2011) appears under the aegis of Joel Beeke, a senior Owen scholar, and reflects the degree of seriousness that is attached to Owen among many Reformed communities in the United States.[71] But the most recent biographical account of Owen appeared outside the religious culture of the "new Calvinism." Tim Cooper's *John Owen, Richard Baxter and the formation of Nonconformity* (2011) made a significant advance on the existing literature by documenting particular aspects of Owen's life over a dozen or so years. Cooper's work, though concentrating on the mid-century period, was detailed and compelling, and its focus was on Owen's relationship with Baxter, identifying telling moments of dissociation between these future leaders of dissent. Cooper's outstanding discussion was sensitive to psychological as well as cultural and theological factors, and opened up an important new approach to Owen's life, to which this book will also make a contribution. For, as Mark Burden properly noted in his review, Cooper's work was "unquestionably the most important study of Owen to have appeared in print."[72]

These many accounts of Owen's life, prepared for different kinds of audiences, perhaps conceal the extent to which their subject continues to challenge his students. Biographers of Owen have long been aware of the challenges they face. Toon began his work by describing his subject as "a man into whose innermost thoughts and feelings it is difficult if not impossible to enter."[73] Toon's response to this emotional deficit was to speculate, imagining, for example, his subject growing up in a home in which "the children were taught to pray, to read the Bible and to obey the commandments": "Each day they sat with the servants listening to their father expound a portion of Holy Scripture and pray for the country, the parish and for each of them individually. At their mother's knee they learned psalms and other portions of the Bible."[74] But the soft focus of Toon's account contrasts Owen's spare autobiography. Owen made little effort at self-fashioning. He did encourage his readers to practice life writing: "for a man to gather up his experiences of God, to call them to mind, to collect them, consider, try, improve them, is an excellent thing,—a duty practised by all the saints, commended in the Old Testament and the New."[75] Yet there is no evidence that he followed his own advice. A prolific but always guarded writer, he left nothing that could be compared to the diary of his exact contemporary and sometime clerical colleague, Ralph Josselin (1617–83).[76] And so, while Toon's comment does reflect the ideal family life that Puritan preachers often emphasized, we can only surmise that it was true of Owen's family in particular. For we need to surmise a great deal about his family: in his millions of published words, Owen made no reference to his mother or to his siblings, and only one reference to his father.[77] This oversight cannot be explained by their obscurity, for, as we will later see, two of his brothers pursued high-profile careers in Cromwellian Ireland, one of them continuing as an MP well into the 1660s, and as a plotter, long thereafter.[78] Neither do we know the names of all of Owen's ten children—each of whom predeceased him. Owen was reticent about referring to himself. He did not preserve any of the standard elements of Puritan life writing—an account of his conversion or call to the ministry, for example, or a diary or a memoir of family providences—though it is possible that these texts may have been lent out, as was common practice among the godly, and subsequently lost.[79] Owen remains, as Geoffrey F. Nuttall has recently noted, "strangely elusive."[80] This was, Owen explained to a theological adversary, a deliberate policy of self-abnegation: "Men are busy, and not so far concerned, I am sure, in me, nor (I am almost persuaded) in you, as to trouble themselves with the perusal of what belongs unto us personally."[81] And, he insisted, the silence was intentional:

> I dare not look upon myself of any such consideration to the world, as to write books to give them an account of myself (with whom they very little trouble their thoughts); to tell them my faith and belief; to acquaint them when I am well and when I am sick; what sin I have mortified most; what books I have read; how I have studied; how I go, and walk, and look; what one of my neighbours says of me, and what another; how I am praised by some and dispraised by others; what I do, and what I would have others do; what diligence, impartiality, uprightness, I use; what I think of other men.[82]

Or, as he later advised Sir John Hartopp, "the reason why I write so seldom unto any of my friends is because I have nothing write; at least nothing that is worth reading in my scribbling."[83] Even the rare moments of self-revelation that remain should not always be taken at face value. Owen's references to himself were always written in a context, and into a context. And so, in the early 1660s, his intense rejection of what he rather euphemistically described as "our late unhappy troubles," or his assertion that he "never had a hand in, nor gave consent unto, the raising of war in these nations, nor unto any political alteration in them," should not necessarily be trusted, as we will later see.[84] These occasional autobiographical references need to be investigated, however challenging may be the attempt to reconstruct their relevant contexts. But the focus of existing scholarship on Owen's ideas may be justified because he committed so little else to posterity.

Owen's autobiographical reluctance existed alongside a strong streak of self-confidence. He was certainly not a deferential reader of other men's work. We cannot access his reception of other writers through his marginalia: it is now impossible to trace the contents of his library and thus to read his noted comments or the evidence of reading strategies that might be contained in his papers.[85] Nor can we do much to trace his engagement with other writers in his footnotes. He clearly felt the expectation to indicate the sources of his ideas, but he generally refused to do so. Owen did not believe himself to be

> inthralled to any man or men, so that it should deserve a note when I dissent from them. Truly, I bless God I am utterly unacquainted with any such frame of spirit or bondage of mind as must be supposed to be in them whose dissent from other men is a matter of such observation. One is my Master, to whom alone my heart and judgment are in subjection.[86]

This would become, as we will later see, a rather pious justification for what might today be recognized as an occasional habit of plagiarism.[87] Nor should this gesturing toward humility be taken at face value. Owen's writing during his term as university vice chancellor reveals his admiration for Thomas Bradwardine (c. 1290–1349), who had also taught theology and held senior administrative positions in Oxford.[88] Owen argued that "there is none of greater name and eminency, for learning, devotion, and subtility" than Bradwardine—and did so even as he represented himself as his modern-day equivalent.[89] But perhaps the most suggestive evidence of Owen's self-regard may be his sitting for portraits. One of these, recently rediscovered in Dr. Williams's Library, London, represents a rather ruddy academic in the red robes of the senior administrator of the University of Oxford, wearing the academic attire that he would attempt to abolish in the later 1650s. We know nothing of the provenance of this portrait, except that, according to an uncatalogued memorandum, it was originally owned by the family of Owen's second wife, Dorothy D'Oyley, and was passed to the Towerton family of Stadhampton, being sold in 1840 to the Reverend John Field of Wallingford, from whom it was purchased by Samuel Morley, in 1858, who immediately presented it to New College, London, by which means it ended up in Dr Williams's Library, London. The other portrait, which has been attributed to John Greenhill (NPG 115, c. 1668), was purchased by the National Portrait Gallery in 1860, and is currently on display at Lyme Hall, Stockport. We know little about the motives behind or the circumstances of this visual text, though the fact that Greenhill is also associated with portraits of John Locke (NPG 3912, c. 1672–76), who had been a student of Owen's, and Anthony Ashley-Cooper, first earl of Shaftesbury (NPG 3893, c. 1672–73), may suggest that Owen's portrait was being made as part of a project to display dissent in the tense environment of Restoration England.[90] Whatever the background to the portraits, it is difficult to believe that Owen had not facilitated their making.

While Owen was reticent about self-disclosure in his published works, therefore, he does not appear to have been a particularly humble man. In a speech to the university community at Oxford in 1657, he acknowledged himself content that "in my forty-second year I have held not the lowest position in the camp, in the senate and in the University—indeed I hold the highest office that a man of my lot and position can attain in our Commonwealth." In fact, he continued, he had "in all things" conducted himself in such a manner that "I am not ashamed or sorry for any of my actions," rounding off this rather rare moment of public self-congratulation by quoting Horace to the effect that "I have lived constantly among the great."[91] But, as this strategic allusion suggests, the issue of audience may have been key to Owen's literary self-fashioning: while he was particularly concerned to reflect an ideal self in his orations to the university, he scrupulously refused to reflect upon himself or his character in his biblical or theological writing, other than during his fragmentantary, confused, and perhaps deliberately misleading response to the Restoration. Owen's reticence about himself, his family, and his cultural and intellectual contexts is unfortunate, for what he refused to provide, in terms of personal detail or ideological provenance, has become the very matter of modern biography. Neither does Owen offer resources to support the "material turn" that has done so much to open up the biographical study of similar subjects, particularly Jonathan Edwards, one century later.[92] While "studies were central to godly identity," we have very little sense of what any of Owen's writing environments might have looked like, or where he stored and how he moved or accessed his library as, after the Restoration, when his vocation became more mobile, it grew to around three thousand volumes.[93] This book will consider those objects associated with Owen that can be found, including his portraits and his gravestone, as part of its concern to engage with its subject in a material and social history of ideas.[94] But this study will necessarily prioritize the literary remains of a writer whose accuracy in self-awareness cannot always be taken for granted.

This lack of biographical data is not particularly unusual in the period, Andrew Hadfield has noted, for we know very little of the lives of most early modern writers.[95] The idea of a "speculation-free biography that simply relies on the facts" is "almost as much a fantasy as the far-fetched and distorted work that collapses fact and fiction," Hadfield has argued, and biographers are "inevitably . . . caught between the Scylla of speculation and the Charybdis of the limited archive."[96] For this reason, as we have noted, previous biographical work on Owen has tended to foreground his ideas and offer hagiographic accounts of his life. The growing body of Owen scholarship, with few notable exceptions, continues to focus on his thinking, sometimes isolating that thinking from any contexts other than those of the "great tradition" of theology in the Christian West. Cooper's work has very helpfully complicated the assumptions upon which much of this recent work has depended, finding new ways of calling attention to Owen's difficulty. This book, following Cooper, finds Owen more complex, subtle, and this-worldly—and ultimately more compelling—than many of the earlier accounts might suggest.

Unlike most of the earlier writing about Owen, therefore, this book will present a critical biography of its subject. And it will do so in terms of which Owen himself would approve. For, as Owen recognized,

> every kind of man has something to admire; every kind of man has also something to cause deserved displeasure: the man about whom we can speak nothing but words of praise does not exist: neither does he who ought to be despised on all accounts. We are men: only he, who feels that wisdom and godliness were born and will die with himself and the champions of the factions he earnestly supports, deserves to be considered to be beneath all other men.[97]

Owen's character evolved alongside aspects of his thinking. Writing about the 1650s, Cooper observed that "the hard part about describing the personality of John Owen is finding it in the first place" (though I would put money on his being a Myers-Briggs type INTJ).[98] Dismissing the idea that Owen's writings in the Cromwellian period reflect his grief over the death of his children, Cooper argues that Owen was "freewheeling and conniving," with a "tendency to anger and even petulance."[99] But those who knew him in later life suggested that his character was changing. Even Richard Baxter, who had many reasons to make a contrary judgement, believed that Owen's later writing demonstrated "more complying mildness, and sweetness, and peaceableness, than ever before."[100] Anthony à Wood described him as "one of the most genteel and fairest writers" among Puritans, "handling his Adversaries with far more civil, decent and temperate Language than many of his fiery Brethren, and by confining himself wholly to the Cause without the unbecoming mixture of personal slanders and reflection."[101] Asty, who had grown up in his congregation, also thought highly of Owen, and offered a pen-portrait that emphasized his nobility:

> as to his person his stature was tall, his visage grave and majestic, and withal comely he had the aspect of a Gentleman, suitable to his birth. . . . As to his temper he was very affable and courteous, familiar and sociable; the meanest person found an easy access to his converse and friendship. He was facetious and pleasant in his common discourse, jesting with his acquaintance, but with sobriety and measure; a great master of his passions especially that of anger: he was of a serene and even temper, neither elated with honour, credit, friends or estate, nor deprest with troubles and difficulties. His carriage was genteel, in nothing mean: He was generous in his favours.[102]

Different writers, focusing on different periods of his life, have offered very different perspectives of their subject. Owen has always divided his biographers: he has been widely respected for his intellectual gifts, but he has not been widely admired.

III

It is for the reasons discussed in the previous section that *John Owen and English Puritanism: Experiences of defeat* concentrates on the development of Owen's ideas in the contexts in which they intervened. This emphasis on the "social history of ideas" borrows its methodological impulses from those intellectual historians whose work has taught scholars of ideas to foreground language, genres, and contexts, and which has recently been advanced within religious history, but which has yet to make much of an impact upon the study of Owen.[103] Paying attention to the significance of the linguistic turn, this book will avoid the errors of idealism, in which Owen's work might be studied without regard to the contexts in which it was written, and realism, in which Owen's work might be explained as being causally determined by its cultural, economic, or personal contexts.[104] It will offer an account of Owen's life within the broader context of the period in which he lived—and, as the events of a life do not necessarily map directly onto moments of political change, will not simply retell a familiar narrative from his perspective. This book's calling attention to the changing circumstances of Owen's publishing career will help readers avoid the tendency—as seen in Perry Miller and, more recently and, ironically, in some new historicist literary critics—of understanding individual texts as speaking on behalf of the society that produced them.[105] Instead, building on the approach of my earlier contribution to this series, *God's Irishmen: Theological debates in Cromwellian Ireland* (2007), this book will pay attention to the disputative contexts in which Owen's work was produced, disseminated, and received, by reconstructing the particular sets of circumstances that his writing addressed, and by paying attention to materiality and to the forms in which these interventions were expressed.

Students of Owen, as we have noted, have found that the temptation to idealism is acute. This temptation reflects a larger difficulty: intellectual historians have often been criticized for wanting to "reduce art and literature to the expression of formal ideas."[106] But I am writing this book as a cultural historian of religious ideas trained in departments of literary studies, and so I share the assumptions of a growing number of scholars across disciplines that the form of an argument, as well as the materiality of the medium in which it is communicated, should be considered alongside its content.[107] Of course, this is certainly the case in terms of genres, but book historians insist that "forms" relating to a text's status as a material object are also essential components of its proper interpretation. This ought to be a particular concern for the study of Owen as it has been developed over the last one hundred and fifty years. For the Goold edition's starkly homogenous formatting of two dozen identical volumes was designed for a mid-Victorian print marketplace, and inevitably concealed the rich material variety of the seventeenth-century editions it purported to represent, as well as their occasional ideological diversity. In addition, Goold's arrangement of Owen's texts can be misleading, as in volumes three and four, for example, which combine six different treatises published at different times under one general title, or as in *Of communion with God*, which provides the text of the first edition with the preface to the second, which was produced in a very different set of political and ecclesiastical circumstances. Goold invites a different method of reading Owen than that advanced in this study in social and biographical theology. Furthermore, Goold often replicates the errors of the earlier editions, errors that Owen himself had lamented.[108] To his credit, Goold did recognize the problem, understanding that the principal difficulty of making an accurate critical edition lay in Owen's habit of quotation from "the Greek and Latin Fathers," and he admitted that problems abounded to "a degree that is a scandal to the British press."[109] But he almost entirely gave up on addressing the problem. Recognizing these difficulties, modern scholars may be tempted to circumvent these text-critical difficulties by downloading facsimiles of early modern publications from the Early English Books Online (EEBO) database. But neither does the extensive use of online archives necessarily solve the problem. Electronic facsimiles provide an illusion of readerly immediacy, but they cannot escape their own standardizing formats in expanding or reducing texts of enormous material variety to the margins of the standard manuscript folio page (A4). Neither can they replicate other conditions of engagement with early modern texts, including binding, varieties of annotation, evidences of usage and ownership, and the often haphazard collecting of materials by multiple authors in single bound editions, which can reveal so much about the conditions and intellectual habits of Owen's first readers. "Protestants *used* their books, dog-earing pages, underlining passages and writing in their margins," Andrew Cambers has recently noted, in his magisterial account of *Godly reading* (2014).[110] The making of marginalia was a particular Puritan practice.[111] This prevalence for readerly intervention makes the very careful preservation of so much of Owen's writing unusual, as in the case of the copies of Owen in Marsh's Library, Dublin, which were owned by Edward Stillingfleet, and presumably were used to research his rebuttal of Owen's ideas. But even when they reveal virtually nothing of the reader's engagement with the text, there can be no substitute for engaging with early modern texts in early modern archives.[112]

This book's aspiration to methodological self-consciousness therefore attempts to move beyond the standard conventions of intellectual biography, a subgenre of biography "rooted in the study of texts," which, Anthony Grafton has observed, has "fused a concentration on context and development with close attention to the text that had formed the center of past intellectuals' lives."[113] It is much less skeptical than Nicholas Tyacke as to the value of biography as a heuristic form, not least because the formal requirements of the genre push the author past historians' tendency to operate within specific periods with discrete historiographies, and allow the author to understand his subject "from the inside out," and in a life cycle that overrules the standard boundary markers of early modern historiography.[114] My own sense in preparing this book is that biography is an especially demanding medium that continually refuses to permit intellectual shortcuts: at times, when I was overwhelmed by the demands of reading Owen's millions of words in their very different contexts, I felt that he could not die soon enough. A number of works have appeared in the last few years to offer a new social perspective on the history of early modern religion, most notably Cooper's *John Owen, Richard Baxter and the formation of nonconformity* (2011) and Alex Ryrie's *Being Protestant in Reformation Britain* (2013). This book follows Cooper in developing social and biographical contexts in an account of historical theology: for all of Owen's reticence about self-disclosure, his biography allows us to see the revolution and its aftermath from the inside out.[115]

This book will therefore approach its task by drawing upon recent interest in the production and consumption of texts. Building on the recent attention paid to the reconstruction of interpretive communities, this book will reconstruct some of the audiences in which Owen's writing was being consumed and reshaped, discussing, for example, Lucy Hutchinson's redaction and translation of *Θεολογουμενα παντοδαπα* (1661), which consistently temper Owen's oppositional rhetorical style for purposes of her own.[116] And this book will pay attention to the different status of a sermon published by Owen within weeks of its delivery and a sermon recorded in an auditor's notebook that finds its way into print after a century of delay had rendered its early contexts forgotten, while remembering that both texts exist at some distance from the "lost acoustic world" of the sermon's first auditors.[117] This book will consider the limited evidence of the circulation through the book trade of his published texts.[118] And, especially in describing his relationship with Andrew Marvell and the coterie of dissenting writers in the later part of the century, this book will suggest strategies by which future scholarship might uncover Owen's broader cultural work in the construction of English political dissent.[119]

IV

As these literary relationships suggest, Owen was an observer of and participant in many of the political, theological, aesthetic, and cultural revolutions of the mid-seventeenth century.[120] Any account of his life necessarily intervenes at a "central and attractive meeting point for many disciplines," at the intersection of print culture, politics, religion, aesthetics, and social nonconformity.[121] Building on Quentin Skinner's arguments in *Reason and rhetoric in the philosophy of Hobbes* (1996), and the related concerns of Richard Muller, this study pays attention to the intellectual contexts in which its subject's ideas were articulated and received, reflecting upon the history of ideas and their discursive locations, while also attending to the semiotic potential of Owen's interventions and to their illocutionary force.[122] This book is unapologetic about focusing on a religious writer to explicate something of the wider cultures of the period, not least because "most early twenty-first-century historians of the civil war would now agree that religious concerns played a major role in causing the breakdown of political stability and the slide towards full-scale internal war in England"—and, we might add, Ireland and Scotland, too, and for many years after the civil war.[123] Owen's age was intractably religious, and even those pushed from its margins to the center and back again can reveal something of its character.

John Owen and English Puritanism therefore offers a new way of reading one of the most important of the seventeenth-century theologians, developing not a systematic exposition of his thought but an account of his religious biography. It develops a broader interest in Owen's texts to offer an interdisciplinary account of a "Renaissance man," describing the cultures in which Owen was acting, writing, and being read. It develops a broader interest in Owen's contexts to offer a richer and socially and culturally complex account of his times, sharing the tendency among historians of early modern ideas to concentrate on themes associated with the emergence of modernity by paying attention to his critical interest in republican ideas and other of the emerging elements of modernity, while also recognizing Owen as a receptor and reformer of the medieval scholastic tradition. This book adopts a broader chronological focus than much of the earlier work, which tended to be most interested in Owen's experience of the Cromwellian period. And this book makes these interventions in a narrative that draws upon the theoretical issues raised in recent historical and literary writing on the period. Above all else, however, this book attempts to be less about sets of ideas than about a person—"ambitious in youth, somewhat depressive and hypochondriac in later years, and conservative and authoritarian throughout his life"—as well as the movement to which this person helped give birth.[124] For this is a book about the texts, cultures, and contexts of John Owen, English Puritanism, and their many experiences of defeat.

I

Apprentice Puritan

BY THE TIME of John Owen's birth in 1616, the Protestant Reformation was poised to enter its second century. Almost one hundred years earlier, Martin Luther's display of 95 theses had begun a revolution in western Christendom. Luther's actions, on 31 October 1517, initiated the social and ecclesiological experiment associated with Protestant reform, unleashing an extraordinary and unprecedented sequence of cultural, political, and military consequences. Throughout the later sixteenth century, the competing imperial aspirations of Protestant and Catholic monarchies were reflected in geopolitical crises and military conflicts. While shifting alliances between rival powers did at times stretch across confessional divisions, they tended to return to sectarian type in moments of pressure. And there were many such periods of tension. For the Protestant Reformation shattered the confessional unity of Europe, called into question the links between early modern believers and the church of the fathers and the saints, and, in widespread attacks on the idea of purgatory, flatly denied traditional assumptions about the connection between the living and the dead. In so doing, the forces of reform radically and traumatically reformulated the political, ecclesiastical, and personal relationships that had underpinned the Christian faith of Europe.

The country into which Owen was born had not escaped the destabilizing forces of religious change. The reformation in England had advanced upon an intensely conservative and elite-centered reorganization of state power and ecclesiastical property, and for many, perhaps most, of its participants, it had not been a distinctly religious affair. Historians are currently re-evaluating the character of English Protestant reform. While older accounts of the period tend to describe the Reformation as a necessary stage en route to the condition of modernity, recent work has argued that the ideas and values of early Protestants were much less modern than has often been assumed, and that their victory was much less immediate, as Englishmen and women clung determinedly to the devotional and ethical habits and theological assumptions of the medieval church.[1] Historians are now generally agreed that "medieval English Catholicism was, up to the very moment of its dissolution, a highly successful enterprise," supporting "a quite remarkable degree of lay involvement and investment," and maintaining "a corresponding degree of doctrinal orthodoxy," which the forces of Protestant reform unexpectedly interrupted.[2] This new perspective on the initial impact of the social aspects of the success of English Catholicism has prompted a reconsideration of the ideology that worked to undermine it. Perhaps inevitably, historians recognize that the "Elizabethan formularies were open to a wide variety of interpretation at both the popular and more elite levels."[3] The new perspective on the English Reformation insists, in short, that it was muddled in its thinking and pragmatic in its policy.

But if its policy was pragmatic, the political implications of Protestant reform were clear. By the end of the sixteenth century, Queen Elizabeth I, old and increasingly unpopular, had not identified an heir. The dynastic politics of the period threatened to impose a new monarch with a Catholic faith on the English population. James VI of Scotland, who was known as a competent Calvinist theologian, came to the throne in London in 1603 to secure the English Protestant succession. His accession benefited from the economic circumstances of the early years of his reign. England enjoyed a trade boom after the end of the Spanish war in 1604. Trade was lifted by a general improvement in agricultural conditions and in a series of better than average harvests in 1618, 1619, and 1620.[4] But the accession of the Scottish king to the English throne also created a series of intractable political crises. James's attempts to style his newly composite monarchy as "Great Britain" failed to gain traction on either side of the Tweed, reflecting Scottish political apathy and English political hostility toward his goal of the "perfect union" of legal, administrative, and religious institutions across his multiple kingdoms. While a large part of the financial difficulty of the period was caused by the spiraling costs of the court, it was not entirely James's fault that the British experiment failed. The difficulty of balancing governmental responsibilities in the contexts of competing institutions in England, Scotland, and Ireland generated the financial, constitutional, and religious tensions between the crown and Parliament that characterized the reign of James and his son, Charles I, and which led, however contingently, to the suspension of Parliament in 1629, the outbreak of civil war in the three kingdoms in 1638, and the chaos that ensued.

Many English Protestants were most concerned by the religious challenges that emerged in the early years of James's reign. By 1603, a substantial network of "Puritans" had organized a vigorous and effective underground movement promoting the further reform of the English church.[5] The hierarchy as a whole had moved from the ambiguity of the early Reformation to embrace the Calvinist theology that had become normative across the church by the end of the sixteenth century. But Puritans wanted to move beyond that ideological consensus to promote further reform in the church's liturgy, sacraments, and practice. Their critique of key practices within the establishment was reflected in hostility to vestments and the use of the prayer book. Toward the end of the sixteenth century, their argument for the reform of the church appeared to have gained significant momentum. But their unease about the new king's religious preferences was rapidly confirmed. For, "shortly after the accession of James I," Nicholas Tyacke has observed, "a darkness seems to descend over the history of Puritanism," as it became increasingly obvious that the "concerted Elizabethan attempt to remodel the English Church along more Protestant lines" were no more likely to succeed under James.[6] James postured at engaging with the Puritan faction by convening the Hampton Court Conference (1604), at which the godly could air their goals for further reform of the church, but he did not advance any of their ecclesiological aspirations.[7] The only clear achievement of the conference—an agreement on the need to publish a new translation of the Bible—turned into a project to remove the language of religious protest from available copies of Scripture. The new translation, which became known as the Authorised Version (1611), made a number of suggestive translation decisions, preferring "church" to "congregation," "bishop" to "elder," and the opacity of nuanced and ambiguous translations to the politically loaded and theologically specific annotations of the old Geneva Bible. James was pushing the church in a direction that reflected entirely different values from those of the Puritans.

Some of the outmaneuvered Puritans plotted a new course toward further reform.[8] William Bradshaw published *English Puritanisme* (1605) in the aftermath of the Hampton Court Conference to consolidate the position of the godly. In the thoroughgoing ecclesiological revolution that he proposed, Christians were to build congregations of "visible saints" within parish structures, and these congregations would recognize no ecclesiastical authority above themselves.[9] Bradshaw developed his new strategy while continuing to minister within the Church of England, and while frequently being harassed for his nonconformity. He denounced separatists, those who took central elements of his argument at face value and moved entirely outside the boundaries of the establishment, moving sometimes to the Low Countries and eventually to the New World in pursuit of religious freedom. Their gesture of defiance was in fact an admission of defeat: the separatists' recognition that they would now operate outside the establishment was indicative of their failure to reform it. The extent to which the world had changed around the Puritans was signaled in the outbreak of the Thirty Years War in 1618, when James refused to enter the conflict in support of his daughter and son-in-law, the beleaguered Protestants Frederick V and Elizabeth of Bohemia. His failure to develop a consistently faith-based foreign policy, even when the security of members of his family hung in the balance, was a very clear signal to many English Protestants that James was not the godly monarch they had anticipated. Nevertheless, most supporters of further reform remained with Bradshaw inside the Church of England, compensating for their outward compromises by nurturing their spiritual life in innovative habits of personal devotion, such as keeping spiritual diaries, while theorizing the ideal shape of a purified church settlement in secret meetings of the godly.[10] Those who paid attention to trends in court and clerical appointments could see that James was becoming much less firmly committed to the Calvinist theology for which he had once been well known.

This was the world of uneasy conformity in which John Owen was raised. He did not grow up in a religious world that was moving inexorably toward the Puritan triumphs of the civil wars, as some accounts of his life have assumed, but in a religious world in which Puritan aspirations for the reform of the Church of England had decisively failed. Owen did not come from a family of radicals.[11] His parents, for example, did not follow the custom of so many others in the period—especially in southeast England—of choosing to provide their children with "godly virtue" names, that curious differentiator of Puritan culture.[12] Neither did they participate in the emigration projects, in which, Owen later appreciatively remembered, some years before he explored the prospect of emigration for himself, "many in this very nation ... many thousands, left their native soil, and went into a vast and howling wilderness in the utmost parts of the world, to keep their souls undefiled and chaste to their dear Lord Jesus."[13] Later in life, he remembered that his father, Henry Owen, had been "a Nonconformist all his days, and a painful labourer in the vineyard of the Lord."[14] Whatever assumptions we make about Owen's childhood experiences, or his very limited reflection on them, we need to remember that they were formed in the home of a moderate Puritan minister, whose "painful labour" endured the bitterness of the compromises that were required by an establishment unsympathetic to his godly ideals. John Owen, in childhood, learned the experience of defeat.

I

Even as England's king, church, and nation rejected Puritan aspirations for their reform, the Oxfordshire family into which John Owen was born maintained a commitment to "religious Puritanism" and to "political loyalty."[15] His father, Henry, appears to have been a student at Oxford and a schoolmaster in Stokenchurch, Oxfordshire, before being ordained as priest by John Bridges, bishop of Oxford, in May 1613. He had moved to the parish in Stadhampton, also known as Stadham, a village several miles south of Oxford, by 1625, where he served as curate, and then as rector, before moving to Hurley and disappearing from the extant documentary record.[16] Owen seems to have admired his father, as well as his strategy of quietly resisting the establishment.[17] It is not clear when Henry married, but his four sons and two daughters were raised in Stadhampton, and John, throughout his life, seems to have regarded the small town as his home.[18]

It may be significant that Owen's recollection of his father's "painful labour" was one of a tiny handful of reflections upon his childhood. Nothing is known of his mother, and very little of the wider family: Owen's published writings make no mention of any family member other than this brief paternal reference. They never reflect upon his childhood experiences, or whether the family enjoyed a "pretty midnight story," which he later remembered would be "told to bring children asleep."[19] The household does not appear to have been wealthy, as the circumstances of Owen's matriculation as a student may suggest, but it did retain some significant connections. He certainly benefited from the family's extended Welsh networks, being named as heir to the estates of the unknown uncle who financed his education: this patronage perhaps augmented the cultural loyalty that would later have Owen address individuals there as "cousin" and appeal to government to support the provision of godly clergy to the principality.[20] Neither do we know much of what life in Stadhampton might have been like, though the village life of Essex, where Owen would fulfill his first pastoral charges, has been artfully illustrated in some of the most exciting historical anthropological work of the last half-century.[21]

Some details of the Owen family are nevertheless clear. John had at least three brothers and two sisters. He and his brothers William (born 1612/13) went up to Queen's College, Oxford, at the same time, graduating with their BA and MA degrees in 1632 and 1635.[22] William subsequently entered pastoral ministry, being ordained as deacon in March 1634 and as priest in May 1635 by John Bancroft, bishop of Oxford, and being licensed to preach in the diocese of Salisbury in September 1635, becoming rector of Remenham between 1648 and 1660, at which point he disappears from the extant documentary record.[23] Philemon and Henry, the two younger brothers, began their careers in the military. This move, when considered alongside their elder brother's unhappy experiences at Oxford, may suggest that their father believed the changing religious expectations of the university required his younger sons to find new opportunities for advancement, or may simply reflect the family's declining financial circumstances, or the widespread militarization of the 1640s and 1650s. Philemon (1622–c. 1651) attended All Souls College, Oxford, sometime after his elder brothers had left the university, and rose to the rank of captain in the New Model Army before his death in Cromwell's Irish campaign was recorded in autumn 1651.[24] Henry (?–fl. 1683), who does not seem to have attended university, progressed from captain to major in the New Model Army, serving in Lord Castlestuart's regiment in Trim, county Meath, in 1648, before joining Commissary-General John Reynolds's regiment of horse, in which he served alongside his brother Philemon, before becoming governor of Maryborough (1651), now Portlaoise, sheriff of Queen's County (1653), now county Laois, and entering Parliament as an Irish MP (1656). It is tempting to speculate that the Owen brothers had particularly close relationships—after all, William and John went to Oxford together, and Henry and Philemon served in the same regiment in Ireland. It might be telling that when Cromwell wanted to persuade Owen to join the Irish expedition, he sent one of the brothers as an advocate.[25] But Henry's later support for the crown being offered to Cromwell indicates that a significant political difference had emerged between himself and John by the mid-1650s, as later chapters of this work will illustrate, and it is not clear that any of the family's other clergymen followed John into Independent congregations.[26] Owen made no comment in any of his publications on his brothers' respectable military and political careers, though he was never reluctant to make capital of his relationships with other strategically placed men in his network: perhaps Owen felt he had nothing to gain from Henry's relational equity as their political inclinations and friendship networks began to diverge. If their paths did diverge, they may have subsequently reconciled, as this book's discussion of later Stuart conspiracy will suggest. It is notable that Henry and his children were to be well provided for in Owen's will—both his son, also called Henry, and his daughter, Heneretta, were to be generously treated.[27]

Owen's sisters, as might be expected, left fewer records. One sister, un-named in the sources, became the mother of John Singleton, who studied in Christ Church, Oxford, while his uncle was dean of the college, and she may have had the most immediate sibling relationship with John during the

1650s.[28] (John Singleton would have studied in Christ Church alongside Roger Puleston, whom Owen recognized as "my young cousin," and whose mother, Lady Elizabeth Puleston, was a patron of another Christ Church student, Philip Henry, the future leader of dissent.[29]) The other sister, Hester, married John Hartcliffe, a curate in her father's church, who became his replacement as the rector of Stadhampton. During the 1660s, Owen's closest sibling relationship may have been with Hester: after the Restoration, as we will see, Owen moved back to Stadhampton, and gathered an Independent congregation in the same village in which his brother-in-law served as parish minister, with his children growing up as neighbors to their cousins. Hartcliffe was ejected in 1662, becoming a Presbyterian nonconformist, while retaining sufficient resources to send his son John to Eton, Oxford, and Cambridge.[30] Owen later wrote a reference to support John's appointment as headmaster of the Merchant Taylor's School.[31] Three of Hester's children, John, Philemon and Samuel, were mentioned in Owen's will.[32] Like those of so many other women in the period—though not, notably, like some of those who most admired their best-known brother—the lives of the Owen sisters remain obscure.

But much of this was in the future when Owen began to attend, at an unknown age, the school that met in a private home in All Saints parish in Oxford under the supervision of Edward Sylvester, a graduate of Balliol College with no obvious Puritan sympathies or clerical status.[33] The school was based five or six miles from the Owen household, and we do not know whether Owen boarded there. It is clear, nevertheless, that Sylvester was teaching a number of students who would go on to assume positions of influence in the religious and political life of the seventeenth century, including William Chillingworth, the godson of William Laud and future author of *The religion of Protestants a safe way to salvation* (1638), who attended the school before 1618.[34] Perhaps it was in this environment that Owen was exposed to the stories that ridiculed his family's convictions: he recalled hearing, "when I was a boy . . . a hundred times," slanderous stories about "Brownists and Puritans," which he later discovered to have been "forgeries of Pagans . . . imposed on the primitive Christians."[35] In the absence of much evidence, we cannot assume that Sylvester's school was confirming the godly predilections of Owen's family. Yet some of his school friendships proved to be enduring, and sometimes in surprising ways. Owen's contemporaries included Henry Wilkinson (1616/17–90), future Presbyterian minister and principal of Magdalen Hall, and John Wilkins (1614–72), a Calvinist theologian who would become warden of Wadham College, brother-in-law of the Protector, and a Restoration bishop.[36] And many of Sylvester's former pupils would appear to have held him in high regard: Owen, Wilkinson, and Wilkins, who each became heads of Oxford colleges, attended the annual dinner held in Sylvester's honor until his death in 1653.[37]

Owen's schooldays came to an end in 1628, when at the age of twelve he began his studies at Queen's College, Oxford. This was not an unusually young age for university entrance in the early seventeenth century, and it reflected the purpose and nature of education in the period. It is not clear why Henry Owen decided to send his sons to Queen's, as it had not been the college that he had attended. Perhaps Henry Owen believed the religious environment of the college would counteract the mixed environment of Sylvester's school. Perhaps he remembered its earlier reputation the "largest college in Oxford" whose provost, Henry Airay (1599–1616), had been "leader of the Calvinist party in the University."[38] Or perhaps he was attracted by its reputation for intellectual vitality: the college's recently appointed provost, Christopher Potter, after his controversial election, had improved discipline, encouraged Greek, Hebrew, and Arabic learning, and homiletic training.[39] Potter had a reputation that would have endeared him to the godly, though by the late 1620s he was moving away from predestinarian theology and was advocating an irenic approach to the discussion of theological differences—positions initially identified with the party of Arminians then rising within the English church.[40] This was part of a wider cultural shift within the university: one fellow of Queen's noted in March 1627 that the vice chancellor of the university had removed himself from Oxford when he should have "censured" a colleague "for his Arminianisme: suspicious."[41] This movement away from Calvinist dogmatism accelerated after Charles forbade discussion of controversial theological subjects such as election to salvation in 1628, and in 1630 appointed William Laud, who by then had become archbishop of Canterbury, as the university's chancellor.

Laud's new statutes for the university consolidated previous pedagogical practice and provide us with clear guidance as to the content of an Oxford undergraduate education in the early seventeenth century. Undergraduates were expected to attend twice weekly lectures on grammar and rhetoric. After the first year, students were expected to attend lectures on logic and moral philosophy, while also attending the disputations. From the third year, students attended lectures by the Regius Professor of Greek on principal classical authors, while also participating in two disputations. Students for the MA were required to continue disputing while also giving six lectures, attending lectures on geometry, astronomy, natural philosophy, metaphysics, history, Hebrew, and Greek.[42] But not everything about Owen's college experience was so enlarging.

If Owen had hoped to find in Queen's an atmosphere congenial to his family's Puritan temperament, he was to be disappointed, for he found himself, in his early teens, at the center of a sharply contested theological and ecclesiastical debate. In December 1628, one fellow of Queen's noted that Potter was being accused, perhaps unfairly, of Arminianism.[43] At the end of Owen's second year of study at Queen's, in June 1630, and, suggestively, as Laud was installed as the new chancellor, Potter's commitment to the new theology was becoming clearer. The college community became embroiled in controversy when Potter recommended that elemental components of Reformed theology and piety should be debated without polemic, indicating that it was no longer essential that these doctrines should be unhesitatingly defended. Potter's push toward the new theology was contested by some of his colleagues: John Langhorne, senior fellow of Queen's, who had refused to support his election as provost, engaged in a contest with Potter that extended over several years before coming to a head in March 1630, when he threatened to "stilletto Mr Provost."[44] In September 1631, another fellow, Edward Cookes, was reported to have condemned Potter as a "dishonest man & persecutor of all goodnes."[45] Some of these colleagues would have understood the implications of Potter's ruling as Owen must have done: Queen's students should no longer assume that these elemental components of international Reformed orthodoxy were upheld in the doctrinal basis of the Church of England.

The ensuing controversy prompted Potter to clarify his approach in a manner that must have astonished the godly, however much it suggests that he was functioning as a stalking horse for the theological and liturgical ambitions of the new chancellor. In late August 1630, Potter rejected the doctrine of reprobation as being "repugnant to ... Scripture, ... contrary to the ... mercy of ... God, ... contrary to the constant judgm[en]t of antiquity, of many reformed Churches, and of plaine reason," and followed this assertion with general critique of the conclusions of the Synod of Dort (1618–19).[46] It is hard to exaggerate the shock this must have been for godly young men like Owen, for whom the canons of Dort had become a touchstone of truth.[47] The Church of England had been represented at the international ecumenical council of Reformed churches at which the canons had been negotiated, after all, and James himself had taken an eager interest in its workings.[48] In fact, its decrees, which offered a thorough rebuttal of the ideas of Jacob Arminius then disturbing the Dutch Reformed churches, had been published, with the volume being dedicated to James. But this progress toward international Reformed orthodoxy, in which James had been a figurehead, had come to a standstill in England, and that by the instruction of the king. The rise of Arminianism in England then became another stage in the collective trauma of the country's religious revolution: the ideals and convictions that had been carefully identified as replacing those of the medieval church, and which had been painstakingly negotiated with European Protestant churches, under the patronage of the monarch, were suddenly redundant. For many Puritans, the rise of the Arminians could mean nothing less than the dismantling of the Reformation.

Potter advanced upon this remarkable attack on the international orthodoxy of the Reformed churches. He covertly prepared a new edition of Jacobus Acontius's *Stratagemata Satanae* (1631), a tract by an Italian Protestant, which argued that the Christian faith should advance with a slim doctrinal basis and a broad toleration of other faiths, though, as his most recent biographer suggests, "much of Oxford would have known Potter was behind this."[49] In February 1629, Laud instigated a public fast, on which meat was forbidden but fish permitted.[50] In April 1629, Potter encouraged Crosfield not to "take upon trust blasphemyes for Catholike doctrines," but to "study & read well before I peremptory resolve," hinting that some who had taken public positions against Arminian theology would change their position if they could do so without loss of honor.[51] Certainly by the summer of 1631, the evidence against Potter was sufficiently damning for Giles Thorne, a fellow of Balliol College, in a sermon to the university community, to denounce him as a full-blown Pelagian.[52] But this repudiation of Potter's interventions succeeded only in demonstrating that he continued to have some very influential supporters. On 22 August, Thorne, with some other "young factious men," was put on trial before Charles I, in a judicial session that met at Woodstock. Potter defended himself against Thorne's accusations of his Pelagianism by explaining that he had encouraged students in the college to read Augustine, among other ancient defenders of orthodoxy. Thorne's accusations were consequently dismissed, and he was expelled from the university.[53] But the attack on the doctrinal basis of the English church continued. In September 1631, the Lincoln College chapel was "dedicated or consecrated to the blessed Virgin Mary & all soules."[54] In the same year, Potter persuaded two of the college fellows, Thomas Crosfield and Francis Coventry, to prepare the translation of Hugo Grotius's *True religion explained*, which was published anonymously in 1632.[55]

Learning from the fate of Giles Thorne, those moving in opposition to Potter took their criticisms underground. In the late summer of 1632, Potter was the subject of a verse satire, entitled "The academicall army of epidemicall Arminians," which circulated in the university. This charge of Arminianism may have been more precise than Thorne's allegations of Potter's Pelagianism. For Potter continued to advance in the affections of William Laud, who was identified as the chief promoter of Arminian ideas in the university community. The archbishop of Canterbury and chancellor of the university encouraged his godson, William Chillingworth, who like Owen had been a pupil in Sylvester's school, to consult Potter in relation to his reversion from Catholicism to the communion of the Church of England, and attempted to advance Potter to a canonry in Windsor. One year later, Potter published *Want of charity in answer to charity mistaken* (1633), by the Jesuit Edward Knott (who published as "Matthew Wilson"). The edition was dedicated to Charles I and claimed to be published "in obedience to your Ma[jes]ties particular commandement," but its sensitivity to and qualified appreciation for the Roman Catholic faith must have surprised many Oxford Protestants. Perhaps this was the context for the anonymous satirical claim made in 1636 that "Dr. Potter is converted and they preach much of the salvation of the Heathens."[56] Meanwhile, Potter continued to press for conformity to the new university statutes and dress codes, which Laud had introduced, and in 1634 praised the beautification of churches and encouraged the Queen's community to bow at the name of Jesus.[57] In November 1634, Crosfield recorded Potter's victory over "ye former faction in our Chapel . . . not bowing at ye name of Jesus & ye Altar, standing up at ye creed & Gospell, wearing of surplesse," and dismissed the protestors as exponents of a "tick tack-conformity."[58] Of course, Owen would also have been learning of the dangers of radical religion. In February 1627, news reached Queen's of a "sect of Edringtonians," led by a "boxmaker" and based in London, and, in 1628, the Queen's community became aware that some "Brownists" had been arrested, "ye leader whereof is not ashamed to call himself one of ye 12 apostles, & ye King subject to him."[59] But Oxford itself was most troubled by the "subtile-close Arminian" threat.[60] It is hardly surprising that Henry Owen sent Philemon elsewhere. Queen's College would have been a tense and unhappy environment for the sons of a "painful" nonconformist.

Whatever the tensions it engendered, a university education could not have been anything other than helpful for a young man in search of connections. The college community into which Owen entered was not large, but it was producing a network of significant figures.[61] Among Owen's contemporaries at Queen's was George Bate (MA, 1629), who became physician to Charles I, Oliver Cromwell, and Charles II; George Benson, future dean of Hereford Cathedral, who began his studies at Queen's in 1627; Robert Napier, who began his studies in 1628, who would become receiver-general and auditor of the duchy of Cornwall under both Charles I and Charles II; John Shaw, who spent a year in the college around 1628 before moving to Brasenose and beginning a career in which he would become known as a firm churchman; Henry Fletcher, a future baronet who raised a regiment for the king and was killed at Rowton Heath in 1645; Sir Edward Turnor, a future judge and speaker of the House of Commons; and John Rushworth, who was a relative of Sir Thomas

Fairfax, and who later acted as a press agent during the Cromwellian invasion of Scotland.[62] Queen's was also producing some notable figures among the godly. Perhaps, from Owen's point of view, the most significant "old boy" of Queen's was Obadiah Sedgwick (matriculated 1616), who in 1639 became vicar of Coggeshall, Essex, and whose later membership in the Westminster Assembly would create the vacancy that Owen would fill in his second pastoral charge.[63]

It is not likely that Owen moved easily among the college's social elite. When he matriculated alongside his brother William on 4 November 1631, he was listed in the college register as a "bateller"—an "undergraduate of a rather low social and financial status."[64] Asty (1721) provides the most information for Owen's years as a student, drawing on the memories of near contemporaries, observing that his finances were provided by a wealthy uncle, and that his rather unhealthy devotion to study was driven by his ambition for a successful career. Owen was a dedicated student, investing long hours in study, and often sleeping little more than four hours per night.[65] This intense devotion to study might have been expected of the son of a "painful nonconformist": reading was "vital to the practice of Puritanism," Cambers has recently asserted, and an intense devotion to study was among the "strategies of alienation" developed by the godly in early seventeenth-century England.[66] But this devotion to study may also have been the means by which Owen coped with the religious tensions of his college, for, "being naturally of an aspiring mind, he applied himself very close to his studies, to accomplish these ends he had so much in view."[67]Whatever their impulse, Owen's studies were clearly formative. His tutor in logic and philosophy was Thomas Barlow, a Calvinist and future Royalist, who became keeper of the Bodleian Library during Owen's tenure as vice chancellor of Oxford and who was later appointed bishop of Lincoln. Barlow schooled Owen in Aquinas's *Summa*, an experience that made a lifelong impression on the appreciative student, profoundly shaping his theological method, as Cleveland's recent work has shown.[68] It is not clear how much Owen benefited from the broader cultural life of the university. His tutor in music was Thomas Wilson: it is difficult to make sense of the long-term value of this aspect of his education.[69] Neither does Owen appear to have been involved in the culture of polite letters associated during this period with the production of university verse anthologies, though Thomas Crosfield, fellow of Queen's, contributed in Latin to *Musarum Oxoniensium pro Rege suo soteria anagramma* (1633), and his former schoolmaster, Edward Sylvester, contributed in Greek to *Musarum Oxoniensium charisteria pro serenissima Regina Maria* (1639).[70] Owen's interest in athletics is better reported: he enjoyed "leaping, throwing the bar, ringing of bells, and such like exercises."[71]

We do not know whether Owen participated in the popular culture of the college: Crosfield's diary entries from this period illustrate the habits of leisure within Queen's, describing the college community's participation in plays, games of cards, bowls, fishing, bull-baiting, and watching a display of human "freaks" ("a dutch-wench all hairy & rough upon her body") and a puppet show of key incidents in biblical history.[72] What is clear is that Owen graduated with his BA on 11 June 1632, one day after Laud's friend John Bancroft was consecrated as bishop of Oxford. Six months later, in December 1632, Bancroft ordained Owen as a deacon.[73] Owen moved into his cycle of advanced study, and graduated with his MA in 1635. John Milton was awarded his Oxford MA in the same year, though not likely at the same ceremony.[74] Owen almost certainly assumed the teaching duties impressed upon MA graduates, and began his long study of divinity.[75] In August 1636, he would have experienced the visit of the court to Oxford, when the sermon in Christ Church celebrating the occasion defended royal power against "ye Anabaptist, puritane & papists."[76]

With the court endorsing the religious transformation of his college, the young divinity student could hardly have missed the writing on the wall. While the Arminian party had been gaining ground in Oxford since his first arrival at the university, especially after Laud became chancellor, it won a significant victory in the summer after Owen's MA graduation, when Laud imposed forms on the university that he could not accept. Alongside an ambitious program of new investments, which led to the establishment of a chair in Arabic and the expansion of the Bodleian Library, the institutions of the university were repurposed to advance the liturgical claims of the Arminian party. In St. Mary's, for example, the communion table was moved into the chancel as part of the increasing emphasis upon sacramental devotion. Religious change was altering the fabric of religious life in Oxford. But Laud's most significant achievement was to rewrite the university statutes, the revised versions of which were published in 1636. The new statutes required students and staff to subscribe to the Thirty-nine Articles and to swear to uphold the royal supremacy and the traditions of the university. It is unlikely that Owen had any difficulty with the doctrinal content of the articles: his publications in the 1640s would enthusiastically endorse the Thirty-nine Articles as being entirely opposed to the new Arminian menace.[77] But he could not swear to observe and uphold the ceremonies that the new statutes imposed, and, as he later put it, "dared not take their prescribed oath in what pertains to ancient ineptitudes."[78]

Owen did not regret all of Laud's activities in the university. Later in life, he remembered meeting Nathaniel Conopius, a Cretan student patronized by Laud who enrolled in Balliol College in 1637 before returning east to become archbishop of Smyrna.[79] Conopius seems to have been something of a flamboyant figure in the university community: John Evelyn remembered his arrival at Balliol, adding that the Cretan was "the first I ever saw drink Coffé [not heard of then in England . . .]."[80] Nor was Conopius a lone figure as an international student. The English universities were witnesses to huge religious and cultural diversity: as John Milton observed in 1644, even the "grave and frugal Transylvanian sends out yearly from as far as the mountanous borders of Russia and beyond the Hercynian wildernes, not their youth, but their staid men to learn our language and our theologic arts."[81] Owen's career in Oxford had been culturally and intellectually enlarging. But he must have struggled with the university's religious life, especially if we take at face value his later claims to have learned his hostility toward episcopacy from his father and to have maintained a nascent commitment to Presbyterian church government throughout his student years. Owen had continued in his father's faith as the university was moving in a different direction. But, in 1637, at the age of 21, as "conscience overcame ambition," Owen abandoned his academic prospects, and left Oxford.[82]

Owen had little doubt that the Laudian reforms represented an unwarranted imposition on the university. It was certainly the case, as recent historians have recognized, that the Laudian party had "failed effectively to reform the religious sensibilities of the grassroots" and, in advancing unpopular innovations, "profoundly alienated large numbers of hitherto conformist puritans."[83] But for Owen, the rejection of Reformed orthodoxy was personal. "If he had once nursed hopes of preferment in church or state, then the loss of his very membership in the university, at the hands of the state and the state church, must have been a crushing disappointment."[84] Owen had worked relentlessly to begin a scholarly life. But, at the age of twenty-one, his ambitions for a career in the church and its educational institutions had been thwarted. As his peers took advantage of their prospects, Owen was being reminded of the experience of defeat.

II

It is difficult to exaggerate the impact of Owen's decision to leave Oxford. It seems to have taken him the best part of the next six years to come to terms with his disappointment. Leaving Oxford, he entered a period of "relative obscurity" from which few documentary traces survive.[85] It is clear, however, that he was ordained as priest in December 1638, once again by John Bancroft, bishop of Oxford.[86] The details of this ordination had been forgotten in many accounts of Owen's life, and perhaps for understandable reasons: Owen's priesting does not fit into the pattern of heroic and principled dissent that has been elaborated in hagiographic accounts of his life. One year after leaving the university because of his refusal to compromise with the demands of its new statutes, Owen submitted himself to the authority of one of the most effective Arminians in the establishment, though, he later claimed, he made no promise of canonical obedience.[87] If his withdrawal from Oxford had reflected radical principle, it was of an occasionally genuflecting sort.

Bancroft, who ordained Owen, was a supporter—and friend—of Laud. His enthusiasm for Arminian reform in and around Oxford had become well known by the later 1630s. Bancroft was a supporter of traditional forms who refused to ordain men he felt unsuited to the clerical life, including a member of the Queen's community, Henry Wilkinson the elder (1610–75), whose Puritanism, Bancroft feared, was too distinct.[88] But Bancroft did ordain Owen, and it is tempting to speculate that this indicates his lack of concern about Owen's convictions. It is certainly possible that Bancroft could have seen Owen as something of a fellow traveler. For, as we will later see, while Owen rejected the Laudian concern to beautify the experience of worship and to rewrite principal themes in Reformed theology, he shared the high view of the sacraments that Arminians felt, perhaps incorrectly, made them distinct.

This apparent compromise with a prominent member of the Arminian hierarchy may have been both cause and consequence of Owen's descent into depression. Asty noted that his despondency continued for around five years after his departure from Oxford, but that it was at its worst for "a quarter of a year; during which time he avoided almost all manner of converse, and very hardly could be induced to speak a word, and when he did speak, it was with such disorder as rendred him a wonder to many." Although the symptoms did not continue at their worst, Owen was "held under very great trouble of mind, and grievous temptations for a long time."[89] It is difficult to know how to interpret this episode, to which Owen himself never referred. Bouts of mental illness were widely reported in the early and middle seventeenth century, and a number of scholars have linked descriptions of such illness to patterns of theological thinking prevalent at the time. Traditionally such episodes were read in terms of the "conviction of sin" expected as part of the standard Puritan morphology of conversion, and scholarship on early modern life writing has therefore been concerned to discriminate between what is likely to be a description of actual experience and what may only be an attempt to mimic it by rehearsing the standard tropes of the conversion narrative genre.[90] John Stachniewski's account of *The persecutory imagination* (1991) argued for a direct link between Calvinism and despair, while Richard L. Greaves's biography of John Bunyan (2002) read its subject in terms of modern psychological theory, with discussions of dysthemia and allied conditions taking the place of Puritan salvific theory. Owen later noted his conviction that episodes of this nature often accompanied regeneration: "God generally takes possession of souls in a cloud; that is, there is some darkness upon them: they cannot tell what their state is;—sometimes they have hopes, and sometimes fears; sometimes they think things are well, and sometimes they are cast down again."[91] It may be significant that Owen, in later life, did not refer to this period of depression as representing a standard component in his morphology of conversion—and that, perhaps reflecting his wider autobiographical reticence, he does not appear to refer to it at all. Owen's silence suggests that he was able, on reflection, to distinguish his medical condition from the spiritual condition that English Puritan theologians described as "conviction of sin." The root cause of Owen's depression may have been spiritual, as his liberation into the assurance of faith in 1642 was to demonstrate. But his depression may have owed as much to the apparent defeat of his career aspirations, or the compromises forced upon him by the ascent of Arminianism within the church, as it did to his anxiety about being one of the elect.

Some biographers have speculated that Owen spent this time of depression at his father's house in Stadhampton.[92] Certainly his first clerical appointment appears to have been occasioned by a network that extended into the town—and even into his father's church. Sir Robert Dormer of Ascot, near Wing, Buckinghamshire, owned property in Stadhampton and had constructed a pew in the parish church. In circumstances that remain obscure, not least given Dormer's reputation for behavioral excess, Catholic religion, and royalist politics, he appointed Owen as chaplain in his home in Great Milton, a neighboring village, and as tutor to his eldest son.[93] Owen's recovery from depression was taking place in familiar circumstances, and close to home. But the position was not to be permanent. Sometime before 1642, and again in obscure circumstances, Owen accepted a similar role in the home of John Lord Lovelace of Hurley, Berkshire. Again, the family connections proved to be important, for it was around this time that Owen's father moved to Harpsden, near Hurley, and his brother William may have become rector in Remenham (though some sources date this to move to 1648).[94] All three Owen clergymen may have been living within a two- or three-mile radius—a perfect environment for Owen's recovery within the support networks of a close-knit family. But the lack of clarity on dates means that we cannot know whether Owen's relocation was a cause or consequence of that of his father and brother, or whether in fact the moves should be related to one another at all. We have no way of reconstructing their new shared life.

Owen's transfer to the Lovelace household must have taken some adjustment. While the household culture has yet to be described and analyzed, it is clear that it was very different from the privileged households with which Owen would already have been familiar.[95] John (1615/16–70), the second Baron Lovelace, had recently married Lady Anne (bap. 1623, d. 1697), the third daughter and eventually co-heir of Thomas Wentworth, earl of Cleveland, and the household had been augmented by the birth of a son, John (c. 1640–93). At the age of 26, Owen was around the same age as his patron and seven years older than his mistress. The Lovelace household, like that of Robert Dormer, was likely a center of Royalist culture and may have provided Owen with many of the most important materials for the early stages of his lifelong study of Arminianism.[96] Owen had begun around 1636 the "more than seven years' serious inquiry" into the key ideas of the theological system that had hijacked his university, developing "a serious perusal of all which I could attain that the wit of man, in former or latter days, hath published in opposition to the truth."[97] This reading project would lead in the short term to *Θεομαχία αυτεξουσιαστικη: or, A display of Arminianisme* (1643) and in the longer term to *Salus electorum, sanguis Jesu: or, The death of death in the death of Christ* (1647). Both texts are replete with evidences of classical learning: while it is difficult to know the theological complexion of the Lovelace household, it is at least conceivable that the library contained some of the books that Owen used to investigate the Arminian menace. The atmosphere in the household was certainly conducive to intellectual life. Like other houses in the period, it was situated at the center of a literary network that included Richard Lovelace, who had contributed a poem on the death of Princess Katherine to the Oxford verse anthology, *Musarum Oxoniensium charisteria pro serenissima Regina Maria* (1639), and who would dedicate his *Lucasta* (1649) to Lady Anne.[98] Yet the Lovelace family network, as it evolved into the later seventeenth century, was to provide Owen with a key political contact in the House of Lords. John, the third Baron Lovelace, who pursued the typical lifestyle of a Restoration rake, promoted the lot of dissenters in the Lords, and regularly met Owen during the turmoil of the exclusion crisis of 1681.[99]

Nevertheless, like other country households, the Lovelaces must have been made anxious by the outbreak of war in the summer of 1642.[100] Perhaps, as they wondered about the possible political, financial, and personal ramifications of the conflict between king and Parliament, they were not particularly concerned by the loss of their family's tutor. Owen appears to have made regular visits elsewhere. In April 1642, he was lodging in the household of Sir Edward Scot, near Ashford, Kent, when Richard Lovelace led as many as 500 supporters to London in order to present a petition in favor of monarchy to the House of Commons, for which pains he was imprisoned, perhaps finding time to write "Stone walls do not a prison make."[101] The Lovelace rebellion was a very clear signal of the breach in English society: Owen later described the event as a "horrid insurrection of a rude, godless multitude."[102] He must have realized that the extended family with which he had found a home was now a danger to the stability of the nation—a conviction that would be confirmed in 1655, when John Lord Lovelace was imprisoned in the Tower on suspicion of plotting against the government.[103] But the decision to leave the Lovelace household was certainly a very significant decision for Owen. Having already abandoned Oxford for the uncertain prospects of a good conscience, Owen declared his support for Parliament, was disinherited by his Welsh uncle, and, when his patron joined the Royalist army, left the household for London.[104]

Owen's work offers no explanation as to why he decided to support the cause of Parliament, having already lost so much for the sake of conscience. His later reflections on the civil war represent it as a struggle for freedom of conscience, rather than for a particular political form. This decision to become politically committed flew in the face of the opinions of those who had done most to create him, including his teachers and patrons. Oxford was a baston of the royalist cause. Owen's two employers, Sir Robert Dormer and John Lord Lovelace, had both declared in favor of the king.[105] Perhaps there was something within the Owen family that drove its members into the conflict: while we have no record of the political opinions of William or the sisters, John, Henry, and Philemon would each serve within the army of the Parliament. But it is not clear why Owen, in 1642, left the proximity of his father and brother, both of whom continued to reside in the Harpsden area. Nor is there any evidence that he returned to the area to visit them, though, during the 1650s, his lodging in Oxford would not be far away.

In the spring of 1642, Owen's journey to London was in many ways a journey into the unknown. The city was, of course, an ideal environment for a young man who wanted to make an impression. London had became the logistical center for the operations of the Parliamentary cause, and the location of a number of well-established congregations of hot Protestants.[106] The clergy of the city were "almost entirely Presbyterian."[107] But Owen does not appear to have developed any significant friendship in the capital before his sudden arrival. For the first time, he may have found himself operating independently of family networks. He found lodgings in Charterhouse Yard, located at the end of Charterhouse Lane, adjacent to Smithfield, in the northeastern part of the city.[108] It must have been an evocative place for Owen to make his new home. Just yards from his new dwelling, the "fires of Smithfield" had consumed a generation of early Protestants in the reign of Mary Tudor. Neither did Charterhouse Yard have a good reputation. In the 1620s, for example, the area had been noted as a center of prostitution.[109] Its "dubious character" was also linked to its being the home of "nonconformist conventicles, currency counterfeiters, republican plotters and illicit printers"—features of the community some of which Owen may have come to appreciate as amenities.[110] The area likely also had financial advantages. Charterhouse was an extra-parochial district, and so its inhabitants were not required to pay tithes or those other rates levied through parish structures. It was a cheap and likely unpleasant place to live, and he stayed in the area for "probably less than a year."[111]

But Owen was cultivating new friendships. His residence in the household of Sir Edward Scot suggests that he was beginning to develop networks of his own. Scot was married to the mother of Thomas Westrow, who had studied with Owen at Queen's, and he may have been the "noble and very dear friend C. Westrow" to whom Owen would refer in the dedication of *The duty of pastors and people distinguished* (1644).[112] Owen enjoyed hospitality in their home, Scot's Hall, in Smeet, near Ashford, Kent, on a number of occasions through this period. A couple of years later, Owen remembered that "twice, by God's providence, have I been with you when your county hath been in great danger to be ruined," both during the earl of Thanet's engagements in Sussex (November–December 1642) and during the Kentish rebellion (1642–43).[113] The family was not known for its piety, and Cook has speculated that its connection with Owen was social rather than religious.[114] Owen, who must have spent considerable time as a houseguest at Scot's Hall, does not appear to have found employment in London.[115] He continued to suffer from bouts of depression, but he was soon to know deliverance. He may have hoped to have made an impression on the religious culture of the capital—but its religious culture would certainly make an impression on him.

Owen's experience of conversion was recorded by Asty, and it is worth quoting in full. One Sunday—and, like much else in the account, we lack the detail of a specific date—Owen went with an unnamed cousin to Aldermanbury Church, hoping to hear a celebrity Puritan preacher, Edmund Calamy:

> He waited for his coming up into the pulpit, but at length it was known that Mr. Calamy was prevented by some extraordinary occasion; upon which many went out of the Church, but Mr. OWEN resolved to abide there, tho' his cousin would fain have persuaded him to go and hear Mr. Jackson, then an eminent preacher in the city; it not being certain whether there would be any person to supply Mr. Calamy's place. Mr. OWEN being well seated, and too much indisposed for any farther

> walk, he resolved after some stay, if no preacher came, to go to his lodgings. At last there came up a country minister to the pulpit, a stranger not only to Mr. OWEN, but to the parish; who having prayed fervently, took for his text these words, *Why are ye fearful, O ye of little faith*, Mat. viii. 26. The very reading of the words surprized Mr. OWEN, upon which he secretly put up a prayer, that God would please by him to speak to his condition; and his prayer was heard; for in that sermon the minister was directed to answer those very objections which Mr. OWEN had commonly formed against himself: and tho' he had formerly given the same answers to himself without any effect, yet now the time was come when God design'd to speak peace to his soul; and this sermon (tho' otherwise a plain familiar discourse) was blest for the removing of all his doubts, and laid the foundation of that solid peace and comfort which he afterwards enjoy'd as long as he liv'd. It is very remarkable that Mr. OWEN could never come to the knowledge of this ministry, tho' he made the most diligent enquiry.[116]

This conversion account is filtered through a series of tropes that would become familiar in later Puritan spiritual narratives, but it does suggest that Owen was continuing to experience ill health ("indisposed for any farther walk"); that he was "sermon gadding" in godly circles in the capital ("expectation of hearing Mr. Calamy"); that these godly circles valued performance in the pulpit over the discipline of listening to preaching ("many went out of the Church"); that this preaching was strongly focused on conversion while running over standard tropes ("directed to answer those very objections which Mr. OWEN had commonly formed against himself . . . tho' he had formerly given the same answers to himself without any effect"); that, unusually, Owen's later experience of assurance of salvation was never troubled ("solid peace and comfort which he afterwards enjoy'd as long as he liv'd"); and that the instrument through which this eminent theologian came to the assurance of salvation was an undated "plain familiar discourse" by an unknown preacher from the country.[117]

The experience was transformative, and from it Owen was launched into the first stages of the literary and pastoral career to which he would dedicate his life. He threw himself into advancing the research and writing projects that he had begun in the mid-1630s, likely gathering key quotations in a commonplace book, which would explain why he recycled so many quotations in his early publications.[118] He appears to have completed his first manuscript, *Tractatu de sacerdotio Christi*, by 1643. Although he never published this text, he did develop what appear to be its principal themes through much of his later writing—including the Reformed view of the work of Christ, and opposition to Arminianism, Socinianism, and Roman Catholicism.[119] And so at the age of twenty-seven, five years after his ordination as priest, under the exhortations of an unknown country preacher, on an unknown date, Owen emerged from the struggles that had "interrupted his program at Oxford, his expectation of an inheritance from his uncle, and his employment in the Lovelace household," and from the experience of defeat.[120] He did not intend to hide his light under a bushel. John Owen was born again.

2

Emerging Theologian

BUOYED UP BY this experience of the assurance of salvation, John Owen launched his literary career in March 1643, with the publication of *Θεομαχία αυτεξουσιαστικη: or, A display of Arminianisme.*[1] Probably prepared for the press while Owen lived in Charterhouse Yard, though drawing on several years of research, the book was designed to call the attention of well-placed patrons to the abilities of its author, who was likely unknown in the capital and, now thrown onto his own resources, almost certainly living in straightened circumstances. *A display of Arminianisme* set out its thesis in its inexpertly Greek title, which might loosely be translated as "the fight of free will against God."[2] Owen's decision to go into print may have surprised members of his immediate circle, most of whom remained unpublished through the period, but it consolidated the traditional link between print and Protestantism even as it reflected the new possibilities of the wider access to media.[3] Until July 1641, English printing had been strictly controlled by the Star Chamber, a court of law that had met in Westminster in circumstances utterly lacking in transparency, and which had become particularly identified with the abuses of royal prerogative. But Parliament had abolished the Star Chamber as part of its long struggle to limit the powers of the crown, and this assertion of parliamentary liberties, which effectively ended censorship, had a sensational impact on the production of print.[4] Owen was an immediate beneficiary of the new situation, and, with a multitude of other authors, printers, and booksellers, he took advantage of new opportunities to shape the emerging public sphere.[5] He must have been the first member of his family and one of the first members of his friendship network to become an author. And he was not alone. Over 2,000 titles would be printed in London in 1643—an almost tenfold increase on the annual average to that point.[6] The situation was overwhelming, and Parliament sought to control the sudden fertility of the English press.

The Licensing Order, passed by Parliament on 14 June 1643, reinstated a program of censorship, and provoked a furious backlash, most famously in John Milton's *Areopagitica* (1644).[7] Writing underwrote the cause of reformation, and Owen's first book appeared only two months before his new freedom to access the technology of print could have been impaired.

A display of Arminianisme was published by Philemon Stephens, in Paul's churchyard, London.[8] It is not clear why Owen decided to publish his first book with this press, or how the publication was financed. Stephens had been publishing since at least 1622. Although he would become best known to posterity for his work with George Herbert, whose *Temple* (1633) was included in the auction catalogue purporting to represent the contents of Owen's library (1684), Stephens's early work had a moderate Puritan and strongly anti-Catholic inflection, and some of his earliest polemical texts were to become his most frequently reprinted. Unusually, given the economics of the early modern book trade, we can assume that Stephens's outputs were a guide to his own convictions, and that he was in close contact with important sections of his market: his shop was a "known meeting place for the godly" in the 1630s.[9] Stephens's publications indicate the kinds of projects that his press could handle and successfully market: his production of Nathaniel Roe's extraordinary *Tabulae logarithmicae, or Two tables of logarithmes the first containing the logarithmes of all numbers from 1, to 100000* (1633), for example, offered a powerful demonstration of his shop's abilities in composition.[10] Stephens was also an innovator, with a keen eye on maximizing returns: his books were some of the earliest to use the blank leaves at the end of text blocks to advertise other titles, and book historians have identified one of his printings of Owen as including one of the earliest examples of this practice.[11] By the early 1640s, Stephens was printing godly works by Nicholas Byfield, John Downame, and Thomas Gataker, and, perhaps more significantly, from Owen's point of view, was moving into a new genre. Since 1640, the Long Parliament had been sponsoring monthly fast-day sermons, inviting rising and established preachers to echo back and very occasionally challenge its sense of divine vocation. Many of these sermons were subsequently published, and Stephens was among the first printers to deal with these texts. Cornelius Burgess's *The first sermon, preached to the Honourable House of Commons now assembled in Parliament at their publique fast* (1641) was followed by Thomas Hill's *The trade of truth advanced* (1642) as Stephens moved to take advantage of the proliferation of this species of political-theological advice.[12] Owen's decision to publish with Stephens was therefore a decision to use a printer whose work was known to Parliament, leveraging for influence by elevating himself above the sudden cacophony of published religious voices. He continued to publish with Stephens until 1649, when Stephens published a collected edition of Owen's works to date. We do not know how many copies of *A display of Arminianisme* were printed by Stephens, or how the text was marketed, though, as we will see, it is likely that sales were slow. But Owen likely had only one audience in mind.

A display of Arminianisme evidenced its author's obvious intention to bring himself to the attention of those best placed to advance his career, and it was advertised as being dedicated to the lords and gentlemen of the parliamentary Committee for Religion, which had been convened to examine all religious innovations introduced since the Reformation.[13] Although Owen was described on the title page as "Master of Arts of Queens Colledge in Oxon," *A display of Arminianisme* was very much a coming-of-age publication. He began his book by invoking the familiar modesty topos, though his protestations may also have reflected something of his earlier struggle with depression. Perhaps considering his unsettled years in Oxford, the shocking impact of war between king and Parliament, his unemployment and his sense of isolation in an unsavory part of the capital, Owen described the book as a "weak endeavour . . . the undigested issue of a few broken hours, too many causes, in these furious malignant days, continually interrupting the course of my studies," and admitted that "the discouragements of these woful days will leave me nothing but a desire that so necessary a work may find a more able pen."[14] He had good cause to worry about his writing. While concerned to "avoid prolixity," Owen still offered several neologisms, including "distortures" and "concreated," with the latter, while hardly a contribution to *belles lettres*, appearing almost twenty years before its first recorded usage in the *Oxford English Dictionary* (*OED*).[15] Ironically, Owen offered these neologisms even as he condemned the "self-coined pretences" of the Arminians: literary style was itself at stake in the contest for orthodoxy.[16] The book's self-conscious learning, awkwardness in expression, and rigidly structured style and format would have done little to warm the hearts of his earliest readers: Owen's first book was "undoubtedly" his "most Thomistic."[17] But Owen's modesty belied his confidence, and in any case he was not intending a devotional effect. With its formal disputational style and intellectual swagger, *A display of Arminianisme* launched a ruthless and relentless attack on a party of "innovators in Christian religion," which, Owen believed, was promoting a "kind of atheism" that "laid the axe to the root of Christianity."[18] This was a strong description from an unemployed chaplain of a theological party then headed by the archbishop of Canterbury with the approval and support of the king.

Perhaps recognizing that it was too dangerous to mount a direct attack on this party's principal English representatives, *A display of Arminianisme* set out to engage with the Continental and Latinate writers who were providing English Arminians with much of their intellectual matériel. It interacted with the works of Jacob Arminius alongside those of his followers among the Dutch Remonstrants, including Johannes Arnoldi Corvinus, Nicolaas Grevinchovius, and Isaac Welsingius.[19] Owen's concern to link the Dutch Remonstrants with the Italian Arian and principal theologian of the Polish Brethren Faustus Socinus reflected the widespread fear among conservative Calvinists that the Arminian threat to soteriology could descend into a full-blown assault on the doctrine of the Trinity.[20] Owen could have made this point more forcefully had he known of the personal and theological links that lay behind the hospitality shown to Socinian refugees by the Arminian community in the Low Countries.[21] But English writers did not entirely escape censure. Owen criticized *A treatise of the divine essence and attributes* (1628), by Thomas Jackson (1579–1640), president of Corpus Christi College, who had been one of the earliest Oxford theologians to move to an anti-Calvinist position, and whose work would have appeared while Owen was a student in a neighboring college. Owen also engaged with work by Edward Reynolds (1599–1676), who was perhaps an unintended target of his vitriol: Reynolds was a solid Calvinist, a member of the Westminster Assembly, who would later be replaced by Owen as dean of Christ Church and vice chancellor of the University of Oxford.[22] But Owen's argument was not inhibited by concern about collateral damage, and he lumped together his antagonists, despite the considerable range of theological opinion they represented. It was a telling strategy, and one that he would continue to deploy: Owen offered his readers a radical simplification of a complex series of intellectual debates, collapsing all nuance into a binary distinction between truth and error. His argument was unhesitating. He described *God's love to mankind* (1633), by Samuel Hoard (1599–1658), as "a book full of palpable ignorance, gross sophistry, and abominable blasphemy, whose author seems to have proposed nothing unto himself but to rake all the dunghills of a few of the most invective Arminians, and to collect the most filthy scum and pollution of their railings to cast upon the truth of God; and, under I know not what self-coined pretences, belch out odious blasphemies against his holy name."[23] Owen's brisk and "misleading" response disguised the extent to which he failed to "engage with Hoard's central thesis" and to recognize its "emotional and pastoral weight."[24] While Continental and Latinate writers may have been Owen's most important targets, he reserved his strongest condemnation for English-language texts, perhaps recognizing that these would be the books most often encountered by those most likely to read his work. Owen denounced English Arminian writers because their theology revived erroneous doctrines that had been destroyed at the Reformation, "that fatal time for idolatry and superstition."[25] Recent work on *A display of Arminianisme* has questioned the accuracy of its representation of the arguments of Owen's antagonists.[26] It may be that Owen was arguing more effectively against Arminian authors than against the theological system they defended. But Owen's argument was not all *ad hominem*. *A display of Arminianisme* mounted a strenuous and often ironic attack on the "old Pelagian idol free-will, with the new goddesse contingency," as the title page put it, contrasting the "maine errors of the Arminians" with the "received doctrine of all the reformed churches," and in particular the "doctrine established in the Church of England."

This invocation of English Protestant orthodoxy was a key move in Owen's argument, for it highlighted his point that prominent individuals in the English hierarchy, including the archbishop of Canterbury, were insufficiently Anglican. The attack upon the institutions of the established church and the simultaneous defense of its constitution are among the more surprising objectives of Owen's first book. Owen wrote as a radically conservative defender of the constitution of "our church," repeatedly contrasting the doctrine of the innovators with that of the Thirty-nine Articles.[27] Thus, he argued, "Arminians" have "apostated from the pure doctrine of the word of God, the consent of orthodox divines, and the confession of this church of England."[28] The "popish-arminian errors" that were being introduced were pushing the Church of England away from catholic tradition.[29] *A display of Arminianisme* therefore sought to appropriate the reasoning of the "ancient fathers and schoolmen" against that of "these bold innovators," who, "with one dash of their pen," have "quite overthrown a sacred verity, an apostolic, catholic, fundamental article of Christian religion"—the doctrine of divine sovereignty.[30] "To prove this to be a heresy exploded by all orthodox and catholic antiquity were to light a candle in the sun," Owen expostulated, fashioning himself as the defender of the Protestant Reformation, Catholic antiquity, and the "more sure testimony" of Scripture (2 Peter 1:19).[31] Perhaps reflecting on his experiences as a student, and the fate of more principled nonconformists in an earlier age, Owen considered that "had a poor Puritan offended against half so many canons as they opposed articles, he had forfeited his livelihood, if not endangered his life."[32] Owen understood the political conflict of the previous decade as emanating from the differences between "Arminians" and "Puritans," and he refused to abandon the Church of England to his opponents.

The substance of Owen's arguments related to the theological innovations of the Arminian party. His book identified the "head and sum of all the controversies between them and us" as being the argument that "several degrees of our salvation" should be "ascribed unto ourselves, rather than God."[33] The debate turned on a simple question, Owen believed, for "all the wrangling disputes of carnal reason against the word of God come at last to this head, Whether the first and chiefest part, in disposing of things in this world, ought to be ascribed to God or man?"[34] For Owen, the freedom of divine and human will were mutually incompatible: if the human will were to operate independently, it would be functionally divine, and, Owen concluded, "Arminians came perilously close to idolatry when they advance the freedom of the will apart from the power and sovereignty of God."[35] Thus "Arminius and his sectaries" were "making Almighty God a desirer that many things were otherwise than they are, and an idle spectator of most things that are done in the world," Owen concluded: they should be recognized as the "emissaries" of Satan.[36]

A display of Arminianisme was much less a comprehensive defense of Reformed orthodoxy than Owen had suggested. For example, the book made no mention of the covenant of redemption—the assumption, which would become foundational to Owen's later thinking, that the persons of the Trinity had made a pact before creation to ensure the redemption of the elect and the renewal of the heavens and earth. The roots of this idea can be traced back to sixteenth-century Protestant theology, but it was first enunciated by the Scottish Presbyterian theologian David Dickson in 1638, and may have come to Owen's attention by way of his readings in Continental theology.[37] Owen certainly hurried to make use of the doctrine in his later writings, outlining its central tenets in his catechisms (1645) and in his later study of the effects of the atonement (1648), as he gradually elaborated the theological framework that would sustain his writing though his spiritual, political, and perhaps mental collapse in the early 1660s.[38]

A display of Arminianisme set out a précis of the doctrine of divine sovereignty that its author had received from the medieval schoolmen, especially Aquinas, and the Reformed writers of the sixteenth century, including Calvin.[39] Owen insisted on the paradox that God determines the free choices of individuals: "God disposeth of the hearts of men, ruleth their wills, inclineth their affections, and determines them freely to choose and do what he in his good pleasure hath decreed shall be performed."[40] For proof of his argument, he invited his readers to "consider the prophecies in Scripture, especially those concerning our Saviour, how many free and contingent actions did concur for the fulfilling of them." Similar arguments could be made from other examples of biblical narrative, he continued, such as the "wasting of Jerusalem by the Babylonians, which though, in regard of God's prescience, it was certainly to come to pass, yet they did it most freely, not only following the counsel of their own wills, but also using divination, or chanceable lots, for their direction, Ezek. xxi. 21."[41] Owen did not deny contingency, but understood all second causes to operate under divine supervision and control, for "oftentimes by things purely contingent and accidental" God executes his purposes, "bestoweth rewards, inflicteth punishments, and accomplisheth his judgements; as when he delivereth a man to be slain by the head of an axe, flying from the helve in the hand of a man cutting a tree by the way."[42] But the attempt to divorce contingency from divine sovereignty was at the root of the Arminian threat, and was "the Helen for whose enjoyment, these thrice ten years, they have maintained warfare with the hosts of the living God."[43]

Owen was aware of the wider implications of the new theory of contingency. It had inevitable implications for the Reformed doctrine of salvation. The Synod of Dort (1618–19) had established an international Reformed consensus, and had agreed, drawing on the conclusions of the medieval scholastic theologian, Peter Lombard, that Christ's death was sufficient for all humanity, but efficient for the salvation of the elect. The new theological trends challenged this international consensus, which drew on important themes in the Catholic past. From Owen's perspective, Arminian theologians could not agree that Christ had died effectively for anyone, and he argued that their appeal to contingency and human volition made it possible that no one would be saved, "so that, when Christ had done all that he could, there was not one man in the world immediately the better for it."[44] Owen responded to this challenge by reiterating the consensus of the Synod of Dort. He agreed with the Arminians that Christ's death could in some senses be considered as of universal value: the blood of Christ "was so exceedingly precious, of that infinite worth and value, that it might have saved a thousand believing worlds," he insisted. "His death was of sufficient dignity to have been made a ransom for all the sins of every one in the world," and "on this internal sufficiency of his death and passion is grounded the universality of evangelical promises."[45] Nevertheless, Owen did not leave his position unqualified. His universalism extended only to the sufficiency of the atonement. Christ's death did not benefit everyone in exactly the same way. Owen recognized that Christ's death was for "all the world" when "the world" was defined as "some of all sorts," rather than all individuals of all sorts.[46] And so Owen mounted an additional argument for the ultimate limitation of the benefits of the cross, for while Christ could have died so as to achieve the salvation of every individual, he did not, but "giveth life to every one for whom he gave his life."[47] His doctrine of its efficiency resolved itself in a narrowly mathematical conclusion.

This extended description of *A display of Arminianisme* may be justified by the fact that it becomes exemplary of Owen's writing through much of the earlier part of his career. In content, defending a high Calvinism, and in method, reducing complex discursive systems into simplified binaries, Owen's work made theology managable. But the book was not an entirely mature statement of his views. Owen's argument in *A display of Arminianisme* made some unexpected moves. Recent historical work has presented Arminianism as being sacramental in a way that the traditional doctrine of the Church of England and the emerging theology of Puritans was not. But Owen's defense of the Reformed doctrine of divine sovereignty was articulated alongside a defense of the power of sacraments. His discussion of baptism rejected the *ex opere operato* sacramental theology, which he associated (not unfairly) with the Laudian party, but refused to move in a Zwinglian direction to argue that sacraments were merely symbols.[48] In one of the most complex passages in *A display of Arminianisme,* Owen insisted that baptism does achieve something: it takes away "that which hinders our salvation; which is not the first sin of Adam imputed, but our own inherent lust and pollution."[49] Owen was arguing that baptism removes the inherent sin of those baptized—that is, the guilt associated with sins that individuals have themselves committed. But it does not remove the guilt of the sin they have inherited from Adam, which continues to be imputed to them, presumably until their regeneration. Owen may well have been aware of the pastoral as well as theological difficulties he was creating. He immediately moved to argue that un-baptized children dying in infancy were not necessarily damned, for God could save them, either on the basis that "their immediate or remote parents" were "believers," or by "his grace of election, which is most free, and not tied to any conditions; by which I make no doubt but God taketh many unto him in Christ whose parents never knew, or had been despisers of, the gospel."[50] It was an unsatisfactory conclusion, which betrayed assumptions that Owen may not have been able to align with other elements of his thinking, and may suggest that he was publishing a doctrine he had not sufficiently considered. It is telling that his future work would never delineate a theology of baptism in similar terms—and that he would condemn the same view in his book on justification (1677).[51]

Nevertheless, Owen's defense of the saving power of baptism has eluded many of his readers, and it suggests something of the complexity of his early theological thinking. His emphasis on the efficacy of baptism reflects that of Cornelius Burgess, whose *Baptismall regeneration of elect infants professed by the Church of England, according to the Scriptures, the primitive Church, the present reformed churches, and many particular divines apart* (1629) was published in Oxford around the same time that Owen began his studies in the city.[52] Even as Burgess complained that he had been "peremptorily censured and condemned by many, as guilty not only of *Arminianisme*, but even of direct *Popery*, and of teaching a *Doctrine of divells*," his book illustrated that a high view of the efficacy of sacraments could be aligned with hostility to Arminian theology.[53] For Burgess, and those who followed him, the conviction that regeneration was effected in the baptism of elect infants was a central tenet of the Church of England, which was supported by the arguments of the best of the Continental Protestant divines. Owen's argument did not immediately map onto Burgess's; however, it anticipated some elements of the later argument of Leonard Van Rijssen (1695).[54] But it indicates the existence of a party within the Church of England that was simultaneously hostile to Arminianism and supportive of the idea that salvation, in certain respects, was effected by baptism—a party that contemporaries described as "Calvinistical, sacramentarian sectaries," within which Owen would admit, on several occasions, that he could be included.[55]

Owen's argument about the efficacy of baptism created an important problem in his analysis. His admission that an unbaptized child who had died without hearing or responding to the gospel could be saved on the basis of the faith of her "immediate or remote parents," or merely by the "grace of election," raised the question of the destiny of other kinds of people who had a similar lack of access to the truth. The claim by Arminians and Socinians that pagans could be saved by paying attention to natural revelation cried out for qualification, for Owen was sure that salvation could not be attained by the "conduct of nature, without the knowledge of Christ."[56] If pagans were to be saved, he concluded, it would be on the basis of special revelation rather than general revelation. And so, not wishing to "straighten the breast and shorten the arm of the Almighty," Owen found himself allowing the possibility that individual pagans could be the recipients of extraordinary revelation, which they could believe and so be saved, outside the boundaries of the visible church.[57] But he never explained how these pagans could be saved without their inherent sin being removed by baptism. Owen's unusual argument about the efficacy of baptism was taking him down some unexpected avenues.

It is easy to overlook these nuances in Owen's writing, for his argument is often driven along by its rhetorical force. His rejection of Arminian theology was unstinting:

> they lay men in Abraham's bosom who never believed in the Son of Abraham; make them overcome the serpent who never heard of the

> Seed of the woman; bring goats into heaven, who never were of the flock of Christ, never entered by him, the door; make men please God without faith, and obtain the remission of sins without the sprinkling of the blood of the Lamb, – to be saved without a Saviour, redeemed without a Redeemer, – to become the sons of God, and never know their elder Brother.[58]

"Having robbed God of his power," he continued, Arminians "leave him so much goodness as that he shall not be troubled at it, though he be sometimes compelled to what he is very loath to do."[59]

Owen's earliest readers could not have missed the political implications of his violent language. *A display of Arminianisme* advertised its status as a political intervention. Owen dedicated his book to the "right honourable The Lords and Gentlemen of the Committee for Religion"; he alluded to the "blood of almost-expiring Ireland," hinting at the memory of the rebellion in 1641, to which theme his later preaching would return; and he lamented the moral condition of the kingdoms, six months into the first civil war, in a retrospective glance that justified the parliamentary war effort in hyperbolic terms.[60] "All agreement without truth is no peace," he insisted, "but a covenant with death, a league with hell, a conspiracy against the kingdom of Christ, a stout rebellion against the God of heaven; and without justice, great commonwealths are but great troops of robbers."[61] But the political point was theological, too, for those who were the "chiefest agents in robbing men of their privileges" in the prelude to the civil war were also those who had "nefariously attempted to spoil God of his providence."[62] Arminianism was the religious style of tyranny, and Laudianism was the royalist party at prayer. And so the spiritual sword of church discipline ought to be unsheathed in the political struggle for English liberties. Arminians were "incapable of our church-communion," Owen argued, for the "sacred bond of peace compasseth only the unity of that Spirit which leadeth into all truth." His intention was to excommunicate the foremost leaders of church and state. Arminians should not be offered the "right hand of fellowship," he insisted, but should occupy the place of the enemy in a relentless "holy war."[63] In this sense, ironically, Owen was more convinced of the importance of the contexts of his writing than have been many of his readers. One of his book's most significant features is its assumption that theology is inescapably political, and that theological ideas have necessarily political implications. The civil war, as Owen understood it, was a war of religion.

Owen's work was being driven by a sense of imminent danger. "Never were so many prodigious errors introduced into a church, with so high a hand

and so little opposition, as these into ours, since the nation of Christians was known in the world," he complained.[64] Developing a metaphor to which he would return in his most important sermon, Owen recognized that "the Prince of Peace hath, by his gospel, sent the sword amongst us," and the "preaching thereof . . . must needs occasion a great shaking of the earth."[65] Owen's language of violence had advanced beyond the rhetoric of Parliament, for his first book, in its call for a "holy war," had moved from an analysis of Arminianism into an apologia for a Puritan crusade.[66]

I

Owen succeeded in gaining the patronage he sought. Shortly after the publication of *A display of Arminianisme*, the Committee on Religion, to whom it had been dedicated, offered Owen the parish of Fordham, in Essex. This offer was immediately followed by another, from Sir Edward Scot, of the parish church in Shepway, Kent.[67] Establishing a pattern that he would repeat in later life, Owen preferred the more powerful of his patrons, and accepted the living in Fordham. The parish church had a long history of hot Protestant preaching. Thomas Upcher, who was rector through most of the later sixteenth century, had been a Marian exile, and may have engineered the removal of the church's stained glass. His ministry was followed by that of Thomas Wither and Robert Cotton, the latter a Puritan who seemed to provoke the hostility of his parishioners, and, by the 1630s, the church fabric was in some state of disrepair.[68] The most recent incumbent, John Alsop, had been an eager supporter of the reforms of William Laud. Owen's first pastoral charge was not likely to be easy.

Owen may have moved quickly—he could take with him only the "small remainder of my poor library," apparently having disposed of some of its content, perhaps to generate income during his difficult days in London.[69] He might not have expected to need many technical works of theology in this rural part of Essex. He may have already known about the library of Samuel Harsnett (d. 1631), which was stored in Colchester, and functioned as a resource for local clergy.[70] Owen may well have surmised that parish life in the traditional heartland of Puritanism was not likely to throw him into theological disputation, even though the living had been sequestered from a chaplain to Archbishop Laud.[71] Owen quickly settled into parish life: a note in the parish register recorded the arrival of "John Owen, Pastor, Anno. Dom. July:16:1643."[72] Almost five years after his ordination as priest by the bishop of Oxford, Owen was installed in his first congregation.

We do not know what Owen thought of his new surroundings. The Fordham parish church was old even in Owen's time: the building dated from 1340, and included Roger Walden (d. 1406), who had become archbishop of Canterbury, among its earlier rectors (it is now an English Heritage grade 1 listed building).[73] Neither do we know how Owen was received into his first living. His neighbor Ralph Josselin, who had been installed minister of the nearby village of Earls Colne in October 1641, complained that, upon his arrival, none of his new parishioners came to welcome him, but he eventually concluded that this reflected local habits of reticence.[74] Nor do we know how Owen conducted his ministry. In November 1646, during a season of bad weather, Josselin recorded that a diet of worship in the Earls Colne church had begun at 11 a.m., and that his preaching had continued for at least four hours, "untill sun was sett."[75] Again, at a public fast day in August 1647, Josselin recorded that he had "expounded, prayed, and preachd, about 5 houres."[76] Josselin seems to have regarded these long services as noteworthy, but we do not know how they compared to those led by his new neighbor in Fordham. Neither do we know much about the content of Owen's preaching in his early days of parish ministry. Again, Josselin's example may be suggestive: he tended to preach on occasional texts, until, in one of his many attempts to develop habits of systematic study, he began on 21 March 1647, the last Sabbath of the year (old style), to "expound the Scriptures beginning. Genesis: 1."[77] It is not clear from his diary how long this habit of consecutive exegesis was continued.[78]

Of course, Owen's silence on these matters may suggest that his transfer into parish ministry happened by accident: in dedicating his first book to the Committee on Religion, he may not have been hoping for a clerical charge. After all, the Westminster Assembly was also meeting for the first time in July 1643. Owen could hardly have expected to be invited to attend this august synod of divines. Still in his mid-twenties, with only one (more than slightly bad-tempered) book behind him, and with no parish experience, Owen would have been an extraordinary candidate for Assembly membership.[79] And yet other young men of Owen's acquaintance did take part, including Henry Wilkinson (1610–75), whom Owen would have known from student days, and his old school friend and exact contemporary, Henry Wilkinson (1616/17–90).[80] But, as his peers settled down to reify the English Reformation in a flagship religious project, Owen was confronted with the challenge of advancing the Reformation in the less auspicious circumstances of Fordham.

As Owen reacquainted himself with village life, leaving behind the challenges of the capital, he realized that the parish was in bad shape. He found that his new parishioners had been badly taught by Alsop, and lamented the village's large number of "grossly ignorant persons."[81] He expressed the weight of his new responsibilities in vividly physical terms: "what a burden upon the shoulders, what a grief unto the soul of a minister . . . is an ignorant congregation."[82] And in this new context the emphasis of his thinking appears to have changed, turning to routinely pastoral concerns, the difficulty of organizing a congregation and teaching the elements of Christian faith. This would certainly have called for effort. Josselin, for example, recorded his enduring struggle to enforce Puritan discipline on the traditional festive culture of the district, but even he continued to share in the local "world of wonders."[83] In November 1644, Josselin heard of a "man in Some, Camb[ridgeshire] that is about 150 yeares old who had 6 wives and 32 children, and very lately carried 2 comes of pease: 2 furlongs: 8 bushels a quarter of a mile"; he later recorded news of a "monster borne about Colchester, first a child, then a serpent, then a toad which lapped," and interviewed a man who claimed to have seen the devil.[84] Josselin was a Puritan, a Cambridge graduate, and a useful reminder of the difference of the mental world that was inhabited by many of the godly—including one of Owen's nearest clerical colleagues. But there was time for domestic pleasures, too. In late 1643, Owen married Mary Rooke (d. 1677), who may have been the daughter of William Rooke, a clothier based in Coggeshall, about five miles from Fordham. He remained characteristically silent about their life together. It is from stray entries in parish records that we must reconstruct their difficult and tragic early years of marriage.[85]

It is likely that Owen's experience of parish life in Fordham influenced his theological formation. Establishing a lifelong habit, Owen made time to write, just as Josselin made time for farming, schoolteaching, and investments.[86] Owen's next few publications show how fully his attention had moved from the Arminian controversy on which he had cut his literary teeth. His next book reflected on the difficulties of establishing functioning church government in the context of a disordered parish, but it also demonstrated the extent to which he had begun to codify his inherited Presbyterian convictions.[87] *The duty of pastors and people distinguished*, which was published by Philemon Stephens in May 1644, was dedicated to Sir Edward Scot, with thanks for some kind of preferment, likely the offer of the parish in Kent. Having addressed the parliamentary Committee on Religion in *A display of Arminianisme*, Owen, ever the diplomat, called attention to the generosity of his other patron in the dedication to second publication.

The duty of pastors and people distinguished was the first text in a series of publications that Owen would develop into a project parallel to that of the Westminster Assembly. From 1644 until 1647, as the Assembly negotiated and published catechisms and a manual of church government, Owen did the same, until the appearance of its confession of faith (1647) formalized the orthodoxy of English Puritanism in a manner not entirely consistent with his earlier stated convictions. *The duty of pastors and people distinguished* reflected its historical moment, and Owen's conviction of the apocalyptic significance of the times. Unlike *A display of Arminianisme*, this book disclaimed any political intentions: "because that the times are troublesome, I have made choice of this messenger. . . . He hath no secret messages prejudicial to the state of church or common-wealth."[88] And in a way, that was true. Owen's only political reflection—a glancing reference to the Court of High Commission, which had been abolished by the Triennial Act (1641), as Satan's "shop on earth to practice his trade in"—confirmed his credentials as a supporter of parliamentary freedoms.[89] But this disclaiming of political intention was perhaps misleading, and the political tensions to which he referred were not just metaphorical. For Owen was deeply conscious of the significance of the times in which he lived, and of the transience of his new medium in light of expected apocalyptic events: "Ambitious I am not of any entertainment for these few sheets, neither care much what success they find in their travel, setting them out merely in my own defence, to be freed from the continued solicitations of some honest, judicious men, who were acquainted with their contents, being nothing but an hour's country discourse, resolved from the ordinary pulpit method into its own principles."[90] After all, he continued, the "glass of our lives, seems to run and keep pace with the extremity of time. The end of those 'ends of the world' which began with the gospel is doubtless coming upon us. . . . Christ shakes the glass, many minutes of that hour cannot remaine."[91] And now, "as if the horoscope of the decaying age had some secret influence into the wills of men to comply with the decrepit world, they generally delight to run into extremes."[92] Owen was settling into Fordham at the chaotic end of the world.

The extremes between which Owen sought to steer in *The duty of pastors and people distinguished* were separatism and unhesitating conformity, establishing his father's moderate Presbyterianism as the *via media* between "democratical confusion" and "hierarchical tyranny."[93] The book's identification of an ecclesiological center revealed the instinctive conservatism of the variety of Puritanism with which Owen had grown up. Owen wrote to defend the Presbyterian system against the "prelaticall or diocesan" and the "independent or congregational."[94] His Presbyterianism reflected the culture of late Elizabethan reform, rather than the more radical Puritanism of the Jacobean period represented in William Bradshaw's *English Puritanisme* (1605), for it was neither radical enough to seek the purity of worship in emigrant congregations, nor complacent enough to fully conform to the expectations of the established church.[95] Although his first book suggested how much his soteriology had been radicalized by his experience of the Arminian advance in Oxford, his second book seemed to be continuing in his father's ecclesiological footsteps.

Again, Owen's writing was a topical reaction to a recent publication, Herbert Thorndike's *Of religious assemblies, and the publick service of God* (Cambridge, 1642), which defended the imposition of non-biblical ceremonies and the use of the Book of Common Prayer.[96] It is not clear where Owen obtained his copy of Thorndike's work, or whether it was bought or borrowed. There was certainly a lively market in secondhand books in the vicinity. In January 1646, for example, Josselin decided to establish his own library by buying secondhand copies of the best theological titles with money raised through gambling.[97] This purpose of selective investment turned out to be astute: several weeks after making his resolution, Josselin bought the library of a deceased clergyman.[98] But Thorndike's *Of religious assemblies* had been very recently published, and was unlikely to have been obtained in the local market for secondhand books. If Owen's concerns about financial supply mirrored those of his clerical colleague—which, given their similar ages, family sizes, and salaries, may well have been the case—we are left to wonder how he could afford to keep up to date with contemporary theological debates. Perhaps he was helped by his younger brother Henry, then living in London, by whom he had already been outpaced in terms of career.[99]

Owen's apparent carelessness about the reception of his second work should not necessarily be taken at face value: his claim that "ambitious I am not of any entertainment for these few sheets, neither care much what success they find" was not obviously borne out. There was, of course, a continuing problem with his writing style. Owen was at points concerned "not to lose myself and reader in this digression," but was prepared to use terminology that many of his readers would have found challenging: "reiglement" was an unusual term that had entered English usage at the end of the sixteenth century, but "inconsutilous" is not once recorded in the *OED*.[100] Owen's casual description of the provenance of his work ("being nothing but an hour's country discourse") was perhaps more believable. For all that it drew on his family convictions, Owen's second book had a provisional quality. Owen was writing without the benefit of a large library, and with an admission that he had perhaps under-utilized the volumes he had in his possession: other matters, he explained, he would "omit until more leisure and an enjoyment of the small remainder of my poor library shall better enable me. For the present . . . although writing without books, I hope I am not beside the truth."[101] In part, this inability to access the relevant scholarly literature provided Owen with an important rhetorical advantage. *The duty of pastors and people distinguished* defended both the priority of preaching and the duty of private interpretation, and balanced the "ancient dignity" of the "sacred calling" with the "Christian liberty" of the "people of God."[102] Owen's inability to consult a wider body of exegetical and theological commentary did not, therefore, invalidate his conclusions. After all, he considered, "he that builds his faith upon preachers, though they preach nothing but truth, and he pretend to believe it, hath indeed no faith at all, but a wavering opinion, build upon a rotten foundation."[103] It was certainly a timely assertion. Six months later, John Milton, during the period in which he was also defending the Presbyterian cause, would make a similar point, warning that "a man may be a heretic in the truth . . . if he believe things only because his pastor says so or the Assembly so determines, without having other reasons, though his belief be true."[104] Milton and Owen agreed: Scripture could speak for itself, if individuals had ears to hear it, and the dull rehearsal of orthodoxy was no substitute for having been persuaded of the truth. Owen complained of those who claimed that the "difference and contrariety among preachers" meant they did "know not what to do nor scarce what to believe": "my answer is, Do but your own duty, and this trouble is at an end. Is there any contrariety in the book of God?"[105] Owen contrasted his intellectual and spiritual independence, which had been forced upon him by his distance from his library, with the tendency of Arminians to defer to one or other variety of authority: "nothing would serve them but a blind submission to the loose dictates of their cobweb homilies."[106] The circumstances of his hasty journey to Fordham provided Owen with the material of rhetorical advantage.

Nevertheless, Owen believed that he had uncovered a high-level conspiracy to undermine the orthodox foundations of the Church of England. He found it impossible not to notice the steady drift of the English establishment: "by their mass have transubstantiated their altars into crosses, their temples into Golgothas, their prelates into Pilates, their priests into hangmen, tormentors of Jesus Christ."[107] In some ways, the Church of England had become comparable to Rome:

> consider what desolate estate the church of God hath been, may be, and at this present in divers places is, reduced to. Her silver may become dross, and her wine be mixed with water, the faithful city becoming a harlot; her shepherds may be turned into dumb, sleeping dogs, and devouring wolves; the watchmen may be turned smiters, her prophets to prophesy falsely, and her priests to bear rule by lies; the commandments of God being made void by the traditions of men, superstition, human inventions, will-worship, may defile and contaminate the service of God; yea, and greater abominations may men possessing Moses' chair by succession do. Now, that the temple of God hath been thus made a den of thieves . . . the abomination of desolation hath been set up in the holy place.[108]

Yet in other respects, Owen continued, the Church of England was in a worse state than that of Rome. Its declension was "unparalleled in any Church, of any age," and could not even be compared to the situation of Catholicism: "what an height of impiety and opposition to Christ the Roman apostacy in a thousand years attained unto," he considered, "and yet I dare aver that never so many errors and suspicions in a hundred years crept into that Church as did into ours of England in sixteen."[109] Writing in 1643, his mathematics hit upon the key date of 1628—the year in which Laud's appointment as bishop of London symbolized the political ascendancy of the Arminians—as the year when the trials of the English church began.

Owen understood that these trials called for a reconsideration of the most fundamental elements of the organization of the English church. In a time of apostasy, he considered, when the church is "collapsed and corrupted . . . when the ordinary teachers are either utterly ignorant and cannot, or negligent and will not perform their duty," the traditional emphasis on ordination could be misplaced. In such times, "gifts in any one to be a teacher, and consent in others by him to be taught, are a sufficient warrant" for the preaching of laymen.[110] But Owen's argument moved from the situation of the English establishment *in extremis* to the constitution of a call to ministry in the ordinary life of the church, when the only "outward call" required to "constitute . . . a preacher of the gospel" was the "consent of God's people to be instructed by him."[111] As in his first book's discussion of baptism, Owen's developing ecclesiology may have had unintended consequences: he set out to defend the church from Arminianism, found himself sidestepping the traditional role of the bishops, and ended up legitimizing the preaching of the laity. Perhaps it was a way to make sense of his own ordination as deacon and priest by the bishop of Oxford—and a way to spare others similar pain.

It is these kinds of claims that made *The duty of pastors and people distinguished* in some ways such a naive publication. Owen concluded his argument with a quotation from "the learned Rutherford" defending Presbyterian government, even though his assumptions entirely contrasted those of Rutherford, whose high Presbyterian ecclesiology could never have countenanced lay preaching in a gathered church.[112] More strategically, *The duty of pastors and people distinguished* "included no discussion of the function and authority of synods as opposed to congregational elders—the issue which many Independents and Presbyterians regarded as their chief point of difference."[113] For all his intention to intervene in a national debate, therefore, Owen rather markedly pulled his punches. The contrast to the vitriol of his first book could not have been greater. It was hardly surprising that *The duty of pastors and people distinguished* was approved by Joseph Caryl, a moderate

Independent and Westminster Assembly member with whom Owen would become closely identified, as representing "much clearness of judgement and moderation of spirit."[114] However he misconstrued other Puritans' arguments, Owen did not want to provoke his brethren. For all that he defended the nascent Presbyterian forms, Owen may already have been leaving them behind.

This strategy of moderation seems to have been successful, for Owen was gaining a reputation as a peacemaker. In April 1644 his name had been listed by residents of Colchester, five miles distant, as a minister who could be consulted in the case of allegations against a local preacher.[115] Owen consolidated this pacific reputation by refusing to take sides in the broader ecclesiological debate. The convening of the Westminster Assembly in the summer of 1643 had begun to highlight the differences between Presbyterians and Independents at a national level, and the publication of *An apologeticall narration* by five "dissenting brethren" in January 1644 had provided an ideological foundation for the emerging party of Independents. But the tone of *An apologeticall narration* was conciliatory, and the movement's earliest days were full of hesitation. It is hardly surprising, therefore, that when Owen was asked to sign a petition demanding that Parliament establish a national system of church government, he did not do so. A national system of church government was a cause he could no longer support.[116]

Reflecting the arguments of the Westminster Assembly's Independents, Owen was coming to conclude in favor of the autonomy of individual congregations. It is not clear whether he read *An apologeticall narration*, but he was very much influenced by another text emanating from the "dissenting brethren." In June, Thomas Goodwin and Philip Nye republished John Cotton's *Keyes of the kingdom of heaven* (1644) as an intervention in the Assembly's debates. It is not clear that the book made much of an impact among the divines, but it had a huge influence on Owen as he read it over the course of the autumn, as the next few years would demonstrate. For, as winter approached and local residents anxiously tracked an outbreak of plague, Owen had become an Independent.[117]

II

Perhaps it was the birth of Owen's first son, John, who was baptized on 20 December 1644, that suggested his next project—a series of texts designed to inculcate the elements of Christian faith to young and unlearned believers.[118] But these texts also responded to a national context. *The principles of the doctrine of Christ* were to be, as the subtitle put it, *Unfolded in two short catechismes, wherein those principles of religion are explained, the knowledge whereof is required by the late ordinance of Parliament, before any person bee admitted to the sacrament of the Lords Supper* (1645). Parliament's new caution about the proper observation of the Eucharist reflected long-standing debates among Puritan theologians about the qualifications for godly communicants. Owen was not alone in preparing instructional materials. Walter Bridges's *A catechisme for communicants* and William Twisse's *A brief catecheticall exposition of Christian doctrine* were also published in 1645. The Westminster Assembly's Directory for Public Worship began to circulate in the early part of the year as a source of liturgical formulae replacing those of the Book of Common Prayer. Ralph Josselin first encountered the Directory in March; by August he had followed its formula for baptism for the first time.[119] But he did not so rapidly follow its guidance regarding the other Protestant sacrament: Josselin had stopped celebrating the Lord's Supper in the early 1640s, and only returned to the practice in 1651.[120] Owen's catechisms, in attempting to prepare his parishioners for the administration of the Lord's Supper, offered an account of parish ministry that was fundamentally different from that of Josselin, reflecting assumptions about the necessity of the Lord's Supper appropriate for a "Calvinist sacramentarian."[121] The differences between the two parishes were fundamental. Both ministers struggled to deal with impenitent parishioners, but while Josselin appears to have assumed that his congregation was unfit for communion, and abandoned the sacrament for the best part of a decade, Owen sought to improve the spiritual condition of his people according to the latest parliamentary ordinance about admission to the Supper, in order to have them commune.[122]

Owen's book of catechisms, also published by Philemon Stephens, suggested the extent to which its author may have adopted his new vocational identity. While it is impossible to know the extent to which Owen was responsible for their content, it is worth noting that the title pages of his first three books change their identification of the author. While the title page on his first book had expanded Owen's academic connections, describing him as a "Master of Arts of Queen's College in Oxon," *The duty of pastors and people distinguished* referred to Owen only as "M.A. of Q. Col. O.," and his book of catechisms described its author simply as "pastor" of the Fordham congregation.[123] This publication was clearly local in origin, though Owen's decision to publish the work with a major London firm suggests that he regarded his parish ministry as something of wider consequence—perhaps a model of clerical activity of which others should take notice—as Richard Baxter would later believe of his own parish ministry. Ironically, the only writer to engage with Owen's model of parish practice would be George Fox, in *The great mystery of the great whore unfolded* (1659).[124]

The catechisms continued Owen's project to publish parallel texts to those of the Westminster Assembly, perhaps in an effort to attract the attention of its members, who were debating the content of their own catechisms during this period. But the ostensible addressees of Owen's third published work were his parishioners. "Brethren, my heart's desire and request unto God for you is, that you may be saved," his preface began, in a series of allusions to the Pauline epistles; "I have great heaviness and continual sorrow in my heart, for them amongst you who, as yet, walk disorderly, and not as beseemeth the Gospel, little labouring to acquaint themselves with the mystery of godliness."[125] And so Owen had his catechisms printed, despite the fact that "the least part of the parish are able to read it in writing."[126] He adverted that he intended to follow his catechisms with an exposition of the Lord's Prayer, the Ten Commandments, and the Apostles' Creed, a promise that was eventually fulfilled, alongside a further catechism, in his primer for children (1652).[127] But his purpose in instructing his parishioners in these classic statements of Christian knowledge appears to have reflected his new responsibility to control access to the Lord's Supper in terms of the doctrinal standards of the recent parliamentary ordinance.

Owen believed that his parishioners should be able to give a good account of the Christian faith as it was understood by the emerging Puritan party. His "Lesser catechism" reduced the principles of the Christian religion to twenty-five chapters, mostly of one question each, in a format not reproduced in the Goold edition. Perhaps significantly, Owen included in the shorter catechism a reference to his high view of the efficacy of baptism, which, he argued, is "a holy ordinance, whereby, being sprinkled with water according to Christ's institution, we are by his grace made children of God, and have the promises of the covenant sealed unto us."[128] Owen's robust sacramentalism, which argued that baptism effects the covenant child's adoption by God, was something he would later abandon, perhaps in part because of its divergence from the account of baptism offered in the Westminster Assembly's Directory for Public Worship. The Directory allowed that baptism could be performed by "pouring or sprinkling," and not, as Owen insisted, only by sprinkling; it argued that the children of believers were already "Christians, and federally holy before Baptisme," and not, as Owen insisted, that they were turned into children of God by baptism.[129] His "Greater catechism" meanwhile organized the principles of faith in twenty-seven chapters, of up to seven questions each. Again, he included in his basic Christian teaching a firm commitment to an idea not shared by the majority of Puritan clergy. One of the most marked features of his catechetical theology is its idiosyncratic view of the Mosaic covenant. For many centuries, theologians had been debating the relationship between the Old and New Testaments. The revival of interest in biblical covenants among Protestant theologians could not disguise the fact that they did not agree on the relationship between the moral law given in Eden, the Ten Commandments given to Moses, and the new law of righteousness given by Jesus Christ. Owen's larger catechism described the covenant of works as the "law that God gave man at first to fulfil," and suggested that this was "the same which was afterwards writen with the finger of God in two tables of stone on Mount Horeb, called the Ten Commandments."[130] It was an idea to which he would later return, arguing throughout his life, though not consistently, that the covenant at Sinai represented a republication of the law given to Adam and Eve in Eden. The idea was current in some Puritan circles. Both *The marrow of modern divinity* (1645) and Samuel Bolton's *The true bounds of Christian freedome* (1645), the latter of which was printed by Philemon Stephens, shared Owen's conviction that the Mosaic covenant was a reprise of the covenant of works that God had made with Adam. Bolton, who in the same year in which he published his book was appointed master of Christ's College, Cambridge, and was later to become vice chancellor of the university, recognized that the issue was among the "the greatest knots in the practicall parts of Divinitie," precisely because, he admitted, "we are not without some places of Scriptures which declare the Law to be abrogated: nor without some againe that speake it yet to be in force."[131] The status of the Mosaic covenant had become "one of the great Disputes in these dayes: whether this be abrogated. Or ... whether Beleevers are freed from the Morall Law."[132] And there were terrible dangers in this time of confusion: "Sathan sought to vent many errors ... it is his best season for merchandizing, at such a time he finds most Chapmen, and in the heat of the market while men are buying truths, he may hope to put off some of his own wares."[133] A similar argument was made in *The marrow of modern divinity*, which was published anonymously by Edward Fisher (fl. 1627–55), a lay theologian who was also a member of the Company of Barber–Surgeons, resident in the parish of St. Sepulchre, London.[134] This interpretative latitude on the Mosaic law was closed down by the divines of the Westminster Assembly, whose confession of faith (1647) described the Mosaic covenant not in relation to the covenant of works but as the legal dispensation of the covenant of grace (WCF 7: 4–6). After its publication, Owen must have found himself in an embarrassing situation, with the key doctrinal statement of the envisaged national Presbyterian settlement, supported by the English Parliament and formally adopted by the Church of Scotland, now ruling out a key principle of the instruction he had presented to his Fordham parishioners as a basic element of Christian knowledge.

But Owen's embarrassment may have been ameliorated by his gradual movement away from the emerging Presbyterian party. When he had arrived at Fordham, in July 1643, Owen had identified himself as a Presbyterian, and as an opponent of the toleration of sects. He was, he later reflected,

> a young man . . . about the age of twenty-six or twenty-seven years. The controversy between Independency and Presbytery was young also, nor, indeed, by me clearly understood, especially as stated on the congregational side. . . . Only, being unacquainted with the congregational way, I professed myself to own the other party, not knowing but that my principles were suited to their judgement and profession, having looked very little farther into those affairs than I was led by an opposition to Episcopacy and ceremonies. . . . Of the congregational way I was not acquainted with any one person, minister or other; not had I, to my knowledge, seen any more than one in my life. My acquaintance lay wholly with ministers and people of the Presbyterian way.[135]

Of course, as we have already noted, Owen's Presbyterianism was of a muted kind, and his account of *The duty of pastors and people distinguished* had not considered the principal difference between the two leading parties among the godly—the question of whether local congregations could be bound by the decisions of a regional synod. The fact that Owen's change of heart came through reading John Cotton suggests that he had not yet come across a copy of Bradshaw's manifesto for congregational autonomy, first published in 1605—another telling indicator of the character of the "painful nonconformity" in which he grew up. We do not know the identity of the Independent apologist whom Owen claimed to have met, or whether this was the individual through whom Owen obtained his copy of Cotton's *Keyes of the kingdom of heaven* (1644). But we do know that Owen read Cotton's work shortly after its publication, and that he found convincing its arguments in favor of congregational autonomy.

III

Owen's conversion to Independent church government in the summer or autumn of 1644 marks one of the most important turning points of his life. This was, perhaps, the moment when he broke ranks with his father and brother, both of whom may have continued to operate in Presbyterian circles.

Owen's interaction with Cotton's book was not slavish, for he rejected its arguments against the toleration of "sects." In *The duty of pastors and people distinguished*, Owen had refused to allow that those who pursue the "true worship of God" but who "wilfully abstain from the public congregations" should be "allowed the benefit of private meetings." If these dissenting Christians were allowed to gather for worship independently of parish structures, the result would be "confused licentiousness."[136] The context for this remark was a private paper that Owen had drawn up, in which he explored the question of whether Arminians should be allowed to convene private meetings for worship, as the Dutch Remonstrants had argued.[137] But Owen was becoming less sure of this position, perhaps because his own theological perspective was increasingly distant from that of the national orthodoxy then being agreed at the Westminster Assembly. As his catechisms emphasized themes in basic Christian knowledge that differed from those of the Westminster divines, Owen found himself slipping into an odd kind of nonconformity. He began to change his mind about the appropriateness of private meetings—a change of mind the significance of which he would later downplay.[138] As the Westminster Assembly codified Christian knowledge in ways that Owen did not, he found himself again considering how best to perpetuate his theological emphases in the experience of defeat.

It was not just his adoption of Independent ecclesiology that would have encouraged his reconsideration of the boundaries of toleration. Although, as Cook observes, "[i]ndependent theory by no means necessitated belief in toleration," English Independents "were a minority and could not expect to survive except under a policy of toleration."[139] The two issues clinched his theological transition. Owen had arrived in Fordham as a Presbyterian who opposed the state's toleration of sects. He had continued to define his understanding of basic Christian knowledge in ways that grew increasingly differentiated from those of the body negotiating the terms of the new religious settlement: Owen could no longer depend on the state's defending his views. Three years later, he emerged (and left the parish) as an Independent whose security depended upon the state's toleration of sects. Of course, as his reading of Cotton had indicated, Independency did not require a commitment to toleration. Owen "never favoured the total separation of church and state."[140] While he was prepared to allow private meetings of those believers whose consciences could not permit them to attend parish worship, he still expected national unity on fundamentals, did not expect that heretics should be allowed to publish their beliefs, and insisted that blasphemy and idolatry were crimes.[141]

Owen developed his ideas about ecclesiology and toleration in written form, and the resultant "country essay" circulated in manuscript within local clerical networks. The paper contributed to a larger debate about the permissible boundaries of toleration. This debate, which was concentrated in the 1640s, precipitated "a bitter family quarrel among puritans," and generated a huge bibliography on the subject, matched "nowhere else in seventeenth-century Europe, with the possible exception of the Netherlands."[142] Owen had come to Fordham as a representative of the Presbyterian party, which saw itself as defending the historic position of the Reformed churches against the opinion that toleration should be extended to those who could not adhere to their confession, a position once held only by Socinians, Arminians, and Anabaptists, but now openly advocated by otherwise conservative Independent clergy. This anti-toleration party was supported by such heresiarchs as Robert Baillie, Samuel Rutherford, Thomas Edwards, John Bastwick, and Ephraim Pagitt, who each campaigned, in Rutherford's phrase, against "pretended liberty of conscience," believing, as John Coffey has put it, that "a nation that prayed together, stayed together."[143] But Owen was breaking from their ranks, and suggesting that toleration should also be extended to those Protestants who adhered to a basic statement of orthodox faith. It took some time for the wider networks of the godly to become aware of his new convictions. He would go public with his new positions on ecclesiology and toleration in an appendix to his next publication, in the spring of 1646. But not all of his readers understood the direction of his arguments. In 1647, William Bartlet, himself an Independent, was still referring to Owen's "Country essay" as reflecting the sentiments of a moderate Presbyterian.[144] Owen continued to consider the biblical ideals for the government of the church and the government of society. But by the age of thirty, he had established the basic positions on ecclesiology, covenant theology, and toleration that he would continue to defend throughout his life. He had not been invited to attend what would become the most significant assembly of Protestant theologians in the seventeenth century, but he was about to be invited to take up a position of influence from which he would advance those ideas—a public career in which, in the short term, he would shape church and state more effectively than would the Westminster Assembly.

3

Frustrated Pastor

OWEN'S MINISTRY IN Fordham continued in a relatively undisturbed part of England. Essex was some distance from the major centers of conflict in the first civil war, and, during much of the conflict, its inhabitants were not subject to the depredations and forced quarter of friendly or hostile soldiers. But Owen was neither ignorant of nor unaffected by the wider political and military situation. Rumors were widely circulated, and local diaries provide evidence of how "news" reached the area, sometimes being corrected and sometimes being confirmed to be true.[1] Stories also circulated in print. The civil war was, after all, one of the first media conflicts, and it provided the context for the emergence of multiple public spheres, in which English society became increasingly demarcated into competing political, social, and religious constituencies. The abolition of the Star Chamber and the collapse of the censorship that had followed it facilitated the proliferation of a new genre of reportage.[2] The newsbooks initially focused on descriptions of rebellion in Ireland but increasingly represented to their readers the progress of the war in England.[3] One of the most important and widely read of these publications was *The moderate intelligencer*, an almost complete run of which, dating from 1645 to 1648, was later included in the catalogue for the sale of Owen's library.[4] *The moderate intelligencer* was promoted as an impartial newspaper of record, which reported on the events of the civil war in the context of a generous selection of foreign stories, and as the sympathies of its editor, John Dillingham, moved from support of Parliament to the Leveller party and finally to the king.[5] If Owen did own the issues that were later sold as part of his estate, he may have collected them during this period, and their representation of current events may have shaped his interpretation of the war. For Dillingham's reporting was judicious. *The moderate intelligencer* made sense of the war by reprinting official documents from both sides of the conflict and by summarizing key events in note form, offering to its readers a collation rather than an interpretation of political data. Dillingham allowed his readers the privilege of sense-making—an editorial latitude that paralleled the role of the state in Owen's developing understanding of the relationship between divine revelation and the limits of religious toleration.

As the war progressed, so too did Owen's career. Sometime in the spring of 1646, he was invited to become the vicar of a more promising neighboring parish. The move was made possible because of confusion as to the legality of Owen's appointment in Fordham. He had been installed in Fordham by the Committee for Plundered Ministers, a subgroup of the Committee to which he had dedicated his first book, on the understanding that its previous incumbent, John Alsop, had fled to the Continent.[6] But rumors that circulated in the area suggested that Alsop had in fact died. Owen must have been unsettled by these stories: if Alsop had died, the rights to present to the parish would have reverted to its patron, Sir John Lucas, who had been imprisoned by Parliament in 1642 for his support of the royalist cause, and who was no friend of Puritans. Owen's ministry in Fordham now lacked legal credibility, and he may have begun to prepare for a move. His last entry in the parish register recorded a baptism that took place in December 1645.[7] It was at this point that his connections to Coggeshall worked to his advantage.

For all their differences, the parishes of Fordham and Coggeshall, which were around five miles apart, were part of the same regional network of churches.[8] On 3 March 1646, elders from both congregations had participated in a meeting of a classis—an arrangement that suggests that local Presbyterian structures were beginning to emerge in advance of Parliament's ruling on the issue at the end of May.[9] Owen, in a gesture that may have reflected his new convictions about congregational autonomy, does not appear to have attended this meeting.[10] But his transfer from Fordham to Coggeshall may have been facilitated by these emerging inter-church links. For, with the support of the earl of Warwick, who was patron of the parish, the Coggeshall congregation invited Owen to become their new pastor.[11]

The situation then grew more confused. It transpired that the rumors had been false: Alsop had not in fact died, the living had not reverted to its patron, but continued to be in the control of the Committee, and Owen could indeed continue as the parish minister of Fordham. The Committee summoned Owen to London, and offered him the choice of both charges. But Owen's hand may have been forced. He had publicly criticized the religious condition of Fordham, and had grown frustrated by its large number of "grossly ignorant persons."[12] It is also possible that his wife wanted to return to her home village. Owen accepted the offer of the parish of Coggeshall.[13] By 2 May 1646, he had been replaced in Fordham by Richard Pulley, who struggled to gain the approbation of the Westminster Assembly committee that examined his suitability for the move, and whose ministry was in keeping with the parish's traditional resistance to the hotter sort of Protestantism. Pulley was replaced by John Bulkley in 1649, but returned to the parish in 1660 and conformed to the new Anglican settlement.[14] Owen had ably judged his first parishioners: his legacy in Fordham was not to be enduring.

Owen's new situation allowed him to move beyond the task of basic Christian instruction, which had occupied his years in Fordham, to consolidate the labors of an incumbent with whom he had far more in common. The previous vicar of Coggeshall, Obadiah Sedgewick, was an established author, most recently of *The doubting believer* (1641); he was a regular preacher to Parliament, a determined Presbyterian who had been called to St. Mildred's, Bread Street, London, when the Long Parliament had convened, and who had been appointed a member of the Westminster Assembly when it convened in 1643.[15] The Coggeshall church would have been "vacant" for some time, and its preaching, before Owen's appointment, had partly been supplied by a neighboring minister, Ralph Josselin.[16] Josselin might have been pleased to hear of Owen's appointment, since the journey from Earls Colne to Coggeshall was "tedious." In early February 1646, he had to travel through country that had just begun to thaw after one of the hardest winters on record, which was represented in his diary by six weeks of "ice of wonderfull thicknes, nigh half a yard in some places," and the freezing over of the Thames.[17] But Owen's move to Coggeshall took some time: while Josselin had noted on 31 March 1646 that such a move was expected, and while the title page of a sermon published in May described Owen as "pastor" of the congregation, he was installed as vicar of the parish only on 18 August 1646.[18]

Whatever the reason for these delays, Owen's move to Coggeshall was in every respect a move for the better. Around two thousand people attended worship in the parish church—though this was perhaps a reflection of the legal requirement to attend public worship.[19] The living offered a comfortable income for a young minister with a small family. Its value of £110 per annum in 1639 compared well with the value of Earls Colne, a neighboring parish, which had been worth £80 per annum when Josselin arrived in 1641.[20] The parliamentary survey of Essex livings in 1650 indicated that "a clergyman's actual income might be very much greater than that given in contemporary ecclesiastical surveys."[21] But Josselin's diary, throughout the 1640s, testifies to his perpetual worries that his income was insufficient: he found it difficult to collect his stipend from his patron and parishioners, and it is possible that Owen faced similar kinds of challenges.[22] The Coggeshall congregation would afford Owen some lifelong friends: one member, Robert Asty, would still be corresponding with him in 1675; and Robert's son, John, who would grow up in Owen's London congregation in the 1670s, would publish an important biography of his pastor in 1721.[23] More important, Owen was leaving the "grossly ignorant" inhabitants of Fordham to serve a congregation that, John Asty would later recall, was "generally sober, religious, and discreet," and which had a direct link to the most important clerical assembly of the time.[24]

It is likely that Owen's move to Coggeshall would have brought him into immediate contact with members of the Westminster Assembly.[25] Parliament had devolved to the Assembly the responsibility to monitor the suitability of clerical candidates, and the divines took this responsibility seriously. Although a full register of their examinations does not appear to have survived, the minutes of the Assembly refer to the names of almost two thousand men who were interviewed in connection with their appointment as schoolmasters, academics, and ministers.[26] Joel Halcomb, who has provided the most detailed account of the means by which clerical transfers were processed, has estimated that the Assembly examined around five thousand men for these positions, including the ministers who replaced Owen in his first two parishes.[27] And their process of examination was not straightforward. The Assembly ensured that all candidates for appointments had subscribed to the Solemn League and Covenant, and tested clerical candidates in a wide-ranging oral examination that assessed their abilities in theology, languages, and philosophy.[28] Clerical appointees had to preach a trial sermon to the Assembly, in an exercise normally scheduled to take place before divines began the main business of the day. Those appointees who passed these rigorous examinations took their paperwork to the Committee for Plundered Ministers, which formalized their new appointment.[29] We might expect that Sedgewick paid particular attention to the Assembly's examination of the candidate who was hoping to become his replacement, but his name does not appear in any of Owen's writing during this period. Neither does Owen's name appear in any of the surviving records of the Assembly, although the records do refer to his replacements in Fordham and Coggeshall. But he could not have avoided the Assembly's examination. Finally—though hardly distinctively, or in the circumstances he might have preferred—he had come to the attention of the divines.

Despite the Assembly's approval of his gifts, however, Owen was a source of some concern to his neighbors. In the parishes immediately surrounding Fordham and Coggeshall there were growing tensions about the issue of church government, which had so disturbed and divided the Westminster divines. In March 1646, Josselin heard William Archer, the lecturer of Halstead, only two miles from Earls Colne, assert that "Presbyterians were all of them proud conceited persons." Josselin immediately defended the honor of his party: "upon which I asking him whether he meant so, he sayd he would not answer mee, but gave mee very unkind words."[30] Josselin was not sure whether Owen would be an effective peacemaker. On 31 March 1646, he noted Owen's change of pastoral situation, and added a note of concern about the growth of ecclesiological innovation: "Mr Owen removes to Coggeshall, he proposed a new project for gathering of churches, nothing but projects, and conceits our devices are best. god [*sic*] give us a good and helpfull(.) neighbour of him."[31] These tensions about church government would have continued into May 1646 when local ministers met to debate congregational autonomy—a meeting from which Josselin asked to be excused.[32] Whatever the concerns of his neighbors, however, Owen was certainly to benefit from his new situation. He had a new living, with financial benefits and fewer pastoral challenges, a new opportunity to gather a fellowship along congregational lines, and he had finally come to the attention of well-placed patrons in London. The weather, too, was full of promise. There was going to be a "very early spring."[33]

I

Owen's move to Coggeshall marked a turning point in his fortunes. Around the same time that Josselin noted his change of circumstances, members of Parliament would have agreed that Owen should preach on their next day of fasting.[34] These monthly devotional exercises for MPs had been inaugurated by the Long Parliament in 1640, with the approval of the king. It is not clear why Charles consented to the scheme, for it "put into the hands of his enemies a means of co-ordination and propaganda to which he himself had no parallel."[35] While the fast-day sermons became an important component of the discursive formation of parliamentary ideology in the mid-1640s, it is difficult to assess their impact. There is "no indication that attendance on the part of the entire membership of the house [of Commons] was expected," for example, and some preachers complained of the inattention of their auditors: there were frequent complaints that MPs came "to judge the Sermon, not to be judged by the Sermon."[36] Similarly, while the sermons articulated a "common ideology (rendered in a religious idiom) which would sustain radical activity and contribute to its coherence," they also evidenced a broad and sometimes contradictory spectrum of mood and aspiration.[37] The first several years of fast-day sermons were dominated by members of the Westminster Assembly, though the Scots Commissioners were not invited to preach to the Commons after July 1644.[38] By the spring of 1646 the program of preaching had entered a "new phase" in which Presbyterian voices were being eclipsed;

its themes became increasingly radical, and its preachers were increasingly recruited from a younger generation of theologians associated with the rising party of the Independents.[39] The "external record of the preaching to parliament thus mirrors the religious changes taking place in the realm."[40] The new direction of the fast-day sermon program was signaled by Hugh Peters, in *Gods doings, and mans duty*, preached on 2 April 1646. And the preaching at the next fast, which was held at the end of that month, illustrated the increasing bifurcation of the religious mood of the Commons: neither of the invited preachers was a member of the Westminster Assembly, and each of them identified with different factions among its divines.

Owen's invitation to address the Commons on 29 April 1646 was another instance of his benefiting from his network of well-placed friends. Invitations to preach to Parliament were "extended personally" by patrons, and Owen had been nominated to preach to the MPs by Sir Peter Wentworth and Thomas Westrow.[41] Wentworth's involvement in making the invitation would have been no great surprise: he was very active in nominating preachers between 1643 and 1648, and may not have known Owen personally.[42] Westrow's involvement was more significant: he had studied with Owen at Queen's, and was the son of Sir Edward Scot, Owen's earlier patron, to whom *The duty of pastors and people distinguished* (1644) had been dedicated.[43] Now an MP, Westrow does not seem to have been particularly active in nominating preachers, so he may have been doing his old college friend a special favor in making these arrangements, perhaps after meeting Owen during his trip to London to be interviewed by the Westminster Assembly.[44] But Westrow may have mistaken his man, for, as Josselin had already noted, Owen's views on the government of church and state were in transition, and there is no record of any further communication between them before Westrow's early death was commemorated by George Wither in *Westrow revived* (1653).

Nevertheless, Owen was provided with the visibility he had long been seeking when the Commons convened for its day of humiliation on 29 April 1646. While the significance of the date could hardly have been anticipated when the Commons invited the unknown preacher to lead their devotions, it did mark the effective end of the civil war. Sir Ralph Hopton and Sir Jacob Astley, the last generals fighting in the royalist cause, had recently surrendered, and at the end of April, in the week immediately preceding the preaching, Charles had escaped from Oxford in a "tacit acknowledgement of defeat," beginning the journey that would end in his surrender to the Scots.[45] But this was not a special service to commemorate these extraordinary events, and they made little impact upon either of the day's sermons: the situation would have looked less conclusive at the time than it has done in retrospect, and contemporary newsbooks wondered whether Charles was in fact fomenting a new conspiracy in London.[46] James Nalton, a local Presbyterian minister, was the first of the day's preachers. His sermon, *Delay of reformation provoking Gods further indignation* (1646), reflected on the "marvailous things that God did for us as *Edge-hill*, at *Newbery*, at *Marston-moore*, at *Nazeby*, famous *Nazeby*, never to be forgotten while we have a tongue to speak the praises of our God, for THERE did *God break the Arrows of the Bow, the shield and the sword, and the battell*."[47] Nalton was worried that God's interventions in favor of Parliament were being squandered. "Our young men have been slain with the edge of the sword, our Widows have bewailed the losse of their husbands, our Orphans have bewailed the losse of their Parents. . . . Villages plundered, houses fired, Brethren imprisoned, Women abused, estates devoured, whole Counties wasted," he considered.[48] Yet the religious condition of England had not improved. Instead, a growing anticlericalism was driving the profileration of new heresies: "I dare boldly say, never was there in any age or Nation under Heaven, a greater contempt cast upon this Ordinance, then there is at this day, especially by subtle and undermining *Sectaries* and Seducers, who cast dirt upon the very paps which they have sucked, villifying those Ministers and that Ministry, whereby they were first enlightened."[49] Warming to his theme, he called upon the Commons to accept the advice of the Westminster Assembly and to renew their commitment to the Solemn League and Covenant.[50] Reflecting on magistrates' duty to legislate against sin, he warned MPs not to "TOLERATE what God would not have TOLERATED" out of "Cowardize or carnall fears, out of sinfull complyance and conformity to the wils of men," for, he continued, "I concieve it worthy the consideration of the wisest, whether the Devill would not thinke he had made a good bargaine, and gained well by the Reformation, if he could exchange the *Prelacie* for an *Universall Liberty*."[51] Nalton's sermon concluded with an admonition for MPs to ensure that "*errours and heresies be discountenanced and suppressed*," and, in what may have been a telling allusion to Thomas Edwards's heresiography, the first installment of which had very recently been published, exhorted MPs to "stop the spreading of this Gangrene, before it over-run the whole body of the Kingdome."[52]

Owen followed Nalton into the pulpit, and, in an example of the ideological variety that characterized the fast-day sermons during their ideological turning point, set about denying his colleague's principal claims. This was in some respects a surprising move, for the men appeared to be similar. Owen would also have subscribed to the Solemn League and Covenant, for this was required of all clergymen appointed by the Committee for Plundered Minsters, and he had spent much of the previous few years trying to attract the attention of members of the Westminster Assembly. Like Nalton, Owen was, at least formally, pastor of a Presbyterian church. But now, having been granted a public voice, and in a forum that provided the opportunity to influence key political and religious networks, he suddenly appeared to sacrifice everything for a new principle. Owen's sermon, *A vision of unchangable free mercy* (1646), advanced a robust critique of the assumptions that underlay Nalton's argument, and took advantage of the Commons' invitation to publish the sermon by appending additional material on the vexed issue of toleration of which MPs may not have approved. Owen was fixing his commitments to the political, if not yet the ecclesiological, principles of the "dissenting brethren," the Independents whose interventions had achieved so little in the Westminster Assembly but whose key ideas were shaping the direction of the civil war by means of their influence in the army.[53]

Owen's first published sermon was a substantial effort, which Goold believed evidenced "a strain of holy fervour and commanding eloquence" to "bear comparison with the best productions of the British pulpit."[54] It was published by Philemon Stephens around one month after its delivery, and it reflected the uncertainty and chaos that followed the king's escape from Oxford. "Whilst the passages of providence are on us, all is confusion," Owen considered, as he reflected on the "day of England's visitation."[55] But his concern was religious rather than political. For "England's troubles" were related to the "almost departing gospel."[56] Like Nalton, Owen worried that "we again in our days have made forfeiture of the purity of his worship, by an almost universal treacherous apostasy; from which the free grace and good pleasure of God hath made a great progress again toward a recovery."[57] The "apostasy" to which Owen was referring was that of the "late hierarchists." Perhaps remembering his close encounter with Arminianism at Oxford, Owen blasted the Laudian threat:

> In worship, their paintings, crossings, crucifixes, bowings, cringing, altars, tapers, wagers, organs, anthems, litany, rails, images, copes, vestments—what were they but Roman varnish, an Italian dress for our devotion, to draw on conformity with that enemy of the Lord Jesus? In doctrine, the divinity of Episcopacy, auricular confession, free-will, predestination on faith, yea, works foreseen, "limbus patrum," justification by works, falling from grace, authority of a church, which none knew what it was, canonical obedience, holiness of churches, and the like innumerable—what were they but helps to Sancta Clara, to make all our articles of religion speak good Roman Catholic?[58]

Arminianism was ultimately destructive of the gospel, Owen concluded: "were a man a drunkard, a swearer, a Sabbath-breaker, an unclean person, so he were no Puritan, and had money . . . the Episcopal heaven was open for them all."[59] Again, he insisted, the civil war was a struggle for true religion.

And so, again like Nalton, Owen believed that the war had illustrated God's concern for England. It "hath made a discovery of England's strength, what it is able to do," he observed. That strength was primarily spiritual, evident not in the "armies it can raise against men" but in the "armies of prayers and tears" by which it could "deal with God." The wars had taught English Christians to pray: "Had not two sorts of people struggled in the womb of this kingdom, we had not sought, nor received, such gracious answers."[60] But the outcome of the conflict still hung in the balance, and all of these gospel blessings could be removed, he continued. Gesturing toward a vast historical panorama, he invited his listeners to consider whether they had ever seen

> the gospel hover about a nation, now and then about to settle, and anon scared and upon wing again; yet working through difficulties, making plains of mountains and filling valleys, overthrowing armies, putting aliens to flight, and at length taking firm root like the cedars of God? Truly if you have not, you are strangers to the place wherein you live.[61]

Yet Owen balanced this concern with a conviction of England's national election. "If now England has received more culture from God than other nations, there is more fruit expected from England than other nations," he considered, as he reflected on the import of Isaiah 5: "For the present, the vineyard of the Lord of hosts is the house of England."[62]

Owen's confidence that the "reformation of England shall be more glorious than of any nation in the world" was made possible by his memory of the reformation.[63] Owen identified himself as a faithful Protestant. When the "kingdom of the beast" was "full of darkness," he remembered, God raised up "reformers, and by them kindles a light, we hope, never to be put out."[64] This reference to the dying words of Thomas Cranmer—at least as reported in the period's most influential and frequently reprinted martyrology, John Foxe's *Acts and monuments* (1563)—was followed by a series of allusions to other sixteenth-century reformers. Owen nodded toward the vision that had confirmed Zwingli in his doctrine of the Lord's Supper, reflecting the interest in extraordinary revelation that extended across several of his early publications, even if Zwingli's symbolic interpretation of the sacraments was something that Owen had already publicly dismissed.[65] He alluded to Calvin in explaining the relationship between divine sovereignty and human sin, arguing that the "sun exhaling a smell from the kennel, is the cause of the smell, but not of its noisomeness."[66] Invoking these theological commonplaces, Owen was in some ways writing himself into the tradition he most valued. His preaching was acutely self-aware, and when during the sermon Owen warned his auditors of the "idol free-will, with the new goddess contingency," he was doing no more than quoting the subtitle of *A display of Arminianisme*.[67] Given his record of self-promotion, and his publisher's later attempt to offload surplus copies of the text, one could be forgiven for imagining that Owen, in the most important sermon of his life to date, was waving around a copy of his first book.

It is difficult to know how much of his sermon can be attributed to performance. We might not be surprised to discover his concern for the progress of the gospel in Wales, as well as in Ireland, France, and the dark corners of the land.[68] But the minister who had complained about and then had chosen to leave the ignorant people of Fordham was less persuasive when he hoped that his colleagues would "flee to those places where, in all probability, the harvest would be great, and the labourers are few or none at all."[69] And while Owen may have sincerely hoped for "less writing, and more praying," as an early beneficiary of the new access to print, he was certainly not among those whose goal it was to "spare perishing paper."[70]

Nevertheless, Owen's parliamentary debut was evidently successful, even though he had admitted that his sermon had caused some difficulty, particularly in terms of his defense of a limited toleration.[71] The Commons asked that the sermon be printed, as most fast-day sermons were, and *A vision of unchangable free mercy* later appeared under the imprint of Philemon Stephens.[72] But Owen took advantage of the sermon's status as a semi-official publication by appending to his text *A short defensative about church-government, (with a countrey essay for the practice of church-government there)*. Always leveraging for influence, Owen explained that his sermon had prompted questions about the extent to which he supported religious toleration, and that he had written the "country essay" to explain his position "at the request of a worthy friend."[73] Continuing the lifelong habit of understating the circumstances of his writing, Owen explained that "after my sermon was printed to the last sheet, I was forced to set apart a few hours, to give an account" of his views on toleration.[74] Its composition was hurried ("the printer stays for every line") and ill-formed ("this unwillingly-exposed embryo and rude abortion") and it may have been this haste that drove Owen to coin terms (like "lenitives") that are not recorded in the *OED*.[75] Of course, his appeal for the evangelization of Wales and other of the nation's "dark corners" had already hinted at his convictions regarding toleration. He had explained, in his sermon, that he would "rejoice" if "Jesus Christ might be preached, though with some defects in some circumstances."[76]

It was this latitude about precise forms that explained why he had not subscribed to recent petitions about church government, no doubt to the chagrin of some of his more committed Presbyterian neighbors.[77] "Let a spade be called a spade," he continued in his longest passage of self-categorization, but let not theologians use hysterical language to abominate the positions of their opponents. The debate about orthodoxy and toleration, though rancorous, was too often uninformed: "Names are in the power of many; things and their causes are known to few."[78] Owen explained that he was not going to be frightened by those, like Nalton, who used rhetorical tricks like assonance to associate "subtle and undermining *Sectaries* and Seducers."[79] Owen would not be cowed by claims that he was a sectary, for the charge could be made against Christians of all kinds:

> I know my profession to the greatest part of the world is sectarism, as Christianity; amongst those who profess the name of Christ, to the greatest number I am a sectary, because a Protestant; amongst Protestants, at least the one half account all men of my persuasion Calvinistical, sacramentarian sectaries; amongst these, again, to some I have been a puritanical sectary, an Arian heretic, because anti-prelatical; yea, and amongst these last, not a few account me a sectary because I plead for presbyterial government in churches . . . therefore, as I find by experience that the horrid names of heretic, schismatic, sectary, and the like, have never had any influence or force upon my judgement . . . so I am persuaded it is also with others.[80]

After all, he concluded, the misuse of names had turned "Christendom" into a "theatre of blood."[81]

The "country essay" was published as an "urgent intervention in a fierce debate."[82] It marked an important stage in Owen's developing thinking about the nature and function of church and state. On the one hand, he was still pleading for "presbyterial government in churches," though gesturing toward the "paucity of positive rules in the Scripture for church government": it is important to note that the plural form of "churches" indicated Owen's belief that individual congregations should be governed by elders (the Independent position), not that these elders should govern groups of churches (the Presbyterian position).[83] On the other hand, he was promoting a much broader public orthodoxy than that allowed by most Presbyterians.[84] John Coffey, one of Owen's most perceptive modern readers, has noticed important similarities between the advocates of toleration in the mid-1640s. "If the rhetoric echoes the radical tolerationists," he explains, "so do [Owen's] arguments."[85]

Owen's "critique of the proponents of coercion" has a "moral or prophetic fervour . . . which could come straight from the pages of the *Bloudy Tenent*"—Roger Williams's definitive defense of toleration (1644).[86] Coffey notes that the "country essay" offers conclusions that Owen would later retract, including the "fallibilist argument," which "stands in contrast to his later theological writings, in which defining heresy with clarity is an overriding concern."[87] And Owen would eventually draw back from his total opposition to executions for heresy.[88] Nevertheless, Coffey concludes, the "country essay" would have "pleased tolerationists far more than their opponents," for the "great bulk of the piece was directed against hardline Presbyterian advocates of uniformity."[89] On a journey from Presbyterianism to Indendependency, and advancing an increasingly broad view of toleration, Owen may have realized that he, too, could become a victim in Christendom's increasingly violent "theatre of blood."[90] The Parliamentarians were dividing in the war about religion.

II

Owen's theology was evolving in Coggeshall as the circumstances of his parishioners grew increasingly difficult. The summer of 1646 ended with exceptionally bad weather and rising food prices, and with the first of the bad harvests that would contribute to the near-famine conditions of the next few years.[91] He noted that his pastoral work and theological reflection were occasionally interrupted, as when an un-named visitor arrived to dispute whether God required an atonement in order to forgive his elect: Owen and his visitor debated the subject before an audience, with Owen remembering the participants' "quietness and sobriety of spirit," which, he noted, "beseemed lovers of and searchers after truth."[92] He kept up his connections with neighboring ministers: Josselin continued to preach occasionally in the village, and took part in a number of clerical discussions on church government throughout 1646 and 1647.[93] The ministers were seriously engaging with the issue of church government. In January 1647, Josselin obtained a copy of the *Jus divinum regiminis ecclesiastici*, which had been published by London Presbyterian ministers less than one month previously.[94] At the end of March 1647, Owen "desird to bee excused in his exchange" with Josselin, likely an agreement to exchange pulpits on a particular Sunday. Josselin reacted badly to the news, which he seems to have interpreted as a rebuff, not least because he had prepared nothing to preach to his own congregation: "I fell to my study, I was wholly unprovided, and my thoughts were disturbed, yett through mercy I went on in my worke."[95] The arrangement, as well as Josselin's response to its failure, suggests that the ministers were sustaining their collegial relationship while diverging in their views of church government. Josselin attended a lecture in Coggeshall on 3 June, and, on 1 July, took part in a conference that was convened in Owen's home.[96] Josselin's Presbyterian convictions remained undiminished. He continued to instruct his parishioners on the subject of church government through the summer of 1647 and regularly signed certificates of qualification for ministry for less experienced clergy.[97] The Essex ministers were continuing to debate ecclesiology, but without conclusion, as Owen's congregational convictions strengthened, even as his reputation among his colleagues continued to grow.[98]

This debate was continuing in increasingly difficult circumstances. In the autumn of 1646 and spring of 1647, Josselin complained that his congregation in Earls Colne was growing increasingly "thin."[99] While there is no reason so suppose that congregants in Coggeshall were also disengaged, it is possible that Owen's parishioners found the debate about church government pastorally sterile. Religious disengagement turned into political disappointment when, in April 1647, Josselin's village quartered "above 60 of Major Desboroughs troope." These defenders of the Parliamentary cause were less godly than many of their supporters might have hoped. Josselin found that while the soldiers were "civill," many of them "cast out evill words, against presbyterians, and ministers particularly."[100] There were widespread fears of the effects of forced quartering, which must also have affected opinion in Owen's parish nearby.[101] And yet, as the army and Parliament began to diverge in their attitudes toward protecting the achievements of the revolution, Owen and Josselin joined a group of ministers that, in June 1647, produced a petition to Fairfax suggesting that the army not be disbanded, requesting that it continue to defend the rights of the people against Parliament.[102] For Parliament was increasingly dominated by a Presbyterian vision of reformation, the first of several conservative turns of the English revolution, and religious uniformity was a key element of their brave new world. Only twelve months after preaching to the Long Parliament, therefore, Owen was concluding that his hopes for religious toleration would be better defended by Independents in the army.

Then tragedy struck. Food prices had been rising since the bad harvest of 1646, and now also reflected the economic disruptions caused by the forced quartering of large numbers of soldiers in the district. Hunger and poor weather brought disease and a summer of horrors: Josselin recorded "great sicknes and illness, agues abounding more then in all my remembrance . . . fruit rottes on the trees as last year though more, and many cattle die of the murraine."[103] In these awful conditions, John and Mary Owen lost two of their three children. Mary, their eldest daughter, was buried on 18 July 1647.[104] One month later, her sister Elizah was buried beside her.[105] We do not know the ages of these children, but they were both younger than John, who had been baptized in December 1644, and so it is possible that these deaths had robbed John and Mary Owen of all but their eldest son, himself less than three years old.[106] Neither do we know how these deaths affected John and Mary, or their only surviving child, though Josselin wrote movingly in his diary of his prolonged grief over the deaths of his children in this period.[107] Josselin noted that the ministers met again in Coggeshall on 5 August, but he made no reference in his diary to his neighbor's bereavements. Neither did Owen.

Nor did Owen mention his own illness, which followed the deaths of his daughters. In late October Josselin noted that Owen was "very ill of the stone, the lord sanctifie his hand and spare him." This illness may have been an occasion for Josselin preaching for Owen on 11 November when he "had conference with 2 troubled soules, and one of them god used mee an instrument to stirre."[108] Owen later lamented the spiritual condition of the Coggeshall parishioners and their lack of response to his preaching—so the impact of Josselin's sermon could have encouraged Owen while also adding to his pastoral disenchantment.[109] As the long winter of hunger and disease passed into spring, both families were united in grief. In February 1648, Josselin buried his 10-day-old son with "teares and sorrowe," while John and Mary buried another child, Thomas, in March, and in unrecorded circumstances.[110] Owen had lost three children in the space of nine months. These were "scarce times," "crazie times," times of worry, illness, and death.[111]

Owen continued to refine his ecclesiological convictions, which he elaborated at the next meeting of ministers, convened in Colchester on 31 March 1648. The network of ministers had agreed to discuss means for the appointment of elders, after the Assembly's publication *Concerning church-government and ordination of ministers* (1647), while Parliament began chasing up noncompliance.[112] In the meeting in Colchester, Josselin "mett Mr Newcomen, and divers other Ministers, wee had much discourse concerning falling into practice . . . seing that elders are to bee chosen." In its efforts to impose a national Presbyterian structure, Parliament had required that all English counties should return a list of elders.[113] Some of the Essex ministers were reluctant to follow this regulation, but those who joined the project appear to have come from across the political spectrum—Thomas Newcomen, for example, was chaplain to Sir John Lucas, a noted royalist, patron of the Fordham parish, and no friend to godly reformation. The results were telling. *The division of the county of Essex into several classes, together with the names of the ministers and others fit to be of each classis* (1648) listed John Bulkley as minister of Fordham, with his patron as ruling elder, but did not list Owen as minister of Coggeshall.

Instead, the incumbent was listed as John Sams, a layman who had recently returned from New England, and who may have been operating as a "teaching elder," working alongside Owen with similar pastoral responsibilities, several years before his formal installation in 1652, in a situation entirely consistent with Owen's beliefs about the pastoral office.[114] In Essex, discussions about the appointment of elders had faltered on the question of procedure. Parliament had recommended that the franchise for the election of elders should include all those who had subscribed to the Solemn League and Covenant. But some of the Essex ministers, including Owen, "conceived this too broad," Josselin reported, "and would have first a separacion to bee made in our parishes; and that by the minister, and those godly that joyne unto him, and then proceed to choosing."[115] It was a telling moment in the local discussions about church government. Owen was not prepared to follow the advice of Parliament and the Westminster Assembly on a fundamental component of local church government, but wanted to identify a congregation of visible saints whose decisions would bind the membership of the broader parish.

Owen was certainly on a rising tide. In his diary, Josselin recorded with dismay the apparently inexorable ascent of Independent ideas. He, too, was attempting to gather together the godly within his parish, but not as a separate congregation. He convened meetings of these visible saints in his home, perhaps in an effort to control opinion, but found the meetings increasingly frustrating, as his parishioners pushed continually against his Presbyterian convictions. The numbers of those attending began to decline: even then, he noted in August 1647, "people are wonderfull backward, and opinionative."[116] One month later, Josselin reported of another meeting in his house that "people drive at an arbitrary maintenance of their ministers and upon their curtesy," as they called for the abolition of compulsory tithes and, presumably, the national church structure that these tithes made possible.[117] Restless spirits within the parish seized upon the opportunities afforded by the quartering of troops in the spring of 1648 to insist that Josselin should lend his pulpit to an army preacher, and in another meeting in Josselin's house argued that "none but reall Saints are to bee in fellowship."[118] Owen's arguments among the ministers were being paralleled by the arguments of "visible saints" in a neighboring parish.

And, at the level of local church government, Owen's tactics may have been successful. By January 1648, Essex had been constituted as an ecclesiastical province and had been divided into fourteen classes, which were interim bodies to oversee the election of elders and the establishment of permanent Presbyterian institutions, but there remains no direct evidence that such ordinations were carried out in the area during this period.[119] The system being promoted by Parliament was unequivocally Erastian, with congregational elders being represented in ecclesiastical courts that ascended from the local congregational session to regional presbytery, provincial synod, national assembly, and finally to Parliament.[120] For Owen and his contemporaries, who were already negotiating competing visions of how best to consolidate the gains of the revolution, the political choice was becoming ever clearer, between "an Erastian Parliament or an Independent Army," and between religious uniformity and a broader toleration.[121] Josselin continued to defend a national Presbyterian settlement and to discountenance any voluntary congregations. He recorded further meetings to discuss baptism and church government during April 1648 but did not indicate whether Owen was in attendance. In April 1648, Josselin subscribed to the Essex petition in support of the London Presbyterian ministers and continued to meet with Newcomen about setting up local Presbyterian institutions.[122] But, he realized, local people "growe weary, and endeavour to give over thoughts of reformacion."[123] It was a challenging time to be promoting a national system of church government: "god hath cast mee into sad times," he worried.[124] In and beyond Essex, the arguments of Owen and the Independents seemed to be carrying the day.

This context of personal suffering and local clerical discussion on the subject of church government contributed to the shape and tone of Owen's next publication.[125] *Eshcol: A cluster of the fruit of Canaan; brought to the borders, for the encouragement of the saints, travelling thither-ward, with their faces towards Syon* had been approved for publication on 30 December 1647, but was published by Philemon Stephens sometime in the late spring of 1648.[126] Goold believed that this book was published soon after Owen had formed an Independent congregation within the Coggeshall parish, and that its advice on church membership was "to this day unsurpassed."[127] Now tired of "this disputing age," and abandoning the scholastic format and polemical tenor of his earlier publications, Owen believed his new book was "savouring . . . little of those ornaments of art or learning which in things that come to public view men desire to hold out."[128] He called for devotional and ethical renewal, arguing that the "foundation of all duties towards God and man" is love.[129] His new tone seemed to reflect his family's bereavements, the "troubles, sorrows, visitations, wants, poverties, persecutions of the saints," and he hoped that his readers would "pity their woundings . . . feel their strokes . . . refresh their spirits, help bear their burdens."[130]

Owen appeared acutely concerned by the challenges faced by pastors. Their work was made difficult by persecution from outside the church and by disloyalty within it. "When persecution ariseth for the word's sake, generally it begins with the leaders, 1 Pet. iv. 17, 18," Owen explained; "the common way to scatter the sheep is by smiting the shepherds."[131] And pastors could also be dismayed when members of their churches "for no cause whatsoever . . . will oftentimes freely leave them and their ministry without any cause at all."[132] Faced with such discouragements, Owen mused, "a pastor's life should be vocal; sermons must be practised as well as preached . . . if a man teach uprightly and walk crookedly, more will fall down in the night of his life than he built in the day of his doctrine."[133]

Owen was also concerned by the growth of religious novelty, which reflected widespread assumptions about the continuity of extraordinary revelation: "some men, yea, very many in our days, have such itching ears after novelty, that they run greedily after every one that lies in wait to deceive with cunning enticing words, to make out some new pretended revelations. . . . Most of the seducers and false prophets of our days are men apparently out of God's way, leaving their own callings to wander without a call, ordinary or extraordinary,—without providence or promise."[134] Nevertheless, he continued to defend lay preaching, perhaps thinking of the work of his apparently unordained fellow elder John Sams, believing that, in confused times, "the not using of such gifts, in an orderly way, according to the rule and custom of the churches, is to napkin up the talent given to trade and profit withal."[135] But he was concerned by the growing habit of "causeless separation from established churches, walking according to the order of the gospel (though perhaps failing in the practice of some things of small concernment)," and believed that this voluntary withdrawal from church fellowship was "no small sin."[136] Of course, he recognized, some Christians had good reasons to leave one congregation for another, and Owen believed that Independent churches should find new ways of managing appropriate removals between congregations, encouraging churches to revive the apostolic practice of providing members in good standing with letters of commendation.[137] Josselin and Owen were now developing rival agendas for settling the order of their congregations. But their attempts to settle the organization of the church were to be disrupted by the outbreak of the second civil war in 1648.

III

In January 1648, Owen's next book was approved for publication, and it is likely that it was published in the early spring. *Salus electorum, sanguis Jesu, or, The death of death in the death of Christ,* was, as its subtitle continued, "a treatise of the redemption and reconciliation that is in the blood of Christ with the merit thereof," which sought to answer "all considerable objections as yet brought to light" to the Reformed doctrine of the atonement. Again, the book was printed by Philemon Stephens, now effectively representing Owen to the wider world from his printing shop in the capital, who included in the prefatory matter a list of the five other texts by Owen that he had already published.[138] *Salus electorum, sanguis Jesu* has become a seminal text in the modern recovery of interest in Owen, largely because, as published under its subtitle, *The death of death*, it became the first recent and widely circulated edition of his work when it was reprinted by the Banner of Truth in 1958. The wide circulation of this text has supported the "common but unhelpful practice of representing Owen's doctrine of the atonement primarily or solely" on the basis of its content.[139] The book was not to become Owen's *magnum opus*, as we will see, but it would certainly have been recognized by contemporary readers as his most significant work to date.

Owen was writing into a context of a spiraling theological debate. During the period of the book's composition, he became involved in a local debate with an individual, "whose name, and all things else concerning him, for the respect I bear to his parts and modesty, shall be concealed."[140] This opponent had defended the proposition that elect sinners did not need to avail of the satisfaction of Christ, which was theirs by right, but merely needed to realize their elect status, and to respond appropriately by faith. Or, as Owen put it, his antagonist asserted "election . . . to the overthrow of redemption."[141] This was a species of high Calvinism that encouraged Owen to include within his book on the atonement a discussion of justification from eternity, a doctrine that Richard Baxter would later accuse him of defending.[142] But *Salus electorum, sanguis Jesu* represented Owen's attempt to leverage for influence in a debate of far greater consequence than this.

For Owen's new book was a contribution to a discussion that centered around a series of publications by Thomas Moore, and which, by 1648, had become well established. Moore, according to Thomas Edwards, was a "great Sectary, that did much hurt in Lincolnshire, Norfolk, and Cambridgeshire; who was famous also in Boston, [King's] Lynn, and even in Holland, and was followed from place to place by many."[143] According to Richard Baxter, however, Moore was a "Weaver . . . of excellent Parts."[144] Like many other tradesmen turned theologians in the period, Moore struggled to move beyond his earlier identity. He "left all other employment to fall a-writing controversies," Owen complained, with a sentiment not entirely supportive of the broadening opportunities of the age.[145] Somehow finding the capital to make it possible, Moore published *The universality of God's free grace* in early April 1646 (not in 1643, as Goold claims), and followed up with *A discovery of seducers that creep into houses* (1646) and *A discourse about the pretious blood and sacrifice of Iesus Christ* (1646).[146] This sequence of texts set out a well-articulated theory of universal redemption, which resisted the nuanced conclusions of high Reformed orthodoxy by arguing that the death of Christ had provided propitiation—that is, had borne God's wrath—for the sins of all humanity. Moore's first book was rapidly answered by Thomas Whitefield's *A refutation . . . of Thomas More* (1646), to which Moore replied in *An uncovering of mysterious deceits by which many are kept from repentance and entring the doore of life* (1647). The debate continued, with the cause of Reformed orthodoxy being defended in John Stalham's *Vindiciae redemptoris* (1647), Obadiah Howe's *The universalist examined and convicted* (1648), and Owen's *Salus electorum, sanguis Jesu* (1648). Owen did not disagree with the earlier refutations of Moore's work, but felt that a more systemic approach was required.[147] It was hardly surprising that Howe complained that "the infirmity of crowding to the Presse is growne Epidemicall."[148] Owen was the fourth author within two years to respond to Moore in print. The speed and frequency of these responses to Moore's first book ironically confirmed that his arguments were far more important than his learned antagonists were prepared to admit.

Owen dedicated his book to the earl of Warwick, his patron in Coggeshall, with thanks for his making possible his move into the parish.[149] The book expanded upon the themes of a chapter in *The display of Arminianisme* and responded to Moore's claims at length and in detail, complaining both of a long list of printers' errors and of its author's ignorance.[150] Owen's work developed in sharp contrast. His work was learned, referring to the "abler pens" that had become involved in the broader discussion of the doctrine of the atonement, and making frequent citations of Samuel Rutherford, the leader of the Scottish and high Presbyterian faction in Westminster Assembly, even as he negotiated his independence from other "great authors" to whose arguments he could not "absolutely adhere."[151] Simultaneously, Owen continued to push back the boundaries of language, using such recently coined terms as "nescience" and "piacular," while deploying "collimed" in a usage predating by several decades its only recorded instance in the *OED*.[152] In such manner Owen preened his scholarly ability, hoping that "some charitable man . . . will undecieve [Moore], by letting him know the meaning of the word εφαπαξ" ("unique")—for, in this flamboyant display of literacy and neologism, Owen would not.[153] Instead, he crammed into his book a much greater number of quotations from classical and medieval authors than had appeared in previous works, reflecting a research base that made sense in terms of Owen's claim that the book was the fruit of "more than seven years' serious enquiry" into the extent and efficiency of the atonement.[154] Even its writing had taken time: Owen, who could and frequently did rush material to press, had spent "some twelve months . . . and upwards" upon its completion.[155] But Owen's arguments were urgent, perhaps reflecting the fact that Arminianism had become a local threat, and was "daily spreading . . . about the parts where I live . . . with the advantage they had obtained by some military abettors."[156] Yet he presented himself as a reluctant controversialist: "I never like myself worse than when faced with a vizard of disputing in controversies," he admitted, even as he took advantage of the outstanding opportunities that early modern theological controversy offered to those who wished to develop and display their rhetorical gifts.[157] Owen complained that Moore's ideological "wildness, in such tattered rags, should find employment, whilst sober truth is shut out of doors," and compared his own work in dismantling Moore's pretensions to that of a farmer in shoveling "dung."[158] Gesturing again to Moore's unpretentious background, and perhaps remembering his own work in Fordham, Owen wondered whether "such bold assertors" were "fitter to be catechised than to preach."[159] It was true that "every age hath its employment in the discovery of truth," Owen noted, as he celebrated the "progress of the last century in unfolding the truths of God." But believers should also lament the byproduct of this "serious enquiry," that craze for novelty in which an author of immature talent "strives to put on beyond his companions in framing some singular artifice."[160] Owen's concluding metaphor clinched his argument: Thomas Moore, the former weaver, should stick to other forms of fabrication.

The contents of *Salus electorum, sanguis Jesu* outlined a basic series of propositions, all intended to disarm the claims of Owen's antagonist.[161] Moore's position was simple, Owen believed: "that there be several and diverse ends of the death of Christ towards several persons, so that some of them belong to all, and all of them belong only to some; which is the πρωτον Ψευδος ["principal falsehood"] of the whole book."[162] Owen recognized, perhaps reflecting on his own spiritual experience, the difficulties that could be engendered by the Reformed doctrines of election and particular redemption. He now understood the apparent pastoral benefit of that false doctrine which argued that "God loves all alike, gave Christ to die for all, and is ready to save all if they will lay hold on him."[163] Moore's Arminianism—like that of the Laudian party at Oxford—seemed to offer an easier route to conversion. But Owen emphatically repudiated the central premise of Moore's argument:

> We deny that all mankind are the object of that love of God which moved him to send his Son to die; God having "made some for the day of evil," Prov. xvi. 4; "hated them before they were born," Rom. ix. 11, 13; "before of old ordained them to condemnation," Jude 4; being "fitted to destruction," Rom. ix. 22; "made to be taken and destroyed," 2 Pet. ii. 12; "appointed to wrath," 1 Thess. v. 9; to "go to their own place," Acts i. 25.[164]

He similarly undermined Moore's doctrine of the extent of the atonement. He admitted that Christ's death was infinitely sufficient, "fit for the accomplishing of any end and the procuring of any good, for all and every one for whom it was intended, had they been millions of men more than ever were created."[165] "If there were a thousand worlds," he continued, "the gospel of Christ might, upon this ground, be preached to them all, there being enough in Christ for the salvation of them all, if so be they will derive virtue from him by touching him in faith."[166] This is what permited Owen to speak in terms of an "offer" of salvation: he was clear that ministers should "command and invite all to repent."[167] But Owen reiterated the scholastic maxim that while Christ's death was sufficient for all, it was efficient only for the elect.[168] This enabled him also to claim that "Christ died not for all and every one—to wit, not for those he 'never knew,' whom he 'hateth,' whom he 'hardeneth,' on whom he 'will not show mercy,' who 'were before of old ordained to condemnation;' in a word, for a reprobate, for the world, for which he would not pray."[169] And so Owen drove toward his unflinching conclusions, that the Arminian system made Christ an unfaithful priest, offering a sacrifice for all while interceding only for his elect.[170] His argument was reduced to a trilemma: "Christ underwent the pains of hell for, either all the sins of all men, or all the sins of some men, or some sins of all men."[171] It was critical to come to the proper conclusion—that Christ had died for "all the sins of some men"—for "to affirm Christ to die for all men is the readiest way to prove that he died for no man, in the sense Christians have hitherto believed, and to hurry poor souls into the bottom of Socinian blasphemies."[172] Calvinism had become Christianity's best defense against Trinitarian heresy, for Arminian ideas were the gateway to a full-scale assault on classical theism.

IV

In reaching that conclusion, Owen had stumbled upon a new theological antagonist, with which he would grapple through the following decade and beyond. Owen would deal with the Socinian menace even as his own thinking continued to develop. *Salus electorum, sanguis Jesu* would not be Owen's final word on the subject of the atonement or its broader theological implications. For all that Owen believed that the book would be the last word in the dispute—"I shall not live to see a solid answer given unto it"—it represented conclusions that he himself would quickly abandon.[173] Owen's reading of Scripture was not to be static, either in terms of exegetical detail or broader theological claims. His argument that "the eternal Spirit" (Hebrews 9:14) referred to the Holy Spirit would be qualified in *Πνευματολογια: or, A discourse concerning the Holy*

Spirit (1674) to refer to Christ's divine nature, for example.[174] Nor would he long continue to argue against the proposition that "God could not have mercy on mankind unless satisfaction were made by his Son"[175]—in fact, this tenet of Moore's argument would become central to Owen's response to Socinian writing in the 1650s, though, as we will see, he chose not to call attention to his theological change of heart.

Of course, it is difficult to estimate how many readers would have noticed these developments in Owen's thinking. Perhaps not many of his early readers were in a position to compare his works. His early books were not rapidly collected. They may have had little impact locally: Ralph Josselin, who was an enthusiastic book collector, did not mention that his neighbor had become an author and does not seem to have read any of his works. Neither were Owen's books making much impact in the capital. His works were not represented in the catalogue of Sion College (1650), for example, the most important clerical library in London.[176] Nor did he seem to be successful in forming around himself an audience. For it is telling that, even some years after Owen had preached to Parliament, Richard Byfield, the Westminster Assembly divine who wrote a recommendation of *Salus electorum, sanguis Jesu*, admitted that he did not know who the author was, even by reputation.[177] Even as the access to print was being democratized, it was difficult to establish a literary reputation in "these times of liberty and error."[178]

But Owen was facing more immediate challenges. At the end of May 1648, he was "very ill with a fever."[179] Meanwhile, the rewewal of civil war had brought an immediate threat to the area, which was increasingly preparing itself for armed conflict. In early June, Josselin was making daily visits to Coggeshall to observe the preparations for the defense of the town against an expected royalist incursion, which came on 12 June.[180] Josselin thought the local militia had behaved well: "no part of Essex gave them so much opposicion as we did. They plundered us, and mee in particular, of all that was portable except, brasse, pewter, and bedding."[181] With his home looted and many possessions destroyed, Josselin escaped to Coggeshall. The despoiled area's recovery was hampered by weather that continued to be disappointing: "flouds every weeke, hay rotted abroad, much was carried away with the flouds, much inned but very durty, and dangerous for catle; corne layd, pulled downe with weeds, wee never had the like in my memory, and that for the greatest part of the summer."[182] Congregations were at least increasing.[183] But the community of the godly was diverging in disturbing and discouraging times.

4

Army Preacher

OWEN'S NEW ECCLESIOLOGICAL principles were pushing him to find a new patron. Thomas Westrow does not appear to have continued to support his old college friend after Owen took advantage of the invitation to address Parliament to advocate radical reform, and, though his commitment to godly politics was strong enough to warrant George Wither's commendation in *Westrow revived* (1653), it is possible the men lost touch after the embarrassment of the "country essay." Perhaps, from Owen's perspective, Westrow had ceased to be useful. The civil wars were pushing apart Parliament's politicians and its military. Owen and other Essex ministers had already addressed Fairfax in a petition, pleading that the army should not be disbanded: despite the twin horrors of anticlericalism and forced quarter, only the army could be trusted to preserve the gains of the revolution.[1] As the second civil war became the cause and consequence of political intransigence, moral ambiguity, and military desperation and self-doubt, Owen responded to the changing circumstances by identifying himself with a powerful new patron, General Fairfax, who would fundamentally redirect the course of his life. For it was at the siege of Colchester, in the summer of 1648, that Owen became a witness to and celebrant of the most extreme and controversial military methods in early modern England.[2] It was in the aftermath of hostilities at Colchester, as Owen became convinced of the political and ecclesiological paradigms that he would guard throughout the rest of his life, that he began to play a "significant role in British national life," becoming the "unofficial preacher-in-chief" of the revolutionary regime, driving toward the crisis that army leaders would use to justify Colonel Thomas Pride's purge of MPs in December 1648 and the consequent trial and execution of the king.[3]

I

The prelude to the siege of Colchester was a rare intrusion into Essex of the conflict of the second civil war.[4] The earl of Norwich, still loyal to the king, had attempted to create one of the series of regional disturbances that constituted the major actions of the second, smaller, and less coordinated royalist war effort. But his lack of experience in military planning pushed him toward the desperate hazard first of taking hostage important members of the Essex county committee, the local administrative body, and then of retreating with them toward a city with inadequate lines of supply and in an unsympathetic region. The local response was immediate. Sir Thomas Honywood, a country committeeman who lived in Coggeshall, set about organizing defenses, assembling two thousand volunteers into fighting units, and stockpiling weapons within the village.[5] These activities were urgently required. Perhaps anticipating the difficulties that they would shortly face, the harried troops of the earl of Norwich showed little mercy to the residents of those villages and towns through which they were pursued: Josselin wrote movingly in his diary of the effect of being plundered by Norwich's soldiers as they retreated through the district. By 12 June 1648, the royalist army had withdrawn into Colchester. On 13 June, Fairfax's forces stormed the city, a style of attack that had been markedly successful elsewhere. But the assault failed and the soldiers of Parliament set about establishing a blockade for which no one had planned. The seige lines they constructed were "probably the most sophisticated . . . of either civil war," and made possible a ten-week blockade marked by long periods of inactivity and sudden episodes of extraordinary and notorious violence.[6] The long blockade, explains its most recent historian, was "exacerbated by the sense of betrayal and desperation that characterised the second civil war . . . a struggle marked by severity, bitterness, and desire for retributive justice."[7] For long weeks things seemed to go quietly, with reports reglarly suggesting the absence of "any great matters."[8] But conflict always continued, with occasional sniping causing more damage than might have been expected: accounts of the seige in *The moderate intelligencer*, the newsbook that Owen may have been collecting throughout this period, reported fears that the royalists were firing bullets that had been daubed in poison for additional effect.[9] The wet weather made for terrible conditions, both within and outside the city walls, and residents were described as stripping the city of dogs and cats, while soldiers ate their horses and looted civilians' homes in their search for supplies. In mid-July, over three hundred houses were burned, with each side blaming the other for arson. An eyewitness described a "terrible red duskye bloody cloud," which "seamed to hang over the Town all night": "many times the flashes mounted aloft far above house, church, or any buildings, and continued with such horror, cracklings heard a mile or two from the town."[10] In a period before light pollution normalized red glows in the night sky, the scene would have been eery, almost apocalyptic. Neither were animals spared the misery. *The Colchester spie*, a short-run royalist newsbook, accused Parliamentarian soldiers of using "burning Bulls"—of setting cattle alight in a bid to create a diversion—while counter-claims of cruelty to cattle were recorded in the parliamentary press.[11] Even by the standards of early modern warfare, the city's residents witnessed and were subject to spectacular suffering. And they were offered little relief, for Fairfax's anti-royalism had noticeably hardened. On 22 August he refused to allow starving noncombatants to leave the city, knowing that any partial evacuation would work to the advantage of its defenders. But those holding the city had little incentive to treat with him. Those royalist officers who had earlier surrendered and had been released on parole were particularly concerned about their future fate—Sir Charles Lucas, for example, had surrendered at Stow-in-the-Wold and had been released on condition that he never again take up arms against Parliament. Fairfax's strategy, observed his most recent biographer, was to encourage royalist soldiers to turn against their officers, and "this was reflected in his terms for surrender. Rank and file soldiers were granted quarter, but senior officers were forced to surrender to Fairfax's mercy."[12]

Fairfax had, to this point, a reputation for strict discipline and for generosity to surrendering enemies, and those who considered surrendering on mercy likely hoped to be released on terms that would be reasonable, if not exactly honorable. And so, on 27 August, the royalist forces released their hostages and capitulated. But, on the following day, the mood of the victors darkened. The parliamentary soldiers—who may earlier have disinterred the corpses of Lucas's relatives from a nearby graveyard to "adorn their hats with bones and hanks of hair"—began to chant for the deaths of the royalist leaders.[13] Lucas and Sir George Lisle were sentenced by a council of war, with the case against Lucas strengthened by evidence that he himself had presided over the execution of twenty prisoners. While Fairfax could claim that he had acted within the terms of martial law, the treatment of Lucas and Lisle by his council of war was "unprecedented and clearly motivated by vengeance"; it reflected the fact that during the long seige the codes of war had been "betrayed." Royalists were "shocked" at Fairfax's sudden reversal of his famous leniency: Lucas and Lisle had surrended, but they were shot to death in cold blood.[14]

Owen appears to have spent a large amount of time with the parliamentary army during the siege. In early July, he spent time with four MPs who were staying in Coggeshall while ensuring the financial supply of the beseiging forces.[15] Taking advantage of the fact that Colchester was only five miles or so from Coggeshall, along the old Roman road of Stane Street, Owen also "seems to have officiated as chaplain" to Fairfax.[16] He was tremendously impressed by Parliament's senior military commander, who was, after all, only four years his senior. Nor was he alone in his estimation of the handsome "black Tom." Ralph Josselin had already met Fairfax, dining with him in March 1647, and was impressed by his modesty.[17] During the Colchester seige, John Milton wrote a sonnet to praise "Fairfax, whose name in arms through Europe rings | Filling each mouth with envy, or with praise."[18] Owen seems to have shared their admiration for the general, while being less impressed by the religious condition of his army. Thomas Edwards's *Gangreana* (1646) had recently painted a bleak picture of the religious life of the soldiers, condemning Fairfax for "failing to enforce religious discipline among his men."[19] However Owen might have criticized aspects of Edwards's book, he would likely have sympathized with his concern to conserve Reformed orthodoxy. This was likely Owen's first sustained contact with the religious radicalism that had come to typify much of its soldiery, toleration for whose opinions he had already defended in principle, and he may have been surprised by his experience of men with "such itching ears after novelty, that they run greedily after every one that lies in wait to deceive with cunning enticing words."[20] Perhaps, like Baxter, Owen's experience of military life encouraged an increasingly conservative approach to the question of the bounds of public orthodoxy. Nevertheless, he assured Fairfax, he accounted it "among those blessings of Providence wherewith the days of my pilgrimage have been seasoned, that I had the happiness for a short season to attend your excellency, in the service of my master, Jesus Christ."[21] Colchester was a turning point, for "the war, and Fairfax with it, had taken a new course."[22] He was "radicalised by his experiences in the second civil war."[23] And Owen—whose patron in Fordham had, after all, been the brother of one of the executed royalists—was similarly transformed.[24]

Owen avoided any reference to the horrific conclusion to the seige, and the war crimes that may have been committed, in his *Eben-ezer: A memoriall of the deliverance of Essex, county, and committee* (1648). The book was a compilation of two sermons, the first preached in Colchester and before Fairfax on 31 August, the day of thanksgiving for the surrender, and the second at Rumford, on 28 September, at another day of thanksgiving, convened by the rescued hostages.[25] After the excitement Owen returned to Coggeshall, where, on 5 October 1648, he dedicated his book to Fairfax, who, the dedicatory preface explained, had heard "part of these ensuing sermons," with a second preface addressed to Sir William Masham and Sir William Rowe, who had been imprisoned in the town, and Sir Henry Mildmay of Wansted and Sir Thomas Honywood, who had been among the forces that had liberated them. Owen emphasized that he was publishing the sermons "upon your request."[26] And he did so as his own publisher. For the first time, Owen did not publish with Philemon Stephens: the sermon was printed in London by W. Wilson, "for the authour," as the title page puts it. It is a revealing moment in Owen's career, in which he sought to justify his self-publication by including two dedicatory prefaces. But it is not clear what might have prompted this decision. Perhaps Stephens no longer wanted to take the financial risk of publishing Owen's work—after all, nine months later, in the summer of 1649, he would be attempting to offload Owen's unsold publications. Owen's decision to self-publish suggests that he was taking upon himself the financial risk of the project—and this after a summer of devastation, poor weather, acute hunger, and in a shattered local economy, in a month in which his neighbors complained that food prices had never been so high.[27] Perhaps he was motivated to take advantage of the events in which he had participated while they were still newsworthy. Whatever the explanation, Owen's decision is powerful evidence that the print culture of the godly continued to expand, even in the most challenging market conditions.

Owen was certainly confident about his interpretation of the significance of the events. He was sure that "the surrender of Colchester . . . [is] a mercy of the first magnitude," for "Essex hath seen more power in a three months' recovery than in the protection of six years."[28] Owen followed this general statement about the importance of the events by reviewing the "shaking times" of recent months.[29] His rhetoric reflected the de-humanizing tone of many publications emanating from the second civil war. After their defeat, he complained, the royalist party had re-emerged as "an enraged, headless, lawless, godless multitude, gathered out of inns, taverns, alehouses, stables, highways, and the like nurseries of piety and pity."[30] Their erstwhile victors now faced dangers from every quarter, and even from their former allies within the capital: "the north invaded, the south full of insurrections, Wales unsubdued, the great city . . . suffering men to lift up their hands against us."[31] The second civil war, which reflected the collapse of old loyalties, represented a crisis of existential proportions, in which providence itself seemed fickle: "Where is the God of Marston Moor, and the God of Naseby?" he wondered.[32] The defeat of the Scots at Preston on 17 August and the end of the siege of Colchester seemed to offer an end to this ambiguity, but the sufferings of east Essex were to continue. Despite Owen's celebratory tone, the area would be further debilitated by Fairfax's imposition of a £12,000 fine upon the townspeople, who would long struggle to rebuild a shattered local economy, alleging their collusion with the beseiged. The damage to the fabric of the town was to be enduring, leading, ironically, to the development of war tourism. In 1656, John Evelyn reported that the city still bore the marks of the seige.[33] As late as 1661, the events were a cause of remarking among foreign tourists: William Schellinks, a Dutch visual artist, recorded his eating an evening meal in the inn in which Sir Charles Lucas had been court-martialed before his execution.[34] But the seige also created opportunities for Owen. Two of the hostages, Sir William Masham and Sir Henry Mildmay, expressed their appreciation for his efforts by inviting him to preach a private sermon and by creating opportunities for him to preach to Parliament.[35]

Eben-ezer turned from this survey of recent history to consider the familiar theme of religious toleration. Its author was doing more than merely riding his hobbyhorse. The situation facing the godly had become urgent. Several months earlier, in May 1648, Parliament had passed its Blasphemy Act, which required that those found guilty of atheism and anti-Trinitarianism be executed, while Arminians, Baptists, antinomians, and universalists should be imprisoned.[36] It was a moment in which the political gains of the Westminster Assembly project should have been consolidated, as a framework for national orthodoxy was used to criminalize religious dissent. Parliament was backing a Presbyterian hegemony that seemed to revoke the idealism of the revolution, even as it ignored the political reality that power increasingly lay with the army. This was exactly the conservative turn that Owen had hoped to avoid, and against which his earlier writing had argued. For while Independents agreed with Presbyterians that the civil magistrate had a duty to suppress heresy and idolatry, they also argued that ecclesiological differences should not constitute a crime.[37] Owen's sermon was urgent because he could see where things were heading in the criminalization of what he regarded as orthodox pieties. "Arguments for persecution are dyed in the blood of Christians," he insisted, hoping that his antagonists could see "in one view all the blood of the witnesses of Christ, which had been let out of their veins by vain pretences," and that they could hear "in one noise the doleful cry of all pastorless churches, dying martyrs, harbourless children of parents inheriting the promise, wilderness-wandering saints, dungeoned believers," understanding that all this agony was "wrested out by pretended zeal to peace and truth."[38] The suffering of the inhabitants of Colchester was to be emblematic of the horror of those who would suffer, at the hands of a Presbyterian Parliament, for their faith. Owen's sermon, far from merely celebrating the victory at Colchester, was calling on the army to make good the gains of the revolution by forcibly revoking laws that had been passed by due process. Having internalized among the Parliamentarians the binary divisions of the war for true religion, he seemed to be calling for a coup.

It was due to the influence of Owen's new allies that the Blasphemy Ordinance was never put into effect. For the crisis between army and Parliament continued to escalate, as tensions focused on disbanding, arrears of pay, and resistance to a hegemonic religious state. On 6 December, Colonel Pride's Regiment of Foot blocked the access to the House of Commons, and allowed entry only to those whose names had been included on a list of approved MPs. Only around two hundred of the more than five hundred seats were to be occupied, in what was soon to become known as the Rump Parliament. Seizing the reins of power, army leaders worked furiously to hammer out their own vision for England. Convening discussions with Levellers in Whitehall in December 1648, Henry Ireton advanced a theory of toleration similar to Owen's, a position with which Oliver Cromwell also largely agreed.[39] In the same month, Bulstrode Whitelock attended "two excellent sermons" that Owen preached in London: he noted that Owen "seemed much to favour" the army, and "spake in dislike of those Members who voluntarily absented themselves from the House."[40] Owen and the army he was addressing had achieved existential clarity. Providence no longer seemed to be ambiguous. With a purged and compliant Parliament, and a shocked public, the army engineered a coup, putting political power firmly in the hands of the Independents. Owen's moral binary was reasserted. Finally the king could be called to account for his crimes in the war against the truth.

II

The trial and execution of Charles I marked a critical turning point both in the wider political, cultural, and religious landscape of England—and in the life of John Owen.[41] In a series of recent publications, Sean Kelsey, John Adamson, and others have offered a new reading of the events leading up to the regicide, emphasizing the reluctance of army leaders to put the king on trial, and illustrating the means by which they sought alternatives to the process that would end with his execution. For five weeks after Pride's Purge, army leaders remained unclear about the best method of progress. Kelsey has argued persuasively that this reluctance continued even into the trial itself, as many commissioners worked to secure a sentence other than execution.[42] These were deeply unsettled weeks, working toward a very unclear conclusion. And they would have been unsettling for Owen. On 30 December 1648, he had been invited to preach at the next fast-day sermon.[43] He must have followed events anxiously as he considered how best to preach to the king's judges.

For Charles was put on trial, found guilty of treason, and was executed on 30 January 1649, on a platform located outside Whitehall, where soldiers and Levellers had been debating the direction of the revolution. His was an iconic death. The crowds that witnessed the regicide were deeply affected by the spectacle of the retributive power of the Rump Parliament. Charles, who spoke clearly, simply, and powerfully from the scaffold, was immediately identified as a martyr by the royalist press and its growing ranks of supporters. In London, his execution was the cause of no popular rejoicing as the new administration redefined the character and intention of government and consolidated its plans for godly rule. Across England, and beyond, the regicide provoked a religious crisis.[44] Individuals searched their consciences for a justification of resistance to the "powers that be." Fairfax, who had been so manipulated that he could not interfere with the execution at the last minute, began his long withdrawal from public life, as royalists circulated pamphlets describing the mental anguish that had since afflicted the executioner of the king.[45] This religious crisis in turn provoked a division among the London clergy. John Price's *Clerico-classicum, or, The clergi-allarum to a third war* (1649), which was published in mid-January, was followed by a series of pamphlets that defined contrasting positions as to the regicide, including John Reading's *Little Benjamin, or Truth discovering error* (1649), which appeared in mid-February as a reply to a statement of forty-seven ministers. The discussion implicated leading Independents, compelling Cornelius Burgess, in *A vindication of the ministers of the Gospel in, and about London* (1649), to defend the network of preachers of which he was a part from the charge that they had been plotting for the king's execution. Across England, those who remained loyal to the old regime and others who had become disaffected with the new launched a series of schemes to return a monarch to the throne.[46] Popular cultural artifacts identified the regicide with the horrors of the second civil war: *The famous tragedy of King Charles I* (1649) described the deaths of Capell and Lucas at Colchester as part of its depiction of recent events.[47] Scottish Presbyterians and Irish Catholics responded with outrage to the execution of their king on the orders of a foreign court of questionable legality, and considered how best to repair their own monarchical government. Across the Continent, *Eikon basilike* (1649), a best-selling memoir attributed to Charles, was translated into several European languages and bore witness to the intensity of a new cult of loyalty and devotion to the late king's cause. As Parliament prepared the legislation that would formalize the new republic and recast its principal institutions, England entered a decade of political experiment and administrative improvisation, which marked a decisive break with centuries of tradition, and which would create extraordinary opportunities for the advancement of the talented, the ambitious, and the mendacious.

It is not clear whether Owen witnessed the king's death, an event that he marked in an ambiguous sermon to Parliament on the day after the regicide. Parliament had not convened any fast-day sermons in the month during which Charles was tried and finally executed, but, on 31 January, it finally found its voice. The scheduling of the regicide had required the regular fast day to be postponed, for the first time, by one day. Three preachers marked the occasion. Stephen Marshall's sermon to the Lords was not printed, but the sermons to the Commons, preached by John Cardell and John Owen, were published.[48] It must have been an extraordinary experience for Owen to preside, with so little pastoral experience and so few political contacts, at the official commemoration of England's first (and only) judicial regicide. It was a telling signal of the significance of his new links with the army.

But Owen's sermon pulled its punches—not least in comparison with Cardell's sermon. Cardell was a well-established minister in London who had acted as a trier for the Westminster Assembly and who would become a Fifth Monarchist.[49] His discussion of the theme of providence developed its recent definition in the Westminster Confession of Faith 5:3: "God hath more ways then one to save his People by, he can do it either by means, or without means, or above means, or contrary to means, as you have been often taught and told."[50] He reminded MPs that God, during the exodus, destroyed the pharaoh and his army, and he invoked Psalm 2 to remind MPs of God's war against kings who conspire against his people.[51] For, he continued, "God will certainly order all the great Affairs of the world in that way, which may chiefly tend unto the advancement of his own Glory, and the good of his own People."[52] By contrast, Owen's sermon was politically timid—but, perhaps, a greater literary success, reflecting the reserve of his closest supporters within the House. Masham and Fairfax refused to sit as the king's judges, and Mildmay, who had served temporarily as a judge, would not sign his death warrant.[53] Owen, not yet the voice of the army republicans, was limited by his patron's hesitations. Nevertheless, *A sermon preached to the Honourable House of Commons, in Parliament assembled: on January 31* (1649) was the first of his best-selling texts, passing through two editions in 1649.[54] Suddenly, his writing had public impact. "No sermon of Owen has excited keener discussion," Goold noted, in its own day or since.[55] Biographers have debated the extent to which the sermon endorsed the revolutionary actions of the previous day—for Owen's language is careful not to reveal too much of his own political position—but it may be significant, as Goold suggests, that while extracts from it were burned in Oxford in 1683, along with other writings by Knox, Buchanan, and Baxter, the order for their burning itself being burned in Oxford in 1710, that Owen was never called to account for his participation in this event.[56] Nevertheless, while his sermon may have been ambiguous, the fact that it was preached at all indicates its author's willingness, however hesitant, to be identified with a revolutionary, regicidal regime.

Owen returned to Coggeshall to face the consequences of his action. His participation in the events of the regicide likely put him in a minority in the area. Not many of the Essex ministers shared his apocalyptic vision, and few were so prepared to publicly identify with the revolutionary cause. Josselin, who did not mention Owen's regicide sermon, recorded in his diary that he was "much troubled with the blacke providence of putting the King to death, my teares were not restrained at the passages about his death . . . the death of the king much talked of, very many men of the weaker sort of christians in divers places passionate concerning it."[57] Other local ministers were openly antagonistic to Owen's views. In early February 1649 a petition against the regicide was circulated among local clergy. Josselin refused to sign it, perhaps reflecting upon the devastating local consequences of his appeal to Fairfax not to disband the army, arguing that ministers should not "intermedle thus in all difficulties of state."[58] But sixty-three other ministers did sign the petition.[59] The text, published as *The Essex watchmen's watchword* (1649), was responding to fears that "Ministers of the Gospel are generally charged . . . as the men that have been the Authors of all the kingdoms Troubles, Fomentors of these unnatural Divisions and Bloody Wars; yea, as men who have had a strong influence unto the contriving and effecting of the Death of our late Soveraign."[60] The petition offered a review of the events leading up to the civil war, a "Story . . . too long and sad for us to relate," lamenting that "a War begun for *The Defence of the King*, even ending in *The Death of the King*; a War begun for *The Defence of the Parliament*, ending in *The Violation of the present, and Mutulation of future Parliaments*."[61] Owen's local credibility had likely already suffered after his celebration of the conclusion of the seige of Colchester, a sermon he chose to self-publish despite the continued sufferings of its inhabitants and the consequent collapse of the local economy. His regicide sermon was not going to foster reconciliation with any offended neighbors. Nevertheless, on 28 February he signed the preface to the text he had reconstructed in his study, "the hasty conception, and, like Jonah's gourd, the child of a night or two."[62] It would be published by Matthew Simmons—he had already published work by John Milton and John Goodwin, two writers whose opinions would have been made illegal under the terms of the old Blasphemy Act (1648)—in a signal of Owen's increasingly radical politics.[63] Owen may have been embarrassed by the company he was keeping in print. He would not rapidly republish with

Simmons, and, in his next sermon to Parliament, made clear that God's new light was "not new doctrines, as some pretend (indeed old errors, and long since exploded fancies)."[64] His politics was moving into uncharted territory as his theology was pulling for home.

Owen dedicated his sermon to the remaining members of the Rump. His mood was grim. "It hath always suited the wisdom of God to do great things in difficult seasons," he explained, for "great works for God will cause great troubles amongst men," the "holy, harmless Reconciler of heaven and earth bids us expect the sword to attend his undertakings for and way of making peace."[65] Neither did Owen expect the situation to improve. Perhaps reflecting on the spectacle of the burning of Colchester and the horrific targetting of its civilian and animal population, he argued that the events of the second civil war and their terrible political necessities could be understood only in light of the apocalypse. "Tumults, troubles, vexations, and disquietness, must certainly grow and increase among the sons of men," he considered, "as the days approach for the delivery of the decree, to the shaking of heaven and earth, and all the powers of the world, to make way for the establishment of that kingdom which shall not be given to another people ... before the consummation of all."[66] The task facing the Rump Parliament was urgent. For God had called the Rump to action "at his entrance to the rolling up of the nation's heavens like a scroll ... in the high places of Armageddon."[67]

Owen began by referring to the king's death. But his approach was nuanced. While he had celebrated the victory at Colchester, he refused to praise the trial and execution of the king. In fact, throughout the sermon, his feelings about the events of the previous day are not clear. He disclaimed any need to comment on the regicide, as politics was "beyond the bounds of my calling," but still identified himself in an allusion to the civil war between David and his rebellious son, denying that, "with Absolom," he had any thought of a "more orderly carrying on of affairs."[68] The allusion worked both ways, with Owen rejecting rebellion against God-given authority—ironically, in the case of David, this was a monarchy—while also implying deference to those whose job it was to make political decisions. Providence was often ambiguous, he explained: "To those that cry, Give me a king, God can give him in his anger; and from those that cry, Take him away, he can take him away in his wrath, Hos xiii. 10, 11."[69] Perhaps he simply was too close to events to make any sense of them.

As in his first sermon to Parliament, Owen appended to his transcript an additional text—inevitably, perhaps, *A discourse about toleration* (1649). He seemed more concerned to announce his theology of toleration than his beliefs about the regicide, for, he believed, the danger to the godly had not passed with the king's death, and "poor England" still "lieth at stake."[70] Owen encouraged Rump MPs to peer behind the rhetoric that was driving conservative and Presbyterian responses to the Independents and their continuing revolution. Those who now sneered at "a parliament of saints, an army of saints," had "sat sometimes and took sweet counsel with us," he remembered.[71] Those who had shared the Independents' "groans for liberty" had, "by the warmth of favour . . . hatched into attempts for tyranny."[72] As long as "superstition and persecution, will-worship and tyranny, are inseparable concomitants," MPs should continue to resist in the "the hell of these times."[73] Yet they should remember that those who, "under God, deliver a kingdom, may have the kingdom's curses for their pains."[74] "All you, then, that are the Lord's workmen, be always prepared for a storm. . . . Be prepared, the wind blows,—a storm may come."[75]

Owen's theory of toleration was certainly considered. He adopted a "measured and judicious approach," which balanced a rejection of Presbyterian ideas of coerced uniformity with a careful statement about the religious duties of the civil magistrate.[76] "By 1649," John Coffey has noticed, "the Presbyterians had been routed . . . and Owen was now almost equally concerned about the threat to religious establishment posed by radical Puritans on his other flank."[77] Against the Presbyterian "houses of blood" and "chambers of death," Owen argued that all sins are not crimes, and that biblical crimes should not always be given biblical punishments, as some of the emerging party of theocrats argued: sins were defined by God, but crimes were those sins that disturbed the public peace.[78] In a tour de force of patristic learning, Owen argued that magistrates did have a religious duty, encouraging, protecting, and financing orthodox preachers, while also providing meeting places for their congregations.[79] And even those who denied this limited role for public authority ought to benefit from it: this provision should be offered to both Presbyterians and Independents, between whom there were only "minute differences."[80] Heretics should not be so facilitated, though their persons ought still to be protected, while wandering preachers should be punished as vagabonds.[81] Owen was growing impatient of Presbyterian "orthodoxism."[82] And others were taking advantage of the loosening of theological parameters: he was condemning the execution of Servetus even as Josselin was finishing his winter campaign of reading anti-Trinitarian writers.[83]

Owen's arguments were developing their own momentum, drawing upon ideas that would become commonplace among the alliance of sometimes competing interests which were promoting policies of broader toleration. His statement that "we had need be cautious what use we make (as one terms it well) of the broom of Antichrist, to sweep the church of Christ" was picked up by an emerging Fifth Monarchist.[84] John Rogers, in 1653, would argue that

> *putting to death* is none of *Christs Ordinance*; and that *fire* and *faggots* are no good *Reformers*. Were a man a *Turk, Saracen, Jew, Heretick*, or what you will? whilst he lives quietly, and peaceably in the *State*; I know not *who*, nor *why* he can be *put to death*. . . . For we must not *sweep* up *Christs* house with Antichrist's broom; nor fight with *his* hands Christs battles, nor with his *weapons* our *warfare*.[85]

Sharing metaphors, as well as ideas, Owen and Rogers agreed that the duty of magistrates was not to persecute peacable heretics, but to ensure the liberty of the saints in "these last evil days of the world."[86] Other radicals agreed. Robert Lilburne, who had signed the king's death warrant, was hoping to circulate copies of Owen's text in occupied parts of Scotland.[87] His inclination suggests something of the sermon's popularity. While we cannot ascertain how many copies were printed, we do know that it was published in two editions in 1649.[88] Owen had preached a sermon that reflected the reserve of his political and military patrons, but found that the symbolic value of the regicide it commemorated meant that the text was appropriated by much more radical voices. Suddenly, Owen had become a spokesman for a radical faction of army leaders. Again he was moving between patrons: as Fairfax began to disengage from the newly republican regime, Owen embraced its opportunities.[89] On 10 April 1649, Josselin took part in "a day of humiliacion at Sr Tho: Honywoods with Mr Owen, Mr Clopton and some others," recording that "the presence in the ordinance was cheerfull."[90] Owen had every reason to be optimistic about the future.

III

After the excitement of the regicide, the exhilaration of the preaching that followed it, and the success of his intervention in the debate about religious toleration, Owen's return to parish life must have been dispiriting. He expressed his disappointment at the quotidian realities of ministry. Three years earlier he had been glad to leave the "grossly ignorant persons" of Fordham; now he began to complain of the "daily troubles, pressures, and temptations" of life among the "poor, numerous, provoking people" of Coggeshall.[91] Perhaps he was discovering that they did not share his enthusiasm for the revolutionary cause—perhaps his joy at the turn of events did not reflect the hardships of local economic collapse or the fears of those, like Josselin, who were shocked by the rapid pace of change. Perhaps Owen was discovering that the legacy of Obadiah Sedgewick was not all that he might have anticipated: the parish's previous incumbent had, after all, promoted a Presbyterian ecclesiology that valorized a mixed congregation of nominal and godly Christians, and this may have frustrated Owen's attempt to establish a congregation of visible saints. Or perhaps, with the victory of what he would have perceived as the party of continuing reformation, he had become impatient with the traditional Puritan project of church reform from within. He was an idealist, searching for a radical simplification of the constitution of true churches, and the regicide had identified an institution by which his vision of a reformation of church—and state—could more rapidly be accomplished. In the months following the execution of Charles I, Owen, like many other English churchmen, was swept up in the expectation that the social and religious changes for which he had prayed, argued, and fought would be immediately realized, as time itself seemed to be "foreshortened."[92] Whatever the reason for this public criticism of his new parish, he could not help but notice the difference between the frustrations of his life as a pastor and the opportunities of the national stage.

But Owen returned to Coggeshall to a family tragedy. The area was sharing "great apprehensions of the famine," and instances of smallpox were recorded in the area in March.[93] It was in these circumstances, sometime in the spring of 1649, that Owen's eldest son, also called John, suddenly died. He was four years old.[94] His death must have been devastating: John and Mary had been married for little more than five years, had already buried two daughters and a son, and John, their firstborn, must have been their only surviving child.[95] It is hard to imagine the impact of this bereavement on the household: Owen did not mention this death, or the deaths of any of his children, in his extant writing, and the only reference to his loss is a record in the parish register. While we cannot date John's death with precision, we do know that his father sought encouragement in the company of other pastors during this period, attending a "day of humiliation" in the home of a local patron on 10 April 1649, which, Josselin noted, was a particularly encouraging meeting.[96] But none of this helped Owen to make sense of his situation. He continued, perhaps confused by the contrast between the responsibilities of parish life, the tragedies of family life, and the opportunities that might be represented by his return to the national stage.

For Owen's was the voice that was increasingly to dominate the parliamentary pulpit. His first parliamentary sermon, *A vision of unchangable free mercy* (1646), had been forgotten, but, in 1649, he was given a second chance: two

MPs who had heard his preaching in Essex engineered his return to parliamentary preaching. Owen's association with the army—initially with its commander-in-chief, Sir Thomas Fairfax, and later with the more radical faction who supported the trial and execution of the king—was pulling him from the ranks of the congregational pastors alongside whom he had served. He had entered the pulpit of St. Margaret's and became the favorite preacher of the army elite at the "very moment when the Independents (by means of their army) achieved supreme power in the English government."[97] With the execution of the king, Parliament began to wind down the program of fast-day sermons. Only nine further sermons to Parliament would be published after his address on the occasion of the regicide—and Owen would be author of four of them.[98] In the spring of 1649 he was being "transformed from a locally known parish minister into ... a figure of national prominence."[99] The king was dead. England had changed. And Owen was becoming a principal spokesperson for the new regime, its prophet of a new world order.

IV

Parliament must have been impressed by Owen's preaching at the end of January 1649, for ten weeks later, as the new administration began to exercise its grip on national affairs, he was invited to preach at the next fast day—the first preacher in the entire decade of fast-day sermons to Parliament to be so rapidly recalled.[100] This fast day had been scheduled for 28 February, but was postponed. In the interim, the office of monarch and the House of Lords were both abolished: England had been constituted as a republic.[101] The rescheduled fast was held on 19 April, when MPs were addressed by Owen and John Warren, from Hatfield Broad Oak, a parish located around ten miles from Coggeshall, in his only appearance before Parliament. The preachers shared an outlook on recent events. Warren's sermon, published as *The potent potter* (1649), set out to "beg a blessing upon good endeavours towards the *settlement of this Nations freedoms*, and to implore the aide of God against the adversaries of our life and peace."[102] Warren's rhetoric trembled with a sense of the eschatological significance of the moment, for, he argued, "those strange Commotions, wherewith the world is filled at this day, speak God about to manifest himself in some more remarkable way than heretofore. ... The wheel of Providence runs swiftly, and one piece of Gods work makes haste in an orderly way to carry forward, and bring on another."[103] Warren drew a lesson from a survey of classical and more recent European history, observing how easily God had "dasht in pieces those voluminous *Monarchies*, which have spred their wings each in his season over the world, whose lofty heads have looked upon themselves as in some need to invade heaven for want of room on earth."[104] Even in the history of England, he continued, forms of government had altered more often than many of his contemporaries had assumed.[105] "Must other Countries be transformed by the *all-changing Providence* of an *unchangable* God, and may not we be changed?" he inquired.[106] For, Warren continued, the reason that God raised "such a dust in breaking down the Kingdomes and Dominions of the world" was that he wanted to "make way for the advancement of his own Kingdome among his Saints."[107] Warren had no doubt as to the identity of the instrument of divine providence: not the Long Parliament, which had so disappointed the godly, but "that first *despised*, then *reviled* Army . . . hath brought you home the spoyles of conquered enemies, in the close of every expedition," for "God hath favoured you, and them, and us with many a remarkable victory."[108]

The sermon by Owen that accompanied Warren's preaching offered a more detailed theological perspective. *Ουρανων ουρανια, The shaking and translating of heaven and earth* (1649) drew on a passage to which Owen had referred in his regicide sermon, to provide an eschatological framework for recent events in a reflection on the revolution of the spring. The sermon illustrated the extent to which he had maintained the remarkable self-confidence that had characterized his earliest printed work.[109] For *Ουρανων ουρανια*—the title translates as "the heavenly things of the heavens," or, in a classical citation, an invocation of "Urania of the heavens"—advertised the fact that its author's reading of the biblical "heavens and earth" differed from that of the standard writers on the subject, including Franciscus Junius, whose notes in the most popular edition of the Geneva Bible had guided the interpretation of several generations of Puritan readers.[110] Owen advanced a metaphorical rather than literal reading of the expression, which, he claimed, referred to national constitutions rather than to the materiality of the created realm.[111] He understood the "heavens of the nations" to refer to "political heights and glory, those forms of government which they have framed for themselves and their own interest, with the grandeur and lustre of their dominions." The "earth," meanwhile, he understood as "multitudes of . . . people, their strength and power, whereby their heavens, or political heights, are supported." The biblical prophets were not predicting the end of the world when they anticipated the collapse of the heavens and earth: it was not the "material heavens and earth" that were to be abolished, or the "Mosaical ordinances" of the Old Testament, as other commentators claimed, but the "political heights and splendour, the popular multitudes and strength, of the nations of the earth, that are thus to be shaken."[112] God "shakes heaven and earth when he shakes all nations," he argued; "that is, he shakes the heaven and earth of the nations."[113] The biblical text was using language redolent of the dissolution of the cosmos to predict a revolution in international government.

Of course, many of Owen's contemporaries were also attempting to understand the extraordinary events of 1649 through the lens of prophetic scripture. Rather than drawing on analogies of doomsday, many of them were weaving into their readings of current affairs an expectation of an impending period of spiritual flourishing, which they described as the "millennium." Owen was careful to distinguish his eschatological expectations from this perspective. He refused to give a date for the "shaking" he expected and disclaimed any commitment to explicitly millennial theory, offering a robust rejection of the anarchic and revolutionary impulse that this theory often supported.[114] But he still advanced a political reading of prophecy, insisting that "the Lord Jesus Christ, by his mighty power, in these latter days, as antichristian tyranny draws to its period," will "shake and translate the political heights, governments, and strength of the nations," so that the nations will become a "quiet habitation for the people of the Most High" and a home for his "peaceable kingdom."[115] Owen believed that the political barrier to the fulfillment of his vision was systemic, in that the "whole present constitution of the government of the nations is so cemented with antichristian mortar, from the very top to the bottom, that without a thorough shaking they cannot be cleansed."[116] The English revolution would be globally exported—in fact, it had to be exported. All the "kings of the earth" had "given their power to Antichrist, endeavouring to the utmost to keep the kingdom of Christ out of the world," and for over seven hundred years they had made it their "main business" to defend the claims of the "man of sin," earning in the process, by the "blood of saints," such titles as "Eldest Son of the Church" and "Defender of the Faith."[117] Consequently, Owen continued, the European nations were so connected to Antichristian power that "no digging or mining, but an earthquake, will cast up the foundation-stones thereof."[118] Reaching for a biblical model for the revolutionary behavior he anticipated, Owen fastened upon the example of Samson, who, "intending the destruction of the princes, lords, and residue of the Philistines, who were gathered together in their idol-temple, effected it by pulling away the pillars whereby the building was supported, whereupon the whole frame toppled to the ground."[119] *Ουρανων ουρανια* was developing an ethical republicanism that justified the global extension of the kingdom of God by means of a crusade of unimaginable intensity: "Tremble, I pray; for you are entering the most purging, trying furnace that ever the

Lord set up on the earth. . . . Babylon shall fall, and all the glory of the earth be stained, and the kingdoms become the kingdoms of our Lord Jesus Christ."[120] The execution of Charles was the first sign of God's intention to refashion the governments of the world.

Owen's expectation of an international revolution moved far beyond that of most of his contemporaries. He may have been aware of the dangers of rhetorical overload: he described one of his sermon's figures of speech as a "pleonasm," a Greek term describing unnecessary rhetorical abundance, which had relatively recently entered vernacular usage.[121] But while his argument was not understated, his reference to Samson as an exemplar of the new ethic of godly imperialism was to become increasingly popular among radical voices in and after the revolutionary decade, most famously in Milton's *Samson agonistes* (1671).[122] The allusion also allowed Owen to talk about himself: Stanley Gower's preface to *Salus electorum, sanguis Jesu* had hailed Owen as a Samson come to deliver God's oppressed people.[123] The invocation of Samson was ultimately ambiguous, given the questionable morality of the biblical hero, but it effectively communicated the need for robust action against overwhelming tyrannical power. However it understood the analogy, Parliament approved of Owen's sermon, and ordered that it be published. Four days later, on 23 April, the monthly fast-day sermons were stopped, ahead of a more general move against the political preaching that had nourished and sustained the cause of Parliament through the most difficult years of the civil wars.[124] As the new regime consolidated, it may have wished to control this important ideological arena. Owen, who may have been aware of the wider significance of the ending of the series of fast-day sermons, rapidly reworked his material, signing his preface from Coggeshall on 1 May, and changed publisher for the third consecutive time, having the sermon distributed by John Cleaver. The title page of the published text indicated that Cleaver was also distributing Owen's self-published Colchester sermons. His gamble had paid off.

Owen was developing his political eschatology as he was continuing to rise in the estimation of his colleagues. On 7 June 1649 he preached again to MPs, who had been gathered by the lord mayor of London to enjoy a banquet in the Grocer's Hall to celebrate the defeat of the Leveller mutiny. Owen and Thomas Goodwin were invited to preach to the party before their meal.[125] In this unpublished sermon, "Human power defeated," Owen's mood was exuberant. Reflecting on the events of the previous year, he considered that "Zion hath been the rise and downfall of all the powers of the world."[126] The Leveller agitators were "rebels from amongst his people" whom God had purged, just as he had "devoted to ruin," like Jehu, Charles I.[127] And his reflections on the regicide moved from criticisms of the Stuarts to launch a principled attack on monarchy itself:

> The breaking of the old monarchies and of papal power is a work meet for the Lord. And in this shall mainly consist the promised glory of the Church of Christ in after days; whose morning star, I doubt not, is now upon us. . . . Look upon all the glorious things that are spoken concerning Zion in the latter days, and you shall find them all interwoven with this still, – the shaking of heaven, the casting down of all thrones, dominions, and mighty ones.[128]

Adopting republican values after Parliament's abolition of monarchy, Owen's fiery rhetoric constructed a purposeful narrative for those soldiers "that shall go for Ireland" to defend the English republic.[129] On 8 June, MPs moved to express their appreciation for the sermons they had enjoyed on the previous evening. Both speakers were invited to publish their sermons—which Owen does not appear to have done. Both were recommended to become heads of Oxford colleges—an appointment that, as we will see, was much more rapidly fulfilled for Goodwin than for his younger colleague. And both were rewarded with an annual pension of £100.[130]

It was likely around this time that Owen met Oliver Cromwell.[131] Leaving London, Owen called upon Fairfax to pay respects. As he waited outside the house, Owen encountered another party who was calling with the same intention. Cromwell recognized Owen: "Sir, you are the person I must be aquainted with," he insisted. Owen's polite—and perhaps reserved—response was that this would be "more to my advantage than yours." The two men entered Fairfax's home together, where Cromwell attempted to persuade the preacher to join his forces for Ireland.[132] Cromwell wrote to Owen's church to encourage them to release their pastor, even as he commanded one of Owen's younger brothers, both of whom served in the military in Ireland, to encourage him to comply.[133] Perhaps Owen, who had exhorted the Irish expeditionary force in his Levellers sermon, had little choice. On 2 July, Parliament ordered him to join the forces preparing for the invasion of Ireland.[134]

Owen likely spent the summer making arrangements for his first extended journey away from home. His routine affairs continued. On 23 July 1649, he hosted a meeting of Josselin and Richard Harlakenden, Josselin's patron, who sought his advice about an oath. Josselin also took the opportunity of attending one of the meetings of the gathered church in Coggeshall, which provided him with a rare opportunity to comment on the practices of the congregation of visible saints that Owen had formed within the structures of the parish. Josselin witnessed a format for Bible study with which he was entirely unfamiliar, in which church members did not sit passively as auditors of a sermon, but actively "discoursed, divers of them of one and the same text of scripture," perhaps encouraged by Owen's defense of lay preaching.[135] Owen, it appears, was developing at a local level some of the freedoms he was anticipating would be enjoyed by the nation as it entered into the liberties of the kingdom of Christ—the revolution he envisaged was not giving way to clerical domination, any more than it supported the domination of lords or kings, but was providing laymen with new opportunities for spiritual leadership. For many things were changing in this new England. The emerging republic was being refashioned as a utopian space in which dreams of equality and human flourishing could be realized. Despite Owen's hostility to political agendas, the impulse that was driving more politically precise iterations in Leveller thinking and Digger practice was also encouraging lay participation in the teaching ministry of the Coggeshall church.[136]

These recent opportunities had allowed Owen to develop a marketable public profile. One indication of his growing significance was the publication by Philemon Stephens of an anthology of his early writings. His regicide sermon had already sold well, having gone into a second impression, and Stephens, who had published all but the last three of Owen's works, sought to capitalize on his earlier relationship with the author by producing *Certaine treatises written by John Owen . . . Formerly published at severall times, now reduced into one volume* (1649). The anthology gathered together *A display of Arminianisme* (1643), *Salus electorum, sanguis Jesu* (1648), and *The duty of pastors and people distinguished* (1644). It suggested that his earlier writings had not sold well: the anthology used the same text blocks for books that Stephens had published as separate volumes, each of the books within the anthology was individually paginated, and they included the same handwritten corrections of errata as those which had earlier been published. The verso of the title page advertised the possibility that *Certaine treatises* would also include Owen's five published sermons, among them sermons that had been published by Stephens's competitors, but they were not included. Stephens's project may have been driven by the need to shift units, but it indicated that Owen was now someone who could make money for his publishers. Aged only 33, Owen had been having a remarkable year, becoming the principal preacher of the new regime and the recipient of a lucrative government pension. He was moving closer to a full-blown republican position as the new regime abolished bishops, lords, and monarchy. It was a token of further elevation to come.

V

Perhaps the most significant evidence of Owen's growing importance to the republican regime was the fact that he was recruited to join the army in a series of invasions. The opportunities for travel that this offered further distinguished Owen's experience from that of Josselin, who, more typical of the age in which he lived, admitted in June 1649 that he had "not rid for above a yeare 10 miles outright."[137] Owen's travels in Ireland and Scotland were the only time of his life in which he lived outside southeast England, but they changed him, even as they reshaped the government of what had been the three Stuart kingdoms.

The Cromwellian intervention in Ireland was the most successful attempt to implement long-standing English political strategies for the island.[138] England's new republican government was compelled to address the threats represented by the various royalist and Catholic armies in Ireland. In the summer of 1649, parliamentary forces opened up territory around Dublin, which facilitated the landing of Oliver Cromwell and some 30,000 fresh troops in the middle of August. These forces immediately began the campaign of total war, which, however closely it parallels other conflicts in the period, continues to be one of the most controversial episodes in Anglo-Irish history. After spending several days in "holy exercises," Cromwell's forces marched north toward Drogheda, where, on 10 September, they enjoyed their most notorious victory, with the siege of the town ending in the deaths of 3,000 royalist soldiers and around 700 townspeople. Cromwell rejoiced in the "righteous judgement of God upon these barbarous wretches, who have imbrued their hands in so much innocent blood," but also hoped that the losses would "tend to prevent the effusion of blood for the future, which are the satisfactory grounds to such actions, which otherwise cannot but work remorse and regret."[139] As news of the invasion circulated in England, Owen joined the campaign. On 16 September, as the events at Drogheda began to be reported, Josselin noted that his neighbor was "going for Ireland," optimistically adding that "the season is very good and gallant, the rate of things continueth dearer and is likely to encrease."[140] Owen's recent sermon to Parliament had projected the need for an "earthquake" to "cast up the foundation-stones" of the European nations to prepare the way for the invading kingdom of God.[141] In Ireland, he would witness this revolution at first hand.

One month after the landing of the New Model Army, and its first decisive battles, Owen left his church and his wife, so recently bereaved of her only surviving child. His journey to Dublin took him outside the southeast of England for the first time in his life. Following the example of the army, and other ministers who traveled to support its work, Owen may have departed to Ireland from Chester. The crossing to Dublin was often rough, was attended by threats from pirates, and must have been extraordinarily demanding for Owen, who was making his first passage by sea.[142] It is not clear exactly when he arrived in Dublin—likely in early October—but he appears to have been based in Dublin Castle, the historic center of English administration, for around four months, throughout the winter of 1649 and the early new year, occasionally preaching in a chapel on Wood Street.[143] Owen's location made sense: Dublin was the logistical center of the invasion. Catholics and suspected royalists had been expelled from the walled towns under English control, and Dublin must have had the aspect of a wartime capital. Owen found the situation in the city harrowing, later remembering the "poor parentless children that lie begging, starving, rotting in the streets, and find no relief; yea, persons of quality . . . seeking for bread, and finding none."[144] And, despite his broad views of toleration, he was shocked by the English radical preachers who had traveled to Ireland to "vaunt themselves to be God . . . in the open streets with detestable pride, atheism, and folly," perhaps recognizing that ideas, like diseases, traveled with the army.[145] But if the situation within the city was discouraging, the situation outside its walls was worse. Owen was well aware of the strength of the forces ranged against the invaders. The soldiers of the English Protestant republic were facing a strange alliance that seemed at times to contradict the sectarian dichotomy of much of the parliamentary rhetoric. The Scottish Presbyterians in Ulster, who as "Covenanted Protestants . . . had sworn, in the presence of the great God to extirpate Popery and prelacy," had joined forces with Irish royalists led by Ormond, who "counted themselves under no less sacred bond for the maintenance of prelates, service books, and the like," and native Catholics, "a mighty number that had for eight years together sealed their vows to the Romish religion with our blood and their own." Owen represented these independently controlled Irish armies as having allied with English royalists, "that party which themselves had laboured to render most odious and execrable, as most defiled with innocent blood," to conceal evidence of the 1641 rebellion and to establish the Catholic faith.[146] The charge was implausible, but typical of Owen's early tendency to lump together everyone to whom he was opposed. He later remembered that the "combined enemy" in Ireland, with its strong logistical base and close links to the Continent, seemed to be "unconquerable," but also that the military strategy of the invaders had been "overswayed by the providence of God."[147] He would have welcomed the successful momentum of the parliamentary campaign, which resulted that autumn in the capture of Wexford (11 October), New Ross (19 October) and Carrickfergus (2 November). These victories secured the east coast of the island and seemed to provide proof of God's blessing on the campaign.[148] Owen may have had a hand in preparing propaganda against the Catholic bishops.[149]

Owen does not appear to have left his base in Dublin. During his four months in the city, he experienced difficulties in terms of workload and health, but also paradoxically his most encouraging experience to date of preaching. "For the present," he explained, he was "by God's providence removed for a season from my native soil, attended with more than ordinary weaknesses and infirmities, separated from my library, burdened with manifold employments." But, after the discouragements of Fordham and Coggeshall, Owen found the people of Dublin enormously responsive to his preaching, and he enjoyed the opportunity of "constant preaching to a numerous multitude of as thirsting a people after the gospel as ever yet I conversed withal."[150] While Josselin preached to the indifferent parishioners of Coggeshall, Owen witnessed the "tears and cries of the inhabitants of Dublin after the manifestations of Christ."[151]

Owen's ministry in Dublin provided the first evidences that his preaching was being attended by conversions. This is not to claim that his earlier ministry had done no good to his parishioners—but that, as far as we can tell, the models of church government that prevailed in Fordham and Coggeshall did not provide the mechanisms by which the circumstances of individual conversion could be recorded. In Dublin, John Rogers gathered a congregation in Christ Church cathedral that required prospective members, both male and female, to publicly narrate an account of their conversion, which he collected, edited, and published.[152] His compendium on church order, *Ohel or Bethshemesh* (1653), demonstrated Owen's importance to the religious life of those believers. One of Rogers's congregants, Andrew Manwaring, recorded that Owen "did me much good, and made *me* see *my misery* in the *want* of *Christ*."[153] Another of Rogers's congregants, Dorothy Emett, stated that "Mr. Owen was the first man by whose means, and Ministry I became sensible of my condition," though she quickly abandoned whatever she had been taught of his views on spirituality, being assured of her salvation by a voice she heard in her sleep.[154] While we have no record of the content of his Irish sermons, it is clear that Owen's experience of preaching in Dublin was happier than it had been in either of his parishes.[155] At last, his ministry as a preacher had been validated by the conversions of auditors "thirsting . . . after the gospel."[156] Ironically, the impact of Owen's preaching was recorded in narratives of conversion of which he could never approve, and by a clerical colleague who became a bitter critic of the policy of his later career.

But Owen's ministry in Dublin also drew him into his first substantial theological dispute—and that with a respondent who was to become one of the most slippery litigants in seventeenth-century religious polemic. Richard Baxter was an emerging controversialist, a self-taught English Presbyterian minister who overwhelmed his antagonists by rhetorical, if not theological, attrition. His attack on Owen began a debate that extended from 1649 to 1657 and initiated "one of the few controversies in which not Baxter himself, but his opponent had the last word."[157] For Baxter, in a poorly considered appendix to his *Aphorisms on justification* (1649), had expostulated upon antinomianism, and made the fatal mistake of finding it in Owen's work.[158] Owen was outraged, and appears to have spent a large part of his time in Dublin preparing a response to Baxter's claims. His research plans were frustrated by the fact that he had traveled lightly, and was, "by the providence of God, in a condition of separation from my own small library," an excuse he had already offered to his readers in *The duty of pastors and people distinguished* (1644).[159] He had likely expected to find the resources he required in local library collections, supreme among which was the library of Trinity College Dublin, which had been very effectively established by the book-buying strategies of James Ussher.[160] But Owen discovered to his surprise that he could not locate an important work by the Polish high Calvinist, Johannes Maccovius.[161] It was, if we take his complaint at face value, another telling moment in his realizing the spiritual needs of Ireland: he assumed he would have ready access to a book that was unavailable to students and scholars in Ireland's only university library, the national seminary of its clergy. He struggled on with his response to Baxter and completed much of his manuscript in Dublin Castle, in which he signed his preface on 20 December 1649.[162] He likely expected to bring the manuscript home and to make final preparations for publication in Essex.

For Owen returned to Coggeshall early in the new year, during another winter of exceptionally high food prices.[163] On Monday 4 February, perhaps en route, Owen appears to have submitted to the Council of State a report on Irish finance, which he had brought with him from Dublin.[164] Back in Coggeshall, he almost certainly met for the first time his new daughter, another Mary, who, likely born in his absence, was baptized on 23 February 1651.[165] But he had no time for a leisurely family reunion, for Owen was immediately plunged into government work. Five days after the baptism of his only surviving child, he was back in London, preparing to preach for Parliament.

This renewed invitation to address MPs provided Owen with an opportunity to reflect upon his experiences in Ireland. His address, *The steadfastness of the promises, and the sinfulness of staggering* (1650), emphasized the need to find English spiritual solutions to Irish political problems. The sermon began by invoking the memory of the 1641 rebellion. Owen encouraged MPs to "look upon the affairs of Ireland" and to witness the "engagement of the great God of revenges against murder and treachery, the interest of the Lord Christ and his kingdom against the man of sin."[166] He was frustrated that so few English Protestants were including the needs of Ireland in their prayers to his "great God of revenges." "Of how many congregations in this nation may the prayers, tears, and supplications for carrying on of the work of God in Ireland, be written with the lines of emptiness!" he considered. "They have forgotten that Ireland was the first of the nations that laid wait for the blood of God's people," and, perhaps thinking of the Amalekites in Numbers 24:20, he remembered that their "latter end shall be to perish for ever."[167] God had permitted the "sworn vassals of the man of sin," the "followers after the beast," to commit crimes that "render them obnoxious unto vengeance, upon such rules of government amongst men as he hath appointed," and so the English forces were entirely justified in giving the Irish a "cup of blood into their hands."[168] But he denied that the pursuit of justice was the only thing that God required of English Protestants:

> How is it that Jesus Christ is in Ireland only as a lion staining all his garments with the blood of his enemies; and none to hold him out as a lamb sprinkled with his own blood to his friends? Is it the sovereignty and interest of England that is alone to be there transacted? . . . I could heartily rejoice, that, innocent blood being expiated, the Irish might enjoy Ireland so long as the moon endureth, so that Jesus Christ might possess the Irish.[169]

Owen reminded MPs that "God's work, whereunto you are engaged, is the propagating of the kingdom of Christ, and the setting up of the standard of the gospel."[170] Moving beyond the rather unspecific political interventions of his earlier sermons to Parliament, he argued that Parliament should provide "one gospel preacher for every walled town in the English possession in Ireland."[171] His first sermon to Parliament had highlighted the spiritual needs of Wales and the darker parts of England, and *The steadfastness of the promises, and the sinfulness of staggering* now made the same appeal for Ireland. "God hath been faithful in doing great things for you," he reminded the MPs; "be faithful in this one,—do your utmost for the preaching of the gospel in Ireland."[172]

His duty performed, Owen returned again to Coggeshall. Even if he was tired by his constant traveling, or by the difficulties of settling back into parish life, he continued to accrue responsibilities. Perhaps responding to his concern for Ireland, Parliament appointed him as a trustee of Trinity College Dublin in March 1650. In early July it requested that he work with Thomas Goodwin, who had recently been appointed as president of Magdalen College,

Oxford, to "seriously consider what laws, rules, orders and constitutions are to be established," and to advise upon "what qualifications are requisite in the admission of persons according to the course now used in the university."[173] At the same time, Parliament appointed Owen to preach every Sunday to the Council of State, with the promise of a £200 salary and accomodation in Whitehall.[174]

These were busy days, and there is some evidence that Owen was looking to cut pastoral corners during the busy spring and early summer of 1650. Josselin heard him preach in Coggeshall on 2 May 1650, noting that his sermon focused on "instructions how to endeavour stablishnednes in believing," phraseology which suggests that Owen had reworked parts of his last parliamentary sermon for his home congregation.[175] For, on top of all his other duties, and in a home with a new baby, Owen was also completing the text of his next theological treatise. As the manuscript that he had completed in Dublin was being printed, Owen discovered that the doctrine he was defending had been challenged by the former bishop of Salisbury, John Davenant (1572–1641), in his treatises on the death of Christ, predestination, and reprobation, which had recently been published.[176] Davenent was, by any estimation, a more worthy opponent than Baxter, a magisterial figure in the evolution of English Calvinism, and so Owen slowed down the printing of the manuscript in order to add new material that dealt more specifically with his arguments. John Sams, meanwhile, likely took up the pastoral slack in Coggeshall.

The expanded book, *Of the death of Christ*, finally appeared on booksellers' stalls in London during May 1650. It was published by Peter Cole, who, in the period, was closely associated with the "dissenting brethren" of Independents at the Westminster Assembly, the regicides, and the radical faction within the army—a clear signal of Owen's shifting politics. *Of the death of Christ* has not received a great deal of attention in scholarship on Owen. This reflects, in part, the attitude of Owen's most influential editor, William Goold, who suggested its lesser importance by printing the text in a very small font in his nineteenth-century edition, which, quite practically, made it extremely difficult to read. But *Of the death of Christ* is a key text in the development of Owen's theology of the atonement, in his relationship with Baxter, and in the emergence of forces that pushed apart prominent voices in the religious leadership of the parliamentary army.[177] Owen explained the background to the project. "About two years since," he reminded his readers, he had published *Salus electorum, sanguis Jesu* (1648), which Baxter had attacked in his *Aphorisms on justification* (1649).[178] Owen was not sure why he had done so. He was mystified by the strength of Baxter's attack, for which he could find "no reason."[179] He believed that Baxter's objections to his arguments focused more on language than ideas, but found that Baxter's own language, which included "such passages of censure as might have been omitted without losing the least grace of his book or style," was not beyond criticism.[180] Equally, he admitted, his own work had been "found to want some grains of accurateness . . . in a scholastical balance."[181] Most seriously, Owen was frustrated by Baxter's lack of rhetorical or formal disputative ability, a loss of control that resulted in there being "scarce more lines than mistakes in this discourse," many of which misrepresented Owen's own position.[182] Baxter had charged that Owen believed in eternal justification, for example, a theological position that Owen parsed as "justification before believing" and rapidly dismissed as heresy. He was clearly frustrated by Baxter's attack: "To have an opinion fastened on me which I never once received nor intimated the least thought of in that whole treatise, or any other of mine, and then my arguments answered as to such an end and purpose as I not once intended to promote by them, is a little too harsh dealing."[183] Perhaps Owen's recent experience of public status had led him to expect better treatment from someone as yet almost entirely unknown.

Owen's response to Baxter's attack revealed some of the principal drivers of his personality. His reaction was prickly, reflecting his sense of seniority and the extent to which he had come to identify with his views of the atonement. After all, he had thought more about this theological issue than about any other: "There have not been many things, in my whole inquiry after the mind of God in his word, which have more exercised my thoughts than the right ordering and distinct disposal of those whereof we treat."[184] And he, at least, had been properly trained, unlike his self-taught opponent. *Of the death of Christ* attempted to settle the question of Owen's orthodoxy by overwhelming Baxter with learning: the text put Baxter's arguments in the context of a wider textual culture, referring repeatedly to Hugo Grotius and Gerardus Vossius, among other eminent humanist scholars. Owen also dabbled in his own variety of guilt by association, linking Baxter, in a charge that was not entirely accurate, and which ultimately underestimated the heterodoxy of his opponent, to the "almost conclamated cause of Arminianism"—in a usage of "conclamated" which anticipates by over a decade the first recorded instance in the *OED*.[185]

Owen was surprised by Baxter's attack and by the divergence of opinion it represented, and his response illustrated the opening up of gaps within the ranks of those parliamentary military chaplains who were supposed to represent the forces of the clerical mainstream. Owen was dismayed by Baxter's attack on his orthodoxy. "It was in our hopes and expectations, not many years ago," he remembered, "that the Lord would graciously have turned back all those bitter streams which, issuing from the pride, unthankfulness, and wisdom of the carnal mind, had many ways attempted to overflow the doctrine of the grace of God, that bringeth salvation." But, "finding now, by experience, that the day of the church's rest from persecution is the day of Satan's main work for seducing and temptation, and that not a few are attempting once more to renew the contest of sinful, guilty, defiled nature, against the sovereign distinguishing love and effectual grace of God," Owen believed that it was "necessary, that the faith once delivered to the saints be contended for and asserted from the word of truth in the like public way wherein it is opposed."[186] He published *Of the death of Christ* with the hope that his arguments could not and would not be answered. But he would have less "rest from persecution" than he might have expected, and would not long continue in a settled pastoral ministry.[187] As the "mild, dry and warme" winter passed into a "forward and fruitfull" spring of 1650, Owen preached again to Parliament on 13 June, a sermon that has not been recorded.[188] Within weeks, he was called to accompany the army on its next international expedition—the invasion of Scotland.[189]

VI

Owen accompanied the army of the English Parliament in its invasion of Scotland in July 1650.[190] The events surrounding the offensive marked a critical turning point in Anglo-Scots relations, and an ironic inversion of the millennial hopes that had been articulated in the preceding decades by many of the leaders of both nations' political and ecclesiastical institutions.[191] Throughout much of the 1640s, the English and Scottish parliaments had espoused a similar political agenda. They had expressed concern at the king's abuse of privilege; they had combined their forces in the first civil war under the (ambiguous) conditions of the Solemn League and Covenant (1643); and their ecclesiastical representatives had hammered out a system of religious uniformity in the terms of the Westminster Confession of Faith (1647), with associated liturgical and catechetical documents. But the political covenant and its religious superstructure could not deliver on the promise of a transnational union of hearts and minds, and the alliance between the Scots and the English Parliament began to crumble.[192] Throughout the later 1640s, tensions had been building between English and Scots theologians at the Westminster Assembly, so that the sympathy toward the English Independents displayed by George Gillespie in *A dispute against the English popish ceremonies* (1637), for example, was reversed by the emergence of the robust, aggressively nationalized and "imperialistic" Presbyterianism advanced by his fellow commissioners: in the year after Gillespie's death, Samuel Rutherford published *A free disputation against pretended liberty of conscience* (1649) to challenge the

Independents' "fecund and broody" evil of congregational autonomy and its correlative, the toleration of religious variety.[193] As the Scots ramped up their rhetoric, they framed their increasingly horrified response to the "teeming freedom" and "teeming truth" of religious toleration in England in covenantal terms, in which the mere existence of Independents became a direct threat to the spiritual and political well-being of Scotland.[194] These views of the Scottish Commissioners were widely shared. David Dickson, in an undated series of sermons probably emanating from this period, argued that "if this land be not humbled the judgment that coms shall be exemplar."[195] And it was to be exemplary. For, despite the invocations by eminent Scottish churchmen and politicians of latter-day glory and unstoppable divine blessing, the nation was invaded and then successfully occupied by forces they believed God had cursed. The struggle between England and Scotland in the summer of 1650 was a "socio-political manifestation of the heady theological debates of the Westminster Assembly"—but one that reversed the Presbyterian victories in the London synod.[196] The Scots in Ulster had already shown their true colors by joining an alliance with "those bloody *Irish Rebells* upon the Kingly Interest."[197] And so, in the summer of 1650, the Church of Scotland and its godly adherents were compelled to come to terms with the "reproach of a Sectarian Army," as regiments of the English Independents advanced ever closer toward the border.[198]

The invasion of Scotland was made possible by new leadership in the New Model Army. Fairfax, its commander-in-chief, had "no love for the Scots," who had "despoiled Yorkshire several times," and after the battle of Preston, he had ordered Cromwell to punish them by "invading Scotland and occupying Edinburgh." But under pressure from his wife to distance himself from the emerging republic, and perhaps fearing that his new illnesses were divine punishment for his activities in war, Fairfax disengaged from the army, surrendering his command, and retired to his family estate at Nun Appleton.[199] His withdrawal left Cromwell in control of the parliamentary forces. The change of leadership represented for Owen an exchange of patrons. And his new patron again put Owen at the center of events.

Like the invasion of Ireland, the invasion of Scotland was driven by theological claims. Scottish readers may have first become aware of the ideals of the English army by means of *A declaration of the army of England upon their march into Scotland* (1650), which was printed in Newcastle, London, and, later, Edinburgh. Its title page advertised that it was "signed in the Name, and by the Appointment of his Excellency the Lord General CROMWELL, and his Councell of Officers," among whose number, Scott Spurlock has suggested, Owen may have been included.[200] It was the first evidence that he had joined the staff of the army. But Owen was also active in representing the events of the invasion to an English audience. In July 1650, he wrote to the Lord Commissioner, John Lisle, a member of the Council of State, summarizing the results of an engagement in which English soldiers, against all expectations, routed superior Scottish forces. Owen reported that the Scottish clergy "told the people before our army came, that they should not need to strike one stroke, but stand still, and they should see the sectaries destroyed."[201] While, as far as we can tell, Owen had played no role in the military campaign in Ireland, he did accompany the army on its march toward Edinburgh, and witnessed its engagements. News of the results of these engagements was quickly circulated. In early August, rumors in Essex suggested that "the Scots were routed and thousands slain."[202] More credible information was reported to Josselin "just when I came downe out of pulpitt" on 8 September, that "4000 weare slain 10000 prisoners: 22 pieces of ordnance taken"—a remarkably accurate assessment of the extraordinary victory at Dunbar, which had taken place only five days earlier.[203] Later in the autumn, Josselin recorded a dream in which he was approached for advice by the grandees of the army in Scotland—perhaps the only indication in his diary of his professional jealousy of Owen.[204] It was a telling example of the elaboration of a code of honor and esteem. But it was Owen's letter, describing the results of the struggle, that was read in Parliament.[205]

Owen, meanwhile, was participating in a vigorous culture of preaching, in which Cromwell and Lambert also seem to have engaged.[206] While his interview in Glasgow with the young Hugh Binning seems to have gone well, his preaching in the Scottish capital does not appear to have been as popular as it had been in Dublin.[207] He preached on at least several occasions in Scotland. His sermon celebrating the success of the English conquest, *The branch of the Lord* (1650), was delivered in part in Berwick on 21 July, and was continued in Edinburgh, where on 26 November it was published by Evan Tyler, who retained his official role as king's printer by working for the new regime.[208] It is not clear how Owen's sermons were received. Rumors about the content of his preaching in Berwick reached Archibald Johnston of Wariston, who recorded in his diary in August 1650 that Owen had warned that "God would bring doun Cromwell and his airmy, who was so proud as to say that at the sight of his face wee would all flye."[209] Nevertheless, in his official publications, if not elsewhere, Owen insisted that he had not joined the invasion with the purpose of engaging in religious controversy. "It was with thoughts of peace, that I embraced my call, to this place, and time of war," he explained in his dedication to Cromwell. He had intended to "pour out a savour of the gospel upon the sons of peace in this place," for "all peace that is from God is precious to my spirit."[210] But *The branch of the Lord* was a very telling publication, for it illustrated that the defense of parliamentary religion could no longer be uncomplicated: the sermon represented the divisions as well as the ambitions of its sponsoring military force, continuing the attack on the Presbyterians that had characterized the literary culture of the invasion, while backpedaling on its earlier defense of religious variety within the army, and, in particular, presenting a much more robust critique of claimants to "inner light."[211] *The branch of the Lord* was one of the earliest signs of the reactionary turn among Independents. Owen presented himself as being entirely opposed to the inflexible claims of the Church of Scotland. He was appalled by the rigor with which Scottish Presbyterians desired to implement their vision of covenanted uniformity.[212] His sermon deconstructed the Scottish Presbyterian consensus, insisting that the Scots should reconsider foundational elements of their ecclesiology. He argued with the zeal of a convert, presenting himself as someone who had only recently abandoned the Presbyterian assumption that the true church required the defense of the state:

> Men looking upon the church, do find that it is a fair fabric indeed, but cannot imagine how it should stand. A few supporters it seemeth to have in the world. . . . Here you have a magistrate, there an army, or so. Think the men of the world, 'Can we but remove these props, the whole would quickly topple to the ground.' Yea, so foolish have I been myself, and so void of understanding before the Lord, as to take a view of some goodly appearing props of this building, and to think, how shall the House be preserved if these should be removed?[213]

Nevertheless, he continued, he was now certain that the church was not composed of believers and their children, as the Scottish confessional tradition claimed, but that it included believers alone. Owen argued that a true gospel church should be constituted only of "elect, believers . . . they alone are built on Christ."[214] There was no room for the ambiguity of a national comprehension, which Rutherford, whose work Owen had so often cited, had defended, in which individuals could not know "whether they are admitted or no."[215] Extending the biblical metaphor, he argued that "there is not one rotten dead stone in all this building."[216]

But, Owen believed, the perennial problem was that believers had a tendency to mistake their own inclinations for the commandments of Jesus Christ. "Many attempts have been to set up light in this house, and not from Christ," he explained. "Some would kindle their traditions for the doctrine of this house; some their prudentials, for the government of it; some their ceremonials, for the worship of it," but these were no more than "candles in the sun." And then he mounted his most searing critique of the Presbyterian position. Earlier in the summer, in *A seasonable and necessary warning*, the Commissioners of the General Assembly of the Church of Scotland had alluded to Jeremiah 9:14 and Isaiah 50:11 when they warned their readers of those who "love to walk in the imaginations of their own hearts, and in the light of their own fire, and in the sparks that they have kindled, corrupting the truth of God, approving errors in themselves, and tolerating them in others."[217] Now, drawing explicitly on the same biblical texts, Owen inquired whether Scottish Presbyterians should "think to compass themselves with sparks, and walk in the light of the fire which themselves have kindled, in the face of the Sun of righteousness? Shall not such men lie down in sorrow? Beloved, take heed of such 'ignes fatui'—foolish, misguiding fires."[218] Of course, there were also "foolish, misguiding fires" among the Cromwellian troops, Owen admitted, as he set out to explain the "true light which lighteth every man" and to resist the "inner light" claims of the radicals. But Owen believed that God would vindicate his English servants, despite their occasional confusion. The Presbyterianism of the Church of Scotland would certainly be destroyed, for "an unjust Usurper had taken possession of this house, and kept it in bondage,—Satan had seized on it, and brought it, through the wrath of God, under his power. He, then, must be conquered, that the Lord Christ may have complete possession of his own house."[219] Satan had conquered the Church of Scotland, but Jesus Christ would be its "great avenger."[220] Owen expected that "he will not lie down until he eat of the prey, and drink the blood of the slain."[221] Owen understood the invasion in terms of God's long war for the liberty of his people. Perhaps remembering John Warren's sermon, *The potent potter* (1649), whose stringent rhetoric he was making his own, Owen argued that God "fearfully broke the old Roman-pagan empire . . . and will as fearfully destroy the antichristian Roman power, with all its adherents," for "sooner or later he will call to an account every instrument of persecution in the world," and "if he be once roused up, he will not couch down, until he eat and drink the blood of the slain."[222] For the "great God of revenges" who had destroyed the alliance of Presbyterians, Episcopalians, and Catholics in Ireland was also the "avenger of this house" in Scotland.[223] "Men may upon various pretences claim this privilege, to such a Land, Nation, or Faction," but "it will in the end appeare to be theirs and only theirs, who are living stones."[224] Those Scots who continued as Presbyterians would have no right to their own land. The war, as Owen explained it, was about ecclesiology—the doctrine of the church. But his antagonists could avoid shameful defeat, for God "beseeches them to be reconciled who have done the wrong, and them to accept of peace who cannot abide the battle."[225]

Owen's apocalyptic register was not untypical of that of the godly. Back in Essex, in the second half of December 1650, Josselin's reading of Thomas Brightman combined with news of the extraordinary achievements of Cromwell's army to prompt him to develop in his diary a series of apocalyptic calculations. He became certain that Charles II would "die an untimely death" before ever being restored to the English throne, that the Jews would be converted by 1654, and that the New Jerusalem would appear by 1665.[226] Josselin noted the "havocke ... made of them in Scotland" who continued to support the antichrist.[227] His fascination with apocalyptic theology continued in March 1651 when his five-year-old daughter dreamed that Jesus told her he should reign on the earth for ten thousand years.[228] Taken out of this private and domestic context, these kinds of ideas had dangerous resonance in the Scottish invasion.

Owen's arguments met with a mixed response. Some Independents appreciated the apologetic value of his work: one officer wrote to Cromwell, wishing that he had copies of Owen's sermons to distribute among the Scots.[229] But many Presbyterians remained unconvinced by his claims. "A News-Letter from Scotland," written in Leith on 31 January 1651, informed its English readers that the "Godly partie" of Rutherford, Wariston, and other "rigid Presbyterian Gentlemen" wanted to "bring all kinde of Government into their owne handes *in ordine ad spiritualia*, to vilifie the proceedings of the Parliament of the Commonwealth of England, and scandalize the practice of the officers of the Army in their most religious performances." The attempt of these Presbyterian leaders to create space for covenanted government amounted to an attempt to "lett them have a liberty to tyrannize both over the bodies and soules of the poore people under pretence of giving them liberty of conscience, which cannot stand with the principles of any who are lovers of true freedome either to their outward or inward man."[230] But some Scots were persuaded by Owen's case. Alexander Jaffray, for example, was captured at Dunbar and imprisoned for six months, during which period, after a series of apparently unrecorded conversations with Owen, Cromwell, and John Fleetwood, he joined the Independents.[231] And one decade later, at the end of the republic, Wariston would become one of Owen's confidants.

News of the campaign was reported in Essex. At the end of November 1650, Josselin noted that he had "heard of the health of ... Mr Owen."[232] In mid-December, he traveled to Coggeshall to be "a helpe to them ... in Mr Owens absence in Scotland."[233] Two months later, on 9 February 1651, he noted weather conditions—dry, cold sunshine—alongside news that Owen had "returned from Scotland," reporting news of "expectacions of some bustles in Ireland and Scotland."[234] One day later, Owen's new daughter,

Elizabeth, was baptized.[235] Her father had already left the army, as a letter from Cromwell on 18 February 1651 suggests.[236] But, once again, he was not long to remain at home. Owen's new patron was offering him a new opportunity. Cromwell, as chancellor of the University of Oxford, was anxious to staff the colleges with reliable hands. On 23 March 1651, Josselin noted that "Mr Owen hath a place of great profitt given him vz. Deane of christ-church."[237] Ireland and Scotland were largely subdued, and Owen's relationship with the army was ending as he was being offered the chance of new conquests—the subjugation of Oxford.

5

Oxford Reformer

OWEN'S RETURN TO Oxford must have been triumphant—and he had time to savor his success. He was appointed as dean of Christ Church, Oxford, in the middle of March 1651, in an unpromising season. The conquests of Ireland and Scotland gave way to military occupation. The army was withdrawing from Oxford in circumstances that seemed to some observers to reflect the ambiguity of the national political situation.[1] "Many suppose our Commonwealth lost," one diarist noted just a couple of weeks afterward: "Spaine and France and Holland against us. Ireland and Scotland heave[y] worke, and not to bee effected, the English divided, and worne out with heavy taxes and burthens, the merchants trade . . . ruined, and so all tending to poverty."[2] Even so, the times were auspicious for Owen.

Of course, he may not immediately have realized that he was Parliament's second choice for the job. The circumstances of his appointment reflected tensions among the godly. Owen was replacing Edward Reynolds, a member of the Westminster Assembly, a supporter of the Solemn League and Covenant, and perhaps an unintended target of Owen's first book, who in 1648 had been appointed as dean of Christ Church and vice chancellor of the university as part of a wave of Presbyterian reform. But, in the aftermath of the regicide, Reynolds had struggled to demonstrate his fealty to the new regime, especially after public servants were required to take the engagement—an oath of allegiance to the republican government, which was first imposed in 1649.[3] Reynolds evaded the consequences of intransigence for several months before he lost his vice chancellorship to Daniel Greenwood in September 1650, and, at the beginning of 1651, was deprived of his position in the college. It was not obvious who would succeed him in Christ Church. Cromwell suggested that Owen should advise how Reynolds could be restored to his position as dean.[4] Parliament initially invited another Westminster divine, the London

Independent Joseph Caryl, to take his place. Reynolds, perhaps realizing the futility of principled resistance to the state, then backtracked and subscribed to the engagement, and Caryl generously offered to step aside in favor of the previous incumbent. But, on 6 February, the parliamentary committee for the reformation of the universities refused to reappoint Reynolds, and Caryl, perhaps embarrassed by the committee's intransigence against his colleague, excused himself from consideration for the post. University staff then intervened in the dispute, submitting to Parliament "The humble Petition of the Vice Chancellor, Doctors, the Proctors, Heads of Houses, and others, of the University of Oxford." Although the contents of this petition are now unclear, MPs moved immediately to offer the position to Owen, who, as the letter from Cromwell on 18 February suggests, had already left the army, and may have been looking for new opportunities.[5] He first heard of his appointment in a newsbook.[6]

Owen had no sooner returned to the southeast of England than he was thrown back into the work of crafting official polemic. On 4 March, nine days before the event, Parliament invited him to preach on its next day of fasting and humiliation. Perhaps reflecting on how little he had been at home since September 1649, for approximately four of the last eighteen months, he declined the invitation, and on 8 March the Council of State permitted him six weeks of badly needed rest.[7] But he was evidently still on the minds of MPs. Owen preached to Parliament on 13 March 1651, and on the next day, MPs voted by the narrow margin of 26 to 19 to offer him the vacancy in Christ Church.[8] Parliament resolved "that it be referred to the Committee for the regulating the Universities, to see this Vote put in Execution, accordingly."[9] Whatever the hesitations of politicians and the rival candidates for the post, the outcome of the process was clear. With the help of supporters in Parliament, Reynolds's hesitance, and Caryl's deference, Owen had been appointed as dean of one of the most significant colleges in Oxford.

Owen had plenty of time to reflect upon the role he might develop in Christ Church, and upon his significant personal advancement. Christ Church had been founded by Cardinal Wolsey in 1525, refounded by Henry VIII in 1546, and was, half a century later, as William Shakespeare had put it, still "famous, | So excellent in art, and still so rising."[10] In 1651, Owen's appointment was a symbolic victory, for he who had preached to commemorate the execution of the king was being invited to officiate in the very deanery which during the civil wars had functioned as Charles's palace, and over the Great Hall in which had been convened the displaced royalist Parliament.[11] The college, which had been at the "centre of civil war Anglicanism," badly needed reform.[12] Having continued to use Latin prayers, and having permitted drinks to the king's health, until immediately before the regicide, it was famously conservative.[13] Its already declining community of academics had been decimated by the board of Visitors, which the Long Parliament had intruded upon the university to promote Presbyterian values. Reynolds was both a member of the Visitors, and their appointee as a college dean. His removal continued the attack on Presbyterian reforms, which had already resulted in the army's purge of the Long Parliament and the subsequent trial and execution of the king.[14] But the college continued to decline after Reynolds's departure. Christ Church had the largest number of academics who were ejected for refusing to take the oath of allegiance to the new regime.[15] One senior member of the college was expelled in September 1651 for having joined the king's army.[16] Dissent was hard to eradicate.

For all that Owen would have found Oxford familiar, therefore, he was moving into a very new world. Academic leadership would present him with challenges that would tax the moral clarity through which he had understood the recent wars. His move into university management required him to negotiate a variety of political, ecclesiastical, and personal loyalties, challenging his skills as a reforming administrator. Christ Church had an unusual system of governance, having been established as "a cathedral and a college within a single institution," with the dean and chapter constituting a single governing body.[17] The college was financially secure, having since its foundation enjoyed extensive powers of patronage, and having developed important relationships with key London schools, electing pupils to Studentships and presenting its graduates to livings.[18] Its pedagogy was well established to the point of being traditional. While the college was to have a stronger emphasis on scientific learning during the Cromwellian period than in the decades following, the undergraduate curriculum would have been very similar to that which Owen had experienced at Queen's one generation before.[19] There is little evidence of provision for education in Hebrew language and literature, despite the insistence by Henry Thurman, a student of Christ Church, in his *Defence of humane learning* (1661), that those who wished to properly understand Scripture should be able to read it in the original languages.[20] But the college had an active intellectual culture, which Owen was to support, sometimes in surprising ways—an environment enhanced by the contributions of talented undergraduates such as John Locke, who, in 1652, composed an "elegant petition" in which he sought admission to the college, and who would later contribute to its anthology of verse eulogizing Protectorate victories (1654).[21] Owen would need to fasten down upon the traditional festive culture of Oxford, and challenge its customary "rites of violence," which he and the heads of houses would condemn in the spring and early summer of

1652.[22] But he would change Christ Church, even as the wider environment of the university would make its mark on him. His appointment as dean was symbolic of his victory over his recent enemies. Displacing its Catholic founders, and its more recent royalist occupants and Presbyterian leaders, Owen had come into his kingdom.

College administration in an institution only seven miles from Owen's childhood home—and his sister Hester and her family—provided his family, with their two baby daughters, with some much-needed stability. The appointment to Christ Church "brought to an end the period in which Owen alternately travelled about with the army and preached to the army-dominated Rump Parliament and Council of State in London."[23] Of course, those demanding months of travel had also made this new appointment possible. His appointment followed the invitation to oversee the reformation of Trinity College Dublin, in July 1650, and Cromwell's letter in February 1651, which sought advice on administrative matters at the university over which he had recently been appointed chancellor, signaling the extent to which Owen's skills as an academic administrator had become appreciated.[24] Owen's new job required the same kind of reformist instinct as these earlier responsibilities, and would involve several of the same allies. He had already been invited to consult with Thomas Goodwin in relation to his ongoing administrative responsibilities in Dublin; Goodwin had recently been appointed by the Rump Parliament as president of Magdalen College, the first of a tranche of new appointments to key roles, including that of Jonathan Godard, Cromwell's physician during the invasion of Scotland, who became warden of Merton College, and John Conant, Edward Reynolds's son-in-law, whose support for the republican regime justified his appointment as rector of Exeter College.[25] Owen and Goodwin were pivotal in this reshuffle and in overseeing its effects beyond the university, for, "through their closeness to Cromwell," they "gave Oxford an influence on the Cromwellian church at least as great as that which it had exerted on the Laudian church before it."[26] After some weeks of rest, and doubtless conscious of his new privileges and responsibilities, Owen took up his new position in the university on 9 May 1651.[27]

These new appointments to key university positions were symbolic of the wider ambitions of the Cromwellian administration. Its political leaders hoped that the universities of England, Scotland, and Ireland would produce the "pious ministry and magistracy that would puritanize, and so stabilize, the land."[28] But there remained some significant barriers to the realization of this goal, including a large body of Presbyterian academics whose loyalty to the republican regime was often ambiguous. Their continued presence was an anomaly. The Oxford colleges had been purged of suspected royalists in 1648, and conservative influences were further disrupted in late 1649, when the Rump Parliament's imposition of the engagement, which required a statement of loyalty to the new regime, resulted in a second round of ejections, led by their newly empowered Independent colleagues.[29] Cromwell, as chancellor of the university, seems to have stayed the full force of these attempts at radical reform, perhaps realizing that he needed the support of the more broadly based community of Presbyterians that the Independents had determined to root out, a move which perhaps anticipated the conservative turn that would mark the later years of his administration. But Cromwell was in some ways out of his depth in academic politics, and, as we have seen, his attempt to prevent the removal of Edward Reynolds did not succeed.[30] In 1651, Henry Stubbe, then a young Christ Church scholar, conveyed to the university another demand for subscription to the engagement, which, he claimed, was the cause of Reynolds and Samuel Fell being "turned out," but which also provided security for other "cavaliers" who wished to remain.[31] Stubbe's intervention created the vacancy that Owen would fill: his appointment to Christ Church marked the conclusion of the drive to put Independents firmly in control of Oxford by the late summer of 1651.[32]

Of course, the extraordinary circumstances of Owen's return to Oxford marked a personal victory over the Arminian domination of the university from which he had fled. He had witnessed the university fall to the Laudians, and that disaster for orthodoxy had been a recurrent theme in his early writings. But now he was being given the opportunity not just to protest against the Arminian captivity of Oxford, but to refashion its culture with the backing of the state. He had models on which to draw, for colleagues were pushing for similar reforms elsewhere in the university. The college that "came closest to meeting the puritan ideal" was Thomas Goodwin's Magdalene.[33] But Owen's measures in Christ Church were far from unsuccessful. Some undergraduates appreciated his vision of reform. Philip Henry, a student in the college who became a future leader of dissent, remembered that "serious godliness was in reputation" as Owen's reforms advanced.[34] His appointment to Christ Church was also welcomed by members of its academic community, including Lewis du Moulin, who celebrated the new dean in the preface to *Oratio auspicalis* (1652). Other members of staff remained unconvinced, however, and, in October 1652, Cromwell directed Owen to negotiate between warring factions among the colleges.[35]

Despite its unpopularity, the new regime offered tangible benefits to the university. Blair Worden has suggested that educational reform was pursued with reasonable success, noting that the new administration attempted to normalize the student body and university environment—reducing, for example, the number of soldiers—while it improved its material conditions.[36] For all of his radical religious convictions, Owen was a very traditional defender of the purpose of the university, having "no sympathy with those root-and-branch critics of the university who saw in its civil war collapse an opportunity to redesign it on first principles."[37] While he displayed no lack of ambition, he also evidenced administrative caution, and statutory reform was "low on Owen's agenda."[38] Royalists and prayer book conformists had much less cause for concern than they might have feared.

For the push for Puritan control was not overwhelmingly welcomed. Owen presided over a vigorously intellectual Puritan community, the members of which included "the dexterous trouble-maker of Christ Church," Henry Stubbe, and, among the students, John Locke, William Penn, and several members of Owen's extended family.[39] But Oxford was the "defeated capital of crown and church." Its "walls sheltered royalist tutors, royalist servants, and royalist conspirators. In the neighbouring countryside there were landowners closely tied both to the university and to the royal cause." This royalist community was resilient, well connected, and intelligent. The university owed much of its distinction to scholars with little sympathy for the new regime: when Owen praised the "outstanding mathematicians" of Oxford, for example, he was drawing attention to the contributions made by some of his more overtly royalist colleagues.[40] The Oxford royalists retreated in order to concentrate their power. Their numbers were centered on Trinity and Queen's—Owen's *alma mater*—and Worden's analysis of the membership of the colleges indicates that "the puritans and the royalists of Cromwellian Oxford often kept themselves apart."[41] But none of this happened by accident. The university administration "connived at the survival of Anglican devotion at Oxford"—including prayer book worship in a house in Merton Street, led by John Fell—perhaps because this devotion was often firmly Calvinistic.[42] But the broader royalist community was often restless. In 1651, a gathered church in the city, which included among the congregants members of the university, was invaded by a mob including students, which insulted men and molested women.[43] These attacks were made possible by the "disgarrisoning" of the city, which improved the university's environment even as it left those loyal to the new regime "vulnerable to threats and assaults."[44] Of course, these kinds of attacks were indicative of the desperation, rather than the strength, of the royalist community.[45] But these events also indicated how little many royalists appreciated their limited toleration within the university. Owen, who was tasked with controlling their behavior, settled into his new role, not by engaging in destructive and polemical faction, but by promoting a Calvinistic piety that transcended the political and cultural division of the university.

I

Owen outlined the qualities of that Calvinistic piety in the summer and autumn of 1651 when he preached, in St. Mary's, Oxford, the material that formed the basis for his later publication, *Of communion with God* (1657).[46] These sermons, directed at the undergraduate population of the city, combined the theological mode with the devotional, and they developed their themes from an allegorical reading of the Song of Solomon. This biblical text had long been a favorite of mystically inclined expositors, and, as Elizabeth Clarke has recently demonstrated, provided for a rich variety of seventeenth-century comment, and that on both sides of the civil war division.[47] While this use of the allegorical mode was conventional enough, the conclusions that Owen drew from his reading of the text were startling: Cook was wrong to argue that the "lectures contained little that would have been controversial in quieter times," and they may also nuance Clarke's claim that the mystical mode developed as Puritan piety was interiorized to reflect disappointment with the direction of the Cromwellian regime in the later 1650s.[48] Instead, this new spirituality was developed by Owen while in his post at Oxford, his most senior administrative role to date, and in terms that would have been familiar to his prayer book and radical auditors, and all this at the beginning of the decade. Clarke is right to point to the sermons' innovation: as some of their earliest readers observed, the sermons initiated a doctrinal revolution, suggesting that believers could commune in highly differentiated ways with the individual persons of the Trinity. Some auditors may have been appalled by Owen's new direction: George Vernon alleged that these sermons encouraged their listeners to become "covetous, concieted, whining and self-seeking hypocrites."[49] But others appealed for the sermons' publication. Owen hesitated to prepare them for the press, deciding instead to improve the material over the next few years, publishing the manuscript shortly before he ended his term as vice chancellor, when, as we will later see, his book provided for the evocative poetry of Faithful Teate's *Ter tria* (1658) and provoked a robustly polemical critique by William Sherlock.[50]

While Owen's earliest auditors would have found his interpretive strategies to be traditional, they would have discovered that his theological emphases were startlingly new. His return to Oxford coincided with a shift in his thinking that was, perhaps, a reflection of the broader range of literary influences upon which he could draw in his new environment: Trueman has noticed that Owen's thinking took on a decidedly Thomist dimension "from the early 1650s," a claim that is given extended and persuasive consideration in Cleveland's study of *Thomism in John Owen* (2013).[51] But Owen was also becoming increasingly experiential: *Of communion with God* was one of the most radical interventions in Trinitarian theology within mid-seventeenth-century Protestant orthodoxy. In one of the best recent readings of the book, Brian Kay has argued that the book "recovers 'three-ness' themes in a way that makes [Owen] perhaps the most explicitly trinitarian writer of his community."[52] Owen's argument that believers should "cultivate a distinct relationship with each person of the Godhead . . . stretched the limits of then current Augustinian assumptions about the unity of the Godhead" by "exploiting underdeveloped and latent allowances in the tradition itself."[53] Kay argues that Owen "breaks new ground" in two ways: first, by "emphasizing the Trinity as the foundational substructure upon which is constructed almost the entirety of Christian soteriology," and second, "by showing how the Christian's devotional response to God takes on a distinctively trinitarian shape."[54] For Owen, "communion is grounded upon union . . . union with Christ is not the end but the beginning of Christian life."[55] Kay explains that the "believer does not simply commune with God, nor even with God-who-is-triune. Owen contends that biblical communion involves a believer relating in distinct ways to each person of the Trinity," so that, "in some sense, the believer's relationship with the Father is different than his relationship to the Son or the Spirit."[56] And, Owen insisted, a realization of the truth of these claims would transform the devotional experience of believers, as he would later note: "they are no more cold in communion; they have not one thought that wanders off from God to eternity. They lose him no more, but always lie down in his bosom, without the least possibility of disturbance."[57] In this affectionate immediacy, Owen's sermons addressed the challenge of a new religious movement that had begun to make its presence felt in the city. Unlike some of his contemporaries, he did not deny that some spiritual benefit could be had in Quaker gatherings. He understood that "edification . . . is attainable in the silent meetings of the Quakers," but, he insisted, "convince any of them of the doctrine of the Trinity, and all the rest of their imaginations vanish into smoke."[58] For all his claims to represent a normative orthodoxy, however, his position differed from that of many of his Puritan peers.[59] While Presbyterians tended to argue that the language of the indwelling of the Spirit should be understood as metynomy, indicating close proximity, Owen wished to take the words at face value.[60] And in doing so, he believed that he had discovered a silver bullet for sanctity.

It is perhaps ironic that Owen could combine the occasional mysticism of the sermons on communion with God with the violent activism of the sermon he preached to celebrate Parliament's victory over the Scots at Worcester on 3 September 1651. News of this victory provoked a wave of riotous iconoclasm in Oxford, as enthusiasts for the republic destroyed symbols of monarchy and the old religious order, including, within Christ Church, stained glass windows, crosses, and ornaments, some of which were trampled upon by Henry Wilkinson, the senior, who must recently have returned from the rather more sedentary experience of the Westminster Assembly.[61] Owen was invited to preach for Parliament on its day of thanksgiving for Cromwell's second significant defeat of the Scottish Presbyterian army (24 October 1651). As Parliament requested that the sermon be published, he appears to have caught the mood of its members. He signed his preface in "my study, Ch[rist] Ch[urch], Oxon.," on 7 November, and published the text as *The advantage of the kingdom of Christ* (1651).[62] The sermon was printed in Oxford, and reprinted in London and Leith: following Lambert's circulation of the regicide sermon, Evan Tyler's edition of Owen's text was a signal that he was being consumed by a Scottish reading public. *The advantage of the kingdom of Christ* was supremely aware of its historical moment and of the providential significance of the victory it celebrated. Just as he had outpaced royalists and Presbyterians in Oxford, so Owen rejoiced that the parliamentary army had successfully avoided the twin dangers of a "tyrant full of revenge"—Charles and the royalist army—and a "discipline full of persecution"—a Scottish Presbyterian hegemony.[63] This rhetorical identification of the middle ground possessed by the Rump Parliament allowed Owen to mount a virulent attack on the Scottish Presbyterians, condemning their "deceivableness of unrighteousness and lies in hypocrisy."[64] Parliament's success was a lesson in the dangers of anticipating providences, he believed, reminding his readers of the enthusiasm with which many of the English Puritans had heralded Scottish involvement in their first civil war—before the Scots switched sides in the second.[65] Owen reflected on the political evolution of the Scottish government, remembering that at Worcester its army had been "shaken and broken with unparalleled destruction, in the maintenance of the interest and cause which at first they prosperously opposed."[66] And his celebration of the English victory was uncomplicated. He reminded MPs that

> of all the times which the Holy One of Israel hath caused to pass over the nations of the world, there hath not any from the days of old been so filled with eminent discoveries of his presence, power, and providence, in disposing of all affairs here below according to the counsel of

> his own will, as the season wherein he hath made you a spectacle unto men and angels, being the instrument in his hand to perform all his pleasure.[67]

The preface was telling, its series of biblical allusions indicating Owen's sense of the ecclesial and almost messianic character of the English state. Lifting expressions from Ephesians 1:11 ("counsel of his own will"), 1 Corinthians 4:9 ("a spectacle unto men and angels"), and Isaiah 53:10 ("the pleasure of the Lord shall prosper in his hand"), his sermon invoked the messianic quality of the political and military executive of the English revolution.

For *The advantage of the kingdom of Christ* defended a divinely sanctioned coup. Owen reminded his hearers that God had a record of changing the forms of government. In a survey of biblical history, he argued that the "seventy elders of the people" had been displaced by a "kingly government in the house of David," which in turn God had destroyed in the exile. He then argued that Hebrew monarchy was "a type of the spiritual dominion of their Messiah . . . a part of their pedagogy and bondage," which the Lord destroyed when his people began to "rest" in its "outward beauty, lustre, and glory . . . to the neglect of the spiritual kingdom of God represented thereby."[68] God, in other words, was also a regicide. And the implication of the sermon was that this divinely sanctioned revolution should be extended internationally as the kingdom of God neared its eschatological realization. The nations were to be "civilly moved, that they may be spiritually established," Owen believed: "Most nations in their civil constitution lie out of order for the bringing in of the interest of Christ;—they must be shaken up and new disposed of, that all obstacles may be taken away."[69] He built upon his earlier arguments about biblical apocalyptic language to advance a preterist reading of Matthew 24, which he explained with reference to the fall of Jerusalem in A.D. 70, and of Revelation 6, which he associated with the fall of Rome. But he argued that the prophecies of Revelation 19–22 were being fulfilled in England's troubles.[70] "I speak not with respect to any engagements of war with foreign nations;—what have I to do with things that are above me?"[71] Owen had already made his position clear. His attempt at nuance could not conceal the fact that he was calling for a global revolution—which, he insisted, had been prophesied in Scripture, as "God in his appointed time will bring forth the kingdom of the Lord Christ unto more glory and power than in former days." That glory and power would be manifest in six things that were "clearly promised," he believed: "fullness of peace unto the gospel and the professors thereof," "purity and beauty of ordinances and gospel worship," "multitudes of converts, many persons, yea, nations," "the full casting out and rejecting of all will-worship," "professed subjection of the nations throughout the whole world unto the Lord Christ," and a "most glorious and dreadful breaking of all that rise in opposition to him."[72] Owen's final exhortation encouraged the members of Parliament to

> believe the promises . . . and you will believe the beast unto destruction, antichrist into the pit, and Magog to ruin. Believe that the enemies of Christ shall be made his footstool, that the nations shall be his inheritance, that he shall reign gloriously in beauty, that he shall smite in pieces the heads over divers nations; – live in the faith of these things, and as it will give you the sweetness of them before they come, so it will hasten their coming beyond the endeavours of thousands, yea, millions of armed men.[73]

Nevertheless, he realized, such war would have its hazards. He may well have been reflecting upon news of the death of his brother, Philemon, in the Irish service. For Philemon's experience of this godly war had not been glorious. In August 1649, the *Commons Journal* had noted that his pay was over £529 in arrears.[74] With his death, sometime before the autumn of 1651, his widow Elizabeth was compelled to petition the Council of State for relief.[75] Philemon had died in England's war to make the "enemies of Christ . . . his footstool," and Owen, almost certainly, had not been able to attend his funeral, an unremarked casuality in the war for the kingdom of Christ.

But Owen was invited to attend, and officiate at, the funeral of another victim of the Irish wars, whose death may have occurred around the same time. This official duty, preaching at the funeral of Cromwell's son-in-law, Henry Ireton, whom Owen may have known since the seige of Colchester, was perhaps his most significant civic responsibility to date. Like Philemon Owen, Ireton had been a victim of the Irish campaign, dying outside Limerick on 26 November 1651. His body had been transferred to London for the funeral, which was held on 6 February 1652 in Henry VII's chapel in Westminster Abbey, and was attended by members of Parliament and the Council of State.[76] It was not widely reported in the newsbooks. Descriptions of the event in *The faithful scout*, for example, made no mention of Owen's contribution.[77] But the event took place amidst extraordinary ceremonies. The funeral functioned to idealize the state, with the mace made for use in Ireland in March 1651 being carried at the head of the cortege, and the "honour codes of the regime and its members" representing "another element in the self-consciously dignified political culture of the English Commonwealth."[78] In these set-piece events, the Cromwellian leadership was developing a "mixture of imagery and spectacle" that would conceal the revolution beneath "layers of respectability which, with time, began to take on the patina of legitimacy."[79] While a distinct form of republican aesthetics did develop during the period, emphasizing utility and modesty, the Cromwellian state also sought to make itself beautiful.[80] Such commemorative events provided the opportunity for the spectacle that was an "expected part of any state's self-legitimisation."[81] But the "creation of Commonwealth pomp ... contributed to the tensions of Commonwealth politics."[82] For aesthetics had been weaponized: some Puritans found the ceremony offensive.[83] Colonel John Hutchinson, a kinsman of the deceased, was not invited to be a pallbearer at Ireton's funeral, and his protest was to attend the event in exaggeratedly bright clothing.[84] The Ireton funeral illustrated some of the "visual priorities" of the regime, as well as those of its critics.[85] It participated in the new state's semiotics of power, and was an important component of its self-fashioning. And preaching was central to this construction of godly memory. Owen does not appear to have been consulted as Parliament drew up new ceremonies and liturgies for this and other major state events.[86] He may have been uncomfortable with certain aspects of the occasion: his sermon's telling silences reflect an emerging republican aesthetic, which required that glory should not be associated too closely with any individual.[87] For the first time, perhaps, he was preaching at an occasion of which he could not entirely approve. It was the first sign of his critical distance from the new regime.

Despite his ambivalence, Owen's sermon had the political task of rescuing the reputation of a member of the Cromwell family from vituperative criticism.[88] His discourse was part of a broader trend of commemoration, as represented in Hugh Peters's *Æternitati sacrum: Terrenum quod habuit, sub hoc pulvere deposuit Henricus Iretonus* (1652), and the anonymous broadsheet, *An elegy (sacred) to the immortal memory of that most renowned, religious, prudent, and victorious commander, Henry Ireton late lord deputy of Ireland* (1652), which combined a rather basic woodcut of Ireton's body lying in state with its claim that "none but IRETON could sad IRELAND save" and "nought but IRELAND could our IRETON kill." Mediating these extremes of high and low culture was Payne Fisher's *Veni, vidi, vici: The triumph of the most excellent & illustrious, Oliver Cromwell ... whereunto is added an elegy upon the death of the late Lord Deputy of Ireland, the much lamented, Henry Ireton* (1652), which presented itself as a translation into English of a Latin original, meditating on the limitations of art and rhetoric to do justice to the achievements of its subject. Owen's sermon, which recuperated the reputation of its subject, developed a reading of Ireton's virtues that confirmed republican modes of heroic description and was published as *The labouring saints's dismission to rest* (1652).

Owen used the printed text of the sermon to dissociate himself from the ceremonialism he had witnessed. Explaining that his duty was to "preach the word, not to carry on a part of a funeral ceremony," he insisted that his "business" was not to eulogize, but to identify those aspects of Ireton's character that would best illustrate the text from which he was preaching.[89] In Owen's discourse, Ireton was a "rare example of righteousness, faith, holiness, zeal, courage, self-denial, love to his country, wisdom, and industry."[90] He praised his "ability of mind, and dexterous industry for the management of human affairs," and reflected upon the "great neglect of self and all self-concernments which dwelt upon him in all his tremendous undertakings."[91] He believed that this man of action had been fulfilling Scriptural prophecies, and reminded his listeners of predictions made in Daniel concerning the "providential alterations, disposing and transposing of states, nations, kingdoms, and dominions," arguing, in pious hyperbole, that what Daniel "had in speculation" was Ireton's to "follow in action."[92] Nevertheless, Ireton's useful life had been suddenly cut short, as he received "his dismission about the age of forty years."[93] And, perhaps reflecting on his recently deceased brother, Owen spoke movingly of the aftermath of a soldier's life, when "tyrants pretend no more title to their kingdom; rebels lie not in wait for their blood; they are no more awakened by the sound of the trumpet, nor the noise of the instruments of death:—they fear not for their relations, they weep not for their friends; the Lamb is their temple, and God is all in all unto them."[94] Philemon was an uncelebrated casualty, but Ireton had become a hero of the long war for the advantage of the kingdom of Christ.

Then, his public responsibilities fulfilled, Owen returned to Coggeshall for a final duty in his congregation. On 18 March 1652, in local and homely circumstances entirely constrasting with those of the state funeral, he oversaw the induction of a new minister. John Sams had gained experience as Owen's assistant in Coggeshall for several years before his responsibilities in the parish were approved by the clerical appointments committee of the Westminster Assembly in February 1652.[95] The service for Sams's installation as "teaching elder" followed the spare and improvisory requirements of the Independent form. Josselin, who attended the service, recorded rather unhappily that Owen "preacht" as Sams was

> sett a part that day with fasting and prayer to be a teaching elder to the church at Coxall. he made a confession of faith, that was no open consent of the church, nor no acceptance of it with any words, nor promise to doe any thing. The messengers viz pastors of 3 churches gave their

> approbation of the act and were witnesses of the churches act one gave an exhortation. 2 prayed for a blessing.[96]

Josselin gave no indication that he had taken part in the service, for his participation would have been entirely inconsistent with his belief that ordinations should be conducted more formally, with public promises, and by presbyteries, following the guidance of the Westminster Assembly.[97] But his attendance at the installation illustrated that neighborly clerical collegiality continued despite ecclesiological differences. Josselin dined again with Owen "at my Lady Honywoods" on 19 March 1652.[98] In Coggeshall, as in Oxford, Owen found it easier to defend his principles in books and public preaching than in table fellowship with the godly.

But Owen was still thinking about Ireton's death and its wider public significance. He signed the preface to the printed version of *The labouring saints's dismission to rest* on 2 April 1652 in Oxford, begging a "candid interpretation unto any thing that may appear not so well digested" in its text: "that which is printed is but the notes which I first took, not having had leisure since to give them a serious perusal."[99] Unusually, he did not revise his manuscript for the press—an incident that may provide privileged access to his habits of sermon preparation, at least in terms of major public events.[100] For Owen was struggling to manage his time. Having traveled between London, Coggeshall, and Oxford, he had entered immediately into another national discussion—about the boundaries of public orthodoxy.

II

On the same day that Owen signed the preface to Ireton's funeral sermon, MPs were thrown into a theological panic as they debated a "Collection of the principal blasphemous Errors" in a recently published anti-Trinitarian book.[101] The debate centered upon *Catechesis ecclesiarum quae in regno Poloniae & magno ducatu Lithuaniae*, a theological statement of late sixteenth-century origin, which had been republished in London in early 1652 (and which was to appear in English translation from a Dutch publisher in June as *The Racovian catechisme*). In late January 1652, John Milton, the state censor, had approved for publication this statement of Socinian convictions.[102] Milton's actions had been entirely legal under the terms of the licensing act, but precipitated a storm of complaint when the catechism was drawn to the attention of MPs on 10 February. With some colleagues, Owen, who had remained in London after Ireton's funeral, presented the catechism to Parliament, along with a warrant, most likely the warrant which two weeks earlier had been issued for the catechism by the Council of State, and a petition, which requested that a committee should be formed for "such proposals as shall be offered for the better propagation of the Gospel," entitled *The humble proposals of Mr. Owen, Mr. Goodwin, Mr. Nye, Mr. Sympson, and other ministers.*[103] It was unlikely to have been a coincidence that their actions coincided with the release, under the terms of the Act of Oblivion, of John Biddle, a notorious anti-Trinitarian agitator, who had been imprisoned since 1646 on the charge of heresy. His release, together with the local publication of the Racovian catechism, seemed to represent an unparalleled attack on traditional Christian orthodoxies. But it also represented a timely opportunity for the religious ideologues of the new regime, who seized the moment to advance the cause of further reformation. Complaining, erroneously, that the Racovian catechism had been "repeatedly printed among us," Owen and his colleagues took full advantage of the moral panic over Socinianism—a panic they had helped foment—to propose a new form of national religious settlement that would replace that of the Westminster Assembly, which had never gained full legal standing, and whose deliberations, as the improvisory character of the ordination of John Sams illustrates, they were increasingly unwilling to accept.[104]

Over the next few months, Owen took advantage of the moral panic by advancing two parallel strategies, which served to make explicit the critique of state policy that had been implicit in the Ireton funeral sermon. On the one hand, he and his colleagues continued to pursue those responsible for the publication of the Racovian catechism: on 21 February, for example, they had Milton appear before a committee of inquiry to explain his role in the event, who claimed, as part of his defense, the principles he had outlined in *Areopagitica* (1644).[105] On 2 April 1652, the committee that had been investigating the catechism, on which Owen had worked alongside Philip Nye, Sydrach Sympson, William Strong, John Dury, William Bridge, William Greenhill, Adoniram Byfield, George Griffiths, and Thomas Harrison, reported its "principal blasphemous Errors" to Parliament. The committee focused on its arguments against the doctrine of the Trinity, which comprised three-quarters of the tract, and "many other gross Errors, concerning Predestination, the Fall of Man, *Christ* adding to the Commandments, Free-will, the Priesthood and Sacrifice of *Christ*, Faith, Justification, Baptism, and the Lord's Supper."[106] The committee's spokesman informed Parliament that it had gathered written examinations of the printer, William Dugard, and others, including Milton, and it presented such evidence as "a Note under the Hand of Mr. *John Milton*, of the 10th of *August* 1650."[107] The result of this inquiry was that MPs voted in April 1652 to burn the *Catechesis ecclesiorum*. Those who favored the broad parameters of the Licensing Act and the Blasphemy Act (1650) were furious. On 29 April, Marchamont Nedham published an editorial in *Mercurius Politicus*, denouncing Owen's plans. In being licensed by Milton, the newsbook may also have been reflecting his anger and frustration: "I fear I have been too large," Nedham explained, "but . . . you have not yet half my mind," in an assault on the plans that extended through the summer.[108] In May, and in the immediate aftermath of the loss of his wife Mary, Milton complained about his treatment by Owen in his sonnet to Cromwell: "Help us to save free Conscience from the paw | Of hireling wolves whose Gospel is their maw."[109] His appeal to Cromwell may have fallen on deaf ears, but it formed part of a chorus of opposition to the new proposals for national orthodoxy, which emanated from a circle of authors associated with the publisher Giles Calvert—a group that Roger Williams described as "champions for the liberty of the soul."[110] The actions of MPs only served to draw attention to the forbidden text: in June 1652, an edition of the Racovian catechism, printed by a Dutch publisher, appeared in an English translation. This suited perfectly the ambitions of those who wished to take advantage of the public outcry.

That panic was a gift to Owen and his committee, for it drew attention to the ambiguity of the boundaries of orthodoxy permitted by the state. For England, perhaps unexpectedly, had no national confession of faith. The only religious statement that had acquired legal standing had been contained in *An ordinance of the Lords and Commons . . . concerning suspention from the sacrament of the Lord's Supper* (1645). The Westminster Confession of Faith (1647) had only ever been partially adopted by Parliament, and its extremely stringent Blasphemy Act (1648) had never been put into effect. But its more lenient replacement, the Blasphemy Act (1650), was found to be insufficient in the face of the Socinian challenge. Shortly after the panic began, therefore, Owen and his clerical colleagues set out to establish a new statement of national orthodoxy, one from which no deviation would be permitted. It was the beginning of a much longer campaign, which resulted in increasingly narrow definitions of permitted opinion. It would consume much of Owen's time and political capital through the rest of the 1650s, as his influence within the regime steadily decreased. Of course, that trend was not obvious in the short term. As a consequence of the petition, he was appointed advisor to the Rump Parliament's Committee for the Propagation of the Gospel, along with some other clergy, and initiated discussions of the new boundaries of orthodoxy by drawing up a list of sixteen one-sentence "fundamentals," each of them supported by nothing more than a catena of biblical citations, which were published in March as *Proposals for the furtherance and propagation of the gospel . . . As also, some principles of Christian religion, without the beliefe of which*

... *salvation is not to be obtained* (1652). These "principles" "defined orthodoxy in Trinitarian and evangelical Protestant terms," from which Socinians and Roman Catholics were excluded.[111] Perhaps surprisingly, given their complaints about the doctrinal content of the Racovian catechism, the committee did not wish to exclude Arminians or Baptists from ministry in the new religious settlement. This recognition that Independents could find ways of working alongside Baptists was to be another significant milestone in Owen's religious and administrative career. Nevertheless, the *Humble proposals* and the *Principles of Christian religion* generated widespread opposition, with notable interventions made by John Milton, Roger Williams, and Sir Henry Vane, and the committee's recommendations were not approved by Parliament.[112] Just as Owen had begun to criticize the aesthetic values of the regime, so the regime was indicating its lack of support for his vision of godly reformation.

All of this committee work was taking up time. Owen was often absent from Christ Church for long periods—from late July until late September 1652, for example, from mid-December 1652 until early February 1653, and from late July until early October 1653.[113] He was being burdened with additional responsibilities. Sometime in 1652, reflecting the fact that a great deal of the theological anxiety of the age was being driven by concerns about the veracity of available copies of Scripture, Owen was appointed to a committee whose task it was to oversee any new publication of Bibles and New Testaments. This committee, on which Owen was to serve alongside the English Baptist Henry Jessey and the Scottish Presbyterian turned Independent John Row, was to be chaired by Thomas Goodwin, Anthony Tuckney, and Joseph Caryl. Its organizational structure paralleled the broad parameters of the discussions about national orthodoxy as Parliament was pushing its divines into broader cooperative ventures—and perhaps to distract some of them from riding their hobbyhorses. Significantly, Owen was not asked to lead this flagship religious project. In the summer of 1652, drawing up statements of national orthdoxy that would never be adopted by Parliament, he may have been moving faster than the political leaders he wished to influence—and in a different direction.[114]

III

Whatever the frustrations involved in these national religious reforms, Owen's institutional ascent continued within Oxford. His existing workload was centered on administration in Christ Church, and regular preaching at St. Mary's. But local duties also began to accumulate. On 1 April 1652, he was appointed to the board of Visitors.[115] This committee had been established in 1647 to oversee the reformation of the university according to the preferences of the then-dominant Presbyterian party. The meeting that admitted him as a member was almost the last for this relic of the old political order. The Independents, who now commanded the apparatus of government, wished to purge the university of their old antagonists. Owen was to be central to the realization of this strategy. After a meeting of the Visitors on 13 April, Owen, Thomas Goodwin, and other leading Oxford Independents petitioned for a new board, a request that Parliament approved in early June, appointing ten members, almost all of whom were Independents.[116]

It is not clear how Owen spent the summer of 1652. His absence from Oxford lasted from late July until late September, and he may have occupied himself in breaks from committee work by preparing *The primer: or, An easie way to teach children the true reading of English, with a necessary catechisme, to instruct youth in the grounds of Christian religion, Also choice places of Scripture.*[117] This pamphlet has not been considered by Owen scholars, most likely because of its absence from the Goold edition, but it is an important text. It included basic material for learning letters. It offered Owen's third attempt at writing a catechism—this one far simpler than either of those he had prepared for his first parishioners. It fulfilled his long-standing promise to complete an exposition of the Ten Commandments and the Lord's Prayer. It showed that he could handle Scripture in as straightforward a manner as the most confirmed biblicist. And, perhaps most significant of all, as Bernard Capp has noted, in its failure to include lists of English monarchs, a feature typical of the genre, *The primer* was advancing a distinctly republican pedagogy.[118]

Nevertheless, after three months of committee work in the capital, Owen returned home to his wife and daughters, both still under the age of three, and to be appointed as vice chancellor of the university on 26 September 1652.[119] In an oration he delivered on the day of his appointment, and in a rare and revealing moment of autobiography, he explained that he had been pressed into the duty against his will, accepting the role because of the "tears and sobs of our ailing *alma mater.*"[120] He allowed that he was not "self-deluded . . . I live not so far from home, nor am I such a stranger to myself" to believe that he was somehow worthy of his new position.[121] In fact, he was not far from home at all—Stadhampton was only a few miles from his new office. "I bring no prodigies," he continued; "from the obscurity of a rural situation, from the din of arms, from journeyings for the sake of the Gospel into the most distant parts of the island and also over the sea, from the bustle of the court I have retreated; unskilful in the government of a University I am come here."[122] Owen, who was always economical with autobiographical material, would reuse this section of writing in his *Diatriba de justitia divina* (1653).[123]

His initial deployment of the familiar modesty topos gave way to observations about the difficulties of academic administration in a period in which learning itself had come under attack by religious ideologues, and in which "a very large section of the students are now—alas!—wandering beyond all bounds of modesty and piety."[124] But he insisted that the Oxford he intended to remodel would have no place for "lazy, drunken, playboys, jesters, mountebanks, despisers of their superiors, law-breakers, night-birds, notorious corrupters of youth, enemies of the good, neglecters of religion or other cancerous sores of such a University."[125] For Owen was in a hurry: "Europe stands agape at the acts of Parliament, the laurels of our soldiers and the enhanced glory, both civil and military, which the parliamentarians and commanding generals to whose care these affairs were entrusted have achieved," and Oxford was to become the training school for leaders of the Protestant republic.[126]

Owen was given further opportunities to realize this ambition. On 16 October, Cromwell delegated to him the chancellor's power to settle disputes, and appointed him to another committee to consider the routine administrative tasks that legally fell to the chancellor. He was now "dean, lecturer, Visitor, vice-chancellor, and two-fold commissioner to act for the chancellor."[127] He was never again to accumulate such administrative power. But his responsibility to lead the university and to manage fundamental change in the face of unrelenting internal and external pressure drove him back to the public arena.

IV

By 13 October 1652, Owen was again in London, preaching to Parliament, a sermon he later published as *Concerning the kingdom of Christ, and the power of the civil magistrate about the things of the worship of God.* The occasion was a day of solemn humiliation during the first naval war with the Dutch, and Owen used the occasion to "bolster support" for his *Humble proposals.*[128] Leveraging providence, arguing that the result of the war would depend upon Parliament's response to the work of his committees, he provided a historical context for the conflicts of the period, and encouraged MPs to remember the

> beginning of the contests in this nation, when God had caused your spirits to resolve that the liberties, privileges, and rights of this nation, wherewith you were intrusted, should not, by his assistance, be wrested out of your hands by violence, oppression, and injustice; this he also put upon your hearts, to vindicate and assert the gospel of Jesus Christ, his ways, and his ordinances, against all opposition, though you were but inquiring the way to Zion, with your faces thitherward. God secretly

> entwining the interest of Christ with yours, wrapped up with you the whole generation of them that seek his face, and prospered your affairs on that account.[129]

But now the enemies of the revolution had expanded to include "Scotland and Holland," two Protestant states, the latter also a republic.[130] "Strange! that Ephraim should join with Syria to vex Judah their brother,—that the Netherlands, whose being is founded merely upon the interest you have undertaken, should join with the great antichristian interest, which cannot possibly be set up again without their inevitable ruin."[131] The Dutch war represented the tragedy of fratricide.

Owen's reading of current affairs was made possible by his biblical theory of history.[132] Returning to some of the texts he had considered at Ireton's funeral, he described Daniel, from whose prophecy he was preaching, as "a man under sad apprehensions of the issues and events of things and the dispensations of God (as many are at this day)."[133] Daniel had foreseen "the four great empires of the world, which had, and were to have, dominion in and over the places of the church's greatest concernments, and were all to receive their period and destruction by the Lord Christ and his revenging hand."[134] The "fourth beast, without name or special form, is the Roman empire," he continued, explaining that his auditors were living during the period in which the Roman empire was finally being destroyed, the period in which it would be replaced by the fifth monarchy—the kingdom of Jesus Christ.[135]

Owen's preaching was infused by confidence about the global expansion of Christianity in the latter days of history, as well as the importance of the religious settlement for which he was pressing. He insisted that the "civil powers of the world, after fearful shakings and desolations, shall be disposed of into a useful subserviency to the interest, power, and kingdom of Jesus Christ."[136] Echoing the conclusions of his earlier sermons to Parliament, he argued that "God will shake the heavens and the earth of the nations round about, until all the Babylonish rubbish, all their original engagements to the man of sin, be taken away."[137] These nations would be "judged and sentenced by the poor creatures whom in this world they continually pursue with all manner of enmity."[138] But the fifth monarchy that the godly would establish would not be like that projected by the radical theocrats. Owen distinguished his position from that of the Fifth Monarchy Men, who, by republishing material associated with the Scottish invasion, were now attempting to appropriate his reputation.[139] Their millennial theories were bankrupt. He reported the "endless and irreconcilable contests" of those who debated

> whether over and beyond all these the Lord Christ shall not bear an outward, visible, glorious rule, setting up a kingdom like those of the world, to be ruled by strength and power; and if so, when or how it shall be brought in,—into whose hands the administration of it shall be committed, and upon what account,—whether he will personally walk therein or no,—whether it shall be clearly distinct from the rule he now bears in the world, or only differenced by more glorious degrees and manifestations of his power. . . . This we find, by woful experience, that all who, from the spirituality of the rule of Christ, and delight therein, have degenerated into carnal apprehensions of the beauty and glory of it, have, for the most part, been given up to carnal actings, suited to such apprehensions.[140]

Owen's concern that belief in an earthly millennium attended and motivated attempts at violent political intervention had some justification. But he remained convinced that the global conquest of Christianity would be signaled by the latter-day conversion of the Jews. This was a theological motif that had gained currency among English Puritans through its inclusions in the annotations on Romans in early editions of the Geneva Bible. It was a theme on which Owen had previously been reticent, preferring to talk about the glorious future of English Protestants. But, he now insisted, "what kingdom soever the Lord Christ will advance in the world, and exercise amongst his holy ones, the beginning of it must be with the Jews."[141] And, he suggested, their conversion would be attended by their restoration to the Promised Land: in an uncharacteristic statement, echoing with Old Testament allusions, he argued that "when the seed of Abraham, being multiplied like the stars of heaven and the sands of the sea-shore, shall possess the gates of their enemies, and shall have peace in their borders,—we may lift up our heads towards the fulness of our redemption."[142] Until then, he continued, it would be an ungrounded assumption to

> dream of setting up an outward, glorious, visible kingdom of Christ, which he must bear rule in, and over the world, be it in Germany or in England. . . . The Jews not called. Antichrist not destroyed, the nations of the world generally wrapped up in idolatry and false worship, little dreaming of their deliverance,—will the Lord Christ leave the world in this state, and set up his kingdom here on a molehill?[143]

Owen's prediction of the global conquest of Protestant Christianity no longer implied a military crusade: "There is nothing more opposite to the spirit of the gospel, than to suppose that Jesus Christ will take to himself a kingdom by the carnal sword and bow of the sons of men. . . . It is by the pouring out of his Spirit in a covenant of mercy."[144] Perhaps reflecting an increasing distrust of the state and his machinery, he argued that there could be no more holy wars. He was moving back from his earlier ebullience.

Nevertheless, Owen could not disguise the fact that his ideas had immediate political consequences. His sermon was exhorting MPs to fulfill the duty that God had pressed upon them, to "act clearly for the good, welfare, and prosperity of the church."[145] Reminding MPs of his attempts to construct a national orthodoxy, he insisted that "error and falsehood have no right or title, either from God or man, unto any privilege, protection, advantage, liberty, or any good thing you are intrusted withal. To dispose that unto a lie, which is the right of and due to truth, is to deal treacherously with Him by whom you are employed."[146] For Owen was also moving away from his earlier and less qualified defense of toleration. As on so many other occasions, Owen used the opportunity of a national political event to drive home his own agenda—this time in support of his program for national orthodoxy—as he attempted to fashion the public sphere in his own image.

V

It is not clear whether Owen was successfully persuading MPs, for the dissolution of the Rump meant that these proposals were set aside. He continued to make his case. At the end of March 1653, and in circumstances of ill health, he signed the preface to his latest book, a work of polemical theology engaging with the issues raised by the moral panic about Socinianism.[147] A number of other English writers had already attacked this controversial new religious movement, including Nicholas Estwick, Edmund Porter, Matthew Poole, Matthew Wren, and Francis Cheynell. But Parliament instructed Owen to prepare a definitive refutation of Socinian ideas. It was another responsibility to add to his long list of duties, and he used *Diatriba de justitia divina* (1653) to reflect upon his workload. "About two years ago," he remembered, "the parliament of the commonwealth promoted me, while diligently employed . . . in preaching the gospel . . . to a chair in the very celebrated university of Oxford."[148] He believed himself to be "unequal to the task," being a person "not far advanced in years, who had for several years been very full of employment, and accustomed only to the popular mode of speaking; who . . . had for some time taken leave of all scholastic studies; whose genius is by no means quick, and who had even forgot, in some measure, the portion of polite learning that he might have formerly acquired."[149] He admitted that he was "a man not wise in the estimation of others,—in his own, very foolish; first called from rural retirement and the noise of arms to this university, and very lately again returned to it from excursions in the cause of the gospel, not only to the extremities of this island, but to coasts beyond the seas," as he rather dramatically described his role in Ireland and Scotland. "Whether any thing exalted or refined can be expected from such a person is easy for any one to determine."[150] He expected opposition from "bantering, saucy, dull-witted, self-sufficient despisers of others," for "no man can either think or speak of me and my works with so much disregard and contempt as I myself . . . both think and speak."[151] And so Owen described *Diatriba de justitia divina* as "a little by-work" emerging from "this most celebrated university."[152] His modesty was not entirely persuasive. He explained that, having "such abundance of various and laborious employment of another kind," he had completed the work in "a few days," in "a few leisure hours stolen from other engagements."[153] The modesty topos was misleading. It had been four months since Owen had turned his attention to the topic of Socinianism in a special lecture in the university.[154] The lecture had gone very well, Owen conceded: "the warmest opposers of what we then maintained were obliged to acknowledge that our arguments are quite decisive," and the "scruples of several" were "removed by a more full consideration of our opinion." Growing in confidence, he was encouraged to "take a deeper view of the subject . . . for the future benefit of mankind."[155] The publication of the *Diatriba de justitia divina* was not, therefore, one of his humbler moments.

But Owen was right—the *Diatriba de justitia divina* was one of his most impressive literary works to date.[156] Advancing upon his earlier tendency to lump together all manner of antagonists, Owen picked his battles, confuting the claims of "Socinians, particularly the authors of the Racovian Catechism, John Crellius, and F. Socinus himself," while moving beyond the attack on false doctrine to expose theological weaknesses among the ranks of the Reformed. For Owen's targets included some "pious, worthy, and very learned divines" who were otherwise "most strictly orthodox," and who continued to argue that God could have forgiven sin without the "satisfaction of Christ."[157] In a rare moment of confessional autobiography, he admitted that he had once held this view himself, but did not explain where he found the idea, or what had influenced him to abandon it.[158] Instead, as the title page made clear, he took aim at such reputable Reformed theologians as Vossius, William Twisse, and Samuel Rutherford. The latter citations were ironic. Owen would supply a commendatory preface to Twisse's *The riches of God's love,* which was published in the same year. Similarly, he had praised Rutherford in his earlier writing, defending at considerable length Rutherford's claim that God could have forgiven sinners by a sheer act of will and without requiring the death of his

Son.[159] But Rutherford had come to epitomize the theocratic Presbyterianism from which Owen had so purposefully turned away. Having previously lauded "the learned Rutherford," he now introduced him to his readers as "a Scotch divine" whose literary style was "very puzzling and harsh," "a mere novice" whose ideas were "falsity and folly."[160] He recognized that the "mighty names of Augustine, Calvin, Musculus, Twisse, and Vossius" opposed the position he now defended, but was glad to be able to cite "Paræus, Piscator, Molinæus, Lubertus, Rivetus, Cameron, Maccovius, Junius, the professors at Saumur, and others" in its defense.[161] The sharp tenor of Owen's rhetoric may reflect anxiety that his allies in this debate were markedly less impressive—and, measured against the Westminster Confession, less orthodox—than those whose opinions he dismissed.

The *Diatriba de justitia divina* began with a dense series of classical citations, perhaps a self-conscious strategy designed to indicate its author's qualifications for his role in the university.[162] Owen's argument moved quickly from a survey of the relevant classical texts to straightforward biblical exposition, dismissing along the way the "triflers" and "bunglers" better known to historians as the medieval schoolmen.[163] Owen was well read in the material he was opposing, and represented the divisions among Socinians as well as their shared assumptions, listing the Racovian catechism among his principal targets.[164] The current crisis was an effect of the recent proliferation of print, he worried: "other theological writings, catechetical, dogmatical, exegetical, casuisitical, and polemical," had so increased that the "world can hardly contain the books that have been written."[165] Despite his concerns about the expansion of print culture, Owen used the dedication to outline his future literary projects, noting that there existed a gap in this scholarly literature on the work of the Holy Spirit, and "almost a total silence" in literature on the believer's communion with God.[166] It was a telling signal of his growing sense of originality, as well as his intention to make a genuine contribution to theological knowledge—for while Owen expected the *Diatriba de justitia divina* to find a ready audience, it was his work on the Holy Spirit and communion with God that would be most widely celebrated in the literary cultures of Puritanism and evangelicalism. Yet the *Diatriba de justitia divina* also contained moments of rhetorical sublimity:

> But if any one, though endowed with the tongues of angels and of men, should attempt to describe this mystery of divine wisdom, whereby it is evident that God exalts his own name, and not only recovers his former honour, but even raises it, manifests his justice, preserves inviolable his right and dominion in pardoning sin, wherewith he is highly pleased

> and incredibly delighted . . . he must feel his language not only deficient, but the eye of the mind, overpowered with light, will fill him with awe and astonishment. That that which is the greatest, yea, the only disgrace and affront to God, should turn out to his highest honour and glory; that that which could not be permitted to triumph without the greatest injury to the justice, right, holiness, and truth of God, should find grace and pardon, to the eternal and glorious display of justice, right, holiness, and truth,—was a work that required infinite wisdom, an arduous task, and every way worthy of God.[167]

The work of salvation was worthy of God, as the task of describing it was worthy of the vice chancellor, whether in the sixteen sentences of his proposed confession of faith, or in the theological attrition of the massive *Diatriba de justitia divina*.

VI

The sense of occasion that shone through the *Diatriba* reflected the growing excitement of the godly in the summer of 1653. In April, the Rump Parliament had been dissolved. Cromwell had grown increasingly frustrated by its inability to produce a constitution, and was extremely worried by its refusal to conclude its work. He called in a troop of soldiers, led by Thomas Harrison, and cleared the House of Commons. Political power was handed to the Independent churches. They were invited to nominate the members of the new Parliament—a process by which this revolutionary body gained its name. The Nominated Assembly was convened in a context of widespread millennial enthusiasm.[168] Modeled after the Jewish Sanhedrin, many of its members hoped that its business would be to prepare the way of the Lord.

The work of reformation continued apace. In July 1653, the new Visitors, including Owen and Goodwin, assessed the quality and integrity of preaching within the university.[169] Shortly afterward, Owen left Oxford to spend the summer in the capital.[170] On 23 August, he preached to the Barebones Parliament, a sermon the text of which has not survived.[171] It is impossible to know whether he addressed the pressure for the abolition of universities, which the more radical MPs advocated as part of their campaign against ungodly institutions. This invitation was a telling sign of his continuing influence: he had preached for the Long Parliament in 1646, the Rump Parliament in 1649, and was now addressing its successor. He was also being expected to lead in resolving conflicts among the godly. *Several proceedings of state affaires* reported at the end of October that Cromwell had called a meeting of leading ministers, including such Independents as Owen, such Presbyterians as Stephen Marshall, and such Baptists as Henry Jessey, to insist that the millenarian preachers associated with Blackfriars should cease their vitriolic criticism of the government and its religious leaders.[172] But Owen's involvement in university administration kept his feet firmly on the ground, and his tenure as vice chancellor was renewed by Cromwell in October 1653.[173] Some of the responsibilities of this position must have been enjoyable, and easy to reconcile with his projects for national reformation. It was during this period that he began to write prefatory material for books that he wanted to support, including a book on divine love by the late William Twisse and William Eyre's book on justification (both published in 1653). Other activities would have been more taxing. In August, the Parliamentary Commissioners in Ireland again wrote to Owen, together with two other ministers, asking for his assistance in recruiting suitable preachers of the gospel.[174] On 10 November, Owen signed a certificate, along with other godly ministers, testifying to the "orthodoxy and good conversation" of Nehemiah Beaton.[175] And on 29 November, Owen required that college heads should report on the quality of the preaching for which their staffs were responsible.[176] These duties were typical of his continuing work to promote godly reformation within the institution. But other of his responsibilities would have been discouraging. In August, Owen was charged with protecting two students, who, it was claimed, had raped the daughter of a poor family.[177] In September, he had to pursue Richard Herbert, second baron Herbert of Cherbury, for unpaid student fees.[178] And in November, he was instructed by the Visitors to oversee the expulsion of John Busbye, a student of Christ Church who had made a blasphemous speech at the funeral of a colleague from Balliol College.[179] But Owen had his reward. On 23 December 1653, he was awarded with a DD in absentia.[180]

The contingencies of university administration paralleled those of the wider political environment. Despite the millennial expectations embedded in its calling, the Barebones Parliament was failing, and the godly were growing in disappointment. Ironically, it was broken by the proposals of the Committee for the Propagation of the Gospel. MPs narrowly defeated the committee's proposal for a national religious settlement on 10 December. Those who had supported Owen's vision of reform ran out of patience. Two days later, they called the assembly to order before most of the radicals had arrived, and voted for its dissolution.[181] Within months, its members had fallen victim to faction, as its religious enthusiasts could brook no contradiction. Attendance in the House dropped as their breach with the moderates became critical. The moderates panicked, and on 8 December 1653 they walked out of the House to present a petition to Cromwell that dissolved the Nominated Assembly. The remaining members were cleared out by soldiers. Once again, the millennium had been postponed, and the Council of State moved immediately to pass the Instrument of Government. On 16 December, under the terms of the Instrument, Cromwell was appointed as Lord Protector, who, with a Council of State, could make law until a new Parliament was assembled in early September. The Independent leaders moved rapidly to announce their loyalty to the Protectorate and to distance themselves from millennial agitation.[182] With the other Independent leaders, Owen untangled himself from some of those who wished to appropriate his reputation, unpicking associations that were not quite alliances, attempting to excuse himself from the embarassment of having an audience of whom he could not approve. For England had just experienced another revolution: the rule of king-in-Parliament had been replaced by the rule of Parliament; and the rule of Parliament was now being replaced by the rule of the army, whose commander-in-chief, Oliver Cromwell, Owen's most useful patron to date, was now the Lord Protector.

6

Cromwellian Courtier

OWEN'S CAREER PEAKED as his new patron was invested as Lord Protector of England.[1] Not everyone was happy with the new constitutional arrangements, and some critics alleged that Cromwell and the military elite were guilty of exactly the luxury and tyranny they had criticized in others.[2] But the new regime recognized its responsibility to promote godliness. The Protectorate was established under the terms of the Instrument of Government (1653)—the first written constitution in English legal history. This required that "the Christian religion, as contained in the Scriptures, be held forth and recommended as the public profession of these nations," and that "able and painful teachers" should be employed for "discovery and confutation of error, heresy, and whatever is contrary to sound doctrine." Those who "profess faith in God by Jesus Christ (though differing in judgement from the doctrine, worship or discipline publicly held forth)" were to be able to practice their religion, "provided this liberty be not extended to Popery or Prelacy, not to such as, under the profession of Christ, hold forth and practise licentiousness."[3] The latter qualifications were the only suggestion that "Christian religion, as contained in the Scriptures," might be any form of non-prelatic Protestantism that disavowed antinomian behavior. In the context of the rapid proliferation of new religious movements, this was hardly adequate—and, oddly, the theology of the Racovian catechism, which had started the theological fuss, had not explicitly been proscribed.

Whatever its ideological ambiguities, the Instrument required sweeping reform of religious institutions. By the end of 1653, the national church structures provided by the Westminster Assembly had largely disappeared, without any new procedures for the ordination of ministers having been established. For all that the revolution had established a marketplace of religious ideas, and had advanced a sudden and often shocking "democratisation of Christianity," individuals were no longer being compelled to attend worship in parish churches, though it is likely that these churches were being better attended than most of the gathered congregations.[4] Lay people and various institutions continued to appoint ministers to livings, and tithes were still being collected as a compulsory tax.[5] These tithes helped to fund the salaries of ministers employed in the parish churches, which had improved under the oversight of the Trustees for the Maintenance of Ministers, while gathered churches continued to elect and provide for their own ministers on an additional and voluntary basis. These improved salaries were, at least in theory, being designated for ministers of proven ability.

One of the principal achievements of the religious policy of the Protectorate was a new facility for adjudicating preachers' merits. The institution of "triers" and "ejectors" developed from suggestions that Owen himself had put forward, with the support of other Independent ministers, in February 1652. The original suggestion was that local committees of "triers" should approve the appointment of preachers, while a centralized body of "ejectors" should consider their removal. These functions were reversed when this process was rolled out, so that the "triers" and "ejectors" evolved to represent a central body that approved candidates for ministry and a series of local committees whose remit it was to deprive unsuitable men.[6] This process mirrored that of the Westminster Assembly, which had recently disbanded, and which had also monitored and approved new clerical appointments, as Owen would have known from first-hand experience. Of course, these institutions could work only if their members could agree to cooperate. On 28 February, Owen and other ministers were called to an audience with the Lord Protector in an effort to promote this kind of reconciliation.[7] Several of these ministers were appointed to the Committee for the Approbation of Public Preachers—as the "triers" were officially known—which was established on 20 March 1654.[8] Its thirty-eight clerical and lay members were "orthodox Calvinists, though they differed considerably in matters of ecclesiology."[9] Most of the group were conservative Independents, including Owen, Joseph Caryl, Philip Nye, Sidrach Simpson, William Greenhill, and William Strong, while others were moderate Presbyterians, including Thomas Manton, Obadiah Sedgewick, and Anthony Tuckney, and a few were moderate Baptists, including Henry Jessey, Daniel Dyke, and John Tombes.[10] Their task was to measure the orthodoxy and piety of ministerial candidates without reference to a formally agreed statement of faith: in effect, "ministerial approbation would be more dependent on the orthodoxy of those doing the examination than on a written confessional standard."[11]

Despite the lack of a clear point of reference, the system worked well, and the "triers" approved over 3,500 ministers by 1659.[12] Its menace was perhaps less significant than many of its critics might have feared: only around fifty ministers had been ejected by mid-1655, a figure that suggests, among other things, that the "persistent godly jeremiads about the wide prevalence of ignorance and scandal within the ministry of the mid 1650s seriously overstated the need for further reform."[13] Owen himself was concerned about a number of attempted ejections, later complaining to John Thurloe, secretary to the Council of State, that "some few men of mean quality and condition" were "casting out on slight and trivial pretence very worthy men." This was a problem he would address later in the year, when ejectors in Berkshire attempted to turn the eminent Orientalist and former Oxford professor Edward Pococke out of his parish church on account of what Owen regarded as "slight and trivial pretences"—that is, Pococke's continued, and criminal, use of the prayer book.[14] Fearing that the local body of ejectors were being too scrupulous, and were being driven by political rather than theological hostilities, Owen traveled to Berkshire with John Wilkins, Seth Ward, and John Walliss, and persuaded the ejectors, "with some warmth . . . of the infinite contempt and reproach which would certainly fall upon them, when it should be said, that they had turned out a man for insufficiency, whom all the learned, not of England only, but of all Europe, so justly admired for his vast knowledge, and extraordinary accomplishments."[15] Even for pious prayer book Anglicans, Owen could be a formidably ally, especially when the opposition to their continued ministry was driven by the same kind of hostility to tithes that was driving much of the criticism of the universities.

Owen's participation in this flagship project of religious settlement, in which he defended a sometimes surprising range of liturgical practice, and worked with individuals, such as Baptists, some of whose beliefs he had cited earlier in the year as being dangerous to the commonwealth, may have encouraged him to reconsider the possibilities for broader ecclesial unity. In early 1654, the parliamentary committee on religion asked a group of theologians for advice on how to understand the "faith in Jesus Christ" referred to in Article 37 of the Instrument of Government. Owen could have regarded participation in the scheme with a jaundiced eye: after all, the pension that had been awarded at Colchester was £200 in arrears.[16] But he joined the group of advisors, along with Philip Nye, Thomas Goodwin, and Sidrach Simpson (all Independents); Richard Vines, Francis Cheynell, and Stephen Marshall (all Presbyterians); and Richard Baxter, who was attending in place of Archbishop James Ussher, who had refused his invitation to join the group.[17] Despite their long-standing literary feud, it was the first time that Owen and Baxter had met.[18] The advisors produced a list of twenty articles of religion, which was privately published for MPs, but which the London bookseller and collector George Thomason added to his collection of printed materials under the title, *A new confession of faith, or the first principles of the Christian religion* (1654).[19] The document was, as John Coffey has put it, "fuller in its wording, and narrower in its theology" than the sixteen sentences of 1653.[20] *A new confession* targeted an expanded range of religious opinions, including those held by Socinians, Quakers, Ranters, and Arminians, but while it was endorsed by MPs on the committee, it was never adopted by Parliament.[21] The completion of the statement was hindered by a long debate between Owen and Baxter as to whether, as the latter unsuccessfully argued, a national confession of faith should use only biblical language.[22] The Commons' rejection of this project signaled its increasing concern to protect freedom of conscience. The frustration of pursuing a politically futile project may have contributed to tensions among the advisors. Richard Baxter remembered that the "over-Orthodox Doctors, Owen and Cheynell," had put "their own Opinions or crude Conceits" into the new "Fundamentals," with Owen being the "great doer of all that worded the Articles," Nye, Goodwin, and Simpson his "assistants," and Cheynell their "scribe."[23]

For Owen's dispute with Baxter was rumbling on, often on proxy fronts. Sometime in 1654, Owen wrote a commendation for William Eyre's *Vindiciae justificationis gratuitae* (1654), a book that defended its author against claims that Eyre had preached in defence of "justification before faith."[24] This charge was almost identical to that which Baxter had made of Owen in his *Aphorisms on justification* (1649), and it was hardly surprising that Owen's commendation should reflect upon his old antagonist, even as they were working together to establish a national orthodoxy.[25] The relationship developed on the basis of mutual distrust, which was not likely alleviated when, in July 1654, Giles Firmin informed Baxter how much Owen was missed from Essex.[26] But Owen's vision for reform had expanded beyond the boundaries of his first parishes. Neither was he content merely to fashion the orthodox faith of England. It was in this period that Owen, having called for the exportation of the English revolution in several of his parliamentary semons, signed a letter to the Protestant churches of Europe, appealing for an international coalition against the forces of Antichrist—another effort that would eventually come to nothing.[27] Owen's grand if impolitic schemes reflected the art of the impossible.

I

The ministers behind *A new confession* may have taken the opportunity to push for a national religious settlement in the absence of a Parliament to oppose it, but the Instrument of Government did require that such an assembly be convened.[28] On 10 June 1654, Owen, as vice chancellor, was instructed to oversee the election of an MP to represent the university.[29] He himself was elected, on 27 June. It is not clear why he wished to serve as an MP in the first Protectoral Parliament: perhaps he had grown frustrated by seeing his religious reforms come to nothing, and thought he could better support them from the floor of the House.

Owen's election as an MP may have provided the occasion for his presentation to the Protector of an anthology of verse in praise of his accomplishments.[30] Of course, this was not the first anthology of panegyric to emerge from Oxford, but it was the first (and only) such collection of verse addressed to Cromwell. This volume, *Musarum Oxoniensium* (1654), which was not represented in the Goold edition but has been generating increasing interest in recent work on Owen and the period, collected the work of a range of university poets with a surprising breadth of political and religious backgrounds.[31] As we noticed in the last chapter, Christ Church had a reputation for poetry.[32] Serious interest in aesthetic form was not universal among Puritans. In the previous year, for example, a floor had collapsed during the performance of *Mucedorus*, an anti-Puritan satire, in Whitney, Oxfordshire, and John Rowe's sermon on the event had sought to represent the tragedy as a providential judgment against the sin of dramatic performance, a sin exacerbated by the fact that the performance was taking place on a fast day.[33] Around the same time, however, the Cromwellian government began to use cultural forms of which it had formerly disapproved, in a shift in aesthetic values that reflected its need to narrate its values to a broader public and to foreign governments.[34] This moment of aesthetic transition may explain Owen's sudden interest in supporting the publication of an anthology of verse that drew on writers from across and beyond the local academic community. The project benefited in this respect from the interest in poetry that was supported at some of its principal feeder schools: John Evelyn reported in 1661 that students from Westminster School, an important source of Christ Church undergraduates, were able to compose poetry in Latin, Greek, Hebrew, and Arabic.[35] *Musarum Oxoniensium* demonstrated the ability and ambition of university poets, whose writing in Latin, Greek, Hebrew, English, Old English, Welsh, and French was published by Leonard Lichfield in Oxford to celebrate the formal end of the first Dutch war in April 1654.[36] The anthology appears to have been printed in June—as suggested by Thomason's note on the edition held in the British Library—and must have been rushed out as the peace treaty was being finalized.[37] Christ Church poets were very well represented in the anthology. In fact, almost every contributor had a Christ Church connection, making the official university celebration of Cromwell's victory over the Dutch actually a display of the polyglot learning of the vice chancellor's college community.

But the volume was not just a display of variety in language. *Musarum Oxoniensium* provides a critical insight into the extraordinary range of political opinion, religious preference, and career experience of the students, graduates, and staff associated with Owen's institution. His role in the project is not clear. It is not evident that he edited the volume, but his poem, "Ad Protectorem," provided its introduction.[38] This sixteen-line neo-Latin eulogy contrasted its author's humble beginnings—"ex humili subitus vate Poeta cano" (line 4)—with a discussion of Augustan qualities of its dedicatee.[39] The imperial language was pointed, and simultaneously lauded the new Protector while tactfully questioning his political style. It was exactly the response that might be expected of someone who felt compelled to praise a patron whom he did not admire. Owen's poem was suggestively ambiguous, supporting Knoppers's claim that "in the very act of representing Cromwell, print made Cromwell vulnerable to misrepresentation and rejection."[40] Nor was Owen's poem alone in its ambivalence. It was followed by work from John Busbye, who had been expelled by the parliamentary Visitors in 1648, was restored in 1650, took his MA in 1652 and was "punished" in 1653, being noted as a "fugitive from Christ Church" in 1655;[41] Thomas Terrent, a tutor in philosophy who may have eulogized the memory of Ben Jonson in verse commending *Jonsonus virbius* (1634);[42] and John Walliss, the Savilian Professor of Geometry, who contributed poems in Latin, Greek, and Hebrew. The medical doctor John Maplet had been the principal of Gloucester Hall before his ejection from office in 1651, and Thomas Lockey had been a college preacher and tutor with an interest in Hobbes until his deprivation by the Visitors.[43] Those contributors who were former students of Christ Church included Richard Bryan, who had been expelled from the college by the Visitors in 1648.[44] Among the current students who contributed to the volume was John Locke, the future philosopher; Edward Bagshawe, an "unruly, intemperate, and provocative undergraduate," who showed "scant regard for authority or tradition," not least when, after graduation, he addressed the vice chancellor while wearing a hat;[45] Robert South, who was attending "illegal services according to the rites of the Church of England which were conducted by three ejected members of Christ Church, Richard Allestree, John Dolben, and John Fell";[46] and William James, an undergraduate of ferocious talent who, in addition to his Latin verse in the university anthology, had already published a Chaldean grammar (1651) and commendatory verse (in English) to John Hoddesdon's *Sion and Parnassus* (1650) and (in Greek) to Henry Stubbes's *Horae subsecivae* (1651), along with multiple unpublished translations, as well as Hebrew-Latin and Arabic-Latin vocabularies.[47] The anthology is evidence of the politically and religiously diverse, and intellectually ambitious, environment of the college community. If Owen's prefatory poem was ambiguous, *Musarum Oxoniensium*, as a collection, also made some unexpected political moves.

But poetry also became a medium through which these claims to theological and poetic ability could be interrogated. Other poets responded to the Oxford anthology—including members of Owen's college. One of the most visceral repsonses to *Musarum Oxoniensium* was provided by Thomas Ireland, who had been a student in Christ Church when his poetry was included, along with that of Christopher Wren and Anthony à Wood, in *Newes from the dead* (1651), a narrative account and anthology of poems commemorating the "execution" and resuscitation of Anne Greene, in Oxford, in December 1650.[48] In 1654, Ireland's *Momus elencticus* used a series of bawdy puns to mock what it described as a "serious piece of Drollerie presented by the Vice Chancellor of Oxon in the name of all his Mirmidons at Whitehall, to expell the Melancholy of the Court, and to tickle its gizzard with a Landskip of dancing Fryars to their own Musick and Numbers."[49] Ireland offered a satirical review of *Musarum Oxoniensium*, with Owen as a principal target. Ireland dismissed the vice chancellor as the author of a "cutted Analysis of Reformation" who "voided a tedious Epistle, | Wherein if you finde one grain of salt, whistle."[50] He mocked Owen's "pittifull Rythme . . . without tune or time."[51] And he made the increasingly familiar charge about Owen's sense of dress:

The first of th' Artillery that did give fire
Was a great Gun of Christ-Church the bigg'st of the Quire,
A welch man I wis by his gate and attire
Well a go to then.

Owen's dress sense had become an issue for many of his critics: while Ireland could satirize his fashion as being rustic and Welsh, other critics would condemn its flamboyance.[52]

John Evelyn, the royalist diarist, made no mention of Owen's attire or his politics when he attended the end of term "Act" later that summer. Evelyn heard Owen "perstringing Episcopacy" on Sunday, 9 July 1654, and the next day listened to him give the vice chancellor's oration, a staple component of a graduation event.[53] There were four doctors graduating in theology and three in medicine—"which was thought a considerable matter, the times consider'd."[54] Evelyn witnessed the "Creation of Doctors, by the Cap, ring, Kisse, &c: those Ceremonies not as yet wholy abolish'd, but retaining the antient Ceremonies & Institution," and considered that George Kendal "performed his Act incomparably well, concluded it with an excellent Oration, abating his Presbyterian animositie." The Act was closed with the "Speech of the V: Chancellor." After a sumptuous dinner in Wadham College, Evelyn visited that "miracle of a Youth, Mr. Christopher Wren"—then a Christ Church student—and "Mr. Barlow . . . of the Bodlean Library, my most learned friend, who shewd me, together with my Wife, The rarities of that famous place, Manuscrips, Medails & other Curiosities."[55] Barlow's tour of the Bodleian collections highlighted its treasures—"no lesse than 1000 MSS: in 19 languages"—as well as tourist curiosities, including "Josephs parti colourd Coat, A Muscovian Ladys Whip, some Indian Weapons, Urnes, Lamps: &: But the rarest, is the Whole Alcoran written in one large sheet of Calico, which is made up in a Priests Vesture of Cape after the Turkish."[56] Evelyn's tour of the library illustrated the variety of its holdings—a topic on which Owen would reflect in 1661, in *Θεολογουμενα παντοδαπα*, the last of his publications to take advantage of the numismatic as well as bibliographical riches of Thomas Barlow's Bodleian. But it also signaled the extent to which Owen had entered a very different world from that of parish and military experience in which he had learned his theological trade.

The rather whimsical nature of Evelyn's tour of the library contrasted with the idealization of republican pedagogical virtues that Owen outlined in his oration. For Owen, the times were dangerous. He had appointed Thomas Barlow—his tutor at Queen's, a former Episcopalian who now "felt closer in ecclesiological matters to the Independents than to the Presbyterians"—to a position in the "most famous library in the world."[57] There Barlow's leadership had been crucial in developing its resources, which, "foiling the prayers of its enemies at home and abroad . . . has remained intact, and has been enhanced and embellished, if not by more learned books, at any rate by a most learned librarian."[58] The survival of the Oxford institutions represented a victory over the "stupidity and barbarity" of the "most distinguished patrons of ignorance" who had been arguing for the "abolition of the Universities."[59] "Let others display their trophies, their spoils taken from the enemy, their brows with chaplets of flowers, the richer fruits of deep peace and tranquil retirement," Owen concluded. "We carry around with us the scars, the dust and sweat, hands raised to heaven, signs of struggle not entirely unworthy of God and of men."[60] And the university's struggle was also that of the republic, led by "our most distinguished Chancellor," who at the head of armies had "trained the wild and roving Nomads of Ireland and has perceived the character, virtue and modesty of the mountain-dwelling Scots."[61] For Oxford was on a war footing. "Do not expect wine merchants, pantomime-girls, and buffoons laid low, beer swillers, night prowlers, debauchers and other human riff-raff brought suppliant on to the stage," or "the trappings of hoods and gowns restored, made famous by honourable names," Owen continued, but "let us adorn the Sparta we have found, let us campaign in earnest, let us burst into the camp of truth, let us make for heaven itself with courage, despairing of nothing, with the Hon. Chancellor raising our standard on high, with Christ our leader and Christ our inspiration."[62] In Owen's Oxford, scholarship was the continuation of war by other means.

At the same time as he was saving the university from extinction, Owen was advancing a prodigious writing career. One of the most substantial of his Cromwellian writings was his treatise on *The doctrine of the saints perseverance* (1654), a massive assault on the claims in John Goodwin's *Redemption redeemed* (1651) that true believers could lose their salvation. Goodwin was an appropriate adversary, "a person whom his worth, pains, diligence, and opinions, and the contests wherein on their account he hath publicly engaged, have delivered from being the object of any ordinary thoughts or expressions. Nothing not great, not considerable, not some way eminent, is by any spoken of him, either consenting with him or dissenting from him."[63] Owen was especially concerned that Goodwin's argument was being driven by analogy rather than exegesis. "Rolling through this field, his expressions swell over all bounds and limits; metaphors, similitudes, parables, all help on the current, though the streams of it being shallow and wide, a little opposition easily turns it for the most part aside," Owen complained, turning to metaphor in an ironic rejection of his antagonist's rhetorical strategy.[64] Owen's own objective was to employ precise, if often unfamiliar, language. He summarized Goodwin's position as assuming a "certain lubricity of the wills of men . . . to propose an intercision of them as to their concatenation and dependence."[65] If readers objected to use his use of terms like "oscitancy," he could at least point them to Goodwin's use of this word in a recent subtitle.[66] But this theological argument offered detailed and nuaced argument that God would preserve those who perservered in using the means of grace. Of all Owen's writing, *The doctrine of the saints perseverance* was most dependent upon Thomas Bradwardine and advanced a robustly Thomistic structure.[67] It did nothing to encourage antinomian complacency. King Hezekiah may have been promised fifteen extra years of life, Owen considered, but he was still required to make every effort to stay alive.[68]

Owen's high regard for Goodwin's abilities might suggest why he spent so much time preparing his reply. The book had been a long time in the making: Robert Abbot was aware that Owen was working on the project in January 1652.[69] Owen had developed his arguments in the intervening years, despite "straits . . . diversions, employments, business of sundry natures. . . . The truth is, no small portion of it owes its rise to journeys, and such like avocations from my ordinary course of studies and employments, with some spare hours, for the most part in time of absence from all books and assistances of that nature whatever."[70] Despite the now familiar gesture toward an inadequate research base, he was not embarrassed by his achievement. Dedicating *The doctrine of the saints perseverance* to "his Highness Oliver," he understood that the "urgency" of "high and important affairs, wherein so many nations are concerned," might prevent Cromwell from having "so much leisure as to take a view of what is here tendered."[71] Some readers might have been surprised by elements of the book's argument. Owen was increasingly hesitant about the use of syllogistic method, and, when Goodwin cited Calvin, was happy to reply with a citation from Paul.[72] In the context of constitutional turmoil, Owen argued that Old Testament monarchs had been elected, and in what may have been more than a passing glance at Cromwell's increasingly monarchical style, argued that "we may very easily be, and often are, decieved in our estimate of righteous persons," who rarely "hold out in the glory of his profession to the end."[73] Owen may not have been thinking only of the recent tragedy in Whitney when he suggested that "that which comes next upon the theatre will, I fear, foully miscarry, and spoil the whole plot of the play."[74] Nevertheless, Owen's sharp rhetoric disguised his tactics. While condemning the "vile conflux of heretics, fanatics and bigots . . . that almost ravishes and violates the bride of Christ even under the holy eyes of the Bridegroom," he was also working to protect them.[75] Quakers began to meet in Oxford in 1654, and were subject to widespread legal and extra-legal opposition, but the fees for the release of at least one imprisoned Quaker were paid by the vice chancellor.[76] Owen's actions were not necessarily consistent with the spirit of the law.

Then, on 3 September, Owen took his seat in the first Protectoral Parliament.[77] Settling into his new situation, he found himself for the first time listening to a sermon to MPs—this delivered by his colleague Thomas Goodwin. Owen's participation in this Parliament has never been recovered. He was certainly keeping interesting company. He wrote a letter from the home of a Mr. Cooke on Pall Mall, perhaps that of the regicide judge, then based in Ireland, and was reported as having dined with John Hildesley, a fellow ejector who had recently been elected as MP for Winchester.[78] Owen may also have aligned himself with a group of old republicans who were hostile to the monarchical tendencies of the new regime. One well-placed observer recorded in his diary that some of the members elected to the new Parliament were "of a contrary judment to Cromwell, as S[ir] Arth[ur] Hazelrig, S[ir] H[enry] Vane, Bradshaw, and withal Doctor Owen."[79] Owen sat in the Commons until October, when he was debarred under the terms of the Clerical Disabilities

Act (1642), and returned to Oxford.[80] But the rumors of his association with republicans provide further evidence that Owen's disenchantment with the regime was being noticed.[81] Perhaps he had overreached himself. His ascent on the national stage ended in the autumn of 1654.

But Owen's power in Oxford was still supreme. In early September, his name was included in the new list of Visitors to the university.[82] This third visitation had a broader and more conservative base than that which had secured the Independents' control of the university in the period immediately after the regicide, including a number of Presbyterians who had not served on the second. For all of its broader base, the third visitation believed itself to have a broader remit, including that of improving the statutes of colleges and of the university. Owen and Goodwin, unlike some of their colleagues, grasped at these powers in an effort to further advance the kind of administrative reforms by which their colleges had already been brought to heel.[83] Their aspiration was in part to promote good piety. On 21 January 1655, the Visitors required that all BA and MA students were to "give an account to a suitable person, chosen by the heads of their respective societies, of sermons heard and religious exercises attended," with the heads of colleges being required to report to the vice chancellor's lodging to certify that the instructions were being observed.[84] Not everyone was persuaded that these activities were realizing their objectives. Henry Bartlett complained to Baxter that Owen was supporting the warden of Wadham College, John Wilkins, even though he had "ejected 2 godly fellows, brought in profane drunkards, scoffers at holiness, & so far discouraged all the godly."[85] Further controversy erupted in January 1655, when the earl of Pembroke invoked his right as a Visitor of Jesus College to settle a university dispute, although the new Visitors to the university protested that this right belonged to them. The details of this dispute are lost to us, but were more likely less significant than the procedural contest it provoked. A committee of protest was formed to defend the traditional rights of the colleges, led by John Wilkins of Wadham, Gerard Langbaine of Queen's, and John Palmer, warden of All Souls. The Visitors, surprised by this turn of events, arranged to meet the protestors in Owen's rooms in Christ Church at 2 p.m. on 9 February. The committee submitted its petition, and was asked to withdraw while the Visitors discussed the case. But they could come to no agreement, and their meeting concluded without further communication with the university committee. It was after 9 p.m. when an Oxford ally, Thankful Owen, to whom John Owen was not related, returned to the premises to let the committee of protest know that the meeting had ended several hours before and that the Visitors did not want to continue the discussion with them. Thus humiliated, the committee of protest consulted colleagues on whether to take the battle to Whitehall, but were persuaded to let the matter lie. The Visitors "learned to treat the colleges more delicately," but their treatment of the protestors betrayed a broader indifference to the traditional rights of the colleges they represented.[86]

II

Owen's tenure as vice chancellor of Oxford had to negotiate changing circumstances, as Commonweath gave way to Protectorate, and as the first Protectoral Parliament gave way to a sequence of royalist risings and the rule of the major-generals. Oxford faced two principal threats in and after 1655—royalists and Socinians. In 1654, following the Independents' campaign against the Socinian menace, Parliament ordered that all copies of John Biddle's *Twelve arguments drawn out of Scripture* (1647) should be destroyed, and appointed Owen to reply to the work. "In hours snatched between committees and on his journeys to London," Owen "composed hundreds of thousands of words" exposing the heresy.[87] His response entirely overwhelmed Biddle's polemic—in content and, especially, in length. *Vindiciae evangelicae* (1655) adopted Thomistic categories in "unusually biting style . . . designed to hold the popular interest."[88] The burden of Owen's response, according to Alan Spence, was to "modify a number of the arguments that the Fathers had used effectively against the Arians a thousand years earlier." His "originality" was to link his defense of orthodox Christology with the Holy Spirit: "Owen incorporated this recognition of the Spirit's work in the life of Jesus within his overview of the Spirit's wider ministry in the life of the Church. He argued that in restoring the image of God to the Church, the Spirit had first to renew it in the human nature of Christ."[89] *Vindiciae evangelicae* was an exercise in polemical Trinitarianism, and likely contributed to Owen's developing understanding of the link between Christian piety and relationships within the Godhead. Owen, drawing upon Irenaeus and Theodore of Mopsuestia, "not only conceded but vigorously affirmed the central element of the Socinian argument—the incarnate Christ was totally dependent on the Holy Spirit in all aspects of his ministry and life." His approach allowed "Christ's life before God to serve as both the ground and paradigm for Christian spirituality."[90]

The royalist threat was equally serious. One of its most dangerous expressions, the Penruddock rising, began in March 1655. Owen coordinated the local military response, advising secretary Thurloe that "there is much riding to and fro in the night in the villages near us; but as yet I cannot learne any certain place of their meetinge, soe keep a continual guard."[91] He raised a troop of sixty scholars, "riding up and down like a spiritual Abeddon," as a critic later recalled.[92] The failure of these risings signaled the end of royalism as an effective military force, but it would hardly have looked like this at the time, for they generated the fears about security that were used to justify the rule of the major-generals, from August 1655 until January 1657.

The rule of the major-generals has often been presented as a military dictatorship, but recent work has argued that they "did not posses anything approaching the exorbitant and unrestricted powers that earlier writers had assumed."[93] This experiment in government saw England divided into twelve districts. Charles Fleetwood, a friend of Owen, was appointed to take care of an area comprising Norfolk, Suffolk, Essex, Hertfordshire, Cambridgeshire and the Isle of Ely, Oxfordshire, and Buckinghamshire.[94] Fleetwood, who remained in London throughout this period, controlled this district through deputies, George Fleetwood (who oversaw Buckinghamshire) and William Packer (who oversaw the rest of the area).[95] Packer would have been the representative of military rule with whom Owen would have been most concerned. He did not have any significant political experience to justify his appointment. He was the "most radical of the major-generals in terms of both his political and religious beliefs," being a noted "anabaptist" lay preacher and a supporter of the Fifth Monarchists, who would shortly be cashiered from the army. He would later regret, in a speech to the Commons in 1659, his actions in this period of non-parliamentary rule.[96] England's new rulers did not present a united, godly front: they related to each other with "unease, suspicion and a good measure of mutual distrust."[97] Nor were they always effective. In September 1656, for example, Packer asked the Oxford corporation to provide him with a copy of the city's charter—which request the corporation refused.[98] Christopher Durston has argued that the major-generals' failure to control local government stymied their efforts at moral reform, though it did effectively contain the royalist military threat.[99] They did not stamp out religious dissent. Quakers were causing problems in Coggeshall during the mid-1650s, and, as we have already noticed, illegal prayer book services were held in Oxford throughout the period.[100] Some major-generals were very hard on religious dissidents.[101] Packer was not likely to have been among them.

But Christ Church, too, was changing. Henry Stubbe returned to his college in 1655 or 1656, after spending two years with the army in Scotland. His arrival back in Oxford coincided with one of the most bitter—and revealing—of the university controversies of the period. Shortly after his return, Stubbe, who was Oxford's "most enthusiastic champion" of Hobbesian theory, began to translate *Leviathan* into Latin.[102] His interest in Hobbes's work developed in parallel with his friendship with the author: Stubbe took Hobbes's side in his prolonged quarrel with John Walliss, the Savilian Professor of Geometry. Hobbes and Stubbe were united in their disapprobation of Walliss's

Presbyterianism, together with its hegemonic political implications.[103] The disdain was mutual: Walliss described Hobbes's work in October 1655 as "nonsense and pure rubbish."[104] Owen was aware of Stubbe's interest in Hobbes's work, and did what he could to discourage it.[105] He was patronizing Stubbe in late 1656, for example, asking the younger man to "study church-government, & a toleration, & so to oppose Presbytery," while offering a post in the library as a reward.[106] The literary work that Owen devolved to Stubbe worried Daniel Cawdrey, who described Stubbe as his patron's amanuensis. Responding to Cawdrey in 1658, Owen emphatically denied the charge: "some five years ago," Stubbe "transcribed about a sheet of paper for me," Owen insisted, "and not one line before or since."[107] But the reality was that Stubbe had continued to act as his research assistant. If he were also acting as an amanuensis, we might better understand how Owen was able to write so much so rapidly—by using dictation and by ventriloquizing the arguments of his assistants. But Stubbe seems not to have taken Owen's hints about his philosophical friend, and attempted—unsuccessfully—to have Hobbes contribute an anonymous "letter" to the book he was writing for Owen.[108] Late in 1656, Stubbes noted that Owen had taken the manuscript to London.[109] It is not clear what became of this work, or whether it was an early draft of Owen's book on schism (1657), but Stubbe was rewarded with his post in the library.[110] He had not sold his loyalty: Stubbe later campaigned against Owen and others in defense of Quaker freedoms and misled Owen by continuing to translate Hobbes into Latin.[111] Owen understood the book's dangers, as Stubbe informed its author: "Hee did speak of yr Leviathan, yt it was a book ye most full of excellent remarques of any, onely you deify the magistrate, & spoyled all by yor kingdome of darknesse."[112]

III

Owen's third oration as vice chancellor, at the end of term event in July 1655, in which the university community took "compensation for the grave labours of the whole year in the joy of one or two brief days," was delivered under a shadow.[113] The Muses were at war, and had fought "more battles for survival than for glory."[114] Reflecting on the attempt by the duke of Savoy to exterminate the Waldensians, a campaign of terror earlier in the spring that had gained international notoriety and had occasioned a sonnet by Milton, Owen recalled that the "the cries of our brothers' recent bloodshed forbid even the Muses from dancing."[115] The university had collected £384 for Waldensian relief.[116] Thinking of their fate, Owen must have been grateful for the distinguishing grace of God, though he remembered that the safety of his own university had only been secured by the "great suffering, the great industry, the many vigils and disturbances, the great expenditure of time and studies and fortunes and friends, the counsel in times of doubt, and the courage in times of crisis."[117] He considered the enthuisiasm with which the university had been militarized in response to the royalist rising led by Penruddock.[118] For the university had been vulnerable. "The rabble was rioting and the military raging and Parliament wavering and the sycophants vigorously maligning her from all directions."[119] His troop of scholars had saved the day.

Meanwhile, Owen was thinking about absent friends, including Joshua Hoyle, the recently deceased Regius Professor of Divinity, "a man who was nearly the first among the leading professors ... on account of his multifarious knowledge and uncommon erudition."[120] Hoyle had been replaced by John Conant, whom Owen praised for his "modesty, eloquence, candour and erudition," despite the opposition of some of the Masters of Arts.[121] And the university had also lost Edward Wood, "a glory to letters, a paragon of virtue," whom Owen had "counted as one bound to me by the closest ties of friendship."[122] He noted the *Vesperia* produced by Edward's younger brother, Anthony à Wood, the future historian of the University of Oxford, who would take quite a different view of his late brother's close friend. Generally, however, the situation of the university was encouraging. Oxford had never "nourished a greater number of innocent and saintly souls than it now does. We do not stand by the censures of visitors, fleeting about for three days amongst the inns, street-corners, squares and taverns, where, perchance, not even the ghost of a student can be seen. We appeal to the Colleges, the libraries, the museums, the schools, the chapels, the churches, the printing presses."[123] In the face of political threat and military violence, the Independents' reform of Oxford had been successful.

IV

Owen became increasingly prominent in the culture of print. In 1655, he was both the dedicatee of Robert Wickens's new concordance and the subject of opprobrium in Thomas Gilbert's *Vindiciae supremi Dei Dominii* (1655), which appeared in response to Owen's *Diatriba de justitia divina*.[124] In the summer of 1655, Owen reported that he was enlarging his sermons on communion with God and preparing *Of temptation*, even as he preached the sermons that would become *Of the mortification of sinne in believers* (1656).[125] Owen's book echoed with the strategies of the pulpit, and included some of his most pithy soundbites: "be killing sin or it will be killing you"; "when sin lets us alone we may let sin alone"; "there is no death of sin without the death of Christ"; and "he that dares to dally with occasions of sin will dare to sin."[126] Owen was worried that "true evangelical mortification is almost lost amongst us," and that the "broad light" and "many spiritual gifts" that had been given to his generation, which had "wonderfully enlarged the bounds of professors and profession," had not been matched by apropriate progress in godliness.[127] And yet for all his exhortations to action, Owen wanted to differentiate his encouragement of mortification from mere moralism: "some men" in "late days have taken upon them to give directions for the mortification of sin, who, being unaquainted with the mystery of the gospel and the efficacy of the death of Christ, have anew imposed the yoke of a self-wrought-out mortification on the necks of their disciples."[128] But this "mortification from a self-strength, carried on by ways of self-invention, unto the end of a self-righteousness, is the soul and substance of all false religion in the world."[129] True sanctification was focused not on the individual's development of self-control, but upon the work of Christ: "Look on him under the weight of our sins, praying, bleeding, dying; bring him in that condition into thy heart; by faith apply his blood so shed to thy corruptions: do this daily."[130]

And his adminstrative activities continued. On 11 September 1655, John Locke, still an undergraduate, noted that Owen had just returned from London, and that he would stay on as vice chancellor for another year "that his honour may be proportionate to his person, and merit": it is not clear whether this statement was tongue-in-cheek.[131] In November 1655, Owen was called to Whitehall to take part in a meeting about the readmission of the Jews.[132] Within the university, he began to campaign against the wearing of academic habits, the next step in his campaign for institutional reformation. In the face of stern opposition, Owen called a meeting of Convocation to discuss this issue on Christmas Day 1655—knowing that many of his adversaries, too committed to festive tradition, would be unable to attend.[133] This action, Tim Cooper has noted, illustrates Owen's "freewheeling and conniving" personality—not least when it is connected with the taking of Owen's portrait, in full academic dress, in unknown circumstances sometime in this period, a portrait that came to be owned by the family of his second wife and is currently in the possession of Dr Williams's Library, London, as the preface noted.[134] But Owen was also under very heavy pressure. Mary and Elizabeth had been joined by other children in the household, but, on 6 March 1656, Ralph Josselin recorded that "gods heavy hand on Dr Owen his 2 eldest sons dead himself neare death," even as he prayed for the vice chancellor's survival.[135] The news was widely reported.[136] It must have been another blow. He had hardly recovered his health when the university's convocation rejected most of his reforms at its meeting on 10 April 1656. He responded by leaving Oxford, returning with the threat of involving a major-general, most likely his ally Charles Fleetwood or the local major-general William Packer, or even Cromwell himself. When he attempted to involve the Visitors, they divided, and Presbyterian members counseled Owen to take a more moderate course.[137] He did not. Nor were his finances in good shape. His Colchester pension of £100 was now "several years" in arrears.[138] In May 1656, he traveled to London to try to attempt its recovery—but, attempting to meet with the Protector, and in inexplicable circumstances, he was briefly arrested.[139] Josselin was worried about his old neighbor, noting in his diary in July 1656 that Owen was attempting to "lay down all the badges of schollers distinction in the universities: Hoods, caps, gowns, degrees, lay by all studdie of philosophy."[140] Josselin recorded that Owen was now a "great scorne ... I feare about him."[141] By pushing his reforms through at speed, and by attacking the use of academic caps and hoods, Owen's actions actually encouraged their fashionability, as Locke observed.[142] His interventions were too often tactless.[143] Even so, his significance continued to grow. He had become a tourist attraction: Johann Zollikofer, a Swiss Reformed minister, visited England, and collected the autographs of those he met, including John Milton, John Dury, Lady Ranelagh, and Owen.[144] In mid-July 1656, as plans were developed for a second Protectoral Parliament, he was again requested to organize the election of an MP to represent the university, and on 17 September he preached the opening sermon to the second Protectoral Parliament.[145]

This sermon, *God's work in founding Zion* (1656), had a "tone of cheerful gratitude," according to one nineteenth-century editor.[146] It is not clear how that could be so. Addressed to Oliver Cromwell, the sermon had the difficult task of defending "the good old cause of England" even as soldiers excluded over one hundred MPs whose republican sympathies were deemed too unsuitable to be represented in the Commons.[147] But Owen sidestepped the issue of executive forms, and insisted that "God hath wrought his mighty works amongst us ... that Zion may be founded, and the general interest of all the sons and daughters of Zion be preserved," that Christians may "live peaceably one with, or, at least, one by another."[148] Owen's celebration of toleration implied a continued critique of the political culture of the Protectorate. He was no longer compelled to defend its political practice—so long as that practice allowed for the toleration of the godly. Religious toleration, not the administration that promoted it, was the chief achievement of the English revolution. Nevertheless, he exhorted MPs, in language that would soon be associated with republican protest, to "be the preservers of the good old cause of England."[149]

Owen's major summer project developed the themes of this sermon. *Of schism* (1656) had no dedication, no preface, and no address to the reader, and did not appear to respond to any particular literary challenge. Its argument was urgent, nevertheless, for "to live in schism is to live in sin; which, unrepented of, will ruin a man's eternal condition. Every one charged with it must either desert his station, which gives foundation to this charge, or acquit himself of the crime in that station."[150] Christendom was shattered, he recognized:

> It is well known how things stand with us in this world. As we are Protestants, we are accused by the Papists to be schismatics; and all other pleas and disputes are neglected. . . . Farther; among Protestants, as being Reformatists, or as they call us, Calvinists, we are condemned for schismatics by the Lutherans, and for sacramentarian sectaries, for no other crime in the world but because we submit not to all they teach.[151]

And yet, he complained, "we are condemned for separation by them who refuse to admit us into union!"[152] The reality was, of course, that "separation from some churches, true or pretended so to be, is commanded in the Scriptures."[153] Nevertheless, he concluded, "I would rather, much rather, spend all my time and days in making up and healing the breaches and schisms that are amongst Christians than one hour in justifying our divisions."[154] And the means by which this would be realized was not the confessions of faith of the first five centuries, but a reformation of the church according to Scripture alone.[155]

Owen's tenure as vice chancellor was renewed by Cromwell in October 1656.[156] Locke recorded that Owen "took ye oath quatenus non contradicit verbo dei, legibus Angliae, principijs conscientiae et judicio proprio"—that is, insofar as it did not contradict the word of God, the laws of England, the principles of conscience, or his own judgment.[157] The qualifications were comprehensive. On 30 October 1656, Owen preached again to Parliament, a sermon entitled *God's presence with a people* (1656). Goold described the sermon as presenting a "vivid picture of the religious state of Wales."[158] Owen's argument was that God's covenant with individuals is unconditional (and so of grace), while his covenant with nations is conditional (and so of works).[159] Owen took advantage of the occasion to reflect upon the reasons for the failure of the first Protectoral Parliament:

> In the last assembly of parliament, how many had no less real intentions to be at work for God than now! God saw that it would not be for the advantage of the people that they should proceed; hence the cloud rested on that assembly, that they could not see how to take one step

> forward. He was still present with us; but it was by a darkening cloud, that we could not journey towards our rest.[160]

This was a starkly revisionist account of the stonewalling which had ensured that not one of the eighty-four bills presented to MPs by the Council of State had passed, and evidence that Owen did not share Cromwell's reluctance to call a parliament. It is hardly surprising that Owen's fall from power occurred rapidly after this sermon had been delivered. The sermon was a providentialist defense of political obstructionism. MPs brought an end to the rule of the major-generals and represented their conservative turn in the new constitution they presented to the Protector in February 1657. The Humble Petition and Advice, England's second and last written constitution, was accompanied with a request that an upper house be re-established and that Cromwell should consider the offer of the crown. The revolutionary tide had turned.

Owen, meanwhile, was shunted into complex diplomatic work with representatives of the Scottish church, which had recently split in two.[161] James Sharp led the Resolutioner delegates and Archibald Johnston of Wariston the Protestors in the discussions in London. It was frustrating work, much more so than the attempts to combine the orthodox English Puritans on a shared statement of faith. Owen's support for the Protestors was evident to all participants. As in his Oxford committees, he was not above bending procedural regularities. In one meeting, for example, he overlooked the absence of a quorum to pass an important report—a resolve that provoked bitter complaint from James Sharp.[162] But Sharp was assured that the Resolutioners had the favor of the court, while the Protestors, and Owen, did not.[163] Even his critics could see that Owen was slipping out of favor. He was also being outmaneuvered in Oxford. John Wilkins, one of his principal antagonists, had married Cromwell's recently widowed sister.[164] The increasingly sinister nepotism of court influence was now extending directly into Oxford. And the Cromwells were watching him. In March 1657, Richard Cromwell advised his brother Henry that "Dr Owen hath been very angry and went in great haste out of London."[165] The radical figures who had appreciated his preaching were now criticizing his temerity.[166] Owen was losing ground on all fronts. His changing fortunes reflected broader changes in the political landscape.[167]

Events were moving quickly. The government toyed with the idea of establishing a new college in Oxford, as a means to extend its influence within the university, as MPs finally acted to resolve Owen's arrears of pay.[168] On 1 May 1657, Parliament awarded Owen lands in Ireland in lieu of his irregularly paid pension.[169] The bill moved through its several readings before being passed on 9 June.[170] At the same time, Owen made one of his most significant—and unpublished—literary interventions. On 8 May, acting as a "ghost writer for certain army officers," Owen prepared a petition requesting that Cromwell not accept the offer of the crown, which had been extended in the Humble Petition and Advice.[171]

Cromwell took the petition seriously, and in Oxford the fallout was almost immediate. On 3 July 1657, he resigned as chancellor of the university.[172] Owen's fourth oration as vice chancellor was likely concurrent with Cromwell's resignation. His frustration with the wider political context boiled over as he complained of the high spirits that attended the Act. Owen had attempted through the previous year to have the non-academic celebrations discontinued and the academic celebrations improved.[173] No longer praising the undergraduate community for its piety, Owen fell upon their lack of respect for their *alma mater*. "It shames me to say with what celebrity—if indeed that can be called celebrated which is shameful to mention—the inept words of drollery and wit are everywhere flung about, while oblivion has obliterated the very traces of things truly worthy of remembrance, and they are suppressed by perpetual silence."[174] Great things had been achieved. The university, which, ten years before, had been "lying almost deserted," could "now boast of the most learned orators, subtle philosophers, acute judges, outstanding mathematicians, pious, acute and forceful heralds of the divine Word, prolific critics."[175] Owen praised the university's theologians, its "most persistent guardians of orthodoxy, to whom it has been of greater importance to serve the divine truth with the humility of spirit that befits it than to attain some reputation for their name and to achieve brilliance through the phantoms of pretty opinions, or the refuse of ancient philosophers, inauspiciously unearthed anew."[176] But many of the undergraduates were out of control: "we have never been able to bring this most celebrated assembly to its end without perforce having to impose silence on someone among the speakers, or, what is much more distressing, to suffer insults."[177] The situation was not quickly to improve. In April 1658, John Locke recorded that students from Owen's Christ Church, "fild with mighty valour and potentiall ale. stormed Corpus christi . . . fought their way in, and beat them all great and small into their chambers and after that the Proctor of the howse comeing into Ch: Ch: something beyond the bounds of his power, found that his authority was not able to preserve him and his squire from being bangd in the enemy quarters."[178] For all of the vice chancellor's attempts at reformation, Oxford, at times, was a riot.

But Owen continued to write. His "well-known vigils" bore immediate fruit in the publication of one of his least-known works of ecclesiological polemic and one of his best-known contributions to the development of

Protestant spirituality. In mid-June 1657, Owen received a copy of Daniel Cawdrey's *Independency a great schism* (1657), a response to Owen's earlier book on schism, and set about to answer it.[179] The debate was broadening. Giles Firmin also contributed to the debate with his *Of schism, parochial congregations, and ordination by the imposition of hands* (1658) and Henry Hammond included "A reply to some passages of the reviewer in his late book on Schism" in one of his pamphlets.[180] Owen did not reply to either of these reponses, but he did reply to Cawdrey, whose book had come into Owen's possession in mid-June 1657.[181] "Coming unto my hands at such a season, wherein, as it is known, I was pressed with more than ordinary occasions of sundry sorts, I thought to have deferred the examination of it until farther leisure might be obtained, supposing that some fair advantage would be administered by it to a farther Christian debate of that discovery of truth and tender of peace which in my treatise I had made. Engaging into a cursory perusal of it, I found the reverend author's design and discourse to be of that tendency and nature as did not require nor would admit of any such delay."[182] And Owen did not delay. His response, of thirty-five thousand words, was drawn up in "the spare hours of four or five days," and he signed the preface three weeks later, on 9 July 1657.[183] Owen's reputation was at stake: "I am, without any provocation intended, and I hope given, reviled from one end of it to the other, and called, partly in down-right terms, partly by oblique intimations, whose reflections are not to be waived, Satan, atheist, sceptic, Donatist, heretic, schismatic, sectary, Pharisee, etc.; and the closure of the book is merely an attempt to blast my reputation, whereof I shall give a speedy account."[184]

This personal attack was clearly very difficult for Owen, for he responded to it with a rare moment of autobiographical reflection. Cawdrey had referred his readers to Owen's early reflection on ecclesiology, *The duty of pastors and people distinguished* (1644), to demonstrate that Owen's position had changed, and that by his own earlier definition he had become guilty of schism. Owen was eager to clear up the misunderstanding: "I was then a young man myself, about the age of twenty-six or twenty-seven years," he explained. "The controversy between Independency and Presbytery was young also, nor, indeed, by me clearly understood, especially as stated on the congregational side." Furthermore, his response reflected personal opinion, not party invective, and responded to "some differences that were then upheld in the place where I lived." But Owen had been writing under a misapprehension: "being unacquainted with the congregational way, I professed myself to own the other party, not knowing but that my principles were suited to their judgment and profession, having looked very little farther into those affairs than I was led by an opposition to Episcopacy and ceremonies." Consequently, "I professed myself of the presbyterian judgment, in opposition to democratical confusion; and, indeed, so I do still, and so do all the congregational men in England that I am acquainted withal." He admitted that he had changed his mind on the appropriateness of private meetings of dissenters. There was no shame in this: "he that can glory that in fourteen years he hath not altered or improved in his conception of some things of no greater importance than that mentioned shall not have me for his rival."[185] That issue aside, Owen concluded, "when I compare what then I wrote with my present judgment, I am scarce able to find the least difference between the one and the other; only, a misapplication of names and things by me gives countenance to this charge."[186]

Owen was right to admit that he was being "pressed with more than ordinary occasions of sundry sorts."[187] For one day after signing the preface to the book on schism, he signed the preface to another, on 10 July, a long-awaited revision of his sermons.[188] *Of communion with God* (1657) appeared shortly before Owen ended his term as vice chancellor. The book itself, he claimed in his preface, was based on material that he had preached to undergraduates in St. Mary's, Oxford, in 1651, which he had promised to publish, but which he had subsequently sought to improve.[189] There were certainly good reasons for his delay. The influence of the Independent party had risen and fallen through the mid-1650s, and Owen's public fortunes had risen and fallen accordingly. His colleagues in the Independent party, with others committed to political and theological principle, were now often regarded as a "sorry company of seditious, factious persons."[190] Trinitarian theology had become thoroughly politicized, with the effort to clamp down upon the tiny Socinian party demanding substantial government resources, as well as the large amounts of Owen's time required for the production of such texts as *Vindicae evangelicae* (1655).[191] Owen's new book was an attempt to turn this political effort into pietistic gain.[192] But for all of his efforts, Owen was underappreciated. His salary was too often in arrears, his students and colleagues too often uncooperative, and the court was now turning against him. He had already buried six of his children—John, the first Mary, Elizah, Thomas, and two baby boys. Perhaps providence was also giving him a warning.

Of communion with God lifted Owen's spiritual interests above his responsibility to govern a restless and uneasy university community and to manage its affairs under a government in perennial turmoil. Owen, who had spent the previous few years articulating his own and his government's concern at the spread of Socinian ideas, did something that few of his readers would have expected, and that has puzzled later historians. His move, to radically distinguish the operations of the divine persons, was made in the context of the Socinian advance, and could easily be misconstrued as reflecting Socinian influence.[193] For *Of communion with God* drew upon Owen's massive biblical and theological learning to expand upon the Western Trinitarian consensus by arguing that Christians could and should cultivate distinct relationships with each of the divine persons. But Owen placed this keen theological intervention at the center of the devotional revolution he hoped to lead. He drew upon the famous opening of Calvin's *Institutes* (1559) to reflect upon the character of the theological task: "the sum of all true wisdom and knowledge" could, he argued, "be reduced to these three heads": "the knowledge of God, his nature and his properties," "the knowledge of ourselves in reference to the will of God concerning us," and, he added, "skill to walk in communion with God."[194]

The third emphasis was vital to Owen's project. The scholastic bent of much mid-seventeenth-century preaching and writing was not producing the godliness that Owen believed it should—and he was not uncritical of the theological tradition in which he participated. He identified in his peers a deficient spirituality, an expectation of Christian life that was insufficiently interested in spiritual experience. Of course, he assumed, unregenerate persons, who can think of God as "hard, austere, severe, almost implacable, and fierce," cannot be expected to "abide with God in spiritual meditations," for they "fix their thoughts only on his terrible majesty, severity and greatness; and so their spirits are not endeared."[195] But Owen feared that the situation was not much better among believers. "How few of the saints are experimentally acquainted with this privilege of holding immediate communion with the Father in love," he lamented.[196] Even "saints" were "afraid to have good thoughts of God. They think it a boldness to eye God as good, gracious, tender, kind, loving."[197] He believed that a fuller grasp of divine revelation would change these opinions: "Would a soul continually eye [God's] everlasting tenderness and compassion, his thoughts of kindness that have been from of old, his present gracious acceptance, it could not bear an hour's absence from him; whereas now, perhaps, it cannot watch with him one hour."[198] "Few can carry up their hearts and minds to this height by faith, as to rest their souls in the love of the Father; they live below it, in the troublesome region of hopes and fears, storms and clouds," he argued. But "all here is serene and quiet . . . the love of the Father is the only rest of the soul."[199]

Of course, Owen's focus on the Song of Solomon, and his method of reading the text, was no novelty in Western spirituality.[200] Owen's novelty was rather his insistence that Christians could have communion with the individual persons of the Trinity. Yet recent scholarship on Owen has not noticed the radical quality of this claim—perhaps because much of this scholarship continues to access Owen through the Goold edition (1850–55), and because Goold's edition of the text includes, without explanation or date, Daniel

Burgess's preface to the second edition of the work (1700). Goold's decision to use the Burgess preface is significant—and particularly so in light of the largely ahistorical quality of so much Owen scholarship. This work, which often evacuates Owen of his contexts and fails to consult early modern editions of his work, has, ironically, missed the innovative quality of this aspect of his thinking. Burgess's preface defends Owen from the charge of novelty, reminding his audience that while "this treatise . . . is the only one extant upon its great and necessary subject," the "doctrine of distinct communion with the Divine Persons" was not "new-fangled" or "uncouth."[201] Nevertheless, Burgess seemed to struggle to find earlier examples of its use. He referred to recent work by Lewis Stuckley (1667), who identified himself as a "soul friend," and by the biblical annotator Samuel Clark (1626–1701), in a sermon on 1 John 1:7, which was undated and possibly unpublished, in that it is not recorded in the Short Title Catalogue.[202] The important thing to note is that Burgess defends *Of communion with God* from the charge of novelty by referring the reader to only two texts, at least one of which was published after the first edition of Owen's work. In fact, Burgess missed the opportunity to refer to one of the most immediate and most interesting evidences of Owen's influence upon the Independent party—a poem on the Trinity, recently recovered, republished, and beginning to attract critical interest, *Ter tria* (1658), by the Irish minister Faithful Teate, which resonates with the new Trinitarian perspective.[203]

Owen had likely little time to consider the impact of his writing as he managed the transition between the old chancellor and his replacement. On 29 July, he delivered another vice chancellor's oration, in a private ceremony at Whitehall, on the occasion of the election of Richard Cromwell as the new chancellor. One newsbook reported on the ceremony.[204] Owen, with the "Heads of Houses in their Scarlets, the Proctors, and a great number of Masters of Arts, representing the Body of the University, came hither to the Lodgings of my Lord Richmond, in their Formalities, the Beadles of the University preceding the Vice-Chancellor." The vice chancellor sat down at the upper end of the room, "where a Table was prepared, and a little beneath the Table two Chairs for the Proctors; the Doctors, and the rest of the University sat in ranke upon Chairs provided on each side of the Roome." Owen opened the proceedings with a short speech in Latin to the effect that the Convocation had assembled to "admit the most Illustrious Lord the Lord Richard Cromwell" to be the new chancellor of the university. Richard, who had yet to enter the room, was then awarded an MA. "Which being done, the University Beadles withdrew into another room, and from thence introduced the most noble Lord, Chancelor elect," dressed in scarlet, who sat beside Owen at the upper end of the room.

The Senior Proctor made a speech in Latin "suitable to the present Occasion." He then read the instrument by which Richard was appointed chancellor, by which he was presented with the "Seal of the University, the Book of Statutes, and the Beadles Staves, the Ensigns of Authority."[205] It was at this point that Owen spoke, "declaring the sense of the University concerning the Election of so illustrious a Lord, the place being vacant upon the voluntary resignation of his most Serene Highness the Lord Protector." Richard, who had never attended either university, was admitted to the Oath of the Chancellor, and "in a short Speech" accepted the honor bestowed upon him by the university, "giving them many noble assurances of his high respects towards men of Learning, with promises of performing whatever lieth in his power, as beomes their Chancellor." The participants then attended banquets "in several Rooms."[206] In the oration that followed, Owen praised "the wisest and most gallant of the men whom this age, rich in heroes, has produced . . . a ruler who had the glory of this island and the respect for religion close to his heart."[207] Addressing Richard, Owen returned to the nautical imagery that occurred so frequently in his university speeches: "After years of dark storm it is perhaps through you, Sire, that the University will look upon the light and sight the harbour."[208]

Owen stayed in London for much of that summer. During late July and early August he was engaged in ecclesiastical diplomacy, advocating the cause of the Protestor party, in an attempt to settle the affairs of the Scottish church.[209] Lacking patience with procedures, and frustrated by the opposition, Owen completed a report and had his committee pass resolutions, despite the fact that it did not have a quorum. "As on previous occasions, Owen had blatantly disregarded procedural niceties in order to accomplish a godly objective."[210] Perhaps his lack of patience with administrative process was being noticed. In early September 1657, Henry Cromwell requested that Owen should advise on the reform of the statutes of Trinity College Dublin, but, in October 1657, Richard Cromwell nominated John Conant as the new vice chancellor of Oxford University, without any recognition of Owen's significant achievements in the role.[211] It was not necessarily a slight—Owen's administration had at some point to end—but it would have been another signal of his declining influence and the changing fortunes of the Independent party whose power he had in some senses come to personify.

Owen picked upon the nautical imagery in his final oration, delivered on 9 October 1657. "After being buffeted by so many storms, all but buried by so many troublesome billows, assailed on all sides by the blasts of adverse winds, surely I am allowed to congratulate myself also, as now at last I come into harbour."[212] Owen looked back upon his five years in office. The first two years, he recalled, "we were a mere rabble and a subject of talk to the rabble," but then the circumstances of the university began to be improved.[213] Alongside increasing numbers of graduations of bachelors, masters and doctors,

> professors' salaries, lost for many years, have been maintained and paid; many offices, by no means negligible ones, sustained; the rights and privileges of the University have been defended against some efforts of its enemies; the treasury is tenfold increased; many of every rank in the University have been promoted to various honours and benefices; new exercises have been introduced and established; old ones have been duly performed; reformation of manners has been diligently undertaken in spite of the grumbling of certain profligate brawlers; labours have been numberless; besides submitting to the most enormous expense, often when brought to the brink of death on your account, I have hated the feeble powers of my body, nearly uncapable of keeping pace with my designs.[214]

And yet, despite the hazards of health and finance, Owen allowed himself a moment of satisfaction, recalling that "in my forty-second year I have held not the lowest position in the camp, in the senate and in the University—indeed I hold the highest office that a man of my lot and position can attain in our Commonwealth—and in all things I have conducted myself in such a manner that I am not ashamed or sorry for any of my actions." He concluded this brief immodesty by quoting Horace: "I have lived constantly among the great."[215] Owen seemed happy: "I am returning to my old work, my well-known vigils, my long-delayed studies," to the "peace and quiet . . . which I do not yet seem to have attained."[216] But it was not to be the retirement that he imagined. Owen was slighted: he and Goodwin were replaced by Presbyterian preachers in the weekly sermons at St. Mary's. The two Independents had no intention of being silenced, and moved almost immediately to convene a competing lecture in St. Peter's in the East. In December, a neighbor in this parish noted that Owen "cannot well digest a private life, and seems angry."[217] Owen was coming into his harbor as the political tide had turned.

Perhaps the only good thing about these demotions was that they were giving Owen more time. His thoughts turned toward a manuscript, a textbook on ecclesiology prepared by John Cotton, which he had possesed for the previous seven months, and now wished to see through to publication. The project allowed Owen to develop a polemic against Daniel Cawdrey, who had responded to Owen in *Independency further proved to be a schism* (1658).[218]

Cawdrey had been involved in a parallel debate with John Cotton, whose defenses of Independency Cawdrey had attacked in *Vindiciæ clavium* (1645) and *The inconsistency of the Independent way with Scripture and itself* (1651). The parallel debates were united when Owen attempted to publish Cotton's work. He had Cotton's manuscript printed, and added his own preface, answering Cawdrey's charges. Owen explained, in his preface to the Christian Reader, why the manuscript had not been published previously, even as he defended himself against Cawdrey's claim that Owen was a lapsed Presbyterian.[219] Owen flatly denied that he had defended "their presbyterian way in the year [16]46," and claimed that

> all the ministers almost in the county of Essex know the contrary, one especially, being a man of great ability and moderation of spirit, and for his knowledge in those things not behind any man I know in England of his way, with whom in that year, and the next following, I had sundry conferences at public meetings of ministers as to the several ways of reformation then under proposal.[220]

This may be a reference to Josselin, with whom Owen was in regular contact throughout the late 1640s, as we have seen. Nevertheless, while admitting that "my judgment is not the same, in this particular, as it was fourteen years ago," Owen was also able to argue that what he had been defending in the mid-1640s was something less than the Presbyterian system that had been negotiated by the Westminster Assembly. He had changed his mind, but not in the way that Cawdrey imagined. "My change I here own ... and in my change I have good company," he insisted. "I shall only say, my change was at least twelve years before the 'Petition and Advice,' wherein the parliament of the three nations is come up to my judgment."[221] Owen was arguing that the second Cromwellian constitution—despite its monarchical trappings to which he was so opposed—was putting in place the church settlement he had invented a decade before.

This was an awkward attempt to idealize and identify with the second Cromwellian constitution, which Owen had already subverted in ghostwriting the army officers' petition against the offer of the crown. But some of the regime's more radical critics may have taken at face value this claim to support the religious agenda of the second Protectoral Parliament. On 5 January 1658, the Fifth Monarchist leader Christopher Feake addressed a meeting at All Hallows, condemning the government as being "as Babylonish as ever, and there is as much of Babylon in the civil state, and the lawyers, and the old popish laws, and the clergy-state, as ever. This power and the old monarchie are one and the same; and this army doth as really support popery, and all the reliques of it, as ever king Charles and the archbishop of Canterbury, and the rest of the bishops did." The national church settlement, with its state-sponsored preachers and committees of triers and ejectors, were no better than what they had replaced. "There is John Owen (you know) dean of Christ church, and the rest; and is it not the army, that upholds and maintains all these?" he expostulated "with a most elated voice," an informer recorded, "and a great deal more, that I wrote not, and cannot recollect."[222] Owen was still being associated with the revolutionary regime from which he was becoming estranged.

Owen's worry about the direction of the revolution was expressed in *Of temptation* (Oxford, 1658), which may have been published in June 1658, according to an inscription on the title page of the edition available on EEBO. *Of temptation* reflected upon the "variety of outward providences and dispensations wherewith I have myself been exercised in this world, with the inward trials they have been attended withal," changes of circumstances that had left a "constant sense and impression of the power and danger of temptations upon my mind and spirit."[223] The times were confusing, Owen admitted, "perplexed and entangled," with the "footsteps of God lying in the deep, where his paths are not known," while "unparalleled distresses and strange prosperities are measured out to men, yea, to professors," with "fearful examples of backsliding, such as former ages never knew," and a "visible declension from reformation seizing upon the professing party of these nations, both as to personal holiness and zeal for the interest of Christ."[224] Owen was thinking, at least in part, of recent events at court. In November 1657, the French ambassador had noted a "different spirit" in Whitehall, as Cromwell's youngest daughters were married, "dances having been held there again during these past days, and the preachers of the older times are withdrawing from it."[225] Owen was not amused. "Would any one have thought it possible that such and such professors, in our days, should have fallen into ways of self, of flesh, of the world," he wondered, "to play at cards, dice, revel, dance?"[226] His criticism of the Cromwell family was becoming ever more overt as his influence in court and university continued to decline.

Nuptial dancing was yet another sign of the court's declension. The court had failed, and his own attempts to reform the university, the success of which he had boasted, were being reversed. Owen could look on his career in university administration only with disappointment. "Go to our several colleges," to inquire for godly young men, he suggested. "What is the answer in respect of many? 'Ah! such a one was very hopeful for a season; but he fell into ill company, and he is quite lost. Such a one had some good beginning of religion, we were in great expectation of him; but he is fallen into temptation.' And so in other places."[227] Owen was losing everything in "these days, wherein all things are shaken."[228] And the situation was not likely to improve. Oliver Cromwell was dying, and Owen was slipping back into the experience of defeat.

7

Defeated Revolutionary

OWEN'S POLITICAL ASCENDENCY ended in the summer of 1658.[1] In the months before the death of Oliver Cromwell, Owen's fortunes, together with those of the army radicals and religious Independents with whom he was most closely associated, went into eclipse. The old republicans "lost power and influence rapidly."[2] "These days wherein we live," Owen reflected, presented "manifold, great, and various temptations wherewith all sorts of persons that know the Lord and profess his name are beset," and he hoped that his new study, *Of temptation*, would be "suited to the times that pass over us."[3] He understood that England was changing, and that to the disadvantage of the godly. Owen had declined in the Protector's estimation after becoming identified with the officers' resistance to the offer of the crown. He had no meetings with his patron as Cromwell's illness worsened over the course of the summer. It was not immediately obvious that Cromwell was dying. But as his illness grew more serious, senior administrators worried about how best to plan for his succession. Owen and his allies in the army were not included in these discussions, and, in the uncertain political maneuverings of the late summer, their tactics grew "necessarily defensive."[4] That defensiveness was made all the more necessary when it became obvious that Richard Cromwell would lead the new administration, and that his policy would favor the Presbyterian party. Owen, who had already been replaced by John Conant as vice chancellor of the university, was in March 1660 replaced by Edward Reynolds as dean of Christ Church, in a move that symbolized the reversal of the Independents' ascendency over Oxford. In the months before the end of his academic career, he found a new position, returning to clerical life as pastor of a gathered church of discontented army officers based in Wallingford House, Charles Fleetwood's home in London. These activities provide one of the few evidences from the 1650s of his being involved in a congregation, but the fellowship would be known more for its political interventions than for its spiritual attainments, and would be blamed for the eventual downfall of Richard's administration. It was from their base in Wallingford House, after all, that the army grandees made their final gambit for a change of government without any anticipation of the political catastrophe to which their actions would lead. As London descended into chaos, as Monck and his army marched south, Owen engaged in a desperate attempt to dissuade his former colleague and fellow Independent from recalling the Parliament that would restore Presbyterian political fortunes, and, it became increasingly clear, the king.

As this last gamble failed, as public order collapsed, and as events moved apparently inexorably toward the restoration of the monarchy, Owen found it difficult to negotiate the vagaries of politics. He was suddenly returned to private life, living quietly through the dangerous days of Presbyterian ascendancy, constitutional restoration, and royalist revenge, and, like many of his former colleagues, surviving by strategies of evasion and misdirection. Like other erstwhile radicals, including his former Christ Church colleague Henry Stubbe, Owen would deny that he had played any significant role in the events of the civil wars, and would proclaim his loyalty to the new king, even as some of those with whom he had been closely identified fled into an uncertain and often dangerous exile. But, even as the government may have offered him episcopal preferment within the restored church, it knew better than to take at face value his protestations of loyalty.[5] In the last months of the republic, Owen bought the second-largest house in Stadhampton. This return to the tiny village in which he had spent his childhood, where his sister Hester lived as wife of the parish minister, John Hartcliffe, and where Owen's daughters could grow up near their cousins, provided the meeting place for a new gathered congregation with a membership that included some of the university's undergraduates, including the young William Penn. But this new church was also suspected of sedition—a suspicion that was not entirely without warrant.[6] In the immediate aftermath of Restoration, Owen may have hoped that a national church settlement along Presbyterian lines would have permitted Independents to engage in public worship, and was perhaps encouraged by the general pardon issued on 24 June 1660. But his hopes and those of the Presbyterians were dashed in August 1662 by the Act of Uniformity and the ejection of two thousand clergy and educators, including his brother-in-law, who had already been suspended for his nonconformity.[7] The triumph of the Presbyterians had been short-lived. Reynolds was again ejected from Oxford as the Cavalier Parliament defined the restored government's attitude to dissent. Like many of his friends and former enemies, Owen returned to the familiar experience of defeat, defending the republic while denying his role in its administration, refining the reformation as England was scheming around him.

I

Cromwell died, famously, on 3 September 1658, on the anniversary of two of his most significant victories at Dunbar (1650) and Worcester (1651). These victories had been won during the period of his closest relationship to Owen. This relationship had moved from the ambiguity of Owen's contribution to *Musarum Oxoniensium* (1654) to the concerns about the diretion of the revolution that were reflected in his association with known republicans in the first Protectoral Parliament. Owen's membership in this Parliament had marked the highpoint of his influence, but he had been ejected from the Commons, perhaps overplaying his hand in so evidently grasping for power. Owen's relationship with Cromwell deterioriated as his political influence declined. The ambiguity of this relationship gave way to Owen's expression of concern, as reflected in the officers' petition against the offer of the crown, and overt criticism, in his final university orations.

Owen did not see his friend and patron in the months before his death. They had gradually become estranged after Owen had supported the officers' protest against the offer of the crown, and Thomas Goodwin had come to take Owen's place as the Protector's spiritual advisor. Owen's loss of status became ever more important in the days following Richard's sudden and, perhaps, unexpected accession. For Richard had been named as successor only three days before his father's death.[8] "Never in English history," Ron Hutton suggested, "has any person approached supreme power with such little practical preparation."[9] His inexperience was to create the vaccuum that the old republicans would seek to exploit. And, "in spite of his avowed desire to keep away from the politics of Richard's Protectorate, Owen became involved with the officers as well as the ministers."[10] These groups combined with results that those who acted to defend the "good old cause" would find disastrous.

In the uncertainty of the late summer of 1658, however, Owen's most immediate concerns were theological. He continued to be the subject of polemical dispute. Thomas Long's *An exercitation concerning the frequent use of our Lords Prayer in the publick worship of God and a view of what hath been said by Mr. Owen concerning that subject* (1658) combined religious with political protest in its complaint that Owen had ejected from the "Sanctuary" this "king of Prayers."[11] Owen did not reply. Now without the luxury of time, he picked his battles carefully, and, as the national political crisis deepened, and his own position became increasingly ambiguous, he moved to defend the most foundational of Protestant doctrines—the sufficiency of Scripture and the reliability of its extant texts. Owen's decision to publish what he described as "several small and hurriedly got-together pieces" in the first few months of an unstable new regime indicates his sense of the theological principles at stake as the national political crisis deepened.[12] These texts significantly advanced Owen's existing critique of the state, arguing that the English republic was failing because it had already betrayed its theological foundations. In the late summer and autumn of 1658, Owen's work on Scripture provided a focus for his concerns about the direction of a republic in turmoil.

The three publications that Owen signed "from my study" on 22 September 1658 were published in November by Henry Hall, the university printer, in a single volume. *Of the divine originall, authority, self-evidencing light, and power of the Scriptures* was accompanied by *A vindication of the purity and integrity of the Hebrew and Greek texts* with some additional "exercitations about the Nature and Perfection of the Scripture, the Right of Interpretation, internall Light, Revelation, &c."[13] These short texts addressed some of the most foundational debates in early modern theology, including the inspiration of Scripture, the emerging science of text criticism, and the accuracy of its English translations, while allowing Owen to map the dogmatic foundations of Protestant scholaticism onto the landscape of contemporary English politics. The doctrine of Scripture had, by the mid-seventeenth century, become a central theme in Protestant scholastic thought.[14] In the mid-1640s, for example, the members of the Westminster Assembly had found the locus of authority not in a duly approved English translation but in the commonly received texts of the Old Testament in Hebrew and the New Testament in Greek, which, they claimed, had been "immediately inspired by God, and, by his singular care and providence, kept pure in all ages," being "authentical; so as, in all controversies of religion, the Church is finally to appeal unto them" (WCF 1:8). Their confidence in Scripture was widely shared, and the qualities that the Westminster divines attributed to the Hebrew and Greek originals were commonly transferred to the English translations. This confidence in the reliability of the manuscripts and their translations explains the mid-century fashion to provide vernacular readers with means toward a searchable sacred text. Throughout the 1640s and 1650s, publishers vied to produce all manner of helps for popular Bible reading, from devotional commentaries and guides to complete the reading of Scripture in one year to scholarly apparatus that offered detailed discussions of textual variants.[15] Owen was heavily involved in this project of biblical science. In 1652, as we have seen, he had been appointed to a committee that was charged with providing quality assurance for new editions of Scripture, though it is not clear how often and to what effect this committee met. His work was appreciated by others who were involved in designing search engines for special revelation. In 1655, for example, Robert Wickens, an old Christ Church student, published *A compleat & perfect concordance of the English Bible composed after a new, and most compendious method, whereby may be readily found any place of canonicall Scripture*, an extraordinary work of textual interrogation, which he had dedicated to Owen as the dean of his *alma mater*. But the emerging "science of order," to which Wickens's concordance was an eminent contribution, also served to enumerate disturbing variants in the sacred text.[16] Bibles were everywhere: around one million copies of Scripture had been published in England before 1640.[17] But for all of this ubiquity, Bible readers were becoming increasingly concerned about the quality and reliability of their English translations, and a growing body of scholarly writing addressed—and sometimes justified—their fears. In 1650, for example, the *Humble proposals concerning the printing of the Bible* proposed that "a fair Copie of the last Translation of the BIBLE, ingrossed either in Parchment or Vellam, in a full Character," and with its accuracy checked by a committee of clergy, should be kept in Sion College, London, "that so all people, upon any doubt, may have recours to the Original, to prove whether their Printed Copies varie, or not."[18] The proposal encoded popular assumptions about the status of the King James translation as an authoritative "original" as much as it reflected older scholarly assumptions about the preferential value of manuscript in an age of unreliable print. Most fundamentally, of course, the proposal highlighted how widespread were doubts about the quality of available printed Bibles.

These doubts about textual accuracy were in some ways a reflection of economic turbulence among London printers. In 1644, the King's Printer, a congomerlate of firms that possessed the monopolopy for the production of Bibles, ceased their publication of Bibles. As the availability of Bibles decreased, so prices began to rise. But the demand for budget editions continued, and was met by Dutch entrepreneurs, whose texts, their critics complained, were "notoriously false, and erroneous."[19] The Bible was too important a book to be sold in poor editions. In the mid-1640s, the divines of the Westminster Assembly took their concerns about the quality of printed Bibles to members of the London book trade, and discovered that the members of the Company of Stationers could not produce an accurate edition of the Bible at a price at which it would be likely to sell.[20] Some entrepreneurs believed that the problems could be resolved, and, when William Bentley began to publish Bibles in accurate editions, prices dropped again. In the summer of 1649, for example, Ralph Josselin purchased a new Bible for one of his children, and noted in his diary that the prices of Bibles had become "very cheape," even outside the capital.[21] But, in 1656, Henry Hills and John Field, Bentley's rivals in trade, obtained a new monopoly on Bible production, driving prices up and his thriving business to failure.[22] Bentley's complaint against the actions of Hills and Field was framed in terms of their insult to Scripture itself, for, he claimed, the copies produced on their presses were of markedly poorer quality than his own Bibles, and contained "many hundreds of . . . dangerous, and pernicious faults and errours," a number of which he listed on a broadside, published in 1656, some of which, he feared, could drive unwary common readers to licentiousness.[23] But even those who read from superior editions of Scripture could not escape this crisis of spiritual confidence. For, as a growing body of literature argued, the problem could be traced back to the original language manuscripts, the scale of which was highlighted in the title of J. T.'s *The reconciler of the Bible* (1655), which attempted to resolve "above two thousand seeming contradictions throughout the Old and New Testament," as the subtitle noted. Improved editions would only underscore the problem—for special revelation, it was feared, was beset with contradictions.

These popular-level concerns about the reliability of Scripture were shared by many scholars. Sometime in 1652, as Parliament sought to limit the production and publication of new and improved translations, Owen had been appointed to a committee of theologians and biblical scholars, not to approve a new and handwritten authoritative fair copy of the Authorised Version, as the authors of *Humble proposals concerning the printing of the Bible* may have hoped, but to assess the quality of some recent translations of Scripture and to approve them for publication.[24] In appointing this committee, Parliament's concerns anticipated those of such scholars as John Biddle, who provided an extraordinary list of textual variants in the copies of the Septuagint in his *In sacra Biblia Graeca ex versione LXX. interpretum scholia simul et interpretum caeterorum lectiones variants* (1653), in an intervention that may have highlighted the links between the new science of text criticism and the unorthodox theology with which he was increasingly associated, while Jean d'Espagne did something similar for English and French translations in his *Shibboleth* (1655). A flood of publications bore witness to the fact that Parliament's efforts had come too late to reassure readers of the quality of their Bibles.[25]

But, from Owen's perspective, the government's concern to support the quality of English Bibles was not convincing. The Council of State was also backing a new project that, in the minds of many conservative Protestants, undercut foundational assumptions about the nature of special revelation. This project was the London Polyglot (1653–57), a nine-language and multivolume text that proved to be the "greatest and last" of the European polyglots and, in printing each of its Bibles on the same page, a "triumph of technology," which has become widely regarded as the most significant product of Cromwellian literary culture.[26] Ironically, the roots of the project were deep in the Laudian past. Brian Walton had developed the idea for the polyglot under the patronage of William Laud, the former archbishop of Canterbury, whose execution in 1645 left the project without substantial ecclesiastical or political support. Walton revived the project in the summer of 1652, around the same time that MPs appointed Owen and his committee to ensure the quality of English Bibles, with support from the Council of State, John Selden, and James Ussher, respectively England's most eminent Hebraist and the archbishop of Armagh, who lent their support to *A brief description of an edition of the Bible* (1652), a prospectus advertising the project. Walton had hoped to produce the text for one-fifth of the price of its closest rival, the Paris Polyglot.[27] For cost was certainly an issue. The French text had bankrupted its publisher, and it was essential that Walton should develop his project on a more secure financial footing. His achievement in funding its publication through subscriptions was both a remarkable evidence of market demand for an edition of Scripture with this level of philological and hermeneutical sophistication and of public support for a volume that formally challenged prevailing assumptions about the fixity of biblical texts. Walton raised £4,000 for the project in its first year, with the Council of State pledging £1,000 and exempting its paper from duty.[28]

The project, which dramatized Walton's theological politics, was certainly controversial. With a generation of other conservative writers, he "saw Europe's civil wars of religion as fuelled by ignorance, sometimes actively abetted by obscurantism," and believed that misinterpretation of Scripture and misunderstanding of its textual character were at the root of contemporary political evils.[29] His project attempted to explode the notion of a single authoritative text by creating a work of extraordinary sophistication, which would simultaneously advertise a sphere of legitimate difference between the competing manuscript traditions and confirm that the textual plurality of sacred Scripture could be resolved by established churches. In one important sense, therefore, the London Polyglot was an exercise in polemical ecclesiology—a project in which the authority of the church would be established as that which would validate or make canonical the plural, sometimes differing, but often equally useful texts of Scripture. This conclusion challenged foundational assumptions that Scripture had to exist in the singular. But it also reversed the consensus of the Reformed churches, which insisted that Scripture gave authority to the church, against the Roman Catholic claim that the church gave authority to Scripture, and so, in the mind of its critics, nourished the revival of medieval theology that Owen and his fellow Calvinists had found so offensive in the Arminian turn of the 1630s. Walton's supplementing the project with two volumes of philological and text-critical commentary could not disguise its profound political and ecclesiological commitments.

Of course, Walton's contribution was extraordinary. The London Polyglot was published alongside similar if not comparable projects, such as Abraham Wheelocke's *Quatuor evangeliorum domini nostri Jesu Christi versio Persica Syriacam & Arabicam suavissimè redolens: ad verba & mentem Graeci textus sideliter & venustè concinnata* (1657), but it rose above the competition to remain a definitive text until its last republication in the early nineteenth century. Its political emphases could not be ignored: the London Polyglot exhibited the variety of multiple and differing texts of Scripture, and assumed that these could be established as credible and canonical only by the authority of the church. Owen feared that sensitive readers of the Polyglot would therefore be faced with a choice between high views of the church, tending to Roman Catholicism, or low views of special revelation, leading to atheism.[30] And he believed that some conscientious Bible readers were already on the horns of this dilemma. He admitted that he had been "affrighted . . . by a little treatise little sent me . . . by my worthy and learned friend Dr Ward," the Savilian professor of astronomy at Oxford. This anonymous text, *Fides divina* (1657), had considered "some principles of this nature," and reprinted the "unwary expressions of some learned men amongst us"—whose names included John Goodwin, Daniel Featley, and Richard Baxter—in order to "eject and cast out as useless the whole Scripture or Word of God."[31] Owen read this book after he had completed the three tracts, but his worst fears were confirmed by the careless utterances of his usual suspects.[32] As the future of the republic grew ever less secure, Brian Walton's Polyglot Bible was pushing beyond breaking point the Protestant doctrine of Scripture. But Owen had waited until the death of the Protector, and the political crisis that followed, to issue his warning about a text-critical project that represented foundational errors in the religious policy of the government.

II

The London Polyglot provided the crucial context for each of the texts published by Owen in the immediate aftermath of the death of Oliver Cromwell and the inauguration of the new regime, for it dramatized his fear that the challenge to the textual reliability and theological infallibility of every "jot and tittle" in Scripture had political as well as religious conseqences. Owen was not opposed in principle to text-critical work. While he accepted as canonical the famously controversial Johannine comma (1 John 5:7–8), he also recognized that gospel writers rearranged their pericopes to make particular theological points, that they reported dominical speeches in different ways, and that inspired writers could use specific Greek terms "improperly."[33] In his response to Walton's project, Owen dismissed the objections of biblical expositors who "understood nothing but Latin," and admitted that "the excellent use of this study . . . cannot be easily expressed." But "the best things are apt to be most abused," he admitted, and "so in particular it hath fallen out with this kind of learning."[34] It was in these terms that Owen addressed Walton's claims and assumptions about the reliability of biblical manuscripts in *Of the divine originall* (1658).[35] This was a focused intervention, which responded principally to Walton's argument that vowel points were a late addition to the Hebrew texts—and therefore that the unpointed texts that were read in Jewish worship over hundreds of years permitted an interpretive latitude than was broader than that recognized by Owen and his conservative colleagues. Owen, as might be expected, insisted that the origins of the vowel points were inspired and that the readings they provided were authentic. The promise as to the reliability of every "jot and tittle" (Matthew 5:18) of the Hebrew vowels had, after all, been made by Jesus Christ, even if it had been undermined by the Council of State.

Owen, who lamented that the text-critical project had "now broken forth among Protestants," had no doubt about the significance of Walton's presuppositions.[36] "Of all the inventions of Satan to draw off the minds of men from the Word of God, this of decrying the authority of the originals seems to me the most pernicious," he explained, for the "whole authority of Scripture in itself depends solely on its divine original."[37] He described Walton's project as printing "the original itself," and then defaming it by "gathering up translations of all sorts, and setting them up in competition with it." Alluding to Isaiah 14:29 and 30:6, Owen argued that Walton's project brought to a conclusion Catholic attempts to undermine the credibility of Scripture: "When Ximenes put forth the Complutensian Bible, Vatablus his, and Arias Montanus those of the king of Spain, this cockatrice was not hatched, whose fruit is now growing to a fiery flying serpent."[38]

It may have been problematic that Owen completed this work before he had actually seen a copy of Walton's edition. Consequently, in citing James Ussher in a long list of Protestant text critics that also included "Beza, Camerarius, Scaliger, Causabon, Drusius, Gomarus . . . Grotius, Heinsius, Fuller, Dieu, Mede, Cameron, Glassius, Cappellus, Amama, with innumerable others," Owen may not have realized that he was referring to one of the project's best-placed supporters.[39] "I have often heard the great Ussher expressing his fear" of what the text-critical project "might yet grow unto," Owen explained, though unhelpfully, he did not explain the circumstances of these conversations.[40] We might assume that the royalist celebrity preacher, who spoke regularly in Lincoln's Inn, London, from 1647 until 1655, was not likely a regular conversation partner for a leading republican divine. But Ussher certainly knew Owen's work, though he left unmarked his copy of *Salus electorum, sanguis Jesu*, and, Locke noted, he had visited Oxford in the summer of 1655.[41] Owen's hints that he had discussed text criticism with the archbishop of Armagh should be read alongside his hopes that there would soon be published lectures on text criticism by his "learned" colleague Grotius—against whom Owen had fulminated in *A review of the Annotations of Hugo Grotius, in reference unto the doctrine of the deity, and satisfaction of Christ* (1656).[42] It may be that his references to the "useful and learned" notes on text criticism prepared by "the learned Mr Pococke" should be taken in a similar way.[43] Although Owen did appreciate the quality of Pococke's scholarship, and had earlier defended the eminent Hebraist from over-zealous ejectors, this appropriation of the reputation of a third theologian with royalist sympathies and links to the University of Oxford perhaps tells us less about Owen's social set than it does about his sense of the best way to respond to Walton's theological politics. His reference to corresponding with Seth Ward about *Fides divina* performed a similar function. Owen was invoking the reputations of the most eminent royalist biblical scholars in an effort to present a united front of famous academics that would intellectually dwarf the relatively unknown editors of the London Polyglot. He may not have realized that some of the colleagues whose names he cited had been among the project's supporters.

Of the divine originall began with a brief survey of the methods of inspiration recorded in Scripture. Owen explained that the human authors of Scripture "were not themselves enabled, by any habitual light, knowledge, or conviction of truth, to declare his mind and will, but only acted as they were immediately moved" by God.[44] They spoke and wrote "no more at their own disposal than the pen is in the hand of an expert writer," and "were but as an instrument of music, giving a sound according to the hand, intention, and skill of him that strikes it."[45] Owen's theory of inspiration as dictation, which assumed that the penmen "took in and gave out without any alteration of one tittle or syllable," was widely supported among Protestant scholastic theologians in the period.[46] The doctrine allowed Owen to claim that "not only the doctrine they taught was the words of truth . . . but the words whereby they taught it were words of truth from God himself," and that it is "required of us, by God himself . . . that we receive the Scriptures not as we do other books . . . but with a divine and supernatural faith."[47] For "without the contribution of help or assistance from tradition, church, or any thing else without themselves," and "upon the penalty of eternal damnation," we are "obliged" to "receive them, with that subjection of soul which is due to the word of God."[48] It was a theory he was later to modify, in *Πνευματολογια, or, A discourse concerning the Holy Spirit* (1674), but it worked to emphasize the divine quality of the inspired text.[49]

Despite the strength of his arguments, Owen recognized that his theory of inspiration as dictation resolved some problems, even as it created others. For, he admitted, whatever the qualities of the originals, although the extant text did remain infallible, it had not remained inerrant. His claims about the qualities of the autographs were claims about texts that almost certainly no longer existed—and which could not be identified if they did. Owen's repsonse to this problem echoed that of Samuel Rutherford, whose work he had earlier commended, in maintaining a theory that the providential preservation of divine revelation was especially focused on those parts of Scripture that were of utmost importance:[50]

> There is no doubt but that in copies we now enjoy of the Old Testament there are some diverse readings. . . . But yet we affirm, that the whole Word of God, in every letter and tittle, as given from him by inspiration, is preserved without corruption. Where there is any variety it is always in things of less, indeed of no, importance. God by his providence preserving the whole entire, suffered this lesser variety to fall out, in or among the copies we have, for the quickening and exercising of our diligence in our search into his Word.[51]

Owen's statement advanced competing arguments—both that the Word of God had been "preserved without corruption" and that the varieties in its extant texts are "in things of less, indeed of no, importance," which have also been preserved for our good. The errors had been introduced to help readers pay attention. Nevertheless, Owen believed, God had not appointed his word to be inscripturated "that so he might destroy its authority."[52] And its authority was guaranteed at the highest level—in other words, by the Bible itself. Individuals would be convinced of the authority of Scripture not by any external authority, or by extraordinary revelation, but by the testimony of the Holy Spirit speaking in Scripture itself:

> When, then, we resolve our faith into the testimony of the Holy Ghost, it is not any private whisper, word, or voice, given to individual persons; it is not the secret and effectual persuasion of the truth of the Scriptures that falls upon the minds of some men, from various

> involved considerations of education, tradition, and the like, whereof they can give no particular account; it is not the effectual work of the Holy Ghost upon the minds and wills of men, enabling them savingly to believe, that is intended; (the Papists, for the most part, pleading about these things, do but show their ignorance and malice;) but it is the public testimony of the Holy Ghost given unto all, of the Word, by and in the Word, and its own divine light, efficacy, and power.[53]

By its very nature, God's word did not need validation by the church. A human organization could never authenticate divine revelation. Anticipating themes that he would develop in *Θεολογουμενα παντοδαπα* (1661), Owen argued that instead of tradition bearing witness to the reliability of Scripture, Scripture bore witness to the unreliability of tradition:

> before the committing of the Scriptures to writing, God had given the world an experiment what keepers men were of this revelation by tradition. Within some hundreds of years after the flood, all knowledge of him, through the craft of Satan and the vanity of the minds of men, which is unspeakable, was so lost, that nothing but as it were the creation of a new world, or the erection of a new church-state by new revelations, could relieve it. After that great trial, what can be further pretended on the behalf of tradition, I know not.[54]

Of course, many Christians did continue to assume that tradition authenticated Scripture. But Owen argued that this could not be the case for Protestants, who, after all, rejected a large number of books in the Roman Catholic canon, a fact which dismayed the common argument that Protestants had simply received the Bible from the medieval church. Nor should the locus of authority be found in extra-biblical evidences. For "evidences" could only be matters of probability, Owen judged, and belief in the inspiration of Scripture was instead a matter of faith.[55] Rather than pointing to evidences, Owen rested his argument about the authority of Scripture on the testimony of the Spirit in Scripture itself—an argument about religious authority that was necessarily and unabashedly circular.

Owen juxtaposed to this study *A vindication of the Hebrew and Greek texts* (1658). This second volume responded specifically to the Prolegomena and Appendix of the London Polylot, and adopted a much more careful tone in dealing with Walton and his associates, not least because Owen had actually now seen the work he was controverting. He described the editors of the Polyglot as "persons of singular worth," and acknowledged the "great usefulness of this work, and am thankful for it," but admitted to having been "somewhat startled with that bulky collection of various readings which the appendix tenders to the view of every one that doth but cast an eye upon it," reiterating his concern that the editors were amending the authentic text on the basis of nothing more than conjecture.[56] Referring once again to his dependence upon Pococke's "excellent Miscellanies" on text-critical problems—which were never to be published—Owen admitted that he had little knowledge of either the subject under dispute or, indeed, of Walton himself:[57]

> I neither profess any deep skill in the learning used in that work, nor am ever like to be engaged in any thing that should be set up in competition with it, nor did I ever know that there was such a person in the world as the chief author of this edition of the Bible but by it. I shall, then, never fail, on all just occasions, to commend the usefulness of this work, and the learning, diligence, and pains, of the worthy persons that have brought it forth.[58]

But Owen also complained of the project's lack of an explicit statement of editorial principles. He worried that Walton and his associates had indicated "no choice made nor judgment used in discerning which may indeed be called various lections," but had "equally given out" whatever differences they had found "in any copies, printed or written. . . . Hence many differences that had been formerly rejected by learned men for open corruptions are here tendered us again."[59] After all, Owen properly considered, "it is not every variety or difference in a copy that should presently be cried up for a various reading."[60] Nor was there any need for anyone to publish a project of this kind, as a canonical text had already been established: sidestepping the debate about the quality of Bible printing, he assured his unlearned readers that the "vulgar copy we use" should "pass for the standard," for it provided a translation of the text which, upon the "invention of printing," had been "in actual authority throughout the world," and had since been in the "public possession of many generations." A critical text was less important than a canonical text, Owen was arguing, and so, if the admirers of Walton's edition compared their ordinary English Bibles to his polyglot, they would, "God assisting, quickly see how little reason there is to pretend such varieties of readings as we are now surprised withal."[61] But Owen did not consider how, if Scripture is self-attesting, why the competing manuscripts that claimed its mantle could not be so as well.

Owen worried that Walton's extraordinary scholarly achievements might have public impact of entirely the wrong sort. Fearing that the appendix, with its detailed linguistic and text-critical apparatus, might provide "some unconquerable objections against the truth of what I had asserted," he prepared some additional material on the subject of the "providence of God in the preservation of the original copies of the Scripture."[62] Again, he admitted that errors had been introduced into the texts during the process of transmission, but he no longer considered them to be useful to promote the diligence of the reader. Instead, he complained that the Walton edition had published these errors "as a fit weapon put into the hands of men of atheistical minds and principles, such as this age abounds withal, to oppose the whole evidence of truth revealed in the Scripture."[63] Owen was prepared to grant that "some of these things may, without any great prejudice to the truth, be candidly debated amongst learned men," but, he continued, the wide circulation of these textual variants could only be an "engine suited to the destruction of the important truth" of the Protestant doctrine of Scripture.[64] For any admission of errors in the original text of Scripture would undermine the claims of the Protestant Reformation while the threat of Catholicism remained: "We went from Rome under the conduct of the purity of the originals; I wish none have a mind to return thither again under the pretence of their corruption."[65] And worse heresies lay in wait. For arguments about the unreliability of Scripture were providing the "foundation of Mohammedanism ... the only pretence of fanatical anti-scripturists, and the root of much hidden atheism in the world."[66]

Of course, as Owen's reference to "fanatical anti-scripturists" had indicated, the Quakers also challenged the reliability of Scripture, and their objections were the subject of his third tract in response to the crisis, *Pro sacris Scripturis exercitationes adversus fanaticosi* (1658).[67] Owen had presented the content of this tract in a lecture to his students as a response to the "fanaticism" that "seems to be spreading on all sides."[68] While he hoped that his students would pay attention to his arguments, Owen was not hopeful that the Quakers would find them convincing. "Such is their folly and error that they at once reject all of the terminology and methodology which I must here employ, and instead offer no more than a deafening babble of confused sounds ... contradicting and refuting each other."[69] This was also, of course, exactly what the subjects of Owen's tract might have said of his decision to publish in Latin. Again, his argument about the character of Scripture was circular. Rather than pulling back from the arguments that had located the evidence for the authority of Scripture in the text of Scripture itself, Owen insisted upon the point. Describing the Bible as the word of God in terms of its source, its subject matter, and its expression, he argued that "the Scriptures demonstrate ... that they are the infallible

Word of God" by "their own Spiritual light, infused by their divine Author alone."[70]

Owen's argument about the self-authenticating character of Scripture provided rhetorical leverage against the claims of Roman Catholic theologians. These apologists were arguing that

> there should be established one visible, public interpreter [of Scripture], and that interpreter should be an infallible one. So they proceed to claim their own church as the one, perfect, independent, visible judge and expositor for all of mankind . . . God was (they say) not unaware of the many difficulties which would arise about the faith of the Church, and so wisely erected this ecclesiastical authority to be the sole arbiter and unfailing judge of all.[71]

Owen frankly admitted the plausibility of the solution—but wondered whether the problem actually existed. "Now, if the situation were really anything like that, all controversy would at once be at an end. . . . If the Sacred Scripture . . . was really itself constantly in need of infallible interpretation, then the best solution would be to have a man or a party vested with sovereign authority to fix its meaning."[72] But, he continued, Protestant theologians held to "two essential points" on this question. First, he explained, "the only unique, public, authentic, and infallible interpreter of Scripture is none other than the Author of Scripture Himself," and that his guidance as to the proper understanding of the Word came "partly through the express words of Scripture and partly by the revelation of God's will contained in the wider context, so that which seems to have been more obscurely spoken may be illuminated by what is plainer until an overall understanding of the divine will is gained."[73] Second, "every person, however private, is called to a knowledge of God as revealed in the Bible, and so it is the duty of all to learn and investigate, to expound and declare, as he is enabled, the mind and will of God in the Scriptures."[74]

But Owen's third tract reflected his specific interest in addressing contexts within the university—and this likely for the benefit of the undergraduates for whom it was first prepared. Consequently, it was less interested in presenting a united front of Oxford academics. Owen, who had praised Grotius's work on text criticism in the first two tracts in the volume, offered a critique of his arguments in the third.[75] But his principal concern was with the Presbyterian party, which was on the ascendency within the university, and which was taking advantage of the moral panic surrounding the Quakers to attack lay preaching, which the Independents had come to defend. Owen therefore made clear that his objection to the Quakers was not based on any hostility to lay preaching. He reiterated his cautious approval of public preaching by men who were not candidates for the ministry, describing preaching by gifted but unordained men as "no intrusion on the ecclesiastical office instituted by Christ," but a "part of the brotherly ministry also established by Him."[76] After all, he continued, the "Spirit of Christ which equips and enables men to be suitable for the edification of others in the knowledge of God" is "not reserved solely for those who have been solemnly set apart for the ministry in some branch of the Church, after undergoing what is usually termed ordination."[77] And, invoking his Independent ecclesiology, which insisted that ordination was only valid within the congregation in which the ordination had taken place, Owen reminded his listeners that all ministers who preached in congregations other than their own did so as laymen.[78] This argument was, of course, anathema to Presbyterians, who recognized that the status recognized by ordination did extend beyond the boundaries of the local church. But Owen went further, arguing that gifted, preaching laymen could even possess infallibility, for as "the Word duly and legitimately interpreted is still the Word of God," so "all correct exposition may thus be said to share in infallibility, so far as it expounds the infallible word."[79]

These were busy days for Owen. As Walton replied in *The considerator considered* (1659), Owen was worrying about the political future, reading Dante, and working on a commentary on Hebrews, the first volume of which would not be published until 1668.[80] But the political crisis of the late republic reflected a spiritual crisis that was undermining English Protestantism, he believed, by attacking foundational convictions about divine revelation. By sponsoring a flagship text critical project, Cromwellian politicians had propelled English Puritans into a battle for the Bible. The dispute highlighted dangerous variety of opinion: all sides in the discussion agreed that English readers should be provided with access to a reliable biblical text, but they disagreed as to what that text would look like, whether it should contain critical apparatus, and from which characteristic or institution its authority would be derived. The Polyglot Bible was an illustration of Owen's increasing divergence from the religious values of the administration by which he had earlier been appointed to oversee the quality of Bible production. All other theological concerns paled beside this. The Protectorate had sponsored a project that had undermined its own credibility and had mounted a serious assault on Scripture. And Owen's critique of its presuppositions was his most serious interrogation to date of the theological principles that were being promoted by the Cromwellian government.

III

Within weeks of finalizing the text of his three publications, Owen led a mobilization of Independent theologians in a project that sought to take advantage of the political vacuum created during Richard's accession by proposing a national religious settlement more detailed and ambitious that anything they had yet achieved.[81] Since the early 1650s, Oliver Cromwell's strategy had been to construct a broad-based toleration of the godly, but, while this aspiration had been encoded in two written constitutions, he had not been able to provide it with an adequate doctrinal foundation. The confession of faith produced by the Westminster Assembly (1647) had never been provided with legal authority, and since 1652, as we have already noticed, Owen had been a member and leader of several committees tasked with the production of a new confession of faith that would provide an adequate balance between orthodoxy and broad-mindedness, and which could be used to police a national established faith. None of the confessions had been granted legal standing. Although Parliament had not found their efforts satisfactory, the divines had made good progress in establishing a system of triers and ejectors in which men from religious communities that might in other circumstances have denounced each other found sufficient common ground to manage and police clerical appointments within a national church structure. But this was not finally satisfactory to those Independent theologians who were beginning to understand the significance of their claims about the character of a local church. And so, in the autumn of 1658, perhaps believing that they were no longer limited by Cromwell's broadly Reformed consensus, a large number of Independent divines mounted their most ambitious effort to settle the structure of the national church.

Their plans may have been developing through the summer. The process had been initiated on 15 June, when Henry Scobell, the clerk of the House of Commons and secretary to the privy council, invited the elders of the Independent churches in London to meet in the home of George Griffith on 21 June—an invitation that had more than the appearance of an official responsibility.[82] The process may have accelerated in July 1658, in the aftermath of a visit to Oxford by Edward Worth, leader of a movement of conservative ministers in Ireland, who had advertised the merits of the Cork association, a network of Presbyterian and Independent ministers in southwest Ireland.[83] In a letter to Henry Cromwell, Worth reported that the heads of both universities had encouraged him to publish the documents of his association, which had recently appeared in Dublin as *The agreement and resolution of severall ministers in the county of Corke for the ordination of ministers* (1657).[84] It seems likely that Owen would have found Worth's arguments compelling, for they mapped out a means by which ministers of different persuasions could work effectively and without compromise in a robustly confessional context and without the theological reductions that were being proposed by Richard Baxter.[85] It is "almost certain" that Worth's visit was the "stimulating effect" that encouraged the English Independents to attempt a similar experiment.[86] But first they had to agree upon a suitable confession of faith.

It was with a view to designing a new confession of faith that the Independent ministers met at the Savoy, former residence of the bishop of London, during the first few weeks of October 1658.[87] The meeting had been well planned. The theologians set aside the twenty sentences of *A new confession* (1654), and returned to the much longer text produced by the Westminster Assembly, ramping up its terms of faith, and drawing up a separate discussion of church government and inter-church relations, which moved away from the Erastianism of the earlier document.[88] The new statement, *A declaration of the faith and order owned and practised in the Congregational Churches in England; agreed upon and consented unto by their elders and messengers in their meeting at the Savoy, Octob. 12. 1658*, was completed in eleven days, and included a preface that was widely attributed to Owen.[89]

The Savoy Declaration made a number of departures from the text of the Westminster Confession. Some of these revisions reflected theological debates that had occurred in the intervening decade. On the authority of the Bible, for example, the Westminster divines had been prepared to confess that "the supreme judge by which all controversies of religion are to be determined, and all decrees of councils, opinions of ancient writers, doctrines of men, and private spirits, are to be examined, and in whose sentence we are to rest, can be no other but the Holy Spirit speaking in the Scripture" (WCF 1:10). The Independents wanted to strengthen this. Reflecting Owen's recent polemic on the subject, they revised the final clauses of the paragraph to emphasize not "the Holy Spirit speaking in the Scripture" but "the holy Scripture delivered by the Spirit; into which Scripture so delivered, our faith is finally resolved" (Savoy 1:10). Similarly, the Independent ministers' revision of the Westminster divines' statement on the Trinity reflected recent emphases in Owen's preaching. The Savoy declaration added to the Westminster formulation the statement that the "doctrine of the Trinity is the foundation of all our communion with God, and comfortable dependence upon him" (Savoy 2:3). The Savoy Declaration also revised the covenant theology of the earlier statement, introducing the language of the covenant of redemption, an idea that had recently appeared in Owen's writing, into the English confessional tradition (8:1). Savoy 9:1 included much stronger language about double imputation to the

Westminster Confession's discussion of justification: a reference to God's justifying believers by "the obedience and satisfaction of Christ" was replaced by a reference to his doing so by "imputing Christ's active obedience to the whole law, and passive obedience in his death for their whole and sole righteousness." Savoy 9:3 introduced into the Westminster Confession statement a claim that Christ's atonement represented an exact payment for the sins of the elect, rather than an equivalent payment—a technical distinction over which Owen and Baxter had spilled much scholarly ink in the previous decade. And, perhaps in a nod to the challenge posed by the claims of religious experience that were circulated by religious radicals, the Savoy Declaration made the primary ground of assurance of salvation objective, directing believers to consider the "blood and righteousness of Christ revealed in the gospel," before turning their attention to the "inward evidences" of election which the Westminster Confession had earlier pushed into the foreground (Savoy 18:2; WCF 18:2).

The Savoy Declaration also projected more radical politics than those of the Westminster Confession. In terms of public policy, it described the "general equity" of the Mosaic judicial laws (WCF 19:4) as having a continuing "moral use" (Savoy 19:4), adopting a much more robust view of the relevance of the Mosaic law for the English state. It entirely rejected the Westminster Confession's commitment to the state's power to govern the church (WCF 23:3; Savoy 24:3). Similarly, the Independent divines omitted a section of the Westminster Confession that had argued that those who "oppose any lawful power . . . resist the ordinance of God" (WCF 20; Savoy 21). This most significant redaction would perhaps reflect the radicalization of the second civil war, and might also explain the activities in which a large number of these conservative Independents were about to engage. As a confession of faith, the Savoy Declaration advanced a more robust Reformed theology, while reserving the right of revolution.

Owen seemed to have been satisfied with his work at Savoy. His later writing hardly ever referred to the Declaration—perhaps a signal that its value was very much of the moment. Nevertheless, he defended the Declaration from a charge by the Oxford theologian Peter du Moulin that it was internally inconsistent, and later cited the text as evidence of the Reformed orthodoxy of the Independent churches.[90] But Owen's dominance of the discussions at Savoy could not precipitate his political rehabilitation. Tellingly, it was Thomas Goodwin who presented the Declaration to Richard on 14 October 1658, with a protestation of loyalty to the new regime from around one hundred Independent churches. Goodwin represented the Declaration as a worthy culmination to the long process of the writing of doctrinal statements that Oliver

Cromwell had sponsored. But, like these earlier attempts at settling the faith and practice of the national church of the republic, the official adoption of the Savoy Declaration was to be overtaken by events—even as these events were being driven by those who framed it. For the Independents were organizing themselves and refining their reformation as the regime they hoped to influence grew weaker and more fractious.

IV

As an employee of the regime, Owen was obliged to attend the state funeral that followed the death of the Lord Protector. Oliver Cromwell was buried in Westminster Abbey on 23 November 1658. His funeral was one of the most emblematic events of the period. The description of the cortege, by John Prestwich, a hostile observer and fellow of All Soul's, Oxford, recorded Owen as proceeding with the commissioners for the approbation of public preachers, who were mostly Independent clergymen, and just ahead of the secretaries for the Latin and French languages, including John Milton, Andrew Marvell, John Dryden, Samuel Hartlib, and Peter Sterry.[91] The mood was careless, with soldiers smoking and drinking as they marched.[92] Owen had no other public function in the event, and lived quietly through the late autumn and winter.

For all of his political eclipse, Owen was not quite yesterday's man. On 24 January 1659, he was in London, where Locke assumed that he was working to prevent a Presbyterian takeover of the university.[93] Whatever his diplomatic ambitions, he was also preparing to preach to the third Protectoral Parliament, which had convened under Richard on 27 January. His sermon, delivered on 4 February, was published as *The glory and interest of nations* (1659). It was notably shorter than most of Owen's other published sermons, being around one-third of their length: as in his previous published sermon, he appears to have spoken from notes that proved so inadequate in his writing up the text that he was forced to rely upon those of auditors, "that I might not preach one sermon and print another."[94] There appears to have been some controversy as to whether the sermon should be published, and, as Tim Cooper has noted, "despite its title . . . there was very little glory about it."[95] But Owen's delay in publishing may also have been politic, for he was witnessing a change of government, and that in a very ambiguous political context, and may have remembered his concern in his regicide sermon not too fully to commit himself to a new regime with an uncertain future. He was certainly quick to conceal the revolutionary impulses that he and other ministers had encoded in the Savoy Declaration just three months before: "there is not any thing—, from the beginning to the ending of this short discourse, that doth really interfere with any form of civil government in the world, administered according to righteousness and equity,—as there is not in the gospel of Christ, or in any of the concernments of it."[96] Owen deployed some rhetorical sleight of hand in claiming that the gospel had no political implications, a claim that was challenged by every sermon he had preached to the Long Parliament, the Rump, and the second Protectoral Parliament, and there was more than a hint of warning to the new assembly in his recollection that "the inhabitants of the earth generally owe all their disturbance, sorrow, and blood to the wise contrivance of a few men" who would not "take the law of their proceedings from the mouth of God," but laid "their deep counsels and politic contrivances in a subserviency to their lusts and ambition."[97] Perhaps remembering the pomp and circumstance of the recent funeral of the Protector, he considered that the "glittering shows of their wealth and riches," the "state and magnificence of their governments," and the "beauty of their laws and order (as they relate to their persons)," are, "in the eye of God, a filthy and an abominable thing,—a thing that his soul loatheth."[98] While Owen may have been employing a republican aesthetic to critique the formalities of the revolutionary regime, he may not have been wise to observe that the "application" of his sermon was "easy unto this assembly"—especially as his students observed that he was gaining his own reputation for vanity.[99] Other well-placed observers were keeping a close eye on his activities: Jerome Sankey, who was informing on Owen for Henry Cromwell, reported that he had preached "very seriously."[100]

Sankey was correct: Owen did consider the situation to be extremely serious.[101] He returned to Oxford, briefly, before getting permission on 26 February for an extended absence from his college. Returning to London, he "gathered a church in the Independent way," as Arthur Annesley informed Henry Cromwell in March 1659, which included among its first members such old republicans as Charles Fleetwood, John Desborough, Colonel Sydenham, James Berry, and William Goffe. There were widespread suspicions as to the new congregation's intentions. For, Annesley continued, Owen's actions in gathering the church had "diverse constructions put upon it and is not, that I can heare, very well liked at Whitehall."[102] Rejecting the "glittering shows" of late Cromwellian politics as that which God considered "filthy" and "abominable," and abandoning the older confessional obligation to support "any lawful power" as "the ordinance of God," Owen was leading his new congregation and the broader community of Independents on a collision course with Richard's government. Gathering his new church in the first week of March in Charles Fleetwood's home in Whitehall, Wallingford House, Owen may have realized how oppositional would be his relationship to the new government.[103] Moving toward Presbyterian forms and visions of religious uniformity, the new Parliament set about its policy of undoing what Owen and his colleagues considered to be the gains of the revolution. "The Independent officers at Wallingford House seemed to be the only saints in England with both the will and the power to prevent such a disaster."[104]

And they did their best to do so. In a rapid and often confusing sequence of events, the army leaders associated with the Wallingford House congregation responded to Richard's support for the Westminster Assembly's documents and the parish-based model of social and religious control to effect a significant change in direction for the revolution.[105] They overthrew the third Protectoral Parliament on 23 April, reinstated the Rump on 6 May, and secured the resignation of the Protector on 25 May.[106]

Owen's response to the coup was literary as much as political. For on 28 May there was published *The throne of David*, a commentary on 2 Samuel by William Guild (1586–1657), a moderate minister of the Church of Scotland who had been provost of King's College, Aberdeen, before being deprived by the Cromwellian authorities in 1651.[107] In his brief preface, Owen noted that the manuscript had been sent to him about a year previously, shortly before its author's death. He had valued the text, appreciating its "handling a subject of great and delightful variety, with a choice mixture of spirituall, morall and politicall observations," and arranged for its publication in Oxford.[108] Unusually, the text of the commentary was prefaced by a two-page appeal for charitable funding by supporters of a new plan for godly community. Referring to examples of good practice from central Europe, the two donors suggested that members of the godly should develop an experiment in self-sufficient living in "one Household government or little Common-wealth" that could support the deserving poor and their neighbors, almost exactly the model of communal living which would provide for the security of Owen's community after the Restoration.[109] Some readers may have been most concerned to understand how the commentary inflected Owen's sense of the political crisis. Guild's discussion of the civil war that followed the accession of David's son, Absolom, certainly lent itself to contemporary political application, but the recommendation of communal living was to become the better reflection of the future situation of the Independents.

Guild's book was a signal of the ambition of the new regime. Led by the Wallingford House officers, it would work to unwind the pragmatic efforts at reconciliation that had been attempted under the Protectorate, and attempt to "revive the constitutional forms of the Commonwealth."[110] The old republicans reinstated the Rump Parliament, but rapidly lost control of the capital—and the country. The London crowds witnessed a chaotic succession of new forms of government—"the army and the Rump, the army without the Rump, and the

Rump without the army"—before radicals pushed the city in the direction of political autonomy and into the vortex of renewed revolution and a third civil war.[111] The chaos engulfed Christ Church, Locke observed, where students "accosted the Cannons with 3 sheets of proposalls very materiall and such as it is supposed had but an ill relish." "A comment on these times is . . . dangerous . . . and therefor fitt for nothing but the fire," Locke observed, in a letter in July 1659.[112] The national situation was almost inexplicable.

Royalists took advantage of the turmoil to advance their own cause. On 1 August, Sir George Booth seized Chester in an effort to begin a national royalist rising. Yet the literature of the rising played down explicitly royalist themes and couched its strategic aims in terms that resonated among many of those who had been affected by the recent downturn in trade. The strategy was successful. London Presbyterians such as Zachary Crofton supported the rising, and others read Booth's proclamation from their pulpits, seeing in the possibility of a royalist revival the means for the suppression of a full-scale assault on orthodoxy, which they believed would accompany the army's unrestricted political power.[113] Booth's actions caused widespread panic. Oxford was again occupied by troops as royalist conspirators became active in colleges—and Owen, despite his best efforts, found himself unable to raise another troop of horse for the defense of the city.[114] He continued to press for the settlement of the issue of the Irish lands he had been granted in lieu of his Colchester pension.[115] At the beginning of September, Owen and many other "divines of chiefest note" and "a great many other persons of quality" met in London to discuss the possibility of a scheme for union.[116] But the Council of State was keeping its friends close, and its enemies even closer. At the end of September, Richard Salwey, president of the Council, wrote to Owen to request that he preach at Whitehall each Sunday in October and November.[117] In the event, Owen hardly had time to begin his series of addresses. The officers were running out of patience with the Rump they had reinstated. On 13 October, soldiers locked MPs out of the chamber, putting power in the hands of an emergency Committee of Safety. General Monck, leading the army in Scotland, was outraged at this attack upon parliamentary government, and intimated that he would march south. Civil war seemed inevitable. Owen and his party had lost their revolution.[118]

As England lurched into constitutional crisis, and faced the prospect of renewed civil war, the intellectual culture of Oxford was changing. In Christ Church, in November, Locke satirized Owen's preaching, playing with a metaphor that he had often used in his orations: "Oh for a Pilot that would steare the tossed ship of this state to the haven of happiness! doe not laugh at this expression for I assure you that I have learnt it out of the pulpit from whence

I heare it every Sunday," he complained.[119] Yet Owen, who despite politicking in London was fulfilling his regular duties in Christ Church, was still being identified with some of the university's most enterprising and intellectually ambitious projects—projects that illustrated the missionary zeal and intellectual capacity of English Puritanism in the late Cromwellian period. Samuel Boguslaw Chyliński's *An account of the translation of the Bible into the Lithuanian tongue* was published in or shortly after November 1659 to illustrate the serious intellectual ambition that continued to drive members of the Oxford University community, even in the face of national political chaos.

Chyliński's was the first translation of the Bible into Lithuanian, and, in a display of Protestant unity, Owen's name came second among those of the supporting divines, following that of John Conant, who had replaced Owen as vice chancellor.[120] Chyliński had come to England with the commendation of Dutch Reformed clergy to pursue his translation project. Unable to return home by renewed conflicts in central Europe, he spent two years in Oxford, evidently enjoying the favor of those who, "arming themselves with Religions buckler," as he put it, "have fought manfully in the cause of God against Sathan and Antichrist, have vindicated the light of truth from out of darknesse, have restored the learned languages and the liberall arts and sciences to their pristine splendour." He believed that "the day of the consummation of all things is at hand . . . many signes whereof we have allready seen, and many more dayly discovering themselves both in heaven and in earth, so that scarce any of them remaine as yet unaccomplished, save that onely, foretold by Christ Math. 24. of preaching the Gospell throughout the world, a testimony to all nations, and then shall the end be."[121] The Bible translation was to be the first stage of an ambitious project to provide Lithuanian Christians with "bookes in that language for the furtherance of the practice of piety." His next project was to translate the Westminster confession and catechisms, and to prepare a metrical version of the Psalms based on the Francis Rous psalter.[122] Despite his preference for statements of faith that some of them wished to replace, the Oxford academics thought highly of Chyliński, and in their advertisement of his project, with its implicit appeal for funds, described him as a "serious and godly person."[123] But his task was never completed, for his supporters were not the only ones "arming themselves with Religions buckler."[124]

In Oxford, dissent was growing behind public displays of unity. Pressure had been bulding for some time, and was expressed in local satirical traditions. F. V., otherwise unidentified, had made obscure allusions to local tensions in *Detur pulchriori, or, A poem in the praise of the University of Oxford* (1658), which described the "Pamphlet bullets" which "fly | About mine ears."[125] In 1659, students had submitted a petition asking for the restoration of sermons in

Latin alongside financial reforms.[126] The traditional culture of Christ Church was also being re-established, and its reputation continued to be appropriated by royalists, including Jasper Mayne, a graduate (MA, 1631), who had enjoyed benefices in several of the college's parishes before the pressures of civil war drove him into seclusion on the Chatsworth estate and into renewed friendship with Thomas Hobbes.[127] Mayne continued to advertise himself as a "student" of Christ Church, not least in the text of his play, *The city match*, which had been presented to the king and queen in Whitehall in 1639, but was finally published in 1659, along with *The amorous warre, A tragi-comoedy*.[128] These plays were published as part of Mayne's attempt at courting patronage—which successfully resulted in his promotion after the Restoration.[129] Tellingly, both plays were printed by Henry Hall, the printer to the university, who was also continuing to work with Owen: Owen was losing control of the Oxford press, even as his party was failing to control the commonwealth. The local cultures of print were illustrating the ambiguity of political fortunes in Oxford: Mayne was not alone in identifying "a sweet change of Times" in the latter months of 1659.[130]

General George Monck, leader of the army in Scotland, and chief opponent of the army republicans, was also busy writing. He had published a declaration to the Independent churches in the three nations, which provoked the response, on 31 October 1659, of Owen and eighteen other leaders of Independent congregations. Meeting in the Savoy, which they may have used as an operational headquarters, they signed a letter to Monck, asking that he receive military officers Edmund Whalley and William Goffe and pastors Joseph Caryl and Matthew Barker to represent the "apprehensions" of the Independent party in the south of England.[131] On 19 November, Owen wrote personally to Monck, warning him both of the dangers represented by the "Comon Enemy" and by "fanatical selfe seeking persons amongst ous." He pleaded with Monck not to let the armies "ingage in blood," fearing a "door of ruine opened to all the sober godly in both Nations," and argued that his old ally should understand that "your principalls and those of your friends here are universally the same." Owen disclaimed any responsibility for or knowledge of the dissolution of the Rump, "being for about five weekes before absent from this place," while also warning Monck that the Parliament could not be reinstated "without the blood of them whose ruine I am perswaded you seeke not." He offered to travel to meet Monck to discuss the situation to "prevent the utter ruine of all that is deare unto you and ous." "Yow shall on all occasions find me a true lover of my countryes liberties, an enemy to all usurpations upon itt, and one resolved to live and dye with the sober godly interest," he protested.[132] Monck's reply to Owen and other Independent clergy, written from Edinburgh on 23 November, was ambiguous, praising the contribution of the Independent churches, whose members "have been eminent Instruments, to labour in Sweat and Blood for these eighteen years past" in defence of "our Laws and Rights as Men," while insisting that only a parliament representing a consenting population could provide a legitimate government.[133]

Six days later, Monck wrote a much longer letter as a personalized covering note for his last item of correspondence—which, for uncertain reasons, he had not sent—thanking Owen for the "satisfaction" that his letter had brought. For Monck, too, was concerned about the "fanaticall and selfe seeking party, which doe threaten much danger to these three nations, for the prevention of whose dominion I dare assert it in the presence of God I have hazarded all that is deare to mee." He reported to Owen how the army dealt with soldiers who advanced heresy, and appealed to Owen to use what influence he had over Fleetwood to bring the army to heel in London. "Being at the heade of a part of the army, I dare not sitt still and let our lawes and liberties go to ruine. . . . I am ingaged in conscience and honnour to see my Country fred (as much as in mee lies) from that intollerable slavery of sword Government," he explained, while also offering the assurance "in the presence of God" that he would oppose the royalist cause "to the last dropp of my bloud." But while Owen and the army leaders were convinced that a strong army provided the best defense against the royalist revival, Monck put his faith in the election of a free parliament.[134] Owen may not have replied to this personal letter, but he did reply with the other Independent ministers and military officers on 13 December 1659. Their response indicated that they were "abundantly satisfied with the intention of the army heere in England . . . which they have manifested in their late resolutions for the speedy calling of Parliament," even as they warned Monck that his actions were encouraging royalists, whose cause was strengthening to the extent that the "people of God" were "in danger now every moment to bee destroyed and slaine by their inraged enemies," and whose deaths would be "laid at your doore."[135] On the same day, an anonymous pamphleteer accused "Dean Owen (so called)" of having conspired, before 1653, with Whalley, Goffe, Cromwell, and a number of other grandees against the Fifth Monarchists.[136] Meanwhile, Monck continued to march south. He replied from Coldstreame, on 22 December, as he prepared to cross the border into England, addressing his letter specifically to Owen, Whalley, and Goffe. He abandoned his earlier ambiguity, and advised the trio that he was not persuaded of the benign intentions of army leaders in London, while offering assurances of his support for the "good old cause and the good people of the Nation," and reminding his addressees that "the cause wee are now contending for is your owne cause, and the cause of all the good people."[137]

As the crisis deepened, Owen rushed out a short pamphlet on tithes and the role of the magistrate in religion, entitled *Unto the questions sent me last night, I pray accept of the ensuing answer, under the title of two questions concerning the power of the supream magistrate about religion, and the worship of God with one about tythes, proposed and resolved* (1659).[138] It was an attempt to position the Independents as being able to maintain religious conservatism without the support of the army in Scotland, and indicative of the extent to which Owen and a tiny number of colleagues found themselves able to bargain for the future of the good old cause against its principal opponent. His was a complicated position, for he, Whalley, and Goffe had, effectively, been attempting to reunite the army the better to resist Parliament.[139] The pamphlet drew a satirical response in *A serious letter to Dr John Owen, sent by a small friend of his* (1659).[140] This single sheet, attributed to "Thomas Truthsbye," offered an ironic account of "the late revolutions" in "this floating and giddy Island," identifying Owen as being the author of much of the chaos of the autumn and winter months:

> your Worship was cried up as high as Tyburn, as well known, and as little trusted; in my Travels Westward they calld you Quaker, Northward Anabaptist, in Oxford a State Independent, in London a Jesuite, beyond Seas a conscience-mender; I can scarce visit a Tavern, or Country Ale-house, but forth comes some of the Learned Works of John Owen, a Servant, &c., as if you were cut out to entertain all sorts of Guests; if I send for Tobacco, your Books are the inclosure of it, and there I finde your name stinking worse than that Indian Weed.

Beyond these insults, the author continued, "how odious you are to all persons, who cannot so sordidly comply with every Government, pray and teach to every Faction, side with all Innovators; . . . you are by all serious men thought the scorn of Religion, a man either of a very wide or seared conscience," with a history of "deceitful promises, and contradictory practices to piety and honesty," and with responsibility for the "downfall of timorous Richard . . . the dissolution of that famous Parliament," and the chaos that followed.[141] It was not a hopeful comment on the likely success of Owen's diplomacy.

War seemed inevitable. Lambert led the army out of London to meet Monck on his long march south. But his force of republicans was critically weakened through desertions. Fleetwood recognized the political realities, and engineered the recall of the Rump, hoping to forestall the threat from Monck by acceeding to his principal demand. But instability continued, with the Corporation of London proceeding to "open rebellion, refusing to pay taxes, encouraging other boroughs to follow in its lead, and preparing to defend itself, by arms if necessary, against all threats to its autonomy."[142] Bloodshed seemed inevitable. Monck kept marching south. And, as Archibald Johnston of Wariston recorded in his diary, "Owen . . . told us all was gon."[143]

V

Owen was right—the revolution was over—and satirists were quick to write its obituary. A parody funeral sermon appeared in January 1660 as *Bradshaws ultimum vale, being the last words that are ever intended to be spoke of him. As they were delivered in a sermon preach'd at his interrment. By J.O. D.D. time-server general of England.* It presented Owen as admitting that "wee Ministers love Mony" and agreeing with the statement that "it is as lawful for to kill a Tyrant, as it is to drink Coffee."[144] This was not the publicity Owen needed when, in February 1660, Monck entered London, with Fairfax's support, and restored the Long Parliament by readmitting those members who had been expelled by Pride's Purge. By bringing back into political favor those MPs who would never have approved the regicide, Monck continued to unwind the revolution. In Oxford, bonfires were lit to celebrate the calling of a "free parliament," while rumps of meat were roasted and thrown at the windows of John Palmer, the warden of All Souls.[145] In March, the Long Parliament ended Owen's tenure in Christ Church and replaced him with Edward Reynolds, revoking the expulsions that had been engineered under the terms of the engagement one decade before.[146] MPs adopted the Westminster Confession of Faith as a national theological statement and ordered that the Solemn League and Covenant be read annually in every parish church, achieving what had been impossible in the later 1640s.[147] Initially the Presbyterians thought they could contain the new Oxford—but they were quickly pushed aside by the rising tide of traditional royalism. The formerly secluded MPs prepared legislation for elections to a free parliament, and voted for the dissolution of the Long Parliament on 16 March. On 23 March, and perhaps confirming his recent status as "time-server general of England," Owen was the first signature of a broadsheet addressed *To His Excellencie the Lord General Monck; the humble gratulation and acknowledgement of Colonel Robert Broughton, and several others his countrey-men* (1660). This jockeying for favor was of no enduring effect. The Convention Parliament was convened on 25 April, with an overwhelmingly royalist membership. Its intention was obvious—to push for the restoration of the Stuarts.

Owen "reacted to the end of Puritan rule with some degree of shock."[148] He and his colleagues "reacted with the despair of men whom God had deserted."[149] Owen went back to Oxfordshire to "watch, hope, and pray."[150] Meanwhile, on 29 May, amidst surging crowds, "such shouting as the oldest man alive never heard," and in a cacophony of trumpets, drums, and church bells, Charles entered London.[151] The revolution was over. The monarchy had been restored.

8

Restoration Politique

THE REVOLUTION WAS over.[1] The Protestant republic, in each of its iterations, had failed. In the chaotic and celebratory aftermath of the king's return, Owen must have found London a strange and dreadful place. Some of the old republicans carried on life as usual, while others, including Whalley and Goffe, with whom Owen had attempted to negotiate with Monck, fled into exile, in locations as far apart as Switzerland and the New World. Those who fled fared best, for the government moved rapidly to make a spectacle of its power. Some of the most vociferous members of the new regime were among those with whom Owen had worked for the old, hoping by their complicity in the punishment of former colleagues to indemnify themselves from a similar fate. The arrests began in early June 1660, and the first executions followed at the end of the summer "amidst the atmosphere of a bear baiting."[2] Thomas Harrison was the first to die, being hung, and drawn and quartered at Charing Cross, on Saturday, 13 October.[3] John Carew was executed in similar circumstances on Monday, 15 October.[4] And on Wednesday, 17 October, at the same location, John Jones, Gregory Clement, Thomas Scott, and Adrian Scrope suffered the same fate.[5] A number of regicides who had fled to the Netherlands were tracked down and arrested by the English ambassador, Sir George Downing, including Miles Corbet, who, along with two others, was hung, and drawn and quartered in April 1662: their degradation continued as the remains were boiled and impaled on stakes at gates to the city.[6] Nor were these things done in a corner: in June 1662, the trial and execution of Sir Henry Vane became an attraction for tourists.[7] Altogether, thirteen regicides were executed, and nineteen were sentenced to life imprisonment. The imprisoned were to be constantly reminded of the possibility of legislated death. In 1661, Lord Monson, Sir Henry Mildmay, and Robert Wallop, three members of the court who had refused to sign the king's death warrant, were sentenced to be removed once every year from the Tower to be dragged in a halter to the gallows at Tyburn.[8] Not even the dead could escape retribution, but were, as Owen put it in another context, "raked out of their graves."[9] On 30 January 1661, the twelth anniversary of his king's death, the corpses of Oliver Cromwell, John Bradshaw, and Henry Ireton, at whose funeral Owen had preached, were disinterred, hung, and mutilated, with their heads displayed at the site of the trial of Charles I in Westminster.[10] Samuel Pepys went to view the heads on 5 February: they were to remain on display until the 1680s.[11] Throughout the 1660s, accounts by contemporary travelers described the public display on stakes of "many limbs of traitors or accomplices of Oliver Cromwell" at the Moorgate entrance to the city, as well as the display of "19 or 20" heads on a bridge.[12] The decaying bodies of old republicans were identified as symbols of rebellion, treason, and the certainty of the monarch's revenge. The threat of retaliation was enduring, and the death lists expanded to include those, like Hugh Peters, by whose side Owen had preached to Richard's parliament in April 1659, who had merely justified the execution of the king. These were frightening times. Supporters of the revolution plotted ways to survive and communicate in a world in which they had never expected to live.[13]

If the actions of the new state were specifically directed toward regicides, the print culture of the early Restoration identified a much larger number of targets. Its satirical and often bawdy wit did not discriminate between the old regime's most vociferous ideologues and others, like the prominent Presbyterian minister Zachary Crofton, who had, after all, been a supporter of Booth's royalist rising. Crofton found himself the target of vicious comedy in *The Presbyterian lash, or, Noctroff's maid whipt* (1661), which alleged that the minister had abused one of his servants.[14] Abraham Cowley's *Cutter of Coleman Street* (1663) developed similar themes of anti-Puritan satire, locating its action around the traditional center of London dissent.[15] And Owen, whose name was popularly associated with the extremes of the republican decade, was widely targeted in the dangerous new world of literary revanche. Some anonymous verse, first published in 1659 but circulating throughout the period, cast "Owen, Caryl, Nye" as the devil's chaplains in an invocation of regicide that must have made its subjects extremely uncomfortable in the larger context of retributive torture.[16] Other satire targeted Owen's theology. In 1660, Samuel Fisher's *Rusticus ad academicos in exercitationibus expostulatoriis, apologeticis quatuor* argued that Puritans would "prate" "Gainst *Truth* . . . | As Dr: *Owens* Doctrine *Does*, | Who heeds not well which way he *Goes*," in another iteration of the charge of Owen's political trimming.[17] Such derisive laughter sustained the social exclusion of the new community of dissenters, the management of which was made possible by legislation undergirding the Restoration's religious settlement, and, at least in the early 1660s, the threat of public and horrific death. While the Cavalier Parliament (1661–79) did contain small but significant Puritan groupings, its association of religious dissent with political threat created a culture of retaliation that proved dangerous for Owen and many others when it was encoded in the raft of legislation described rather inexactly as the Clarendon Code (1661–65).[18] While W. K. Jordan has argued that the "mass of men" and all "reasonable opinion" accepted the necessity of toleration by 1660, large parts of England's religious and political elites still idealized the principle of religious uniformity, and during the quarter-century following, as John Coffey has observed, "England witnessed a persecution of Protestants by Protestants without parallel in seventeenth-century Europe."[19] It was in this context of social exclusion, political retaliation, and horrific spectacle of death that Owen would make some of his most significant theological contributions—but it was a context in which he would first need to learn how to survive.

Owen did adapt to the new condition of England, while having for much of the 1660s and 1670s "no constant home," "no continuous employment," and some very powerful friends, sometimes of an unexpected political provenance. His strategy was to "talk about old times as little as possible. Personal reflections were missing in most of his writings," which, through much of the period, were "abstract treatises defending gospel truths and short pamphlets designed to influence specific policies," and not always in a transparent way.[20] He had no intention of becoming a martyr. His preferred method of avoiding that fate was to occlude himself in plain view. Owen's writing had always guarded against unnecessary personal reference, but now his distaste for the confessional mode became a vital principle, with several of his books appearing anonymously, and some advancing arguments that seemed entirely alien to the religious and constitutional causes that he had earlier defended. As he slipped out of the public eye, lodging with rich and well-connected friends, he left fewer documentary traces. After the early 1660s, his religious biography turns largely into a history of ideas stripped of personal context—a fact reflected in the structure of this book, and in the content and focus of its latter chapters, which focus less on the published materials, which are often circumspect, and more on manuscript recollections of his preaching.

Nevertheless, Owen's writing in this period illustrates the variety of English religion in the later seventeenth century. His ability to develop a literary career in such unpromising circumstances complicates older assumptions about the hegemony of Anglican ideas, and points to a vibrant and often well-capitalized culture of nonconformist print, which could negotiate new relationships to a hostile government while also memorializing the revolution in subtle and sometimes misleading strategies of resistance and celebration.[21] Owen's writing also reflects the divisions that beset "nonconformity," which was "not a party or even a community, but manifested . . . variously as a culture, a social experience and a spiritual activity."[22] But his writing also bears witness to personal disappointment. Experiencing militia raids and occasional arrest, Owen endured this long period of seclusion by dividing up his family, sending his wife and more often his children to safety elsewhere while he devoted himself to literary work and, when possible, to preaching. He was almost certainly busier than ever, publishing relatively little in the early to mid-1660s but likely continuing to prepare the massive multivolume commentary on Hebrews and the several substantial monographs that would appear in rapid succession after 1668.

It was not the writing retreat he would have preferred, but perhaps Owen felt that he had some catching up to do. After all, he had little to show for his several decades of hard work. His attempts to improve the parishes of Fordham and Coggeshall had failed, and his reformation of Christ Church and the University of Oxford was to be undone as part of the broader unwinding of the English revolution. In his old college, public prayers were being made in Latin by summer 1660, weekly communion was being revived, and by November 1661, the canons and students had begun to wear surplices.[23] Nor had Owen enjoyed the spoils of the revolution: while he had been awarded large salaries in a series of senior positions, they had often been unpaid, and Owen had never obtained the funds that he had been promised in the grant of Irish land, which he had pursued through the latter 1650s, an income stream which he would, in any case, have lost with the change of government. With the Restoration, Owen returned to the experience of defeat. But at least he now knew how to respond.

I

In the immediate aftermath of the Restoration, Owen gathered a church in his new home in Stadhampton. It is not likely that this was a large fellowship, but it was likely ideologically coherent, and attracted among its adherents several students from Oxford, among them William Penn, the future Quaker leader, who regularly rode the seven miles to the village to join the congregation in worship. In mid-January 1661, just days after the abortive Fifth Monarchist rising in London, members of the Oxfordshire militia surprised Owen's congregation and confiscated a half-dozen cases of pistols.[24] While no one was arrested, the congregation was clearly being watched, and perhaps for good reason. Owen lived quietly after the election of the Cavalier Parliament in

April 1661, preparing for publication the text of his most significant intellectual project to date.

Θεολογουμενα παντοδαπα (1661) was the final output of Owen's academic career, a gathering together of his lectures on the history of theology, which provides the clearest evidence of his immediate respose to the Restoration.[25] He had been working on the project since the late summer of 1658, when he had noted his hopes that the lectures would be published by Henry Wilkinson.[26] In the event, they were published by the university printer, Henry Hall, who in the previous year had also published plays by Jasper Mayne, which had lampooned the Puritan regime. But Owen was careful to emphasize the scholarly nature of his endeavor, and included in the text a dedicatory poem, also in Latin, likely written by his old Oxford ally, Thomas Goodwin: it was the only occasion in which his work would be recommended in a prefatory poem. The small amount of scholarship published on *Θεολογουμενα παντοδαπα* has tended to read the text in relation to emerging debates about theological method among European Protestant scholastic theologians.[27] The often technical arguments of these publications offer a helpful reminder that *Θεολογουμενα παντοδαπα* is not, after all, a "biblical theology," as its most recent translation into English is entitled, but is in fact an almost encyclopedic historical account of the history of ideas associated within Owen's doctrine of revelation: the book offers an expansive account of the history of language, literature, and culture to support its argument that the original knowledge of God given to Adam and Eve slowly dissipated, except among the descendants of Abraham, among whom it was gradually corrupted.[28] It was the expansiveness of this argument that perhaps attracted the attention of Lucy Hutchinson, who in the early 1670s translated sections of the text into English: *Θεολογουμενα παντοδαπα* offered her both a rationale for her interest in Lucretius, whose work she had translated, as well as an explanation of contemporary theological trends.[29] For, as David Norbrook has argued, *Θεολογουμενα παντοδαπα* represented Owen's prescient attempt to challenge opinions that "seemed likely" to become the "ideological foundations" of the restored monarchy, while also taking aim at ideas that he anticipated would become the ideological foundations of the new church settlement by mounting a "stringent onslaught on the idea of a 'natural theology' that might provide a common ground for belief outside either Scripture or the traditions of the church."[30] This reading of the text, emphasizing its continuity with Owen's earlier political and theological commitments, has obvious merits, especially insofar as he is seen to be advancing a considered theological and political platform in the changing circumstances of the Restoration.

But *Θεολογουμενα παντοδαπα* highlights discontinuities as well as continuities with Owen's earlier theological and political positions, and represents a complex new stage in the development of his thinking. It offers the first evidences that he had begun to study the work of Johannes Cocceius (1603–69), for example: the structure of Owen's work reflects that of the Dutch theologian's *Summa doctrinae de foedere et testamento Dei* (1648), and it also developed the concept of the *pactum salutis*, which projected Reformed ideas of covenant onto the Trinity to argue for a pre-creation covenant of redemption established among the persons of the Godhead.[31] Owen, as we have noted, appears to have learned this doctrine in his reading of Continental theologians, rather than those of the Scottish church among whom it first emerged.

The structural and thematic influences of the Dutch high Calvinist perhaps underplayed the extent to which *Θεολογουμενα παντοδαπα* is a troubled text. It reflected Owen's impressive knowledge of the archival holdings of the University of Oxford, as well as his changed circumstances, now living under the threat of government reprisal. He had lost much of his earlier confidence: the text's first signal of retreat was his explanation in his preface to the reader that "I am worth nothing and live quietly and in obscurity," being "thoroughly weary of controversy."[32] That intellectual retreat continued as he refused to enter the debate about the hypothetical universalist theory of the atonement, a debate in which he had previously spilled much ink but which he now regarded as a "matter of irrelevance."[33] Instead, *Θεολογουμενα παντοδαπα* constructed a theology of culture, offering a global and interdisciplinary history of Christian theology in its myriad linguistic, geographical, and cultural contexts. Owen's project was to demythologize the religions of classical antiquity, proving them to be corruptions of the natural revelation given by God to Adam and Eve. Part of his argument was developed in a discursive analysis of poetry, from both antique and more recent English authors, including Chaucer, which took seriously some of their most fantastic claims about ghosts and vampires to construct a critique of the religious-rhetorical foundations of social control from antiquity to the late medieval period.[34] But, as Hutchinson and other readers may have realized, the work reflected the strategic ambiguities and rhetorical gambits required of old republicans engaged in literary work in the early 1660s.

The timing of the publication of *Θεολογουμενα παντοδαπα* was not auspicious. The events of the Restoration had likely dealt a serious blow to the fortunes of the scholarly and godly reading public that would have been Owen's most obvious audience.[35] The book was not an immediate commerical success. In July 1665, for example, the trustees of Chetham's Library, Manchester, bought a copy of *Θεολογουμενα παντοδαπα* as part of parcel of books that included standard medical, legal, literary, and theological texts, including the works of Chaucer. It was one of the cheapest in the shipment of 116 items, costing 6 shillings and sixpence against the shipment average of approximately £1 8s.[36] Owen's most challenging book to date would find a more appreciative audience elsewhere, exercising substantial influence on the composition of Lucy Hutchinson's *Order and disorder* (1679), and being reprinted for Continental audiences in Bremen (1684) and Frankfurt (1700). But, in the immediate aftermath of its publication, the English market for secondhand books was fixing its own value on his work: there was not a sufficient demand for Owen's most serious account of cultural and intellectual history to push its value any higher.

Owen, meanwhile, adopted a studied political ambiguity. He continued his pastoral work in Stadhampton while the congregation and its supporters continued to be monitored. The authorities were also tracking Owen's readers: in December 1661, for example, an informer noted that Lady Wariston had recently received one of Owen's books.[37] Books were being circulated to preserve the networks of the godly, for reading could take the place of meeting. In the spring of 1662, several students who were discovered to be attending Owen's congregation were fined for nonconformity and expelled from the university. In late April 1662, Sir William Penn shared with Samuel Pepys a letter addressed by Owen to his son, who, the diarist complained, had been "much perverted in his opinion," having been among the disciplined undergraduates.[38] This letter, in which Owen encouraged Penn to continue to dissent from the religious, political, and educational establishment, illustrates the extent to which its author was beginning to dissimulate. It would have been written as Owen was upholding the rights of the extemperous freedom of worship preferred by the Independents in the final drafts of *A discourse concerning liturgies, and their imposition*, which was most likely published in the early summer. This was around the same time that he was also upholding the rights of the monarchy and religious establishment in the final drafts of his *Animadversions on Fiat Lux*, which was published in June, while planning his "remove out of the Land," and working under the protection of the earl of Oxford, Aubrey de Vere, who during the 1650s had twice been imprisoned in the Tower for his adventures in royalist conspiracy.[39] Defending the cause of the Independents, as well as that of the ecclesiastical establishment, while under the care of a former enemy, and exploring the possibility of emigration, Owen was playing a very deep game.[40]

Those historical theologians who have noticed that *Θεολογουμενα παντοδαπα* represents a significant methodological reversal in Owen's work have not often considered its broader context. In the early 1660s, he was reconsidering his previously held opinions in political and personal contexts that can best be described as opaque. Much of the writing that he produced in the period was entirely uncharacteristic of his former intellectual, theological, and political confidence. It is possible that Owen may have experienced something of an intellectual breakdown. Perhaps his "experience of defeat" had become almost pathological. Perhaps his commitment to understanding contemporary events through the lens of providence had provoked a much greater degree of self-scrutiny and self-criticism than his biographers have generally imagined, as his polemical providentialism proved to be entirely insufficient in explaining the situation of the godly. Or perhaps, like some other nonconformists within the context so superbly outlined in Neil Keeble's study of *The literary culture of nonconformity* (1987), he was simply advancing a deliberate campaign of sustained literary subterfuge.

II

In the early 1660s, Owen preferred to publish anonymously. He had good reason to do so in relation to his defense of extemporaneous prayer, *A discourse concerning liturgies, and their imposition* (1662). This text was most likely published in the early summer of 1662, almost certainly before the imposition of the Act of Uniformity on 24 August, and intended to shore up the fragments of the ruined Independent party in advance of a serious legal threat. Appearing without any information about its publisher, and in defiance of the licensing laws of the new government, the discourse resonated with themes from Owen's recent writing, defending the use of confessions of faith, which it described as "preservations against . . . danger," and associating the liturgical practice of the Church of England with that of the Church of Rome.[41] The book was a long defense of what Reformed theologians described as the "regulative principle of worship"—the proposition that "the will of God is the sole rule of his worship."[42] Owen located the "worship wars" in early modern England as reflecting the perennial difficulty of sinful humanity to accept that the only way to worship God was in forms that he himself had prescribed: "such is the corrupt nature of man, that there is scarce any thing whereabout men have been more apt to contend with God from the foundation of the world. That their will and wisdom may have a share (some at least) in the ordering of his worship, is that which of all things they seem to desire."[43] *A discourse concerning liturgies, and their imposition* therefore cast the liturgical conflict in the English church in absolute and binary terms, as a contest between the worship styles of the old and new covenants: Owen was returning to the simplifying dualities of his earliest polemical work. He described the worship of Old Testament Israel as being dominated by liturgical functions that were undermined by the ministry of Christ and his apostles, and ultimately "buried in the ruins of the city" in 70 A.D., when the "main occasion" of liturgical worship was "utterly taken away" in the Roman desctruction of the Temple.[44] But the attraction of liturgy remained. Owen surveyed the "golden fragments of antiquity" to illustrate the slow return to Old Testament modes of worship in the writings of the church fathers.[45] Their influence had been pervasive, he explained, to the extent that the medieval church had "reduced things . . . to the very state and condition wherein they were in Judaism."[46] His long account of the reformation of the English church described the pragmatism of the first reformers, who preserved erroneous liturgical forms even as they adopted clearer understandings of the gospel.[47] One century later, the struggle in the Church of England was merely the latest iteration of the long war against the forms of worship that had been instituted by Christ. For, he continued, it was Christ, not Moses, who should determine the content of new covenant worship: "He, being the Head, Lord, and only Lawgiver of his church, coming from the bosom of his Father to make the last revelation of his mind and will," should "determine and appoint that worship of God . . . which was to continue to the end of the world."[48] Christ equips his pastors with gifts, not liturgies, Owen argued, and the demand for liturgies was being driven by those clergy who did not have the gifts necessary for the responsibilities with which they had been entrusted.[49] His conclusion that English law should preserve the "liberty given by Christ unto his chuch" seemed "not immodest."[50] For any requirement to attend liturgical worship was tantamount to a legislative duty to sin.[51] Owen was doing his utmost to hold the Independents together. But his book illustrated the complexity of his response to the crisis of impending ejection: he was critiquing the religious establishment in uncompromising terms, even as he was preparing to uphold its rights in a contemporaneous publication. But its conclusion that the government was preparing to compel Christians to sin was hardly encouraging for those who continued to monitor Owen's network.

III

Much of Owen's writing in and after the summer of 1662 must have dismayed his admirers and friends. *A discourse concerning liturgies, and their imposition* may have appealed to the old verities of the Independent party, but *Θεολογουμενα παντοδαπα* had already illustrated Owen's movement away from scholastic theological method, and the texts that followed it represented a much broader social and political shift, even as other key figures in the revolutionary regime found opportunities for advancement within the restored government. These texts represented an entirely different genre of theological polemic, and were by far the wittiest and most playful of his writing to date (that alone should make us suspicious of their purpose). But this shift in genre and tone reflected some of the broader literary strategies of dissent in and after the troubled summer of 1662, and should not necessarily be taken at face value. Henry Stubbe, for example, whom Owen had patronized at Christ Church, developed similar techniques of evasion: formerly known as a radical Hobbesian Independent, and a troublemaker, Stubbe published *The Indian nectar, or A discourse concerning chocolata* (1662) to contribute to what Steve Zwicker has described as a nonconformist "language of disguise."[52] Stubbe's literary corpus in the 1660s was "marked by subterfuge and replete with double meanings," features that have "misled" many readers of his work, who have taken his arguments at face value, imagining that he abandoned his earlier principles, and underestimating the extent to which his subtle and allusive work continued to offer a serious critique of the circumstances in which he wrote.[53] Owen developed a similar strategy, when he prepared *Animadversions on a treatise entitled 'Fiat lux'* (1662) and *A vindication of the Animadversions on 'Fiat lux'* (1664) as anonymous responses to a recent work of Catholic apologetic by John Vincent Cane (1661).[54]

The background to the production of the *Animadversions* is obscure, but it appears that Edward Hyde, who had recently been elevated as the first earl of Clarendon, may have lent Cane's *Fiat lux* to Owen for a "few days," requesting that he should respond to its claims.[55] Hyde's link with Owen is perhaps surprising; however, it may be explained by the even more surprising fact of Owen's being under the protection of the earl of Oxford.[56] In early 1660, as events progressed toward Restoration, Hyde had been attempting to find a church settlement that the Puritan majority would find acceptable, and had further indicated his sympathy for Presbyterians and Independents during the Convention Parliament's discussion of the post-Restoration religious settlement.[57] But his own position was made particularly difficult around October 1660 when his daughter, Anne, admitted her affair with James, duke of York, the brother of the king and the court's leading Catholic: the surprise discovery that Anne was pregnant was followed by the shock that she and James had been secretly married.[58] As Hyde called for his daughter to be put on trial, the royal family rushed to patch up the union. James publicly recognized his wife as duchess of York and the king offered her father, then still Baron Hyde, the earldom of Clarendon.[59] In the aftermath of the scandal, the details of Hyde's preference for the toleration of Protestant dissenters were lost in a blizzard of allegations about his sympathy for Catholics and his attempt to inveigle his way into the royal family. But Clarendon's nadir was represented by the publication of Cane's *Fiat lux*, an apology for Catholicism that opened and closed by quoting his own words and thus appropriated his reputation for a cause he claimed to abominate.[60] If Clarendon wished to re-establish his reputation as a vigorous Protestant, he would have found Owen a useful tool over whom he could easily wield influence. The task may have been related to Clarendon's broader and entirely unscruplous pattern of exacting protection money from clients and old friends.[61] Perhaps there were good reasons that Owen should want to please him—as he managed to do, if Asty's account of Owen's audience with Clarendon and the consequent offer of episcopal preferment is credible.[62] Clarendon appears to have lent *Fiat lux* to Owen for a "few days," in circumstances now impossible to reconstruct. Whatever the circumstances or the details of the arrangements, a "few days" was long enough for Owen, who habitually exaggerated the speed at which he wrote, to compose a response of several hundred thousand words in length.

Owen's responses to Cane in the *Animadversions* and *A vindication* clearly served Clarendon's interests. His defense of the rights of the "chief families" of England was balanced by steady loyalty to the king and by support of the cause of generic Protestantism: Owen remained convinced that "the most ready way to go out of the catholic [church] is to go into the Roman."[63] But these texts also represented what may be a dramatic change in Owen's beliefs. He used the texts to continue his retreat from his previously held convictions. He continued the attack on scholastic theology, which he had begun in *Θεολογουμενα παντοδαπα*: the schoolmen are those, he claimed, who "out of a mixture of philosophy, traditions, and Scripture, all corrupted and perverted, have hammered that faith which was afterward confirmed under so many anathemas at Trent."[64] Nor was this merely an attack on Catholic scholasticism, as some of his commentators have claimed. The niggling doubts about method that had surfaced occasionally in his writing in the later 1650s had come to full fruit. Scholastic method was to be abominated wherever it was found: "Some learn their divinity out of the late and modern schools, both in the Reformed and Papal church," he worried, but "many things . . . give me cause to doubt" that it "hath any better success in the Reformed churches."[65]

Owen combined this uncertainty about the validity of Reformed education with some sense of embarrassment about his earlier political commitments. He denied that the previous two decades of strife had been at all indicative of the fissiparous character of Reformed religion, and abominated what he rather euphemistically described as "our late unhappy troubles."[66] He denied any involvement in civil war or revolution, stating that he "never had a hand in, nor gave consent unto, the raising of war in these nations, nor unto any political alteration in them,—no, not to any one that was amongst us during our revolutions." Instead, he claimed, he had "lived and acted under them the things wherein he thought his duty consisted," and challenged "all men to charge him with doing the least personal injury to any"—a challenge that he may have imagined to be particularly effective in the circumstances of an anonymous publication. Nevertheless, Owen continued, he was "amongst them who bless God and the king for the act of oblivion."[67] He insisted that he "doth, and ever did, abhor swords, and guns, and crusades, in matters of religion and conscience, with all violence," and that he "ever thought it an uncouth sight to see men marching with crosses on their backs to destroy Christians."[68] He insisted that he knew "no party among Christians that is in all things to be admired, nor any that is in all things to be condemned," but slipped in a positive reference to the church polity of the Independents, whom he evidently still supported.[69]

Owen, in other words, was using the invitation to defend Clarendon's reputation to consolidate his own. But this was a markedly revisionist, and more than slightly oblique, program of self-fashioning, for Owen had published the *Animadversions* anonymously. His authorship was widely suspected—not least by the author of *Fiat lux*, whose response to Owen's text was vociferous and highly personal. "I have been told of late," Cane explained in 1663, "that the Authour of the *Animadversions* upon *Fiat lux* is one Doctour *O N*." Cane had seen through Owen's defense of a generic Protestantism, and pushed back against the arguments of one whom he considered to have been "a Protestant against Popery which you found down, a Presbyterian against Protestancy which you threw down, an Independent against Presbyterianry which you kept down," thus reinscribing the familiar charge of Owen's opportunistic careerism.[70] Cane's exposure of the identity of his antagonist made many of Owen's claims of innocence appear to be ironic, and Owen abandoned his anonymity in his response.

But Owen used the *Animadversions* and *A vindication*, which followed it in 1664, to position himself as a defender of monarchy.[71] He described Charles I as "our late king, of glorious memory," and celebrated the reign of Charles II, under which, while "our present sovereign sways the sceptre of this land," Owen believed himself to be secure from the dangers of "fire and fagot," and hoped that "our posterity may be so under his offspring for many generations" to come.[72] Charles II, he continued, was "not only the greatest Protestant but the greatest potentate in Europe . . . it is no small satisfaction unto me to contemplate on the heavenly principle of gospel peace planted in the noble soil of royal ingenuity and goodness; when fruit may be expected to the great profit and advantage of the whole world."[73] The rhetoric must have been astonishing for some early readers of the work—not least those who complained of the morals of the court and those old republicans who were still being hunted down in places as far apart as Massachussets and Lake Geneva as part of the king's revenge.[74] He was writing as if the revolution had never occurred—and seemed almost entirely credulous about the future of religious toleration that Clarendon was attempting to promote—but in a fashion commensurate with the Independents' expressions of gratitude for his interventions in their favor.[75]

Owen's defense of monarchy in these texts had obvious implications for his construction of the religious establishment. He upheld the historic claim of the English monarchy to be "head" of the English church, for example, and positioned himself likewise as a defender of the Church of England and its statement of faith.[76] In the Thirty-nine Articles, he argued, "the practical truths of the gospel . . . are maintained and asserted in the church of England, and by all Protestants."[77] Consequently, he continued, in a futher invocation of his theological position in the early 1640s, "I embrace the doctrine of the church of England, as declared in the Thirty-Nine Articles, and other approved writings of the most famous bishops and other divines thereof."[78] After all, he explained, differences between Protestants were only verbal, and English Christians had to look beyond the Reformation to earlier models of church life: "it was not Luther nor Calvin, but the word of God, and the practice of the primitive church, that England proposed for her rule and pattern in her reformation."[79] Therefore, he continued, English Christians should not be burdened with subscription to detailed confessions of faith: "He that believeth that whatever God reveals is true, and that the holy Scripture is a perfect revelation of his mind and will (wherein almost all Christians agree), need not fear that he shall be burdened with multitudes of particular articles of faith, provided he do his duty in sincerity, to come to an acquaintance with what God hath so revealed."[80] In fact, he concluded, perhaps reflecting on the frustrations of his work for a Cromwellian religious settlement, confessions of faith were no more than "a Procrustes' bed to stretch them upon, or crop them unto the size of, so to reduce them to the same opinion in all things." The effort to impose a confession of faith would be "vain and fruitless . . . that men have for many generations wearied themselves about, and yet continue so to do. . . . When Christians had any unity in the world, the Bible alone was thought to contain their religion. . . . Nor will there ever, I fear, be again any unity among them until things are reduced to the same state and condition."[81] It was an extraordinary conclusion at which England's principal defender of high Calvinism had arrived:

> In a word, leave Christian religion unto its primitive liberty, wherein it was believed to be revealed of God, and that revelation of it to be contained in the Scripture, which men searched and studied, to become themselves, and to teach others to be, wise in the knowledge of God

> and living unto him, and the most of the contests that are in the world will quickly vanish and disappear. But whilst every one hath a confession, a way, a church, and its authority, which must be imposed on all others . . . we may look for peace, moderation and unity, when we are here no more, and not sooner.[82]

Owen's biographers have not explained this extraordinary passage in his career. His statements are astonishing. On the one hand, they suggest that Owen had rethought his rejection of Baxter's argument that confessions of faith should only contain biblical language.[83] On the other hand, these words demonstrate the variety of loyalty in the Restoration, if we take them at face value. And some may have so taken these statements: Asty records that Clarendon offered Owen preferment within the Church of England on the basis of this performance, an offer that could have been part of Charles II's policy of building an inclusive administration, paralleling the membership of four ex-Cromwellians in his first privy council.[84] But these words need not be taken at face value—for, as Owen admitted in these works, "nothing likes us more than dissimulation."[85]

This stylistically awkward admission of a preference for dissimulation may provide a key to the proper interpretation of these texts—as well as a warning for that substantial body of scholarship that reads Owen's arguments without due regard to context. For, throughout this period, and beyond, the claims advanced in Owen's writing did not always cohere, nor did they always correspond to his deeds. And yet Owen's rejection of confessions of faith as Procrustean beds in the *Animadversions* and his celebration of confessions of faith as "preservations against . . . danger" in *A discourse concerning liturgies, and their imposition* may ultimately make sense.[86] His admission of the lack of value of confessions of faith may reflect his despair at being able to gain public acceptance for even the simplest statement of religious "fundamentals" during the 1650s. But his obsession in the 1650s with excluding Catholics from the public practice of religion sat awkwardly with his claim, in the early 1660s, that he could "neither approve nor justify" their being persecuted, at this point appealing to the king and duke of York, whose aspirations to toleration for Catholics and other dissenters were not widely shared by MPs.[87] As this book has repeatedly argued, Owen's thinking was never static. But this reading of his writing in the early 1660s demonstrates that any scholarly focus that reads his books on their own terms, and outside their historical contexts, runs the danger of underestimating the extent to which Owen participated in and constructed the contexts in which he wrote.

Owen's work in the early 1660s spoke to the confusion of the times. "The present face of Christianity makes the world a wearisome wilderness," he explained, "nor should I think any thing a more necessary duty than it would be for persons of piety and ability to apologize for the religion of Jesus Christ, and to show how unconcerned it is in the ways and practices of the most that profess it."[88] And his satisfaction with the rule of Charles II was not so complete that he refused to consider emigration: in 1664, he was involved in negotiations about the purchase of land in New England, where, he may have realized, his old colleagues Whalley and Goffe were still in hiding, though the conveyancing was never completed.[89] While he was arguing in print that he had accepted the Restoration settlement, he was actively working to evade its rigor, and to escape its jurisdiction in an area friendly to other refugees. It may now be impossible to reconstruct the incident out of which Owen's wittiest and most politically troubled writing emerged, but it is clear that *Θεολογουμενα παντοδαπα*, the *Animadversions*, and its subsequent *A vindication* represent a brief capitulation to some of the central intellectual concerns of early Restoration culture. But, he explained, as his concluded his response to *Fiat lux*, "my pen is dull."[90] He seemed tired—daunted by the new world he had entered and perhaps at this stage lacking the courage to publicly confront it.

IV

Despite Owen's best efforts at influencing public debate in *A discourse concerning liturgies, and their imposition* and in the *Animadversions*, the Act of Uniformity was passed, without the qualifications that some dissenters were expecting, the Book of Common Prayer was imposed, and two thousand ministers and educators were ejected from the established church in late August 1662.[91] "Newes we have none but whats evill," Owen advised his friend John Thornton in a letter dated around September. He was distressed that a number of his colleagues had conformed, and reflected on the providential punishments meted out to one of their number, who had died "sadly and desperately." "I hope the cryes of many 1000 soules in England for the bread of life will pierce the heavens."[92] He may have overestimated the number of those who had been convinced by the ecclesiological arguments of the previous two decades: while a substantial proportion of the clergy left the established church, the community of dissenters would be a tiny proportion of the population at large.

After all his protestations against its imposition, Owen may have been surprised by the degree of popular support for the new Book of Common Prayer.

One diarist reported that eager crowds had "almost torn his clothes off [the] back" of a man who was distributing copies of the text.[93] The new emphasis on liturgical propriety had also led to an explosion of interest in newly revived rites of passage: candidates were confirmed in scenes of extraordinary enthusiasm "by the hundred, without any examination or distinction," for example.[94] Amidst the rejoicing crowds were some individuals whose royalist piety had quietly been observed, such as the man who, "when he heard that the king had been beheaded, vowed that he would not let his beard be cut until England had another king again; his was 3/4 ell long."[95] But others greeted the Act of Uniformity with dismay. Not all the ministers who conformed to the new church structures did so with enthusiasm. One diarist noted

> so many black-coats or parsons that we did not know what to make of it. Some smoked a little pipe on their horses, others hung their heads. Some were cheerful, others looked very melancholic, some had the newly printed book of common prayer in their hands. . . . These parsons or preachers had come there to damn, so that they should not be damned, that is to say, to swear the oath of uniformity.[96]

But others did not take the oath. Outside Emmanuel College, Cambridge, a professor packed his "books and household goods on to a cart . . . he had lost his post because he would not agree to conform with the acts of the bishops."[97] Across England, ministers preached "farewell sermons," and left their congregations in tears.[98]

Although Owen was already preaching to a gathered congregation outside the national church structure, he too was affected by the ejection, becoming part of a community of dissenters that was one-quarter of a million strong, and "far from being a cohesive party."[99] Not being a parish minister, he had no need to preach a farewell sermon. But he continued to preach, even as such action was politicized and criminalized in the new legislative environment.[100] Nevertheless, like other dissenting ministers, he discovered that "notable puritan families, who retained considerable influence in many localities, were not only able to provide pensions and employment for indigent ministers, but could, in many cases, still offer a measure of political protection."[101] And so, he discovered, as he gradually moved his base of operations to Middlesex, could notable families with no reputation for vigorous religion, including that of the former royalist conspirator, the earl of Oxford. Owen continued to exhort tiny household congregations, while braver or more ambitious nonconformists, preaching in the capital from as early as 1663, commanded audiences of thousands.[102] Their number included a friend of Owen who "did preach in

Publique at London a fortnight since and tells me of many others of the same predicament that still doe the like."[103] Perhaps Owen knew that he was still being watched. Around December 1662, Henry Bennet, the earl of Arlington, was informed of the movements of several "suspicious persons," including Thomas Goodwin and John Owen, "who now scruple at the surplice, but used to wear velvet cassocks, and to receive from 500l. to 700l. a year from their churches," an almost certainly inprobable claim, given that we do not know whether Owen was even associated with a congregation during this period.[104] Nevertheless, while less well-connected dissenters could suffer the full force of the law, Owen merely brushed against legal infirmities while building links that would eventually introduce him into the most elevated ranks of English society. He continued, all the while, to write. As he wrote, he quietly renewed his earlier commitments. His later writing was much less witty than his work in the early 1660s, and gradually returned to his earlier methods and convictions. He took time to develop the literary and intellectual strategies required by those who would endure the experience of defeat.

V

Meanwhile, Owen's family had been divided. He was working as a household chaplain for Lady Abney, the daughter of Joseph Caryl, and was preaching regularly in her house at Theobalds while suffering from serious eye trouble.[105] At least three of his children were still alive—Mary, now in her early teens, and Judith and Matthew, who must have been much younger.[106] From his correspondance, it appears that his children were sent to live in Hanslope, possibly with the family of Sir Thomas Tyrell. John and Mary Owen found it difficult to visit the children, being obliged to remain with "our Lady"—presumably Sarah Caryl—who required her chaplain to move with her to London. John Thornton, Owen's correspondent, lived about ten miles from Hanslope, at Woburn Abbey, and Owen hoped that he might visit the children on their parents' behalf.[107] In spring 1663, he requested Thornton to "step to Hanslope and see the children, seeing we are not like to see them God knowes when."[108] The Owen family was clearly discomfited by the separation.

For all of its disruption of family life, Lady Abney's move to London in the early part of 1663 allowed Owen to reconnect with other Independent ministers. Their movements were being observed by spies, who reported that Owen was meeting regularly with Thomas Goodwin and Henry Jessey, and that he was living "in ye Fields on ye left hand neer Moregate where ye Quarters hang"—within sight, in other words, of the decaying carcasses of his friends.[109] Little wonder that Owen was also pursuing opportunities that could have led to emigration. For good opportunities existed. He had been invited to become president of Harvard College and also to follow John Cotton and John Norton as minister of First Church in Boston.[110] Neither would he have been without friends in the new world—some of the members of his Wallingford House congregation had fled to Massachusetts, though as fugitives they could not easily correspond with old friends.[111] And so, in London, in 1664, he met John Pyncheon, of Springfield, Massachusetts Bay, to discuss the purchase of land in New England, "particularly about the River of Piscataqua, now called N. Hampshire, for between one and two hundred pounds," though nothing came of the negotiations.[112]

Owen retreated from his hope for geographical distance, and adopted a tone of ironic distance instead. By the autumn of 1663, he had returned to Lady Abney's home at Theobalds, and was living with Matthew, and perhaps other of his children.[113] Writing to Thornton, he explained that his papers, perhaps including the manuscript for a forthcoming book, were lodged with Henry Oldenburg, a member of the Royal Society, who, it seems, was pretending to be too busy with the scientific advances of his colleagues to do anything to promote Owen's literary career. Owen's response to this sidelining of theological knowledge was scathing, striking out at the utilitarian direction of the new Society's deliberations:

> I hope they are upon some serious consultations for the benefit of mankind, how a hen may sit on her eggs and addle none, how oysters may be so geometrically layd that in stead of 200 or 300, an oyster wench may lay 8 or 900 in her basket at once and sell them all without tearing her throat or tyring her head, how his majestys bears may be taught to bite none but fanatickes and that without hurting their teeth, besides many other devices for the promoting of trade, the preventing the Dutch, and the ruine of Gayland [Guinea?] and all which are under deliberation.[114]

But Owen was also observing the fate of dissenters. "The Anabaptists here at Theobalds and the quakers in London [are] more numerous than ever," he reported to a correspondent. "A troop (viz. the county troop) came to Theobalds last Lords day thinking to catch the Anabaptists at their meeting, but you would not thinke how many came to warne them of it, so they dispersed and though the troopers stood gazing 3 or 4 hours on high ground to watch their rendezvous, yet they escaped their sight and met in a wood undiscovered."[115]

Perhaps it was concerns about security that led Owen to move into the household of Charles Fleetwood in Stoke Newington. Fleetwood had lived very quietly since the Restoration, and had largely been left alone. His household was a large one, centered around his children by his first two wives; the children of his new wife, Mary Hartropp, by her first husband; and the new family they started together, after their wedding in January 1664. The happy couple—and their three sets of children—were almost immediately joined by the Owen family. It was in the Fleetwood home that Judith Owen, whose birth date is not recorded, may have died in May 1664.[116] The move to Stoke Newington allowed Owen and his family to regroup, and provided for the regathering of his most trusted circle of friends, who had been associated with the congregation that had met in Fleetwood's earlier home in Whitehall. Owen began to regain confidence in his ministry. By the early months of 1665, he was traveling occasionally to Stadhampton, where he was discovered preaching in contravention of the law to a congregation of around thirty.[117] But family tragedies continued, and were perhaps related to the outbreak of plague in London (1665–66): Matthew died in April 1665, and was buried at Stoke Newington.[118] The family may have moved back home. For it was from Stadhampton, on 13 April 1666, that his only surviving child, Mary Owen, aged 17, married Roger Kynaston of Llanfechain, who was five years her senior and a gentleman.[119] Perhaps Owen wondered whether the fire and plague in London, and the recent and ominous series of comets, had personal as well as national significance. Mary would return to live with her parents, likely separating from Kynaston, joining the Leadenhall Street congregation in March 1675, and, like each of her siblings, dying before her father.[120]

Emigration was still a possibility. Appeals to come to Boston arrived as late as August 1665.[121] By the summer of 1666, Owen had decided that these invitations should be refused. It is not clear why he made this decision: early rumors that the king himself had forbidden the move have given way to suggestions that Owen realized that the situation of the godly was no more secure in Massachusetts, which was after all an English colony, than at home.[122] And things were changing for the better: by the end of 1666, dissenting gatherings in London were "as safe as they had been under the republic," as the legislation that had driven persecution was less frequently invoked and approached its expiration.[123] By 1666, Owen had found his feet in the old world. He had formed a little church, based principally around the Fleetwood household, representing a regathering of many of the members of the congregation that had met in Wallingford House: Sarah Cook calculated that by 1673 sixteen members of this church were related by "long friendship, employment, blood, or marriage" with the Fleetwood family and the Wallingford House congregation.[124] Owen had found his calling: he would serve this congregation for the rest of his life.

VI

It was the prospect of an indulgence for public worship by dissenters, and, perhaps, a series of discussions on the subject with the earl of Clarendon, which stimulated Owen and other dissenters to revive their literary careers in 1667.[125] Ironically, Owen followed his recent rejection of articles of faith with a text designed as a catechism, and his recent defense of generic Protestantism with a book specifically designed to promote Independent principles. *A brief instruction in the worship of God, and discipline of the churches of the New Testament* (1667) was published illegally, without an ascription either of author or of publisher, but circulated widely enough to warrant the appearance of subsequent editions in 1676 and 1688.[126] Owen's last attempts at writing catechisms and a volume on ecclesiology had appeared in the mid-1640s and in *A primer* (1652). The new catechism was a much more substantial discussion, which focused on principles relating to public worship and congregational administration as they had been developed among Independents in the ensuing two decades and likely reflected the practice of the congregation that gathered in Stoke Newington. Its biblicism was set out in the answer to the first question, which insisted that Christians should worship God "in and by the ways of his own appointment."[127] The longest section of the catechism was focused upon establishing this regulative principle for public worship, and, as in *A discourse concerning liturgies, and their imposition,* Owen's development of the idea was stringent. He insisted that all "inventions" in worship were "needless and useless, and, because forbidden, unlawful to be observed."[128] Neither could a church excuse itself from the full performance of its obligations by citing the penalties of the Clarendon Code: "No opposition, no persecution, can give the church a dispensation wholly to omit and lay aside the use of any thing that the Lord Christ hath commanded to be observed in the worship of God."[129] For, Owen continued,

> Some duties of obedience there are which the world neither doth nor can discern in believers; such are their faith, inward holiness, purity of heart, heavenly-mindedness, sincere mortification of indwelling sin; some whose performance ought to be hid from them, as personal prayer and alms, Matt. vi. 2–6; some there are which are very liable to misconstruction amongst men, as zeal . . . but this conscientious observation of instituted worship, and therein avowing our subjection unto

> the authority of God in Christ, is that which the world may see and take notice of, and that which, unless in case of persecution, ought not to be hid from them, and that which they can have no pretence of scandal at: and therefore hath God appointed that by this means and way we shall honour and glorify him in the world; which if we neglect, we do evidently cast off all regard unto his concernments in this world.[130]

Some of Owen's comments in *A brief instruction* were predictable, such as his call for a shared confession of faith to enable churches to confess a common creed—in which discussion, oddly, he did not mention the Savoy Declaration.[131] Other of his comments reflected new positions, such as his advocacy of the weekly celebration of the Lord's Supper, and his concern that the Authorised Version of the Bible, the reliability of which he had defended in his discussions of the London Polyglot, was supporting Anglican arguments in its mistranslation of key ecclesiastical terms.[132]

Despite its anonymity, Owen's responsibility for the book was widely recognized. Benjamin Camfield, the rector of Whitby, Debyshire, attacked the theological content of the catechism in *A serious examination of the Independents catechism* (1669), while the anonymous author of *A letter to a friend concerning some of Dr Owen's principles and practices* (1670) extended the critique also to Owen's record of administration in Oxford. Richard Baxter seized upon Owen's discussion of the office of ruling elder to imagine that he was drifting back toward Presbyterianism, a misunderstanding of Owen's position that nevertheless raised the tantalizing possibility of reapprochement with his old antagonist, initiating an extended correspondence in which nothing was ultimately achieved. As the several published responses suggest, Owen's book circulated outside narrow denominational audiences: the copy of *A brief instruction in the worship of God* held in the Folger Library, for example, came from Kimbolton Castle, the home of Robert Montagu, third earl of Manchester, who would be associated with Shaftesbury's opposition party during the exclusion crisis at the end of the 1670s.[133]

Indulgence and toleration considered in a letter unto a person of honour (1667) was also published anonymously. It is not clear to whom the letter was addressed, although Goold speculates that it may have been Sir Thomas Overbury, a correspondent of Owen who shared his views on these controversial subjects.[134] It was a letter of "hasty thoughts," around ten thousand words in length, which may have been designed for publication.[135] Owen was writing in response to "discourses sent me, published lately, about Indulgence and Toleration."[136] Although he did not mention which titles he had seen, he was clearly responding to those texts that were arguing for the continued suppression of nonconformity. He claimed to be surprised by the number of recent publications on the subject, explaining rather disengenously that he did not understand "the reason of their multiplication at this time, nor what it was that made them swarm so unseasonably."[137] He certainly found them wanting, complaining in particular of their arguments from history, in which, he complained,

> stories are told of things past and gone; scattered interest, dissolved intrigues, buried miscarriages, such as never can have any aspect on the present posture of affairs and minds of men in this nation, are gathered together and raked out of their graves, to compose mormoes for the affrightment of men from a regard to the ways of peace and moderation. This they enlarge upon with much rhetoric and some little sophistry.[138]

Owen's complaint was that his enemies were too ready to remember the civil wars and revolution as part of their invention of religious monsters, but his reference to ideas being "raked out of their graves" was a clear invocation of the body parts besides which he had lived in Moorgate.

The revolution cast a long shadow over his letter. After all, Owen was still appealing to "the fundamentals of Christian religion," which he and his committee had attempted to settle during much of the 1650s.[139] He hinted that Anglicans should remember how generously they had been tolerated in the republic, and appealed for them to abandon their "wrath, envy, and revenge."[140] He warned that the insistence on ecclesiastical uniformity was putting the security of the monarchy at stake. Owen was now pursuing his own revisionist history, inverting the parties in the civil wars, describing dissenters as the true friends of the king and Anglicans as those whose commitment to their own religion was so radical and absolute that they would gamble the security of the monarchy to preserve it. For Owen realized that the toleration of the dissenters was more likely to be promoted by Charles than by his Parliament: "I cannot but hope that his majesty will re-assume those blessed counsels of peace . . . for all those who desire an indulgence, though differing in themselves in some things, do jointly cast their expectations and desires into a dependence on his majesty, with advice of his parliament."[141] Owen presented his hopes as more than a reflection of party interest. For, if the government abandoned the indulgence, and attempted to "build the interest of a nation on a uniformity of sentiment and practices," it would find itself "continually tossed up and down."[142] Owen was invoking the memory of civil war to threaten its return.

Owen's argument in *Indulgence and toleration considered* entirely sidestepped biblical exposition and theological discussion to appeal to economics. He worried that the persecution of diligent and productive Christians was contributing to the downturn in trade: "hands . . . by this means are taken off from labour, the stocks from employment, the minds from contrivances of industry in their own concerns," and "poverty . . . is brought on families—in all which the common good hath no small interest."[143] Give dissenters leave to worship in freedom, he seemed to be arguing, and they would think less about theology and more about the practical contrivances of enlightenment and the creation of wealth. After all, he concluded, "there is no nation under heaven wherein such an indulgence or toleration as is desired would be more welcome, useful, acceptable, or more subservient to tranquility, trade, wealth, and peace."[144]

Owen's appeal for the toleration of Protestant dissenters was continued in *A peace-offering in an apology and humble plea for indulgence and libertie of conscience* (1667). This text also appeared illegally, without information about its author or publisher, and also contained an argument from economics, describing dissenters as "mostly of that sort and condition of men in the commonwealth upon whose industry and endeavours . . . the trade and wealth of the nation do much depend."[145] But it also included a long defense of the theology of the Independents, as outlined in the Savoy Declaration. After surveying European Reformed confessions, Owen insisted that the Independents "fully embrace" the doctrinal parts of the Thirty-nine Articles, arguing that "there is not any proposition in our whole confession which is repugnant unto any thing contained in the articles, or is not by just consequence deductable from them."[146] "We have no new faith to declare," he continued, "no new doctrine to teach, no private opinions to divulge, no point or truth do we profess, no not one, which hath not been declared, taught, divulged and esteemed as the common doctrine of the Church of England, ever since the Reformation."[147] The real problem, as he saw it, was that his antagonists were not familiar with the Savoy Declaration, and, "if men will take to themselves the liberty of entertaining evil and groundless surmises, it is impossible for us or any living to set bounds to their imaginations."[148] Owen was clearly frustrated by the level of theological discussion during the indulgence crisis.

Of course, the danger of Owen's reference to the Savoy Declaration was that it rooted the development of Independent theology in the events of the revolutionary period. This was a fact that Owen's antagonists had already noted. But he dismissed their invocation of "the late troubles in these nations" with a reminder that "his majesty's clemency and grace" had put the events of the rebellion "into legal oblivion for ever."[149] In any case, Owen claimed, not at this point anticipating the conclusions of modern historians, and entirely contradicting the claims of his earliest publications, the civil wars could not have been wars of religion, as Independent principles bore "absolute freedom . . . from any such tendency" to rebellion.[150] He imagined that the present suffering of dissenters reflected God's judgment upon them, and imagined their future in terms of quietistic passivity.[151] Even if dissenters were to be "scattered over the face of the earth, we shall yet pray for the prosperity of his majesty and the land of our nativity."[152] For, he insisted, "magistracy" was "the ordinance of God, and his majesty as the person set over us by his providence in the chief and royal administration thereof," and so the role of the dissenting subject was to render religious obedience to the king. But this was a claim, encoded in the Westminster Confession, which the Savoy Declaration had refused to confirm. Perhaps, he might have reflected, it was just as well that his antagonists had not read his community's principal statement of faith.

But some of his critics did not understand the direction of his argument. Richard Perrinchief responded to Owen's *Peace offering*, as well as John Corbet's *The second discourse of the religion in England*, in *Indulgence not justified* (1668). Perrinchief was mystified by the provenance of the anonymous text: "what sort or party of Protestants" were responsible for the tract "it leaves us to conjecture. Some passages in it perswade us that they are Independents," though that label could include "Anabaptists, Socinians, Antinomians." Clearly ignoring Owen's appeal to the Savoy Declaration, Perrinchief admitted that "we are still in the dark what sort of men they are; therefore we can take no notice of the great kindness they show to themselves, in being free in their own commendations."[153] He constructed his own argument from church history, to conclude that the apostles, the fathers, with the Christian emperors of antiquity and modern Europe were all opposed to the indulgence of dissenting consciences. Owen's literary occlusion, for some of his readers, may have been too successful.

VII

For all that Owen was eager to conceal his literary identity, however, he did sit for a portrait by one of the most fashionable artists of the late 1660s. John Greenhill was an up-and-coming protégé of Peter Lely, the principal artist for the court, whose work to date had featured a series of eminent actors and dramatists, as well as political figures of both court and country factions, including some of the politicians with whom Owen would come to be idenfitied in the 1670s. Greenhill was an emerging celebrity, whose work would be praised in verse both by John Locke, who sat for him on two occasions, and by his friend, Aphra Behn.[154] Owen's sitting for Greenhill provides further evidence that "royalists and parliamentarians patronised the same artists, and were rendered in the same styles," as court-country divisions in politics gave way to ambiguous loyalties in cultural work.[155] Like so much of Owen's biography in this period, however, it is impossible to reconstruct the events that led up to the making of this portrait, or its broader significance within the literary and religious environment of the period. Nor is there anything to which the portrait can be compared in an effort to ascertain its versimilitude—though, as Owen was over fifty years old, and with a long history of medical complaints, it may represent an idealized version of its subject, who looked older and thinner than in the portrait taken in Oxford. It is possible that the portrait was commissioned by Philip Lord Wharton, and that Owen felt obliged to sit for it: he does not refer to the portait in his writing, and seems to peer from the canvas disdainfully on the viewer—or, perhaps, upon the artist, whose increasingly dissolute lifestyle would lead to an alcohol-related death less than a decade later.[156] Whoever commissioned the painting, it was purchased by the National Museum of Wales in 1971, and ended up in the collection of Lyme Park, Stockport.

It is ironic that Owen's portrait should be taken during the period of his greatest literary occlusion. But the irony reflects broader strategies at work in the writing he completed during the 1660s. These texts simultaneously concealed and revealed his intentions, encoding dissenting ambitions in texts that differed in ideology according to the audience they were intended to address. But his tactics could not account for the fact that his work could also be read by the wrong kind of readers. Critics of the Independents could read and respond to *A discourse concerning liturgies, and their imposition*, just as other readers, like Perrinchief, could make points about the existence of competing communities among dissenters as part of his complaint about the uncertain provenance of the *Peace offering*. Owen knew that his best hopes for toleration did not lie with the Cavalier Parliament, or in the sympathies of the broader culture of print, but he would need to project a much clearer literary persona if he were to gain the attention of the king.[157]

9

Nonconformist Divine

OWEN'S SITTING FOR the Greenhill portrait was, perhaps, an indication of his renewed confidence. By the end of the 1660s, with the expiration of the Conventicles Act between 1668 and 1670, and, presumably, with the protection of well-placed patrons, he was ready to come out of hiding, to rise "in the esteeme & affection of this Country," and to become one of its most considerable and most prolific literary voices.[1] Revitalizing his writing career with recovered purpose, he established himself as a principal leader of nonconformists, publishing a huge volume of texts in multiple genres and in varying lengths, addressing a wide variety of themes, and almost consistently under his own name. At the same time, he intervened, sometimes in unexpected ways, in the turbulent political and cultural life of the period, facilitating the publishing careers of Andrew Marvell and John Bunyan while providing vital material for cultural work by Lucy Hutchinson, as he and his readers continued to be observed, and as his own literary and political network continued to expand.

Owen's publications in the latter period of his life reflected the distinctive cadences of his theology, which had long been established, and his politics and scholastic method, confidence in which he had begun to recover. They bore witness to his increasing tendency to distinguish his private and speculative readings of providence from his public and scholarly contributions to biblical studies and political debate.[2] From the late 1660s until his death, Owen's writing would include some of the most important of his scholarly and intellectual achievements, and many of the books for which he would become best known among dissenters and, later, evangelicals. This would also be the period in which his earlier books were most often reprinted, as Owen became a marketable author in the expanding cultures of dissenting print: twenty-six of the forty Owen titles that went into at least a second impression were first published in the last fifteen years of his life, though the number of impressions through which his books went never competed with the most successful of his peers within his literary culture.[3] The pricing of Owen's works in this period generally matched the value attributed to comparable texts published by other dissenting ministers.[4] His status within this world of nonconformist print would be consolidated by increasingly frequent opportunities to recommend the works of others in prefaces and commendatory material. While his later writing reflects his settled theological and political positions, its intellectual complexity increases in inverse proportion to the availability of relevant biographical data. After the late 1660s, as relevant sources grow scarce, Owen's religious biography offers less in terms of ideas in context, and must transpose either into a fuller history of his expanding congregation, supported by extensive auditor's notes, or a more spartan history of his ideas, developing themes from his printed texts. Even in terms of the latter, Owen's later work demands more detailed study than is possible within the confines of this book. Reflecting its aspirations in biographical theology, this chapter will describe major themes in the work of these later years, after his long and troubled formation, the often frustrating years of achievement, and the more recent panic of self-doubt. Sharply dividing his public writing and his private preaching, and being closely identified with some of the most well-known conspiracies of the period, Owen re-established his reputation as the most formidable and sometimes unpredictable of nonconformist divines—and one of the most significant theologians in the religious history of early modern England.

I

In uncertain circumstances, Owen returned to publication under his own name with his mammoth commentary on Hebrews, the first folio of which appeared in 1668. This volume would be the first of an almost encyclopedic expository series, with further installments published in 1674, 1680, and 1684. Its two million or so words would surely constitute one of the longest commentaries ever published on any New Testament epistle. It is possible that the commentary was based on lectures that Owen had given at Oxford.[5] He certainly seems to have been working on the project for over a decade, and had likely continued his research and writing during the nervous but sometimes quiet years of the early Restoration, despite his frequent and disrupting changes of location.[6] His interest in one of the most significant themes of the epistle had been reflected in the title of his first book, *Tractatu de sacerdotio Christi*, which he had written in the early 1640s, but which he had never published.[7] He had sustained this thematic focus through much of the rest of his writing: the long controversy with the Arminians was, at one level, a sustained dispute about Christ's priestly office, and the relationship between his intercession (which, following John 17, most Protestants limited to the elect) and his offering of atonement (which strict Calvinists argued was presented on behalf of the elect and which others argued was presented on behalf of humanity more generally). The *Exercitations on the epistle to the Hebrews . . . with an exposition and discourses on the two first chapters* (1668) was, Owen explained, the culmination of the "whole course" of his studies. David Clarkson, in his sermon following Owen's funeral, described the commentary as his *magnum opus*: "he said, Now his Work was done, it was time for him to die." If only in terms of sheer bulk, this was undoubtedly his "greatest work."[8]

The commentary resonated with familiar themes. Owen's interest in the priesthood of Christ had been reflected in his earlier writings. He had preached from Hebrews in April 1646 to describe the "shaking and translating of heaven and earth." His work on the Sabbath developed from his reading of Hebrews 4, and his work on apostasy was rooted in his reading of Hebrews 6.[9] If the contents of his posthumous library catalogue are taken at face value, he may have owned around fifty commentaries on Hebrews, so he was certainly aware of the need to justify the publication of another.[10] Of course, he was able to relate the content of the epistle to the challenge of Socinian theology, but his principal concern was to use the epistle to address the "past, present, and future condition of the . . . church of the Jews."[11] The commentary was packed with Hebraic learning, and drew freely on a wide range of rabbinical literature. The first volume included a substantial prolegomena, considering such issues as the epistle's authorship and occasion of writing (Owen argued that it was written by Paul before the end of Temple worship in 70 A.D.), as well as sustained discussion of Jewish theories as to the coming of the Messiah, and why these could have been fulfilled only in Jesus Christ.

If these conclusions were to be expected, Owen's decision to dedicate the first volume of the commentary to Sir William Morrice, a member of the Privy Council and secretary of state, was more surprising. Morrice was an unexpected patron, an MP excluded by Pride's Purge who had more recently assisted in the Restoration, but who had apparently encouraged Owen's literary work earlier in the decade, in a manner it is now impossible to reconstruct, while also protecting John Milton from the full rigors of the law.[12] Owen was grateful that Morrice had allowed some earlier treatises to "pass freely into the world," for the activity of writing was the "only way of left me to serve the will of God and the interest of the church in my generation." He insisted that his writings in the earlier part of the decade had "nothing in them tending to the least disadvantage unto those whose concernment lies in peace and truth in these nations."[13] But he also wanted to remind his readers of the challenging circumstances in which dissenters were pursuing their literary work:

> I must beg also of the learned reader a consideration of the state and condition wherein, through the good providence of God, I have been during the greatest part of the time wherein these Exercitations were written and printed; and I shall pray, in requital of his kindness, that he may never know by experience what impressions of failings, mistakes, and several defects in exactness, uncertainties, straits, and exclusion from the use of books, will bring and leave upon endeavours of this kind.[14]

It was a diplomatic description of the doubt and, possibly, the duplicity that had been reflected in Owen's writing in the earlier part of the decade. Of course, the complaint of being without books had been repeated through his earliest writings, and, not for the first time, he attempted to turn this to his advantage: "I must now say, that, after all searching and reading, prayer and assiduous meditation on the text have been my only reserve, and far most useful means of light and assistance."[15] This was, however, a "means of light and assistance" that two million words of exposition would deny to his readers.

For all that Owen was claiming to enjoy the support of Sir William Morrice, the difficulty of finding an appropriate publisher was pushing him into other unexpected alliances. *The nature, power, deceit, and prevalency of the remainders of indwelling-sin in believers* (1668) was published by Elizabeth Calvert, the widow of one of the most radical publishers of the Cromwellian period, whose shop had been notorious for its support of antinomian authors.[16] This choice of publisher was ironic, for Owen's book emphasized the authority of divine law, its inscription on human conscience, and the power of the sin that it prompted.[17] He was worried about antinomianism, lamenting the "apostasies and backslidings of many, the scandalous sins and miscarriages of some, and the course and lives of the most."[18] Declension was, of course, an important theme in Hebrews, and Owen may have figured his readers as being tempted, like the addressees of the epistle about which he was also thinking, to slip back into an easier pattern of religious conformity, even as many of his fellow travelers in revolution had so apostasized as now to lead the persecution of the godly. Believers had to be careful. Sin "feeds upon itself," he explained; "the more men sin, the more they are inclined unto sin."[19] Perhaps reflecting on his own experience in the early 1660s, he considered that "the life of temptation lies in deceit," and remembered that "the profession of many hath declined in their old age or riper time."[20] He was conscious of apostasy among those erstwhile revolutionaries who "look upon their former zeal as folly," and reminded his readers of the hostility of those who had planned the "ruin of some of us . . . a thousand times."[21] But godly readers should not to fall victim to despair about the declension of old comrades or obstruction and persecution of the government. God can "stop their fury when he pleaseth," he remembered, quoting Psalm 76:12: God " 'shall cut off the spirit of princes: he is terrible to the kings of the earth.' . . . Some he will cut off and destroy, some he will terrify and affright. . . . He can knock them on the head, or break out their teeth, or chain up their wrath; and who can oppose him?"[22] Owen's exhortation alluded to the regicide. Memories of the revolution should provide believers with spiritual confidence in their struggle against indwelling sin. It is unclear what Morrice would have made of this bold and dangerous critique of the policy of the Parliament of which he was a member.

Owen's theological work continued to echo his political concerns. It was likely around this period that he preached to his small congregation the sermon that has been collected under the title "The furnace of divine wrath." The text, a version of which would be published in Owen's posthumous study of the mortification of sin in believers (1721), affords a privileged glimpse into the ideological formation of Owen's church community. His private preaching continued to enunciate the prophetic analysis that had dominated in his public preaching in earlier decades, but which had almost entirely been occluded from his published writing in the 1660s. At the end of that troubled decade, Owen was increasingly distinguishing the private voice of the prophet from the public voice of the scribe. It was another of his strategies for survival.

In "The furnace of divine wrath," Owen was reflecting upon events in the mid-1660s, which many of his contemporaries regarded as providential indicators. Two spectacular comets (1664 and 1665) had been followed by the loss of 25 percent of the population of London in the outbreak of bubonic plague (1665–66), and the destruction of the homes of around 70,000 citizens in the great fire of London (September 1666).[23] Owen lamented the hard-heartedness of English Christians, who were unresponsive to such signs: "The plague, the fire, have not done it; signs in the heavens above and in the earth beneath have not done it; the sincere preaching of the gospel, though in weakness, hath not done it; entreaties, beggings, exhortations, hath not done it; our prayers have not done it; we cleave unto the world still." Owen recognized that "a woful and a wicked corruption and profaneness of life" had "grown upon the generality of the nation," a fact that made so inexplicable the tendency of so many of the godly to identify with and wish to succeed within it. And his little church would not escape the fiery trial. "I have been speaking of it to this congregation for some years, that we are all going into the same furnace," he explained, frustrated that his concerns that providential warnings were being disregarded.[24] This sermon, like much of Owen's preaching throughout this period, offered a much more immediate account of his concern about the circumstances of English dissent than did the comments that he was prepared to publish for friendly and unfriendly scrutiny.

For Owen would preach to his small congregation messages that he could not dare commit to print, messages that experimented with prognostication and the sometimes politically charged interpretation of providence. We have been provided with extensive access to the private world of this conventicle. The notes for "The furnace of divine wrath" were taken by Sir John Hartopp, the son-in-law (and stepson) of Owen's old friend and recent patron Charles Fleetwood, and a member of the Exclusion Parliaments (1679–81), who, around this period, began the monumental task of transcribing the sermons, by various ministers, that were preached to his congregation. Owen's preaching features heavily in this record, and Hartopp's notes are detailed and convincing. His method was to takes notes in shorthand, and then to expand these notes in fair copy in bound notebooks, several of which he appears to have used simultaneously. Hartopp did not hide the limits of his record: he did not conceal the moment in which his late arrival in church meant that he missed the beginning of Owen's sermon, for example, nor do his notes always make complete sense, even after his expanding them in fair copy.[25] Consequently, the sermons recorded in Hartopp's notebooks have become an important (if unauthorized) part of the Owen canon. The editions of Owen's sermons that appeared in 1721, 1756, and 1760 each claimed to reprint materials from notebooks that had been preserved by Hartopp's family.[26] In 1854, Goold discovered a further volume of sermon notes, still in the possession of Hartopp's family, and included them in volume seventeen of his edition, sometime after the sermons from the eighteenth-century editions had been collected in his volumes eight and nine.[27] The notebooks used by these earlier editors seem to have disappeared, but three further notebooks, as yet unpublished, are held in Dr. Williams's Library, London. The relationship between these notebooks is not clear. It appears that there is minimal duplication between the sermon notebooks that have already been published and those still held in Dr. Williams's Library: the published and unpublished notebooks both contain sermons on Romans 1:16, dating from May 1670, but there does not appear to be any other significant overlap. The existence of multiple notebooks for the same period suggests that Hartopp was writing up his notes in parallel texts, perhaps with a view to circulating one notebook while making fair copies of more recent sermons in another. Taken alongside the records of Owen's congregation, which exist from 1673, these sermon notes allow us a privileged insight into the conditions in which he was working after the late 1660s.[28]

Hartopp's notes describe the culture of worship within Owen's congregation. At some points, his notes provide a detailed record of the activities of the church and the locations in which Owen was preaching. They reveal that, for much of the late 1660s, he was routinely preparing two or three substantial sermons every week; that the congregation was observing the Lord's Supper on a weekly basis for at least part of this period; that Owen's habit of preaching extended series of sermons ended in 1673, when, as we will see, the members of Joseph Caryl's congregation joined his church; and that Owen's regular routine of biblical exposition was accompanied by seasonal series in topical and doctrinal concerns. The detailed nature of many of these accounts means that we have a far greater knowledge of Owen's pastoral experiences at this point than in any other stage of his career—and makes staggering his concurrent literary output.

For Owen was incredibly busy. Living quietly throughout most of 1669, he was preaching to his small congregation from Hebrews 3 and 4, with occasional sermons in the second half of the year on the doctrine of the everlasting covenant.[29] Hartopp's notes from later in the year suggested that the congregation was meeting on a monthly basis for the celebration of the Lord's Supper, in a sequence of meetings focusing on preparation, administration, and thanksgiving, all without explanation as to why the frequency of sacramental observation had changed from Owen's advocacy of weekly communion in the late 1660s.[30] In addition to this full calendar of congregational preaching, and as his confidence grew and networks were re-established within the wider community of dissenters, Owen was able to join with other Independent and Presbyterian ministers, including Philip Nye, Thomas Brooks, Thomas Watson, William Bates, and Peter Sterry, in a public lecture at Hackney.[31] This early sign of dissenting cooperation may have drawn Owen into occasional ecclesiastical diplomacy. On 25 March 1669, with other Independent clergy, he signed a letter to the governor of Massachusetts, complaining of the colony's treatment of Baptists, investing the reputational currency of his recent invitations to its college and best-known church in the principles of toleration that he had long defended.[32] And in the early summer of 1669, Owen wrote to the Independent church in Hitchin, Hertfordshire, attempting to heal divisions that had been caused by the withdrawal of five members who had become convinced of believers' baptism, even as another faction in the church began to appeal to Richard Baxter, who declined to become involved in the dispute.[33]

At the same time, Owen also made time for several substantial literary contributions. This may have been underwritten by his inheriting £500 from a relative, Martyn Owen, who died in March 1669, perhaps his first substantial income for some time.[34] These texts were designed for a popular audience, for he had become concerned by the activity of those members of new religious movements who had become "exceedingly sedulous in scattering and giving away, yea, imposing *gratis* ... their small books which they publish, upon all sorts of persons promiscuously."[35] Consequently, *A practical exposition on the 130th Psalm* (1669) offered no spectacular displays of its author's learning. Writing for a popular audience, Owen sought to develop pithy modes of expression, insisting that "he that hath slight thoughts of sin had never great thoughts of God," while reminding his readers that God "remembers the duties which we forget, and forgets the sins which we remember."[36] As in his private sermons, he cited the fire and plague as providential warnings that ought to drive sinners to repentance, though in a much less dramatic fashion.[37] The book concluded with an unusually long section of evangelistic appeal, for he had grown frustrated by those who ignored the solemn warnings of his preaching, who left the meetings "shaking their heads, and striking on their breasts," before forgetting everything they had heard by the time they arrived home.[38] The gospel demanded more than this, for it "cost no less than the price of the blood of the Son of God," he insisted, before concluding the volume by cursing all those readers who still would not believe his message.[39] Perhaps he was remembering the frustrations of parish life in the 1640s—or perhaps he was lamenting the lack of engagement of contemporary Independents.

Owen continued to address a popular audience in *A brief declaration and vindication of the doctrine of the Trinity: As also of the person and satisfaction of Christ* (1669). This short handbook, which had been "written in a few hours ... without the least design or diversion of mind towards accuracy or ornament," included several lists of proof texts, which were designed to "give every ordinary reader an instance how fully and plainly what he is to believe in this matter is revealed in the Scripture."[40] But *A brief declaration and vindication* understated the significance of its own contribution. Its discussion of Christ's satisfaction was one of the fullest accounts of this theme in Owen's writing, and its appendix offered a sequence of supporting linguistically technical arguments.[41] The book also made some unexpected moves, arguing, for example, that the binding of Satan, which in Revelation 20 was associated with the beginning of the thousand-year reign of Christ, was to be expected in the future—a standard trope of the millennial theory that Owen had earlier rejected, and a position that significantly advanced upon his earlier expectations of an undefined latter-day glory for the church.[42] Owen's move toward an explicitly post-millennial paradigm is further evidence to support the claim that dissenters were not abandoning the eschatological impulses that had driven their earlier work, but were modifying their earlier claims, often making them ever more precise.[43] He could no longer consider that the devil had been bound, as his earlier arguments against millennial theory had assumed: perhaps the horrors of the last decade could only be explained in diabolical terms. But, far from fearing the future, Owen's millennial theory was anticipating a period of unique blessing for the godly.

Even as he saw these publications through the press, Owen was also becoming involved in supporting the literary work of others. He prepared a preface for James Durham's *Clavis cantici* (1669), which defended the allegorical interpretation of the Song of Solomon as being consistent with the New Testament. This hermeneutical approach was confirmed by Henry Lukin's *An introduction to the holy Scripture* (1669), to which Owen also contributed a preface, which listed "the several tropes, figures, proprieties of speech used therein," as the subtitle noted, another activity which suggests that Owen did not take his hermeneutic for granted.[44] And, as Catholicism became fashionable at court, he ramped up his Protestant credentials. He used his preface for *The true idea of Jansenism* (1669), by Theophilus Gale, to argue for the existence of theological variety among Catholics: "there is not one point in which they differ from Protestants, wherein they are agreed among themselves."[45] For all that he sympathized with the Augustinian emphases of Jansenist theology, Owen was most concerned to use their history to make polemical points about Rome.

This long list of responsibilities might help to explain the failure of Richard Baxter's attempt to initiate ecumenical discussions with Owen. Baxter's project was in some senses surprising, for Owen's recent publications on the issue of toleration had rankled Presbyterians. They wanted their congregations to be comprehended within the national church, and had been lobbying, not without success, to achieve this goal. But Owen was unsympathetic, and, having abandoned the idea of a single national church, had been arguing instead that those congregations that maintained an orthodox Protestant faith should be tolerated outside its boundaries. This debate was played out in the complex and often ambiguous political environment of the court, where both sides were lobbying powerful patrons. Owen, as so often before, knew how to gain political influence. In September 1668, the Presbyterian leader Thomas Manton informed Baxter that "the comprehension thought of by some, and endeavoured by our friends in Court, was wholly frustrated by Dr Owen's proposal of a toleration."[46] But the discussion continued. Baxter's reading of *A brief instruction in the worship of God* had encouraged him to believe that Owen had moderated his Independent ecclesiology, particularly in terms of admitting that the members of a church did not themselves have the power of the keys, as we have already noted. He believed that this revision of Independent ecclesiology offered a sufficient platform for cooperation between the two communities, so he wrote to his old rival to begin an extended correpondence relating to a possible agreement for cooperation between Independent and Presbyterian ministers.[47] Owen, at first, seemed enthusiastic: "could I contribute any thing towards the Accomplishment of so holy, so necessary a Work, I should willingly spend my self, and be spent in it."[48] The two men met, perhaps for the first time since the difficulties of the 1650s, when in the winter of 1668 Baxter made a series of visits to Owen's home to discuss how the proposals could be refined. In January 1669, Owen wrote to Baxter to express his approval of his "essay": "Upon the whole matter, I judge your proposals worthy of great consideration; and the most probable medium of the attainінge the end aymed at, that yet I have perused."[49] But Baxter's response was prickly, and remembered old quarrels.[50] His subsequent letters and visits to Owen achieved nothing. Baxter was clearly frustrated by what he regarded as Owen's pointless delays.[51] He felt slighted, and perhaps he had been: in a culture that valued precise exchanges of honor, Owen had failed to visit him, and had written a letter to Baxter that he failed to post.[52] But the slighting may have been unintentional: perhaps Owen was involved in so many other activities that he did not have time or energy to commit to the project. He did not have the health to support an ever-increasing workload. At the end of 27 February, he abandoned preaching to his congregation before his sermon was completed, apologizing that "my strength is gone."[53] For all of his conviction that "God gives us enough time for all that he requires of us," Owen, in 1669, was working at—perhaps even beyond—full capacity.[54] But Owen's difficulties in managing his workload may have further contributed to Baxter's suspicions that he could not be trusted.

Owen's activities may have slowed down as the second and more stringent Conventicles Act (1670) took effect.[55] He had responded directly to the new legislation, and in terms that MPs could understand. *The state of the kingdom with respect to the present bill against conventicles* (1670) made economic arguments in favor of the toleration of religious dissenters.[56] The debates that this Act provoked may have propelled Owen into direct action of resistance: rumors circulated that he had engineered the placing of some of his books in the lodgings of MPs in an effort to gain influence.[57] He already had influence: George Vernon placed Owen at the center of a network that included John Wilkins, bishop of Chester, Thomas Barlow, bishop of Lincoln, the earl of Orrery, the earl of Anglesea, Lord Willoughby, Lord Wharton, and others.[58] But these attempts to intervene failed, and the Act was put into effect from 10 May 1670. Owen responded to the crisis in *The present distresses on Nonconformists examined* (1670), making no effort to conceal the fact that he did not intend to obey the new law.[59] At the end of May, an informer explained to Henry Bennet, baron Arlington, a senior politician, that he had consulted Owen, Goodwin, Manton, Harrison, and Tombes, and had discovered that the dissenters "intend to continue their assemblies, and to submit to the penalties of the Act, if taken."[60]

And so Owen continued to fulfill his congregational responsibilities. From February until October 1670, he was preaching to his congregation a long series on John 3:3.[61] During the spring, he was talking about religious liberty to Bulstrode Whitelocke, whose safety had been secured by bribery on a massive scale, in a conversation network that also included Lady Ranelagh and Lord Willoughby.[62] In May, Owen preached several sermons to his congregation on Romans 1:16, remembering that he had "lived in days wherein it hath been so far from being a shame to be counted a Christian, that it hath been a shame for a man to be counted no Christian."[63] One week later, continuing his exposition of the text into a second sermon, he considered that the power of the gospel "hath this power upon the souls of men,—to convince them, convert them, draw them home to God," but also to "expose them to all troubles in this world; to make them let go their reputation and livelihood, and expose themselves even to death itself."[64]

Owen was becoming ever more conscious of death. In November 1670, in a letter to Charles Nichols, he complained that "I have daily warnings from my age, being now about fifty four and many infirmities to be preparing for my dissolution."[65] Preaching to his congregation in the same month, he remembered that he could not know how death "may approach us, and how soon this will be." But, he continued, "when all this state and frame of things shall vanish, and we prove to have an utter unconcernment in things below; when the curtain shall be turned aside, and we shall look into another world; the soul's relief lies in God's immutability,—that we shall find him the same to us in death as he was in life, and much more."[66]

Owen would certainly need this kind of encouragement as the gospel continued to expose him to "all troubles in this world."[67] Some of his difficulties came from those whom he might have expected to be his allies. Much of the attention from New England, for example, was positive. In the first half of 1671, John Hull, who had sailed across the Atlantic, was a regular attender at Owen's meetings.[68] In August 1671, the magistrates and ministers of Massachusetts wrote to the leaders of the English Independents to appeal for help in refurbishing the college in Cambridge, and in recruiting new staff and students.[69] Six months later, the English ministers replied by advising the Americans of "the straits and troubles the ministers and churches of Christ are here wrestling with," the "exhausted purses of those that are most able to contribute," and of the "impoverished families" that could not afford to send their sons to study there.[70] But some of the colonial contacts were discouraging. Around the same time, Owen wrote to John Eliot, the veteran missionary to native Americans. This was a much more personal letter, responding to Eliot's recent criticism of Owen's *Exercitations concerning the name, original, nature, use and continuance of a day of sacred rest* (1671), a substantial exposition of Hebrews 4. Eliot had used some "severe expressions" in responding to Owen's discussions of the Sabbath, and Owen had been stung by his assertions that his work was likely to undermine biblical standards of holiness. He was wounded by the charge: "I suppose there is scarce any one alive in the world who hath more reproaches cast upon him than I have; though hitherto God has been pleased in some measure to support my spirit under them. . . . I do acknowledge unto you that I have a dry and barren spirit." The cause was not self-pity: "that I should now be apprehended to have given a wound unto holiness in the churches . . . is one of the saddest frowns in the cloudy brows of Divine Providence." Owen wondered whether this same providence was now calling him to "surcease from these kinds of labours."[71] He was ready to give up writing. And he was ill. In letters dating from the same period, Owen complained of a relapse into dysentry, "with such violence that I had the sentence of death in my selfe."[72] And the "reproaches" continued. Samuel Parker, a senior Anglican, attacked Owen in his *Defence and continuation of the Ecclesiastical Polity* (1671), citing his record of preaching against toleration and casting up the record of his activities during the revolution to argue for his mendacity, as Roger L'Estrange, who policed publications, threatened the life of one party who intended to intervene.[73]

But Owen stuck it out. By the end of 1671, he had begun a long series of sermons on Hebrews 12:14, a text on which he would continue to preach until May 1673, returning to the passage later that summer.[74] His movement into the public sphere continued in the spring of 1672. In the early part of the year, he was continuing to preach to his congregation, with Hartopp taking notes on sermons on 5 and 9 January.[75] These sermons may have been occasional texts, as other manuscript evidence suggests that Owen had begun an extended series on Hebrews 12:14, which would stretch from November 1671 until May 1673.[76] At the end of January and in early February, he developed a short series of studies on the doctrine of conversion.[77]

Finally there was a glimmer of respite: he must have been heartened by the king's promise that the hegemony of the established church would cease, and encouraged by several interviews with representatives of the crown.[78]

Owen and the other Independents had long realized that their political hopes for toleration lay with the king, rather than his parliament. On 15 March 1672, Charles issued an indulgence that allowed dissenters to meet for public worship.[79] It was a triumph for Owen's arguments, though perhaps a policy driven by other concerns, and he was pushed to the foreground in conveying the gratitude of his community. On the morning of 28 March, Owen and other Independent ministers addressed the king in Lord Arlington's residence. Shortly afterward, Charles provided Owen with one thousand guineas to alleviate the suffering of dissenters.[80] The extraordinary experience of meeting the king, whose father's death he had commemorated in 1649, must have been as overwhelming as the opportunity to begin the public worship for which dissenters had long waited. Owen led—and to some extent coordinated—the rush for licenses for public worship. On 16 April he applied for a license to preach in the Society of Leathersellers, which may never have been granted.[81] Owen used his new home, in Charterhouse Yard, the site of his first home in London, as a collection point for licenses for those Independents coming in from the country, including representatives of the Independent fellowship he had established in Coggeshall.[82]

Of course, the opportunity to organize was pushing dissenters—and their divisions—into the public sphere. Owen's response was to publish, in June or July 1672, *A discourse concerning evangelical love.*[83] The theme had not dominated his earlier writing, and was not obviously supported by his new metaphor of choice. Several times in his exposition of Psalm 130 and in the *Brief declaration* he had invoked the image of Samson, who, though late in life and in discouraging circumstances, had scored his greatest victory against the Philistines in an act of self-sacrifice that ensured the mass death of his enemies.[84] The account of Samson was becoming increasingly common in the print culture of dissent: Milton's *Samson agonistes* (1671) was certainly not the only text to invoke the specter of strategic self-destruction in the face of overwhelming odds. And others were recognizing Owen's potential for danger, including Samuel Parker, who seemed to epitomize the "apostasies and backslidings" about which Owen had worried.[85] Once a precisian student in Cromwellian Oxford, and now an enthusiastic opportunist and rising star within the Church of England, Parker had described his former vice chancellor as "the greatest Pest and Most Dangerous Enemy of the Commonwealth."[86] He had thrown down a gauntlet. The stage was set for one of the period's principal literary debates, which provoked some unexpected antagonists and illuminated some very unexpected alliances.

II

In September 1672, Owen was standing in Nathaniel Ponder's printing shop in London, reading the proofs of an anonymous political satire, *The rehearsal transpros'd*, a response to Samuel Parker's series of vitriolic attacks on nonconformity.[87] Owen and his former student had a very long history. Parker's *Discourse of ecclesiastical politie* (1669) had been met by Owen's *Truth and innocence vindicated* (1669). Parker's response, his *Defence and continuation of the Ecclesiastical Politie* (1671), ramped up the "vociferous abuse" of his former vice chancellor, citing as evidence of his danger the sermons that he had preached in the 1650s.[88] Parker continued his assault in his *Preface to Bishop Bramhall's vindication* (1672), describing Owen as a "great Scribler," who was also "the great Bell-weather of Disturbance and Sedition."[89] Parker's language was extreme: "it were a notorious Calumny to paint anything but the Devil himself in blacker Colours."[90] This was fighting talk from a senior figure in the Restoration church.

But Owen had his allies. His task in Ponder's printing shop was to protect the identity of the author of *The rehearsal transpros'd*—his friend, Andrew Marvell. It is not clear when this friendship developed: although Marvell and Owen both served in the Cromwellian administration, and processed next to each other at Cromwell's funeral, it most likely that their friendship developed after the younger man came out of the influence of his former colleague, and Owen's esrtwhile nemesis, John Milton. Marvell had managed to survive the purges of the Restoration to represent Hull as a member of the Cavalier Parliament.[91] *The rehearsal transpros'd* was a witty and often scurrilous riposte to Parker's charges. Owen must have appreciated Marvell's concern: if the contents of his posthumous library sale can be taken at face value, he may have owned two copies of Marvell's text.[92] But in its ribaldry and politically charged wit, *The rehearsal transpros'd* was a most unlikely object for his care.

Marvell's response to Parker was designed, in part, to rescue Owen's reputation. It was another attempt to identify the cause of dissent with that of the court. Marvell complained that Parker had meddled "with the King, the Succession, the Privy-Council, Popery, Atheism, Bishops, Ecclesiastical Government, and above all with Nonconformity, and *J. O.*"[93] He complained that Parker had made Owen a peculiar target of his literary energy, "either in broad meanings or in plain terms," and speculated that the difficulties in their relationship could be traced back to problems during the period in which Parker was a student.[94] But, Marvell complained, his attack on Owen was entirely without proportion, and was driven by inappropriate energy: "there was no holding him. Thus it must be, and no better, when a man's Phancy is up, and his Breeches are down."[95] Marvell's bawdy wit attacked Parker's reputation with a combination of ideology and innuendo.

The debate escalated as other participants joined the discussion, and as Parker replied to Marvell in *A reproof to The rehearsal transpros'd*, which Marvell answered in the second part of his text. The exchange prompted a generous range of replies, including *Rosemary and Bayes* (1672), by the ever unreliable Henry Stubbe, which critiqued both sides represented in the argument. While defending Owen's reputation, Marvell argued the case for the toleration of dissenters. As in Owen's responses to *Fiat lux*, Marvell spoke highly of the character of the king, who remained the best hope for securing religious toleration. And the king also appears to have admired Marvell's work, twice reading his riposte to Parker. It was the kind of work he enjoyed. For, in Marvell's writing, theology had become sexualized. And thus it continued in Parker's response, *The transproser rehears'd* (1673), which cast the satirist and the theologian as lovers. Parker imagined the scene, as Marvell,

> being passionately in Love (you may allow him to be an Allegorical Lover at least) with old I[J]oan (not the Chandlers, but Mr. Calvins Widow) walks discontentedly by the side of the Lake Lemane, sighing to the Winds and calling upon the Woods; not forgetting to report his Mistresses name so often, till he teach all the Eccho's to repeat nothing but I[J]oan; now entertaining himself in his Solitude, with such little Sports, as loving his Love with an I[J], and then loving his Love with an O, and the like for the other Letters.[96]

Parker's attack on Owen continued as MPs pushed for and achieved the revocation of the indulgence in March 1673.[97] The king had been outflanked. Dissenters were again endangered, and perhaps more so, after a year of liberty had brought their networks into public view. Owen found himself occasionally in danger. In Oxfordshire, he evaded capture by the cunning ruse of being in bed when his host informed the troopers that he had already left the premises.[98] His circumstances grew more dangerous, but his pastoral work continued.

III

Owen's ministry entered a new phase on 5 June 1673, when his small congregation amalgamated with the church that had been led by Joseph Caryl, who had recently died, with a stated meeting place in the larger group's premises in Leadenhall Street, London.[99] The two ministers had a long association. Caryl had likely first encountered Owen by means of *The duty of pastors and people distinguished* (1644), which he had recommended for publication: ironically, given that the merger was between two Independent congregations, this was a book in which Owen had presented himself as a Presbyterian. The two men had first met on 19 April 1649, when they preached on the same occasion to Parliament. Their names were increasingly associated during the late spring and early summer of 1650, by which time they had been appointed by Cromwell to accompany the army in its invasion of Scotland. Their friendship had continued into the second generation: Owen's host at Theobalds in the early 1660s had been Caryl's daughter, Sarah Caryl. With this extended friendship between their pastors, the two congregations were not likely to be strangers to each other, though their memberships were strikingly different. At the point of amalgamation, Owen's congregation comprised around thirty-five individuals, most of whom are identifiable as wealthy individuals with strong links to the fellowship that had met in Wallingford House. At the center of Owen's congregation was a network of disappointed revolutionaries, many of whom had a direct link to the Cromwell family. Their number included Charles Fleetwood and his wife, Mary; Sir John Hartopp, with others of their children; and Cromwell's brother-in-law, Colonel John Desborough, who had spent the early 1660s in exile on the Continent, planning an invasion of England and a third civil war, before returning home to spend a year in the Tower of London. Cromwell Fleetwood, a son of Charles and Bridget, joined the combined church in June 1673. Samuel Lee, formerly an Oxford academic, was the author of *Israel redux* (1677), which argued for the future restoration of the Jews to the Promised Land. By contrast, the congregation that had been led by Joseph Caryl numbered around 135 and represented a more diverse population, with few of the names, according to the early twentieth-century editor of the church book, being of any "public interest."[100]

Moving to London in the spring of 1673, Owen's pastoral responsibilities must suddenly have multiplied. We have a good sense of the circumstances of this combined congregation from its church book, which lists the membership of both churches at the point of amalgamation, and adds details of losses and gains into the early eighteenth century. The church gained 111 new members in the decade between the combination of the churches and Owen's death. Their number included Mary Kennington, Owen's last surviving daughter, who joined the church in March 1674 and died in April 1682, and the Countess of Anglesey, who joined the church in October 1680, and whose husband, Sir Arthur Annesley, was a senior government official. The church book gives no hint of the tensions that his position might have introduced into the fellowship, though the fact that John and Mary Owen had frequently dined with the Annesleys during the previous decade may suggest that his influence in dissent was benign.[101] Around fifteen members of those originally belonging to Owen's church died in the period 1673–83, including Mary, his wife. A number of members of the combined group were dismissed, with their new places of residence sometimes being noted, while others left the church to join the Baptists and Quakers. There do not appear to have been any excommunications during Owen's ministry.[102] Perhaps the most important addition to the new church in its first year was Isaac Loeffs, who became a member of the church on 26 December 1673 and was installed as Owen's assistant on Friday, 23 January 1674.[103] Loeffs would be the first of three assistants, serving alongside Owen from 1673 until 1682. He would be followed by Robert Ferguson, a convert from the Church of Scotland who had acted as a government spy in the 1660s before becoming a Whig hack, and an agent of the earl of Shaftesbury, who would serve alongside Owen from 1674 until *circa* 1679, while becoming involved in regicidal conspiracies, and who would, after Owen's death, convert to the Church of England and become a Jacobite conspirator. Owen's last assistant—and replacement—would be David Clarkson, who would lead the Leadenhall Street congregation from 1682 until 1686.[104] The move to London also situated Owen with the broader cultures of the Independent churches. John Bunyan's congregation in Bedford released members who moved to the capital on condition that they join the Leadenhall Street church, for example; Bunyan himself claimed that Owen had endorsed the arguments of his *Differences in judgement about water baptism, no bar to communion* (1673), though he ultimately preferred not to write a commendation, supposedly on the advice of several London Baptists.[105] By 1673, therefore, Owen had entered into his final responsibility, as pastor of a substantial, well-connected, and growing Independent church in London.

Owen marked the amalgamation of the churches in a sermon on "Gospel charity." He was clearly worried that the members of the new church might downplay the significance of their relationships with each other by paying excessive attention to him, perhaps as the means by which they had come and would be held together.[106] But loyalty to the pastor was insufficient—and in fact was a structural weakness in a context in which ministers could easily be displaced. "I had rather see a church filled with love a thousand times, than filled with the best, the highest, and the most glorious gifts," Owen explained, for it was mutual love, rather than extraordinary preaching, that would sustain the life of the congregation.[107] "Love is the means of communion between all the members of the mystical body of Christ," he continued, "as faith is the instrument of their communion with their head, Jesus

Christ."[108] Perhaps it was around this time that Owen supplied a preface for *The nature and principles of love* (1673), written, appropriately enough, by the late Joseph Caryl.

The sermon on "Gospel charity" is a good reflection of the extent to which Owen's later preaching reflected new and pastoral themes, even as it developed new techniques of presentation. For, from 1673, Owen appears to move away from long series of sermons to preach each week on isolated texts.[109] Perhaps the larger part of his new congregation had developed a distaste for series of sermons after the extraordinary concentration of their previous pastor, Joseph Caryl, whose homiletic project on the Old Testament book of Job consumed twelve volumes of printed text and fifteen years of his life (1651–66).[110] Owen's sermons contrast entirely with those that he had published during the 1640s and 1650s, being much shorter and much simpler, and addressing the very specific conditions of a small group of people that he likely knew extremely well. But many of the themes were enduring. It was only one month after the combination of the two churches, on Friday, 11 July 1673, that Owen reminded the fellowship of the providential warnings that England had received in the form of fire and plague.[111] Perhaps thinking of Mrs. Loyd, a congregant who died in the same month, Owen considered that "our things, and other men's things, the things of the nation, are the things of families, so far as they are in and of this world, are liable to a destructive dissolution. . . . There is a dissolution lies at the door between you and your estates, between you and your wives, between you and your children."[112] "Wives, children, husbands, may be dead, our houses may be fired and all consumed," he continued. "There is only this, the word of God, that abides for ever; the promises of God fail not."[113] He was speaking from experience.

Owen's literary work continued. His duties in 1673 included writing prefaces for *A new and useful concordance*, by Vavasor Powell, as well as Edward Polhill's *The divine will considered in the eternal decrees*, and a new edition of the metrical psalter that had been recommended by the Westminster Assembly. Owen's name was third on the long list of supporting ministers, alongside that of Thomas Manton, in a preface which admitted that while "spiritual songs of meer humane composure may have their use," devotion would be "best secured, where the matter & words are of immediately Divine inspiration; and to us Davids Psalms seem plainly intended by those terms of Psalms and Hymns and Spiritual Songs, which the Apostle useth, Ephes. 5. 19. Col. 3. 16."[114] Nevertheless, the preface acknowledged, only some of those ministers recommending the psalter had actually been using it—an extraordinary illustration of the limited impact of Westminster Assembly documents in the later seventeenth century.[115]

Of course, Owen was not the only member of the Leadenhall Street church to engage in literary work. The best-known literary figure associated with the congregation does not appear to have become a member. Lucy Hutchinson, the memoirist of the civil wars who had followed the loss of her husband by undertaking substantial projects of translation, was attending the congregation regularly in 1673, and may around this period have begun her translation of Owen's *Θεολογουμενα παντοδαπα* (1661), a text that appears to have influenced her epic poem, *Order and disorder* (1679).[116] It is not clear why Hutchinson did not join the congregation—perhaps her belief in believers' baptism made this impossible. There is much about Owen's relationship with Hutchinson that remains opaque. It is possible that their acquaintance pre-dated the Restoration, though Hutchinson's memoir of her husband's life provides no evidence to substantiate the possibilities: John Hutchinson, who signed the king's death warrant, may have attended the sermon that Owen preached to Parliament on the day after the regicide, and, given the rather small numbers of those committed to the revolutionary regime in its earliest years, it is likely that the two men knew each other. Hutchinson engaged Robert Ferguson, who joined the church in 1674 and later acted as Owen's pastoral assistant, as a Latin tutor for her son.[117] Her close friend, Lady Annesley, wife of the earl of Anglesey, the anti-regicide judge who would hold the office of Lord Privy Seal after 1673, would become a member of the church in 1680.[118] But Owen never refers to Hutchinson, although she attended his preaching and spent considerable time translating one of his most demanding works. Hutchinson's decision to follow her translation of Lucretius and Calvin with detailed and analytical work on Owen's most difficult book to date illustrates something of the place of women in the strongly cerebral, if ideologically versatile, subcultures of the godly in the later Restoration.[119] Hutchinson's project to translate large sections of Owen's *Θεολογουμενα παντοδαπα* is one of the most remarkable evidences of the manner in which women readers were engaging with his work. Hutchinson would have found in the text a rationale for thinking about Lucretius, an author about whom she and Owen had both written.[120] Hutchison may also have read Owen's text as illustrative of the means by which dissenting literary activity could circumvent the horrific circumstances of the 1660s. Remembering her own vacillations, which preserved her husband's life in the period immediately following the Restoration, she may have understood better than many of Owen's modern readers the strategic ambiguities and rhetorical gambits required of old republicans engaged in literary work in the dangerous world of the 1670s.[121]

IV

By the mid-1670s, Owen had established the pattern of the last years of his life. Now in his late fifties, dogged by illness and likely concerned about the health of his wife, Owen focused his work on preaching, pastoral care, and writing for publication. Yet, in literary terms, the last decade of his life was one of his most productive. Some of this work was occasional, as in his interactions with William Sherlock (1674) and Edward Stillingfleet (1680, 1681), two Anglican theologians who challenged the literary, theological, and political quality of Owen's work. Sherlock was concerned by Owen's treatise on communion with God, and published *A discourse concerning the knowledge of Jesus Christ and our union and communion with him* (1674) to offer an "ironic imitation" of the non-conformist appropriation of the medieval mystical tradition. He exposed the "accumulation of hyperbole" in dissenting readings of the Song of Solomon as representing no more than "empty word association."[122] "Christ is Lovely, because he is rich and powerful," Sherlock continued in his parody of dissenting exposition, "and he is powerful, because he is rich, and lovely, and Rich, because he is powerful and lovely."[123] His argument was that the dissenters' reading of the Song attributed "too much substantive meaning to a rhetorical strategy."[124] And the charge stung: Owen's assistant, Robert Ferguson, also replied to Sherlock in *The interest of reason in religion* (1675). But Owen addressed Sherlock's concerns in a weightly series of linguistically and critically advanced theological and expository studies.

His most significant works in this period were his volumes of commentary on Hebrews (1674, 1680, 1684), to which was appended *The nature of apostasie from the profession of the Gospel, and the punishment of apostates declared, in an exposition of Heb. 6. 4, 5, 6* (1676). His greatest innovations in this latter part of his writing career were included in a sequence of works developing new insights in the work of the Holy Spirit, including *Πνευματολογια, or, A discourse concerning the Holy Spirit* (1674), which continued to engage with the "scurrilous, clamorous writings" of Samuel Parker, and *A discourse of the work of the Holy Spirit in prayer* (1682), with additional work appearing after his death.[125] This work was purposefully new: advancing upon and clarifying his earlier work in the area, Owen explained that he "knew not of any who ever went before me" in preparing such a detailed pneumatology, and that consequently he had "no rule, nor guide, nor any thing to give us assistance but pure revelation," though it is not the case, as has been claimed, that Owen was recognizing the "primary authority" of experience in this text.[126] Much of Owen's writing in this period restated central tenets of Protestantism, as in *The reason of faith: or*

An answer unto that enquiry, wherefore we believe the Scripture to be the word of God (1677), *The doctrine of justification by faith through the imputation of the righteousness of Christ* (1677), *Σύνεσις πνευματική, or, The causes, waies & means of understanding the mind of God* (1678), and, most polemically of all, *The Church of Rome no safe guide* (1679) and anonymous interventions, including *A brief and impartial account of the nature of the Protestant religion* (1682). This return to foundational doctrines reflected his increasing sense of the fragility of the English Reformation, as James, the openly Catholic duke of York, waited in the wings to succeed his brother to the throne. *Some considerations about union among Protestants* (1680) and *The case of present distresses on non-conformists, examined* (1682), the latter of which was published anonymously, maintained his interest in discussing the political situation of his community. Owen returned to meditate upon deity in *Ξριστολογια, or, A declaration of the glorious mystery of the person of Christ, God and Man* (1679), and returned to pastoral theology, for which he had become well known, in *Φρονεμα του πνευματος, or, The grace and duty of being spiritually-minded* (1681). In the view of his reading public, Owen had become a scribe, developing large-scale expositions of biblical texts and theological themes, sticking largely to safe ground to make the mature contributions that would be so frequently reprinted in succeeding centuries and which have attracted fine theological analysis in recent work. Owen retained the old prophetic impulse, but it rarely broke into public view. *An humble testimony unto the goodness and severity of God in his dealings with sinful churches and nations* (1681) was one of the few occasions in which the providential analysis of his private sermons was reflected in the culture of print.

For it is Owen's work within his congregation that reveals most about his religious life in this period. His concern for his congregants reflected the griefs that he had earlier endured. Around May 1674, Owen wrote to Lady Elizabeth Hartopp, who was mourning the death of her infant daughter. "Your dear infant is in the eternal enjoyment of the fruits of all our prayers," Owen assured the grieving mother, "for the covenant of God is ordered in all things, and sure." It was, perhaps, an occasion for him to think of the deaths of his own children. "God in Christ will be better to you than ten children"—alluding to the Old Testament story of Hannah but also, perhaps, thinking of his own ten children, only one of whom was still alive.[127] Writing to Charles Fleetwood in July 1674, Owen reported that his wife's health had improved, and considered that "there is more than ordinary mercy in every days preservation."[128] By the end of the summer, Owen was concerned that "the great change of the weather in this moist place hath stirred up my old distemper," a discomfort about which he was still concerned in March of the following year.[129] In May 1675 he was reflecting on the dangers attending dissenters' business interactions: godly "traders and dealers ... can scarce touch upon a business ... but they must be compelled to hear swearing, cursing, filthy discourses, that are not convenient, and all manner of profaneness. There is peril in this."[130] But there was peril in the churches, too: preaching to the Leadenhall Street congregation on 1 January 1676, Owen reminded his listeners that the great fire, one decade earlier, had been a providential warning.[131] He was worried that his congregants had become passive observers of divine activity, waiting for God's revenge upon their persecutors, instead of sharing in his pain over their display of sin. In early November 1676, he noted that

> we have been almost well contented that men should be as wicked as they would themselves, and we sit still and see what would come of it. Christ hath been dishonoured, the Spirit of God blasphemed, and God provoked against the land of our nativity; and yet we have not been affected with these things. . . . There is no one of us can have any evidence that we shall escape outward judgements that God will bring for these abominations.[132]

Owen was ever more convinced that the dissenting churches were failing. He feared that "the minds of professors" had "grown altogether indifferent as to the doctrine of God's eternal election, the sovereign efficacy of grace in the conversion of sinners, justification by the imputation of the righteousness of Christ." He was increasingly nostalgic: "I bless God I knew something of the former generation, when professors would not hear of these things without the highest detestation."[133] Owen believed that "there was not a more glorious profession for a thousand years upon the face of the earth, than was among the professors of the last age in this nation."[134] There was no hint of regret for the actions in which the "professors of the last age in this nation" had engaged. Looking at London in the mid-1670s, all he could see was declension. It was hardly surprising, in February 1676, that an informer described the Leadenhall Street congregation as "praying and preaching to the decrying of the present power and all authority to them contrary."[135]

Owen's personal griefs continued. Mary Owen, to whom he had been married for three decades, died on 28 January 1677.[136] He made no reference to her death in any of his sermons in this period. He carried on relentlessly. Owen continued his literary work, perhaps recommending that his publisher should take on John Bunyan's *The pilgrim's progress* (1677) while preparing commendatory prefaces for Patrick Gillespie's *The ark of the covenant opened* and Samuel Corbyn's *An awakening call* on 22 March.[137] Through this period, he was working simultaneously on his book on justification and the next installment of his commentary on Hebrews—a fact that explains their substantial duplication of content.[138] He was also remembered as having taken advantage of links to Thomas Barlow, his former tutor and Oxford librarian, who as bishop of Lincoln was still working for the benefit of dissenters, to secure the release from prison of John Bunyan, on 21 June.[139] And then, suddenly, on the same day, and in unknown circumstances, Owen was licensed to marry Dorothy D'Oyley, a widow from within the congregation who would outlive him by twenty years. He was described as living in St. Andrew Undershaft, possibly, as Cook suggests, in a house on Leadenhall Street rented for him by his brother Henry.[140] But marriage did little to lift his spirits. At the end of the summer, William Hooke informed Increase Mather that Owen was "valetudinarious and crazy," and "often down."[141] One year later, he continued to be dismayed by the spiritual condition of the gathered congregations: "I tell you freely," he advised his congregation on 6 September 1678, "my fears are, that if we were to gather churches again, as we did thirty years ago, we should have but a small harvest."[142] Idealizing the past, while despairing of the future, Owen was struggling to make sense of the present.

It is this sense of failure that dominates Owen's private preaching in the latter years of his life. On 11 April 1679, Sir John Hartopp arrived late at the meeting, and missed taking notes on the early part of Owen's sermon.[143] But he was able to record his pastor's jeremiad: "Is there not a confluence of all sorts of sins among us whereof mankind can contract guilt, especially of those sins upon the commission of which God pronounces a nation ruined,—atheism and profaneness, blood and murder, adultery and uncleanness, and pride?"[144] Remembering the warnings of the fire and plague, Owen concluded that "London will be undone and England will fall, and there will be no deliverance."[145] The city had turned into a scene from a nightmare. The discipline involved in the production of technical theological writing that took up so much of his time could not distract Owen from the reality that London was a theater of torture, in which gates, walls, and posts were "hung like shambles with the limbs of slaughtered persons," and "the ground around ... strewn with the bones and ashes of men burned to death."[146] Yet these horrors, so visible to all who gathered for the preaching, pointed to worse horrors to come: "for many years ... without failing," he reminded his congregation on 9 April 1680, "I have been warning you continually of an approaching calamitous time, and considering the sins that have been the causes of it."[147] Later in the month, his prognostications grew more specific: "I have had a great persuasion that the clouds that are gathering will, at least in their first storm, fall upon the people of God. I must repeat it again and again; I have been warning you some years, and telling you it would be so. ... I have not sat studying for things to speak, but only tell you the experience of my own heart."[148] In early May, he reported to the congregation that "half the talk of the world" was about the possibility that Catholicism would return to England.[149] Toward the end of the month, he had become more hopeful, that "when God hath accomplished some ends upon us, and hath stained the glory of all flesh, he will renew the power and glory of religion among us again, even in this nation."[150] All hope was not lost.

And then God's ends—and plots—began. On Thursday, 15 July 1680, Owen and other ministers were summoned by Sir Lionell Jenkins to "speak with him that afternoon about some matters of great consideration."[151] Twenty years after the Restoration, and at the age of sixty-three, Owen was still considered a threat to the stability of the regime, whose downfall he was predicting. And for good reason: Owen may have been involved in conspiracies with Henry Owen, his brother, and Robert Ferguson, his assistant pastor, in the febrile aftermath of the discovery of the so-called "Popish Plot" to murder Charles II.[152] The interrogation did not discourage Owen. Several months later, he preached a fast-day sermon for his church.[153] This was to become the first sermon to his congregation to be published, appearing as *Seasonable words for English Protestants* (1690). Owen set out to "represent ... the state of the nation wherein we live, and the only way and means for our deliverance from universal destruction."[154] His discussion of the biblical text returned to themes that he had developed in *Θεολογουμενα παντοδαπα* (1661), arguing that idolatry began in Babylon. His premise was that the Old Testament denunciations of Babylon should be applied to the Roman Catholic church.[155] He recognized that he wrote in unpromising times for the future of English Protestants, and frankly admitted that "no man doth more despond."[156] He fashioned himself after the prophet Isaiah: "Methinks sometimes I see by faith the Lord high lift up upon his throne, and his train filling the temple with his glory, and holding the balance of this nation in his hand, and [that he] can turn it to mercy or judgement, as seems good unto him."[157] Owen reckoned that the plague, the great fire, the second Dutch war, and "the prodigious appearances in heaven above" were all signs of the times—especially "that which at present hangs over us, as an ensign of God's supernal host."[158] This comet was one of a sequence that generated widespread discussion in the political and scientific literature of the period.[159] Owen's reference was not to Halley's comet, as Goold suggests, which only came into view in the late summer of 1682, but to the "Great Comet," which was visible from the middle of November 1680 until the middle of March 1681, and which, in December 1680, was increasing in intensity.[160] Owen believed that Titus Oates's discovery of the "Popish Plot" was an indication that God was still being merciful to England (though the plot turned out to be a fabrication).[161] But the threat of a Catholic king was real: just as the revolution had been undone, so the reformation could be reversed. Owen realized the limits of what an old and infirm man could contribute to the defense of the Protestant faith: "I wish I had strength."[162]

For it was all too obvious that he was part of a declining generation. In September 1680, Owen lamented "this dying time, especially among good ministers, one or another [dying] almost every day."[163] On 3 October he reflected upon the very recent death of a member of the church with whom he had enjoyed "thirty years' acquaintence and friendship, and half that time in church-fellowship"—William Steele, who must have joined the Stoke Newington congregation in the mid-1660s before transferring to the Leadenhall Street church.[164] Owen felt his loss. "The seat before my eyes is very much changed in a short time."[165] But the loss was fruitful. Owen continued his meditations on death on 10 October 1680, and developed the material for later use in his book on the glory of Christ.[166] Meanwhile, deaths in the congregation continued. Owen did not explain this simply on the basis of the age profile of the church. His long-standing habit of providential interpretation pushed him to consider these deaths as evidence of divine displeasure. "I cannot look before me, I cannot look behind me, but I see the footsteps of death. It hath been here, it hath been there, upon the right hand and upon the left," he explained in July 1681.[167] Reporting that he had sat by the bedside of a dying church member, Owen admitted the principal failing of his ministry: "I do not know that [God] hath given me a greater rebuke, in the whole course of my ministry, than that I have been labouring in the fire to discover the causes of God's withdrawing from us without any success."[168] He was worried and frustrated by the loss of old friends, the decline of eminent ministers, and political powerlessness. In his earliest clerical appointments, he had blamed his failures on his parishioners. But now he was willing to recognize his own responsibility. "I have seen too many days of humiliation without reformation," he explained to his congegation in the spring of 1681; "I have now been very long, though very unprofitable, in the ministration of the word. . . . I am ready to faint, and give over, and to beg of the church they would think of some other person to conduct them in my room, without these disadvantages."[169] He had given his people too many sermons that he could describe as "poor, weak . . . and perhaps . . . quickly forgotten."[170] Owen was ending his long career as a minister of the word by acknowledging another experience of defeat.

Owen retired to the country, lodging with Philip, Lord Wharton, in Woodburn, but his plotting may have continued. Always a schemer, and always pushing for providence to lead in the direction he preferred, Owen may have spent his last years developing a series of conspiracies. Traveling in and out of London, he was regularly in trouble with the law. On 21 November 1681, he was required to appear in the Crown Office with ten other ministers, including Robert Ferguson, on charges which warranted the fine of £4,840, which it is not clear was ever paid.[171] On 12 December, he was included in another list of dissenting ministers against whom incriminating information had been lodged.[172] In an undated letter to the Leadenhall Street church, he admitted that "the continuance of my painfull infirmities and the increase of my weaknesses will not allow me at present to hope that I should be able to bear the journey" to London.[173] He was glad that the work of preaching was "well supplied by my brother in the ministry," his pastoral assistant, and encouraged the believers to remember that "the shame and loss we may undergo for the sake of Christ and the profession of the Gospel, is the greatest honour which, in this life, we can be made partakers of." But he also remembered the state of the church—that "every trial of our faith towards our Lord Jesus Christ is also a trial of our love toward the brethren," and so encouraged the church to take care of itself while it was unsafe for its ministers to be seen in public. Owen advised the church to "appoint some among your selves, who may continually as their occasions will admit, goe up and down from house to house and apply themselves peculiarly unto the weake, the tempted, the fearful, those who are ready to despond, or to halt, and to encourage them in the Lord."[174] The church had no ruling elders to support the work of its ministers, and, as in the congregation in Coggeshall, the responsibility for pastoral care would have to fall upon laymen. But Owen was also in need of encouragement. In a later letter to Thomas Whitaker, he reported that he was "labouring with age, infirmities, temptations, and troubles," and admitted that he had "dreadful apprehensions of the present state of things in the world," for God was "withdrawing his presence from His Churches and other professors of the gospel."[175] He was still writing: he had finished the second part of *The true nature of a gospel church and its government*, but did not know when it would be published (it eventually appeared in 1689). And he still had sufficient influence to have his nephew, John Hartcliffe, from Stadhampton, appointed as headmaster of the Merchant Taylors' School.[176]

But Owen faced one final family tragedy. Mary, his only surviving child, who had joined the church in 1674, died.[177] It must have been a terrible blow for a discouraged old man. In August, Owen wrote to Charles Fleetwood, complaining that he was experiencing "soe much deadness, soe much unspirituality, soe much weakness in faith, coldness of love, instability in holy meditations," while recognizing that he could also be "overwhelmed" by "great . . . glorious . . . inexpressible" thanksgiving.[178] In early September, he appointed his pastoral successor, preaching an ordination sermon for David Clarkson.[179] "Christ hath instituted a beautiful order in his church, if it were discovered and improved," he considered; "I have wished sometimes I could live to see it; but I do not think I shall." It was an opportunity for Owen to offer a retrospective view of his long and troubled career: "I have the advantage of most here present in this," he explained, "that I know the contest we had for the truths of the gospel before our troubles began, and was an early person engaged in them; and knew those godly ministers that did contend for them as for their lives and souls." But the clarity and urgency of the exposition of the gospel—and the wars fought in its defense—had given way to weakness, ambiguity, and confusion among believers. Owen, who had written millions of words to clarify Protestant theology, could not understand the evil days on which he had fallen:

> Who would have thought that we should have come to an indifferency as to the doctrine of justification, and quarrel and dispute about the interest of works in justification; about general redemption, which takes off the efficacy of the redeeming work of Christ; and about the perseverance of the saints.[180]

Despite his best efforts, his extraordinary project of refining the Reformation had failed. He had published millions of words in the defense and development of doctrines that now met with indifference.

Perhaps it was this sense of corporate and individual failure that drove Owen to consider other means by which to defend the Protestant constitution of England and the freedom of dissenting believers. Legal pressure continued to be brought to bear upon him and his colleagues, who were prosecuted under the terms of the Corporation and Conventicle acts in late October and early November 1682, even as Owen may have engaged in "the great final climax" of his career—the Rye House Plot (1682–83).[181]

The Rye House Plot emerged out of the tensions that had been created by the attempt of some MPs in the Oxford Parliament (1681) to exclude James, the duke of York, from the royal succession. This Exclusion Bill reflected their fear that James, whose Catholicism had been revealed in 1673, would upon his accession to the throne overturn the Protestant liberties of the kingdom. But the bill was never enacted—Charles dissolved the Oxford Parliament before his brother could be legally barred from becoming king. There was now no legitimate means of protecting the Protestant constitution of England.

The plotters proposed a simple solution to the problem. Charles and James would be assassinated near Rye House, Hertfordshire, as they returned from the races at Newmarket on 1 April 1683, and a Protestant dynstasy would be re-established. Like almost every plot in the period, however, the Rye House

Plot was exposed, and the political backlash drove the renewed persecution of dissenters. Henry Owen and Robert Ferguson were alleged to be heavily involved in this attempted regicide.[182] Owen may have supported them. Cook has suggested that "the question of Owen's possible complicity in the plot is one of the most important, difficult, and sensitive issues his biographer must face."[183] For he was named by several informers and participants, including the Duke of Monmouth himself, as being among the plotters.[184] He had, after all, already been involved in at least one coup d'état. Though all of the evidence against him was circumstantial, and though he denied the charge, his involvement would have been neither implausible nor out of character. Owen may have been evasive to the end of his complex career.

Perhaps he had other concerns. Writing his *Meditations and discourses on the glory of Christ, Gospel grounds and evidence of the faith of God's elect,* and *A treatise on the dominion of sin and grace,* his thoughts were fixed on eternal matters. For Owen was in acute pain. In January 1683, his doctor, Edmund King, wrote to advise him that he had "a stone too big to pass."[185] He continued to support the literary work of younger colleagues. On 14 February 1683, he signed his preface to Samuel Clark's annotated New Testament, tracing the history of these texts from the Geneva Bible to the present day, perhaps not anticipating that his commendation would be followed by that of Richard Baxter, dated in August.[186] On 23 March, he updated his will. In April 1683, he was once again prosecuted for holding a conventicle.[187] On Wednesday, 27 June, "Dr. Owen was sent for to Whitehall ... and a Message was sent out to him that he must go before Judge Jones, he did so, the Judge gave him the Oath of Allegiance &c and so he went to his own house."[188] Owen explained that he had come into London with the purpose of visiting his doctor, and that he knew of the recent plot only by means of the public proclamation. But, on the same day, Robert Quary of Dublin testified before the court that he had recently heard Henry Owen refer to "80 or 100 thousand fighting men in the city of London, Dissenters, besides women and children and that the King lost considerably by putting the laws in execution against Dissenters ... and that, since the laws were put in execution against them, it was so far from lessening their number that there were two to one of what there were before."[189] It was an inauspicious coincidence—and, ironically, possible evidence that the situation of dissenters was not as hopeless as Owen had feared. But on 21 July 1683, members of the University of Oxford presented to the king their *Judgement and decree ... against certain pernicious books and damnable doctrines, destructive to the sacred persons of princes their state and government, and of all humane society,* listing Owen's regicide sermon among those texts advancing the "damnable doctrine" that "possession and strength give a right to Govern, and successe in a cause or enterprise proclaimes it to be Lawfull and just; To pursue it, is to comply with the will of God, because it is to follow the conduct of his Providence," a rather Hobbesian and entirely inaccurate interpretation of Owen's providential analysis and political theology.[190]

But Owen was dying. On 22 August 1683, he wrote again to Charles Fleetwood. "I am very desirious to speak one word to you more in this world," he advised his old friend. Writing "by the hand of my wife," in a new home in Ealing, and suffering from "strong pains" and an "intermitting fever," Owen recognized that he was in "my dying hour. I am going to him whom my soul hath loved, or rather who hath loved me with an everlasting love." Returning to the nautical imagery of so many of his sermons and university orations, he worried about the congregations he was leaving behind: "I am leaving the ship of the church in a storm, but whilst the great Pilot is in it the loss of a poore under-rower will be inconsiderable. Live and pray and hope and waite patiently and doe not despair," he encouraged his comrade, for "the promise stands invincible and he will never leave thee nor forsake thee."[191] It was the culmination of a busy and disciplined career. Fleetwood may have remembered his pastor's exhortation that "it is not a long life, but public service for God, that we are to esteem a blessing in this world. A little time filled up with service and duty is inexpressibly to be preferred before a multitude of days spent in unprofitableness and vanity."[192] With his wife by his side, and with old friends in mind, Owen looked back on a life of "service and duty," in which religious faith had been pitted against political doubt, and in which every success had been undone in defeat. Two days later, he was dead.

Conclusion

JOHN OWEN DIED on 24 August 1683, at the age of sixty-seven. Throughout his long life, he had been no stranger to the thought of death, having buried his first wife and all of his children. His constant illnesses had encouraged him to consider his own mortality, even during the period that must in retrospect have appeared to be the apex of his career, his time as vice chancellor of Oxford. "Do not expect learned groans, or erudite death-cries," he had warned his colleagues in an annual address to the university community; "he who has learnt to rely on a good conscience during his lifetime will have no need of elegance at the point of death."[1] If his death was not elegant, it was certainly timely. Owen died on the twenty-first anniversary of the imposition of the Act of Uniformity. The Latin inscription on his gravestone linked the two events, stating that Owen "left the world on a day dreadful for the Church by the cruelties of men."[2] He died believing that the English Reformation was facing greater threats than it ever had before. He died as he had so regularly lived—in the experience of defeat.

Owen was buried on Thursday, 9 September, in Bunhill Fields, London, a graveyard for dissenters.[3] By the late seventeenth century, Bunhill Fields had become a "powerful rallying point and symbol for high-ranking nonconformists."[4] The ground had never been consecrated—in fact, it had been opened for mass burials during the plague outbreak, almost twenty years before—and so dissenters could inter the bodies of their friends without any need to use the liturgy of the established church.[5] But Bunhill Fields was not a place of ignominy. Owen's funeral was a public occasion, and it was very well attended. One observer suggested that the carriages of sixty-seven nobles and gentlemen were present, while an anonymous biographer offered a higher estimate, recording that Owen's funeral was attended by "near a hundred Noblemens, Gentlemens, and Citizens Coaches with six Horse each, and a great number of Gentlemen in Mourning on Horseback."[6] Whatever the grandeur of the mourners, Owen's interment was marked by the erection of a plain, unornamented gravestone.[7]

As was common in the cultures of Puritans and nonconformists, Owen's burial was not the occasion of a religious ceremony. Instead, on the Sunday following his interment, David Clarkson, Owen's pastoral colleague since 1682, preached a commemorative sermon to the Leadenhall Street church.[8] The sermon, which considered Philippians 3:21, was not included in *Sermons and discourses on several divine subjects*, an anthology of Clarkson sermons that appeared in 1696, but it eventually appeared as a volume in 1720, and was reprinted one year later in *A complete collection of the sermons of . . . John Owen* (1721). Clarkson admitted his "unhappiness that I had so little and late acquaintance" with Owen, and believed he was "not competent" to provide an adequate view of his life: "the account that is due to the world, requires a volume, and a better hand than mine, which I hope it will meet with in time." He hailed Owen as "that excellent person . . . that great worthy," and described his former colleague as a "great light . . . one of eminency for holiness and learning and pastoral abilities." Clarkson's brief paean on Owen's personal and spiritual qualities gave way to an extended consideration of his abilities as a writer—for, as his relatively recent appointment to the church suggested, Clarkson had known the deceased better as an author than a colleague. He noted that Owen's commentary on Hebrews had "gain'd him a name and esteem, not only at home, but in foreign countries. When he had finished it (and it was a merciful providence that he lived to finish it) he said, Now his work was done, it was time for him to die." But his writing would live on, for, "if holiness, learning, and a masculine unaffected stile can command any thing, his practical discourses cannot but find much acceptation with those who are sensible of their soul concerns, and can relish that which is divine, and value that which is not common or trivial." Clarkson concluded the sermon by repeating Owen's final words to him, a prayer "that the Lord would double the Spirit upon us, that he would not remember against us former iniquities; but that his tender mercies may speedily prevent us, for we are brought very low."[9]

Others among Owen's admirers were less pessimistic about the future. The anonymous author of *An elegy on the death of that learned, pious, and famous divine, Doctor John Owen* (1683) believed that its subject had "rais'd himself a Monument of his Own, | Which will out-last those of the hardest Stone." The poem, which was printed as a folio broadside within a month of his death, praised Owen's contribution to the literary culture of nonconformity, lamenting "this Rev'rend Father in our Israel" whose "Name's above

Applause," while worrying about the lack of immediate poetic response to his death.[10]

Tho' Verse was silent, there's no doubt but those
Who knew him well, made Elegies in Prose:
And wrote 'em on their Hearts; and we may think,
If writ elsewhere, they us'd their Tears for Ink.[11]

If the writer of the elegy had been aware of Owen's earlier concerns about the effectiveness of his preaching ministry, he did not show it, arguing that

Many a Spiritual Orphan here Remains,
That owe their Birth to his Religious Pains;
And many more that have by him been Fed,
Instructed, Helpt, Rais'd, Cur'd and Comforted.[12]

The anonymous poet had other concerns, worrying, as Sharon Achinstein has put it, "what omen the loss of such an eminent man would mean to the community as a whole."[13] But Owen's legacy would continue:

H'has rais'd himself a Monument of his Own,
Which will out-last those of the hardest Stone.
His Fame will Live to lat'st Posterity,
In [hi]'s Theo-Christo-Pneumatology:
And various Volumes more; where we may find
How in [hi]'s Great Soul, Rich Gifts and Grace were joyn'd.[14]

Though Owen's voice was "Silenc'd now," his "Pious Pen, | Do's and will Preach to Multitudes of Men."[15]

Nevertheless, the poem continued, the loss of Owen "may well apprehend some Ill to come."[16] *An elegy* represented Owen's death as a "surrogate for the feared end of the world," with the deceased becoming the "means by which to project diverse fears and hopes about the community's survival."[17] Clarkson's funeral sermon had made a similar point, arguing that "it portends evil . . . *For the righteous are taken away from the evil to come.* When those that stand in the gap are removed, there is wrath breaking in upon that people without any remedy."[18] The theme had been persistent in the funeral sermons that Owen had preached for members of his congregation, but Clarkson and the anonymous elegist agreed: while his books would most effectively perpetuate his memory, Owen's death was, for many of his followers, a sign of the end of an age—if not the end of the world.

I

Owen's death confirmed his public status. Within the ranks of dissenting ministers, he was, of course, extremely well connected. His most immediate connections may have been demonstrated by the terms of his two wills.[19] His first of these, dated 29 June 1678, had been made within a week of his marriage to Dorothy D'Oyley, and may have been required to protect her substantial property. The beneficiaries of this will included his daughter Mary, who died in 1682.[20] The will stipulated that if Mary did not bear children, her bequest should go to Owen's brother Henry and his heirs.[21] Other beneficiaries had included John Desborough, a former major-general, who had died in 1680; and Richard King, an otherwise unknown figure in Owen's life who may have been a supporter of Vavasor Powell.[22] Unlike many others of the godly, Owen did not refer to any bequests of books.[23] The second will, made on 23 March 1683, was a more considered affair, and provided Owen with the opportunity of showing generosity to an extended network of family and friends while updating his family situation and financial affairs. For Owen had sold the lands in Soulderne that had been brought to the marriage by Dorothy, who was now to receive his lands in Eaton, Berkshire. As his daughter Mary had died, the remaining property was to be divided between his "only brother," Henry, with his son and daughter, Henry and Heneretta, and Mary Hall, wife of Bartholomew Hall of Harpsden, Henley, where Owen's brother had been a minister. It is possible, given the preferential ordering of names of the will, that Mary was his neice.[24] In terms of cash payments, the second will reached out to encompass a broader family circle, promising £200 to Doyley Michell, Dorothy's nephew, upon his attaining the age of 16, and a further £200 to pay off debts accrued by John, Philemon, and Samuel Hartcliffe, the sons of his sister Hester, to their uncles, Henry Owen and Roger Kynaston. Mary Hall was to be provided with £100; Daniel Fogge of Oxford was to be given £40; Owen's servants, Mary Lint and Elizabeth Meech, were provided with £30 and £20, respectively; John Collins, an Independent minister in London, was to be given £20;[25] James Bury of Battersey, Surrey, and Jeffrey Eliston, who may have had a link to Coggeshall, were bequeathed £10; and Dorothy was to have £40 to disburse as she pleased. Sums of £5 were to be given to Owen's three pastoral assistants in the Leadenhall Street congregation: Isaac Loeffs

(1673–82), Robert Ferguson (1674–*c.* 1679), despite the fact that his plotting had forced him into exile, and David Clarkson (from 1682).[26] The terms of the will may indicate those members of Owen's network of friends and family members whom he particularly valued—or to whom he felt particularly obligated—at the end of his life. Some of the executors and beneficiaries were well-established friends. We do not know anything about Owen's relationships with Fogge, Collins, Bury, or Eliston: perhaps it was simply that Owen knew they were in financial need.

Nevertheless, each of the terms of the will was prospective. The assignments of property were premised on the assumption that the estate would recover bonds worth £1,332 10s, which had been taken out in the name of Thomas Owen, one of the witnesses of the will. These bonds were to be recovered from Ursula Cartwright, a widow who had bought the land in Soulderne, which had been settled on Dorothy D'Oyley when she had married Owen; from Jane Hussey, a spinster; and from William Hussey, a merchant. The fact that Owen's entire legacy was bound up in loans that had been taken out in someone else's name suggests something of the complexity of the financial situation faced by nonconformists in late seventeenth-century England. And it is not clear whether these bonds were successfully recovered. The decision to sell three thousand volumes from Owen's library in May 1684—a decision presumably made by Dorothy, who had been appointed the "full and sole Executrix" of Owen's estate—may have been a means to raise additional capital, though it is likely that Edward Millington, the auctioneer, also sought to profit from the dispersal of such a well-known scholarly library, through the relatively recently established practice of coffee shop auctions.[27] Dorothy may also have been involved in facilitating the publication of Owen's works after his death, perhaps for financial benefit: the final volume of the commentary on Hebrews (1684) was followed by *Meditations and discourses on the glory of Christ* (separate parts were published in 1684 and 1691), *A treatise of the dominion of sin and grace* (1688), *The true nature of a gospel church and its government* (1689), *Seasonable words for English Protestants* (1690), *A guide to church-fellowship and order* (1692), *Two discourses concerning the Holy Spirit* (1693), and *Gospel grounds and evidences of the faith of God's elect* (1695). The posthumous publication project was significant in that some of these texts advanced exegetical and theological arguments that Owen had long since abandoned.[28] But Dorothy had her own concerns. She sold her home in Ealing to her distant relative, the Quaker John Wilmer, in 1685, but likely remained in the area, continuing as a member of the Leadenhall Street church until her death on 18 January 1704.[29]

II

The terms of the will, however insecure, reflected relationships similar to those from which Owen himself had benefited. He had depended upon a wide network of friends, patrons, and supporters in his forty years as a minister, administrator, and theologian. Once a young and restless Calvinist in search of promotion, who continually found his patrons disappointing, he had become a colleague of Thomas Fairfax and an intimate of Oliver Cromwell, the manager of a galaxy of Oxford stars, a beneficiary of the notice of the earl of Clarendon and the protection of the earl of Oxford, a friend of John Bunyan and Andrew Marvell, and had enjoyed personal audiences with Charles II and his brother the duke of York.[30] Despite the horrors of the Restoration, Owen may have had more cause in the early 1680s than in the late 1650s to believe that he had "lived constantly among the great."[31] But his high connections did not prevent his being attacked as a representative of a certain kind of Restoration nonconformity, as in Samuel Butler's *Hudibras*, the first complete edition of which appeared in the year after Owen's death.[32] The publication of *Hudibras* reignited a pamphlet debate as to the value of Owen's contribution to the religious and political life of the previous decades. If some of the interventions were vitriolic, others verged on the hagiographical. *A vindication of Owen . . . by a friendly scrutiny* (1684) suggested that its subject displayed "much of heaven and love to Christ, and saints and all men; which came from him so seriously and spontaneously, as if grace and nature were in him reconciled, and but one thing."[33] Socially and politically well-connected, but always the subject of critique, Owen and his friendship network epitomized and simultaneously undermined the cultural marginality of nonconformity in the late seventeenth century.

Owen certainly had his critics: almost as many books were written against him as by him. His later critics tended to attack his theological ideas and political vacillations, rather than (as in the 1650s) his lifestyle or appearance. Most of these interventions were concerned about his theology. Within the circles of nonconformity, Richard Baxter—whose relationship with Owen was always complex—thought highly of his intellectual ability but described him as an "over-Orthodox Doctor," lamenting his unbending commitment to the emerging orthodoxies of Reformed scholasticism.[34] In the closing years of the century, Baxter sought to bring closure to his troubled relationship with Owen, confessing with something not quite approaching regret that "I medled too forwardly with Dr. Owen, and one or two more that had written some Passages too near to Antinomianism."[35] Baxter admitted that he "should have considered what a temptation it would prove to the Passions of such a man" to engage in "personal opposition to Dr. Owen's Errours."[36] He also criticized a later stage of Owen's career, claiming that "Owen and his Assistants" in the gathered church in Wallingford House "did the main Work" in organizing republican opposition in the late 1650s, and arguing that Owen had been the "greater persuader of Fleetwood, Desborough and the rest of the Officers of the Army who were his Gathered Church, to Compel Rich[ard] Cromwell to dissolve his Parliament," with fatal consequences for the Protectorate and the freedoms of the godly.[37] Nevertheless, Baxter remembered, not without some degree of self-regard, Owen "grew more humble and orthodox before he died."[38] For Baxter wanted to control Owen's reputation. In the immediate aftermath of Owen's death, he attempted unsuccessfully to obtain his papers from Stephen Lobb, an Independent minister with whom Owen had been associated.[39] And he attempted his own biography project. Sometime after Baxter's death, however, his literary editor, Matthew Sylvester, who was "deeply concerned about the credibility of Baxter's views in *Reliquiae Baxterianae*," wrote to Owen's widow "with tender and affectionate respect and reverence to the Doctors Name and Memory" to "desire her to send me what she could, well attested, in favour of the Doctor, that I might insert it in the Margent, where he is mentioned as having an hand in that Affair at Wallingford House."[40] But Dorothy was unable or unwilling to help—she had, after all, married Owen two decades after the events in question. Sylvester responded by occluding Baxter's most vociferous criticism of her late husband from the version of the text that he published.[41] Others criticized the influence of Owen's religious ideas on politics—including some of those with whom he had once been closely identified. Sometime after Owen's death, one of his most important former patrons took his revenge. Edward Hyde, the earl of Clarendon, who may have commissioned Owen to write *Animadversions on Fiat Lux* (1662), denounced him as a traitor whose influence had worked to "corrupt the judgement of the People, and to take off the bonds of Conscience towards His Majesty, by advancing the Houses of Parliament above the King."[42] Royalists also remembered Owen's role in the fall of Richard Cromwell, but were perhaps less appreciative of his intervention than they should have been.[43] Perhaps Owen's strange and disturbing claims of enduring loyalty to the house of Stuarts in *Animadversions on Fiat Lux* had not been sufficiently persuasive—even to Hyde, who may have commissioned the volume, and who may have sought to reward its author.

III

Nevertheless, for all that Owen's admirers regarded his extraordinary learning and ability as being "eminent" and "worthy to be remembered in all ages,"

Owen made no distinctive and enduring contribution to English or Reformed theology.[44] His taut, precise, and often abbreviated writing was unusually demanding, even in terms of Puritan literary culture: in terms of the knowledge he expected of those for whom he wrote, he was his own ideal reader. Nevertheless, as David Clarkson admitted in his funeral sermon, Owen "did not affect singularity; they were old truths that he endeavoured to defend, those that were transmitted to us by our first reformers, and owned by the divines of the Church of England."[45] As Robert Letham has more recently argued, Owen was "not so much an innovator as a brilliant synthesizer."[46] A number of his works added extraordinary detail to conventional loci, such as his work on the Holy Spirit.[47] Others of his works pushed the theological consensus on conventional loci to the boundaries of orthodoxy, such as his work on communion with the individual persons of the Trinity, which was regularly reprinted, but made little enduring impact on the popular culture of evangelicalism. There is no "center" to Owen's theology, such as historical theologians have attempted to identify in other religious writers: Trueman has recognized that "the intellectual content of Owen's thought defies simplistic reduction to one or two key themes."[48] Owen developed his theological insights on almost all fronts.

Owen's theological contribution has generally been understood in terms of the theological loci within which he worked. Recent studies, as the Introduction noted, have tended to consider Owen's work in terms of its particular contribution to theology proper, Christology, covenant theology, ecclesiology, and so on. This approach has been institutionalized in Owen studies—not least because the Goold edition, which remains the only substantial edition of Owen in print, has preferred a thematic to a chronological arrangement for Owen's works. Indeed, the one text by Owen that might have done most to challenge this preference for single-themed study—his massive statement of prolegomena, *Θεολογουμενα παντοδαπα* (1661)—has until very recently remained on the periphery of the scholarly literature. By contrast, this biography has attempted to read Owen's works in chronological order and across the thematic range. In doing so, it has highlighted the fact that Owen was not a synthetic thinker, and that he preferred to treat each theme individually—though often with an extraordinary capacity for detail.[49] But Owen's preference for thematic discretion has created difficulties for his readers. His discussions of sanctification took place apart from his discussions of ecclesiology, for example, and so those who listened most carefully to his advice on the means by which to pursue holiness could have understood that piety could be pursued without reference to the church or its sacraments.[50]

Perhaps Owen realized that there were difficulties in his method. After all, throughout much of his life, he remained a disappointed churchman. He complained of the large number of "grossly ignorant persons" in Fordham, and of the "daily troubles, pressures, and temptations" of life among the "poor, numerous, provoking people" of Coggeshall.[51] References to the large number of people attending his preaching during this period should be understood in light of the legal requirement to attend public worship: the large numbers of auditors were no evidence that Owen's preaching was being sucessful. His journey to Dublin gave him the opportunity of preaching to a "numerous multitude of as thirsting a people after the gospel as ever yet I conversed withal," but he stayed in the city for only a few months, and returned home only to be sent to Scotland and then into university administration, in a period in which his involvement in congregational life cannot be traced before his gathering of the congregation of republicans in Wallingford House.[52] When, in the aftermath of the Restoration, Owen gathered a small congregation in his home, he was still, in some senses, an inexperienced pastor. And, for much of the later period, for all that his admirers lauded his abilities as a theologian and a preacher, his church did not count more than forty members. The move to Leadenhall Street increased the number of his auditors, but some of this congregation's most gifted adherents, like Lucy Hutchinson, could not be persuaded to join. By the end of his career, Owen had come to believe that his writing had failed to protect orthodox religion; that his preaching had made little impact upon his hearers; that Independent churches had failed to preserve true piety; and that his own greatest failing was his inability to explain the situation of dissenters by means of the providentialist framework that had provided the infrastructure for his earliest and most politically significant sermons.[53] By the 1670s, Owen believed, the churches were in ruins. This enduring sense of failure may explain his increasing tendency to prioritize the subjective over the objective, and to isolate the pursuit of holiness from life in the church and participation in its sacraments. For all that Owen developed a polemical ecclesiology, he abandoned his early sacramentalism and later failed systematically to root the Christian life within the church's means of grace. In making this move, he was subverting, not epitomizing, the Reformed theological tradition that he is often believed to personify.

Owen's legacy was not what he may have expected it to be. His theology has been considered as "the last, finely tooled and sophisticated hurrah of a thoughtful, learned, articulate theological tradition which was about to collapse."[54] But it now seems clear that his emphasis on subjectivist piety was participating in that reimagining of the Christian life that would come to full fruition in the revivalist evangelicalism that blossomed in and after the 1730s.[55] Owen's fear in later life that his millions of published words had failed to protect Reformed doctrine was somewhat misplaced—for new readers would come to understand his contributions in new ways. Owen would become a darling of evangelical readers from the mid-eighteenth century, after John Wesley included his work within the *Christian library* (1750), even as the congregation that had formerly met in Leadenhall Street was led by Isaac Watts into unorthodox Trinitarian speculation.[56] Owen's legacy would be appreciated by William Wilberforce in the 1790s; developed and disputed by English Baptists and Scottish Presbyterians in the nineteenth century, including C. H. Spurgeon and John McLeod Campbell; promoted in the twentieth century by independent Baptists, including A. W. Pink, and Welsh Congregationalists, including Martyn Lloyd-Jones; remembered among "Plymouth" Brethren, including William Kelly, who praised the "excellent and learned Dr. John Owen," and the missionary martyr Jim Elliot, a reader of Owen who died shortly before the Banner of Truth republished *The death of death* (1958).[57] The republication project that began in the 1950s has done much to popularize Owen's works to the "new Calvinists" who have again reinvented his legacy. As they turned to his analyses of religious experience, rather than his treatises on political theology or intra-Puritan polemic, "new Calvinists" have found in Owen a tool for their self-fashioning—to the extent that, in the late twentieth and early twenty-first century, all kinds of products would be branded with Owen's image, from a theological study center and a chain of bookshops to mugs, T-shirts, and neckties, with the consumers of which entirely missing the irony of his decorative status in light of his concern for sartorial modesty.[58] Contemporary evangelicals celebrate Owen for his investigations of spiritual experience, rather than for the achievements with which he was most satisfied, including his defenses of Trinitarianism and his commentary on Hebrews. Owen's works would shape the interior world of evangelicals over several centuries, but their reading preferences would identify new kinds of significance in his work.

This is not a biographical context that suggests great achievement. Nevertheless, in this book's account, Owen emerges as the genius of English Puritanism—its preeminent thinker, and a formative influence on successive generations of evangelicals. Owen's work represents the best of the intellectual and spiritual achievements of that generation of English Protestants who could no longer tolerate the ambiguity and frustration of their parents' relationship to the established church. No longer prepared to occasionally conform, they imagined and then created a new world in their own image. But even in the 1650s, when that new world seemed to become most real, these believers could not escape the ethical and moralistic imperative that had driven their parents' response to the uncertain situation of the English establishment. Teasing apart the responsibilities of congregational life and those of the life of holiness, these English Puritans drove an individualistic and subjectivist turn within popular Protestantism, and did more than most historians have realized to lay the theoretical foundation for the new religious movement that would emerge in the 1730s. It is, perhaps, to John Owen and his fellow English Puritans that the very substantial global community of evangelicals must trace its difficult beginning.[59] It would not have been the legacy for which Owen might have wished—but evidence, perhaps, of the providence that guided and made purposeful his many experiences of defeat.

Notes

EPIGRAPH

1. Owen, *The works of John Owen*, ed. William H. Goold, 24 vols. (Edinburgh: Johnstone & Hunter, 1850–55), 8: 353.

PREFACE

1. Owen, *Works*, 13: 253.
2. Owen, *Works*, 11: 12–13.
3. Owen, *Works*, 8: 33.
4. Owen, *Works*, 10: 110.
5. Sebastian Rehnman has claimed that the translation is of "such inferior quality that it cannot be used for serious study"; *Divine discourse: The theological methodology of John Owen* (Grand Rapids, MI: Baker, 2002), p. 17 n. 3. Nevertheless, I use it with gratitude. Part of *Θεολογουμενα παντοδαπα* appeared as *Evangelical theology: A translation of the sixth book of Dr. Owen's Latin work entitled Theologoumena*, trans. John Craig (Edinburgh, 1837).
6. Owen, *Works*, 8: 163.
7. Owen, *Works*, 11: 7.
8. Owen, *Works*, 11: 7.
9. Owen, *Works*, 6: 230, 10: 8.
10. Anthony à Wood, *Athenae Oxonienses*, 4 vols. (Oxford, 1813), 4: 98.
11. Owen, *Works*, 6: 188.
12. Owen, *Works*, 8: 434.
13. Owen, *Works*, 8: 434; 10: 35.

INTRODUCTION

1. Carl Trueman has argued persuasively that Owen's work should be read in the context of European Protestant scholasticism, but, as Ryan McGraw and others

have recognized, Owen describes himself as a "puritan," and engaged most extensively in debates that were particular to English Puritans; Carl R. Trueman, *John Owen: Reformed Catholic, Renaissance man* (Aldershot, UK: Ashgate, 2007), pp. 5–6; Ryan M. McGraw, *A heavenly directory: Trinitarian piety, public worship and a reassessment of John Owen's theology* (Bristol, CT: Vandenoeck & Ruprecht, 2014), pp. 13–14. See also Christopher Cleveland, *Thomism in John Owen* (Farnham, UK: Ashgate, 2013), pp. 5–11.

2. Dewey D. Wallace, *Shapers of English Calvinism, 1660–1714: Variety, persistence, and transformation* (Oxford: Oxford University Press, 2011), p. 5.
3. John Owen, "Fifth oration" (9 October 1657), in *The Oxford orations of John Owen*, ed. Peter Toon (Callington, Cornwall, UK: Gospel Communication, 1971), pp. 45–46.
4. John W. Tweeddale, "John Owen's commentary on Hebrews in context," in Kelly M. Kapic and Mark Jones (eds.), *The Ashgate research companion to John Owen's theology* (Farnham, UK: Ashgate, 2012), p. 50.
5. Richard Baxter, *Reliquiae Baxterianae, or, Mr. Richard Baxters narrative of the most memorable passages of his life and times faithfully publish'd from his own original manuscript by Matthew Sylvester* (1696), p. 8.
6. Vincent Alsop, *A vindication of the faithful rebuke to a false report against the rude cavils of the pretended defence* (1698), p. 10; see also *An address to the Church of England: Evidencing her obligations both of interest and conscience, to concurr with his gracious Majesty in the repeal of the penal laws and tests* (1688), p. 8.
7. For the auction catalogue that purported to represent the content of Owen's library, see Edward Millington, *Bibliotheca Oweniana* (1684), and the discussion in Crawford Gribben, "John Owen, Renaissance man? The evidence of Edward Millington's *Bibliotheca Oweniana* (1684)," *Westminster Theological Journal* 72:2 (2010), pp. 321–32.
8. Rolf Engelsing, *Der Börger als Leser: Lesergeschichte in Deutschland, 1500–1800* (Stuttgart: Metzler, 1974); Andrew Cambers, *Godly reading: Print, manuscript and Puritanism in England, 1580–1720* (Cambridge: Cambridge University Press, 2011), p. 36.
9. Dr. Williams's Library NCL, MS L6/2, 3, 4, with a handlist in Mark Burden, *John Owen, Learned Puritan* (Oxford University CEMS website, 2013), http://www.cems-oxford.org/projects/lucy-hutchinson/john-owen-learned-puritan, accessed 7 November 2014. Earlier volumes in this series of manuscripts were published in Owen, *Works*, vols. 9 and 16.
10. Among the more recent examples of this popularizing trend are John Owen, *Sin and temptation: The challenge of personal holiness*, ed. James M. Houston (Minneapolis, MN: Bethany, 1983); John Owen, *Thinking spiritually* [from *The grace and duty of being spiritually minded*] (London: Grace Publications, 1989); John Owen, *Communion with God*, ed. R. J. K. Law (Edinburgh: Banner of Truth,

1991); John Owen, *Apostasy from the Gospel*, ed. R. J. K. Law (Edinburgh: Banner of Truth, 1992); John Owen, *Christians are forever* [from *The doctrine of the saints' perseverance explained and confirmed*], ed. H. Lawrence (Darlington: Evangelical Press, 1993); John Owen, *The glory of Christ*, ed. R. J. K. Law (Edinburgh: Banner of Truth, 1994); John Owen, *Hebrews*, eds J. I. Packer and Alister McGrath (Wheaton, IL: Crossway, 1998); John Owen, *The Holy Spirit*, ed. R. J. K. Law (Edinburgh: Banner of Truth, 1998); Kris Lundgaard, *The enemy within: Straight talk about the power and defeat of sin* (Phillipsburg, NJ: P & R, 1998); Kris Lundgaard, *Through the looking glass: Reflections on Christ that change us* (Phillipsburg, NJ: P & R, 2000); John Owen, *The Spirit and the Church*, R. J. K. Law (Edinburgh: Banner of Truth, 2002); and Kelly M. Kapic and Justin Taylor, *Overcoming sin and temptation* (Wheaton, IL: Crossway, 2006).

11. In this, Owen's reception mirrors that of Samuel Rutherford, who is remembered for the devotional content of his letters, rather than for the scholastic theological interventions; John Coffey, *Politics, religion and the British revolutions: The mind of Samuel Rutherford* (Cambridge: Cambridge University Press, 1997), p. 1.
12. Owen, *Works*, 10: 494. The Goold edition is kept in print by the Banner of Truth Trust, although their edition does not include the Latin writings that were published as Johnstone & Hunter's vol. 17; the Banner of Truth edition of vol. 16 includes some material that originally appeared in Johnstone & Hunter's vol. 17. The notes will indicate where I have used the Banner of Truth edition of vol. 16 to access material contained in the Johnstone & Hunter edition of vol. 17.
13. Richard Baxter, *Aphorismes of justification* (The Hague, 1655), p. 301.
14. For an outstanding study of markings, see William H. Sherman, *Used books: Marking readers in Renaissance England* (Philadelphia: University of Pennsylvania Press, 2008).
15. Folger Shakespeare Library, O737.2.
16. Andrew Thomson, "Life of Dr Owen," in Owen, *Works*, 1: xxi–cxxii.
17. William H. Goold, "General preface," in Owen, *Works*, 1: vii.
18. *DNB*, s.v.
19. J. I. Packer, "Introductory essay," in John Owen, *The death of death* (Edinburgh: Banner of Truth, 1959), p. 25. These comments contrast Sinclair B. Ferguson's appreciative observation of Owen's "passionate relentlessness. He will not let go of a theme until he has exhausted it"; *The Trinitarian devotion of John Owen* (Sanford, FL: Reformation Trust, 2014), p. 50.
20. Owen, *Works*, 10: 61.
21. John Owen, *A defense of sacred Scripture against modern fanaticism*, trans. Stephen P. Westcott (Grand Rapids, MI: Soli Deo Gloria, 1994), p. 821. This is a translation into English of *Exercitationes adversus fanaticos*, which appeared in Johnstone & Hunter's vol. 17.
22. Owen, *A defense of sacred Scripture against modern fanaticism*, p. 822.

23. See, for example, the suspiciously well-preserved copies of Owen's works in Chetham's Library, Manchester, and Marsh's Library, Dublin. The volumes in Chetham's are well preserved despite the regular use of other godly texts by such clergy as John Rastrick, Henry Newcome, and John Worthington; Cambers, *Godly reading*, p. 150.
24. Trinity College Dublin CC.k.65; Richard Snoddy, *The soteriology of James Ussher: The act and object of saving faith* (Oxford: Oxford University Press, 2014), p. 245.
25. Cambers, *Godly reading*, p. 15; Michael Hunter and Annabel Gregory (eds.), *An astrological diary of the seventeenth century: Samuel Jeake of Rye, 1612–1699* (Oxford: Clarendon Press, 1988), pp. 102, 104.
26. Folger Shakespeare Library, 137959q.
27. *The correspondence of John Owen (1616–83)*, ed. Peter Toon (Cambridge: James Clarke, 1970), p. 117.
28. George Hunsinger, "Justification and mystical union with Christ: Where does Owen stand?" in Kelly M. Kapic and Mark Jones (eds.), *The Ashgate research companion to John Owen's theology* (Farnham, UK: Ashgate, 2012), p. 204.
29. See, for example, *Marweiddiad pechod mewn credinwyr* ([Shrewsbury], 1796), a Welsh translation of Owen's study, *Of the Mortification of Sinne in Believers* (1656); and a translation into Dutch of his commentary on Hebrews, *Eene uitlegginge van den sendbrief van Paulus den apostel aen de Hebreen*, 4 vols., ed. Commincq (Rotterdam, 1733–40); Kapic, *Communion with God*, pp. 18–20.
30. James Moffatt, *The golden book of John Owen* (London: Hodder and Stoughton, 1904), pp. x, xii.
31. For a theological biography of Packer, see Alister McGrath, *J. I. Packer: A biography* (Grand Rapids, MI: Revell, 1998); for Owen's impact on Packer, see Don J. Payne, *The theology of the Christian life in J. I. Packer's thought: Theological anthropology, theological method, and the doctrine of sanctification* (Milton Keynes, UK: Paternoster, 2009). On the use of history within this emerging Reformed theological community, see John Coffey, "Lloyd-Jones and the Protestant past," in Andrew Atherstone and David Ceri Jones (eds.), *Engaging with Martyn Lloyd-Jones* (Nottingham, UK: Apollos, 2011), pp. 293–326.
32. J. I. Packer's "Introductory essay," which first appeared in John Owen, *The death of death in the death of Christ* (London: Banner of Truth, 1959), was republished in *A quest for godliness: The Puritan vision of the Christian life* (1994; rpt. Wheaton, IL: Crossway, 2014); but its robust defense of Calvinist soteriology seems hard to equate with his defense of his support for "Evangelicals and Catholics together"; J. I. Packer, "Why I signed it," *Christianity Today* 38:14, 12 December 1994.
33. Packer, "Introductory essay," p. 2.
34. Packer, "Introductory essay," p. 1.

35. Payne, *The theology of the Christian life in J. I. Packer's thought*, passim.
36. A new translation of Owen's Latin works is being prepared; see https://www.logos.com/product/28651/the-latin-works-of-john-owen-in-english, accessed 7 November 2014.
37. Christopher Hill, *The experience of defeat: Milton and some contemporaries* (1984; rpt. London: Bookmarks, 1994), pp. 164–72; Christopher Hill, *A tinker and a poor man: John Bunyan and his church, 1628–1688* (New York: Albert A. Knopf, 1989), pp. 167–68.
38. Unfortunately, Westcott's book prefers not to provide citations for its quotations, the language of which it also updates, making it extremely difficult to locate the passages to which it refers (p. x). This is particularly problematic in terms of its interesting discussion of Owen's experience of army life (p. 25).
39. Edwin E. M. Tay, *The priesthood of Christ: Atonement in the theology of John Owen (1616–1683)* (Milton Keynes, UK: Paternoster, 2014), p. 7.
40. Rehnman, *Divine discourse*, pp. 25, 125.
41. Edward Holberton, *Poetry and the Cromwellian Protectorate: Culture, politics, and instititutions* (Oxford: Oxford University Press, 2008), pp. 61–86; Gráinne McLaughlin, "The idolater John Owen? Linguistic hegemony in Cromwell's Oxford," in Richard Kirwan (ed.), *Scholarly self-fashioning and community in the early modern university* (Farnham, UK: Ashgate, 2013), pp. 145–66.
42. These positions are subjected to critique in McGraw, *A heavenly directory*, pp. 56–63.
43. Cambers, *Godly reading*, p. 10.
44. Carl R. Trueman, *The claims of truth: John Owen's Trinitarian theology* (Carlisle, UK: Paternoster, 1998), p. 1.
45. J. I. Packer, "Foreword," in Kelly M. Kapic, *Communion with God: The divine and the human in the theology of John Owen* (Grand Rapids, MI: Baker, 2007), p. 9.
46. Richard A. Muller, *After Calvin: Studies in the development of a theological tradition* (Oxford: Oxford University Press, 2003), p. 47.
47. Owen, *Works*, 13: 227.
48. Joel Beeke, *The quest for full assurance: The legacy of Calvin and his successors* (Edinburgh: Banner of Truth, 1999), pp. 165–66, argues that Owen's early theology of assurance of salvation followed Calvin in arguing that assurance was an "integral part of faith," while the later Owen modified this position "in response to the Westminster Confession," though Beeke admits that Owen "seldom quoted the Confession directly on assurance." I have not found any such direct quotations.
49. This claim is made in Francis Lee, *John Owen represbyterianized* (Edmonton, Canada: Still Waters Revival Books, 2000); but see the more nuanced analysis in Stephen P. Westcott, *By the Bible alone! John Owen's theology for today's church* (Fellsmere, FL: Reformation Media & Press, 2010), pp. 518–37.

50. Tay, *The priesthood of Christ*, pp. 164–66.
51. Ironically, these early opinions, which Owen had to revise, were articulated in his first book on the atonement, making *The death of death* (1959), the book that launched the modern Owen revival, in some important ways unrepresentative of his mature views.
52. Owen, *Works*, 8: 253.
53. Owen, *Hebrews*, 6: 520–29.
54. Owen, *Works*, 14: 108.
55. Sarah Gibbard Cook, "A political biography of a religious Independent: John Owen, 1616–1683" (unpublished PhD thesis, Harvard University, 1972), pp. 285–86; Owen, *Works*, 14: 193.
56. Owen, *Works*, 14: 314.
57. In an undated letter, written after 1658, Owen did defend the Savoy Declaration against the charge of internal inconsistency made by Peter du Moulin; *The correspondence of John Owen*, ed. Toon, pp. 165–68.
58. Alec Ryrie, *Being Protestant in Reformation Britain* (Oxford: Oxford University Press, 2013), p. 1.
59. Andrew Marvell, *The Rehearsal Transpros'd and The Rehearsal Transpros'd the second part*, ed. D. I. B. Smith (Oxford: Clarendon Press, 1971), p. 38.
60. Cotton Mather, *Magnalia Christi Americana, or The ecclesiastical history of New-England*, 2 vols. (1702; rpt. Hartford: Silus Andrus and Son, 1853), 1: 524–25.
61. Anonymous, "The life of . . . . John Owen," in *Seventeen sermons preach'd by the Reverend Dr. John Owen: With the dedications at large. Together with the Doctors life*, 2 vols. (London, 1720), 1: iii–iv.
62. The year of Owen's birth was listed as 1618, instead of 1616; Anonymous, "The life of . . . . John Owen," in *Seventeen Sermons*, i. v.
63. A likely "first draft" of Asty's memoir can be found in a commonplace book held in the library of New College, Edinburgh; University of Edinburgh, New College MS Comm 2. The manuscript is identified by Tim Cooper, in *John Owen, Richard Baxter and the formation of Nonconformity* (Farnham, UK: Ashgate, 2011), p. 259 n. 3. Cook characterizes Asty's biography as "unreliable hearsay"; Cook, "Political biography," p. 9.
64. Andrew Thomson, "Life of Dr Owen," in *The Works of John Owen*, ed. William H. Goold (Edinburgh: Johnstone & Hunter, 1850–55), 1: xxi.
65. Cook, "Political biography," p. 14; Thomson, "Life of Dr Owen," 1: xxii.
66. Cook, "Political biography," pp. 13, 19.
67. Cook, "Political biography," p. 1.
68. Cook, "Political biography," p. 17.
69. *Time* magazine, 12 March 2009.
70. Irene Howatt, *Ten boys who made history* (Fearn, Ross-shire, UK: Christian Focus Press, 2003), pp. 21–33.

71. Simonetta Carr, *John Owen* (Grand Rapids, MI: Reformation Heritage Books, 2010). See also the biographical account of Owen included in Joel R. Beeke and Randall J. Pederson, *Meet the Puritans: With a guide to modern reprints* (Grand Rapids, MI: Reformation Heritage Books, 2006), pp. 455–63.
72. Mark Burden, review of Tim Cooper, *John Owen, Richard Baxter and the formation of nonconformity*, in *Congregational History Society Magazine* 6:5 (2012), pp. 279–81.
73. Peter Toon, *God's statesman: The life and work of John Owen, pastor, educator, theologian* (Exeter, UK: Paternoster, 1971), p. vii.
74. Toon, *God's statesman*, p. 2.
75. Owen, *Works*, 6: 45.
76. *The diary of Ralph Josselin, 1616–1683*, ed. Alan Macfarlane, Records of Social and Economic History (Oxford: Oxford University Press, 1976).
77. Toon, *God's statesman*, p. 3.
78. History of Parliament, s.v.
79. For a discussion of the circulation of Puritan life writing, see Cambers, *Godly reading*, pp. 69–71.
80. Geoffrey F. Nuttall, "Foreword," in *The correspondence of John Owen*, ed. Toon, p. vii.
81. Owen, *Works*, 14: 479.
82. Owen, *Works*, 12: 594.
83. *The correspondence of John Owen*, ed. Toon, p. 160.
84. Owen, *Works*, 14: 8.
85. For a broader discussion of this theme, see Kevin Sharpe, *Reading revolutions: The politics of reading in early modern England* (New Haven, CT: Yale University Press, 2000); H. J. Jackson, *Marginalia: Readers writing in books* (New Haven, CT: Yale University Press, 2001); Sherman, *Used books* (2008).
86. Owen, *Works*, 13: 248.
87. See, for example, Owen, *Works*, 3: 47; Cleveland, *Thomism in John Owen*, pp. 134, 146. Samuel Parker ridiculed Owen as a "famous Writer ... that abounds with Rabbinical Quotations, all of which if you would trace them, are trivial in Modern Authors"; *A defence and continuation of the Ecclesiastical Politie* (1671), p. 153. See James R. Jacob, *Henry Stubbe, radical Protestantism and the early Enlightenment* (Cambridge: Cambridge University Press, 1983), p. 132.
88. Brian Kay, *Trinitarian spirituality: John Owen and the doctrine of God in Western devotion* (Milton Keynes, UK: Paternoster, 2007), pp. 95–97.
89. Owen, *Works*, 9: 69–70; Kay, *Trinitarian spirituality*, p. 96.
90. David Saywell and Jacob Simon, *National Portrait Gallery, London: Complete illustrated catalogue* (London: Third Millennium Publishing, 2004), p. 473.
91. Owen, "Fifth oration" (9 October 1657), in Toon (ed.), *Oxford orations*, p. 45.

92. See, for example, Wilson H. Kimnach and Kenneth P. Minkema, "The material and social practices of intellectual work: Jonathan Edwards' study," *William and Mary Quarterly* 69:4 (2012), pp. 683–730.
93. Cambers, *Godly reading*, p. 74.
94. Owen's grave is discussed in Sharon Achinstein, *Literature and dissent in Milton's England* (Cambridge: Cambridge University Press, 2003), p. 46. On the "social history of ideas," see Robert Darnton, "In search of the Enlightenment: Recent attempts to create a social history of ideas," *Journal of Modern History* 43:1 (1971), pp. 113–32; Quentin Skinner, *Visions of politics*, vol. 1: *Regarding method* (Cambridge: Cambridge University Press, 2002); and Anthony Grafton, "The history of ideas: Precept and practice, 1950–2000 and beyond," *Journal of the History of Ideas* 67 (2006), p. 26.
95. Andrew Hadfield, *Edmund Spenser: A life* (Oxford: Oxford University Press, 2012), pp. 1–15.
96. Hadfield, *Edmund Spenser*, p. 11.
97. Owen, "Fifth oration" (9 October 1657), in Toon (ed.), *Oxford orations*, p. 45.
98. Tim Cooper, "Owen's personality: The man behind the theology," in Kelly M. Kapic and Mark Jones (eds.), *The Ashgate research companion to John Owen's theology* (Aldershot, UK: Ashgate, 2012), p. 215.
99. John Piper, in *Contending for our all: Defending truth and treasuring Christ in the lives of Athanasius, John Owen, and J. Gresham Machen* (Wheaton, IL: Crossway, 2011), p. 87, argues that Owen was shaped by his grief. This claim is denied in Cooper, "Owen's personality: The man behind the theology," pp. 215, 221–22.
100. Richard Baxter, *An account of the reasons why the twelve arguments said to be Dr John Owen's change not my judgement about communion with parish-churches* (1684), sig. M4r, in Richard Baxter, *Catholick communion defended* (1684).
101. Wood, *Athenae Oxoniensis*, 2: 740.
102. John Asty, "Memoirs of the Life of John Owen," in *A complete collection of the sermons of the reverend and learned John Owen D.D.* (London: John Clark, 1721), pp. 33–34.
103. J. G. A. Pocock, "The history of political thought: A methodological enquiry," in Peter Laslett and W. G. Runciman (eds.), *Philosophy, politics and society*, second series (Oxford: Blackwell, 1962), pp. 183–202; John Dunn, "The identity of the history of ideas," in Peter Laslett, Quentin Skinner, and W. G. Runciman (eds.), *Philosphy, politics and society*, fourth series (Oxford: Blackwell, 1982), pp. 158–73; Quentin Skinner, *Visions of politics*, vol. 1: *Regarding method*, pp. 103–27; Grafton, "The history of ideas: Precept and practice, 1950–2000 and beyond," p. 4; Alister Chapman, John Coffey, and Brad S. Gregory (eds.), *Seeing things their way: Intellectual history and the return of religion* (South Bend, IN: University of Notre Dame Press, 2009).

104. For a discussion of this approach, see John Patrick Diggins, "Arthur O. Lovejoy and the challenge of intellectual history," *Journal of the History of Ideas* 67:1 (2006), p. 184; Mark Goldie, "Obligations, utopias and their historical context," *Historical Journal* 26 (1983), pp. 727–46.
105. Grafton, "The history of ideas: Precept and practice, 1950–2000 and beyond," p. 15.
106. Grafton, "The history of ideas: Precept and practice, 1950–2000 and beyond," p. 8.
107. It is striking to note the extent to which the field of "Puritan studies" has been shaped by the approaches of literary scholars, from William Haller and Perry Miller to Philip Gura, Janice Knight, and Sarah Rivett, though this trend is more marked in American than in British or Irish contexts.
108. William H. Goold, "General preface," in Owen, *Works*, 1: xiii, quoting the appendix to *Salus electorum, sanguis Jesu*. For a comparison with editions of the works of Thomas Goodwin, see Mark Jones, *Why heaven kissed earth: The Christology of the Puritan Reformed Orthodoxy theologian, Thomas Goodwin (1600–1680)*, Reformed Historical Theology (Oakville, CT: Vandenhoeck & Ruprecht, 2010), pp. 16–21.
109. Goold, "General preface," in Owen, *Works*, 1: xiv.
110. Cambers, *Godly reading*, p. 3; see also David Cressy, "Books as totems in seventeenth-century England and New England," *Journal of Library History* 21 (1986), pp. 92–106.
111. Cambers, *Godly reading*, p. 35.
112. On early modern habits of reading, see Lisa Jardine and Anthony Grafton, "'Studied for action': How Gabriel Harvey read his Livy," *Past and Present* 129 (1990), pp. 30–78; Sharpe, *Reading revolutions*.
113. Grafton, "The history of ideas: Precept and practice, 1950–2000 and beyond," p. 14.
114. Nicholas Tyacke, "Introduction," in Nicholas Tyacke, *Aspects of English Protestantism, c. 1530–1700* (Manchester: Manchester University Press, 2001), p. 20. On literary history as pushing against periodisation within the historiography of early modern England, see Cambers, *Godly reading*, pp. 8, 14.
115. Ryrie, *Being Protestant in Reformation Britain*, p. 12.
116. *The works of Lucy Hutchinson*, vol 2: *Theological writings*, eds Elizabeth Clarke, David Norbrook and Jane Stevenson (Oxford: Oxford University Press, forthcoming); Anne Goldgar, *Impolite learning: Conduct and community in the Republic of Letters, 1680–1750* (New Haven, CT: Yale University Press, 1995); Jonathan Israel, *Radical Enlightenment: Philosophy and the making of modernity, 1650–1750* (Oxford: Oxford University Press, 2001); Noel Malcolm, *Aspects of Hobbes* (Oxford: Clarendon Press, 2002); Cambers, *Godly reading*.
117. David J. Appleby, *Black Bartholomew's Day: Preaching, polemic and Restoration nonconformity* (Manchester: Manchester University Press, 2007), p. 69.

Ian Green's comments on the study of sermons are particularly helpful; *Continuity and change in Protestant preaching in early modern England*, Friends of Dr. Williams Library, Sixtieth Lecture (London: Dr Williams Library, 2009).

118. For more on this process, see Daniel Woolf, *Reading history in early modern England* (Cambridge: Cambridge University Press, 2000); idem, *The social circulation of the past: English historical culture, 1500–1730* (Oxford: Oxford University Press, 2003); Sherman, *Used books.*
119. R. I. V. Hodge, *Foreshortened time: Andrew Marvell and 17th century revolutions* (Cambridge: D. S. Brewer, 1978), pp. 18–19.
120. For a discussion of these aesthetic revolutions, see Laura Lunger Knoppers, *Constructing Cromwell: Ceremony, portrait, and print, 1645–1661* (Cambridge: Cambridge University Press, 2000).
121. Grafton, "The history of ideas: Precept and practice, 1950–2000 and beyond," p. 30.
122. Quentin Skinner, *Reason and rhetoric in the philosophy of Hobbes* (Princeton, NJ: Princeton University Press, 1996); Richard A. Muller, "Reflections on persistent Whiggism and its antidotes in the study of sixteenth- and seventeenth-century intellectual history," in Alister Chapman, John Coffey, and Brad S. Gregory (eds.), *Seeing things their way: Intellectual history and the return of religion* (South Bend, IN: Notre Dame University Press, 2009), pp. 134–53.
123. Christopher Durston and Judith Maltby, "Introduction: Religion and revolution in seventeenth-century England," in Christopher Durston and Judith Maltby (eds.), *Religion in Revolutionary England* (Manchester: Manchester University Press, 2006), p. 2.
124. Cook, "Political biography," p. 23.

CHAPTER 1

1. See, for example, Ulinka Rublack, *Reformation Europe* (Cambridge: Cambridge University Press, 2005); Eamon Duffy, *The voices of Morebath: Reformation and rebellion in an English village* (New Haven, CT: Yale University Press, 2001); Eamon Duffy, *The stripping of the altars: Traditional religion in England, c. 1400–c. 1580*, second edition (New Haven, CT: Yale University Press, 2005).
2. Duffy, *The Stripping of the altars*, p. xviii.
3. Tyacke, "Introduction," *Aspects of English Protestantism, c. 1530–1700*, p. 27.
4. W. G. Hoskins, "Harvest fluctuations and English economic history, 1480–1619," *Agricultural History Review* 12 (1964), pp. 28–46; W. G. Hoskins, "Harvest fluctuations and English economic history, 1620–1759," *Agricultural History Review* 16 (1968), pp. 15–31; C. J. Harrison, "Grain price analysis and harvest qualities, 1465–1634," *Agricultural History Review* 19 (1975), pp. 135–55.

5. Patrick Collinson, *The Elizabethan Puritan movement* (London: Jonathan Cape, 1967); John Craig, "The growth of English Puritanism," in John Coffey and Paul C.-H. Lim (eds.), *The Cambridge companion to Puritanism* (Cambridge: Cambridge University Press, 2008), pp. 34–47.
6. Nicholas Tyacke, "The fortunes of English Puritanism, 1603–40," *Aspects of English Protestantism, c. 1530–1700* (Manchester: Manchester University Press, 2001), p. 111; see, more generally, W. B. Patterson, *William Perkins and the making of a Protestant England* (Oxford: Oxford University Press, 2014).
7. These aspirations were listed in the Millenary Petition (1603); J. P. Kenyon, *The Stuart constitution: Documents and commentary*, second edition (Cambridge: Cambridge University Press, 1986), pp. 117–19.
8. Tom Webster, "Early Stuart Puritanism," in John Coffey and Paul C.-H. Lim (eds.), *The Cambridge companion to Puritanism* (Cambridge: Cambridge University Press, 2008), pp. 48–66; Paul C.-H. Lim, "Puritans and the Church of England: Historiography and ecclesiology," in John Coffey and Paul C.-H. Lim (eds.), *The Cambridge companion to Puritanism* (Cambridge: Cambridge University Press, 2008), pp. 223–40.
9. Tyacke, "The fortunes of English Puritanism, 1603–40," p. 113.
10. For more on the cultures of the godly in this period, see Polly Ha, *English Presbyterianism, 1590–1640* (Stanford, CA: Stanford University Press, 2010), passim.
11. Classic discussions of the Puritan family include Edmund S. Morgan, *The Puritan family: Religion and domestic relations in seventeenth-century New England*, revised edition (New York: Harper, 1966), and Levin L. Schücking, *The Puritan family: a social study from the literary sources*, trans. Brian Battershaw (New York: Schocken Books, 1969). For a summary of recent work on the history of the Puritan family, see Cambers, *Godly reading*, pp. 83–84.
12. C. W. Bardsley, *Curiosities of Puritan nomenclature* (London: Chatto & Windus, 1880); Scott Smith-Bannister, *Names and Naming patterns in England, 1538–1700* (Oxford: Clarendon Press, 1997).
13. Owen, *Works*, 2: 151. Owen may have been reading the divisions of the later period back into his childhood. For a caution about this habit, see Ryrie, *Being Protestant in Reformation Britain*, p. 8.
14. Owen, *Works*, 13: 224.
15. Cook, "Political biography," p. 25. For more on this context, see Anthony Milton, *Catholic and Reformed: The Roman and Protestant Churches in English Protestant thought, 1600–1640* (Cambridge: Cambridge University Press, 1995).
16. Clergy of the Church of England database, ref 14409, accessed 1 June 2015. For the context of English Puritanism in the 1630s, see Peter Lake, "'A Charitable Christian Hatred': The Godly and their enemies in the 1630s," in Christopher Durston and Jacqueline Eales (eds.), *The culture of English Puritanism, 1560–1700*

(New York: Palgrave Macmillan, 1996), pp. 145–83, and Tom Webster, *Godly clergy in early Stuart England: The Caroline Puritan movement, c. 1620–1643* (Cambridge: Cambridge University Press, 1997).

17. Owen, *Works,* 13: 224; Clergy of the Church of England database, ref 14409, accessed 1 June 2015.
18. Cook, "Political Biography," pp. 26, 28. On village life in early modern England, see Margaret Spufford, *Constrasting communities: English villagers in the sixteenth and seventeenth centuries* (Cambridge: Cambridge University Press, 1974); Keith Wrightson and David Levine, *Poverty and piety in an English village: Terling, 1525–1700* (Oxford: Oxford University Press, 1979); and the large literature on Earls Colne, Essex, including, most recently, Dolly MacKinnon, *Earls Colne's early modern landscapes* (Farnham, UK: Ashgate, 2014), passim.
19. Owen, *Works,* 14: 153.
20. Toon, *God's statesman,* p. 12; Bodleian MS Eng Lett c 29, f. 145, and *Diaries and letters of Philip Henry,* p. 32, reprinted in *The correspondence of John Owen,* ed. Toon, pp. 103–4.
21. Earls Colne records: http://linux02.lib.cam.ac.uk/earlscolne/, accessed 1 June 2015. See also Alan MacFarlane, *The family life of Ralph Josselin* (New York: Norton, 1973); Robert von Friedeburg, "Reformation of manners and the social composition of offenders in an East Anglian cloth village: Earls Colne, Essex, 1531–1642," *Journal of British Studies* 29 (1990), pp. 347–85; H. R. French and R. W. Hoyle, "English individualism refuted—and reasserted: The land market of Earls Colne (Essex), 1550–1750," *Economic History Review* 56 (2003), pp. 595–622; and MacKinnon, *Earls Colne's early modern landscapes.*
22. The religious history of the University of Oxford in this period lacks the detail provided by David Hoyle's account of *Reformation and religious identity in Cambridge, 1590–1644,* The History of the University of Cambridge: Texts and Studies (Woodbridge, UK: Boydell, 2007).
23. Some records suggest that William moved to Remenham in 1638. See William A. Shaw, *A history of the English church during the civil wars and under the Commonwealth, 1640–1660,* 2 vols. (London: Longmans, Green, 1900), 2: 361; Clergy of the Church of England database, refs 14411, 31043, and 2068, accessed 1 June 2015.
24. On Puritan attitudes toward education, see John Morgan, *Godly learning: Puritan attitudes towards reason, learning and education, 1540–1640* (Cambridge: Cambridge University Press, 1986). Philemon Owen may have been a friend of James Whitelocke, son of Bulstrode Whitelocke; Ruth Spalding, *The improbable Puritan: A life of Bulstrode Whitelocke 1605–1675* (London: Faber and Faber, 1975), p. 122.
25. Asty, "Memoirs," p. ix.

26. The History of Parliament database, s.v. "Henry Owen," forthcoming. I am grateful to Stephen Roberts for sharing this record with me in advance of publication.
27. "The will of Dr John Owen," in *The correspondence of John Owen*, ed. Toon, p. 184.
28. Cook, "Political Biography," p. 28.
29. Bodleian MS Eng Lett c 29, f. 145, and *Diaries and letters of Philip Henry*, p. 32, reprinted in *The correspondence of John Owen*, ed. Toon, pp. 103–4.
30. C. S. Knighton, "Hartcliffe, John (1651/2–1712)," *ODNB*, provides details of its subject's father.
31. C. S. Knighton, "Hartcliffe, John (1651/2–1712)," *ODNB*.
32. "The will of Dr John Owen," in *The correspondence of John Owen*, ed. Toon, p. 184.
33. Cook, "Political biography," pp. 28–29; Sylvester is not listed in the Clergy of the Church of England database.
34. Warren Chernaik, "Chillingworth, William (1602–1644)," *ODNB*.
35. Owen, *Works*, 8: 197.
36. Wood, *Athenæ Oxonienses*, 2: 505, 849; Jim Spivey, "Wilkinson, Henry (1616/17–1690)," *ODNB*. This Henry Wilkinson should be distinguished from his tutor of the same name; contra Toon, *God's statesman*, p. 3.
37. Cook, "Political biography," p. 29.
38. *The diary of Thomas Crosfield*, ed. Frederick S. Boas (London: Oxford University Press, 1935), p. xviii.
39. *The diary of Thomas Crosfield*, ed. Boas, p. xix; John R. Magrath, *The Queen's College*, 2 vols. (Oxford: Clarendon Press, 1921), vol. 1, passim.
40. A. J. Hegarty, "Potter, Christopher (1590/91–1646)," *ODNB*.
41. *The diary of Thomas Crosfield*, ed. Boas, p. 11.
42. Bill, *Education at Christ Church, Oxford*, pp. 195–96, 207; Mordechai Feingold, "The humanities," in *The history of the University of Oxford*, vol. 4: *The seventeenth century*, ed. Nicholas Tyacke (Oxford: Oxford University Press, 1997), pp. 211–357.
43. "Præpositus conqueritur se falsò accusari à vulgo pro Arminianismo, qui per 14 annos sedulò versatus in istis controversijs defendere Calvinum contra Arminium"; *The diary of Thomas Crosfield*, ed. Boas, p. 31.
44. *The diary of Thomas Crosfield*, ed. Boas, pp. 4, 41.
45. *The diary of Thomas Crosfield*, ed. Boas, p. xx.
46. MS Rawl. C. 167, 227r.
47. Owen, *Works*, 10: 84.
48. Queen's College, Oxford, MS 390, 51v; *The British delegation at the Synod of Dort (1618–1619)*, ed. Anthony Milton (Woodbridge, UK: Boydell, 2005).
49. Hegarty, "Potter, Christopher (1590/91–1646)," *ODNB*.
50. *The diary of Thomas Crosfield*, ed. Boas, p. 50.
51. *The diary of Thomas Crosfield*, ed. Boas, p. 51.

52. Anthony à Wood, *The history and antiquities of the University of Oxford*, 2 vols. (Oxford, 1796), 1: 375; Clergy of the Church of England database, ref 15662, accessed 1 June 2015.
53. *The diary of Thomas Crosfield*, ed. Boas, p. 56. For Thorne's future career, see *The diary of Robert Woodford*, ed. John Fielding, Camden fifth series (Cambridge: Cambridge University Press, 2013), p. 310 n. 708.
54. *The diary of Thomas Crosfield*, ed. Boas, p. 57.
55. Hegarty, "Potter, Christopher (1590/91–1646)," *ODNB*; *The diary of Thomas Crosfield*, ed. Boas, p. 59.
56. University of Nottingham Library, MS C1. c, 84b.
57. Hegarty, "Potter, Christopher (1590/91–1646)," *ODNB*.
58. *The diary of Thomas Crosfield*, ed. Boas, p. 74.
59. *The diary of Thomas Crosfield*, ed. Boas, pp. 9, 20; see also Christopher Marsh, *The family of love in English society, 1550–1630* (Cambridge: Cambridge University Press, 1994) and Peter Lake, *The Boxmaker's revenge: "Orthodoxy," "heterodoxy" and the politics of the parish in early Stuart London* (Manchester: Manchester University Press, 2001), passim.
60. *The diary of Thomas Crosfield*, ed. Boas, p. 25.
61. For a general description of Queen's College in this period, see Magrath, *The Queen's College*, 1: 242–76.
62. Joad Raymond, "Rushworth, John (c. 1612–1690)," *ODNB*; Crawford Gribben, "Polemic and apocalyptic in the Cromwellian invasion of Scotland," *Literature and History* 23:1 (2014), pp. 1–18.
63. Magrath, *The Queen's College*, 1: 268–73, with additional information from Elizabeth Lane Furdell, "Bate, George (1608–1668)," *ODNB*; Stephen Wright, "Napier, Robert (1610/11–1686)," *ODNB*; Andrew J. Hopper, "Shaw, John (1612/13–1689)," *ODNB*; John Callow, "Turnor, Sir Edward (1616/17–1676)," *ODNB*; Joad Raymond, "Rushworth, John (c. 1612–1690)," *ODNB*; Barbara Donagan, "Sedgwick, Obadiah (1599/1600–1658)," *ODNB*.
64. Cook, "Political biography," p. 31.
65. Asty, "Memoir," p. iii.
66. Cambers, *Godly reading*, pp. 7, 22. Countering suspicions of relentless Puritan graft, Cambers suggests that much of this reading was done in bed (p. 54).
67. Asty, "Memoirs," p. iii.
68. John Spurr, "Barlow, Thomas (1608/9–1691)," *ODNB*; Suzanne McDonald, "Beholding the glory of God in the face of Jesus Christ," in Kelly M. Kapic and Mark Jones (eds), *The Ashgate research companion to John Owen's theology* (Farnham, UK: Ashgate, 2012), p. 144; Rehnman, *Divine discourse*, pp. 32–39; Trueman, *John Owen*, pp. 9–12; Cleveland, *Thomism in John Owen*.
69. Richard L. Greaves, "Owen, John (1616–1683)," *ODNB*.

70. *Musarum Oxoniensium pro Rege suo soteria anagramma* (Oxford, 1633), pp. 29–30; *Musarum Oxoniensium charisteria pro serenissima Regina Maria* (Oxford, 1639), sig. Cv.
71. Asty, "Memoirs," p. iii.
72. *The diary of Thomas Crosfield*, ed. Boas, pp. xxi–xxv, 54.
73. Nicholas W. S. Cranfield, "Bancroft, John (1574–1641)," *ODNB*. Cook was not aware of the dates of Owen's ordinations; Cook, "Political biography," p. 33. Details of the ordinations in Greaves, "Owen, John (1616–1683)," *ODNB*, are corrected in The Clergy of the Church of England database, ref. 14413, accessed 1 June 2015; I am grateful to Kenneth Fincham for this reference.
74. Cook, "Political biography," p. 31; Greaves, "Owen, John (1616–1683)," *ODNB*; *Life records of John Milton, 1608–1674*, ed. J. Milton French, 2 vols. (New Brunswick, NJ: Rutgers University Press, 1949–1950), 1: 291; Gordon Campbell and Thomas N. Corns, *John Milton: Life, work, and thought* (Oxford: Oxford University Press, 2008), pp. 86–87; Edward Jones, *John Milton: The emerging author, 1620–1642* (Oxford: Oxford University Press, 2012), p. 30.
75. Toon, *God's statesman*, p. 6; Trueman, *John Owen*, p. 2.
76. *The diary of Thomas Crosfield*, ed. Boas, p. 91.
77. See, for example, Owen, *Works*, 10: 6, 53, 65, 122–23.
78. Owen, *Oxford orations*, ed. Toon, p. 32.
79. Owen, *Works*, 14: 472.
80. *The diary of John Evelyn*, ed. Guy de la Bédoyère (Woodbridge, UK: Boydell, 1995), p. 26; see also Wood, *Athenæ Oxonienses*, 4: 808.
81. John Milton, *Areopagitica* (1644), in *The complete poetry and essential prose of John Milton*, ed. Willliam Kerrigan, John Rumrich, and Stephen M. Fallon (New York: The Modern Library, 2007), p. 957; Graeme Murdock, *Calvinism on the frontier, 1600–1660: International Calvinism and the Reformed Church in Hungary and Transylvania* (Oxford: Clarendon Press, 2000), pp. 49–51.
82. Cook, "Political biography," p. 36.
83. Christopher Durston and Judith Maltby, "Introduction: Religion and revolution in seventeenth-century England," in Christopher Durston and Judith Maltby (eds.), *Religion in revolutionary England* (Manchester: Manchester University Press, 2006), p. 3. Owen would make exactly the same kinds of mistakes in his attempts to reform the university in the 1650s.
84. Cook, "Political biography," p. 37.
85. Cook, "Political biography," p. 38.
86. Cranfield, "Bancroft, John (1574–1641)," *ODNB*. The Clergy of the Church of England database, ref. 14413, accessed 1 June 2015; I am grateful to Kenneth Fincham for this reference.
87. Owen, *Works*, 13: 286, 16: 276.

88. Jim Spivey, "Wilkinson, Henry (1610–1675)," *ODNB*; Cranfield, "Bancroft, John (1574–1641)," *ODNB*.
89. Asty, "Memoirs," p. iv.
90. See, for example, John Stachniewski, *The persecutory imagination: English Puritanism and the literature of religious despair* (Oxford: Clarendon Press, 1991); Crawford Gribben, "Lay conversion and Calvinist doctrine during the English Commonwealth," in D. W. Lovegrove (ed.), *The rise of the laity in Evangelical Protestantism* (London: Routledge, 2002), pp. 36–46; Crawford Gribben, "Puritan subjectivities: The conversion debate in Cromwellian Dublin," in Michael Brown, Charles Ivar McGrath, and Tom P. Power (eds.), *Converts and conversions in Ireland, 1650–1850* (Dublin: Four Courts, 2005), pp. 79–106; Kathleen Lynch, *Protestant autobiography in the seventeenth-century Anglophone world* (Oxford: Oxford University Press, 2012).
91. Owen, *Works*, 9: 292–93.
92. Cook, "Political biography," p. 39.
93. Wood, *Athenæ Oxonienses*, 2: 737; Ian Roy, "Dormer, Robert, first earl of Carnarvon (1610?–1643)," *ODNB*.
94. Cook, "Political biography," p. 39; Shaw, *A history of the English church during the civil wars and under the Commonwealth*, 2: 361. But note that Henry Owen's name is not listed in connection with Harpsden on The Clergy of the Church of England database, location ref. 1462, accessed 1 June 2015.
95. Matthew Dimmock, Andrew Hadfield, and Margaret Healy (eds.), *The intellectual culture of the English country house, 1500–1700* (Manchester: Manchester University Press, 2015), does not refer to the Lovelace household.
96. Manfred Weidhorn, *Richard Lovelace* (New York: Twayne, 1970); C. H. Hartman, *The Cavalier spirit: And its influence on the life and work of Richard Lovelace* (1925; rpr. New York: Haskell House, 1973); F. J. Levy, "How information spread among the gentry, 1550–1640," *Journal of British Studies* 21 (1982), pp. 11–34; Nicholas McDowell, *Poetry and allegiance in the English civil wars: Marvell and the cause of wit* (Oxford: Oxford University Press, 2008), chapter 3.
97. Owen, *Works*, 10: 149.
98. Dennis Kay, *Melodious tears: The English formal elegy from Spenser to Milton* (Oxford: Clarendon Press, 1990), pp. 222, 224. Lovelace's "Elinda's Grove" is "filled with images of horror based on Royalist experience of land expropriation and expulsion in the 1640s"; Anthony Low, *The reinvention of love: Poetry, politics and culture from Sidney to Milton* (Cambridge: Cambridge University Press, 1993), p. 155. See also McDowell, *Poetry and allegiance in the English civil wars*, p. 114.
99. David Hosford, "Lovelace, John, third Baron Lovelace (c. 1640–1693)," *ODNB*.
100. Martyn Bennett, *The civil wars in Britain and Ireland, 1638–1651* (Oxford: Blackwell, 1997), pp. 125–26.

101. Raymond A. Anselment, "Lovelace, Richard (1617–1657)," *ODNB*; Nigel Smith, *Literature and revolution in England, 1640–1660* (New Haven, CT: Yale University Press, 1994), p. 253.
102. Owen, *Works*, 13: 3.
103. David Hosford, "Lovelace, John, third Baron Lovelace (c. 1640–1693)," *ODNB*.
104. Asty, "Memoirs," p. iv; Wood, *Athenæ Oxonienses*, 2: 737. On the emergence of royalism, see Anthony Milton, "Anglicanism and royalism in the 1640s," in John Adamson (ed.), *The English civil war* (New York: Palgrave Macmillan, 2009), pp. 61–81.
105. Ian Roy, "Dormer, Robert, first earl of Carnarvon (1610?–1643)," *ODNB*.
106. Francis J. Bremer, *Lay empowerment and the development of Puritanism* (New York: Palgrave Macmillan, 2015), p. 46.
107. Shaw, *A history of the English church during the civil wars and under the Commonwealth*, 2: 137.
108. See the Agas map of London, http://mapoflondon.uvic.ca/map.htm?section=B4, accessed 1 June 2015.
109. *Middlesex county records*, ed. J. C. Jeaffreson, 4 vols. (London: Middlesex County Record Society, 1888), 3: 13.
110. Adrian Johns, *The nature of the book: Print and knowledge in the making* (Chicago: University of Chicago Press, 1998), p. 73.
111. Cook, "Political biography," p. 40.
112. Joseph Foster, *Alumni Oxonienses* (Oxford: Oxford University Press, 1891), "Thomas Westrow"; Cook, "Political biography," p. 43; Owen, *Works*, 13: 4. Scot shared in the work of the parliamentary County Committee; A. M. Everitt, *The Community of Kent and the Great Rebellion* (Leicester, UK: Leicester University Press, 1966), pp. 49, 53, 108, 115, 144, 147–48.
113. *Correspondence of John Owen*, ed. Toon, p. 12.
114. Cook, "Political biography," p. 43.
115. Owen, *Works*, 13: 3.
116. Asty, "Memoirs," p. v.
117. Compare Owen's conversion to that of C. H. Spurgeon; Peter J. Morden, *Communion with Christ and his people: The spirituality of C. H. Spurgeon* (Eugene, OR: Pickwick, 2013), pp. 48–55.
118. Cook, "Political biography," p. 42; see, for an example of Owen's recycling of quotations, Owen, *Works*, 10: 99, 171.
119. Owen, *Works*, 13: 2, 18 n. 2.
120. Cook, "Political biography," p. 42.

CHAPTER 2

1. This was Owen's earliest publication. The catalogue of Chetham's Library, Manchester, mistakenly links the subject of this biography to the "J. O." who

wrote the preface to J. H[umphrey], *The obligation of human laws discussed* (1641); for similar instances of misidentification of "J. O.," see *The correpondence of John Owen*, ed. Toon, p. 179 n. 1–2.

2. I am grateful to Dion Smythe, Queen's University Belfast, and Pavlos Karageorgi, Westminster Theological Seminary, for advice on Owen's idiosyncratic Greek usage.
3. Cambers, *Godly reading*, p. 2. See also Roger Chartier, *The cultural uses of print in early modern France*, trans. Lydia G. Cochrane (Princeton, NJ: Princeton University Press, 1987); Tessa Watt, *Cheap print and popular piety, 1550–1640* (Cambridge: Cambridge University Press, 1991); Jean-François Gilmont (ed.), *The reformation and the book*, trans. Karin Maag (Aldershot, UK: Ashgate, 1998); Alexandra Walsham, *Providence in early modern England* (Oxford: Oxford University Press, 1999); Nigel Smith, "Non-conformist voices and books," in John Barnard and D. F. Mackenzie (eds), *The Cambridge history of the book in Britain*, 6 vols. (Cambridge: Cambridge University Press, 1999–2014), 4: 410–30; Ian Green, *Print and Protestantism in early modern England* (Oxford: Oxford University Press, 2000); Peter Lake with Michael Questier, *The Antichrist's lewd hat: Protestants, papists and players in post-reformation England* (New Haven, CT: Yale University Press, 2002); Brian Cummings, *The literary culture of the reformation: Grammar and grace* (Oxford: Oxford University Press, 2002); Joad Raymond, *Pamphlets and pamphleteering in early modern Britain* (Cambridge: Cambridge University Press, 2003); Andrew Pettegree, *Reformation and the culture of persuasion* (Cambridge: Cambridge University Press, 2005).
4. Kenyon, *The Stuart constitution*, pp. 204–5.
5. Peter Lake and Steve Pincus, "Rethinking the public sphere in early modern England," *Journal of British Studies* 45 (2006), pp. 270–92.
6. Figures of over 2,000 were generated by a search on EEBO of titles published in London during 1643, when titles of uncertain date were eliminated. On the explosion of print, see David Zaret, *Origins of democratic culture: Printing, petitions, and the public sphere in early-modern England* (Princeton, NJ: Princeton University Press, 2000), and David Cressy, *England on edge: Crisis and revolution, 1640–1642* (Oxford: Oxford University Press, 2006).
7. Crawford Gribben, *The Puritan millennium: Literature and theology, 1550–1682* (Dublin: Four Courts, 2000), pp. 127–48.
8. On Philemon Stephens, see Daniel W. Doerksen, "The Laudian interpretation of Herbert," *Literature and History* 3:2 (1994), pp. 36–54, at pp. 40–42; Daniel W. Doerksen, *Picturing religious experience: George Herbert, Calvin and the Scriptures* (Newark: University of Delaware Press, 2011), pp. 35–36. Stephens is not mentioned in Cyprian Blagden, *The Stationers' Company: A history, 1403–1959* (London: Allen & Unwin, 1960).

9. Jacqueline Eales, "A road to revolution: The continuity of Puritanism, 1559–1642," in Christopher Durston and Jacqueline Eales (eds.), *The culture of English Puritanism, 1560–1700* (Basingstoke, UK: Palgrave 1996), p. 199.
10. Cambers argues that we ought to take printers' convictions more seriously; Cambers, *Godly reading*, pp. 192–210.
11. Archer Taylor, *Book catalogues: Their variety and uses* (Chicago: Newberry Library, 1957), pp. 83–84.
12. See John F. Wilson, *Pulpit in Parliament: Puritanism during the English civil wars, 1640–1648* (Princeton, NJ: Princeton University Press, 1969), passim.
13. Owen, *Works*, 10: 4–5; Shaw, *A history of the English church during the civil wars and under the Commonwealth*, 2: 176–79.
14. Owen, *Works*, 10: 8–9.
15. Owen, *Works*, 10: 54, 79, 86. "Distortures" is not in the *OED*, and the earliest usage of "concreated" dates from 1661.
16. Owen, *Works*, 10: 61.
17. Owen, *Works*, 10: 49; Cleveland, *Thomism in John Owen*, pp. 33, 37.
18. Owen, *Works*, 10: 19, 27, 108.
19. Owen, *Works*, 10: 17, 66.
20. Owen, *Works*, 10: 27.
21. Sarah Mortimer, *Reason and religion in the English revolution: The challenge of Socinianism* (Cambridge: Cambridge University Press, 2010), pp. 25, 38.
22. Owen, *Works*, 10: 17, 76; Sarah Hutton, "Thomas Jackson, Oxford Platonist, and William Twisse, Aristotelian," *Journal of the History of Ideas* 39:4 (1978), pp. 635–52.
23. Owen, *Works*, 10: 61.
24. Tim Cooper, *John Owen, Richard Baxter and the formation of nonconformity* (Farnham, UK: Ashgate, 2011), p. 69.
25. Owen, *Works*, 10: 115.
26. See, for example, R. Glynne Lloyd, *John Owen* (Pontypridd, UK: Modern Welsh Publications, 1972), p. 46; Trueman, *Claims of truth*, p. 23, and Cooper, *John Owen, Richard Baxter and the formation of nonconformity*, pp. 69–72. Geoffrey F. Nuttall similarly suspected that Owen was not responding to Fox's arguments, but rather responding to what he would have meant if he had been using Fox's language; *The Holy Spirit in puritan faith and experience*, p. 42.
27. Owen, *Works*, 10: 6, 53, 65, 122–23.
28. Owen, *Works*, 10: 69. The earliest *OED* reference to the usage of "apostated" dates from 1642.
29. Owen, *Works*, 10: 6.
30. Owen, *Works*, 10: 45, 70.
31. Owen, *Works*, 10: 62.
32. Owen, *Works*, 10: 9.

33. Owen, *Works*, 10: 6.
34. Owen, *Works*, 10: 11.
35. Cleveland, *Thomism in John Owen*, p. 40.
36. Owen, *Works*, 10: 8, 12, 99.
37. Tay, *The priesthood of Christ*, p. 34. For an account of the scholarly debate about Owen's construction of the covenant of redemption, see Laurence R. O'Donnell, "The Holy Spirit's role in John Owen's 'covenant of the mediator' formulation: A case study in Reformed Orthodox formulations of the *pactum salutis*," *Puritan Reformed Journal* 4:1 (2012), pp. 95–97.
38. Tay, *The priesthood of Christ*, pp. 34–35.
39. For the context of reformation scholasticism, see Carl R. Trueman and R. S. Clark (eds), *Protestant scholasticism: Essays in reassessment* (Carlisle, UK: Paternoster, 1999), and Willem van Asselt et al., *Introduction to Reformed scholasticism* (Grand Rapids, MI: Reformation Heritage Books, 2011).
40. Owen, *Works*, 10: 42.
41. Owen, *Works*, 10: 29.
42. Owen, *Works*, 10: 35.
43. Owen, *Works*, 10: 38.
44. Owen, *Works*, 10: 96.
45. Owen, *Works*, 10: 89.
46. Owen, *Works*, 10: 90.
47. Owen, *Works*, 10: 88.
48. For a general account of the doctrine and practice of baptism in the period, see Will Coster, *Baptism and spiritual kinship in early modern England* (Aldershot, UK: Ashgate, 2002).
49. Owen, *Works*, 10: 80.
50. Owen, *Works*, 10: 81.
51. Owen, *Works*, 5: 21.
52. *The diary of Thomas Crosfield*, ed. Boas, p. 38.
53. Cornelius Burgess, *Baptismall regeneration of elect infants professed by the Church of England, according to the Scriptures, the primitiue Church, the present reformed churches, and many particular divines apart* (Oxford, 1629), p. 4.
54. Heinrich Heppe, *Reformed dogmatics*, trans. G. T. Thomson (London: Allen & Unwin, 1950), p. 619.
55. Owen, *Works*, 8: 47; 13: 94.
56. Owen, *Works*, 10: 14, 111.
57. Owen, *Works*, 10: 111.
58. Owen, *Works*, 10: 110.
59. Owen, *Works*, 10: 16.
60. Owen, *Works*, 10: 6.
61. Owen, *Works*, 10: 5.
62. Owen, *Works*, 10: 5.

63. Owen, *Works*, 10: 7.
64. Owen, *Works*, 10: 8.
65. Owen, *Works*, 10: 6.
66. Owen, *Works*, 10: 7.
67. Owen, *Works*, 10: 3.
68. "Fordham: Church," *A history of the county of Essex*, vol. 10: *Lexden Hundred (part) including Dedham, Earls Colne and Wivenhoe* (London: Victoria County History, 2001), pp. 215–17.
69. Owen, *Works*, 13: 16. Cambers notes the frequency in the 1640s of scholars complaining about the fate of their libraries; Cambers, *Godly reading*, p. 122.
70. Cambers, *Godly reading*, p. 147.
71. Toon, *God's statesman*, p. 17.
72. Toon, *God's statesman*, p. 17.
73. http://list.english-heritage.org.uk/resultsingle.aspx?uid=1239789, accessed 1 June 2015; R. G. Davies, "Walden, Roger (*d.* 1406)," *ODNB*.
74. Macfarlane, *The family life of Ralph Josselin*, p. 150. One member of Josselin's parish was the sister of Samuel Rogers; *The diary of Samuel Rogers, 1634–1638*, ed. Tom Webster and Kenneth Shipps, Church of England Record Society (Woodbridge, UK: Boydell, 2004), p. xxii.
75. *The diary of Ralph Josselin*, ed. Macfarlane, p. 76.
76. *The diary of Ralph Josselin*, ed. Macfarlane, p. 101.
77. *The diary of Ralph Josselin*, ed. Macfarlane, p. 89.
78. On this practice of *lectio continua*, see Green, *Continuity and change in Protestant preaching in early modern England*, pp. 36–39; Arnold Hunt, *The art of hearing: English preachers and their audiences, 1590–1640* (Cambridge: Cambridge University Press, 2010).
79. Scholars continue to assume the contrary: Robert Letham describes Owen as "probably the greatest English-speaking theologian at the time of the Assembly, but a few years too young to have been considered for membership in it"; Robert Letham, *The Westminster Assembly: Readings its theology in historical context* (Phillipsburg, NJ: P & R, 2009), p. 235.
80. Jim Spivey, "Wilkinson, Henry (1616/17–1690)," *ODNB*; Jim Spivey, "Wilkinson, Henry (1610–1675)," *ODNB*.
81. Owen, *Works*, 1: 465.
82. Owen, *Works*, 13: 47.
83. Macfarlane, *The family life of Ralph Josselin*, pp. 17, 189–91.
84. *The diary of Ralph Josselin*, ed. Macfarlane, pp. 27, 60, 67.
85. Toon, *God's statesman*, p. 17.
86. Macfarlane, *The family life of Ralph Josselin*, passim.
87. On the development of English Presbyterianism in the mid-century period, see Claire Cross, "The church in England, 1646–1660," in G. E. Aylmer (ed.), *The Interregnum: The quest for settlement* (London: Macmillan, 1972), pp. 99–120;

John Morrill, "The Church of England, 1642–1649," in John Morrill (ed.), *The nature of the English revolution* (Harlow, UK: Routledge, 1993), pp. 148–75; Elliot Vernon, "'A ministry of the gospel': The Presbyterians during the English revolution," in Christopher Durston and Judith Maltby (eds.), *Religion in revolutionary England* (Manchester: Manchester University Press, 2006), pp. 115–36; Ha, *English Presbyterianism.*

88. Owen, *Works*, 13: 3.
89. Owen, *Works*, 13: 28.
90. Owen, *Works*, 13: 3.
91. Owen, *Works*, 13: 5.
92. Owen, *Works*, 13: 5.
93. Owen, *Works*, 13: 5.
94. Owen, *Works*, 13: 39.
95. Ha, *English Presbyterianism*, passim.
96. W. B. Patterson, "Thorndike, Herbert (*bap.* 1597?, *d.* 1672)," *ODNB.*
97. *The diary of Ralph Josselin*, ed. Macfarlane, pp. 53–54, 78.
98. *The diary of Ralph Josselin*, ed. Macfarlane, p. 55.
99. Henry Owen seems to have been the "Colonel Owen" named in "An ordinance for the speedy establishing of a Court Martiall, within the Cities of London, Westminster, or Lines of Communication, together with the names of such Commissioners as are appointed for the Execution thereof," dated 16 August 1644; *Acts and ordinances of the Interregnum, 1642–1660*, eds. C. H. Firth and R. S. Rait, 3 vols. (London: His Majesty's Stationery Office, 1911), 1: 486.
100. Owen, *Works*, 13: 19, 24.
101. Owen, *Works*, 13: 16.
102. Owen, *Works*, 13: 5.
103. Owen, *Works*, 13: 41.
104. Milton, *Areopagitica* (1644), in *The complete poetry and essential prose of John Milton*, p. 952.
105. Owen, *Works*, 13: 40.
106. Owen, *Works*, 13: 42.
107. Owen, *Works*, 13: 27.
108. Owen, *Works*, 13: 37.
109. Owen, *Works*, 13: 27.
110. Owen, *Works*, 13: 18.
111. Owen, *Works*, 13: 38.
112. Owen, *Works*, 13: 49; Coffey, *Politics, religion and the British revolutions*, passim.
113. Cook, "A political biography," p. 51.
114. Owen, *Works*, 13: 2.
115. T. W. Davids, *Annals of evangelical nonconformity in the county of Essex* (London, 1863), p. 224.

116. Owen, *Works*, 8: 45–46.
117. *The diary of Ralph Josselin*, ed. Macfarlane, pp. 15–21, 31, 35.
118. Toon, *God's statesman*, p. 17; Essex County Records Office, Microfiche D/P 372/1/1; Steve Griffiths, *Redeem the time: Sin in the writings of John Owen* (Fearn, Ross-shire, UK: Mentor, 2001), p. 249 n. 9.
119. *The diary of Ralph Josselin*, ed. Macfarlane, pp. 37, 44.
120. John Walter, "Josselin, Ralph (1617–1683)," *ODNB*.
121. Owen, *Works*, 8: 47; 13: 94.
122. *The diary of Ralph Josselin*, ed. Macfarlane, pp. 77, 236.
123. *The principles of the doctrine of Christ* was published in a second edition in 1684.
124. W. C. Braithwaite, *The beginnings of Quakerism*, second edition (Cambridge: Cambridge University Press, 1961), p. 300.
125. Owen, *Works*, 1: 465, citing Romans 9:2 and 2 Thessalonians 3:6, 11.
126. Owen, *Works*, 1: 465.
127. Owen, *Works*, 1: 466.
128. Owen, *Works*, 1: 469.
129. [Westminster Assembly,] *A directory for the publique worship of God in the three kingdomes* (1645), p. 20.
130. Owen, *Works*, 1: 476.
131. Samuel Bolton, *The true bounds of Christian freedome* (1645), p. 64.
132. Bolton, *The true bounds of Christian freedome*, p. 73.
133. Bolton, *The true bounds of Christian freedome*, "To the Christian reader," n.p.
134. Stephen Wright distinguishes two Edward Fishers in Stephen Wright, "Fisher, Edward (*b.* 1611/12, *d.* in or after 1656)"; see also Christopher E. Caughey, "Puritan responses to antinomianism in the context of Reformed covenant theology, 1630–1696" (unpublished PhD thesis, Trinity College Dublin, 2013), pp. 74–100.
135. Owen, *Works*, 13: 222–23.
136. Owen, *Works*, 13: 47.
137. Owen, *Works*, 13: 47–48.
138. Owen, *Works*, 13: 227.
139. Cook, "A political biography," p. 55.
140. Cook, "A political biography," p. 56.
141. Owen, *Works*, 8: 59, 10: 426–27.
142. John Coffey, "The toleration controversy during the English revolution," in Christopher Durston and Judith Maltby (eds.), *Religion in Revolutionary England* (Manchester: Manchester University Press, 2006), pp. 42–43.
143. Coffey, "The toleration controversy during the English revolution," pp. 45–46.
144. William Bartlet, *Ichnographia, or, A model of the primitive congregational way* (1647), p. 23.

CHAPTER 3

1. Josselin's diary records how news reached the area, and how it was often immediately corrected: see, for example, rumors about the taking of Chester; *The diary of Ralph Josselin*, ed. Macfarlane, p. 46. Similarly, on 31 January 1649, Josselin "heard K[ing] C[harles] was executed, but that was uncertaine" (p. 155). Josselin was right, but for the wrong reasons, as the rumor anticipated the event of the regicide by several days.
2. On the evolution of reportage, see Joad Raymond, *The invention of the newspaper: English newsbooks, 1641–1649* (Oxford: Clarendon Press, 1996), and Andrew Pettegree, *The invention of news: How the world came to know about itself* (New Haven, CT: Yale University Press, 2014).
3. See, for example, David O'Hara, *English newsbooks and Irish rebellion, 1641–1649* (Dublin: Four Courts, 2006).
4. Edward Millington, *Bibliotheca Oweniana* (1684), p. 28.
5. Raymond, *The invention of the newspaper*, passim; Joad Raymond, "Dillingham, John (*fl.* 1639–1649)," *ODNB*.
6. Shaw, *A history of the English church during the civil wars and under the Commonwealth*, 2: 177–79, 185–87.
7. Toon, *God's statesman*, p. 19.
8. For an account of the village's history, see B. Dale, *The annals of Coggeshall, otherwise Sunnedon, in the county of Essex* (Coggeshall, 1863).
9. Davids, *Essex*, p. 293, 294, 306. The participation of Fordham and Coggeshall in the local classis, as of 3 March 1646, is recorded in Shaw, *A history of the English church during the civil wars and under the Commonwealth*, 2: 1, 388, 392.
10. Neither the parish of Fordham nor that of Coggeshall were represented by a minister at this meeting; Shaw, *A history of the English church during the civil wars and under the Commonwealth*, 2: 388.
11. Davids, *Essex*, p. 398; Asty, "Memoirs," pp. vi–vii.
12. Owen, *Works*, 1: 465.
13. *Journals of the House of Lords*, 8: 467.
14. Shaw, *A history of the English church during the civil wars and under the Commonwealth*, 2: 327; *Commons letters and journals*, 8: 291; *The minutes and papers of the Westminster Assembly, 1643–1652*, ed. Chad van Dixhoorn, 5 vols. (Oxford: Oxford University Press, 2012), 4: 165 n. 2; Pat Lewis, *All Saints Church, Fordham, Essex: Notes on the rectors from 1198*, available at www.fordhamchurch.org.uk/assets/docs/fordham-rectors.pdf, accessed 1 June 2015.
15. *The minutes and papers of the Westminster Assembly*, ed. van Dixhoorn, 1: 136.
16. *The diary of Ralph Josselin*, ed. Macfarlane, pp. 16, 41.
17. *The diary of Ralph Josselin*, ed. Macfarlane, pp. 52–53.

18. *The diary of Ralph Josselin*, ed. Macfarlane, p. 57; Shaw, *A history of the English church during the civil wars and under the Commonwealth*, 2: 33; *Commons letters and Journals*, 8: 467.
19. Toon, *God's statesman*, pp. 25–26; Cooper, *John Owen, Richard Baxter and the formation of nonconformity*, p. 40.
20. Barbara Donagan, "Sedgewick, Obadiah (1599/1600–1658), "*ODNB; The diary of Ralph Josselin*, ed. Macfarlane, p. 17.
21. *The diary of Ralph Josselin*, ed. Macfarlane, p. 76; cf. Christopher Hill, *Economic problems of the church* (Oxford: Oxford University Press, 1963), p. 113.
22. *The diary of Ralph Josselin*, ed. Macfarlane, p. 17.
23. *The correspondence of John Owen*, ed. Toon, p. 161 n. 1.
24. Owen, *Works*, 1: 465; Asty, "Memoirs," p. vii.
25. Joel Halcomb, "The examination of ministers," in *The minutes and papers of the Westminster Assembly, 1643–1652*, ed. Chad Van Dixhoorn, 5 vols. (Oxford: Oxford University Press, 2012), 1: 217–26.
26. Halcomb, "The examination of ministers," p. 216.
27. Halcomb, "The examination of ministers," p. 218; *The minutes and papers of the Westminster Assembly*, 4: 165 n. 2, 4: 882 n. 7.
28. Halcomb, "The examination of ministers," pp. 219–20.
29. Halcomb, "The examination of ministers," pp. 222–23.
30. *The diary of Ralph Josselin*, ed. Macfarlane, p. 56.
31. *The diary of Ralph Josselin*, ed. Macfarlane, p. 57.
32. *The diary of Ralph Josselin*, ed. Macfarlane, p. 61.
33. *The diary of Ralph Josselin*, ed. Macfarlane, p. 61.
34. Wilson indicates that these invitations were generally agreed upon at the previous preaching; Wilson, *Pulpit in Parliament*, p. 62.
35. Hugh Trevor-Roper, "Fast sermons," in *Religion, the reformation and social change* (London: Secker and Warburg, 1967), p. 306.
36. Wilson, *Pulpit in Parliament*, p. 44; James Nalton, *Delay of reformation provoking Gods further indignation* (1646), p. 12.
37. Wilson, *Pulpit in Parliament*, p. 51.
38. Wilson, *Pulpit in Parliament*, pp. 7, 65, 78, 85.
39. Wilson, *Pulpit in Parliament*, pp. 87, 89.
40. Wilson, *Pulpit in Parliament*, pp. 89–90.
41. Wilson, *Pulpit in Parliament*, p. 62.
42. Wilson, *Pulpit in Parliament*, p. 104.
43. Foster, *Alumni Oxonienses*, "Thomas Westrow."
44. *CJ* 4: 489, 526.
45. Tim Cooper, "Owen's personality: The man behind the theology," in Kelly M. Kapic and Mark Jones (eds.), *The Ashgate research companion to John Owen's theology* (Farnham, UK: Ashgate, 2012), p. 217.

46. *The moderate intelligencer* 61, 30 April–7 May 1646, p. 420.
47. Nalton, *Delay of reformation*, p. 15.
48. Nalton, *Delay of reformation*, p. 29.
49. Nalton, *Delay of reformation*, p. 16.
50. Nalton, *Delay of reformation*, sig. A3r, p. 35.
51. Nalton, *Delay of reformation*, pp. 25–26, 38.
52. Nalton, *Delay of reformation*, p. 41.
53. Ian Gentles, "The politics of Fairfax's army, 1645–9," in John Adamson (ed.), *The English civil war* (New York: Palgrave Macmillan, 2009), pp. 175–201; Paul Lim, "*Adiaphora*, ecclesiology and reformation: John Owen's theology of religious toleration in context," *Westminster Theological Journal* 67:2 (2005), pp. 206–22.
54. Owen, *Works*, 8: 2.
55. Owen, *Works*, 8: 6, 18.
56. Owen, *Works*, 8: 16–17.
57. Owen, *Works*, 8: 27.
58. Owen, *Works*, 8: 28.
59. Owen, *Works*, 8: 29.
60. Owen, *Works*, 8: 19.
61. Owen, *Works*, 8: 15.
62. Owen, *Works*, 8: 39.
63. Owen, *Works*, 8: 27.
64. Owen, *Works*, 8: 12.
65. Owen, *Works*, 8: 8.
66. Owen, *Works*, 8: 11; John Calvin, *Institutes of the Christian religion*, ed. John T. McNeill (Philadelphia, PA: Westminster Press, 1960), i, xvii, 5.
67. Owen, *Works*, 8: 12.
68. Owen, *Works*, 8: 30, 40, 41.
69. Owen, *Works*, 8: 40.
70. Owen, *Works*, 8: 33, 43.
71. Owen, *Works*, 8: 44.
72. *CJ* 4: 526.
73. Owen, *Works*, 8: 47.
74. Owen, *Works*, 8: 44.
75. Owen, *Works*, 8: 44, 48.
76. Owen, *Works*, 8: 41.
77. Owen, *Works*, 8: 45.
78. Owen, *Works*, 8: 47.
79. Nalton, *Delay of reformation*, p. 16.
80. Owen, *Works*, 8: 47.
81. Owen, *Works*, 8: 47.

82. John Coffey, "John Owen and the Puritan toleration controversy, 1646–59" in Kelly M. Kapic and Mark Jones (eds.), *The Ashgate research companion to John Owen's theology* (Farnham, UK: Ashgate, 2012), p. 231.
83. Owen, *Works,* 8: 48.
84. Lim, "*Adiaphora,* ecclesiology, and reformation: John Owen's theory of religious toleration in context," p. 281.
85. Coffey, "John Owen and the Puritan toleration controversy," p. 232.
86. Coffey, "John Owen and the Puritan toleration controversy," p. 232.
87. Coffey, "John Owen and the Puritan toleration controversy," p. 233.
88. Owen, *Works,* 8: 63–66.
89. Coffey, "John Owen and the Puritan toleration controversy," p. 232.
90. Owen, *Works,* 8: 47.
91. *The diary of Ralph Josselin,* ed. Macfarlane, pp 69, 73.
92. Owen, *Works,* 10: 274.
93. *The diary of Ralph Josselin,* ed. Macfarlane, p. 64; Owen, *Works,* 13: 301.
94. *The diary of Ralph Josselin,* ed. Macfarlane, p. 82.
95. *The diary of Ralph Josselin,* ed. MacFarlane, p. 90.
96. *The diary of Ralph Josselin,* ed. Macfarlane, pp. 95, 98.
97. *The diary of Ralph Josselin,* ed. Macfarlane, pp. 70, 98.
98. *The diary of Ralph Josselin,* ed. Macfarlane, p. 95.
99. *The diary of Ralph Josselin,* ed. Macfarlane, pp. 70, 93.
100. *The diary of Ralph Josselin,* ed. Macfarlane, pp. 91–93.
101. *The diary of Ralph Josselin,* ed. Macfarlane, p. 94.
102. *The diary of Ralph Josselin,* ed. Macfarlane, pp. 97–98; *Four petitions to his excellency Sir Thomas Fairfax* (1647).
103. *The diary of Ralph Josselin,* ed. Macfarlane, p. 101.
104. Essex County Records Office, Microfiche D/P 36/1/1; cited in Griffiths, *Redeem the time,* p. 249 n 9.
105. Essex County Records Office, Microfiche D/P 36/1/1; cited in Griffiths, *Redeem the time,* p. 249 n. 9.
106. Essex County Records Office, Microfiche D/P 372/1/1; cited in Griffiths, *Redeem the time,* p. 249 n. 9. In the neighboring parish of Earles Colne, the minister Ralph Josselin baptized his children as soon as one day and as late as one month after their birth; Macfarlane, *The family life of Ralph Josselin,* p. 88.
107. Macfarlane, *The family life of Ralph Josselin,* pp. 100–101.
108. *The diary of Ralph Josselin,* ed. Macfarlane, p. 107.
109. Owen, *Works,* 1: 465; 8: 245.
110. *The diary of Ralph Josselin,* ed. Macfarlane, pp. 113–14; Essex County Records Office, Microfiche D/P 36/1/1; cited in Griffiths, *Redeem the Time,* p. 249 n. 9.
111. *The diary of Ralph Josselin,* ed. Macfarlane, pp. 103, 108.

112. Shaw, *A history of the English church during the civil wars and under the Commonwealth*, 2: 15.
113. Shaw, *A history of the English church during the civil wars and under the Commonwealth*, 2: 13–15.
114. *The division of the county of Essex into several classes, together with the names of the ministers and others fit to be of each classis* (1648); Shaw, *A history of the English church during the civil wars and under the Commonwealth*, 2: 388. Owen would later appoint a chaplain to Christ Church, Oxford, despite the fact that he had never been ordained; E. G. W. Bill, *Education at Christ Church, Oxford, 1660–1800* (Oxford: Clarendon Press, 1988), p. 26. On John Sams, see *The minutes and papers of the Westminster Assembly, 1643–1652*, ed. Chad van Dixhoorn, 5 vols. (Oxford: Oxford University Press, 2012), 4: 707n, 882.
115. *The diary of Ralph Josselin*, ed. Macfarlane, p. 121.
116. *The diary of Ralph Josselin*, ed. Macfarlane, p. 102.
117. *The diary of Ralph Josselin*, ed. Macfarlane, p. 104.
118. *The diary of Ralph Josselin*, ed. Macfarlane, p. 105.
119. Shaw, *A history of the English church during the civil wars and under the Commonwealth*, 2: 22, 29, 30.
120. Shaw, *A history of the English church during the civil wars and under the Commonwealth*, 2: 21.
121. Shaw, *A history of the English church during the civil wars and under the Commonwealth*, 2: 100.
122. *The diary of Ralph Josselin*, ed. Macfarlane, p. 122.
123. *The diary of Ralph Josselin*, ed. Macfarlane, p. 123.
124. *The diary of Ralph Josselin*, ed. Macfarlane, p. 124.
125. Owen, *Works*, 13: 53.
126. John Owen, *Eschol* (1648), [A6r].
127. Goold, "Prefatory note," in Owen, *Works*, 13: 52.
128. Owen, *Works*, 13: 54.
129. Owen, *Works*, 13: 62.
130. Owen, *Works*, 13: 73.
131. Owen, *Works*, 13: 61.
132. Owen, *Works*, 13: 61.
133. Owen, *Works*, 13: 57.
134. Owen, *Works*, 13: 78.
135. Owen, *Works*, 13: 70.
136. Owen, *Works*, 13: 69.
137. Owen, *Works*, 13: 78.
138. John Owen, *Salus electorum, sanguis Jesu* (1648), sig. A4r.
139. Tay, *The priesthood of Christ*, p. 8.
140. Owen, *Works*, 10: 274.

141. Owen, *Works,* 10: 274.
142. Owen, *Works,* 10: 276.
143. Thomas Edwards, *Gangreana,* 3 vols (1646), 1: 96.
144. Richard Baxter, *Reliquiae Baxterianae* (1696), 1: 50.
145. Owen, *Works,* 10: 377.
146. "Prefatory note," in Owen, *Works,* 10: 140.
147. Tay, *The priesthood of Christ,* p. 11.
148. Obadiah Howe, *The universalist examined and convicted* (1648), sig. A2r.
149. Owen, *Works,* 10: 145.
150. Owen, *Works,* 10: 371.
151. Owen, *Works,* 10: 155, 197, 347, 409.
152. Owen, *Works,* 10: 194, 201, 267.
153. Owen, *Works,* 10: 372.
154. Owen, *Works,* 10: 149.
155. Owen, *Works,* 10: 155.
156. Owen, *Works,* 10: 156.
157. Owen, *Works,* 10: 155.
158. Owen, *Works,* 10: 187, 189.
159. Owen, *Works,* 10: 189.
160. Owen, *Works,* 10: 151.
161. Tay, *The priesthood of Christ,* p. 12.
162. Owen, *Works,* 10: 199.
163. Owen, *Works,* 10: 154.
164. Owen, *Works,* 10: 227.
165. Owen, *Works,* 10: 231.
166. Owen, *Works,* 10: 297.
167. Owen, *Works,* 10: 300.
168. Owen, *Works,* 10: 296.
169. Owen, *Works,* 10: 245.
170. Owen, *Works,* 10: 183.
171. Owen, *Works,* 10: 173.
172. Owen, *Works,* 10: 290.
173. Owen, *Works,* 10: 156.
174. Tay, *The priesthood of Christ,* p. 55.
175. Owen, *Works,* 10: 205.
176. Owen's work is not represented in *Catalogus universalis librorum omnium in Bibliotheca Collegii Sionii apud Londinenses* (1650).
177. Owen, *Works,* 10: 148.
178. Owen, *Works,* 10: 316.
179. *The diary of Ralph Josselin,* ed. Macfarlane, p. 126.
180. *The diary of Ralph Josselin,* ed. Macfarlane, pp. 127–28.

181. *The diary of Ralph Josselin*, ed. Macfarlane, p. 128.
182. *The diary of Ralph Josselin*, ed. Macfarlane, p. 129.
183. *The diary of Ralph Josselin*, ed. Macfarlane, p. 129.

CHAPTER 4

1. *The diary of Ralph Josselin*, ed. Macfarlane, pp. 97–98; *Four petitions to his excellency Sir Thomas Fairfax* (1647).
2. For a recent account of the Colchester seige that pays attention to the laws of war, see Barbara Donogan, *War in England, 1642–1649* (Oxford: Oxford University Press, 2008), pp. 312–88; see also Brian Lyndon, "Essex and the King's cause in 1648," *Historical Journal* 29 (1986), pp. 17–39. Perhaps thinking of an earlier period, Cooper has argued that Owen was "relatively untouched by the war"; *John Owen, Richard Baxter and the formation of nonconformity*, p. 50.
3. Hill, *The experience of defeat*, p. 165; Cook, "Political biography," p. 24.
4. For a notable recent history of this conflict, see Robert Ashton, *Counter-revolution: The second civil war and its origins, 1646–8* (New Haven, CT: Yale University Press, 1994).
5. John Rushworth, *Historical collections of private passages of state*, 8 vols. (1721), 7: 1150, 1153.
6. Donagan, *War in England, 1642–1649*, p. 322.
7. Donagan, *War in England, 1642–1649*, p. 312.
8. *The moderate intelligencer*, 176, 27th July–3rd August 1648.
9. *The moderate intelligencer*, 173, 6th–13th July 1648.
10. *Mercurius elencticus*, 34, 12–19 July 1648, p. 268; *Colchesters teares*, pp. 13–14; Donagan, *War in England, 1642–1649*, pp. 332–33.
11. *The Colchester spie*, 1, 11 August 1648; *Mercurius Anglicus*, 1, 27 July–3 August, sig. A3v; Donagan, *War in England, 1642–1649*, p. 325 n. 48.
12. Andrew Hopper, *'Black Tom': Sir Thomas Fairfax and the English Revolution* (Manchester: Manchester University Press, 2007), p. 86.
13. P. R. Newman, *The old service: Royalist regimental colonels and the Civil War, 1642–1646* (Manchester: Manchester University Press, 1993), pp. 183, 224.
14. Hopper, *'Black Tom'*, pp. 86–89; Donagan, *War in England, 1642–1649*, p. 385.
15. *CJ* 5: 619; Asty, "Memoirs," p. viii; Rushworth, *Historical collections*, 7: 1172.
16. Owen, *Works*, 8: 72.
17. *The diary of Ralph Josselin*, ed. Macfarlane, p. 90.
18. John Milton, "On the Lord General Fairfax, at the Seige of Colchester," ll. 1–2, in *The complete poetry an essential prose of John Milton*, eds. William Kerrigan, John Runrich, and Stephen M. Fallon (New York: The Modern Library, 2007), p. 152.
19. Hopper, *'Black Tom'*, p. 194.

20. Owen, *Works*, 13: 78.
21. Owen, *Works*, 8: 74.
22. Hopper, *'Black Tom'*, p. 87.
23. Hopper, *'Black Tom'*, p. 94.
24. John Walter, "Lucas, John, first Baron Lucas of Shenfield (1606–1671)," *ODNB*; Barbara Donagan, "Lucas, Sir Charles (1612/13–1648)," *ODNB*.
25. Donagan, *War in England, 1642–1649*, p. 385. The date for the Rumford sermon is in the published subtitle.
26. Owen, *Works*, 8: 76.
27. Josselin complained that he had never paid more for food than during October 1648; *The diary of Ralph Josselin*, ed. Macfarlane, p. 140.
28. Owen, *Works*, 8: 107, 115.
29. Owen, *Works*, 8: 76, 116–18.
30. Owen, *Works*, 8: 124.
31. Owen, *Works*, 8: 125.
32. Owen, *Works*, 8: 88.
33. *The diary of John Evelyn*, ed. Guy de la Bédoyère (Woodbridge, UK: Boydell, 1995), p. 101.
34. *The journals of William Schellinks' travels in England, 1661–1663*, trans. and ed. Maurice Exwood and H. L. Lehmann (London: Royal Historical Society, 1993), p. 33.
35. CJ 6: 107, 152, 217, 374, 544; 7: 13.
36. Coffey, "The toleration controversy during the English revolution," p. 48.
37. Coffey, "The toleration controversy during the English revolution," p. 49.
38. Owen, *Works*, 8: 97.
39. Coffey, "The toleration controversy during the English revolution," p. 51; J. C. Davis, "Cromwell's religion," in John Morrill (ed.), *Oliver Cromwell and the English revolution* (London: Longman, 1990), pp. 181–208; Blair Worden, "Oliver Cromwell and the sin of Achan," in David L. Smith (ed.), *Cromwell and the Interregnum* (Oxford: Blackwell, 2003), pp. 39–59.
40. Bulstrode Whitelock, *Memorials of the English affairs*, new ed. (London, 1732), p. 356.
41. For an excellent account of this period, see Ronald Hutton, *The British republic, 1649–1660* (New York: Macmillan, 1990), despite its claim that Owen and other Independents worked for a "less stringent definition of orthodoxy than the presbyterians" (p. 29).
42. John Adamson, "The frighted junto: Perceptions of Ireland, and the last attempts at settlement with Charles I," in Jason Peacey (ed.), *The regicides and the execution of Charles I* (New York: Palgrave Macmillan, 2001), pp. 36–70; Elliot Vernon, "The quarrel of the Covenant: The London Presbyterians and the regicide," in Jason Peacey (ed.), *The regicides and the execution of Charles*

I (New York: Palgrave Macmillan, 2001), pp. 202–24; Sean Kelsey, "The death of Charles I," *Historical Journal* 45:4 (2002), pp. 727–54; Sean Kelsey, "The trial of Charles I," *English Historical Review* 118:477 (2003), pp. 583–616; John Adamson, *The noble revolt: The overthrow of Charles I* (London: Weidenfeld and Nicolson, 2007).

43. *CJ* 6: 107.
44. John Morrill and P. Baker, "Oliver Cromwell, the regicide and the sons of Zeruiah," in David L. Smith (ed.), *Cromwell and the interregnum* (Oxford: Blackwell, 2003), pp. 17–36.
45. Hopper, *'Black Tom'*, pp. 93–105; Richard Brandon, *The confession of Richard Brandon the hangman (upon his death bed) concerning his beheading His Late Majesty, Charles the First, King of Great Brittain, and his protestation and vow touching the same, the manner how he was terrified in conscience* (1649).
46. See, for a general survey, David Underdown, *Royalist conspiracy in England, 1649–1660* (New Haven, CT: Yale University Press, 1971).
47. Janet Clare, "General introduction," in *Drama of the English Republic, 1649–60* (Manchester: Manchester University Press, 2002), p. 17.
48. Wilson, *Pulpit in Parliament*, p. 95.
49. R. L. Greaves and R. Zaller (eds.), *Biographical dictionary of British radicals in the seventeenth century*, 3 vols. (Brighton: Harvester, 1982–84), 1: 124–25.
50. John Cardell, *Gods wisdom justified, and mans folly condemned, touching all maner of outward providential administrations* (1649), p. 10.
51. Cardell, *Gods wisdom justified*, p. 12.
52. Cardell, *Gods wisdom justified*, p. 6.
53. *CJ* 6: 126; *The writings and speeches of Oliver Cromwell*, ed. W. C. Abbott, 4 vols. (Cambridge, MA: Harvard University Press, 1947), 1: 728, 742; George Yule, *The Independents in the English civil war* (Cambridge: Cambridge University Press, 1958), pp. 84, 97, 108, 109; M. F. Keeler, *The Long Parliament, 1640–1641* (Philadelphia, PA: American Philosophical Society, 1954), p. 269.
54. See the *Short Title Catalogue*.
55. Owen, *Works*, 8: 128.
56. Owen, *Works*, 8: 128.
57. *The diary of Ralph Josselin*, ed. Macfarlane, p. 155.
58. *The diary of Ralph Josselin*, ed. Macfarlane, p. 157.
59. *The diary of Ralph Josselin*, ed. Macfarlane, p. 157 n. 1.
60. *The Essex watchmen's watchword* (1649), sig. A2r.
61. *The Essex watchmen's watchword*, pp. 3–4.
62. Owen, *Works*, 8: 130.
63. Coffey, "John Owen and the Puritan toleration controversy," p. 234; Ian Gadd, "Simmons, Matthew (*b.* in or before 1608, *d.* 1654)," *ODNB*.
64. Coffey, "John Owen and the Puritan toleration controversy," p. 235; Owen, *Works*, 8: 274.

65. Owen, *Works*, 8: 129.
66. Owen, *Works*, 8: 129.
67. Owen, *Works*, 8: 129.
68. Owen, *Works*, 8: 130.
69. Owen, *Works*, 8: 135.
70. Owen, *Works*, 8: 138.
71. Owen, *Works*, 8: 147.
72. Owen, *Works*, 8: 147.
73. Owen, *Works*, 8: 137, 160.
74. Owen, *Works*, 8: 139.
75. Owen, *Works*, 8: 161–162.
76. Coffey, "John Owen and the Puritan toleration controversy," p. 235.
77. Coffey, "John Owen and the Puritan toleration controversy," p. 236.
78. Owen, *Works*, 8: 164–69.
79. Owen, *Works*, 8: 189–91.
80. Owen, *Works*, 8: 193.
81. Owen, *Works*, 8: 192, 197.
82. Owen, *Works*, 8: 176.
83. Owen, *Works*, 8: 180; *The diary of Ralph Josselin*, ed. Macfarlane, p. 153.
84. Owen, *Works*, 8: 180.
85. John Rogers, *Ohel or Bethshemesh* (1653), p. 179.
86. Owen, *Works*, 8: 191.
87. R. Scott Spurlock, *Cromwell and Scotland: Conquest and religion, 1650–1660* (Edinburgh: John Donald, 2007), p. 46.
88. See the *Short Title Catalogue*.
89. Hopper, *'Black Tom'*, p. 109.
90. *The diary of Ralph Josselin*, ed. Macfarlane, p. 163.
91. Owen, *Works*, 1: 465, 8: 245.
92. On this concept, see Hodge, *Foreshortened time*.
93. *The diary of Ralph Josselin*, ed. Macfarlane, pp. 161, 163.
94. Essex County Records Office, Microfiche D/P 372/1/1; Griffiths, *Redeem the time*, p. 249 n. 9.
95. Essex County Records Office, Microfiche D/P 36/1/1; Griffiths, *Redeem the time*, p. 249 n. 9.
96. *The diary of Ralph Josselin*, ed. Macfarlane, p. 163.
97. Cook, "Political biography," p. 70.
98. Wilson, *Pulpit in Parliament*, pp. 273–74.
99. Cook, "Political biography," p. 70.
100. Wilson, *Pulpit in Parliament*, pp. 237–54.
101. S. R. Gardiner (ed.), *The constitutional documents of the Puritan revolution, 1625–1660*, third edition (Oxford: Clarendon Press, 1936), pp. 384–88; Kenyon, *The Stuart constitution*, pp. 306–7.

102. John Warren, *The potent potter* (1649), p. 5.
103. Warren, *The potent potter*, sig. A3r.
104. Warren, *The potent potter*, p. 8.
105. Warren, *The potent potter*, p. 13.
106. Warren, *The potent potter*, p. 13.
107. Warren, *The potent potter*, p. 20.
108. Warren, *The potent potter*, p. 14.
109. Achinstein, *Literature and dissent in Milton's England*, p. 73.
110. Gribben, *The Puritan millennium*, pp. 67–79. I am grateful to Pavlos Karageorgi for his advice on this translation.
111. Owen, *Works*, 8: 252.
112. Owen, *Works*, 8: 253.
113. Owen, *Works*, 8: 253.
114. Owen, *Works*, 8: 256–266. Tai Liu, *Discord in Zion: The Puritan divines and the Puritan revolution, 1640–1660* (The Hague, The Netherlands: Martinus Nijhoff, 1973), pp. 48–49, and Daniels, *The Christology of John Owen*, p. 443, which provide otherwise excellent accounts of their subjects, are nevertheless too quick to identify explicitly millennial themes in Owen's early writing.
115. Owen, *Works*, 8: 260.
116. Owen, *Works*, 8: 274.
117. Owen, *Works*, 8: 263.
118. Owen, *Works*, 8: 266.
119. Owen, *Works*, 8: 267.
120. Owen, *Works*, 8: 279.
121. Owen, *Works*, 8: 253; the term is first noted by the *OED* in 1610.
122. Samson and other Hebrew Bible figures were to become central to a developing political language. As Kevin Killeen has noted, "many biblical actors—kings, judges, priests, and generals—who featured in the vast biblical discourse that constituted a major, though now largely invisible, language of political thought" in early modern England tend not to feature in our "maps of civil war exemplarity;" Kevin Killeen, "Hanging up kings: The political Bible in early modern England," *Journal of the History of Ideas* 72:4 (2011), p. 550.
123. Owen, *Works*, 10: 147.
124. Wilson, *Pulpit in Parliament*, p. 96.
125. *CJ* 7: 217, 2267; Wood, *Athenae Oxonienses*, 2: 738; Asty, "Memoirs," p. viii.
126. Owen, *Works*, 9: 199.
127. Owen, *Works*, 9: 200, 210–11.
128. Owen, *Works*, 9: 206–7.
129. Owen, *Works*, 9: 216.
130. *CJ* 6: 226–228. Cromwell was also rewarded; Ian Gentles, *Oliver Cromwell: God's warrior and the English revolution* (New York: Palgrave Macmillan, 2011), p. 107.

131. Donald Leggett has questioned the likelihood that this was the first occasion for a meeting between Owen and Cromwell; "John Owen as religious advisor to Oliver Cromwell, 1649–1659" (unpublished MPhil thesis, University of Cambridge, 2006), p. 12.
132. Asty, "Memoirs," p. ix, misdates this meeting; Cook, "Political biography," p. 99.
133. Asty, "Memoirs," pp. ix–x.
134. Whitelock, *Memorials*, p. 411; *CJ* 6:248.
135. *The diary of Ralph Josselin*, ed. MacFarlane, p. 174.
136. Hopper, *'Black Tom'*, pp. 111–12; Crawford Gribben, "Millennialism and the renewal of nature: Thomas Fairfax, the Diggers and Andrew Marvell's 'Upon Appleton House,'" in Helen Cooney and Mark Sweetnam (eds.), *Enigma and revelation in Renaissance literature: Essays in honour of Eiléan Ní Chuilleanáin* (Dublin: Four Courts, 2012), pp. 183–98.
137. *The diary of Ralph Josselin*, ed. Macfarlane, p. 170.
138. Crawford Gribben, *God's Irishmen: Theological debates in Cromwellian Ireland* (Oxford: Oxford University Press, 2007), pp. 3–53.
139. *Writings and speeches of Oliver Cromwell*, ed. Abbott, 2: 127.
140. *The diary of Ralph Josselin*, ed. MacFarlane, p. 179; O'Hara, *English newsbooks and Irish rebellion*, p. 202.
141. Owen, *Works*, 8: 266.
142. For John Murcot's journey from Chester to Dublin, and his escape from pirates, see [J. G.], *Moses in the mount, or The beloved disciple leaning on Jesus' bosom. Being a narrative of the life and death of Mr. John Murcot* (1657), passim.
143. This location is noted in Sandra Hynes, "Mapping friendship and dissent: The letters from Joseph Boyse to Ralph Thoresby, 1680–1710," in Ariel Hessayon and David Finnegan (eds.), *Varieties of seventeenth- and eighteenth-century English radicalism in context* (Farnham, UK: Ashgate, 2011), p. 211.
144. Owen, *Works*, 8: 237.
145. Owen, *Works*, 8: 236.
146. Owen, *Works*, 8: 232–33.
147. Owen, *Works*, 8: 232.
148. Gribben, *God's Irishmen*, p. 26.
149. Austin Woolrych, *Britain in revolution, 1625–1660* (Oxford: Oxford University Press, 2002), p. 473.
150. Owen, *Works*, 10: 479.
151. Owen, *Works*, 8: 237; *The diary of Ralph Josselin*, ed. Macfarlane, p. 187.
152. Gribben, *God's Irishmen*, pp. 55–78.
153. Rogers, *Ohel*, p. 412 [inset pagination, p. 3].
154. Rogers, *Ohel*, p. 412. Note the errors in pagination in this part of the book.

155. Owen C. Watkins claims that Owen made "frequent use of the personal testimony," but did not provide supporting evidence; *The puritan experience* (London: Routledge and Kegan Paul, 1972), p. 30.
156. Owen, *Works*, 10: 479.
157. Hans Boersma, *A hot pepper corn: Richard Baxter's doctrine of justification in its seventeenth-century context of controversy* (Vancouver, BC: Regent College Publishing, 2003), p. 43.
158. Tay, *The priesthood of Christ*, pp. 136–50.
159. Owen, Works, 13: 16.
160. Alan Ford, *James Ussher: Theology, history, and politics in early-modern Ireland and England* (Oxford: Oxford University Press, 2007); Elizabethanne Boran, "The libraries of Luke Challoner and James Ussher, 1595–1608," in H. H. W. Robinson-Hammerstein (ed.), *European universities in the age of the Reformation* (Dublin: Four Courts, 1998), pp. 75–115.
161. Owen, *Works*, 10: 471; W. J. van Asselt, M. D. Bell, and R. Ferwerda, ed. and trans. *Scholastic discourse: Johannes Maccovius (1588–1644) on theological and philosophical distinctions and rules* (Apeldoorn, The Netherlands: Instituut voor Reformatieonderzoek, 2009).
162. Owen, *Works*, 10: 479.
163. *The diary of Ralph Josselin*, ed. Macfarlane, pp. 185–86.
164. *CSPD* (1649–1650), p. 506; *CJ* 6: 357.
165. Essex County Records Office, Microfiche D/P 36/1/1; Griffiths, *Redeem the time*, p. 249 n. 9; *The correspondence of John Owen*, ed. Toon, p. 24.
166. Owen, *Works*, 8: 230–31.
167. Owen, *Works*, 8: 231.
168. Owen, *Works*, 8: 235.
169. Owen, *Works*, 8: 235.
170. Owen, *Works*, 8: 235.
171. Owen, *Works*, 8: 236.
172. Owen, *Works*, 8: 235.
173. *Acts and ordinances of the Interregnum*, eds. Firth and Rait (1911), 2: 355; *CJ* 6: 343–44; Robert Dunlop (ed.), *Ireland under the Commonwealth*, 2 vols. (Manchester: Manchester University Press, 1913), 1: 10–11.
174. *CSPD* 1650, p. 30.
175. *The diary of Ralph Josselin*, ed. MacFarlane, p. 199.
176. Owen, *Works*, 10: 432, 479.
177. Cooper, *John Owen, Richard Baxter and the formation of nonconformity*, pp. 94–98.
178. Owen, *Works*, 10: 435. For a full description of this incident, see Cooper, *John Owen, Richard Baxter and the formation of nonconformity*, pp. 88–94.
179. Owen, *Works*, 10: 437.
180. Owen, *Works*, 10: 435–36.

181. Owen, *Works*, 10: 435; Cooper, *John Owen, Richard Baxter and the formation of nonconformity*, p. 74.
182. Owen, *Works*, 10: 459.
183. Owen, *Works*, 10: 449.
184. Owen, *Works*, 10: 436.
185. Owen, *Works*, 10: 433. For Baxter's challenge to the Reformed doctrine of justification, see Tim Cooper, *Fear and polemic in seventeenth-century England: Richard Baxter and antinomianism* (Aldershot, UK: Ashgate, 2001), pp. 74–75.
186. Owen, *Works*, 10: 431.
187. Owen, *Works*, 10: 431.
188. *CJ* 6: 412, 423.
189. *The diary of Ralph Josselin*, ed. Macfarlane, p. 198.
190. For a fuller account of the invasion, see Gribben, "Polemic and apocalyptic in the Cromwellian invasion of Scotland," pp. 1–18.
191. For the theological background to this conflict, see Crawford Gribben, "The Church of Scotland and the English apocalyptic imagination, 1630–1650," *Scottish Historical Review* 88:1 (2009), pp. 54–56; Crawford Gribben, "'Passionate desires, and confident hopes': Puritan millenarianism and Anglo-Scottish union, 1560–1644," *Reformation & Renaissance Review* 4:2 (2002), pp. 241–58.
192. Frances Dow, *Cromwellian Scotland, 1651–1660* (Edinburgh: John Donald, 1979), pp. 2–12.
193. Hunter Powell, "The Dissenting Brethren and the power of the keys, 1640–44" (unpublished PhD thesis, University of Cambridge, 2011); Spurlock, *Cromwell and Scotland*, p. 9; Samuel Rutherford, *A free disputation against pretended liberty of conscience* (1649), p. 15; see Crawford Gribben, "Samuel Rutherford and liberty of conscience," *Westminster Theological Journal* 71:2 (2009), pp. 355–73.
194. John Warr, *The corruption and deficiency of the laws of England* (1649), quoted in Christopher Hill, *Milton and the English revolution* (London: Faber and Faber, 1977), p. 67; John Milton, *The doctrine and discipline of divorce* (1643), in D. M. Wolfe (ed.), *The complete prose works of John Milton* (New Haven, CT: Yale University Press, 1953–1982), 2: 224.
195. Glasgow University Library, Ms Gen 3, "Sermons on Lamentations by David Dickson," p. 17.
196. Spurlock, *Cromwell and Scotland*, p. 13.
197. *A declaration of the army of England upon their march into Scotland*, p. 12.
198. *A declaration of the army of England upon their march into Scotland*, p. 17.
199. Hopper, *'Black Tom'*, p. 114.
200. *A declaration of the army of England upon their march into Scotland*, title page; R. Scott Spurlock, "'Anie Gospell Way': Religious Diversity in Interregnum Scotland," *Records of the Scottish Church History Society* 37 (2007), pp. 89–119; Spurlock, *Cromwell and Scotland*, pp. 20–30; R. Scott Spurlock, "The politics of

eschatology: Baptists in Interregnum Scotland," *Baptist Quarterly* 44:2 (2010), pp. 324–46.

201. *Original memoirs written during the Great Civil War; being the life of Sir Henry Slingsby, and memoirs of Capt. Hodgson* (Edinburgh, 1806), pp. 244–45.
202. *The diary of Ralph Josselin*, ed. Macfarlane, p. 212.
203. *The diary of Ralph Josselin*, ed. Macfarlane, p. 215.
204. *The diary of Ralph Josselin*, ed. Macfarlane, p. 219.
205. *Original memoirs written during the Great Civil War*, pp. 244–45.
206. Henry Reece, *The army in Cromwellian England, 1649–1660* (Oxford: Oxford University Press, 2013), p. 119.
207. Lloyd, *John Owen*, p. 72.
208. See R. Scott Spurlock, "Cromwell's Edinburgh press and the development of print culture in Scotland," *Scottish Historical Review* 90:2 (2011), pp. 179–203.
209. *Diary of Sir Archibald Johnston of Warison*, ed. D. H. Fleming, 3 vols. (Edinburgh, 1919–1940), 2: 16.
210. Owen, *Works*, 8: 283.
211. Glasgow University Library, Ogilvie 728.
212. See, for example, Gribben, "Samuel Rutherford and liberty of conscience," pp. 355–373.
213. Owen, *Works*, 8: 292–93.
214. Owen, *Works*, 8: 287.
215. Owen, *Works*, 8: 301.
216. Owen, *Works*, 8: 287.
217. Owen, *Works*, 8: 296; *A seasonable and necessary warning* (1650), p. 7.
218. Owen, *Works*, 8: 296.
219. Owen, *Works*, 8: 298.
220. Owen, *Works*, 8: 308.
221. Owen, *Works*, 8: 308.
222. Owen, *Works*, 8: 308.
223. Owen, *Works*, 8: 230–31, 308.
224. Owen, *Works*, 8: 299.
225. Owen, *Works*, 8: 283.
226. *The diary of Ralph Josselin*, ed. Macfarlane, pp. 223–25, 228.
227. *The diary of Ralph Josselin*, ed. Macfarlane, p. 227.
228. *The diary of Ralph Josselin*, ed. Macfarlane, p. 237.
229. John Nickolls, *Original letters and papers of state, addressed to Oliver Cromwell* (London, 1743), pp. 48–49.
230. "A News-Letter from Scotland," in C. H. Firth (ed.), *Scotland and the Commonwealth: Letters and papers* (Edinburgh: Scottish History Society, 1895), p. 33.
231. Dow, *Cromwellian Scotland*, p. 16; Coffey, *Politics, theology and the British revolutions*, p. 221; John Coffey, "Jaffray, Alexander (1614–1673)," *ODNB*, s.v.; Woolrych, *Britain in revolution*, p. 492.

232. *The diary of Ralph Josselin*, ed. Macfarlane, p. 220.
233. *The diary of Ralph Josselin*, ed. Macfarlane, p. 223.
234. *The diary of Ralph Josselin*, ed. Macfarlane, p. 234.
235. *The correspondence of John Owen*, ed. Toon, p. 24.
236. *The writings and speeches of Oliver Cromwell*, ed. Abbott, 4: 947.
237. *The diary of Ralph Josselin*, ed. Macfarlane, p. 239.

CHAPTER 5

1. Reece, *The army in Cromwellian England*, p. 121.
2. *The diary of Ralph Josselin*, ed. Macfarlane, p. 243.
3. "Deans of Christ Church, Oxford," *Fasti Ecclesiae Anglicanae, 1541–1857*, vol. 8: *Bristol, Gloucester, Oxford and Peterborough dioceses*, ed. Joyce M. Horn (London: Institute for Historical Research, 1996), pp. 80–83. On the engagement controversy, see Glenn Burgess, "Usurpation, obligation, and obedience in the thought of the Engagement controversy," *Historical Journal* 29:3 (1986), pp. 515–36; Edward Vallance, "Oaths, casuistry, and equivocation: Anglican responses to the Engagement controversy," *Historical Journal* 44:1 (2001), pp. 59–77.
4. *Writings and speeches of Oliver Cromwell*, ed. Abbott, 4: 947.
5. *Writings and speeches of Oliver Cromwell*, ed. Abbott, 4: 947.
6. Asty, "Memoirs," p. x.
7. *CJ* 6: 544, 549; *CSPD* (1651), p. 74.
8. *Severall proceedings in Parliament*, 77, 13–20 March 1651, pp. 1163, 1165.
9. *CJ* 6: 548–49.
10. William Shakespeare, *Henry VIII*, 4:2:61–62, in *The Norton Shakespeare*, eds. Stephen Greenblatt et al. (New York: Norton, 1997). For a general account of the history of the college, see Judith Curthoys, *The Cardinal's college: Christ Church, chapter and verse* (London: Profile, 2012).
11. Frederick John Varley, *The siege of Oxford: An account of Oxford during the civil war, 1642–1646* (Oxford: Oxford University Press, 1932), p. 128.
12. Blair Worden, "Politics, piety, and learning: Cromwellian Oxford," in *God's instruments: Political conduct in the England of Oliver Cromwell* (Oxford: Oxford University Press, 2012), p. 93.
13. Worden, "Politics, piety, and learning," p. 95.
14. Worden, "Politics, piety, and learning," pp. 96–98.
15. Worden, "Politics, piety, and learning," p. 104.
16. Worden, "Politics, piety, and learning," p. 105.
17. Bill, *Education at Christ Church, Oxford*, p. 17.
18. Bill, *Education at Christ Church, Oxford*, p. 17.
19. Bill, *Education at Christ Church, Oxford*, pp. 196, 307.
20. Bill, *Education at Christ Church, Oxford*, pp. 301–2.

21. Bill, *Education at Christ Church, Oxford*, pp. 94, 251; *The correspondence of John Locke*, 8 vols., ed. E. S. de Beer (Oxford: Clarendon Press, 1976), 1: no. 5.
22. The untitled proclamations are recorded as Wing o863B (22 March 1651[2]) and Wing o903B (5 July 1652); Worden, "Politics, piety, and learning," pp. 104–5. For "rites of violence," see Natalie Zemon Davis, *Society and culture in early modern France* (Stanford, CA: Stanford University Press, 1975), pp. 152–88; see also Graeme Murdock, Penny Roberts, and Andrew Spicer (eds.), *Ritual and violence: Natalie Zemon Davis and early modern France, Past & Present* Supplement 7 (Oxford: Oxford University Press, 2012).
23. Cook, "Political biography," p. 117.
24. *Writings and speeches of Oliver Cromwell*, ed. Abbott, 4: 947; *Ireland under the Commonwealth*, ed. Dunlop, 1: 10–11; *The correspondence of John Owen*, ed. Toon, p. 51.
25. *CJ* 8 Jan 1650; Worden, "Politics, piety, and learning," pp. 118–19.
26. Worden, "Politics, piety, and learning," p. 119.
27. "Deans of Christ Church, Oxford," *Fasti Ecclesiae Anglicanae*, pp. 80–83.
28. Worden, "Politics, piety, and learning," p. 123.
29. Worden, "Politics, piety, and learning," pp. 114–15.
30. Worden, "Politics, piety, and learning," pp. 113–14.
31. Quoted in Jacob, *Henry Stubbe, Radical Protestantism and the early Enlightenment*, p. 9; Worden, "Politics, piety, and learning," pp. 113–14.
32. Worden, "Politics, piety, and learning," pp. 113–19.
33. Worden, "Politics, piety, and learning," p. 174.
34. *An account of the life and death of Mr Philip Henry* (1712), p. 19.
35. *The correspondence of John Owen*, ed. Toon, pp. 51–52, 52–53.
36. Worden, "Politics, piety, and learning," p. 152.
37. Worden, "Politics, piety, and learning," p. 151.
38. Worden, "Politics, piety, and learning," p. 157.
39. Worden, "Politics, piety, and learning," pp. 154; see, more generally, Jacob, *Henry Stubbe, Radical Protestantism and the early Enlightenment*.
40. *Oxford orations*, ed. Toon, pp. 15, 24–25, 34–35.
41. Worden, "Politics, piety, and learning," p. 182.
42. Nuttall, *The Holy Spirit in Puritan faith and experience*, p. 129.
43. OUA SP/E/4, fos 45, 47, 102a; *CSPD* 1651–1652, pp. 81–82.
44. Reece, *The army in Cromwellian England*, pp. 121, 132.
45. Worden, "Politics, piety, and learning," pp. 92–93.
46. Owen, *Works*, 2: 1–274, 6: 3, 13: 225; 16: 275; Kay, *Trinitarian spirituality*, pp. 113–84.
47. Elizabeth Clarke, *Politics, religion and the Song of Songs in seventeenth-century England* (New York: Palgrave, 2011).
48. Cook, "Political biography," p. 126; Clarke, *Politics, religion and the Song of Songs in seventeenth-century England*, pp. 179–80.

49. Vernon, *Letter to a friend*, p. 4.
50. Owen, *Works*, 2: 2–3.
51. Trueman, *The claims of truth*, p. 113.
52. Kay, *Trinitarian spirituality*, p. 109.
53. Kay, *Trinitarian spirituality*, pp. 6–7.
54. Kay, *Trinitarian spirituality*, pp. 113–14.
55. Kay, *Trinitarian spirituality*, pp. 118–19.
56. Kay, *Trinitarian spirituality*, p. 120.
57. Owen, *Works*, 8: 360.
58. Kay, *Trinitarian spirituality*, pp. 46–47, citing Owen, *Works*, 3: 66, 4: 331.
59. Kay, *Trinitarian spirituality*, pp. 175–76.
60. Kay, *Trinitarian spirituality*, p. 176.
61. Anthony à Wood, *The history and antiquities of the University of* Oxford, 2 vols. (Oxford, 1786), 2: 648–49; Abraham Wright, *Parnassus biceps* (1656), pp. 3–12 n. 168; Foster, *Alumni Oxonsiensis*, "Henry Wilkinson."
62. Owen, *Works*, 8: 314.
63. Owen, *Works*, 8: 326.
64. Owen, *Works*, 8: 313.
65. Gribben, "The Church of Scotland and the English apocalyptic imagination, 1630–1650."
66. Owen, *Works*, 8: 328.
67. Owen, *Works*, 8: 313.
68. Owen, *Works*, 8: 316–17.
69. Owen, *Works*, 8: 321.
70. Owen, *Works*, 8: 321–22.
71. Owen, *Works*, 8: 322.
72. Owen, *Works*, 8: 334.
73. Owen, *Works*, 8: 335.
74. *CJ*, 6: 280–282.
75. *CJ*, 7: 37–40.
76. Ian J. Gentles, "Ireton, Henry (*bap.* 1611, *d.* 1651)," *ODNB*; see also Holberton, *Poetry and the Cromwellian Protectorate*, pp. 143–62, for the wider context of Cromwellian ceremonialism.
77. *The faithful scout*, 6 February–13 February 1652, p. 433.
78. Sean Kelsey, *Inventing a republic: The political culture of the English Commonwealth, 1649–53* (Manchester: Manchester University Press, 1997), pp. 91, 141.
79. Kelsey, *Inventing a republic*, p. 2.
80. Knoppers, *Constructing Cromwell*, pp. 3–4.
81. Kelsey, *Inventing a republic*, p. 58.
82. Kelsey, *Inventing a republic*, p. 152.
83. Kelsey, *Inventing a republic*, p. 170.

84. Kelsey, *Inventing a republic*, p. 54, citing *Writings and speeches of Oliver Cromwell*, ed. Abbott, 2: 504; Lucy Hutchinson, *Memoirs of the Life of Colonel Hutchinson*, ed. C. H. Firth, 2 vols. (London, 1885, 1906), 2: 186–88.
85. Kelsey, *Inventing a republic*, pp. 58, 73.
86. These ceremonies are parsed in Knoppers, *Constructing Cromwell*.
87. Kelsey, *Inventing a republic*, p. 75.
88. Knoppers, *Constructing Cromwell*, p. 29.
89. Owen, *Works*, 8: 363.
90. Owen, *Works*, 8: 343.
91. Owen, *Works*, 8: 348, 350.
92. Owen, *Works*, 8: 351.
93. Owen, *Works*, 8: 355, 359.
94. Owen, *Works*, 8: 361.
95. Macfarlane, *The family life of Ralph Josselin*, p. 186 n. 1; *The minutes and papers of the Westminster Assembly*, ed. van Dixhoorn, 4: 882.
96. *The diary of Ralph Josselin*, ed. MacFarlane, p. 274.
97. *The form of church government* (1645), issued by the Westminster Assembly, included a full description of the process of ordination, from which Owen's practice significantly diverges—including the requirement that men being ordained make promises to the congregation, which should in turn indicate its support of his call.
98. *The diary of Ralph Josselin*, ed. MacFarlane, p. 274.
99. Owen, *Works*, 8: 343.
100. Nuttall suggested that Owen used techniques of memorization to prepare for preaching; *The Holy Spirit in Puritan faith and experience*, p. 82.
101. *CJ* 7: 113–114; Ryan Kelly, "Reformed or reforming? John Owen and the complexity of theological codification for mid-seventeenth-century England," in Kelly M. Kapic and Mark Jones (eds.), *The Ashgate research companion to John Owen's theology* (Aldershot, UK: Ashgate, 2012), pp. 3–29.
102. For an exposition of Socinian positions, see Cooper, *John Owen, Richard Baxter and the formation of nonconformity*, pp. 64–66.
103. *CJ*, 7: 85–86; Michael Lawrence, "Transmission and transformation: Thomas Goodwin and the Puritan project" (unpublished PhD thesis, University of Cambridge, 2002), p. 145; Mortimer, *Reason and religion in the English revolution*, pp. 196–204; Blair Worden, *Literature and politics in Cromwellian England: John Milton, Andrew Marvell, Marchamont Nedham* (Oxford: Oxford University Press, 2007), pp. 247–249.
104. On the history of the "fundamentals," see Carolyn Polizotto, "The campaign against *The humble proposals* of 1652," *Journal of Ecclesiastical History* 38 (1987), pp. 569–81; Richard Muller, *Post-Reformation Reformed dogmatics*, 4 vols. (Grand Rapids, MI: Baker, 2003), 1: 406–30; Jeffrey Collins, "The church settlement

of Oliver Cromwell," *History* 87 (2002), pp. 18–40; Ann Hughes, "'The public confession of these nations': The national church in Interregnum England," in Christopher Durston and Judith Maltby (eds.), *Religion in revolutionary England* (Manchester: Manchester University Press, 2006), pp. 93–114; Ryan Kelly, "Reformed or reforming?" pp. 3–30; Owen, *Works*, 10: 561.

105. Campbell and Corns, *John Milton*, p. 245.
106. CJ 7: 113–114; Tay, Priesthood of Christ, p. 61.
107. *CJ* 7: 113–14.
108. *Mercurius Politicus*, 29 April 1652, pp. 1553–56; *Mercurius Politicus*, 12 August 1652, pp. 1785–90; Hill, *Milton and the English revolution*, p. 184; Worden, *Literature and politics in Cromwellian England*, p. 253.
109. Milton, "To the Lord General Cromwell, May 1652, on the proposals of certain ministers at the Committee for Propagation of the Gospel," in *The complete poetry and essential prose of John Milton*, eds. Kerrigan, Rumrich, and Fallon, pp. 153–54; Campbell and Corns, *John Milton*, p. 245.
110. Polizzotto, "The campaign against *The Humble Proposals* of 1652," pp. 569–81; Mario Caricchio, "*News from the New Jerusalem*: Giles Calvert and the radical experience," in Ariel Hessayon and David Finnegan (eds.), *Varieties of seventeenth- and eighteenth-century English radicalism in context* (Farnham, UK: Ashgate, 2011), p. 85.
111. John Coffey, "Defining heresy and orthodoxy in the puritan revolution," in David Loewenstein and John Marshall (eds.), *Heresy, literature and politics in early modern English culture* (Cambridge: Cambridge University Press, 2006), p. 120.
112. Coffey, "Defining heresy and orthodoxy in the Puritan revolution," p. 120.
113. Oxford, Christ Church, Archive, Chapter book, p. 54.
114. *CSPD* 26: 1–74.
115. *The register of the visitors of the University of Oxford, from AD 1647 to AD 1658*, ed. M. Barrows (London, 1881), p. 353; Wood, *Athenae Oxonienses*, 2: 738.
116. *The register of the visitors of the University of Oxford*, ed. M. Barrows.
117. Oxford, Christ Church, Archive, Chapter book, p. 54.
118. B. C. Capp, *England's culture wars: Puritan reformation and its enemies in the Interregnum, 1649–1660* (Oxford: Oxford University Press, 2012), p. 17.
119. Worden, "Politics, piety, and learning," pp. 118–19; Toon, *God's statesman*, p. 63.
120. *Oxford orations*, ed. Toon, p. 5.
121. *Oxford orations*, ed. Toon, pp. 5–6.
122. *Oxford orations*, ed. Toon, p. 6.
123. Owen, *Works*, 10: 492, 494; Mortimer, *Reason and religion in the English revolution*, pp. 208–10, argues that in *Diatriba de justitia divina* Owen was much less skeptical of the possibility of the "natural knowledge of God" than he had been in his work in the 1640s.

124. *Oxford orations*, ed. Toon, p. 5.
125. *Oxford orations*, ed. Toon, p. 7.
126. *Oxford orations*, ed. Toon, p. 8.
127. Cook, "Political biography," p. 146.
128. Owen, *Works*, 8: 367; Coffey, "John Owen and the Puritan toleration controversy," p. 239.
129. Owen, *Works*, 8: 381.
130. Owen, *Works*, 8: 381.
131. Owen, *Works*, 8: 382.
132. Owen, *Works*, 8: 367.
133. Owen, *Works*, 8: 368.
134. Owen, *Works*, 8: 368–89.
135. Owen, *Works*, 8: 369.
136. Owen, *Works*, 8: 374.
137. Owen, *Works*, 8: 374.
138. Owen, *Works*, 8: 372.
139. *A declaration of several of the churches of Christ, and the godly people in and about the citie of London* (1654); Nuttall, *The Holy Spirit in Puritan faith and experience*, p. 110.
140. Owen, *Works*, 8: 373.
141. Owen, *Works*, 8: 375.
142. Genesis 22:17, 26:4.
143. Owen, *Works*, 8: 376.
144. Owen, *Works*, 8: 376.
145. Owen, *Works*, 8: 389.
146. Owen, *Works*, 8: 394–95.
147. Owen, *Works*, 10: 485. Owen cites the old style date for 25 March 1653.
148. Owen, *Works*, 10: 492.
149. Owen, *Works*, 10: 492–93.
150. Owen, *Works*, 10: 494.
151. Owen, *Works*, 10: 489.
152. Owen, *Works*, 10: 484.
153. Owen, *Works*, 10: 486, 489.
154. Owen, *Works*, 10: 486.
155. Owen, *Works*, 10: 486.
156. The book was translated into English by Hamilton (1794), a translation that was corrected for the Goold edition as *A dissertation on divine justice* (1653).
157. Owen, *Works*, 10: 506.
158. Owen, *Works*, 10: 508.
159. Owen, *Works*, 10: 155, 197, 347, 409.
160. Owen, *Works*, 13: 49; 10: 507, 539, 562, 612.

161. Owen, *Works*, 10: 488.
162. Owen, *Works*, 10: 496–98.
163. Owen, *Works*, 10: 501–2.
164. Owen, *Works*, 10: 505–6.
165. Owen, *Works*, 10: 490.
166. Owen, *Works*, 10: 490–1.
167. Owen, *Works*, 10: 624.
168. Lynch, *Protestant autobiography in the seventeenth-century Anglophone world.*
169. *The register of the visitors of the University of Oxford*, ed. Barrows, pp. 359–60.
170. Oxford, Christ Church, Archive, Chapter book, p. 54.
171. *CJ* 7: 297, 308.
172. *Several proceedings of state affaires*, 27 October–3 November 1653; Cook, "Political biography," p. 155; Austin Woolrych, *Commonwealth to Protectorate* (Oxford: Clarendon Press, 1982), pp. 324–25; Woolrych, *Britain in revolution*, p. 555.
173. *The correspondence of John Owen*, ed. Toon, pp. 62–63.
174. *Ireland under the Commonwealth*, ed. Dunlop, 2: 371; *The correspondence of John Owen*, ed. Toon, p. 59.
175. *CSPD* 66: 381–426.
176. *The register of the visitors of the University of Oxford*, ed. Barrows, pp. 370–75; Wood, *History and antiquities*, 2: 656.
177. Oxford University Archives, W.P.a.23 (12), reprinted in *The correspondence of John Owen*, ed. Toon, p. 121.
178. Bodleian Tanner MS 52, fol. 48, cited in *The correspondence of John Owen*, ed. Toon, pp. 61–62.
179. "Chapter book of Christ Church," p. 63, cited in *The correspondence of John Owen*, ed. Toon, p. 63.
180. Wood, *Fasti*, p. 104.
181. Woolrych, *Commonwealth to Protectorate*, pp. 312–52.
182. Cook, "Political biography," p. 160; Bodleian MS Carte, 81 ff. 16r–17r; in *The correspondence of John Owen*, ed. Toon, pp. 66–68.

CHAPTER 6

1. Christopher Durston, *Cromwell's major-generals: Godly government during the English revolution* (Manchester: Manchester University Press, 2001), p. 2. S. R. Gardener's *History of the Commonwealth and Protectorate, 1649–1656*, 4 vols. (London, 1903), is the last detailed account of the early Protectorate.
2. Kelsey, *Inventing a republic*, p. 186.
3. "Instrument of Government" (1653), paras 35, 37, in Gardiner (ed.), *The constitutional documents of the Puritan revolution*, p. 416.

4. For more on this concept, see Nathan O. Hatch, *The democratization of American Christianity* (New Haven, CT: Yale University Press, 1991).
5. Hughes, "The public profession of these nations," pp. 96–97.
6. Hughes, "The public profession of these nations," p. 97.
7. *Severall proceedings of state affaires*, 23 February–2 March 1654, p. 3671.
8. *Acts and ordinances of the Interregnum*, eds. Firth and Rait, 2: 855–58; *CSPD* (1654), pp. 37–69.
9. Coffey, "Defining heresy and orthodoxy in the Puritan revolution," p. 121.
10. Hughes, "The public profession of these nations," p. 99; *CJ* 7: 361.
11. Kelly, "Reformed or reforming?" p. 7.
12. Hughes, "The public profession of these nations," p. 98.
13. Hughes, "The public profession of these nations," p. 99; Durston, *Cromwell's major-generals*, p. 161.
14. *The correspondence of John Owen*, ed. Toon, p. 83; *A collection of the state papers of John Thurloe*, ed. Thomas Birch, 7 vols. (London, 1742), 3: 281.
15. Leonard Twells, *The life of … Dr Edward Pocock* (London, 1816), p. 129–38, 151–75.
16. *CSPD* (1653–54), p. 360.
17. *CSPD* (1653–54), p. 360; Coffey, "Defining heresy and orthodoxy in the Puritan revolution," p. 121.
18. Cooper, *John Owen, Richard Baxter and the formation of nonconformity*, p. 140.
19. This manuscript is available on EEBO as Thomason E.826[3].
20. Coffey, "Defining heresy and orthodoxy in the Puritan revolution," p. 121.
21. Coffey, "Defining heresy and orthodoxy in the Puritan revolution," p. 122; Mortimer, *Reason and religion in the English revolution*, pp. 220–25.
22. Cooper, *John Owen, Richard Baxter and the formation of nonconformity*, pp. 140–54, 177–88.
23. Coffey, "The toleration controversy during the English revolution," p. 53; Coffey, "Defining heresy and orthodoxy in the Puritan revolution," p. 121, citing Baxter, *Reliquiae Baxterianae*, 2: 197–98.
24. *Calendar of the correspondence of Richard Baxter*, eds. Keeble and Nuttall, 1: 96.
25. Tay, *The priesthood of Christ*, pp. 141–42.
26. *Calendar of the correspondence of Richard Baxter*, eds. Keeble and Nuttall, 1: 150.
27. The only extant copy of this letter is found in the Staatsarchiv, Zurich, E. II. 457 b, f. 1; with an English translation provided in *The correspondence of John Owen*, ed. Toon, pp. 68–70.
28. Wariston, *Diary*, 2: 214.
29. Register of Convocation, p. 249, reprinted in *The correspondence of John Owen*, ed. Toon, pp. 70–71.
30. Thomas Ireland, *Momus elencticus* (1654), p. 1.

31. David Norbrook, *Writing the English republic: Poetry, rhetoric and politics, 1627–1660* (Cambridge: Cambridge University Press, 1999), p. 301.
32. *The life and poems of William Cartwright*, ed. R. Cullis Goffin (Cambridge: Cambridge University Press, 1918), p. xvi; Bill, *Education at Christ Church, Oxford*, p. 247.
33. Clare, "General introduction," in *Drama of the English Republic*, pp. 7–8.
34. Clare, "General introduction," pp. 1–2.
35. *The diary of John Evelyn*, ed. de la Bédoyère, p. 121.
36. For an extended discussion of this collection, see Gerald M. Maclean, *Time's witness: Historical representation in English poetry, 1603–1660* (Madison: University of Wisconsin Press, 1990), pp. 236–39; Holberton, *Poetry and the Cromwellian Protectorate*, pp. 61–86; and McLaughlin, "The idolater John Owen?" pp. 145–66.
37. [Richard Moon], *Perfect and impartial intelligence*, 3, 26 May–2 June 1654, pp. 17–19.
38. McLaughlin has claimed that Owen edited the collection; "The idolator John Owen?" p. 145.
39. Owen's poem is reprinted in *The correspondence of John Owen*, ed. Toon, pp. 78–79. For a discussion of its nuances, see Holberton, *Poetry and the Cromwellian Protectorate*, pp. 84–86.
40. Knoppers, *Constructing Cromwell*, p. 5.
41. *Alumni Oxonienses*, s.v.
42. *CSPD* (1631–33), pp. 370–84.
43. G. Le G. Norgate, "Maplet, John (1611x15–1670)," rev. Patrick Wallis, *ODNB*; E. T. Bradley, "Lockey, Thomas (1602?–1679)," rev. Nigel Ramsay, *ODNB*.
44. *Alumni Oxonienses*, s.v.
45. Bagshawe became an Independent minister and was buried in Bunhill Fields, with an inscription that Owen reportedly composed; N. H. Keeble, "Bagshaw, Edward (1629/30–1671)," *ODNB*.
46. Burke Griggs, "South, Robert (1634–1716)," *ODNB*.
47. Hugh de Quehen, "James, William (*c.* 1634–1663)," *ODNB*.
48. Richard Watkins, *Newes from the dead* (1651), pp. 12, 13–14, 20–21.
49. Ireland, *Momus elencticus*, p. 1.
50. Ireland, *Momus elencticus*, p. 2.
51. Ireland, *Momus elencticus*, p. 2.
52. Cooper, *John Owen, Richard Baxter and the formation of nonconformity*, pp. 110–11; McGraw, *A heavenly directory*, p. 106; Worden, "Politics, piety, and learning," p. 163 n. 482.
53. *The diary of John Evelyn*, ed. de la Bédoyère, p. 88.
54. *The diary of John Evelyn*, ed. de la Bédoyère, p. 88.
55. *The diary of John Evelyn*, ed. de la Bédoyère, p. 88.
56. *The diary of John Evelyn*, ed. de la Bédoyère, pp. 88–89. Similar objects were put on display at Chetham's in Manchester; Cambers, *Godly reading*, p. 118.

57. Jacob, *Henry Stubbe, radical Protestantism and the early Enlightenment*, p. 23.
58. "Second oration," in *Oxford orations*, ed. Toon, p. 11.
59. "Second oration," in *Oxford orations*, ed. Toon, p. 11.
60. "Second oration," in *Oxford orations*, ed. Toon, p. 10.
61. "Second oration," in *Oxford orations*, ed. Toon, p. 12.
62. "Second oration," in *Oxford orations*, ed. Toon, pp. 10, 18.
63. Owen, *Works*, 11: 13. On Goodwin, see John Coffey, *John Goodwin and the Puritan revolution: Religion and intellectual change in 17th-century England* (Woodbridge, UK: Boydell, 2006).
64. Owen, *Works*, 11: 14.
65. Owen, *Works*, 11: 151.
66. Owen, *Works*, 11: 30; John Goodwin, *An answer to a printed paper: Wherein . . . the predominant designe of it fully evinced to be, either an unscholarlike oscitancie and mistake, or else somewhat much worse* (1649).
67. Kay, *Trinitarian spirituality*, p. 95; Cleveland, *Thomism in John Owen*, pp. 46–52. In October 1656, the trustees of Chetham's Library, Manchester, paid 7s for Owen's *The doctrine of the saints perseverance* (1654), which shows no signs of use; Matthew G. Yeo, "The acquisition of books by Chetham's Library, 1655–1700: A case study in the distribution and reception of texts in the English provinces in the late seventeenth century," 2 vols. (unpublished PhD thesis, University of Manchester, 2009), 1: 148, 2: 333; Matthew Yeo, *The acquisition of books by Chetham's Library, 1655–1700* (Leiden, The Netherlands: Brill, 2011), p. 141.
68. Owen, *Works*, 11: 172.
69. *Calendar of the correpondence of Richard Baxter*, eds. Keeble and Nuttall, 1: 72–73.
70. Owen, *Works*, 11: 16.
71. Owen, *Works*, 11: 5–6.
72. Owen, *Works*, 11: 16, 215.
73. Owen, *Works*, 11: 38, 79, 85.
74. Owen, *Works*, 11: 112.
75. "Second oration," in *Oxford orations*, ed. Toon, p. 16.
76. *"The first publishers of truth," being early records (now first printed) of the introduction of Quakerism into the counties of England and Wales*, supplements 1–5, *Journal of the Friends Historical Society*, ed. N. Penney (1907), pp. 210–12, 214.
77. *The correspondence of John Owen*, ed. Toon, p. 119.
78. Bodleian Tanner MS 69, f. 182; reprinted in *The correspondence of John Owen*, ed. Toon, pp. 74–75; *Calendar of the correpondence of Richard Baxter*, eds. Keeble and Nuttall, 1: 158; *History of Parliament*, s.v.
79. Wariston, *Diary*, 2: 287, 310.
80. Oxford, Christ Church, Archive, Chapter book.
81. Cook, "Political biography," pp. 184–85.

82. *Acts and ordinances of the Interregnum*, eds. Firth and Rait, pp. 1026–29.
83. Worden, "Politics, piety, and learning," p. 129.
84. Christ Church Archives, Oxford, DP ii.c.1, f. 52.
85. *Calendar of the correpondence of Richard Baxter*, eds. Keeble and Nuttall, 1: 152.
86. Worden, "Politics, piety, and learning," p. 132.
87. Worden, "Politics, piety, and learning," p. 159; Mortimer, *Reason and religion in the English revolution*, pp. 225–30.
88. Cook, "Political biography," p. 166; Cleveland, *Thomism in John Owen*, pp. 52–67; Spence, "The significance of John Owen for modern Christology," pp. 178–82.
89. Spence, "The significance of John Owen for modern Christology," p. 180.
90. Spence, "The significance of John Owen for modern Christology," pp. 181–82.
91. *State papers of John Thurloe*, ed. Birch, 3: 281.
92. *Perfect Proceedings* 29 March–5 April 1655, p. 4569; George Vernon, *A letter to a friend concerning some of John Owen's principles* (1670), p. 13.
93. Durston, *Cromwell's major-generals*, pp. 10, *passim*.
94. Durston, *Cromwell's major-generals*, pp. 22, 27, 29.
95. Durston, *Cromwell's major-generals*, pp. 31, 38.
96. Durston, *Cromwell's major-generals*, pp. 43, 50–51.
97. Durston, *Cromwell's major-generals*, p. 74.
98. Durston, *Cromwell's major-generals*, p. 90.
99. Underdown, *Royalist conspiracy in England*, pp. 169–78; Durston, *Cromwell's major-generals*, pp. 87, 148.
100. Macfarlane, *The family life of Ralph Josselin*, pp. 26–27; Durston, *Cromwell's major-generals*, pp. 165–66.
101. Durston, *Cromwell's major-generals*, pp. 138–39.
102. Jacob, *Henry Stubbe, radical Protestantism and the early Enlightenment*, pp. 10, 17.
103. Jacob, *Henry Stubbe, radical Protestantism and the early Enlightenment*, pp. 10–11, 17–24; Jeffrey R. Collins, *The allegiance of Thomas Hobbes* (Oxford: Oxford University Press, 2007), pp. 120–22.
104. John Wallis, *Johann Wallisii ... elenchus geometriae Hobbianae* (1655); an English translation is provided in *The correspondence of John Owen*, ed. Toon, pp. 86–88.
105. BL Add. MS 32553, fol. 14, 18; Jacob, *Henry Stubbe, radical Protestantism and the early Enlightenment*, p. 20.
106. BL Add. MS 32553, fol. 7; Jacob, *Henry Stubbe, radical Protestantism and the early Enlightenment*, p. 19.
107. Owen, *Works*, 13: 300.
108. BL Add. MS 32553, fol. 10–11; Jacob, *Henry Stubbe, radical Protestantism and the early Enlightenment*, p. 19.

109. BL Add. MS 32553, fol. 12; Jacob, *Henry Stubbe, radical Protestantism and the early Enlightenment*, p. 19; Thomas Hobbes, *The correspondence*, ed. Noel Malcolm, 3 vols. (Oxford: Clarendon Press, 1994), 1: 338.
110. Hobbes, *The correspondence*, ed. Malcolm, 1: 334.
111. Jacob, *Henry Stubbe, radical Protestantism and the early Enlightenment*, p. 38.
112. Hobbes, *The correspondence*, ed. Malcolm, 1: 459.
113. "Third oration," in *Oxford orations*, ed. Toon, p. 20.
114. "Third oration," in *Oxford orations*, ed. Toon, p. 21.
115. "Third oration," in *Oxford orations*, ed. Toon, p. 20.
116. R. S. Paul, *The Lord Protector* (Grand Rapids, MI: Eerdmans, 1955), pp. 336–37.
117. "Third oration," in *Oxford orations*, ed. Toon, p. 21.
118. *The correspondance of John Owen*, ed. Toon, p. 83.
119. "Third oration," in *Oxford orations*, ed. Toon, pp. 22–23.
120. "Third oration," in *Oxford orations*, ed. Toon, p. 23.
121. "Third oration," in *Oxford orations*, ed. Toon, p. 23. See Anthony à Wood, *Annals of the University of Oxford*, ed. John Gutch, 2 vols. (Oxford, 1792–96), for the years 1655–56.
122. "Third oration," in *Oxford orations*, ed. Toon, p. 28.
123. "Third oration," in *Oxford orations*, ed. Toon, p. 24.
124. *The correspondence of John Owen*, ed. Toon, pp. 89–91; on Wickens, see Crawford Gribben, "The commodification of Scripture, 1640–1660: Politics, ecclesiology and the cultures of print," in Kevin Killeen et al. (eds), *The Oxford handbook of the Bible in early modern England* (Oxford: Oxford University Press, 2015), pp. 224–36, and Crawford Gribben, "Reading the Bible in the Puritan revolution," in Robert Armstrong and Tadhg O'Hannrachain (eds.), *The English Bible in the early modern world*, St. Andrews Studies in Reformation History (Farnham, UK: Ashgate, forthcoming).
125. Owen, *Works*, 6: 3, 29.
126. Owen, *Works*, 6: 9, 11, 33, 62.
127. Owen, *Works*, 6: 14.
128. Owen, *Works*, 6: 3.
129. Owen, *Works*, 6: 7.
130. Owen, *Works*, 6: 85.
131. *The correspondence of John Locke*, ed. de Beer, 1: 30.
132. *CSPD* (1655), p. 23.
133. Cooper, "Owen's personality," pp. 219–21; Bodliean Library, OUA SP/E/4 f. 91r–93v; Walter Pope, *The life of the Right Reverend Father in God, Lord Bishop of Salisbury* (London, 1697), pp. 41–42.
134. Cooper, "Owen's personality," p. 221. This portrait is used on the cover of this book.
135. *The diary of Ralph Josselin*, ed. MacFarlane, p. 363.

136. *Report on the manuscripts of the earl of Egmont*, 2 vols. (London: Historical Manuscripts Commission, 1905), vol. 1 part 2, p. 576.
137. Worden, "Politics, piety, and learning," pp. 134–35.
138. *CSPD* (1653–54), pp. 344–80; *CSPD* (1655–56), pp. 245–304.
139. *CSPD* (1655–56), p. 319.
140. *The diary of Ralph Josselin*, ed. MacFarlane, p. 374.
141. *The diary of Ralph Josselin*, ed. Macfarlane, p. 374; see also *The register of the visitors of the University of Oxford*, ed. Barrows, p. xli.
142. *The correspondence of John Locke*, ed. de Beer, 1: 54.
143. Worden, "Politics, piety, and learning," pp. 132–35.
144. *Calendar of the correpondence of Richard Baxter*, eds. Keeble and Nuttall, 2: 38.
145. Register of Convocation, p. 289; reprinted in *The correspondence of John Owen*, ed. Toon, p. 93; Owen, *Works*, 8: 401.
146. Owen, *Works*, 8: 398.
147. Owen, *Works*, 8: 399–400, 425; *The diary of Ralph Josselin*, ed. MacFarlane, p. 381.
148. Owen, *Works*, 8: 405, 418–19.
149. Owen, *Works*, 8: 425.
150. Owen, *Works*, 13: 94.
151. Owen, *Works*, 13: 94.
152. Owen, *Works*, 13: 94.
153. Owen, *Works*, 13: 110.
154. Owen, *Works*, 13: 95.
155. Owen, *Works*, 13: 192.
156. Register of Convocation, p. 290; reprinted in *The correspondence of John Owen*, ed. Toon, p. 94.
157. Hobbes, *The correspondence*, ed. Malcolm, 1: 311–12; 1: 314 n 10.
158. Owen, *Works*, 8: 428.
159. Owen, *Works*, 8: 436.
160. Owen, *Works*, 8: 441–42.
161. For the broader context to this dispute, see Cook, "Political biography," pp. 221–28.
162. *Consultations*, ed. Stephen, 2: 74.
163. *Consultations*, ed. Stephen, 2: 88–89.
164. Toon, *God's statesman*, pp. 98–99.
165. *The correspondence of Henry Cromwell, 1655–1659*, ed. Peter Gaunt (Cambridge: Cambridge University Press, 2007), p. 221.
166. John Rogers, who had praised Owen in *Ohel or Bethshemesh* (1653), attacked him in the preface to John Canne's *The time of the end* (1657).
167. Cooper, *John Owen, Richard Baxter and the formation of nonconformity*, p. 122.

168. R. A. Beddard, "A projected Cromwellian foundation at Oxford and the 'true reformed Protestant interest,' c. 1657–8," *History of Universities* 15 (1999), pp. 155–192.
169. For the background to this, see Cook, "Political biography," p. 230; *CJ* 7: 529.
170. *The diary of Thomas Burton*, ed. J. T. Rutt, 4 vols. (London, 1828), 2: 94–101; *CJ* 7: 532, 534–36, 551–53.
171. Cook, "Political biography," p. 233; Ludlow, *Memoirs*, 2: 25.
172. Register of Convocation, p. 305; reprinted in *The correspondence of John Owen*, ed. Toon, pp. 98–99.
173. See Wood, *Annals of the University of Oxford*, for the years 1656–57.
174. "Fourth oration," *Oxford orations*, ed. Toon, p. 30.
175. "Fourth oration," *Oxford orations*, ed. Toon, p. 34.
176. "Fourth oration," *Oxford orations*, ed. Toon, p. 35.
177. "Fourth oration," *Oxford orations*, ed. Toon, p. 31.
178. *The correspondence of John Locke*, ed. de Beer, 1: 60–62.
179. Owen, *Works*, 13: 209.
180. Owen, *Works*, 13: 208.
181. Owen, *Works*, 13: 209.
182. Owen, *Works*, 13: 209.
183. Owen, Works, 13: 209.
184. Owen, *Works*, 13: 214.
185. Owen, *Works*, 13: 227.
186. Owen, *Works*, 13: 222–23.
187. Owen, *Works*, 13: 209.
188. Owen, *Works*, 2: 3; 13: 209–10, 267.
189. Owen, *Works*, 2: 2–3; Cook, "Political biography," pp. 240–41; Kapic, *Communion with God*, passim; Joel R. Beeke and Mark Jones, *A Puritan theology: Doctrine for life* (Grand Rapids, MI: Reformation Heritage Books, 2012), pp. 101–16.
190. Owen, *Works*, 2: 38.
191. Philip Dixon, *Nice and hot disputes: The doctrine of the Trinity in the seventeenth century* (London: T & T Clark, 2003), pp. 34–65; Mortimer, *Reason and religion in the English revolution*, passim.
192. Paul C. H. Lim, *Mystery unveiled: The crisis of the Trinity in early modern England* (Oxford: Oxford University Press, 2012), pp. 174–203.
193. Mortimer, *Reason and religion in the English revolution*, passim.
194. Owen, *Works*, 2: 80.
195. Owen, *Works*, 2: 32, 35.
196. Owen, *Works*, 2: 32.
197. Owen, *Works*, 2: 35.
198. Owen, *Works*, 2: 32.
199. Owen, *Works*, 2: 23.

200. Owen's reading of the Song, and the context of controversy, is discussed in Clarke, *Politics, religion and the Song of Songs in seventeenth-century England*, pp. 177–81.
201. Owen, *Works*, 2: 4.
202. Lewis Stucley, "To the Reader," in Theophilus Polwheile, *Of quencing the spirit the evill of it, in respect both of its causes and effects* (1667), sig. A3.
203. Faithful Teate, *Ter tria*, ed. Angelina Lynch (Dublin: Four Courts, 2007). On Teate's Trinitarianism and its relationship to Owen's, see Crawford Gribben, "Poetry and piety: John Owen, Faithful Teate and communion with God," in Ian Clary and Steve Weaver (eds.), *The pure flame of devotion: The history of Christian spirituality: Essays in honour of Michael A. G. Haykin* (Toronto, ON: Joshua Press, 2013), pp. 197–215.
204. *Mercurius politicus* 373 (July 1657), pp. 7957–58.
205. *Mercurius politicus* 373 (July 1657), pp. 7957–58.
206. *Mercurius politicus* 373 (July 1657), pp. 7957–58.
207. "Sixth oration," *Oxford orations*, ed. Toon, p. 47.
208. "Sixth oration," *Oxford orations*, ed. Toon, p. 48.
209. For a nuanced account of these events, see Cook, "Political biography," pp. 245–48.
210. Cook, "Political biography," p. 247.
211. BM Landsdowne MS 833, f. 179; reprinted in *The correspondence of John Owen*, ed. Toon, pp. 100–1, and *The correspondence of Henry Cromwell*, ed. Gaunt, pp. 316–17. Register of Convocation, p. 309; reprinted in *The correspondence of John Owen*, ed. Toon, p. 101.
212. "Fifth oration," *Oxford orations*, ed. Toon, p. 40.
213. "Fifth oration," *Oxford orations*, ed. Toon, p. 41.
214. "Fifth oration," *Oxford orations*, ed. Toon, pp. 45–46.
215. "Fifth oration," *Oxford orations*, ed. Toon, p. 45.
216. "Fifth oration," *Oxford orations*, ed. Toon, pp. 40, 46.
217. *CSPD* (1657–58), p. 216.
218. Owen, *Works*, 13: 279.
219. Owen, *Works*, 13: 279.
220. Owen, *Works*, 13: 301.
221. Owen, *Works*, 13: 294–95.
222. *State papers of John Thurloe*, ed. Birch, 5: 748–61.
223. Owen, *Works*, 6: 89.
224. Owen, *Works*, 6: 89–90.
225. *The writings and speeches of Oliver Cromwell*, ed. Abbott, 4: 670; Holberton, *Poetry and the Cromwellian Protectorate*, pp. 143–62.
226. Owen, *Works*, 6: 111
227. Owen, *Works*, 6: 150.
228. Owen, *Works*, 6: 89.

CHAPTER 7

1. Henry Reece has noted that we lack a detailed narrative history of the period from Oliver Cromwell's death to the return of the king; *The army in Cromwellian England*, pp. 2–3 n 3.
2. Cook, "Political biography," p. 253.
3. Owen, *Works*, 6: 89.
4. Cook, "Political biography," p. 253.
5. Asty, "Memoirs," p. xxiv.
6. *A history of the county of Oxford*, vol. 7 (1962), pp. 81–92; Wood, *Athenae*, 4: 96–102.
7. Appleby, *Black Bartholemew's day*, p. 2; Matthews, *Calamy revised*, p. 251.
8. Ronald Hutton, *The Restoration: A political and religious history of England and Wales, 1658–1667* (Oxford: Oxford University Press, 1985), p. 18.
9. Hutton, *The Restoration*, p. 18.
10. Cook, "Political biography," p. 253.
11. Thomas Long, *An exercitation concerning the frequent use of our Lords Prayer in the publick worship of God and a view of what hath been said by Mr. Owen concerning that subject* (1658), "Preface," n.p.
12. John Owen, *A defense of sacred scripture against modern fanaticism*, in *Biblical theology: The history of theology from Adam to Christ*, trans. Stephen P. Westcott (Grand Rapids, MI: Soli Deo Gloria, 1994), p. 775.
13. Owen, *Works*, 16: 293. The EEBO edition has "November" written on its title page; *Of the divine original, authority, self-evidencing light, and power of the Scriptures* (1658), title page.
14. Muller, *Post-Reformation Reformed dogmatics*, vol. 2, passim.
15. Gribben, "The commodification of Scripture, 1640–1660," passim; Gribben, "Reading the Bible in the Puritan revolution," passim.
16. For the "science of order," see Michel Foucault, *The order of things: An archaeology of the human sciences* (London: Pantheon Books, 1970).
17. Christopher Hill, *The English Bible and the seventeenth-century revolution* (London: Penguin, 1993), p. 18.
18. *Humble proposals concerning the printing of the Bible* (1650), single sheet.
19. *William Bentley printer at Finsbury near London, touching his right to the printing of Bibles and Psalms* (1656), single sheet.
20. *William Bentley printer at Finsbury near London, touching his right to the printing of Bibles and Psalms*, single sheet; *To all Printers, Booke-sellers, Booke-binders, Free-men of the Company of Stationers* (1645).
21. *The diary of Ralph Josselin*, ed. Macfarlane, p. 173.
22. David Daniell, *The Bible in English: Its history and influence* (New Haven, CT: Yale University Press, 2003), p. 459.
23. The background to this contest was explained in a series of broadsides. *The case of William Bentley printer at Finsbury near London, touching his right to the printing*

of Bibles and Psalms (1656) was answered by *A Short Answer to a Pamphlet, Entituled, The Case of William Bentley* (1656), published by the Company of Stationers, which roundly rejected his story, while *A true state of the case of John Field and Henry Hills, the Parliaments Printers* (1656), responding to attacks by William Kilburne, defended their monopoly and denied that they were responsible for the inflation of prices, for which they claimed booksellers should take responsibility. Further information on this context is provided in *The London printer, his lamentation: or The press oppressed, and overpressed* (1660). This text is reprinted in *The Harliean miscellany: or, A collection of scarce, curious, and entertaining pamphlets and tracts* (London, 1745), 3: 277–82.

24. *CSPD* (1652–1653), pp. 1–74.
25. David Norton, *A textual history of the King James Bible* (Cambridge: Cambridge University Press, 2005), pp. 89–98.
26. Peter N. Miller, "The 'antiquarianization' of Biblical scholarship and the London Polyglot Bible (1653–57)," *Journal of the History of Ideas* 62:3 (2001), p. 467. For a broader context, see the essays gathered in Ariel Hessayon and Nicholas Keene (eds.), *Scripture and scholarship in early modern England* (Aldershot, UK: Ashgate, 2006).
27. British Library, Additional Manuscripts 32,093, fol. 333r.
28. Miller, "The 'antiquarianization' of Biblical scholarship and the London Polyglot Bible," pp. 468–69; Owen, 16: 282.
29. Miller, "The 'antiquarianization' of Biblical scholarship and the London Polyglot Bible," p. 470.
30. Owen, *Works*, 16: 286.
31. Owen, *Works*, 16: 289.
32. Owen, *Works*, 16: 289.
33. Owen, *Works*, 3: 155; 11: 82; 12: 419; 15: 13. See Michael Strickland, "Seventeenth-century Puritans and the synoptic problem," *Puritan Reformed Journal* 6:1 (2014), pp. 31–42.
34. Owen, *Works*, 16: 285, 289.
35. Owen, *Works*, 16: 293.
36. Owen, *Works*, 16: 287.
37. Owen, *Works*, 16: 285, 297.
38. Owen, *Works*, 16: 286.
39. Owen, *Works*, 16: 289.
40. Owen, *Works*, 16: 289.
41. Ford, *James Ussher*, pp. 268, 270; *The kingdom's weekly intelligencer*, 18–25 January 1648, p. 816; TCD shelf mark CC.k.65; Snoddy, *The soteriology of James Ussher*, p. 245; *The correspondence of John Locke*, ed. de Beer, 1: 31.
42. Owen, *Works*, 16: 290.
43. Owen, *Works*, 16: 291.

44. Owen, *Works*, 16: 298.
45. Owen, *Works*, 16: 298–99.
46. Owen, *Works*, 16: 299; Muller, *Post-Reformation Reformed dogmatics*, 2: 242–250.
47. Owen, *Works*, 16: 305–6.
48. Owen, *Works*, 16: 307.
49. Owen, *Works*, 3: 145.
50. Rutherford, *A free disputation against pretended liberty of conscience*, p. 366; Gribben, "Samuel Rutherford and liberty of conscience," pp. 366–67.
51. Owen, *Works*, 16: 301.
52. Owen, *Works*, 16: 318.
53. Owen, *Works*, 16: 328.
54. Owen, *Works*, 16: 334; see also 16: 310.
55. Owen, *Works*, 16: 337.
56. Owen, *Works*, 16: 347, 348 n. 2, 374.
57. Owen, *Works*, 16: 362.
58. Owen, *Works*, 16: 349.
59. Owen, *Works*, 16: 364.
60. Owen, *Works*, 16: 364.
61. Owen, *Works*, 16: 366.
62. Owen, *Works*, 16: 347.
63. Owen, *Works*, 16: 353, 355.
64. Owen, *Works*, 16: 352.
65. Owen, *Works*, 16: 370.
66. Owen, *Works*, 16: 348.
67. Owen, *Works*, 16: 348. This pamphlet has been translated into English as *A defense of sacred scripture against modern fanaticism*, in John Owen, *Biblical theology: A history of theology from Adam to Christ*, trans. Stephen P. Westcott (Grand Rapids, MI: Soli Deo Gloria, 1994), pp. 769–854.
68. Owen, *A defense of sacred scripture*, trans. Westcott, p. 775.
69. Owen, *A defense of sacred scripture*, trans. Westcott, p. 775.
70. Owen, *A defense of sacred scripture*, trans. Westcott, pp. 777, 787–88.
71. Owen, *A defense of sacred scripture*, trans. Westcott, p. 794.
72. Owen, *A defense of sacred scripture*, trans. Westcott, p. 795.
73. Owen, *A defense of sacred scripture*, trans. Westcott, p. 797.
74. Owen, *A defense of sacred scripture*, trans. Westcott, p. 797.
75. Owen, *A defense of sacred scripture*, trans. Westcott, p. 786.
76. Owen, *A defense of sacred scripture*, trans. Westcott, pp. 799–800.
77. Owen, *A defense of sacred scripture*, trans. Westcott, p. 802.
78. Owen, *A defense of sacred scripture*, trans. Westcott, p. 803.
79. Owen, *A defense of sacred scripture*, trans. Westcott, p. 816.
80. Owen, *Works*, 16: 328, 376.

81. Cook, "Political biography," p. 253. Joel Halcomb, "A social history of congregational religious practice during the Puritan revolution" (unpublished PhD thesis, University of Cambridge, 2009), pp. 207–42.
82. Sean Kelsey, "Scobell, Henry (*bap.* 1610, *d.* 1660)," *ODNB*.
83. Gribben, *God's Irishmen*, pp. 38, 117–21.
84. *The correspondence of Henry Cromwell*, ed. Gaunt, p. 394.
85. Tim Cooper, *Fear and polemic in seventeenth-century England: Richard Baxter and antinomianism* (Aldershot, UK: Ashgate, 2001), pp. 155–60, suggests that the Savoy Declaration was a rebuff of Baxter's plans for the extension of local associations; see also Paul C.-H. Lim, *In pursuit of purity, unity, and liberty: Richard Baxter's Puritan ecclesiology and its seventeenth-century context* (Leiden, The Netherlands: Brill, 2004), pp. 156–89.
86. Shaw, *A history of the English church during the civil wars and under the Commonwealth*, 2: 168.
87. Cooper, *John Owen, Richard Baxter and the formation of nonconformity*, pp. 236–40.
88. Ryan Kelly, "Reformed or reforming?" pp. 3–29.
89. Cook, "Political biography," p. 257.
90. *The correspondance of John Owen*, ed. Toon, pp. 165–68; Owen, *Works*, 13: 546, 551.
91. *The diary of Thomas Burton*, 2: 516–30; Knoppers, *Constructing Cromwell*, pp. 139–46.
92. Hutton, *The Restoration*, p. 25.
93. *The correspondence of John Locke*, ed. de Beer, 1: 66–67.
94. Owen, *Works*, 8: 455.
95. Cooper, *John Owen, Richard Baxter and the formation of nonconformity*, p. 235.
96. Owen, *Works*, 8: 455.
97. Owen, *Works*, 8: 461.
98. Owen, *Works*, 8: 463.
99. Owen, *Works*, 8: 457; *The correspondence of John Locke*, ed. de Beer, 1: 70–71.
100. *The correspondence of Henry Cromwell*, ed. Gaunt, p. 449.
101. Cooper offers the best account of Owen's activities in 1659; Cooper, *John Owen, Richard Baxter and the formation of nonconformity*, pp. 227–57.
102. *The correspondence of Henry Cromwell*, ed. Gaunt, p. 475. Ironically, Annesley's wife would become a member of Owen's congregation in the 1670s; T. G. Crippen, "Dr Watts's church-book," *Transactions of the Congregational Historical Society* 1 (1901–4), p. 29.
103. Cook, "Political biography," p. 264.
104. Cook, "Political biography," pp. 264–65.
105. Hutton, *The Restoration*, p. 35.
106. Hutton, *The Restoration*, pp. 35–41.

107. R. P. Wells, "Guild, William (1586–1657)," *ODNB*; 28 May is the date on the title page of the copy stored on EEBO.
108. John Owen, "To the reader," in William Guild, *The throne of David* (Oxford, 1659), n.p.
109. I. S. and W. R., "A letter," in William Guild, *The throne of David* (1659), sig. E2r.
110. Gary S. De Kray, *London and the Restoration, 1659–1683* (Cambridge: Cambridge University Press, 2005), pp. 19–20.
111. De Krey, *London and the Restoration*, p. 14.
112. *The correspondence of John Locke*, ed. de Beer, 1: 83–84.
113. Hutton, *The Restoration*, pp. 58–59; De Kray, *London and the Restoration*, p. 26.
114. Worden, "Politics, piety, and learning," p. 187.
115. *CJ* 7: 778–779.
116. *Calendar of the correpondence of Richard Baxter*, eds. Keeble and Nuttall, 1: 409.
117. *CSPD* (1649/60), p. 221; reprinted in *The correspondence of John Owen*, ed. Toon, pp. 104–5.
118. Hutton, *The Restoration*, p. 67.
119. *The correspondence of John Locke*, ed. de Beer, 1: 125.
120. Samuel Boguslaw Chyliński, *An account of the translation of the Bible into the Lithuanian tongue* (Oxford, 1659), p. 8; S. L. Greenslade, *The Cambridge history of the Bible*, vol. 3: *The West, from the Reformation to the Present Day* (Cambridge: Cambridge University Press, 1995), p. 134.
121. Chyliński, *An account of the translation of the Bible into the Lithuanian tongue*, p. 3.
122. Chyliński, *An account of the translation of the Bible into the Lithuanian tongue*, p. 4.
123. Chyliński, *An account of the translation of the Bible into the Lithuanian tongue*, pp. 7–8.
124. Greenslade, *The Cambridge history of the Bible*, 3: 134–35; Chyliński, *An account of the translation of the Bible into the Lithuanian tongue*, p. 3.
125. F. V., *Detur pulchriori, or, A poem in the praise of the University of Oxford* (1658), p. 1.
126. Christ Church Archives, Oxford, DP ii.c.1, f. 68.
127. Dennis Flynn, "Mayne, Jasper (1604–1672)," *ODNB*.
128. John R. Elliott, "Drama," in Nicholas Tyacke (ed.), *The history of the University of Oxford*, vol. 4: *Seventeenth-century Oxford* (Oxford: Clarendon Press, 1997), p. 653.
129. R. A. Beddard, "Restoration Oxford," in Nicholas Tyacke (ed.), *The history of the University of Oxford*, vol. 4: *Seventeenth-century Oxford* (Oxford: Clarendon Press, 1997), p. 823.
130. Jasper Mayne, *The amorous warre, A tragi-comoedy* (Oxford, 1659), p. 1.
131. *The Clarke papers: Selections from the papers of Sir William Clarke*, ed. C. H. Firth, 4 vols. (London: Camden Society, 1904), 4: 81–82; Hutton, *The Restoration*, p. 74.
132. *The Clarke papers*, ed. Firth, 4: 121–24.

133. *A collection of letters written his Excellenecy General George Monck*, ed. John Toland (London, 1714), no. xii.
134. *The Clarke Papers*, ed. Firth, 4: 151–54.
135. *The Clarke Papers*, ed. Firth, 4: 184–86.
136. *A faithfull searching home word* (1659), pp. 14, 16. For broader context, see Woolrych, *Commonwealth to Protectorate*, pp. 120–22.
137. *The correspondence of John Owen*, ed. Toon, pp. 114–16; Hutton, *The Restoration*, p. 79.
138. This text is reprinted in Goold's edition as *Two questions concerning the power of the supreme magistrate about religion* (1659); Owen, *Works*, 13: 507.
139. Hutton, *The Restoration*, pp. 85–87.
140. Thomas Truthsbye, *A serious letter to Dr John Owen, sent by a small friend of his* (1660), single sheet.
141. Truthsbye, *A serious letter to Dr John Owen*, single sheet.
142. De Krey, *London and the Restoration*, p. 5.
143. Wariston, *Diary*, 3: 160.
144. *Bradshaws ultimum vale* (1660), pp. 10, 12.
145. Worden, "Politics, piety, and learning," p. 188.
146. Worden, "Politics, piety, and learning," p. 188.
147. *CJ* 7: 862; Hutton, *The Restoration*, p. 101.
148. Cook, "Political biography," p. 281.
149. Cook, "Political biography," p. 278.
150. Cook, "Political biography," p. 279.
151. *The diurnal of Thomas Rugg, 1659–61*, ed. W. L. Sachse (London: Camden Society, 1961), pp. 89–90, quoted in De Krey, *London and the Restoration*, p. 3. See also Hutton, *The Restoration*, pp. 125–26.

CHAPTER 8

1. Hutton argues that the republic ended principally because those who had defended it no longer wished to do so; *The Restoration*, p. 116.
2. Hutton, *The Restoration*, p. 134.
3. Ian J. Gentles, "Harrison, Thomas (bap. 1616, d. 1660)," *ODNB*.
4. J. T. Pearcey, "Carew, John (1622–1660)," *ODNB*.
5. Stephen K. Roberts, "Jones, John (*c.* 1597–1660)," *ODNB*; J. T. Pearcey, "Clement, Gregory (*bap.* 1594, *d.* 1660)," *ODNB*; C. H. Firth, rev. Sean Kelsey, "Scott, Thomas (*d.* 1660)," *ODNB*; John Wroughton, "Scrope, Adrian (1601–1660)," *ODNB*.
6. *The journals of William Schellinks' travels in England, 1661–1663*, trans. and ed. Maurice Exwood and H. L. Lehmann (London: Royal Historical Society, 1993), p. 83; Sarah Barber, "Corbet, Miles (1594/5–1662)," *ODNB*.

7. *The journals of William Schellinks' travels in England*, pp. 92–93.
8. *The journals of William Schellinks' travels in England*, p. 72; J. T. Pearcey, "Mildmay, Henry (*c.* 1594–1664/5?)," *ODNB*; J. T. Pearcey, "Wallop, Robert (1601–1667)," *ODNB*.
9. Owen, *Works*, 13: 521.
10. John Morrill, "Cromwell, Oliver (1599–1658)," *ODNB*; Sean Kelsey, "Bradshaw, John (*bap.* 1602, *d.* 1659)," *ODNB*; Ian J. Gentles, "Ireton, Henry (*bap.* 1611, *d.* 1651)," *ODNB*.
11. *The diary of Samuel Pepys*, eds. Robert Latham and William Matthews (London: Bell, 1970), 2: 31 (5 February 1661).
12. *The journals of William Schellinks' travels in England*, pp. 48, 51.
13. N. H. Keeble, *The literary culture of nonconformity in later seventeenth-century England* (Leicester, UK: Leicester University Press, 1987), pp. 25–67. For a recent discussion of Restoration print culture, and its legal contexts, see Lois G. Schwoerer, *The ingenious Mr Henry Care, Restoration publicist* (Baltimore, MD: Johns Hopkins University Press, 2001), passim.
14. *The Presbyterian lash, or, Noctroff's maid whipt* (1661), p. 1; Gribben, *God's Irishmen*, pp. 53–55.
15. Adrian Johns, "Coleman Street," *Huntington Library Quarterly* 71:1 (2008), pp. 33–54. Coleman Street had also been a center of Lollard activity; Bremer, *Lay empowerment and the development of Puritanism*, p. 11.
16. Anonymous, *The arraignment of the divel, for stealing away President Bradshaw, To the tune of, Well-a-day, well-a-day* (1659), number 9. The same verse was included in Alexander Brome's *Rump, or, An exact collection of the choycest poems and songs relating to the late times by the most eminent wits from anno 1639 to anno 1661* (1662), p. 137.
17. Samuel Fisher, *Rusticus ad academicos in exercitationibus expostulatoriis, apologeticis quatuor The rustick's alarm to the rabbies, or, The country correcting the university and clergy* (1660), p. 47.
18. Ian Green, *The re-establishment of the Church of England, 1660–1663* (Oxford: Oxford University Press, 1978), p. 179.
19. Coffey, "The toleration controversy during the English revolution," p. 60.
20. Cook, "Political biography," p. 281.
21. On Anglican hegemony, see J. C. D. Clark, *English society, 1688–1832: Ideology, social structure and political practice during the Ancien Regime* (Cambridge: Cambridge University Press, 1985).
22. Appleby, *Black Bartholomew's Day*, p. 47.
23. Bill, *Education at Christ Church, Oxford*, p. 29.
24. *CSPD* (1660–61), p. 473; Matthews, *Calamy revised*, p. 376.
25. John Owen, *Θεολογουμενα παντοδαπα: Sive De natvra, ortv, progressv, et stvdio verae theologiae libri sex* (Oxford, 1661). An English-language "version" of this

text is published as *Biblical theology*, trans. Westcott. Rehnman has expressed concern about this translation, in *Divine discourse*, p. 17 n. 3, but I am using it with gratitude.

26. Owen, *Works*, 16: 293.
27. The most comprehensive discussion of the text is provided by Renhman, *Divine discourse*.
28. *Θεολογουμενα παντοδαπα* was included in volume 17 of Owen, *Works*, ed. Goold, but was not included in the subsequent reprinting of this edition by the Banner of Truth Trust.
29. See Lucy Hutchinson, *On the principles of the Christian religion, addressed to her daughter; and on theology* (London, 1817). David Norbrook is currently editing a critical edition of this text.
30. Norbook, "*Order and Disorder*: The poem and its contexts," p. xix.
31. Owen, *Biblical theology*, trans. Wescott, pp. 205–6; van Asselt, "Covenant theology as relational theology," pp. 67, 69. See also Owen, *Works*, 17: 382 for another reference. While scholars have generally agreed that the *pactum salutis* concept was developed by Cocceius, another Dutch Reformed theologian writing at the end of the century, Herman Witsius, traced its origins to Owen's commentary and his *Exercitationes* on Hebrews; van Asselt, "Covenant theology as relational theology," pp. 69, 73–74. Five of Cocceius's works were listed in *Bibliotheca Oweniana* (1684), Edward Millington's auction catalogue purporting to represent the contents of Owen's library, including a large commentary on Hebrews (1659), though the credibility of the catalogue as a reflection of the content of Owen's library is disputable; Gribben, "John Owen, Renaissance man?" pp. 321–32; Trueman, *John Owen*, pp. 86–87.
32. Owen, *Biblical theology*, trans. Wescott, pp. xlviii, 89.
33. Owen, *Biblical theology*, trans. Wescott, p. 48.
34. Owen, *Biblical theology*, trans. Wescott, pp. 128, 133. On Owen's broader interest in and influence upon contemporary English poetry, see Gribben, "Poetry and piety: John Owen, Faithful Teate and communion with God," pp. 197–215.
35. Theophilus Gale recorded his appreciation of the work; Wallace, *Shapers of English Calvinism*, p. 105.
36. Yeo, "The acquisition of books by Chetham's Library, 1655–1700," 2: 370–80.
37. *CSPD* (1661–62), p. 593. I owe this reference to David Norbrook.
38. *The diary of Samuel Pepys*, eds. Latham and Matthews, 3: 72–73 (28 April 1662).
39. Massachussetts Historical Society, *Collections*, fourth series, vol. 8 (Boston, 1868), p. 195; *CSPD* (1661–62), p. 593.
40. For the broader context of dissenting writing during this period, see Keeble, *The literary culture of nonconformity*, pp. 93–126.
41. Owen, Works, 15: 28, 33; for the new licensing laws, see Hutton, *The Restoration*, p. 156.

42. Owen, *Works*, 15: 38.
43. Owen, *Works*, 15: 40.
44. Owen, *Works*, 15: 7.
45. Owen, *Works*, 15: 22.
46. Owen, *Works*, 15: 7.
47. Owen, *Works*, 15: 29–32.
48. Owen, *Works*, 15: 4–5, 8.
49. Owen, *Works*, 15: 10–12.
50. Owen, *Works*, 15: 17.
51. Owen, *Works*, 15: 55.
52. Jacob, *Henry Stubbe, radical Protestantism and the early Enlightenment*, p. 45; Steven N. Zwicker, "Language as disguise: Politics and poetry in the late seventeenth century," *Annals of Scholarship* 1 (1980), pp. 47–67. During the 1640s and 1650s, royalists had developed similar strategies of literary occlusion: Lois Potter, *Secret rites and secret writings: Royalist literature, 1641–1660* (Cambridge: Cambridge University Press, 1989).
53. Jacob, *Henry Stubbe, radical Protestantism and the early Enlightenment*, p. 3.
54. *Aminadversions* was likely published in June 1662; Owen, *Works*, 14: 184.
55. Asty, "Memoirs," p. xxiii, notes that a "Person of Honour" provided Owen with a copy of *Fiat lux*, requesting that he reply to it. Goold argues that this "Person of Honour" was Hyde; "Prefatory note," Owen, *Works*, 14: 2. Christopher Hill's discussion of Hyde's religion is still relevant: "Lord Clarendon and the Puritan revolution," in *Puritanism and revolution: Studies in interpretation of the English revolution of the 17th century* (London: Secker & Warburg, 1958), pp. 181–94.
56. *CSPD* (1661–62), p. 593.
57. See, for example, Hutton, *The Restoration*, p. 108.
58. Hutton, *The Restoration*, pp. 149–50.
59. Hutton, *The Restoration*, p. 154.
60. Owen, *Works*, 14:8; J[ohn] V[incent] C[ane], *Fiat lux* (n.p., 1662), pp. 8–9, 366–68.
61. Spalding, *The improbable Puritan*, p. 233; Hutton, *The Restoration*, p. 164.
62. Asty, "Memoirs," pp. xxiii–xxiv.
63. Owen, *Works*, 14: 89, 334, 395.
64. Owen, *Works*, 14: 49. Owen had offered criticisms of the scholastic theologians in the 1650s; Owen, *Works*, 12: 42.
65. Owen, *Works*, 14: 315.
66. Owen, *Works*, 14: 8.
67. Owen, *Works*, 14: 190.
68. Owen, *Works*, 14: 193.
69. Owen, *Works*, 14: 304, 395.

70. [J.V.C.], *An epistle to the authour of the Animadversions upon Fiat lux in excuse and justification of Fiat lux against the said animadversions* (Douay?, 1663), p. 108. See also J. V. C., *Three letters declaring the strange odd preceedings of Protestant divines when they write against Catholicks: by the example of Dr Taylor's Dissuasive against popery, Mr Whitbies Reply in the behalf of Dr Pierce against Cressy, and Dr Owens Animadversions on Fiat lux* (1671).
71. Owen, *Works*, 14: 33.
72. Owen, *Works*, 14: 108, 169.
73. Owen, *Works*, 14: 254.
74. Hutton, *The Restoration*, pp. 186–87; Don Jordan and Michael Walsh, *The king's revenge: Charles II and the greatest manhunt in British history* (Lonon: Little, Brown, 2012).
75. Hutton, *The Restoration*, pp. 175–76, 196–97.
76. Owen, *Works*, 14: 107.
77. Owen, *Works*, 14: 65.
78. Owen, *Works*, 14: 196.
79. Owen, *Works*, 14: 53, 109.
80. Owen, *Works*, 14: 251.
81. Owen, *Works*, 14: 314.
82. Owen, *Works*, 14: 314–15.
83. Cooper, *John Owen, Richard Baxter and the formation of nonconformity*, pp. 140–54.
84. Asty, "Memoirs," p. xxiv; Roger Lockyer, *Tudor and Stuart Britain* (1964; 3rd edition, Harlow, UK: Pearson Education, 2005), p. 393.
85. Owen, *Works*, 14: 197.
86. Owen, Works, 15: 28, 33.
87. Owen, *Works*, 14: 119.
88. Owen, *Works*, 14: 312.
89. *Calendar of State Papers Colonial, America and West Indies, Volume 18: 1700* (1910), pp. 354–80.
90. Owen, *Works*, 14: 171.
91. Hutton, *The Restoration*, p. 176.
92. Bodleian Rawlinson Letters 109, f. 87; reprinted in *The correspondence of John Owen*, ed. Toon, pp. 129–30.
93. *The journals of William Schellinks' travels in England*, p. 128.
94. *The journals of William Schellinks' travels in England*, p. 140.
95. *The journals of William Schellinks' travels in England*, p. 130. An "ell" is approximately 18 inches in length.
96. *The journals of William Schellinks' travels in England*, p. 127.
97. *The journals of William Schellinks' travels in England*, p. 153.
98. *The journals of William Schellinks' travels in England*, p. 129.
99. Appleby, *Black Bartholomew's Day*, p. 37.

100. Appleby, *Black Bartholomew's Day*, p. 55.
101. Appleby, *Black Bartholomew's Day*, p. 40.
102. Appleby, *Black Bartholomew's Day*, p. 57.
103. Bodleian Rawlinson Letters 109, f. 85–86; reprinted in *The correspondence of John Owen*, ed. Toon, pp. 132–34.
104. *CSPD* (1661–1662), vol. 2: June 1661–Dec 1662, citing SP 29/65 f. 17. Vol. LXV, 10, p. 594.
105. *The correspondence of John Owen*, ed. Toon, p. 131.
106. Cook, "Political biography," p. 289.
107. *The correspondence of John Owen*, ed. Toon, pp. 130–31.
108. Bodleian Rawlinson Letters 109, f. 87; reprinted in *The correspondence of John Owen*, ed. Toon, pp. 130–31.
109. G. L. Turner, "Williamson's spy book," *Transactions of the Congregational Historical Society* 5 (1912), pp. 247–53, 314; G. L. Turner, *Original records of early non-conformity under persecution and indulgence* (London: Unwin, 1911), 1: 89, 3: 514; Walter Wilson, *The history and antiquities of dissenting churches and meeting houses in London, Westminster, and Southwark*, 4 vols. (London, 1808–14), 3: 69; Matthews, *Calamy revised*, p. 377.
110. John Hull, "Diary," *Archaeologia Americana: Transactions and collections of the American Antiquarian Society* 3 (1857), pp. 173, 207–10; *Collections*, Massachusetts Historical Society, 2nd series, 2: 265–67, reprinted in *The correspondence of John Owen*, ed. Toon, pp. 135–36.
111. Christopher Durston, "Goffe, William (*d*. 1679?)," *ODNB*.
112. *Calendar of State Papers Colonial, America and West Indies, Volume 18: 1700* (1910), pp. 354–80.
113. *The correspondence of John Owen*, ed. Toon, pp. 133–35.
114. Bodleian Rawlinson Letters 109, f. 85–86; reprinted in *The correspondence of John Owen*, ed. Toon, pp. 132–34.
115. Bodleian Rawlinson Letters 109, f. 85–86; reprinted in *The correspondence of John Owen*, ed. Toon, pp. 132–34.
116. Cook, "Political biography," p. 296, refers to a passage in the manuscript of Toon's biography that did not make it into the published volume.
117. *CSPD* (1664–65), p. 222; Vernon, *Letter to a friend*, p. 39; Owen, *Works*, 16: 274. Baxter argued that Owen had fled from London during the plague; *Reliquiae Baxterianae*, 3: 19; Jones, *Why heaven kissed earth*, p. 51 n.
118. *The correspondence of John Owen*, ed. Toon, p. 135 n. 14; Hutton, *The Restoration*, pp. 225–30.
119. *Chirk Castle Accounts, A.D. 1666–1753*, ed. William Martial Myddelton (Manchester: Manchester University Press, 1931), p. 25.
120. Orme, "Memoir," p. 25; Crippen, "Dr Watts's church book," p. 29.
121. Hull, "Diary," pp. 215, 218.

122. Cook, "Political biography," pp. 298–99.
123. Hutton, *The Restoration*, p. 263.
124. Cook, "Political biography," p. 301. In 1680, Owen stated that he had been in church fellowship with the individual he was burying for about fifteen years; Owen, *Works*, 9: 341.
125. De Krey, *London and the Restoration*, pp. 96, 100.
126. Russell's edition of Owen's works reprints the first edition, and Goold's the second edition.
127. Owen, *Works*, 15: 447.
128. Owen, *Works*, 15: 467.
129. Owen, *Works*, 15: 463.
130. Owen, *Works*, 15: 474.
131. Owen, *Works*, 15: 530.
132. Owen, *Works*, 15: 496, 512.
133. Folger 0721.
134. Owen, *Works*, 13: 518.
135. Owen, *Works*, 13: 524.
136. Owen, *Works*, 13: 519.
137. Owen, *Works*, 13: 519.
138. Owen, *Works*, 13: 521.
139. Owen, *Works*, 13: 522.
140. Owen, *Works*, 13: 533, 536.
141. Owen, *Works*, 13: 535.
142. Owen, *Works*, 13: 531.
143. Owen, *Works*, 13: 523.
144. Owen, *Works*, 13: 540.
145. Owen, *Works*, 13: 571.
146. Owen, *Works*, 13: 551–52.
147. Owen, *Works*, 13: 552.
148. Owen, *Works*, 13: 546–47.
149. Owen, *Works*, 13: 548.
150. Owen, *Works*, 13: 548.
151. Owen, *Works*, 13: 573.
152. Owen, *Works*, 13: 549.
153. Richard Perrinchief, *Indulgence not justified* (1668), p. 4.
154. Diana Dethloff, "Greenhill, John (1644?–1676)," *ODNB*; Jacob Simon, *National Portrait Gallery: Complete illustrated catalogue* (London: National Portrait Gallery, 2004), p. 473. Selby Whittingham is currently writing a monograph on Greenhill, which may provide more detailed comment on this aspect of Owen's biography. I am grateful to Dr. Whittingham for advice on this portrait.
155. Kelsey, *Inventing a republic*, p. 55.

156. See, more generally on political painting in this period, Kevin Sharpe, *Image wars: Promoting kings and Commonweaths in England, 1603–1660* (New Haven, CT: Yale University Press, 2010).
157. De Krey, *London and the Restoration*, p. 122.

CHAPTER 9

1. *Calendar of the correpondence of Richard Baxter*, eds. Keeble and Nuttall, 2: 86.
2. Paul Helm has suggested that we should distinguish between Owen's public, "scribal" interventions from his private, "prophetic" interventions; private correspondence to the author, 22 May 2015.
3. Keeble, *The literary culture of nonconformity*, pp. 128–29.
4. Keeble, *The literary culture of nonconformity*, pp. 133–35.
5. Tweeddale, "John Owen's commentary on Hebrews in context," p. 52; Rehnman, *Divine discourse*, p. 18; Kelly Kapic, "Typology, the Messiah, and John Owen's theological reading of Hebrews," in J. Laansma and D. Treier (eds.), *Christology, hermeneutics, and Hebrews: Profiles from the history of interpretation* (Edinburgh: T & T Clark, 2012), pp. 135–54. For a publication history of this commentary, see Lee Gatiss, "Adoring the fullness of the Scriptures in John Owen's commentary on Hebrews" (unpublished PhD thesis, University of Cambridge, 2013), pp. 1–7.
6. Owen, *Works*, 16: 328, 376.
7. Tweeddale, "John Owen's commentary on Hebrews in context," p. 53.
8. Owen, *Works*, 18:5, 8–9; Tweeddale, "John Owen's commentary on Hebrews in context," p. 52. Note that this quotation is occasionally and erroneously rendered in the first person; David Clarkson, "A funeral sermon . . . ," in *Seventeen sermons preach'd by the late reverend and learned John Owen, D.D.* (London, 1720), 1: lxxiii.
9. Owen, *Works*, 18: 16, 267; Henry M. Knapp, "John Owen's interpretation of Hebrews 6:4–6," *Sixteenth Century Journal* 34 (2003), p. 44.
10. Knapp, "Understanding the mind of God," p. 106 n. 221; Tweeddale, "John Owen's commentary on Hebrews in context," p. 57 n. 31.
11. Owen, *Hebrews*, 1: 6–7.
12. Toon, *God's statesman*, p. 128; Barbara K. Lewalski, *The life of John Milton* (Oxford: Blackwell, 2000), p. 400.
13. Owen, *Hebrews*, 1: 3–4.
14. Owen, *Hebrews*, 1: 8.
15. Owen, *Hebrews*, 1: 9.
16. Caricchio, "News from the New Jerusalem," pp. 69–86.
17. Owen, *Works*, 6: 165.
18. Owen, *Works*, 6: 155.

19. Owen, *Works*, 6: 170.
20. Owen, *Works*, 6: 174, 215.
21. Owen, *Works*, 6: 267, 282.
22. Owen, *Works*, 6: 269.
23. *The diary of Samuel Pepys*, eds. Latham and Matthews, 5: 352–57 (21–27 December 1664); 6: 48 (1 March 1665); 6: 75 (6 April 1665); John Gadbury, *De cometis* (1665); Paul Slack, *The impact of plague in Tudor and Stuart London* (Oxford: Oxford University Press, 1995); A. Lloyd Moote and Dorothy C. Moote, *The great plague: The story of London's most deadly year* (Baltimore, MD: The Johns Hopkins University Press, 2004); Kathleen Miller, *The print culture of plague in early modern England* (New York: Palgrave Macmillan, forthcoming); Adrian Timmiswood, *By permission of heaven: The story of the Great Fire of London* (London: Jonathan Cape, 2006), pp. 4, 101.
24. Owen, *Works* [Banner of Truth edition], 16: 428, 431.
25. Owen, *Works*, 9: 587; [Banner of Truth edition], 16: 480.
26. Owen, *Works*, 9: 18, 408, 519–20.
27. Owen, *Works* [Banner of Truth edition], 16: 424–25.
28. Crippen, "Dr Watts's church-book," pp. 26–38.
29. Dr. Williams's Library, NCL, MS L6/2, unpaginated. Owen, *Works*, 9: 409, 420.
30. Owen, *Works*, 9: 521, 523, 529, 538, 541, 544, 555.
31. *A history of the county of Middlesex*, vol. 10: *Hackney* (1995), pp. 130–44.
32. Mather, *Magnalia Christi Americana*, 2: 534.
33. Joseph Ivimey, *History of the English Baptists* (London, 1814), 2: 189–91; *Calendar of the correpondence of Richard Baxter*, eds. Keeble and Nuttall, 2: 111–12.
34. Francis Peck, *Desiderata curiosa: or, A collection of divers scarce and curious pieces relating chiefly to matters of English history* (London, 1779), p. 547.
35. Owen, *Works*, 2: 372.
36. Owen, *Works*, 6: 394, 603.
37. Owen, *Works*, 6: 576, 628, 632.
38. Owen, *Works*, 6: 396.
39. Owen, *Works*, 6: 518, 541.
40. Owen, *Works*, 2: 424, 439.
41. Tay, *The priesthood of Christ*, p. 21.
42. Owen, *Works*, 2: 371.
43. Warren Johnston, *Revelation restored: The apocalypse in later seventeenth-century England* (Woodbridge, UK: Boydell, 2011), pp. 15, 104, 156, 174, 177.
44. Kay, *Trinitarian spirituality*, p. 165.
45. John Owen, "Preface," in Theophilus Gale, *The true idea of Jansenism* (1669), [sig. A2r].
46. *Calendar of the correpondence of Richard Baxter*, eds. Keeble and Nuttall, 2: 65.
47. Baxter, *Reliquiae Baxterianae*, 3: 61.

48. Dr. Williams's Library, Richard Baxter Letters 59.5.18, reprinted in *The correspondence of John Owen*, ed. Toon, pp. 136–38.
49. *Calendar of the correpondence of Richard Baxter*, eds. Keeble and Nuttall, 2: 71.
50. *Calendar of the correpondence of Richard Baxter*, eds. Keeble and Nuttall, 2: 72.
51. Dr. Williams's Library, Richard Baxter Letters 59.5.18, reprinted in *The correspondence of John Owen*, ed. Toon, pp. 136–38; Baxter, *Reliquiae Baxterianae*, 3: 64.
52. Baxter, *Reliquiae Baxterianae*, 3: 62–73.
53. Owen, *Works* [Banner of Truth edition], 16: 439.
54. Owen, *Works*, 6: 230.
55. Kenyon, *Stuart constitution*, pp. 356–59.
56. Owen, *Works*, 13: 583–86.
57. Vernon, *Letter to a friend*, p. 66.
58. Vernon, *Letter to a friend*, p. 34; Cooper, *John Owen, Richard Baxter and the formation of nonconformity*, pp. 272–73.
59. Owen, *Works*, 13: 579–82.
60. *CSPD* (1670), p. 231.
61. Dr Williams's Library, NCL, MS L6/2, unpaginated.
62. Spalding, *The improbable puritan*, p. 243.
63. Owen, *Works*, 9: 224, 217–37; Dr. Williams's Library, MS NCL MS L6/2.
64. Owen, *Works*, 9: 235.
65. *The correspondence of John Owen*, ed. Toon, p. 148.
66. Owen, *Works*, 9: 248.
67. Owen, *Works*, 9: 235.
68. Hull, "Diary," pp. 141–250.
69. *Transactions of the Colonial Society of Massachusetts* 11 (1906–7), pp. 338–41, 370; reprinted in *The correspondence of John Owen*, ed. Toon, pp. 149–51.
70. Thomas Hutchinson, *A collection of original papers relative to the history of the colony of Massachusetts-Bay* (Boston, 1769), pp. 429ff; reprinted in *The correspondence of John Owen*, ed. Toon, pp. 151–53.
71. Mather, *Magnalia Christi Americana*, 1: 536–37; reprinted in *The correspondence of John Owen*, ed. Toon, pp. 153–55.
72. Bodleian Rawlinson MS 63.f.19 (62); reprinted in *The correspondence of John Owen*, ed. Toon, pp. 156–67.
73. Keeble, *The literary culture of nonconformity*, p. 105.
74. Dr. Williams's Library, NCL, MS L6/2, unpaginated.
75. Owen, *Works* [Banner of Truth edition], 16: 440–55.
76. Dr. Williams's Library NCL, MS L6/2, "Contents," unpaginated.
77. Owen, *Works*, 9: 359–64.
78. *CSPD* (1671), p. 264.
79. Kenyon, *Stuart constitution*, pp. 382–83.
80. Asty, "Memoirs," p. xxix.

81. Cook, "Political biography," p. 334; *CSPD* 1671–72, pp. 328–427, 433.
82. Cook, "Political biography," p. 334–35.
83. Owen, *Works*, 15: 57–185.
84. Owen, *Works*, 2: 372; 6: 344, 368.
85. Owen, *Works*, 6: 155.
86. Samuel Parker, *Preface to Bishop Bramhall's vindication* (1672), n.p. [civ]; Jon Parkin, "Parker, Samuel (1640–1688)," *ODNB*.
87. *Report on the manuscripts of the late Allan George Finch, esq., of Burley-on-the-Hill, Rutland*, ed. S. C. Lomas (London: H. M. Stationery Office, 1913), 2:10.
88. "Introduction," Andrew Marvell, *The rehearsal transpros'd and The rehearsal transpros'd the second part*, ed. D. I. B. Smith (Oxford: Clarendon Press, 1971), p. xii.
89. Parker, "A Preface to the Reader," *Bishop Bramhall's vindication of himself and the Episcopal clergy from the Presbyterian charge of Popery* (1672), sig. $A2^{v}$, a^{r}, n.p.
90. Parker, "A Preface to the Reader," *Bishop Bramhall's vindication*, n.p.; Jason P. Rosenblatt, *Renaissance England's chief rabbi: John Selden* (Oxford: Oxford University Press, 2006), p. 113.
91. See McDowell, *Poetry and allegiance in the English civil wars.*
92. Nigel Smith, *Andrew Marvell: The chameleon* (New Haven, CT: Yale University Press, 2010), p. 253. The contents of Owen's library were auctioned by Edward Millington, who published a catalogue for the event, *Bibliotheca Oweniana* (1884). See Gribben, "John Owen, Renaissance man?" for discussion of the content of this catalogue as a guide to reconstructing Owen's library.
93. Marvell, *The rehearsal transpros'd*, ed. Smith, pp. 5–6.
94. Marvell, *The rehearsal transpros'd*, ed. Smith, pp. 40–41.
95. Marvell, *The rehearsal transpros'd*, ed. Smith, p. 7.
96. [Samuel Butler], *The transproser rehears'd* (1673), pp. 137–38.
97. Kenyon, *Stuart constitution*, pp. 383–84.
98. Asty, "Memoirs," p. xxv.
99. Owen, *Works*, 9: 271.
100. Crippen, "Dr. Watts's church-book," pp. 26–38; Toon, *God's statesman*, pp. 152–55.
101. Toon, *God's statesman*, p. 126.
102. Crippen, "Dr. Watts's church-book," pp. 26–38.
103. Crippen, "Dr. Watts's church-book," p. 29; Owen, *Works*, 9: 431–41.
104. Barry Till, "Clarkson, David (*bap.* 1622, *d.* 1686)," *ODNB*.
105. Richard Greaves, *John Bunyan and English nonconformity* (London: Hambledon Press, 1992), pp. 64, 160; Greaves, *Glimpses of glory*, pp. 297, 301.
106. Owen, *Works*, 9: 266.
107. Owen, *Works*, 9: 268.
108. Owen, *Works*, 9: 258.

109. Dr. Williams's Library, NCL, MS L6/2, unpaginated.
110. P. S. Seaver, "Caryl, Joseph (1602–1673)," *ODNB*.
111. Owen, *Works* [Banner of Truth edition], 16: 464.
112. Owen, *Works* [Banner of Truth edition], 16: 456; Crippen, "Dr. Watts's church-book," p. 28.
113. Owen, *Works* [Banner of Truth edition], 16: 460.
114. "To the Reader," Francis Rous, *The psalms of David in meeter* (1673), sig. A5r–v.
115. "To the Reader," Rous, *The psalms of David in meeter*, sig. A5v.
116. David Norbook, "*Order and Disorder*: The poem and its contexts," p. xviii; N. H. Keeble, "'But the Colonel's shadow': Lucy Hutchinson, women's writing, and the civil war," in Thomas Healy and Jonathan Sawday (eds.), *Literature and the English Civil War* (Cambridge: Cambridge University Press, 1990), pp. 227–47; David Norbrook, "Memoirs and oblivion: Lucy Hutchinson and the Restoration," *Huntington Library Quarterly* 75 (2012), pp. 233–82; Achinstein, *Literature and dissent in Milton's England*, p. 69; David Norbook, "Chronology," p. xi; Hutchinson, *On the principles of the Christian religion, addressed to her daughter; and on theology*; David Norbrook, "Introduction," in Lucy Hutchinson, *Order and disorder*, ed. David Norbrook (Oxford: Blackwell, 2001), pp. xix–xx; Katherine Narveson, "The sources for Lucy Hutchinson's *On Theology*," *Notes and Queries*, n.s., 36 (1989), pp. 40–41.
117. David Norbook, "Hutchinson [*née* Apsley], Lucy (1620–81)," *ODNB*; Crippen, "Dr. Watts's church-book," p. 29.
118. Norbook, "Chronology," p. xi; Norbook, "*Order and disorder*: The poem and its contexts," pp. xix; Elizabeth Scott-Baumann, *Forms of engagement: Women, poetry and culture, 1640–1680* (Oxford: Oxford University Press, 2013), p. 194; Crippen, "Dr. Watts's church-book," p. 29.
119. Norbook, "*Order and disorder*: The poem and its contexts," p. xvi; Norbook, "Chronology," p. xi.
120. Owen, *Biblical theology*, trans. Wescott, pp. 105, 111.
121. For more on this context, see Annabel Patterson and Michael Dzeleainis, "Marvell and the earl of Anglesey: A chapter in the history of reading," *Historical Journal* 44 (2001), pp. 703–26.
122. Clarke, *Politics, religion and the Song of Songs in seventeenth-century England*, p. 183.
123. Sherlock, *A discourse concerning the knowledge of Jesus Christ and our union and communion with him*, p. 117.
124. Clarke, *Politics, religion and the Song of Songs in seventeenth-century England*, p. 183.
125. Owen, *Works*, 3: 121, 213.
126. Owen, *Works*, 3: 7, 105. Sinclair B. Ferguson notes that Owen's doctrine of the sealing of the Holy Spirit changes between 1667 and 1674; "John Owen and

the doctrine of the Holy Spirit," in Robert W. Oliver (ed.), *John Owen: The man and his theology* (Phillipsburg, NJ: P & R, 2002), p. 122. This claim about the "primary authority" of experience is made in Nuttall, *The Holy Spirit in Puritan faith and experience*, p. 7.

127. *The correspondence of John Owen*, ed. Toon, pp. 157–58.
128. *The correspondence of John Owen*, ed. Toon, pp. 159–60.
129. *The correspondence of John Owen*, ed. Toon, p. 161; Owen, *Works*, 9: 298.
130. Owen, *Works* [Banner of Truth edition], 16: 476.
131. Owen, *Works* [Banner of Truth edition], 16: 519, 525.
132. Owen, *Works*, 9: 325.
133. Owen, *Works*, 9: 327.
134. Owen, *Works*, 9: 329.
135. *CSPD* (1675–76), p. 571.
136. Crippen, "Dr Watts's church-book," pp. 28–29; *The correspondence of John Owen*, ed. Toon, p. 181.
137. Owen, *Works*, 9: 612; Greaves, *Glimpses of glory*, p. 226.
138. Tay, *The priesthood of Christ*, p. 129, notes similarities between Owen's comments on Hebrews 7:22 (in *Works*, 21: 499–504, 507–8) and *The doctrine of justification* (in *Works*, 5: 182–87, 187–88).
139. Asty, "Memoirs," p. xxx; Hutton, *The Restoration*, p. 279; Greaves, *Glimpses of glory*, pp. 44–46.
140. Cook, "Political biography," p. 351.
141. William Hooke to Increase Mather, in *Collections of the Massachusetts Historical Society*, 4th series, 8: 584.
142. Owen, *Works* [Banner of Truth edition], 16: 479.
143. Owen, *Works* [Banner of Truth edition], 16: 480.
144. Owen, *Works* [Banner of Truth edition], 16: 481–82.
145. Owen, *Works* [Banner of Truth edition], 16: 482.
146. Owen, *Works*, 14: 493.
147. Owen, *Works*, 9: 491.
148. Owen, *Works*, 9: 499.
149. Owen, *Works*, 9: 505.
150. Owen, *Works*, 9: 514.
151. *The entring book of Roger Morrice*, ed. Mark Goldie et al., 6 vols. (Rochester, NY: Boydell and Brewer, 2007), 2: 235.
152. Cook, "Political biography," pp. 363–66.
153. Goold claims this sermon was preached in December 1681; however, Owen's reference to the "Great Comet" then in display suggests that the sermon was actually preached in December 1680; Owen, *Works*, 9:2.
154. Owen, *Works*, 9: 3.
155. Owen, *Works*, 9: 4.

156. Owen, *Works*, 9: 6.
157. Owen, *Works*, 9: 9. The allusion is to Isaiah 6.
158. Owen, *Works*, 9: 11.
159. William E. Burns, *An age of wonders: Prodigies, politics and providence in England, 1657–1727* (Manchester: Manchester University Press, 2002), pp. 97–124.
160. Owen, *Works*, 9: 11.
161. Owen, *Works*, 9: 13.
162. Owen, *Works*, 9: 16.
163. Owen, *Works*, 9: 336.
164. Owen, *Works*, 9: 341; Crippen, "Dr Watts's church-book," p. 27.
165. Owen, *Works*, 9: 342.
166. Owen, *Works*, 9: 350.
167. Owen, *Works* [Banner of Truth edition], 16: 488.
168. Owen, *Works* [Banner of Truth edition], 16: 490, 492.
169. Owen, *Works*, 9: 405.
170. Owen, *Works*, 9: 332.
171. *CSPD* (1680–81), pp. 592, 613; *CSPD* (1682), pp. 86, 104, 610.
172. *CSPD* (1680–81), pp. 596–654.
173. *The correspondence of John Owen*, ed. Toon, pp. 170–72.
174. *The correspondence of John Owen*, ed. Toon, pp. 170–72.
175. *The works of John Owen*, ed. T. Russell (1826), 1: 423; *The correspondence of John Owen*, ed. Toon, p. 172.
176. C. S. Knighton, "Hartcliffe, John (1651/2–1712)," *ODNB*.
177. Crippen, "Dr Watts's church-book," p. 29.
178. Owen, *Works*, 9: 453; *The correspondence of John Owen*, ed. Toon, pp. 172–73.
179. Crippen, "Dr Watts's church-book," p. 29.
180. Owen, *Works*, 9: 459.
181. Cook, "Political biography," p. 374.
182. *CSPD* (1684–1685), p. 258; Melinda Zook, "Ferguson, Robert (*d.* 1714)," ODNB.
183. Cook, "Political biography," p. 374.
184. Cook, "Political biography," pp. 375–76.
185. *The correspondence of John Owen*, ed. Toon, pp. 173–74.
186. *The New Testament of our Lord and Saviour Jesus Christ with annotations*, ed. Samuel Clark (1683), n.p.
187. Cook, "Political biography," p. 382.
188. *The entring book of Roger Morrice*, ed. Goldie et al., 2: 374.
189. *CSPD* (1683), pp. 284–390.
190. *The entring book of Roger Morrice*, ed. Goldie et al., 2: 377.
191. Asty, "Memoir," p. xxxii; *The correspondence of John Owen*, ed. Toon, p. 174.
192. Owen, *Works* [Banner of Truth edition], 16: 502.

CONCLUSION

1. "Fifth oration" (9 October 1657), in *Oxford orations*, ed. Toon, p. 41.
2. This translation is provided in Achinstein, *Literature and dissent in Milton's England*, p. 46.
3. Lynch, *Protestant autobiography in the seventeenth-century Anglophone world*, pp. 228–29.
4. Achinstein, *Literature and dissent in Milton's England*, p. 43.
5. Achinstein, *Literature and dissent in Milton's England*, p. 43.
6. Anon, "Life of Owen," p. xxxvii; Wood, *Athenae Oxoniensis*, 2: 747; Achinstein, *Literature and dissent in Milton's England*, p. 46.
7. Achinstein, *Literature and dissent in Milton's England*, p. 46.
8. David Clarkson, *Funeral sermon* (1720), p. lxxi. Reference to the Sunday after the burial is found in David Clarkson, "A funeral sermon on Dr John Owen," in *A complete collection of the sermons of ... John Owen* (1721), n.p. [first page of the Clarkson sermon in a footnote].
9. Clarkson, "A funeral sermon on Dr John Owen," n.p.
10. Anonymous, *An elegy on the death of that learned, pious, and famous divine, Doctor John Owen, who dyed the 24th. of August, 1683* (1683), single sheet. The EEBO copy is marked 22 September 1683.
11. Anonymous, *An elegy on ... John Owen*, single sheet.
12. Anonymous, *An elegy on ... John Owen*, single sheet.
13. Achinstein, *Literature and dissent in Milton's England*, p. 35.
14. Anonymous, *An elegy on ... John Owen*, single sheet.
15. Anonymous, *An elegy on ... John Owen*, single sheet.
16. Anonymous, *An elegy on ... John Owen*, single sheet.
17. Achinstein, *Literature and dissent in Milton's England*, p. 35.
18. Clarkson, "A funeral sermon on Dr John Owen," n.p.
19. "The will of Dr John Owen," in *The correspondence of John Owen*, ed. Toon, pp. 181–85.
20. Crippen, "Dr Watts's church-book," pp. 26–38; Orme, "Memoirs," p. 25.
21. Crippen, "Dr Watts's church-book," pp. 26–38.
22. "The will of Dr John Owen," in *The correspondence of John Owen*, ed. Toon, p. 181 n. 2.
23. Cambers, *Godly reading*, p. 124.
24. "Harpsden," in *The Henley guide* (Henley-on-Thames: Hickman and Stapledon, 1826), pp. 57–59.
25. Caroline L. Leachman, "Collins, John (1632?–1687)," *ODNB*.
26. Barry Till, "Clarkson, David (*bap.* 1622, *d.* 1686)," *ODNB*; Toon, *God's statesman*, p. 157.
27. "The will of Dr John Owen," in *The correspondence of John Owen*, ed. Toon, p. 185; Gribben, "John Owen, Renaissance man?"

28. Crawford Gribben, "John Owen, baptism and the Baptists," forthcoming.
29. Joseph Joshua Green, "The Puritan family of Wilmer: Their alliances and connections," *Transactions of the Congregational History Society* 4:3 (1909), pp. 11, 19. Crippen, "Dr Watts's church-book," pp. 26–38.
30. Asty, "Memoirs," p. xxix.
31. "Fifth oration" (9 October 1657), in Toon (ed.), *Oxford orations*, p. 45.
32. Samuel Butler, *Hudibras in three parts* (1684), p. 118.
33. *A vindication of Owen by a friendly scrutiny* (1684), p. 34.
34. Baxter, *Reliquiae Baxterianae*, p. 199.
35. Baxter, *Reliquiae Baxterianae*, p. 107. Cooper's *John Owen, Richard Baxter and the formation of nonconformity* remains the preeminent account of the relationship between its subjects.
36. Richard Baxter, *Richard Baxter's penitent confession and his necessary vindication in answer to a book called The second part of the mischiefs of separation, written by an unnamed author with a preface to Mr. Cantianus D. Minimis, in answer to his letter which extorted this publication* (1691), p. 25.
37. Baxter, *Reliquiae Baxterianae*, 3: 42, 101.
38. Baxter, *Richard Baxter's penitent confession*, p. 25.
39. *Calendar of the correpondence of Richard Baxter*, eds. Keeble and Nuttall, 2: 260–63.
40. Baxter, *Reliquiae Baxterianae*, 3: 5; Lynch, *Protestant autobiography in the seventeenth-century Anglophone world*, p. 275.
41. Lynch, *Protestant autobiography in the seventeenth-century Anglophone world*, p. 237.
42. Edward Hyde, earl of Clarendon, *Transcendent and multiplied rebellion and treason, discovered, by the lawes of the land* (n.d.), p. 16.
43. William Baron, *A just defence of the royal martyr, K. Charles I, from the many false and malicious aspersions in Ludlow's Memoirs and some other virulent libels of that kind* (1699), p. 25.
44. John Brown, *The life of justification opened, or, A treatise grounded upon Gal. 2, II wherein the orthodox doctrine of justification by faith, & imputation of Christ's righteousness is clearly expounded, solidly confirmed, & learnedly vindicated from the various objections of its adversaries, whereunto are subjoined some arguments against universal redemption* (Holland, 1695), p. 5.
45. Clarkson, *Funeral sermon*, p. lxxi.
46. Letham, "John Owen's doctrine of the Trinity in its catholic context," p. 190.
47. Tay, *The priesthood of Christ*, pp. 72–79.
48. Trueman, *Claims of truth*, p. 45. Peter de Vries searches for such a center in "Union and communion with Christ in the theology of John Owen," *Reformed Theological Journal* 15 (1999), pp. 77–96, and "The significance of union and communion with Christ in the theology of John Owen (1616–1683)," *Reformed Theological Journal* 17 (2001), pp. 75–89.

49. Daniels, *The Christology of John Owen*, p. 294.
50. Ecclesiological and sacramental themes are noticably absent from the books collected in Owen, *Works*, vol. 6.
51. Owen, *Works*, 1: 465; Owen, *Works*, 8: 245.
52. Owen, *Works*, 10: 479.
53. Martyn C. Cowan, "The prophetic preaching of John Owen from 1646 to 1659 in its historical context" (unpublished PhD thesis, University of Cambridge, 2012), pp. 157–80.
54. Trueman, *John Owen*, p. 127.
55. David W. Bebbington, *Evangelicalism in modern Britain: A history from the 1730s to the 1980s* (London: Unwin Hyman, 1989), pp. 49–55; W. R. Ward, *Early evangelicalism: A global intellectual history, 1670–1789* (Cambridge: Cambridge University Press, 2006), pp. 119–39; John Coffey, "Puritan legacies," in John Coffey and Paul C.-H. Lim (eds.), *The Cambridge companion to Puritanism* (Cambridge: Cambridge University Press, 2008), pp. 327–45.
56. Daniels, *The Christology of John Owen*, p. 161.
57. William Wilberforce, *A practical view of the prevailing religious system of professed Christians* (1797; rpt. London, 1830), pp. 240–41; *Letters of A. W. Pink* (Edinburgh: Banner of Truth, 1978), p. 55; William Kelly, Appendix to the Notice of the *Achill Herald* Recollections, http://www.stempublishing.com/authors/kelly/8_Bt/achill2.html, accessed 15 June 2015; *The journals of Jim Elliot*, ed. Elizabeth Elliot (Grand Rapids, MI: Fleming H. Revell, 1978), pp. 149, 294, 327; Iain H. Murray, *D. Martyn Lloyd-Jones: The fight of faith, 1939–1981* (Edinburgh: Banner of Truth, 1990), p. 363. Alan Spence believes that elements of Owen's Christology map onto those advanced in very controversial circumstances by Edward Irving; *Incarnation and inspiration*, p. 53.
58. For the John Owen Centre, at London Theological Seminary, and the Wesley Owen chain of Christian bookshops, see Kapic, *Communion with God*, p. 15. The mugs, T-shirts, and neckties are widely available online at the time of writing.
59. See Crawford Gribben, "Becoming John Owen," forthcoming.

Bibliography

This bibliography builds on the invaluable contributions made by John W. Tweeddale, "A John Owen bibliography," in Kelly M. Kapic and Mark Jones (eds.), *The Ashgate research companion to John Owen's theology* (Farnham, UK: Ashgate, 2012), pp. 297–328, and Mark Burden, "John Owen, learned Puritan," available at http://www.cems-oxford.org/projects/lucy-hutchinson/john-owen-learned-puritan, accessed on 1 June 2015. This bibliography does not include entries in standard reference works, including the *Oxford Dictionary of National Biography* and the *Calendar of State Papers*. Unless otherwise noted, all items are published in London.

MANUSCRIPTS

Christ Church Archives, Oxford

Deanary Papers ii.c.

Dean and Chapter i.b.3

Dr. Williams's Library, London

NCL, MS L6/2

NCL, MS L6/3

NCL, MS L6/4

Glasgow University Library

Ms Gen 3, "Sermons on Lamentations by David Dickson"

Ogilvie 728

University of Edinburgh, New College

New College Comm 1

New College Comm 2

University of Nottingham Library

MS C1. c, 84b

University of Oxford, Bodleian Library

OUA SP/E/4

Primary Sources
By John Owen

———, *Θεομαχία αυτεξουσιαστικη: or, A display of Arminianisme* (1643).
———, *The duty of pastors and people distinguished* (1644).
———, *The principles of the doctrine of Christ unfolded in two short catechismes* (1645).
———, *A vision of unchangeable free mercy* (1646).
———, *Eshcol, a cluster of the fruit of Canaan* (1647).
———, *Eben-ezer: a memoriall of the deliverance of Essex, county, and committee* (1648).
———, *Salus electorum, sanguis Jesu; or The death of death in the death of Christ* (1648).
———, *A sermon preached to the Honourable House of Commons, in Parliament assembled: on January 31* (1649).
———, *Certaine treatises written by John Owen M.A. Sometimes of Queens College in Oxford, now pastor of the church at Coggsehall in Essex. Formerly published at severall times, now reduced into one volume* (1649).
———, *Ουρανων ουρανια, The shaking and translating of heaven and earth* (1649).
———, *The branch of the Lord, the beauty of Sion: or, The glory of the Church, in its relation unto Christ* (1650).
———, *Of the death of Christ, the price he paid, and the purchase he made* (1650).
———, *The stedfastness of promises, and the sinfulness of staggering* (1650).
———, *The advantage of the kingdome of Christ in the shaking of the kingdoms of the world: or Providentiall alterations in their subserviency to Christ's exaltation* (1651).
———. "The Epistle Dedicatory," in Henry Whitfield, *Strength out of weakness; or a glorious manifestation of the further progress of the gospel among the Indians in New England* (1652).
———, *The labouring saints dismission to rest. A sermon preached at the funeral of the Right Honourable Henry Ireton Lord Deputy of Ireland* (1652).
———, *The primer: or, An easie way to teach children the true reading of English. With a necessary catechisme, to instruct youth in the grounds of Christian religion* (1652).
———, *The humble proposals of Mr. Owen, Mr. Tho. Goodwin, Mr. Nye, Mr. Sympson, and other ministers, who presented the petition to the Parliament, and other persons, Febr. 11. under debate by a committee this 31. of March, 1652. for the furtherance and propagation of the Gospel in this nation* (1652).
———, *A sermon preached to the Parliament, Octob. 13. 1652* (1652).
———, *Diatriba de justitia divina* (1653).
———, "Preface," in William Twisse, *The riches of God's love unto the vessells of mercy, consistent with his absolute hatred or reprobation of the vessells of wrath* (Oxford, 1653).
———, *The doctrine of the saints perseverance, explained and confirmed* (1654).
———, "Preface," in George Kendall, *Sancti sanciti, or, The common doctrine of the perseverance of the saints* (1654).
———, "To the Reader," in William Erye, *Vindiciæ justificationis gratuitæ* (1654).

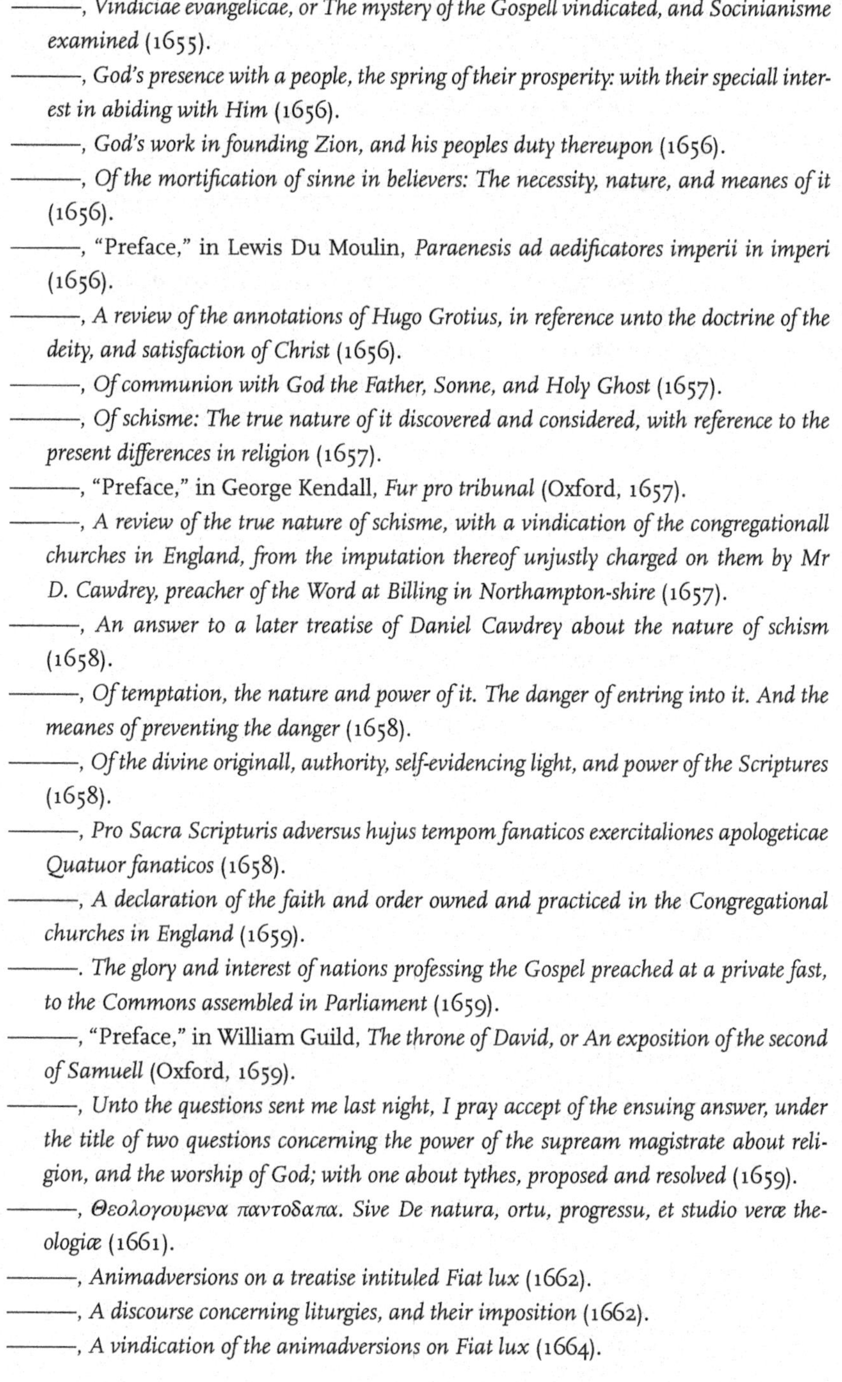

———, *Vindiciae evangelicae, or The mystery of the Gospell vindicated, and Socinianisme examined* (1655).

———, *God's presence with a people, the spring of their prosperity: with their speciall interest in abiding with Him* (1656).

———, *God's work in founding Zion, and his peoples duty thereupon* (1656).

———, *Of the mortification of sinne in believers: The necessity, nature, and meanes of it* (1656).

———, "Preface," in Lewis Du Moulin, *Paraenesis ad aedificatores imperii in imperi* (1656).

———, *A review of the annotations of Hugo Grotius, in reference unto the doctrine of the deity, and satisfaction of Christ* (1656).

———, *Of communion with God the Father, Sonne, and Holy Ghost* (1657).

———, *Of schisme: The true nature of it discovered and considered, with reference to the present differences in religion* (1657).

———, "Preface," in George Kendall, *Fur pro tribunal* (Oxford, 1657).

———, *A review of the true nature of schisme, with a vindication of the congregationall churches in England, from the imputation thereof unjustly charged on them by Mr D. Cawdrey, preacher of the Word at Billing in Northampton-shire* (1657).

———, *An answer to a later treatise of Daniel Cawdrey about the nature of schism* (1658).

———, *Of temptation, the nature and power of it. The danger of entring into it. And the meanes of preventing the danger* (1658).

———, *Of the divine originall, authority, self-evidencing light, and power of the Scriptures* (1658).

———, *Pro Sacra Scripturis adversus hujus tempom fanaticos exercitaliones apologeticae Quatuor fanaticos* (1658).

———, *A declaration of the faith and order owned and practiced in the Congregational churches in England* (1659).

———. *The glory and interest of nations professing the Gospel preached at a private fast, to the Commons assembled in Parliament* (1659).

———, "Preface," in William Guild, *The throne of David, or An exposition of the second of Samuell* (Oxford, 1659).

———, *Unto the questions sent me last night, I pray accept of the ensuing answer, under the title of two questions concerning the power of the supream magistrate about religion, and the worship of God; with one about tythes, proposed and resolved* (1659).

———, *Θεολογουμενα παντοδαπα. Sive De natura, ortu, progressu, et studio veræ theologiæ* (1661).

———, *Animadversions on a treatise intituled Fiat lux* (1662).

———, *A discourse concerning liturgies, and their imposition* (1662).

———, *A vindication of the animadversions on Fiat lux* (1664).

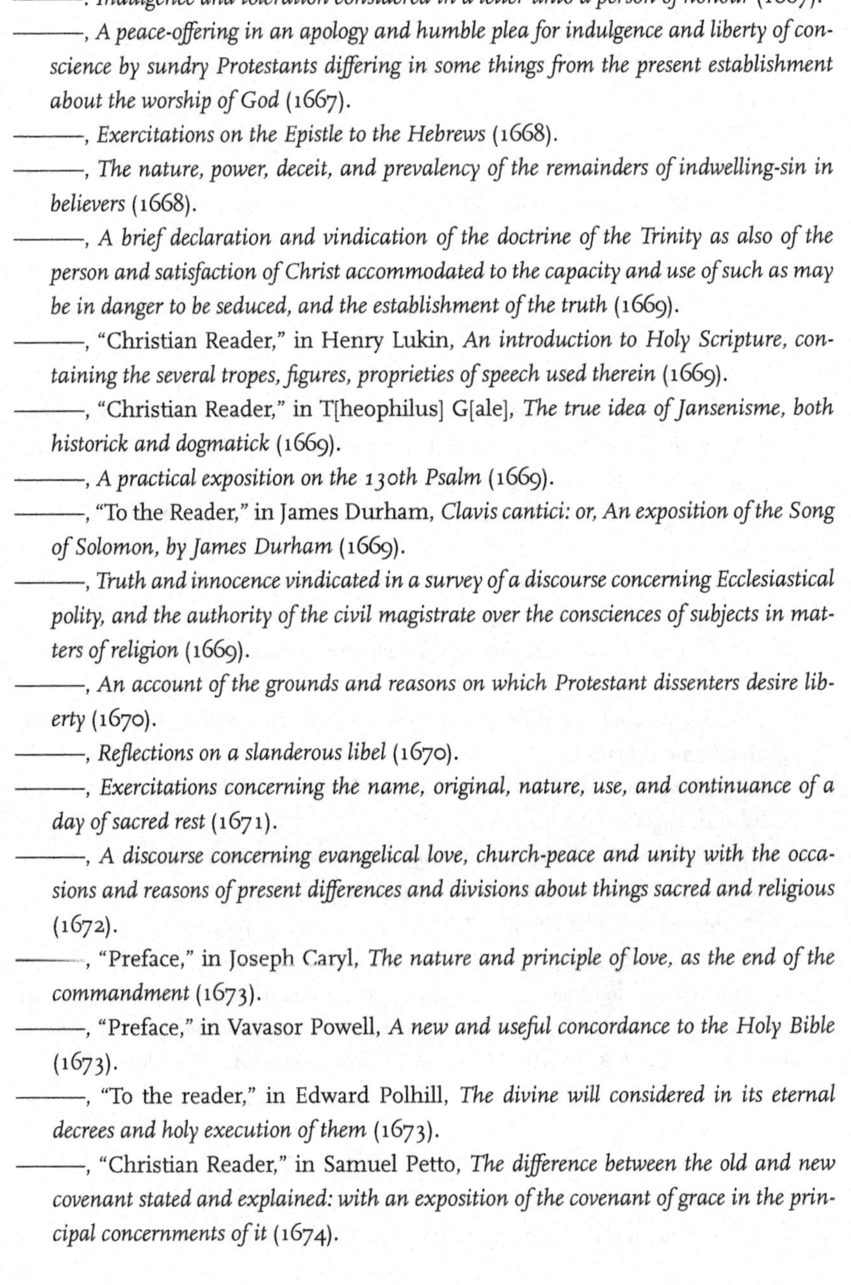

———. *A brief instruction in the worship of God, and discipline of the churches of the New Testament, by way of question and answer with an explication and confirmation of those answers* (1667).

———. *Indulgence and toleration considered in a letter unto a person of honour* (1667).

———, *A peace-offering in an apology and humble plea for indulgence and liberty of conscience by sundry Protestants differing in some things from the present establishment about the worship of God* (1667).

———, *Exercitations on the Epistle to the Hebrews* (1668).

———, *The nature, power, deceit, and prevalency of the remainders of indwelling-sin in believers* (1668).

———, *A brief declaration and vindication of the doctrine of the Trinity as also of the person and satisfaction of Christ accommodated to the capacity and use of such as may be in danger to be seduced, and the establishment of the truth* (1669).

———, "Christian Reader," in Henry Lukin, *An introduction to Holy Scripture, containing the several tropes, figures, proprieties of speech used therein* (1669).

———, "Christian Reader," in T[heophilus] G[ale], *The true idea of Jansenisme, both historick and dogmatick* (1669).

———, *A practical exposition on the 130th Psalm* (1669).

———, "To the Reader," in James Durham, *Clavis cantici: or, An exposition of the Song of Solomon, by James Durham* (1669).

———, *Truth and innocence vindicated in a survey of a discourse concerning Ecclesiastical polity, and the authority of the civil magistrate over the consciences of subjects in matters of religion* (1669).

———, *An account of the grounds and reasons on which Protestant dissenters desire liberty* (1670).

———, *Reflections on a slanderous libel* (1670).

———, *Exercitations concerning the name, original, nature, use, and continuance of a day of sacred rest* (1671).

———, *A discourse concerning evangelical love, church-peace and unity with the occasions and reasons of present differences and divisions about things sacred and religious* (1672).

———, "Preface," in Joseph Caryl, *The nature and principle of love, as the end of the commandment* (1673).

———, "Preface," in Vavasor Powell, *A new and useful concordance to the Holy Bible* (1673).

———, "To the reader," in Edward Polhill, *The divine will considered in its eternal decrees and holy execution of them* (1673).

———, "Christian Reader," in Samuel Petto, *The difference between the old and new covenant stated and explained: with an exposition of the covenant of grace in the principal concernments of it* (1674).

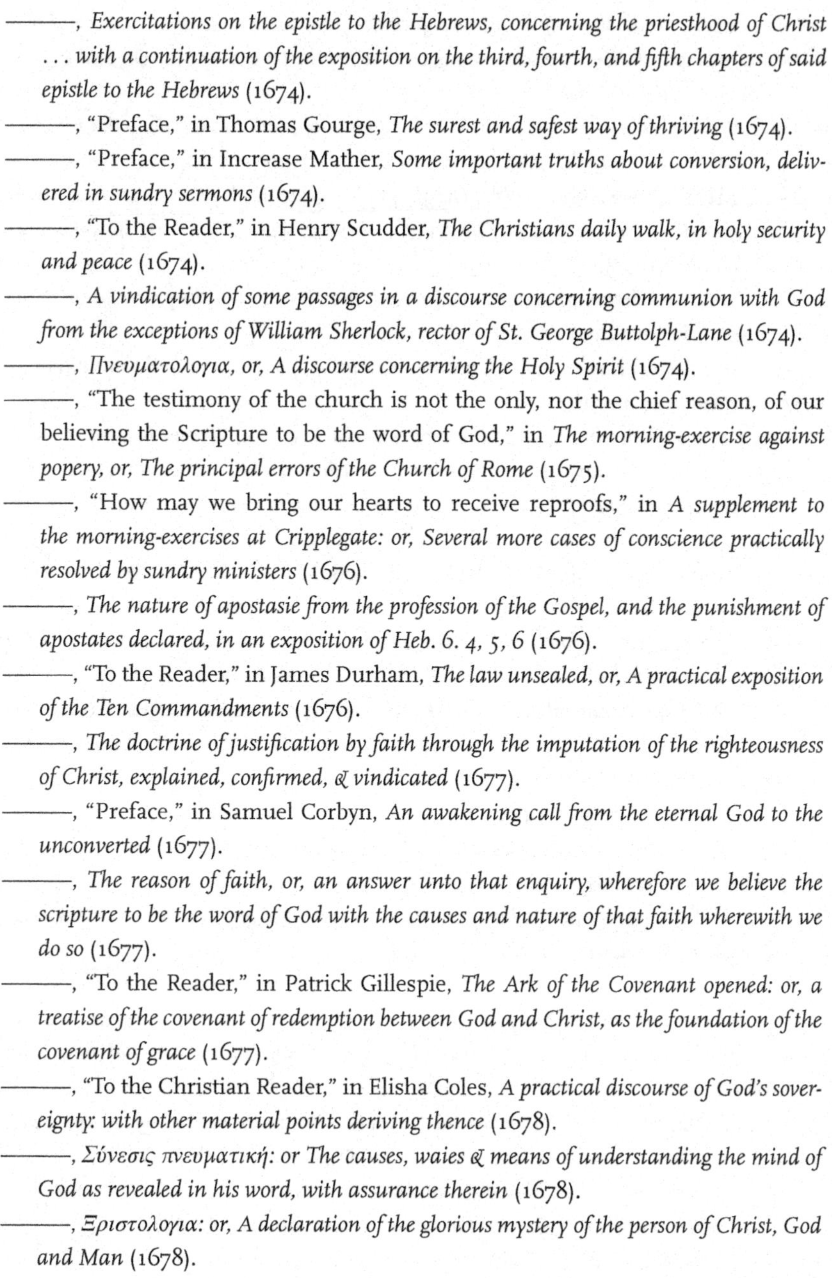

———, *Exercitations on the epistle to the Hebrews, concerning the priesthood of Christ . . . with a continuation of the exposition on the third, fourth, and fifth chapters of said epistle to the Hebrews* (1674).

———, "Preface," in Thomas Gourge, *The surest and safest way of thriving* (1674).

———, "Preface," in Increase Mather, *Some important truths about conversion, delivered in sundry sermons* (1674).

———, "To the Reader," in Henry Scudder, *The Christians daily walk, in holy security and peace* (1674).

———, *A vindication of some passages in a discourse concerning communion with God from the exceptions of William Sherlock, rector of St. George Buttolph-Lane* (1674).

———, *Πνευματολογια, or, A discourse concerning the Holy Spirit* (1674).

———, "The testimony of the church is not the only, nor the chief reason, of our believing the Scripture to be the word of God," in *The morning-exercise against popery, or, The principal errors of the Church of Rome* (1675).

———, "How may we bring our hearts to receive reproofs," in *A supplement to the morning-exercises at Cripplegate: or, Several more cases of conscience practically resolved by sundry ministers* (1676).

———, *The nature of apostasie from the profession of the Gospel, and the punishment of apostates declared, in an exposition of Heb. 6. 4, 5, 6* (1676).

———, "To the Reader," in James Durham, *The law unsealed, or, A practical exposition of the Ten Commandments* (1676).

———, *The doctrine of justification by faith through the imputation of the righteousness of Christ, explained, confirmed, & vindicated* (1677).

———, "Preface," in Samuel Corbyn, *An awakening call from the eternal God to the unconverted* (1677).

———, *The reason of faith, or, an answer unto that enquiry, wherefore we believe the scripture to be the word of God with the causes and nature of that faith wherewith we do so* (1677).

———, "To the Reader," in Patrick Gillespie, *The Ark of the Covenant opened: or, a treatise of the covenant of redemption between God and Christ, as the foundation of the covenant of grace* (1677).

———, "To the Christian Reader," in Elisha Coles, *A practical discourse of God's sovereignty: with other material points deriving thence* (1678).

———, *Σύνεσις πνευματική: or The causes, waies & means of understanding the mind of God as revealed in his word, with assurance therein* (1678).

———, *Ξριστολογια: or, A declaration of the glorious mystery of the person of Christ, God and Man* (1678).

———, *The church of Rome, no safe guide, or, Reasons to prove that no rational man, who takes due care of his own eternal salvation, can give himself up unto the conduct of that church in matters of religion* (1679).

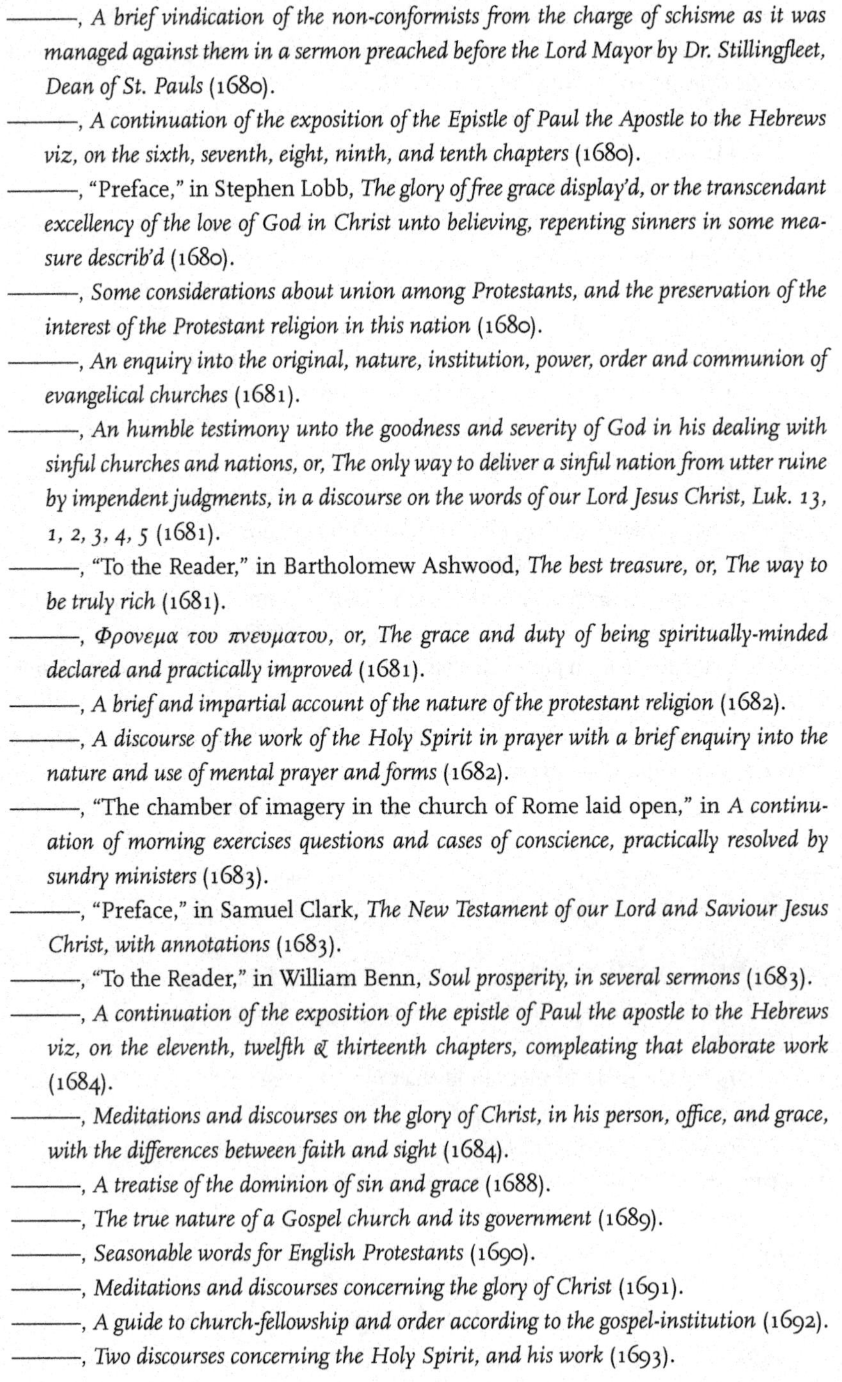

———, *A brief vindication of the non-conformists from the charge of schisme as it was managed against them in a sermon preached before the Lord Mayor by Dr. Stillingfleet, Dean of St. Pauls* (1680).

———, *A continuation of the exposition of the Epistle of Paul the Apostle to the Hebrews viz, on the sixth, seventh, eight, ninth, and tenth chapters* (1680).

———, "Preface," in Stephen Lobb, *The glory of free grace display'd, or the transcendant excellency of the love of God in Christ unto believing, repenting sinners in some measure describ'd* (1680).

———, *Some considerations about union among Protestants, and the preservation of the interest of the Protestant religion in this nation* (1680).

———, *An enquiry into the original, nature, institution, power, order and communion of evangelical churches* (1681).

———, *An humble testimony unto the goodness and severity of God in his dealing with sinful churches and nations, or, The only way to deliver a sinful nation from utter ruine by impendent judgments, in a discourse on the words of our Lord Jesus Christ, Luk. 13, 1, 2, 3, 4, 5* (1681).

———, "To the Reader," in Bartholomew Ashwood, *The best treasure, or, The way to be truly rich* (1681).

———, *Φρονεμα του πνευματου, or, The grace and duty of being spiritually-minded declared and practically improved* (1681).

———, *A brief and impartial account of the nature of the protestant religion* (1682).

———, *A discourse of the work of the Holy Spirit in prayer with a brief enquiry into the nature and use of mental prayer and forms* (1682).

———, "The chamber of imagery in the church of Rome laid open," in *A continuation of morning exercises questions and cases of conscience, practically resolved by sundry ministers* (1683).

———, "Preface," in Samuel Clark, *The New Testament of our Lord and Saviour Jesus Christ, with annotations* (1683).

———, "To the Reader," in William Benn, *Soul prosperity, in several sermons* (1683).

———, *A continuation of the exposition of the epistle of Paul the apostle to the Hebrews viz, on the eleventh, twelfth & thirteenth chapters, compleating that elaborate work* (1684).

———, *Meditations and discourses on the glory of Christ, in his person, office, and grace, with the differences between faith and sight* (1684).

———, *A treatise of the dominion of sin and grace* (1688).

———, *The true nature of a Gospel church and its government* (1689).

———, *Seasonable words for English Protestants* (1690).

———, *Meditations and discourses concerning the glory of Christ* (1691).

———, *A guide to church-fellowship and order according to the gospel-institution* (1692).

———, *Two discourses concerning the Holy Spirit, and his work* (1693).

———, *Gospel grounds and evidences of the faith of God's elect* (1695).
———, *An answer unto two questions: by the late judicious John Owen, D.D.* (1720).
———, *Seventeen sermons preach'd by the late reverend and learned John Owen, D. D.* (1720).
———, *A complete collection of the sermons of the reverend and learned John Owen, D.D. Formerly published: with an addition of many others never before printed. Also several valuable tracts, now first published from manuscripts: and some others, which were very scarce. To which are added his Latin orations, whilst vicechancellor of Oxford, taken from his own copies. And to the whole are prefix'd memoirs of his life: some letters written by him upon special occasions: and his funeral sermon, preach'd by Mr. David Clarkson* (1721).
———, *The works of the late reverend and learned John Owen, D.D.* (1721).
———, *Eene uitlegginge van den sendbrief van Paulus den apostel aen de Hebreen*, ed. Simon Commincq, 4 vols. (Rotterdam, 1733–1740).
———, *Thirteen sermons preached on various occasions. By the reverend and learned John Owen, D.D.* (1756).
———, *Twenty-five discourses suitable to the Lord's Supper, delivered just before the administration of that sacred ordinance* (1760).
———, *A treatise on the extent of the death of Christ. Being an abridgement of Dr. Owen's Death of death in the death of Christ, with a recommendatory preface by the Rev. Charles de Coetlogon* (1770).
———, *An exposition of the epistle to the Hebrews; with the preliminary exercitations, by John Owen, D. D., revised and abridged, with a full and interesting life of the author*, ed. Edward Williams, 4 vols. (1790).
———, *Marweiddiad pechod mewn credinwyr* (Mwythig, 1796).
———, *An exposition of the epistle to the Hebrews, with the preliminary exercitations*, ed. George Wright, 7 vols. (Edinburgh, 1812–14).
———, *The works of John Owen*, ed. Thomas Russell, 21 vols. (London, 1826).
———, *Evangelical theology: A translation of the sixth book of Dr. Owen's Latin work entitled Theologoumena*, trans. John Craig (Edinburgh: M. Paterson, 1837).
———, *The works of John Owen*, ed. William H. Goold, 24 vols. (Edinburgh: Johnstone and Hunter, 1850–55).
———, *The works of John Owen*, ed. William H. Goold, 23 vols., reprint (Edinburgh: Banner of Truth, 1965 [vols. 1–16]; 1991 [vols. 1–7 of Hebrews commentary]).
———, *The Oxford orations of John Owen*, ed. Peter Toon (Callington, Cornwall, UK: Gospel Communications, 1971).
———, *Biblical theology: The history of theology from Adam to Christ*, trans. Stephen P. Westcott (Morgan, PA: Soli Deo Gloria, 1994).

Modern Editions

———, *Hebrews: The epistle of warning*, ed. M. J. Tryon (Grand Rapids, MI: Kregel, 1953).

———, *The Holy Spirit: His gifts and power, exposition of the Spirit's name, nature, personality, dispensation, operations and effects* (Grand Rapids, MI: Kregel, 1954).

———, *The death of death in the death of Christ* (Edinburgh: Banner of Truth, 1959).

———, *The correspondence of John Owen (1616–1683): With an account of his life and work*, ed. Peter Toon (Cambridge: James Clarke, 1970).

———, *Sin and temptation: The challenge of personal godliness*, ed. James M. Houston (Portland, OR: Multnomah, 1983).

———, *Hebrews*, eds. Alister McGrath and J. I. Packer (Wheaton, IL: Crossway, 1988).

———, *Thinking spiritually* [from *The grace and duty of being spiritually minded*] (London: Grace Publications, 1989).

———, *Communion with God*, ed. R. K. Law (Edinburgh: Banner of Truth, 1991).

———, *Apostasy from the gospel*, ed. R. J. K. Law (Edinburgh: Banner of Truth, 1992).

———, *Christians are forever* [from *The doctrine of the saints' perseverance explained and confirmed*], ed. H. Lawrence (Darlington: Evangelical Press, 1993).

———, *The glory of Christ*, ed. R. J. K. Law (Edinburgh: Banner of Truth, 1994).

———, *The mortification of sin: A Puritan's view of how to deal with sin in your life* (Fearn, Ross-shire, UK: Christian Heritage, 1996).

———, *The Holy Spirit*, ed. R. J. K. Law (Edinburgh: Banner of Truth, 1998).

———, *The Spirit and the Church*, ed. R. J. K. Law (Edinburgh: Banner of Truth, 2002).

———, *The Holy Spirit: His gifts and power* (Fearn, Ross-shire, UK: Christian Heritage, 2004).

———, *Meditations on the glory of Christ* (Fearn, Ross-shire, UK: Christian Heritage, 2004).

———, *The doctrine of justification by faith: With an introductory essay by Carl R. Trueman* (Grand Rapids, MI: Reformation Heritage Books, 2006).

———, *Overcoming sin and temptation: Three classic works by John Owen*, eds. Kelly M. Kapic and Justin Taylor (Wheaton, MI: Crossway, 2006).

———, *Communion with God* (Fearn, Ross-shire, UK: Christian Heritage, 2007).

———, *Communion with the Triune God*, eds. Kelly M. Kapic and Justin Taylor (Wheaton, IL: Crossway, 2007).

———, *Spiritual-mindedness*, ed. R. J. K. Law (Edinburgh: Banner of Truth, 2009).

———, *The priesthood of Christ* (Fearn, Ross-shire, UK: Christian Heritage, 2010).

Other Primary Sources

An account of the life and death of Mr Philip Henry (1712).

Acts and ordinances of the Interregnum, 1642–1660, eds. C. H. Firth and R. S. Rait, 3 vols. (London: His Majesty's Stationery Office, 1911).

Alsop, Vincent, *A vindication of the faithful rebuke to a false report against the rude cavils of the pretended defence* (1698).

The arraignment of the divel, for stealing away President Bradshaw, To the tune of, Well-a-day, well-a-day (1659).

Asty, John, "Memoirs of the Life of John Owen, D. D.," in *A complete collection of the sermons of the Reverend and learned John Owen, D. D.* (1721).

Baron, William, *A just defence of the royal martyr, K. Charles I, from the many false and malicious aspersions in Ludlow's Memoirs and some other virulent libels of that kind* (1699).

Bartlet, William, *Ichnographia, or, A model of the primitive congregational way* (1647).

Baxter, Richard, *Aphorismes of justification* (The Hague, 1655).

———, *Catholick communion defended* (1684).

———, *Richard Baxter's penitent confession and his necessary vindication in answer to a book called The second part of the mischiefs of separation, written by an unnamed author with a preface to Mr. Cantianus D. Minimis, in answer to his letter which extorted this publication* (1691).

———, *Reliquiae Baxterianae, or, Mr. Richard Baxters narrative of the most memorable passages of his life and times faithfully publish'd from his own original manuscript by Matthew Sylvester* (1696).

Bellarminus junior enervatus: or The insufficiency of Mr. Richard Baxter's answer to Dr. Owen's twelve arguments about divine worship detected (1684).

Bolton, Samuel, *The true bounds of Christian freedome* (1645).

Bradshaws ultimum vale (1660).

Brandon, Richard, *The confession of Richard Brandon the hangman* (1649).

The British delegation at the Synod of Dort (1618–1619), ed. Anthony Milton (Woodbridge, UK: Boydell, 2005).

Brome, Alexander, *Rump, or, An exact collection of the choycest poems and songs relating to the late times by the most eminent wits from anno 1639 to anno 1661* (1662).

Brown, John, *The life of justification opened* (Holland, 1695).

[Butler, Samuel], *The transproser rehears'd* (1673).

———, *Hudibras in three parts* (1684).

Burgess, Cornelius, *Baptismall regeneration of elect infants professed by the Church of England, according to the Scriptures, the primitiue Church, the present reformed churches, and many particular divines apart* (Oxford, 1629).

Catalogus universalis librorum omnium in Bibliotheca Collegii Sionii apud Londinenses (1650).

Calvin, John, *Institutes of the Christian religion*, ed. John T. McNeill (Philadelphia, PA: Westminster Press, 1960).

C[ane], J[ohn] V[incent], *Fiat lux* (n.p., 1662).

———, *An epistle to the authour of the Animadversions upon Fiat lux. In excuse and justification of Fiat lux against the said Animadversions* (1663).

C[ane], J[ohn] V[incent], *Three letters declaring the strange odd proceedings of Protestant divines when they write against Catholicks: by the example of Dr Taylor's Dissuasive against popery, Mr Whitbies Reply in the behalf of Dr Pierce against Cressy, and Dr Owens Animadversions on Fiat lux* (1671).

Cardell, John, *Gods wisdom justified, and mans folly condemned, touching all maner of outward providential administrations* (1649).

Cawdrey, Daniel, *Independencie a great schism: Proved against Dr. Owen his apology in his tract Of Schism* (1657).

Chauncy, Isaac, *A theological dialogue: Containing the defence and justification of Dr. John Owen from the forty two errors charged upon him by Mr. Richard Baxter* (1684).

Chirk Castle accounts, A.D. 1666–1753, ed. William Martial Myddelton (Manchester: Manchester University Press, 1931).

Chyliński, Samuel Boguslaw, *An account of the translation of the Bible into the Lithuanian tongue* (Oxford, 1659).

Clagett, William, *A discourse concerning the operations of the Holy Spirit: with a confutation of some part of Dr. Owen's book upon that subject* (1678).

The Clarke papers: Selections from the papers of Sir William Clarke, ed. C. H. Firth, 4 vols. (London: Camden Society, 1904).

Clarkson, David, "A funeral sermon of the much lamented death of the late reverend and learned divine John Owen, D. D.," in *Seventeen sermons preach'd by the late reverend and learned John Owen, D. D.*, 2 vols. (1720).

A collection of the state papers of John Thurloe, ed. Thomas Birch, 7 vols. (London, 1742).

Collier, Thomas, *A compendious discourse about some of the greatest matters of Christian faith* (1682).

The correspondence of John Locke, 8 vols., ed. E. S. de Beer (Oxford: Clarendon Press, 1976).

Crippen, T. G., "Dr Watts's church-book," *Transactions of the Congregational Historical Society* 1 (1901–4).

Cromwell, Henry, *The correspondence of Henry Cromwell, 1655–1659*, ed. Peter Gaunt (Cambridge: Cambridge University Press, 2007).

Cromwell, Oliver, *The writings and speeches of Oliver Cromwell*, ed. W. C. Abbott, 4 vols. (Cambridge, MA: Harvard University Press, 1947).

A declaration of several of the churches of Christ, and the godly people in and about the citie of London (1654).

A dialogue between the Pope and the Devil, about Owen and Baxter (1681).

The diary of John Evelyn, ed. Guy de la Bédoyère (Woodbridge, UK: Boydell, 1995).

The diary of Ralph Josselin, 1616–1683, ed. Alan Macfarlane, Records of Social and Economic History (Oxford: Oxford University Press, 1976).

The diary of Robert Woodford, ed. John Fielding, Camden fifth series (Cambridge: Cambridge University Press, 2013).

The diary of Samuel Pepys, eds. Robert Latham and William Matthews (London: Bell, 1970).

The diary of Samuel Rogers, 1634–1638, eds. Tom Webster and Kenneth Shipps (Woodbridge, UK: Boydell, 2004).

The diary of Sir Archibald Johnston of Wariston, ed. D. H. Fleming, 3 vols. (Edinburgh, 1919–40).

The diary of Thomas Burton, ed. J. T. Rutt, 4 vols. (London, 1828).

The diary of Thomas Crosfield, ed. Frederick S. Boas (London: Oxford University Press, 1935).

The diurnal of Thomas Rugg, 1659–61, ed. W. L. Sachse (London: Camden Society, 1961).

The division of the county of Essex into several classes, together with the names of the ministers and others fit to be of each classis (1648).

Edwards, Thomas, *Gangreana*, 3 vols. (1646).

An elegy on the death of that learned, pious, and famous divine, Doctor John Owen (1683).

Elys, Edmund. *Animadversions upon some passages in a book entituled The true nature of a gospel-church and its government written (as it is said by the publisher) by John Owen* (1690).

The entring book of Roger Morrice, ed. Mark Goldie et al., 6 vols. (Rochester, NY: Boydell and Brewer, 2007).

The Essex watchmen's watchword (1649).

F. V., *Detur pulchriori, or, A poem in the praise of the University of Oxford* (1658).

A faithfull searching home word (1659).

"The first publishers of truth," being early records (now first printed) of the introduction of Quakerism into the counties of England and Wales, supplements 1–5, *Journal of the Friends Historical Society*, ed. N. Penney (1907).

Fisher, Samuel, *Rusticus ad academicos in exercitationibus expostulatoriis, apologeticis quatuor* (1660).

Four petitions to his excellency Sir Thomas Fairfax (1647).

Gadbury, John, *De cometis* (1665).

Gale, Theophilus, *The true idea of Jansenism* (1669).

Goodwin, John, *An answer to a printed paper: Wherein . . . the predominant designe of it fully evinced to be, either an unscholarlike oscitancie and mistake, or else somewhat much worse* (1649).

———, *Triumviri . . . Together with some brief touches (in the preface) upon Dr. John Owen, Mr. Thomas Lamb (of the Spittle), Mr. Henry Jeanes, Mr. Obadiah How, and Mr. Marchamond Needham, in relation to their late writings against the author* (1658).

Guild, William, *The throne of David* (Oxford, 1659).

Hammond, Henry, *An answer to the animadversions on the dissertations touching Ignatius's epistles, and the episcopacie in them asserted* (1654).

Hammond, Henry, *A continuation of the defence of Hugo Grotius, in an answer to the review of his annotations* (1657).

A history of the county of Essex, vol. 10: *Lexden Hundred (part) including Dedham, Earls Colne and Wivenhoe* (London: Victoria County History, 2001).

The holy and profitable sayings of that learned and reverend divine, Dr. John Owen, who departed this life August 1683, and left behind him these excellent sentences, very useful for all families, for the benefit and instruction of the ignorant, and those that have not time or opportunity to peruse the practical treatises of divinity abroad in the world; together with his last prayer before he departed (1683).

Horn, John, *Thyra aneogmene. The open door for mans approach to God . . . In answer to a treatise of Master John Owen* (1650).

———, *Independency further proved to be a schism, or, A survey of Dr Owens review of his tract of schism* (1658).

Hotchkis, Thomas, *A discourse concerning the imputation of Christ's righteousness to us, and our sins to him; with many useful questions, thereunto pertaining, resolved. Together with reflections more at large upon what hath been published concerning that subject by Mr. Robert Ferguson in his Interest of reason in religion; and by Dr. John Owen in his book styled Communion with God* (1675).

———, *A postscript, containing the authors vindication of himself and the doctrine from the imputations of Dr. John Owen* (1678).

Howe, Obadiah, *The universalist examined and convicted* (1648).

Hull, John, "Diary," *Archaeologia Americana: Transactions and collections of the American Antiquarian Society* 3 (1857).

Humble proposals concerning the printing of the Bible (1650).

Humfrey, John, *Peaceable disquisitions: which treat of the natural and spiritual man, preaching with the demonstration of the Spirit, praying by the Spirit. Assurance, the Arminian grace, possibility of heathens salvation, the reconciliation of Paul and James, the imputation of Christ's righteousness; with other incident matters. In some animadversions on a discourse writ against Dr. Owen's Book of the Holy Spirit* (1678).

Hutchinson, Lucy, *On the principles of the Christian religion, addressed to her daughter; and On theology* (London, 1817).

———, *Memoirs of the life of Colonel Hutchinson*, ed. C. H. Firth, 2 vols. (London, 1885, 1906).

———, *Order and disorder*, ed. David Norbrook (Oxford: Blackwell, 2001).

———, *The works of Lucy Hutchinson*, vol. 2: *Theological writings*, eds. Elizabeth Clarke, David Norbrook, and Jane Stevenson (Oxford: Oxford University Press, forthcoming).

Hyde, Edward, earl of Clarendon, *Transcendent and multiplied rebellion and treason, discovered, by the lawes of the land* (n.d.).

I[reland?], T[homas?]. *Momus elencticus or A light come-off upon that serious piece of drollerie presented by the Vice Chancellor of Oxon in the name of all his mirmidons at*

Whitehall, to expell the melancholy of the court, and to tickle its gizzard with a land-skip of dancing fryars to their own musick and number (1654).

[J. G.], *Moses in the mount, or The beloved disciple leaning on Jesus' bosom. Being a narrative of the life and death of Mr. John Murcot* (1657).

The life and poems of William Cartwright, ed. R. Cullis Goffin (Cambridge: Cambridge University Press, 1918).

Long, Thomas, *An exercitation concerning the frequent use of our Lords Prayer in the publick worship of God. And a view of what hath been said by Dr. Owen concerning that subject* (1658).

Marvell, Andrew, *The rehearsal transpros'd and The rehearsal transpros'd the second part*, ed. D. I. B. Smith (Oxford: Clarendon Press, 1971).

Mather, Cotton, *Magnalia Christi Americana*, 2 vols. (1702; rpt. Hartford: Silus Andrus and Son, 1853).

Mayne, Jasper, *The amorous warre, A tragi-comoedy* (Oxford, 1659).

Middlesex county records, ed. J. C. Jeaffreson, 4 vols. (London: Middlesex County Record Society, 1888).

Millington, Edward, *Bibliotheca Oweniana* (1684).

Milton, John, *The complete poetry and essential prose of John Milton*, ed. William Kerrigan, John Rumrich, and Stephen M. Fallon (New York: The Modern Library, 2007).

———, *Life records of John Milton, 1608–1674*, ed. J. Milton French, 2 vols. (New Brunswick, NJ: Rutgers University Press, 1949–50).

———. *The complete prose works of John Milton*, ed. D. M. Wolfe (New Haven, CT: Yale University Press, 1953–82).

Monck, George, *A collection of letters written his Excellency General George Monck*, ed. John Toland (London, 1714).

Musarum Oxoniensium (1654).

Musarum Oxoniensium charisteria pro serenissima Regina Maria (Oxford, 1639).

Musarum Oxoniensium pro Rege suo soteria anagramma (Oxford, 1633).

Nalton, James, *Delay of reformation provoking Gods further indignation* (1646).

The New Testament of our Lord and Saviour Jesus Christ with annotations, ed. Samuel Clark (1683).

Original memoirs written during the Great Civil War; being the life of Sir Henry Slingsby, and memoirs of Capt. Hodgson (Edinburgh, 1806).

Orme, William, *Memoirs of the life, writings, and religious connexions, of John Owen, D. D., vice-chancellor of Oxford and dean of Christ Church, during the Commonwealth* (London: T. Hamilton, 1820).

———, "Memoirs of the life and writings of Dr John Owen," in *The works of John Owen*, ed. Thomas Russell (London: Paternoster, 1826), vol 1.

Parker, Samuel, *A defence and continuation of the ecclesiastical politie, by way of letter to a friend in London* (1671).

Parker, Samuel, *Bishop Bramhall's Vindication of himself and the episcopal clergy from the Presbyterian charge of Popery* (1672).

———, *Preface to Bishop Bramhall's Vindication* (1672).

Perrinchief, Richard, *Indulgence not justified: being a continuation of the Discourse of toleration* (1668).

Pope, Walter, *The life of the Right Reverend Father in God, Lord Bishop of Salisbury* (London, 1697).

The Presbyterian lash, or, Noctroff's maid whipt (1661).

The register of the visitors of the University of Oxford, from ad 1647 to AD *1658*, ed. M. Barrows (London, 1881).

Rogers, John, *Ohel or Bethshemesh* (1653).

Rolle, Samuel, *An impartial vindication of the clergy of England. In a letter to a friend, in which are intermixt several passages, which may serve as a reply to Dr. Owen's and Mr. Baxter's late answers to Dr. Stillingfleet's sermon, entituled the mischief of separation* (1680).

Rutherford, Samuel, *A free disputation against pretended liberty of conscience* (1649).

Ryland, John, *Contemplations on the eternal and immutable justice of God, from the Latin dissertations of Dr. John Owen* (1787).

Schellinks, William, *The journals of William Schellinks' travels in England, 1661–1663*, trans. and ed. Maurice Exwood and H. L. Lehmann (London: Royal Historical Society, 1993).

Scottow, Joshua, *A narrative of the planting of the Massachusetts colony anno 1628. With the Lord's signal presence the first thirty years. Also a caution from New-Englands apostle, the great Cotton, how to escape the calamity, which might befall them or their posterity. And confirmed by the evangelist Norton with prognosticks from the famous Dr. Owen* (1694).

A seasonable and necessary warning (1650).

Sellers, William, *An examination of a late book published by Doctor Owen, concerning a sacred day of rest* (1671).

Shakespeare, William, *The Norton Shakespeare*, ed. Stephen Greenblatt (New York: Norton, 1997).

Teate, Faithful, *Ter tria*, ed. Angelina Lynch (Dublin: Four Courts, 2007).

To all printers, booke-sellers, booke-binders, free-men of the Company of Stationers (1645).

Vernon, George, *A letter to a friend concerning some of John Owen's principles* (1670).

A vindication of Owen by a friendly scrutiny (1684).

Wallis, John, *Johann Wallisii . . . elenchus geometriae Hobbianae* (1655).

Walton, Brian, *The considerator considered: or, A brief view of certain considerations upon the Biblia polyglotta, the prolegomena and appendix thereof* (1659).

Warren, John, *The potent potter* (1649).

Watkins, Richard, *Newes from the dead* (1651).

[Westminster Assembly,] *A directory for the publique worship of God in the three kingdomes* (1645).

———, *The minutes and papers of the Westminster Assembly, 1643–1652*, ed. Chad van Dixhoorn, 5 vols. (Oxford: Oxford University Press, 2012).

Whitehead, George, *The divinity of Christ, and unity of the three that bear record in heaven* (1669).

Whitelock, Bulstrode, *Memorials of the English affairs*, new ed. (London, 1732).

William Bentley printer at Finsbury near London, touching his right to the printing of Bibles and Psalms (1656).

Woodward, Ezekias, *A treatise of prayer* (1656).

Wright, Abraham, *Parnassus biceps* (1656).

Vernon, George, *A letter to a friend concerning some of Dr. Owens principles and practices* (1670).

A vindication of the late reverend and learned John Owen D.D. By a friendly scrutiny into the merits, and manner of Mr. Rich. Baxters opposition to twelve arguments concerning worship by the lyturgy, said to be Dr. Owens (1684).

Y. J., *Animadversions on the late very reverend Mr. Corbet's remains, and humble endeavour. As also, concerning justification, against the late worthy Mr. Gibbons, Mr. Truman, and Dr. Owen* (1685).

Young, Arthur (ed.), *Oweniana: or, Select passages from the works of Owen* (London: J. Hatchard, 1817).

Secondary Sources

Achinstein, Sharon, *Literature and dissent in Milton's England* (Cambridge: Cambridge University Press, 2003).

Adamson, John, "The frighted junto: Perceptions of Ireland, and the last attempts at settlement with Charles I," in Jason Peacey (ed.), *The regicides and the execution of Charles I* (New York: Palgrave Macmillan, 2001).

———, *The noble revolt: The overthrow of Charles I* (London: Weidenfeld and Nicolson, 2007).

Appleby, David J., *Black Bartholomew's Day: Preaching, polemic and Restoration nonconformity* (Manchester: Manchester University Press, 2007).

Ashton, Robert, *Counter-revolution: The second civil war and its origins, 1646–8* (New Haven, CT: Yale University Press, 1994).

Baker, Wayne J., "Church, state, and toleration: John Locke and Calvin's heirs in England, 1644–1689," in W. Fred Graham (ed.), *Later Calvinism: International perspectives* (Kirksville, MO: Sixteenth Century Journal Publishers, 1994).

Barcellos, Richard C., "John Owen and New Covenant theology," *Reformed Baptist Theological Review* 1 (2004).

Barcellos, Richard C. *The family tree of Reformed biblical theology: Geerhardus Vos and John Owen* (Owensboro, KY: Reformed Baptist Academic Press, 2010).

Bardsley, C. W., *Curiosities of Puritan nomenclature* (London: Chatto & Windus, 1880).

Barraclough, Peter, *John Owen, 1616–1683* (London: Independent Press, 1961).

Barrett, Matthew, and Michael A. G. Haykin, *Owen on the Christian life: Living for the glory of God in Christ* (Wheaton, IL: Crossway, 2015).

Bebbington, David W., *Evangelicalism in modern Britain: A history from the 1730s to the 1980s* (London: Unwin Hyman, 1989).

Beddard, R. A., "Restoration Oxford," in Nicholas Tyacke (ed.), *The history of the University of Oxford*, vol. 4: *Seventeenth-century Oxford* (Oxford: Clarendon Press, 1997).

———, "A projected Cromwellian foundation at Oxford and the 'true reformed Protestant interest,' c. 1657–8," *History of Universities* 15 (1999).

Beeke, Joel R., *Assurance of faith: Calvin, English Puritanism, and the Dutch Second Reformation* (New York: Peter Lang, 1991).

———, *The quest for full assurance: The legacy of Calvin and his successors* (Edinburgh: Banner of Truth, 1999).

———, and Randall J. Pederson, *Meet the Puritans: With a guide to modern reprints* (Grand Rapids, MI: Reformation Heritage Books, 2006).

———, and Mark Jones, *A Puritan theology: Doctrine for life* (Grand Rapids, MI: Reformation Heritage Books, 2012).

Bennett, Martyn, *The civil wars in Britain and Ireland, 1638–1651* (Oxford: Blackwell, 1997).

Bill, E. G. W., *Education at Christ Church, Oxford, 1660–1800* (Oxford: Clarendon Press, 1988).

Blagden, Cyprian, *The Stationers' Company: A history, 1403–1959* (London: Allen & Unwin, 1960).

Boersma, Hans, *A hot pepper corn: Richard Baxter's doctrine of justification in its seventeenth century context of controversy* (Zoetermeer: Uitgeverij Boekencentrum, 1993).

Boran, Elizabethanne, "The libraries of Luke Challoner and James Ussher, 1595–1608," in H. H. W. Robinson-Hammerstein (ed.), *European universities in the age of the Reformation* (Dublin: Four Courts, 1998).

Braithwaite, W. C., *The beginnings of Quakerism*, second edition (Cambridge: Cambridge University Press, 1961).

Bremer, Francis J., *Lay empowerment and the development of Puritanism* (New York: Palgrave Macmillan, 2015).

Burden, Mark, review of Tim Cooper, *John Owen, Richard Baxter and the formation of nonconformity*, in *Congregational History Society Magazine* 6:5 (2012).

———, "A biographical dictionary of tutors at the dissenters' private academies, 1660–1729," Dr. Williams's Centre for Dissenting Studies (2013), available at http://www.english.qmul.ac.uk/drwilliams/pubs/dictionary.html, accessed 1 June 2015.

Burgess, Glenn, "Usurpation, obligation, and obedience in the thought of the Engagement controversy," *Historical Journal* 29:3 (1986).

Burns, William E., *An age of wonders: Prodigies, politics and providence in England, 1657–1727* (Manchester: Manchester University Press, 2002).

Cambers, Andrew, *Godly reading: Print, manuscript and Puritanism in England, 1580–1720* (Cambridge: Cambridge University Press, 2011).

Campbell, Gordon, and Thomas N. Corns, *John Milton: Life, work, and thought* (Oxford: Oxford University Press, 2008).

Capp, B. S. *England's culture wars: Puritan reformation and its enemies in the Interregnum, 1649–1660* (Oxford: Oxford University Press, 2012).

Caricchio, Mario, "*News from the New Jerusalem*: Giles Calvert and the radical experience," in Ariel Hessayon and David Finnegan (eds.), *Varieties of seventeenth- and eighteenth-century English radicalism in context* (Farnham, UK: Ashgate, 2011).

Carr, Simonetta, *John Owen* (Grand Rapids, MI: Reformation Heritage Books, 2010).

Caughey, Christopher E., "Puritan responses to antinomianism in the context of Reformed covenant theology, 1630–1696" (unpublished PhD thesis, Trinity College Dublin, 2013).

Chapman, Alister, John Coffey, and Brad S. Gregory (eds.), *Seeing things their way: Intellectual history and the return of religion* (South Bend, IN: University of Notre Dame Press, 2009).

Chartier, Roger, *The cultural uses of print in early modern France*, trans. Lydia G. Cochrane (Princeton, NJ: Princeton University Press, 1987).

Clare, Janet (ed.), *Drama of the English republic, 1649–60* (Manchester: Manchester University Press, 2002).

Clark, J. C. D., *English society, 1688–1832: Ideology, social structure and political practice during the Ancien Regime* (Cambridge: Cambridge University Press, 1985).

Clarke, Elizabeth, *Politics, religion and the Song of Songs in seventeenth-century England* (New York: Palgrave, 2011).

Cleveland, Christopher, *Thomism in John Owen* (Farnham, UK: Ashgate, 2013).

Clifford, Alan C., *Atonement and justification: English evangelical theology, 1640–1790* (Oxford: Clarendon Press, 1990).

Coffey, John, *Politics, religion and the British revolutions: The mind of Samuel Rutherford* (Cambridge: Cambridge University Press, 1997).

———, "Defining heresy and orthodoxy in the Puritan revolution," in David Loewenstein and John Marshall (eds.), *Heresy, literature and politics in early modern English culture* (Cambridge: Cambridge University Press, 2006).

———, *John Goodwin and the Puritan revolution: Religion and intellectual change in 17th-century England* (Woodbridge, UK: Boydell, 2006).

Coffey, John, "The toleration controversy during the English revolution," in Christopher Durston and Judith Maltby (eds.), *Religion in revolutionary England* (Manchester: Manchester University Press, 2006).

———, "Puritan legacies," in John Coffey and Paul C.-H. Lim (eds.), *The Cambridge companion to Puritanism* (Cambridge: Cambridge University Press, 2008).

———, "Lloyd-Jones and the Protestant past," in Andrew Atherstone and David Ceri Jones (eds.), *Engaging with Martyn Lloyd-Jones* (Nottingham: Apollos, 2011).

———, "John Owen and the Puritan toleration controversy, 1646–59," in Kelly M. Kapic and Mark Jones (eds.), *The Ashgate research companion to John Owen's theology* (Farnham, UK: Ashgate, 2012).

Collins, Jeffrey R., "The church settlement of Oliver Cromwell," *History* 87 (2002).

———, *The allegiance of Thomas Hobbes* (Oxford: Oxford University Press, 2007).

Collinson, Patrick, *The Elizabethan Puritan movement* (London: Jonathan Cape, 1967).

Cook, Sarah Gibbard, "A political biography of a religious Independent: John Owen, 1616–1683" (unpublished PhD thesis, Harvard University, 1972).

Cooper, Tim, *Fear and polemic in seventeenth-century England: Richard Baxter and antinomianism* (Aldershot, UK: Ashgate, 2001).

———, "State of the field: John Owen unleased: Almost." *Conversations in Religion and Theology* 6 (2008).

———, "Why did Richard Baxter and John Owen diverge? The impact of the First Civil War." *Journal of Ecclesiastical History* 61 (2010).

———, *John Owen, Richard Baxter, and the formation of nonconformity* (Farnham, UK: Ashgate, 2011).

———, "Owen's personality: The man behind the theology," in Kelly M. Kapic and Mark Jones (eds.), *The Ashgate research companion to John Owen's theology* (Aldershot, UK: Ashgate, 2012).

Coster, Will, *Baptism and spiritual kinship in early modern England* (Aldershot, UK: Ashgate, 2002).

Cowan, Martyn C., "The prophetic preaching of John Owen from 1646 to 1659 in its historical context" (unpublished PhD thesis, University of Cambridge, 2012).

Craig, John, "The growth of English Puritanism," in John Coffey and Paul C.-H. Lim (eds.), *The Cambridge companion to Puritanism* (Cambridge: Cambridge University Press, 2008).

Cressy, David, "Books as totems in seventeenth-century England and New England," *Journal of Library History* 21 (1986).

———, *England on edge: Crisis and revolution, 1640–1642* (Oxford: Oxford University Press, 2006).

Cross, Claire, "The church in England, 1646–1660," in G. E. Aylmer (ed.), *The Interregnum: The quest for settlement* (London: Macmillan, 1972).

Cummings, Brian, *The literary culture of the reformation: Grammar and grace* (Oxford: Oxford University Press, 2002).

Curthoys, Judith, *The Cardinal's college: Christ Church, Chapter and verse* (London: Profile, 2012).

Dale, B., *The annals of Coggeshall, otherwise Sunnedon, in the county of Essex* (Coggeshall, 1863).

Daniell, David, *The Bible in English: Its history and influence* (New Haven, CT: Yale University Press, 2003).

Daniels, Richard W., *The Christology of John Owen* (Grand Rapids, MI: Reformed Heritage Books, 2004).

Darnton, Robert, "In search of the Enlightenment: Recent attempts to create a social history of ideas," *Journal of Modern History* 43:1 (1971).

Davids, T. W., *Annals of evangelical nonconformity in the county of Essex* (London, 1863).

Davis, J. C., "Cromwell's religion," in John Morrill (ed.), *Oliver Cromwell and the English revolution* (London: Longman, 1990).

Davis, Natalie Zemon, *Society and culture in early modern France* (Stanford, CA: Stanford University Press, 1975).

de Vries, Peter, "Union and communion with Christ in the theology of John Owen," *Reformed Theological Journal* 15 (1999).

———, "The significance of union and communion with Christ in the theology of John Owen (1616–1683)," *Reformed Theological Journal* 17 (2001).

De Kray, Gary S., *London and the Restoration, 1659–1683* (Cambridge: Cambridge University Press, 2005).

Diggins, John Patrick, "Arthur O. Lovejoy and the challenge of intellectual history," *Journal of the History of Ideas* 67:1 (2006).

Dimmock, Matthew, Andrew Hadfield, and Margaret Healy (eds), *The intellectual culture of the English country house, 1500–1700* (Manchester: Manchester University Press, 2015).

Dixon, Philip, *Nice and hot disputes: The doctrine of the Trinity in the seventeenth century* (London: T & T Clark, 2003).

Doerksen, Daniel W., "The Laudian interpretation of Herbert," *Literature and History* 3:2 (1994).

———, *Picturing religious experience: George Herbert, Calvin and the Scriptures* (Newark: University of Delaware Press, 2011).

Donogan, Barbara, *War in England, 1642–1649* (Oxford: Oxford University Press, 2008).

Dow, Frances, *Cromwellian Scotland, 1651–1660* (Edinburgh: John Donald, 1979).

Duffy, Eamon, *The voices of Morebath: Reformation and rebellion in an English village* (New Haven, CT: Yale University Press, 2001).

———, *The stripping of the altars: Traditional religion in England, c. 1400–c. 1580*, second edition (New Haven, CT: Yale University Press, 2005).

Dunlop, Robert (ed.), *Ireland under the Commonwealth*, 2 vols. (Manchester: Manchester University Press, 1913).

Dunn, John, "The identity of the history of ideas," in Peter Laslett, Quentin Skinner, and W. G. Runciman (eds.), *Philosphy, politics and society*, fourth series (Oxford: Blackwell, 1982).

Durston, Christopher, *Cromwell's major-generals: Godly government during the English revolution* (Manchester: Manchester University Press, 2001).

———, and Judith Maltby (eds), *Religion in revolutionary England* (Manchester: Manchester University Press, 2006).

Eales, Jacqueline, "A road to revolution: The continuity of Puritanism, 1559–1642," in Christopher Durston and Jacqueline Eales (eds.), *The culture of English Puritanism, 1560–1700* (Basingstoke, UK: Palgrave 1996).

Elliott, John R., "Drama," in Nicholas Tyacke (ed.), *The history of the University of Oxford*, vol. 4: *Seventeenth-century Oxford* (Oxford: Clarendon Press, 1997).

Engelsing, Rolf, *Der Bürger als Leser: Lesergeschichte in Deutschland, 1500–1800* (Stuttgart, Germany: Metzler, 1974).

Everitt, A.M., *The Community of Kent and the Great Rebellion* (Leicester, UK: Leicester University Press, 1966).

Fasti Ecclesiae Anglicanae, 1541–1857, vol. 8: *Bristol, Gloucester, Oxford and Peterborough dioceses*, ed. Joyce M. Horn (London: Institute for Historical Research, 1996).

Ferguson, Sinclair B., *John Owen on the Christian life* (Edinburgh: Banner of Truth, 1987).

———, "John Owen and the doctrine of the Holy Spirit," in Robert W. Oliver (ed.), *John Owen: The man and his theology* (Phillipsburg, NJ: P & R, 2002).

———, "John Owen and the doctrine of the person of Christ." in Robert W. Oliver (ed.), *John Owen: The man and his theology* (Phillipsburg, NJ: P & R, 2002).

———, *The Trinitarian devotion of John Owen* (Sanford, FL: Reformation Trust, 2014).

Feingold, Mordechai, "The humanities," in *The history of the University of Oxford*, vol. 4: *The seventeenth century*, ed. Nicholas Tyacke (Oxford: Oxford University Press, 1997).

Firth, C. H. (ed.), *Scotland and the Commonwealth: Letters and papers* (Edinburgh: Scottish History Society, 1895).

Foord, Martin, "John Owen's gospel offer: Well-meant or not?" in Kelly M. Kapic and Mark Jones (eds.), *The Ashgate research companion to John Owen's theology* (Aldershot, UK: Ashgate, 2012).

Ford, Alan, *James Ussher: Theology, history, and politics in early-modern Ireland and England* (Oxford: Oxford University Press, 2007).

Foster, Joseph, *Alumni Oxonienses* (Oxford: Oxford University Press, 1891).

Foucault, Michel, *The order of things: An archaeology of the human sciences* (London: Pantheon Books, 1970).

French, H. R., and R. W. Hoyle, "*English individualism* refuted—and reasserted: The land market of Earls Colne (Essex), 1550–1750," *Economic History Review* 56 (2003).

Gardiner. S. R. *History of the Commonwealth and Protectorate, 1649–1656*, 4 vols. (London, 1903).

——— (ed.), *The constitutional documents of the Puritan revolution, 1625–1660*, third edition (Oxford: Clarendon Press, 1936).

Gatiss, Lee, *From life's first cry: John Owen on infant baptism and infant salvation* (London: Latimer Trust, 2008); partially reprinted as "From life's first cry: John Owen on infant baptism and infant salvation," in Kelly M. Kapic and Mark Jones (eds.), *The Ashgate research companion to John Owen's theology* (Aldershot, UK: Ashgate, 2012).

———, "Adoring the fullness of the Scriptures in John Owen's commentary on Hebrews" (unpublished PhD thesis, University of Cambridge, 2013).

Gentles, Ian, "The politics of Fairfax's army, 1645–9," in John Adamson (ed.), *The English civil war* (New York: Palgrave Macmillan, 2009).

———, *Oliver Cromwell: God's warrior and the English revolution* (New York: Palgrave Macmillan, 2011).

Gleason, Randall C., *John Calvin and John Owen on mortification: A comparative study in Reformed spirituality* (New York: Peter Lang, 1995).

Goldgar, Anne, *Impolite learning: Conduct and community in the Republic of Letters, 1680–1750* (New Haven, CT: Yale University Press, 1995).

Goldie, Mark "Obligations, utopias and their historical context," *Historical Journal* 26 (1983).

Gilmont, Jean-François (ed.), *The reformation and the book*, trans. Karin Maag (Aldershot, UK: Ashgate, 1998).

Grafton, Anthony, "The history of ideas: Precept and practice, 1950–2000 and beyond," *Journal of the History of Ideas* (2006).

Greaves, Richard, *John Bunyan and English nonconformity* (London: Hambledon Press, 1992).

Greaves, R. L., and R. Zaller (eds.), *Biographical dictionary of British radicals in the seventeenth century*, 3 vols. (Brighton: Harvester, 1982–84).

Green, Ian, *The re-establishment of the Church of England, 1660–1663* (Oxford: Oxford University Press, 1978).

———, *Print and Protestantism in early modern England* (Oxford: Oxford University Press, 2000).

———, *Continuity and change in Protestant preaching in early modern England* (London: Dr. Williams's Library, 2009).

Green, Joseph Joshua, "The Puritan family of Wilmer: Their alliances and connections," *Transactions of the Congregational History Society* 4:3 (1909).

Greenslade, S. L., *The Cambridge history of the Bible*, vol. 3: *The West, from the Reformation to the present day* (Cambridge: Cambridge University Press, 1995).

Gribben, Crawford, *The Puritan millennium: Literature and theology, 1550–1682* (Dublin: Four Courts, 2000).

Gribben, Crawford, "Lay conversion and Calvinist doctrine during the English Commonwealth," in D. W. Lovegrove (ed.), *The rise of the laity in Evangelical Protestantism* (London: Routledge, 2002).

———, "'Passionate desires, and confident hopes': Puritan millenarianism and Anglo-Scottish union, 1560–1644," *Reformation & Renaissance Review* 4:2 (2002).

———, "Puritan subjectivities: The conversion debate in Cromwellian Dublin," Michael Brown, Charles Ivar McGrath, and Tom P. Power (eds.), *Converts and conversions in Ireland, 1650–1850* (Dublin: Four Courts, 2005).

———, *God's Irishmen: Theological debates in Cromwellian Ireland* (Oxford: Oxford University Press, 2007).

———, "The Church of Scotland and the English apocalyptic imagination, 1630–1650," *Scottish Historical Review* 88:1 (2009).

———, "Samuel Rutherford and liberty of conscience," *Westminster Theological Journal* 71:2 (2009).

———, "John Owen, Renaissance man? The evidence of Edward Millington's *Bibliotheca Owenia* (1684)," *Westminster Theological Journal* (2010).

———, "Millennialism and the renewal of nature: Thomas Fairfax, the Diggers and Andrew Marvell's 'Upon Appleton House,'" in Helen Cooney and Mark Sweetnam (eds.), *Enigma and revelation in Renaissance literature: Essays in honour of Eiléan Ní Chuilleanáin* (Dublin: Four Courts, 2012).

———, "Poetry and piety: John Owen, Faithful Teate and communion with God," in Ian Clary and Steve Weaver (eds.), *The pure flame of devotion: The history of Christian spirituality: Essays in honour of Michael A. G. Haykin* (Toronto, ON: Joshua Press, 2013).

———, "Polemic and apocalyptic in the Cromwellian invasion of Scotland," *Literature and History* 23:1 (2014).

———, "The commodification of Scripture, 1640–1660: Politics, ecclesiology and the cultures of print," in Kevin Killeen et al. (eds), *The Oxford handbook of the Bible in early modern England* (Oxford: Oxford University Press, 2015).

———, "Reading the Bible in the Puritan revolution," in Robert Armstrong and Tadhg O'Hannrachain (eds.), *The English Bible in the early modern world*, St. Andrews Studies in Reformation History (Farnham, UK: Ashgate, forthcoming).

———, "John Owen, baptism and the Baptists," in Ronald S. Baines, Richard C. Barcellos, and James P. Butler (eds.), *By common confession: Essays in honor of James M. Renihan* (Palmdale, CA: RBAP, 2015).

———, "Becoming John Owen," forthcoming.

Griffiths, Steve, *Redeem the time: Sin in the writings of John Owen* (Fearn, Ross-shire, UK: Mentor, 2001).

Ha, Polly, *English Presbyterianism, 1590–1640* (Stanford, CA: Stanford University Press, 2010).

Hadfield, Andrew, *Edmund Spenser: A life* (Oxford: Oxford University Press, 2012).

Halcomb, Joel, "A social history of congregational religious practice during the puritan revolution" (unpublished PhD thesis, University of Cambridge, 2009).

Harrison, C. J., "Grain price analysis and harvest qualities, 1465–1634," *Agricultural History Review* 19 (1975).

Hartman, C. H., *The Cavalier spirit: And its influence on the life and work of Richard Lovelace* (1925; rpt. New York: Haskell House, 1973).

Hatch, Nathan O., *The democratization of American Christianity* (New Haven, CT: Yale University Press, 1991).

Haykin, Michael A. G., "John Owen and the challenge of the Quakers," in Robert W. Oliver (ed.), *John Owen: The man and his theology* (Phillipsburg, NJ: P & R, 2002).

———, "The Calvin of England: Some aspects of the life of John Owen (1616–1683) and his teaching on Biblical Piety," *Reformed Baptist Theological Review* 1 (2004).

———, and Mark Jones (eds.), *Drawn into controversie: Reformed theological diversity and debates within seventeenth-century British Puritanism* (Göttingen: Vandenhoeck & Ruprecht, 2011).

The Henley guide (Henley-on-Thames: Hickman and Stapledon, 1826).

Heppe, Heinrich, *Reformed dogmatics*, trans. G. T. Thomson (London: Allen & Unwin, 1950).

Hessayon, Ariel, and Nicholas Keene (eds.), *Scripture and scholarship in early modern England* (Aldershot, UK: Ashgate, 2006).

Hill, Christopher, *Puritanism and revolution: Studies in interpretation of the English revolution of the 17th century* (London: Secker & Warburg, 1958).

———, *Economic problems of the church* (Oxford: Oxford University Press, 1963).

———, *Milton and the English revolution* (London: Faber and Faber, 1977).

———, *The experience of defeat: Milton and some contemporaries* (London: Faber & Faber, 1984).

———, *A tinker and a poor man: John Bunyan and his church, 1628–1688* (New York: Albert A. Knopf, 1989).

———, *The English Bible and the seventeenth-century revolution* (London:Penguin, 1993).

Hodge, R. I. V., *Foreshortened time: Andrew Marvell and 17th century revolutions* (Cambridge: D. S. Brewer, 1978).

Holberton, Edward, *Poetry and the Cromwellian Protectorate: Culture, politics, and institutions* (Oxford: Oxford University Press, 2008).

Hopper, Andrew, *'Black Tom': Sir Thomas Fairfax and the English revolution* (Manchester: Manchester University Press, 2007).

Hoskins, W. G., "Harvest fluctuations and English economic history, 1480–1619," *Agricultural History Review* 12 (1964).

———, "Harvest fluctuations and English economic history, 1620–1759," *Agricultural History Review* 16 (1968).

Howatt, Irene, *Ten boys who made history* (Fearn, Ross-shire, UK: Christian Focus Press, 2003).

Howson, Barry H., "The Puritan hermeneutics of John Owen: A recommendation," *Westminster Theological Journal* 63 (2001).

Hoyle, David, *Reformation and religious identity in Cambridge, 1590–1644* (Woodbridge, UK: Boydell, 2007).

Hughes, Ann, "'The public confession of these nations': The national church in Interregnum England," in Christopher Durston and Judith Maltby (eds.), *Religion in revolutionary England* (Manchester: Manchester University Press, 2006).

Hunsinger, George, "Justification and mystical union with Christ: Where does Owen stand?" in Kelly M. Kapic and Mark Jones (eds.), *The Ashgate research companion to John Owen's theology* (Farnham, UK: Ashgate, 2012).

Hunt, Arnold, *The art of hearing: English preachers and their audiences, 1590–1640* (Cambridge: Cambridge University Press, 2010).

Hunter, Michael, and Annabel Gregory (eds.), *An astrological diary of the seventeenth century: Samuel Jeake of Rye, 1612–1699* (Oxford: Clarendon Press, 1988).

Hutchinson, Thomas, *A collection of original papers relative to the history of the colony of Massachusetts-Bay* (Boston, 1769).

Hutton, Ronald, *The Restoration: A political and religious history of England and Wales, 1658–1667* (Oxford: Oxford University Press, 1985).

———, *The British republic, 1649–1660* (New York: Macmillan, 1990).

Hutton, Sarah, "Thomas Jackson, Oxford Platonist, and William Twisse, Aristotelian," *Journal of the History of Ideas* 39:4 (1978).

Hyde, Daniel R., "'The fire that kindleth all our sacrifices to God': Owen and the work of the Holy Spirit in prayer," in Kelly M. Kapic and Mark Jones (eds.), *The Ashgate research companion to John Owen's theology* (Aldershot, UK: Ashgate, 2012).

Hynes, Sandra, "Mapping friendship and dissent: The letters from Joseph Boyse to Ralph Thoresby, 1680–1710," in Ariel Hessayon and David Finnegan (eds.), *Varieties of seventeenth- and eighteenth-century English radicalism in context* (Farnham, UK: Ashgate, 2011).

Israel, Jonathan, *Radical Enlightenment: Philosophy and the making of modernity, 1650–1750* (Oxford: Oxford University Press, 2001).

Ivimey, Joseph *History of the English Baptists* (London, 1814).

Jackson, H. J., *Marginalia: Readers writing in books* (New Haven, CT: Yale University Press, 2001).

Jacob, James R., *Henry Stubbe, radical Protestantism and the early Enlightenment* (Cambridge: Cambridge University Press, 1983).

Jardine, Lisa, and Anthony Grafton, "'Studied for action': How Gabriel Harvey read his Livy," *Past and Present* 129 (1990).

Johns, Adrian, *The nature of the book: Print and knowledge in the making* (Chicago: University of Chicago Press, 1998).

———, "Coleman Street," *Huntington Library Quarterly* 71:1 (2008).

Johnston, Warren, *Revelation restored: The apocalypse in later seventeenth-century England* (Woodbridge, UK: Boydell, 2011).

Jones, Edward, *John Milton: The emerging author, 1620–1642* (Oxford: Oxford University Press, 2012).

Jones, Mark, *Why heaven kissed earth: The Christology of the Puritan Reformed Orthodox theologian, Thomas Goodwin (1600–1680)* (Oakville, CT: Vandenhoeck & Ruprecht, 2010).

Jordan, Don, and Michael Walsh, *The king's revenge: Charles II and the greatest manhunt in British history* (London: Little, Brown, 2012).

The journals of Jim Elliot, ed. Elizabeth Elliot (Grand Rapids, MI: Fleming H. Revell, 1978).

Kapic, Kelly M., *Communion with God: The divine and the human in the theology of John Owen* (Grand Rapids, MI: Baker Academic, 2007).

———, "Owen, John (1616–1683)," in *Dictionary of major Biblical interpreters*, ed. Donald K. McKim, second edition (Downers Grove: IVP, 2007).

———, "The Spirit as gift: Explorations in John Owen's pneumatology," in Kelly M. Kapic and Mark Jones (eds.), *The Ashgate research companion to John Owen's theology* (Aldershot, UK: Ashgate, 2012).

———, "Typology, the Messiah, and John Owen's theological reading of Hebrews," in J. Laansma and D. Treier (eds.), *Christology, hermeneutics, and Hebrews: Profiles from the history of interpretation* (Edinburgh: T & T Clark, 2012).

———, and Randall C. Gleason (eds.), *The devoted life: An invitation to the puritan classics* (Downers Grove, IL: IVP, 2004).

Kay, Brian K., *Trinitarian spirituality: John Owen and the doctrine of God in western devotion* (Milton Keynes, UK: Paternoster, 2007).

Kay, Dennis, *Melodious tears: The English formal elegy from Spenser to Milton* (Oxford: Clarendon Press, 1990).

Keeble, N. H., *The literary culture of nonconformity in later seventeenth-century England* (Leicester, UK: Leicester University Press, 1987).

———, "'But the Colonel's shadow': Lucy Hutchinson, women's writing, and the civil war," in Thomas Healy and Jonathan Sawday (eds.), *Literature and the English civil war* (Cambridge: Cambridge University Press, 1990).

Keeler, M. F., *The Long Parliament, 1640–1641* (Philadelphia, PA: American Philosophical Society, 1954).

Kelly, Ryan, "Reformed or reforming? John Owen and the complexity of theological codification for mid-seventeenth-century England," in Kelly M. Kapic and Mark Jones (eds.), *The Ashgate research companion to John Owen's theology* (Aldershot, UK: Ashgate, 2012).

Kelly, William, Appendix to the Notice of the *Achill Herald* Recollections, http://www.stempublishing.com/authors/kelly/8_Bt/achill2.html, accessed 15 June 2015.

Kenyon, J. P., *The Stuart constitution: Documents and commentary*, second edition (Cambridge: Cambridge University Press, 1986).

Kelsey, Sean, *Inventing a republic: The political culture of the English Commonwealth, 1649–53* (Manchester: Manchester University Press, 1997).

———. "The death of Charles I," *Historical Journal* 45:4 (2002).

———. "The trial of Charles I," *English Historical Review* 118:477 (2003).

Killeen, Kevin, "Hanging up kings: The political Bible in early modern England," *Journal of the History of Ideas* 72:4 (2011).

Kimnach, Wilson H., and Kenneth P. Minkema, "The material and social practices of intellectual work: Jonathan Edwards' study," *William and Mary Quarterly* 69:4 (2012).

King, David M., "The affective spirituality of John Owen," *Evangelical Quarterly* 68 (1996).

Knapp, Henry M., "Augustine and Owen on perseverance," *Westminster Theological Journal* 62 (2000).

———, "John Owen's interpretation of Hebrews 6:4–6: Eternal perseverance of the saints in puritan exegesis," *Calvin Theological Journal* 34 (2003).

———, "John Owen, on schism and the nature of the church," *Westminster Theological Journal* 72 (2010).

Knoppers, Laura Lunger, *Constructing Cromwell: Ceremony, portrait, and print, 1645–1661* (Cambridge: Cambridge University Press, 2000).

Lake, Peter, "'A charitable Christian hatred': The godly and their enemies in the 1630s," in Christopher Durston and Jacqueline Eales (eds.), *The culture of English Puritanism, 1560–1700* (New York: Palgrave Macmillan, 1996).

———, *The boxmaker's revenge: "Orthodoxy," "heterodoxy" and the politics of the parish in early Stuart London* (Manchester: Manchester University Press, 2001).

———, and Steve Pincus, "Rethinking the public sphere in early modern England," *Journal of British Studies* 45 (2006).

———, with Michael Questier, *The Antichrist's lewd hat: Protestants, papists and players in post-reformation England* (New Haven, CT: Yale University Press, 2002).

Lawrence, Michael, "Transmission and transformation: Thomas Goodwin and the puritan project" (unpublished PhD thesis, University of Cambridge, 2002).

Lee, Francis, *John Owen re-Presbyterianized* (Edmonton, AB: Still Waters Revival, 2000).

Leggett, Donald, "John Owen as religious advisor to Oliver Cromwell, 1649–1659" (unpublished MPhil thesis, University of Cambridge, 2006).

Letham, Robert, *The Westminster Assembly: Readings its theology in historical context* (Phillipsburg, NJ: P & R, 2009).

———, "John Owen's doctrine of the Trinity in its catholic context," in Kelly M. Kapic and Mark Jones (eds.), *The Ashgate research companion to John Owen's theology* (Aldershot, UK: Ashgate, 2012).

Letis, Theodore P., *The majority text: Essays and reviews in the continuing debate* (Grand Rapids, MI: Institute for Biblical Textual Studies, 1987).

Letters of A. W. Pink (Edinburgh: Banner of Truth, 1978).

Levy, F. J., "How information spread among the gentry, 1550–1640," *Journal of British Studies* 21 (1982).

Lewalski, Barbara K., *The life of John Milton* (Oxford: Blackwell, 2000).

Lewis, Pat, *All Saints Church, Fordham, Essex: Notes on the rectors from 1198*, available at www.fordhamchurch.org.uk/assets/docs/fordham-rectors.pdf, accessed 1 June 2015.

Lim, Paul C.-H., *In pursuit of purity, unity, and liberty: Richard Baxter's Puritan ecclesiology and its seventeenth-century context* (Leiden, The Netherlands: Brill, 2004).

———, "The Trinity, *adiaphora*, ecclesiology, and reformation: John Owen's theory of religious toleration in context," *Westminster Theological Journal* 67 (2005).

———, "Puritans and the Church of England: Historiography and ecclesiology," in John Coffey and Paul C.-H. Lim (eds.), *The Cambridge companion to Puritanism* (Cambridge: Cambridge University Press, 2008).

———, *Mystery unveiled: The crisis of the Trinity in early modern England* (Oxford: Oxford University Press, 2012).

Liu, Tai, *Discord in Zion: The Puritan divines and the puritan revolution, 1640–1660* (The Hague, The Netherlands: Martinus Nijhoff, 1973).

Lloyd, R. Glynne, *John Owen* (Pontypridd, UK: Modern Welsh Publications, 1972).

Lockyer, Roger, *Tudor and Stuart Britain* (1964; third edition, Harlow, UK: Pearson Education, 2005).

Low, Anthony, *The reinvention of love: Poetry, politics and culture from Sidney to Milton* (Cambridge: Cambridge University Press, 1993).

Lynch, Kathleen, *Protestant autobiography in the seventeenth-century Anglophone world* (Oxford: Oxford University Press, 2012).

Lyndon, Brian, "Essex and the King's Cause in 1648," *Historical Journal* 29 (1986).

MacFarlane, Alan, *The family life of Ralph Josselin* (New York: Norton, 1973).

MacKinnon, Dolly, *Earls Colne's early modern landscapes* (Farnham, UK: Ashgate, 2014).

Maclean, Gerald M., *Time's witness: Historical representation in English poetry, 1603–1660* (Madison, WS: University of Wisconsin Press, 1990).

Magrath, John R., *The Queen's College*, 2 vols. (Oxford: Clarendon Press, 1921).

Malcolm, Noel, *Aspects of Hobbes* (Oxford: Clarendon Press, 2002).

Marsh, Christopher, *The Family of Love in English society, 1550–1630* (Cambridge: Cambridge University Press, 1994).

Mayor, Stephen, "The teaching of John Owen concerning the Lord's Supper," *Scottish Journal of Theology* 18 (1965).

McDonald, Suzanne, "The pneumatology of the 'lost' image in John Owen," *Westminster Theological Journal* 71 (2009).

McDonald, Suzanne, "Beholding the glory of God in the face of Jesus Christ," in Kelly M. Kapic and Mark Jones (eds.), *The Ashgate research companion to John Owen's theology* (Farnham, UK: Ashgate, 2012).

McDowell, Nicholas, *Poetry and allegiance in the English civil wars: Marvell and the cause of wit* (Oxford: Oxford University Press, 2008).

McGrath, Alister, *J. I. Packer: A biography* (Grand Rapids, MI: Revell, 1998).

McGrath, Gavin J., "Puritans and the human will: Voluntarism within mid-seventeenth English Puritanism as seen in the works of Richard Baxter and John Owen" (unpublished PhD thesis, Durham University, 1989).

McGraw, Ryan M., "John Owen on the Holy Spirit in relation to the Trinity, the humanity of Christ, and the believer," in Joel R. Beeke and Joseph A. Pipa (eds.), *The beauty and glory of the Holy Spirit* (Grand Rapids, MI: Reformation Heritage Books, 2012).

———, *A heavenly directory: Trinitarian piety, public worship and a reassessment of John Owen's theology* (Bristol, CT: Vandenoeck & Ruprecht, 2014).

McKim, Donald K., "John Owen's doctrine of Scripture in historical perspective," *Evangelical Quarterly* 45 (1973).

McKinley, David J., "John Owen's view of illumination: An alternative to the Fuller-Erickson dialogue," *Bibliotheca Sacra* 154 (1997).

McLaughlin, Gráinne, "The idolater John Owen? Linguistic hegemony in Cromwell's Oxford," in Richard Kirwan (ed.), *Scholarly self-fashioning and community in the early modern university* (Farnham, UK: Ashgate, 2013).

Miller, Kathleen, *The print culture of plague in early modern England* (New York: Palgrave Macmillan, forthcoming).

Miller, Peter N., "The 'antiquarianization' of Biblical scholarship and the London Polyglot Bible (1653–57)," *Journal of the History of Ideas* 62:3 (2001).

Milton, Anthony, *Catholic and Reformed: The Roman and protestant churches in English protestant thought, 1600–1640* (Cambridge: Cambridge University Press, 1995).

———, "Anglicanism and royalism in the 1640s," in John Adamson (ed.), *The English civil war* (New York: Palgrave Macmillan, 2009).

Moffatt, James (ed.), *The golden book of John Owen* (London: Hodder and Stoughton, 1904).

Moote, A. Lloyd, and Dorothy C. Moote, *The great plague: The story of London's most deadly year* (Baltimore, MD: The Johns Hopkins University Press, 2004).

Morden, Peter J., *Communion with Christ and his people: The spirituality of C. H. Spurgeon* (Eugene, OR: Pickwick, 2013).

Morgan, Edmund S., *The Puritan family: Religion and domestic relations in seventeenth-century New England*, revised edition (New York: Harper, 1966).

Morgan, John, *Godly learning: Puritan attitudes towards reason, learning and education, 1540–1640* (Cambridge: Cambridge University Press, 1986).

Morrill, John, "The Church of England, 1642–1649," in John Morrill (ed.), *The nature of the English revolution* (Harlow, UK: Routledge, 1993).

———, and P. Baker, "Oliver Cromwell, the regicide and the sons of Zeruiah," in David L. Smith (ed.), *Cromwell and the Interregnum* (Oxford: Blackwell, 2003).

Mortimer, Sarah, *Reason and religion in the English revolution: The challenge of Socinianism* (Cambridge: Cambridge University Press, 2010).

Muller, Richard, *After Calvin: Studies in the development of a theological tradition* (Oxford: Oxford University Press, 2003).

———, *Post-Reformation Reformed dogmatics*, 4 vols. (Grand Rapids, MI: Baker, 2003).

———, "Reflections on persistent Whiggism and its antidotes in the study of sixteenth- and seventeenth-century intellectual history," in Alister Chapman, John Coffey, and Brad S. Gregory (eds.), *Seeing things their way: Intellectual history and the return of religion* (South Bend, IN: Notre Dame University Press, 2009).

Murdock, Graeme, *Calvinism on the frontier, 1600–1660: International Calvinism and the Reformed Church in Hungary and Transylvania* (Oxford: Clarendon Press, 2000).

———, Penny Roberts, and Andrew Spicer (eds.), *Ritual and violence: Natalie Zemon Davis and early modern France, Past & Present* supplement 7 (Oxford: Oxford University Press, 2012).

Murray, Iain H., *D. Martyn Lloyd-Jones: The fight of faith, 1939–1981* (Edinburgh: Banner of Truth, 1990).

Najapfour, Brian G., "'That it might lead and direct men unto Christ': An analysis of John Owen's view of the Mosaic covenant," *Scottish Bulletin of Evangelical Theology* 29 (2011).

Narveson, Katherine, "The sources for Lucy Hutchinson's *On Theology*," *Notes and Queries*, n.s., 36 (1989).

Newman, P. R., *The old service: Royalist regimental colonels and the Civil War, 1642–1646* (Manchester: Manchester University Press, 1993).

Nickolls, John, *Original letters and papers of state, addressed to Oliver Cromwell* (London, 1743).

Norbrook, David, *Writing the English republic: Poetry, rhetoric and politics, 1627–1660* (Cambridge: Cambridge University Press, 1999).

———, "Memoirs and oblivion: Lucy Hutchinson and the Restoration," *Huntington Library Quarterly* 75 (2012).

Norton, David, *A textual history of the King James Bible* (Cambridge: Cambridge University Press, 2005).

Nuttall, Geoffrey F., *The Holy Spirit in Puritan faith and experience* (Oxford: Basil Blackwell, 1946).

O'Donnell, Laurence R., "The Holy Spirit's role in John Owen's 'covenant of the mediator' formulation: A case study in Reformed Orthodox formulations of the *pactum salutis*," *Puritan Reformed Journal* 4:1 (2012).

O'Hara, David, *English newsbooks and Irish rebellion, 1641–1649* (Dublin: Four Courts, 2006).

Oliver, Robert W. (ed.), *John Owen: The man and his theology* (Phillipsburg, NJ: P & R, 2002).

———, "John Owen: His life and times," in Robert W. Oliver (ed.), *John Owen: The man and his theology* (Phillipsburg, NJ: P & R, 2002).

Packer, James I., "Introductory essay," in John Owen, *The death of death in the death of Christ* (Edinburgh: Banner of Truth, 1959).

———, *A quest for godliness: The Puritan vision of the Christian life* (Wheaton, IL: Crossway, 1990).

———, "Why I signed it," *Christianity Today* 38:14, 12 December 1994.

Patterson, W. B., *William Perkins and the making of a Protestant England* (Oxford: Oxford University Press, 2014).

Patterson, Annabel, and Michael Dzeleainis, "Marvell and the earl of Anglesey: A chapter in the history of reading," *Historical Journal* 44 (2001).

Paul, R. S., *The Lord Protector* (Grand Rapids, MI: Eerdmans, 1955).

Payne, Jon D., *John Owen on the Lord's Supper* (Edinburgh: Banner of Truth, 2004).

Peck, Francis, *Desiderata curiosa: or, A collection of divers scarce and curious pieces relating chiefly to matters of English history* (London, 1779).

Pettegree, Andrew, *Reformation and the culture of persuasion* (Cambridge: Cambridge University Press, 2005).

———, *The invention of news: How the world came to know about itself* (New Haven, CT: Yale University Press, 2014).

Piper, John, *Contending for our all: Defending truth and treasuring Christ in the lives of Athanasius, John Owen, and J. Gresham* (Wheaton, IL: Crossway, 2006).

Pocock, J. G. A., "The history of political thought: A methodological enquiry," in Peter Laslett and W. G. Runciman (eds.), *Philosophy, politics and society*, second series (Oxford: Blackwell, 1962).

Potter, Lois, *Secret rites and secret writings: Royalist literature, 1641–1660* (Cambridge: Cambridge University Press, 1989).

Polizotto, Carolyn, "The campaign against *The humble proposals* of 1652," *Journal of Ecclesiastical History* 38 (1987).

Powell, Hunter, "The Dissenting Brethren and the power of the keys, 1640–44" (unpublished PhD thesis, University of Cambridge, 2011).

Raymond, Joad, *The invention of the newspaper: English newsbooks, 1641–1649* (Oxford: Clarendon Press, 1996).

———, *Pamphlets and pamphleteering in early modern Britain* (Cambridge: Cambridge University Press, 2003).

Reece, Henry, *The army in Cromwellian England, 1649–1660* (Oxford: Oxford University Press, 2013).

Rehnman, Sebastian, *Divine discourse: The theological methodology of John Owen* (Grand Rapids, MI: Baker, 2002).

———, "John Owen: A Reformed Scholastic at Oxford," in Willem J. van Asselt and Eef Dekker (eds.), *Reformation and scholasticism: An ecumenical enterprise* (Grand Rapids, MI: Baker Academic, 2001).

———, "John Owen on faith and reason," in Kelly M. Kapic and Mark Jones (eds.), *The Ashgate research companion to John Owen's theology* (Aldershot, UK: Ashgate, 2012).

Report on the manuscripts of the earl of Egmont, 2 vols. (London: Historical Manuscripts Commission, 1905).

Report on the manuscripts of the late Allan George Finch, esq., of Burley-on-the-Hill, Rutland, ed. S. C. Lomas (London: H. M. Stationery Office, 1913).

Rigg, J. M. "Owen, John, D. D. (1616–1683), theologian," *Dictionary of National Biography* (1896).

Rogers, Jack B., and Donald K. McKim (eds.), *The authority and interpretation of the Bible* (New York: Harper & Row, 1979).

Rosenblatt, Jason P., *Renaissance England's chief rabbi: John Selden* (Oxford: Oxford University Press, 2006).

Rublack, Ulinka, *Reformation Europe* (Cambridge: Cambridge University Press, 2005).

Rushworth, John, *Historical collections of private passages of state*, 8 vols. (1721).

Ryrie, Alec, *Being Protestant in Reformation Britain* (Oxford: Oxford University Press, 2013).

Saywell, David, and Jacob Simon, *National Portrait Gallery, London: Complete illustrated catalogue* (London: Third Millennium Publishing, 2004).

Schücking, Levin L., *The Puritan family: A social study from the literary sources*, trans. Brian Battershaw (New York: Schocken Books, 1969).

Schwoerer, Lois G., *The ingenious Mr Henry Care, Restoration publicist* (Baltimore, MD: The Johns Hopkins University Press, 2001).

Scott-Baumann, Elizabeth, *Forms of engagement: Women, poetry and culture, 1640–1680* (Oxford: Oxford University Press, 2013).

Sharpe, Kevin, *Reading revolutions: The politics of reading in early modern England* (New Haven, CT: Yale University Press, 2000).

———, *Image wars: Promoting kings and Commonweaths in England, 1603–1660* (New Haven, CT: Yale University Press, 2010).

Shaw, William A., *A history of the English church during the civil wars and under the Commonwealth, 1640–1660*, 2 vols. (London: Longmans, Green, 1900).

Sherman, William H., *Used books: Marking readers in Renaissance England* (Philadelphia: University of Pennsylvania Press, 2008).

Skinner, Quentin, *Reason and rhetoric in the philosophy of Hobbes* (Princeton, NJ: Princeton University Press, 1996).

Skinner, Quentin, *Visions of politics*, vol. 1: *Regarding method* (Cambridge: Cambridge University Press, 2002).

Slack, Paul, *The impact of plague in Tudor and Stuart London* (Oxford: Oxford University Press, 1995).

Smith, Christopher R., "'Up and be doing': The pragmatic Puritan eschatology of John Owen," *Evangelical Quarterly* 61 (1989).

Smith, Nigel, *Literature and revolution in England, 1640–1660* (New Haven, CT: Yale University Press, 1994).

———, "Non-conformist voices and books," in John Barnard and D. F. Mackenzie (eds.), *The Cambridge history of the book in Britain*, 6 vols. (Cambridge: Cambridge University Press, 1999–2014).

———, *Andrew Marvell: The chameleon* (New Haven, CT: Yale University Press, 2010).

Smith-Bannister, Scott, *Names and naming patterns in England, 1538–1700* (Oxford: Clarendon Press, 1997).

Snoddy, Richard, *The soteriology of James Ussher: The act and object of saving faith* (Oxford: Oxford University Press, 2014).

Spalding, Ruth, *The improbable puritan: A life of Bulstrode Whitelocke, 1605–1675* (London: Faber and Faber, 1975).

Spence, J. Alan, "John Owen and Trinitarian agency," *Scottish Journal of Theology* 43 (1990).

———, "Christ's humanity and ours: John Owen," in C. Schwöbel and Colin Gunton (eds.), *Persons, divine and human* (Edinburgh: T & T Clark, 1991).

———, *Incarnation and inspiration: John Owen and the coherence of Christology* (London: T & T Clark, 2007).

———, "The significance of John Owen for modern Christology," in Kelly M. Kapic and Mark Jones (eds.), *The Ashgate research companion to John Owen's theology* (Aldershot, UK: Ashgate, 2012).

Spufford, Margaret, *Contrasting communities: English villagers in the sixteenth and seventeenth centuries* (Cambridge: Cambridge University Press, 1974).

Spurlock, R. Scott, "'Anie Gospell Way': Religious diversity in Interregnum Scotland," *Records of the Scottish Church History Society* 37 (2007).

———, *Cromwell and Scotland: Conquest and religion, 1650–1660* (Edinburgh: John Donald, 2007).

———, "The politics of eschatology: Baptists in Interregnum Scotland," *Baptist Quarterly* 44:2 (2010).

———, "Cromwell's Edinburgh press and the development of print culture in Scotland," *Scottish Historical Review* 90:2 (2011).

Stachniewski, John, *The persecutory imagination: English Puritanism and the literature of religious despair* (Oxford: Clarendon Press, 1991).

Strickland, Michael, "Seventeenth-century puritans and the synoptic problem," *Puritan Reformed Journal* 6:1 (2014).

Tay, Edwin E. M., "Christ's priestly oblation and intercession: Their development and significance in John Owen," in Kelly M. Kapic and Mark Jones (eds.), *The Ashgate research companion to John Owen's theology* (Aldershot, UK: Ashgate, 2012), pp. 159–169.

———, *The priesthood of Christ: Atonement in the theology of John Owen (1616–1683)* (Milton Keynes, UK: Paternoster, 2014).

Taylor, Archer, *Book catalogues: Their variety and uses* (Chicago: Newberry Library, 1957).

Timmiswood, Adrian, *By permission of heaven: The story of the Great Fire of London* (London: Jonathan Cape, 2006).

Toon, Peter, *God's statesman: The life and work of John Owen* (Exeter, UK: Paternoster, 1971).

——— (ed.), *Puritans, the millennium, and the future of Israel: Puritan eschatology, 1600–1660* (Cambridge: James Clarke, 1970).

Trevor-Roper, Hugh, *Religion, the reformation and social change* (London: Secker and Warburg, 1967).

Troxel, A. Craig, "'Cleansed once for all': John Owen on the glory of gospel worship in Hebrews," *Calvin Theological Journal* 32 (1997).

Trueman, Carl R., *The claims of truth: John Owen's Trinitarian theology* (Carlisle, UK: Paternoster, 1998).

———, "Faith seeking understanding: Some neglected aspects of John Owen's understanding of Scriptural interpretation," in A. N. S. Lane (ed.), *Interpreting the Bible: Historical and theological studies in honour of David F. Wright* (Leicester, UK: Apollos, 1997).

———, "John Owen as a theologian," in Robert W. Oliver (ed.), *John Owen: The man and his theology* (Phillipsburg, NJ: P & R, 2002).

———, *John Owen: Reformed Catholic, Renaissance man* (Aldershot, UK: Ashgate, 2007).

———, and R. S. Clark (eds.), *Protestant scholasticism: Essays in reassessment* (Carlisle, UK: Paternoster, 1999).

Turner, G. L., *Original records of early non-conformity under persecution and indulgence* (London: Unwin, 1911).

Tweeddale, John W., "John Owen's commentary on Hebrews in context," in Kelly M. Kapic and Mark Jones (eds.), *The Ashgate research companion to John Owen's theology* (Aldershot, UK: Ashgate, 2012).

———, "A John Owen bibliography," in Kelly M. Kapic and Mark Jones (eds.), *The Ashgate research companion to John Owen's theology* (Aldershot, UK: Ashgate, 2012).

Twells, Leonard, *The life of . . . Dr Edward Pocock* (London, 1816).

Tyacke, Nicholas, *Aspects of English Protestantism, c. 1530–1700* (Manchester: Manchester University Press, 2001).

Underdown, David, *Royalist conspiracy in England, 1649–1660* (New Haven, CT: Yale University Press, 1971).

van Asselt, Willem, et al., *Introduction to Reformed scholasticism* (Grand Rapids, MI: Reformation Heritage Books, 2011).

van Asselt, Willem J., "Covenant theology as relational theology: The contributions of Johannes Cocceius (1603–1669) and John Owen (1618–1683) to a living Reformed theology," in Kelly M. Kapic and Mark Jones (eds.), *The Ashgate research companion to John Owen's theology* (Aldershot, UK: Ashgate, 2012).

van Asselt, W. J., M. D. Bell, and R. Ferwerda, ed. and trans. *Scholastic discourse: Johannes Maccovius (1588–1644) on theological and philosophical distinctions and rules* (Apeldoorn, The Netherlands: Instituut voor Reformatieonderzoek, 2009).

van den Brink, Gert, "Impetration and application in John Owen's theology," in Kelly M. Kapic and Mark Jones (eds.), *The Ashgate research companion to John Owen's theology* (Aldershot, UK: Ashgate, 2012).

Vallance, Edward, "Oaths, casuistry, and equivocation: Anglican responses to the Engagement controversy," *Historical Journal* 44:1 (2001).

Varley, Frederick John, *The siege of Oxford: An account of Oxford during the civil war, 1642–1646* (Oxford: Oxford University Press, 1932).

Vernon, Elliot, "The quarrel of the Covenant: The London Presbyterians and the regicide," in Jason Peacey (ed.), *The regicides and the execution of Charles I* (New York: Palgrave Macmillan, 2001).

———, "'A ministry of the gospel': The Presbyterians during the English revolution," in Christopher Durston and Judith Maltby (eds.), *Religion in revolutionary England* (Manchester: Manchester University Press, 2006).

von Friedeburg, Robert, "Reformation of manners and the social composition of offenders in an East Anglian cloth village: Earls Colne, Essex, 1531–1642," *Journal of British Studies* 29 (1990).

Wallace, Dewey D., *Puritans and predestination: Grace in English Protestant theology, 1525–1695* (Chapel Hill: North Carolina University Press, 1982).

———, "Owen, John (1616–1683)," in Francis J. Bremer and Tom Webster (eds.), *Puritans and Puritanism in Europe and America: A comprehensive encyclopedia* (Santa Barbara, CA: ABC-Clio, 2006).

———, *Shapers of English Calvinism, 1660–1714: Variety, persistence, and transformation* (Oxford: Oxford University Press, 2011).

Walsham, Alexandra, *Providence in early modern England* (Oxford: Oxford University Press, 1999).

Ward, W. R., *Early evangelicalism: A global intellectual history, 1670–1789* (Cambridge: Cambridge University Press, 2006).

Watkins, Owen C., *The Puritan experience* (London: Routledge and Kegan Paul, 1972).

Watt, Tessa, *Cheap print and popular piety, 1550–1640* (Cambridge: Cambridge University Press, 1991).

Webster, Tom, *Godly clergy in early Stuart England: The Caroline Puritan movement, c. 1620–1643* (Cambridge: Cambridge University Press, 1997).

———, "Early Stuart Puritanism," in John Coffey and Paul C.-H. Lim (eds.), *The Cambridge companion to Puritanism* (Cambridge: Cambridge University Press, 2008).

Weidhorn, Manfred, *Richard Lovelace* (New York: Twayne, 1970).

Westcott, Stephen P., *By the Bible alone! John Owen's Puritan theology for today's church* (Fellsmere, FL: Reformation Media & Press, 2010).

Wilberforce, William, *A practical view of the prevailing religious system of professed Christians* (1797; rpt. London, 1830).

Wilson, John F., *Pulpit in Parliament: Puritanism during the English civil wars, 1640–1648* (Princeton, NJ: Princeton University Press, 1969).

Wilson, Walter, *The history and antiquities of dissenting churches and meeting houses in London, Westminster, and Southwark*, 4 vols. (London, 1808–14).

Worden, Blair, "Oliver Cromwell and the sin of Achan," in David L. Smith (ed.), *Cromwell and the Interregnum* (Oxford: Blackwell, 2003).

———, *Literature and politics in Cromwellian England: John Milton, Andrew Marvell, Marchamont Nedham* (Oxford: Oxford University Press, 2007).

———, "Politics, piety, and learning: Cromwellian Oxford," in *God's instruments: Political conduct in the England of Oliver Cromwell* (Oxford: Oxford University Press, 2012).

Woolf, Daniel, *Reading history in early modern England* (Cambridge: Cambridge University Press, 2000).

———, *The social circulation of the past: English historical culture, 1500–1730* (Oxford: Oxford University Press, 2003).

Woolrych, Austin, *Commonwealth to Protectorate* (Oxford: Clarendon Press, 1982).

———, *Britain in revolution, 1625–1660* (Oxford: Oxford University Press, 2002).

Wrightson, Keith, and David Levine, *Poverty and piety in an English village: Terling, 1525–1700* (Oxford: Oxford University Press, 1979).

Yeo, Matthew G., "The acquisition of books by Chetham's Library, 1655–1700: A case study in the distribution and reception of texts in the English provinces in the late seventeenth century," 2 vols. (unpublished PhD thesis, University of Manchester, 2009).

———, *The acquisition of books by Chetham's Library, 1655–1700* (Leiden, The Netherlands: Brill, 2011).

Yule, George, *The Independents in the English civil war* (Cambridge: Cambridge University Press, 1958).

Zaret, David, *Origins of democratic culture: Printing, petitions, and the public sphere in early-modern England* (Princeton, NJ: Princeton University Press, 2000).

Zwicker, Steven N., "Language as disguise: Politics and poetry in the late seventeenth century," *Annals of Scholarship* 1 (1980).

Index

CPSIA information can be obtained
at www.ICGtesting.com
Printed in the USA
BVOW03s0534180817
492323BV00003B/10/P